Foundations of Information Systems

Foundations of Information Systems

VLADIMIR ZWASS

Fairleigh Dickinson University

Boston, Massachusetts   Burr Ridge, Illinois   Dubuque, Iowa
Madison, Wisconsin   New York, New York   San Francisco, California   St. Louis, Missouri

Irwin/McGraw-Hill

*A Division of The **McGraw·Hill** Companies*

FOUNDATIONS OF INFORMATION SYSTEMS

Copyright 1998 by The McGraw-Hill Companies, Inc. All right reserved. Printed in the United States of America. Except as permitted under the United States Copyright Act of 1976, no part of this publication may be reproduced or distributed in any form or by any means, or stored in a data base or retrieval system, without the prior written permission of the publisher.

This book is printed on acid-free paper.

1 2 3 4 5 6 7 8 9 0 VH/VH 9 0 9 8 7

ISBN 0-697-13312-5

Editorial director: *Michael W. Junior*
Senior sponsoring editor: *Rick Williamson*
Developmental editor: *Christine Wright*
Editorial coordinator: *Carrie Berkshire*
Marketing manager: *James Rogers*
Project manager: *Gladys True*
Production supervisor: *Scott Hamilton*
Interior designer: *Becky Lemna*
Cover image: *Ed Honowitz, courtesy of Tony Stone Images*
Photo research coordinator: *Keri Johnson*
Compositor: *Interactive Composition Corporation*
Typeface: *10/12 Minion*
Printer: *Von Hoffmann Press, Inc.*

Library of Congress Cataloging-in-Publication Data

Zwass, Vladimir.
    Foundations of information systems / Vladimir Zwass.
        p.   cm.
    Includes indexes.
    ISBN 0-697-13312-5
    1. Management information systems.   I. title.
    T58.6.Z848 1997
    658.4'038'011—dc21   97- 596

http://www.mhhe.com

For my son, Josh,
        as he enters college

Preface

Information systems have become a key to the effectiveness and success of organizations. Knowing how to acquire, use, and manage information systems to satisfy your own and your firm's requirements is a key to *your* effectiveness as a manager and a knowledge worker. Understanding the business role of information systems is a vital part of a manager's education. The purpose of this book is to lead you to this understanding. The text has been designed for the foundations course in information systems, to introduce you both to their fundamental concepts and to their applications in business life. It is my firm belief that the discipline has matured enough to call for such a foundations book.

The foundations course in information systems (IS) is a stepping-stone to other courses in the business curriculum. Information systems have become far too important to organizations and far too ingrained in the professional life of all of us to be left to the IS professionals. The foundations course also serves as an introduction to a more advanced study of information systems in organizations.

ABOUT THIS TEXT

This textbook has been written to take the student into the 21st century. Utmost attention is paid to integrate the current business and management ideas with the deployment of new information technologies. Yet, the book is rooted in the concepts that have emerged over the decades of development of the IS discipline.

The important subjects of a foundations course are presented in proper depth, rather than treated with a perfunctory paragraph. This is accomplished through chapter coverage, numerous minicases and vignettes that illustrate their subject with real-life practices of many companies around the globe, and with serious case studies that accompany each chapter. Careful attention is paid to small entrepreneurial firms, so often the source of new ideas.

A major distinguishing feature of the text is also a consistent development of several principal themes throughout the entire book. These themes reflect the demands of the contemporary business environment. The themes are:

Transformation of Business Processes with Information Systems

The capabilities offered by IS present an opportunity to redesign business processes of a firm in order to reach for new levels of performance. Introduced early in Chapter 1, business process redesign is discussed again in Chapter 3, in the context of the strategic deployment of IS, and in Chapter 7, when we see how telecommunications may be used in the redesign. Transformation of business processes is also presented at length in Chapter 13 and placed in the context of international business in Chapter 18. It is the subject of several case studies and multiple vignettes.

Strategic Use of Information Systems

Innovative uses of information technology to achieve a superior long-term competitive position are illustrated throughout the text. Chapter 3 of the book devotes extensive coverage to the subject, both with a strong conceptual framework and with numerous examples, leading up to the development of a virtual value chain for the firm. Other chapters continue to present strategic IS. The cases and examples of strategic IS are drawn not only from the practice of major corporations but also from many small companies. You will encounter a family-run winery in Napa Valley that is a leader in the use of information technologies, and you will read about Texas Instruments as well.

Support of Knowledge Work and of Organizational Knowledge Management

Information systems are a lever of knowledge work. Personal productivity software and professional support systems assist an individual in processing information, solving business problems, developing new products, and creating new knowledge. As business teams are becoming the nodal work units in organizations, creative problem solving and knowledge work in teams find support in intranets, groupware, workflow systems, and group decision support systems. The need to exploit IS capabilities to preserve and enhance organizational knowledge is discussed early in Chapters 1 and 3. A systematic discussion of IS supporting knowledge work will be found in Chapter 8 of the text, accompanied by a coverage of creativity techniques in group problem solving. Multiple vignettes and minicases deal with organizational learning.

The Advance of Internet-Based Electronic Commerce

Electronic commerce is the sharing of business information, maintaining business relationships, and conducting business transactions by means of computer telecommunications networks. With the development of the Internet's World Wide Web, electronic commerce has been changing both the ways organizations deal with one another and the way internal corporate processes are carried out with the assistance of intranets. The book has been written to incorporate the coverage of electronic commerce and the Internet throughout, some of it based on the author's work in the field. An extensive discussion of electronic commerce is offered in Chapters 7 and 9.

The Use of Information Systems in Business Globalization

Many examples, vignettes, and cases throughout the text have been drawn from the international business areas. The text culminates with Chapter 18 that provides an exceptionally extensive and integrated presentation of innovating with information systems for global reach. A section of the chapter illustrates business process redesign in a global corporation. A major case focusing on Nestlé, headquartered in beautiful Vevey on Lake Geneva, was developed by visiting the firm.

Total Quality Management

Global competition has called forth a pursuit of uncompromising quality of products and services through new management techniques. You will read how information systems serve in this task in Chapter 12, and you will learn how to develop quality information systems in Part Five of the text. As an exceptional feature, Chapter 15 will introduce to you the software development process from the point of view of quality management.

The text offers an integrated discussion of the acquisition of information systems. Today, information systems come into corporate service from multiple sources. End-user computing has been integrated by leading firms into the overall organizational computing. Many applications are acquired from their specialized vendors and customized for specific use. IS outsourcing has become a part of life for a number of firms. Chapter 13 presents an integrated view of these multiple sources of information system acquisition, setting them in the context of developing a general IS architecture for a firm.

Ethical issues that arise during the development and use of information systems are introduced early—in fact, in Chapter 1 of the text. Each subsequent chapter focuses on the relevant ethical problems in the Issues for Discussion included at the chapter's conclusion. A thorough discussion of ethical and societal issues in information systems is offered in Chapter 17.

The dynamics of the current corporate environment permeate the text. Virtual organizations (some on a global scale), teamwork, customer-supplier linkages, mass customization, agile manufacturing, database marketing, group problem solving, innovation, and creativity are some of the concepts that appear in chapter contents, vignettes, and cases. The core new technologies are set in this business context. They include object-oriented development, client/server computing, data warehouses and data mining, the use of Java, intelligent agents, wireless networks and nomadic computing, asynchronous transfer mode for multimedia networking , public-key encryption, push technology for the Web, hypermedia, and virtual reality—to name just a few information technologies whose creative business use is covered in the text.

The text relies on integrating the discussion of fundamental concepts with showing their practical application in many vignettes, interviews with leaders and practitioners, extensive cases, and in-text examples. Literature references have been carefully selected to enable the student to delve into the best—and accessible—work in the field. An extensive glossary and several indexes will help in working with the text.

A basic objective was to make the text interesting and to show the excitement of bringing information systems into the service of business initiatives, from beating global competitors to enabling a customer to design a special window for a new house on a computer screen, and rushing the design electronically into production and forwarding the window to the building site.

STRUCTURE OF THE TEXT

The book is designed in a modular fashion, to give the instructor total flexibility in teaching the course. The diagram in Figure I shows this design. As you can see, any of the other parts of the text may follow the presentation of Part One. Let us briefly review the six parts of the text.

Part One presents the business capabilities of information systems in action in operations, management, knowledge work, and business competition. The core concepts of information systems are introduced and immediately set to work in the competitive environment of our information society. This part introduces the principal themes of the text, combining the explanation of concepts with the presentation of practice.

Part Two presents the contemporary and emerging information technologies. The instructor may elect to discuss only some of the five chapters of this part or assign some of this material as readings. The presentation of IS hardware concludes with showing how to enrich business systems with multimedia. The discussion of software includes the coverage of personal productivity software, fourth-generation languages supporting end-user computing, and the explanation of object-oriented programming. Database management is described both from the technological and managerial points of view. Telecommunications have become the driving technology of organizational integration and an extensive chapter presents the foundations of business networking. A thorough presentation of the facilities of the Internet and the World Wide Web in the context of electronic commerce and intranets is provided. The part culminates with a discussion of information system

Figure I

Modular structure of the text

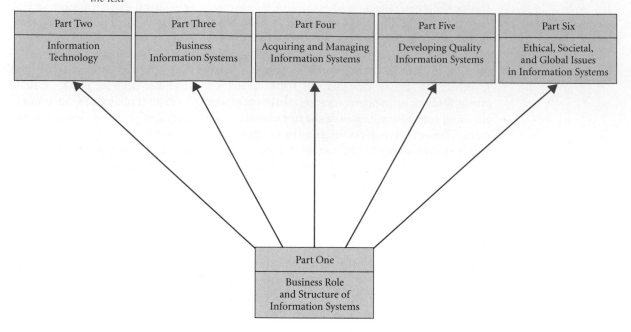

Part Two	Part Three	Part Four	Part Five	Part Six
Information Technology	Business Information Systems	Acquiring and Managing Information Systems	Developing Quality Information Systems	Ethical, Societal, and Global Issues in Information Systems

Part One
Business Role and Structure of Information Systems

architecture and shows how telecommunications are used to redesign business processes and to compete in the marketplace.

Part Three offers an extensive presentation of business information systems. Chapter 8 discusses support of knowledge work with professional support systems and office information systems. Electronic document management, workflow systems, electronic message handling, teleconferencing, electronic meeting systems, and groupware are given proper coverage. Chapter 9 describes transaction processing systems and management reporting systems. It devotes close attention to electronic data interchange (EDI) that evolves into electronic commerce. Chapter 10 discusses decision support and executive information systems, including group decision support systems. Chapter 11 concentrates on expert systems, while also introducing other technologies of applied artificial intelligence, such as neural networks, fuzzy logic, robotics, and computerized speech recognition. Chapter 12 provides an integrated view of information systems supporting the business functions of marketing, manufacturing, accounting and finance, and human resource management. The coverage is deeply rooted in the best business practices of today and illustrated with many examples.

Part Four shows how to acquire and manage information systems. Business reengineering, information systems planning, assessing a system's business value, life cycle-based system development, prototyping, end-user development, purchase, and outsourcing of information systems are all given due attention. No system can be successful without the buy-in and support of the people who will use and manage it: System implementation measures to achieve this success are discussed at length. The available options in organizing the information systems function in a firm are presented. Threats to IS security, including the specific Internet context, IS controls, and IS auditing are covered in depth. This reflects the present corporate needs in the face of pervasive dependence on a properly functioning and secure IS.

Part Five will be studied when a more extensive coverage of IS development is desired. It begins by discussing the role of information systems in Total Quality Management and shows how the principles of total quality can be applied to IS themselves. Concepts, tools, and techniques of structured systems development are explained and illustrated. System maintenance and project management are discussed. Computer-aided software engineering (CASE) and object-oriented development are presented.

Part Six discusses ethical, societal, and global issues in IS. The fundamental ethical issues involved in building and using information systems are analyzed. Practical scenarios show how ethical decisions can be made in the light of ethical principles and codes of ethics. Impacts of information technology in the workplace are described. The exceptionally comprehensive concluding chapter of the text shows how companies can exploit information systems to innovate and succeed in the global marketplace.

Irwin/McGraw-Hill will maintain an active site on the World Wide Web to enhance the printed text with supplementary material and to keep up the exceptional currency of the textbook. The site's locator is available from the publisher's representative.

ACKNOWLEDGEMENTS

As the Editor-in-Chief of a leading journal in the field of management information systems and a consultant, I have benefited from many discussions with the leading thinkers, teachers, and practitioners in the United States and abroad. Their insights and comments have helped me refine my own thinking on the role of information technology in modern business and, indeed, in our information society. My students have helped me over the years to understand how to help them in learning information systems. It is impossible to thank all of them here. However, I would like to express my special gratitude to the book's reviewers:

Marvin Albin
Morehead State University

Joseph Brady
University of Delaware

Jane Carey
Arizona State University West

Drew Cobb
Johns Hopkins University & College of Notre Dame

Edouard Desautels
University of Wisconsin

Charles Downing
Boston College

Nancy Johnson
Metropolitan State University

James LaSalle
University of Arizona

William Leigh
University of Central Florida

Jay Lightfoot
University of Northern Colorado

C. Stuart McKelvie
University of Manitoba

Leah Pietron
University of Nebraska at Omaha

Leonard Presby
William Paterson State College

Conrad Royksund
Luther College

Teresita Salinas
Washburn University

Ann Theis
Adrian College

Robert Trent
University of Virginia

The development and production of a major textbook calls upon many talents to assist the author. It is my privilege to acknowledge the efforts of the professionals at Irwin/Mc-Graw-Hill who helped me. Rick Williamson has been an outstanding and highly discerning senior sponsoring editor. Christine Wright and Carrie Berkshire have expertly guided the book through the development. Gladys True made the production go smoothly and swiftly. Keri Johnson and Randall Nicholas conducted the photo research with a sure hand. To all of them go my sincere thanks.

All of us hope you will find the text not only instructive but enjoyable as well.

Vladimir Zwass

Brief Contents

Contents

PART THREE

Business Information Systems   *287*

CHAPTER EIGHT

Support of Individual and Group Knowledge Work   *288*

CHAPTER NINE

Transaction Processing and Management Reporting Systems   *324*

PART SIX

Ethical, Societal, and Global Issues in Information Systems   *609*

CHAPTER SEVENTEEN

Ethical and Societal Issues in Information Systems   *610*

FOCUS MINICASE: You May Be Well, But Will It
Be Good For You?   *611*

CHAPTER EIGHTEEN

Innovating with Information Systems for Global Reach   *638*

FOCUS MINICASE: Global Business Calls for
Global Suppliers   *639*

Business Role and Structure of Information Systems

Part One of the text will tell you how to achieve business results using information systems and will introduce their fundamental concepts. We will stress the use of information systems for business transformation and for competition in the global marketplace.

Chapter One will discuss what information systems are and the information system literacy you will acquire using this text. Computers and telecommunications—the two interrelated enabling technologies of information systems—will be introduced. You will see how these technologies make possible new ways to build organizations and new ways to work. We will describe the principal capabilities of information systems and show how to deploy them for business results. We will also take an initial look at the human side of the pervasive use of information systems.

Chapter Two will present the fundamental concepts of information and systems as applied to the informational needs of management and organizations. Five principal components of information systems will be introduced. We will also describe the specific types of information systems that enterprises use to support their operations, management, and knowledge work.

Chapter Three will characterize the competitive environment of our information society and show how information systems have evolved to help organizations compete in this environment. Business globalization will be portrayed as a principal characteristic of today's competition. The major thrusts in using strategic information systems to seek competitive advantage will be discussed. Strategies, forces, and tactics in competitive markets will be related to the deployment of strategic information systems. A firm's value chain will be used to identify opportunities for implementing strategic information systems, in some cases by creating a virtual value chain of information.

The first part of the book as a whole will introduce the principal themes of the text:

- Strategic use of information systems in business competition.
- Transformation of business processes with information systems.
- Movement to electronic commerce by using the rapidly growing resources of the Internet.
- Deployment of information technology in business globalization.
- Knowledge work and the management of organizational knowledge with information systems.
- Total quality management in supporting business with information.

CHAPTER ONE

Introduction to Information Systems and Their Capabilities

OBJECTIVES

After you complete this chapter, you will be able to:

1. Demonstrate understanding of what an information system is and why you need information systems literacy.
2. Identify the types of information systems used in organizations.
3. Specify the business results that can be achieved with properly implemented information systems.
4. Explain how the emerging virtual organizations differ from traditional organizational structures.
5. Discuss the advantages and the drawbacks of telecommuting, and its relationship to information technologies.
6. Specify the 10 principal capabilities of information systems.
7. Understand how information systems capabilities can be used to redesign business processes in order to achieve business results.
8. State and explain the principal ethical issues involved in the development and use of information systems.

OUTLINE

What Can Information Systems Do for You if You Run the Largest Commercial Port in the World?

The Port of Rotterdam in the Netherlands is the largest commercial port in the world. The port is on the New Meuse River near its mouth on the North Sea. Some 30,000 ocean-going vessels and 150,000 river boats pass through every year (see Photo 1.1). With nearly 300 million tons of cargo shipped and with $35 billion in revenues a year, the port faces fierce competition from other ports in Northwest Europe, including Antwerp, Hamburg, and Le Havre. Running a port here is a highly competitive business indeed. As the European economies encounter protracted difficulties, the competition gets keener. This has spurred the Port of Rotterdam authorities to develop Plan 2010, a program to strengthen the port's competitive position and make it the central distribution center of Europe. The plan calls for a 15-year investment of about $23 billion. A significant part of the sum will be spent on information systems, in recognition of their vital role in the business of the port.

"Port business is becoming very dependent on quick information exchange between the companies," says Koos van der Steenhoven, director of strategic planning for the port. Thousands of independent firms that patronize the port and provide services there, such as large oil companies, medium-size freight forwarders, or small customs brokers, need to have their information systems connected with those of the port for fast exchange of cargo manifests, import permits, and other business documents. In the future paper-based documentation will be exchanged in digital form, between the

Photo 1.1

The Port of Rotterdam, the largest commercial port in the world, is embarking on an ambitious plan to use information technology for competitive advantage. (From Richard Pastore, "First Port of Call," CIO, October 15, 1995, p. 52.)

computers of the interested parties. The port must provide the central node for this system and support the informational efforts of all its business partners.

There are examples of success that the Port of Rotterdam can emulate. It is thanks to a similar system of electronic data interchange (EDI) that the Port of Singapore in the South China Sea has been able to reduce the processing of typical ship's trade documents from a minimum of two days and as many as four days to as little as 15 minutes. Keeping a ship in dock an extra day costs its owners dearly, and the computerization of document exchange saves the port's patrons many millions of dollars. In addition, Singapore's system, known as TradeNet, has enabled that port to cut its document processing staff by 75 percent, while the volume of shipments doubled. Thus, the economies of the EDI system benefited both the customers and the port. Rotterdam is eager to learn from the success of Singapore.

As a pilot program, 10 trucking companies already use EDI from their offices to schedule freight pickup and dropoff at the Port of Rotterdam. When container-handling companies join this interorganizational information system, it will be possible to prepare the appropriate freight just in time for the truck arrival. For now, the system has cut in half the average one and three-quarter hours the trucks would previously spend at the terminal; this period will eventually be reduced to 15 to 20 minutes. Even a small company, such as Ammerlaan Transportation, has its trucks stopping at the port 50 to 55 times a day and stands to save significant amounts of money. The pilot program has already made a competitive difference, since other ports in the area have no comparable capability.

The port is also modernizing its integrated Vessel Traffic Management System, an information system that provides traffic controllers with a complete overview of traffic in the port 24 hours a day. Along with providing current information, the system maintains historical data on seagoing ships. The accumulated extensive database helps the port's managers control its current operations as well as plan for the future. The data are available over computer networks spread out in a 62-mile radius. As the computer hardware is replaced and the software modified under Plan 2010, the Port of Rotterdam expects to lower its annual information systems costs, while acquiring significant business benefits from this system.

Operating in a way as a private company and in a way as a government agency, the port has initiated a long-range plan with Rotterdam's Erasmus University to enhance the information systems education there. The port will need superior information systems specialists to help it use the new technologies for competitive advantage. It will also need business managers who know how to use information systems to achieve business results.

Based on Richard Pastore, "First Port of Call." *CIO*, October 15, 1995, pp. 50–54; Teo, Hock Hai and others, "Organizational Transformation Using Electronic Data Interchange: The Case of TradeNet in Singapore," *Journal of Management Information Systems*, 13, no. 4 (Spring 1997); and the World Wide Web site of the Port of Rotterdam http://www.MediaPort.org/uk/port.

Today's organizations cannot be operated or managed effectively without information systems that are built using a range of information technologies. The result of this is that your performance as a manager, a professional, or an entrepreneur will depend on your information systems literacy—on your ability to exploit the capabilities of information systems to achieve business results.

1.1   WHAT ARE INFORMATION SYSTEMS?

An **information system** is an organized set of components for collecting, transmitting, storing, and processing data in order to deliver information for action. In business firms and other organizations, this information is necessary for both operations and management. Most information systems in today's organizations are built around the information technologies of computers and telecommunications—they are computer-based information systems. As you read in the Focus Minicase, the Port of Rotterdam's expanding information systems help the organization run its day-to-day business, and also plan for the future. They also help the port to cooperate with its business partners and compete in the marketplace.

In the next chapter, we will look more closely at the concepts involved in the definition of information systems. But before we do that, here is an example of why every manager and professional today must be proficient with these systems.

Let us say you become a newly minted sales representative. You will need to manage your accounts with an information system that helps you identify promising leads, maintain information about ongoing relationships with your clients, make current product information available to these clients, and perform the necessary corporate reporting. Information will reach you through a number of systems. You will communicate with your clients over wide area computer networks such as the Internet and interact over local area networks of personal computers with the teammates who will work with you on projects. You will need to access external information bases and work with the corporate marketing and sales system. Using your notebook computer, you will prepare your budgets and client presentations, wherever you are at the time. You can easily see that your professional performance will depend on your understanding of information systems in the context of your business.

As a manager or an entrepreneur, you may seek competitive advantage for your firm by exploiting the potential of information systems. In this text you will encounter many examples of small entrepreneurial companies that successfully compete in this way. In the global environment of today's business, your reach may easily cross national boundaries. A privately held travel agency, Rosenbluth Travel in Philadelphia, reached the pinnacle of its business segment by collecting and processing information in order to give corporate travelers the best deals. It then allied itself with travel agencies across the globe, creating by means of telecommunications a virtual corporation. A world traveler can deal with any allied local agency as though he or she were dealing directly with Rosenbluth. Customer loyalty is very high (Miller 1993). In recent years, Internet's World Wide Web has attracted much entrepreneurial energy and ingenuity. Read about it in the vignette on the next page.

As we approach the twenty-first century, information technology emerges as the fundamental technology of business. It enables efficient operations of a small business or a large corporation; it makes possible effective management; and it supports the search for competitive advantage in the marketplace. Economic growth, that is, growing productivity of resources, is based on moving to newer and more advanced technologies.

With the economic unification of Western Europe, the exceptionally high economic growth rates in the Pacific Rim, and the progressive entry into the market economy of the countries of Eastern Europe and the former Soviet Union, the world is becoming a global economy. This global division of labor is expected to lead to greater productivity throughout the world. Information technologies enable and drive this progress. Information technologies make global cooperation possible. Along with the relatively free flow of capital and other tangible resources throughout the world, the flow of information has emerged as a

IN THE SPOTLIGHT

Becoming an Information System Entrepreneur

Photo 1.2

Jeff Bezos, the founder and chief executive officer of Amazon.com. (From Fast Company, October/November 1996, p. 132.)

Jeff Bezos (pictured in Photo 1.2) has founded the largest bookstore in the world—with no store and few books in stock. Bezos's bookstore, Amazon.com, is on the Internet's World Wide Web. Customers can search the company's book database by title, subject, author, or keyword. Payment is by credit card, either by phone or via a secured Web transaction. Once ordered via the Web site, the book is shipped by the distributor to Amazon.com's warehouse and the customer usually receives it within five days of ordering.

A Wall Street trader when he ventured into electronic commerce, Bezos promptly realized the potential of the Internet's explosive growth for on-line retailing. Just a few months after he raised the start-up capital from private investors, his Web-based bookstore was open for business. It has been attracting customers and highly favorable attention from the business world ever since its inception in 1994. Let's learn from some of the opinions of its founder:

Why is Amazon.com flourishing? Because we're delivering a value proposition that can't be delivered any other way . . . When the Web first caught my attention, I made a list of 20 product categories [that could be retailed on the Web]—books,

music, computer hardware and software—and investigated the merits of selling them on-line. Books were far and away the best category.

What's special about books? There are so many of them! There are 1.5 million English-language books in print, 3 million books in all languages worldwide. This volume defined the opportunity . . . The biggest phenomenon in retailing is the big-format store—the "category killer"—whether it's selling books, toys, or music.

But the largest physical bookstore in the world has only 175,000 titles. We have 1.1 [more recently 2.5] million titles. And you can't offer our selection in a catalog. If you printed the Amazon.com catalog, it would be the size of seven New York City phone books. The only way to build a 1.1 million-title bookstore is on the Web.

You've explained the competitive opportunity. How do you create competitive advantage against potential rivals? People who just scratch the surface of Amazon.com—"oh, you sell books on the Web"—don't understand how hard it is to actually be an electronic merchant. We're not just putting up a Web site. There are very few off-the-shelf tools that help do what we're doing. We've had to develop lots of our own [information] technologies . . . In a way, this is good news. There are lots of barriers to entry.

Based on William C. Taylor, "Who's Writing the Book on Web Business? (. . . Amazon.com)," *Fast Company,* October/November 1996, pp. 132–33; and Michael Martin, "The Next Big Thing: A Bookstore?" *Fortune,* December 9, 1996, pp. 168–70. You may visit the company's Web site at http://www.amazon.com.

major factor in the globalization of business. Information technologies are also a principal factor in global competition through which each nation can seek a higher standard of living.

The globalization of business and pervasive technological change bring challenges to national economies and to the lives of all of us. As corporations compete in the global environment, jobs can be moved to countries with lower labor costs, with information technologies facilitating the necessary communication and collaboration. Information technologies may also become an enabler of changes leading to downsizing companies and

IN THE SPOTLIGHT

You May Not Choose a Career in Information Systems, But…

Let Michele Chocholek tell you why she chose a career in information systems (IS)—and you will understand better what information systems literacy is. With an MBA from the University of Minnesota and two years' experience in IS, Chocholek is a systems analyst with the 3M Corporation. Here are some of her responses:

Why a career in IS? Three primary reasons are the ability to provide technology solutions to business problems, the dynamic nature of technology, and the need for a communications link between business professionals and technology professionals.

Rewards? The greatest reward has been witnessing the application of technology to solve a problem, more than just applying technology for the sake of technology.

Challenges? The toughest thing for me is understanding the business needs without having done the job. It requires learning to ask the right questions of the right people. Another challenge is understanding the capabilities of technology.

You and IS in 10 years? IS is [becoming] a driving force in the business world, yet it is still far from being a major player. In the next 10 years, I think IS will hold its own in the marketing, finance, production, and [other] functional areas of today. IS will more directly shape the direction of the business world. I see myself involved with IS; however, since I am a business-oriented person, I see myself in a role that is more involved with strategic planning, applying the functional abilities of IS to finance and production.

Based on Melanie Menagh, "Newcomers Expectations and Challenges," *Computerworld Best Places to Work,* June 15, 1994, p. 26.

people needing retraining. It is vital to understand the potential effects of new technologies and utilize them for the greatest possible benefit.

As you may conclude, information systems literacy (and not just computer literacy!) is necessary to perform your job as a manager or a professional, to conduct a firm's activities, and to seek opportunities in the marketplace for the products of a firm or of a nation. As a computer-literate person, you may be able to select the personal computer equipment you need, and you will then use your computer system effectively in many pursuits, from managing your investments to interacting with others over the Internet. Information systems literacy goes well beyond that. **Information systems literacy** gives you the knowledge you need to apply information technology in a business setting to support your own work, the work of your team, and the operations of the organization at large in pursuit of its competitive goals (as you can read in the above vignette). Since information-systems thinking pervades all organizational activities, information technology has become too important to be left to the information systems specialists. All of us who want to contribute to economic activity need information systems literacy. Let us proceed to acquire it.

1.2   WHAT DO INFORMATION SYSTEMS DO FOR ORGANIZATIONS?

Information systems in organizations include systems that support business operations of the firm, systems that support its management, and systems that assist general **knowledge work,** that is, work with abstract information rather than with tangible materials. For example, in Wal-Mart Stores, the point-of-sales system supports the operations conducted at sales registers. An information system automatically triggers electronic orders for store merchandise to be replenished, that go from Wal-Mart's computers directly to

Figure 1.1

Information systems in organizations

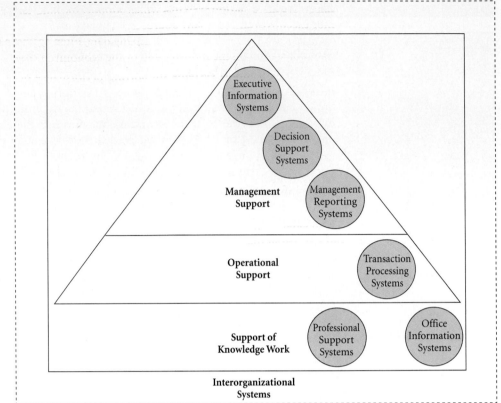

the computers of the firm's suppliers. The massive volume of data acquired daily by these operational information systems from billions of sale transactions are processed to provide the firm's managers with the ability to plan the development of new stores and make sure that the existing ones are properly operated. Using this information and supported in their knowledge work by specialized information systems for market research, the company's marketing specialists can plan cost-effective advertising campaigns for the coming season.

Organizational information systems are shown in Figure 1.1. The outside frame indicates that these systems are frequently interconnected with systems of other firms into interorganizational systems (remember the electronic orders Wal-Mart's system sends to the suppliers' systems?).

Specifically, information systems include:

- **Transaction processing systems** necessary for operational data processing, for example, to register customer orders, and to produce invoices and payroll checks. Each transaction is an elementary business activity, such as a sale or a shipment of goods.

- **Management reporting systems**[1] capable of producing reports for specific time periods, designed for managers responsible for specific functions or processes in a firm. Using these reports, managers are able to control their area of responsibility.

- **Decision support systems,** expressly designed for the support of individual and collective decision making. Such a system can help you to decide, for example, how much money you should budget for your sales team in Florida over the next quarter, considering the current sales forecast.

- **Executive information systems,** which support the long-term, strategic view that senior executives and company boards need to take of the business. These systems provide easy access to summarized company data, often against a background of external information on the industry and of the economy at large.

- **Professional support systems** supporting performance of tasks specific to a given profession. Such systems support lawyers in performing legal research and assembling legal documents, architects in designing the exteriors and interiors of buildings, designers in modeling a new automobile model, commercial artists in producing an advertising campaign, or biologists who are developing a new pharmaceutical product. All of these tasks are examples of knowledge work. A graphical report produced by a system supporting a bank's business analysts is shown in Figure 1.2.

- **Office information systems,** which support and help coordinate knowledge work in an office environment by handling documents and messages in a variety of forms—text, data, image, and voice.

You will study the capabilities, structures, and uses of all these types of information systems in this text. As operational support systems, transaction processing systems assist in the day-to-day activities of the enterprise by keeping track of its resources and commitments. Through such systems, a manufacturing company can track the inventory of finished goods, a bank can maintain the status of demand deposits for its customers, and a distributor's system can answer customer queries regarding orders. The primary function of operational support systems is thus transaction processing.

Management support systems assist the various levels of management in controlling their business units. Through management reporting systems, managers are able to obtain summary reports on past, current, and projected activity within their areas of responsibility. Decision support systems allow managers to consider various courses of future action and see projected results in order to plan future activities. With an executive information

Figure 1.2

A report produced by a professional support system that uses geographical information software The report shows the comparative use of tellers and automatic teller machines (ATMs) in the area of the owner bank's operations. This report has been placed on the corporate network and is seen in a Netscape browser screen. (Courtesy of MapInfo, Troy, New York) (From *InformationWeek,* November 4, 1996, p. 104.)

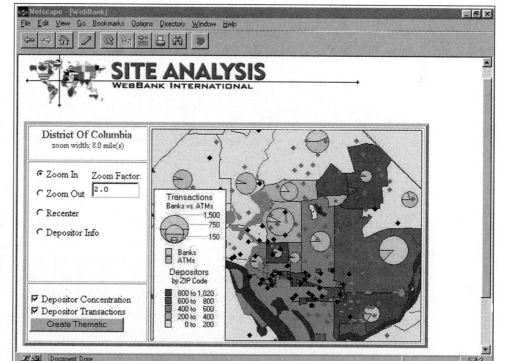

system, executives are able to get an overview of the company's operations, compare company performance with competitors, and obtain detailed information on any aspect they want to review in depth.

Office information systems and professional support systems help with diverse aspects of individual and group knowledge work. The range of this type of support is broad and growing. An individual may maintain his or her business calendar and communicate with co-workers through electronic mail; in some systems you can send images and voice messages along with text. In an insurance company, the flow of paper policies may be replaced by electronic documents processed with an information system. Corporate lawyers rely on external and internal databases of case law and on boilerplate templates to produce briefs and other legal documentation. Using the resources of the Internet's World Wide Web, a team of collaborators widely dispersed in space and working at different times can complete a project faster than people working side by side. Taken together, information systems are transforming the way organizations are managed and the way they operate (Jarvenpaa and Ives 1994).

In many cases, the information systems of an organization become connected to those of its suppliers, customers, and business partners, or to the providers of information about the external environment in which the firm operates. All of these are increasingly connected into **interorganizational systems** that help several firms share information in order to coordinate their work, collaborate on common projects, or sell and buy products and services. Such a shared system may, for example, permit a hotel chain and an airline to sell bundled flight tickets and hotel reservations and then identify and reward their best customers. The facilities of the Internet are increasingly deployed to create such systems. In the Focus Minicase, you encountered an interorganizational system in the making which is helping the Port of Rotterdam to work with its business partners. Interorganizational systems speed the flow of information between companies and may give the participants a competitive edge.

Indeed, it is increasingly common to develop certain information systems to help firms compete in the marketplace. A transaction processing system for ordering your products, with terminals installed at thousands of client sites, which satisfies the specialized requirements of each client, is an example of a strategic information system. A **strategic information system** assists a firm in realizing its long-term competitive goals. We will see many examples of such systems in the text.

Since the implementation of an information system is a considerable investment on the part of the owner firm, the system should pay for itself in business results. We will show how to calculate tangible business outcomes in Section 13.3. However, the most important benefits that can stem from a properly implemented information system are listed in Table 1.1. As you may conclude from the table, some of these outcomes are directly re-

Table 1.1	
Possible business results from information systems	1. Enhanced competitive position (increased market share or profits).
	2. Increased productivity (lower costs per unit of output).
	3. Improved quality of products or services leading to higher customer satisfaction.
	4. Improved decision-making ability.
	5. Ability to respond faster to the demands of the marketplace.
	6. Enhanced ability to communicate and collaborate within the firm and with customers and suppliers.
	7. Enhanced goodwill of employees.

IN THE SPOTLIGHT

Information Systems for Business Results

McDonnell Douglas Helicopter Systems of Mesa, Arizona, sells commercial aircraft with many customized features. The paper-based purchasing process used to take 48 days and try the customer's patience with errors and omissions. To solve this problem, a multimedia sales-support system was implemented. Salespeople are now outfitted with portable Macintosh PowerBooks from Apple Computer, equipped with portable printers. Each notebook computer's memory contains full-motion video, animation, and graphics that help the customer visualize the helicopter. The sales support system helps customers design their own instrument panel layout for the cockpit and select the color scheme. The entire configuration of the craft is checked out by a computerized expert system. When it is found satisfactory, a legal purchase document can be printed out at the customer's site in minutes. This instant check-out and pricing are possible thanks to the central database (kept on the more powerful server computer at the office), where preapproved prices for all possible options and configurations are stored. The portables can access the database by linking with a modem and the AppleTalk remote access software into the Ethernet local area network at the McDonnell Douglas office right from the customer's site. Salespeople can run several what-if scenarios for customers to enable them to fit their budget.

The sales cycle takes 8 days—down 83 percent from the 48 days that the selling based on paper brochures and verbal price negotiating used to take. The worldwide sales staff was cut from 74 to 18 people, with nearly four times the number of purchase agreements produced per employee. New product lines are now being introduced without staffing up. The total cost of the sales support system over the three years of its development and operation was $230,000. Benefits due to saved labor and avoiding rework (which used to be necessary because of errors in the produced helicopter specifications) for the same three years are estimated at $840,000. But benefits go well beyond these numbers. "It's difficult to quantify the financial impact of being more responsive and conveying a professional image," says the manager of business development for McDonnell Douglas, Alan Neugebauer, "but customers are impressed by the fact that none of our competitors have a system like ours."

Telogy Inc. of Menlo Park, California, is a privately held 250-employee firm that competes with such giants as General Electric, Hewlett-Packard, and Japan's Anritsu in the global electronic test equipment market. The firm doesn't manufacture its own equipment but customizes devices made by others or refurbishes used devices for sale, rent, or long-term lease. Telogy's annual revenues (about $100 million) grow by 24 percent, far surpassing the industry average growth of 4 percent—a clear sign of competitive advantage.

Over a period of three years, the company streamlined its business processes (sales, order fulfillment, customer support customizing the equipment) and then acquired and customized off-the-shelf software packages to support them. The new processes rely on teams that are fully responsible for them. The packages include a sales and marketing system from Aurum Software and a manufacturing resource planning system from TXbase Systems. Run in a client/server configuration with Sun Microsystems servers, the distributed system provides access to the users working on their personal computers through a Windows client interface. In other words, computational tasks are divided between the more powerful server computers and the client computers—the users' PCs. All the components of the system access a central database. Some of the marketing information is being moved to the World Wide Web on the Internet.

Thanks to the business processes redesigned around the teamwork and use of the database, customer-order fulfillment has been reduced from 11 to 3 days. The sales department now has detailed account histories for each client and can customize the sales pitch. Customers can check the status of their order by calling a voice-activated 24-hour automated order-tracking system, unique to this market.

Management support systems help spot trends quickly through the analysis of new orders. This enables the firm to compete in the rapidly changing marketplace, where it is easy to accumulate large inventories of outdated equipment. The company does business

Continued

globally and the system links all the sites. This means that the international headquarters in Brussels receives a price update the instant it is entered in a California office. Indeed, the system development process itself was accelerated by hiring contractors in India for well-defined parts of the work, thereby enabling around-the-clock development at a moderate cost.

The company calculates that the investment of $5.8 million in the development of the system will return over $3 million annually

for at least five years. The increased sales and reduced inventories are tangible benefits; the ability to compete globally against far larger companies is certainly as important a business result.

Based on Megan Santosus, "Birds on a Wire," *CIO,* February 1, 1996, pp. 28–30; Peter Fabris, "Orders of Magnitude," *CIO,* February 1, 1996, pp. 52–54; and Tom Field, "Covering New Territory," *CIO,* September 15, 1996, pp. 66–74.

lated to business competition, while others such as improved decision-making ability or enhanced employee goodwill, make your firm a stronger competitor indirectly.

Consider what business results were achieved by the two very different companies described in the preceding vignette.

The two companies described in the vignette are no exception. Since 1991, corporate investment on information technology in the United States outpaces capital spending on all other types of machinery. U.S. business corporations typically spend 4 percent of their annual revenue on information systems. In particular, financial corporations such as banks, brokerage houses, or insurance companies, are far more dependent on their information systems than are manufacturing concerns. After all, the "visible" assets of a financial company amount to bit patterns in computer storage, representing investments, cash on hand, or insurance premiums. Thus, small banks spend approximately 7 percent, and large banks up to 13 to 16 percent, of their budgets on information systems. On the average, business firms now earn impressive returns on their investment in information systems (Brynjolfsson and Hitt 1996). Spending on information systems bears, on average, higher returns than other types of capital investment. In the vignette on page 13, the words of one of the most experienced information systems managers and thinkers will tell you that it takes knowledge and effort to achieve these business results.

1.3 | THE ENABLING TECHNOLOGIES: COMPUTERS AND TELECOMMUNICATIONS

Information systems today are largely computer-based. Although variety of information technologies are deployed in building these systems, the principal information technologies relate to computers and telecommunications.

A **computer** is an electronic general-purpose information processor. As a matter of fact, computers are used to search for data more frequently than they are used to compute. Further along in this chapter, we will study the capabilities that computer-based information systems offer organizations, and we will see how far they go beyond "computing." Computer programs, also called **software,** adapt general-purpose computers to the task at hand. For example, expert systems are a software technology that offers advice in specific classes of problems, such as diagnosing equipment malfunction or evaluating an investment. Computer **hardware** consists of the physical devices employed in computer systems. It is the software that makes the hardware useful.

People, Not Information Systems, Produce Business Results

"After 20 years of research, I have found that computers indeed add a great deal of value to well-managed companies. But computers aren't an unqualified blessing. Identical machines with identical software will make things worse if the enterprise is mismanaged. . . . Computers are only the catalysts. Business values are created by well-organized, well-motivated, knowledgeable people who understand what to do with the information that shows up on computer screens."

Paul A. Strassman, who served as the chief information officer (CIO) to several major organizations, including Xerox and the Pentagon, in "Computers Don't Make Money. People Do." *Computerworld*, February 19, 1996, p. 72.

Most information systems comprise multiple computers. They range from supercomputers, costing millions of dollars and processing billions of instructions per second, to inexpensive micro-processors embedded, for example, in point-of-sale terminals. The large machines can sift through a customer database to find prospects for a new service. They can also run elaborate economic forecasting models to position the company's products for the next two years, relying on the massive data accumulated in the sales database. The point-of-sale terminals may simply collect and transmit data about the items being sold. Indeed, one of the tasks of an information system comprising both of these computer categories is to collect the details of all the sales into a database that will help in marketing and in the long-term demand forecasting for product inventory. Information systems encompass many personal computers that are networked workstations of end users—people who use computers to perform their work.

In the information systems of today, computer technology is virtually inseparable from **telecommunications:** electronic transmission of information over distances. Most information systems are distributed locally or geographically, and it is the telecommunications technology that unifies them. Indeed, in our example, remote point-of-sale terminals are connected through a telecommunications network to a central computer that enters the transactional data into a database and processes the data as needed. This system of computers and telecommunications is a **computer network.** Organizations deploy a variety of such networks to match their structure and business goals.

A public computer network known as the **Internet,** which is actually a network of networks without any central control, has become the essential worldwide information utility. The Internet offers its users such facilities as electronic mail (E-mail), Telnet (for running programs on remote computers), and FTP (a *file transfer protocol* used to transfer large collections of data, text, and images). The most widely used facility of the Internet has become the **World Wide Web**—a collection of multimedia (text, numbers, photos, graphics, voice, moving images) databases stored in computers known as servers located all over the world. The components of these databases are interlinked and form so-called hypermedia that the user can navigate (surf) using programs known as browsers. We will discuss the Internet facilities in more depth in Chapter 7.

When looked at in more detail, information systems draw on a variety of information technologies. Videoconferencing via the screens of their personal computers helps team-members at different sites to communicate and work together. Digital image processing replaces paper-based information with digitized images that can be entered into computer systems and manipulated and communicated as needed. Virtual reality systems make their users feel part of an artificial world created with computer graphics—say, for example, while testing a prototype car that exists only in the computer's memory. These and many other technologies will be discussed in this text.

Information technologies are used by organizations to further organizational goals, such as increasing sales, speeding up order processing, or improving teamwork. Let us now turn our attention to the new organizational environment and new ways of working enabled by information technologies. We will then study the specific capabilities that information systems offer organizations.

1.4   NEW ORGANIZATIONAL ENVIRONMENT AND NEW WAYS TO WORK

Information technologies are widely deployed in the organizations structured in the traditional fashion, that is, built of relatively fixed, hierarchical, and specialized units. At the same time, information technologies are enabling a change toward new types of business organizations, often called virtual organizations. These firms have flexible boundaries, as many of the firms' functions are actually performed by specialized business partners. Equally flexible are the basic business units of a virtual organization, as it is formed of clusters of project-oriented teams. By allowing people to work away from the office, information technologies are a foundation of new working arrangements, such as telecommuting from a virtual workplace.

Traditional Organizational Structures

To function, organizations have to be structured into subdivisions that take responsibility for their own results and together contribute to corporate objectives. Traditionally, a business organization has been structured along functional or divisional lines.

In a **functional structure,** people who perform similar activities are placed together in formal units and thus the organization is subdivided in accordance with the functions of the enterprise. Any firm that provides goods or services has several functions to perform: marketing and sales (developing markets for the company's products and selling them); production (creating or adding value by manufacturing goods or offering services); accounting and finance (managing the funds of the enterprise); and human resources (attracting and developing a quality workforce). Depending on the nature of the firm, additional functional units may be included, such as research and development (R&D) and logistics (warehousing and distributing the inventory).

A diagram presenting the arrangement of work positions in an organization is called an **organization chart.** A chart for a company with a functional structure is shown in Figure 1.3a.

Although functional structure helps to develop strong skills within various functional units, it suffers from significant disadvantages. These drawbacks include poor coordination of effort across functions—with many decisions referred up the corporate hierarchy—and the lack of clear responsibility for the overall product or service. All of this slows down the innovation necessary to respond to the rapidly changing competitive environment of today.

An alternative is the **divisional structure** in which company divisions are formed based on the groups of products or services they deliver, geographic region they cover, or customer segment they serve. A divisional structure based on product groups is shown in Figure 1.3b. Divisional structures display a greater flexibility in responding to the competitive demands of the marketplace. They often suffer, however, from duplicating resources

Figure 1.3

Organization charts of companies with traditional structures

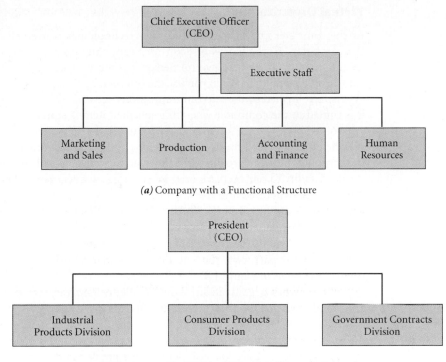

(a) Company with a Functional Structure

(b) Company with a Divisional Structure (by product group)

and efforts across divisions (marketing people, for example, have to be spread around several geographic divisions) and from less developed functional expertise.

The traditional organizational structures are defined by clear and lasting assignment of roles to all members, clear lines of responsibility and command, and clear setting of the boundaries of the firm against the environment. Stability is the hallmark. Multilayered organization charts define the longlasting hierarchical structure of such an organization. The reliance on traditional organizational structures has significant general drawbacks, however. Relative permanence and rigidity of both functional and divisional structures often lead to a lack of coordination across the corporation's units and to units pursuing their own, as opposed to organizational, goals. Multiple layers of management separate the line workers from the top managers; layers of middle managers carry information up the hierarchy and decisions down to the "troops." The process is slow and distortions (self-serving, perhaps, on the part of some managers) may result.

Information systems are widely used within the traditional hierarchical functional or divisional structures, which still prevail in organizational design. In Chapter 12 we will see how information systems are employed to support the various functions of an enterprise. Indeed, information systems may be deployed to reinforce any desired corporate structure, from highly centralized to decentralized (George and King 1991). However, the highly competitive environment of today has led to the development of alternative organizational forms aimed at innovation and flexibility. Shrinking lifetimes of product and services and the need to satisfy specific demands of individual customers call for these objectives. These new kinds of business organizations, enabled by information technology, are known as virtual organizations.

Virtual Organizations

As the computer and telecommunications technologies converged, "the network became the computer," in the words of Scott McNealy, chief executive of Sun Microsystems, the leading manufacturer of powerful personal computers known as technical workstations. Consider what happens when you use the Internet: Your request for information is sent into cyberspace, formed by the telecommunications networks, and managed by computers until it is routed to the computer where the specified item is stored. Then that item is accessed and routed back to you. You may also wish to use the Telnet facility of the Internet to run a specific program on a remote computer. It is as though the varied information resources of the computer network are directly connected to your personal computer.

The ability to rely on computer networks has opened new vistas for the way organizations can be structured and the way people in these organizations can work. A **virtual organization** is an organization whose structure is to a large degree created by using information systems rather than following organization charts[2]. Virtual organizations no longer rely on bricks and mortar for containing and shaping them (Goldman 1995). These organizations can depart from the traditional hierarchical organizations in two principal respects, illustrated in Figure 1.4.

In a **network organization,** shown in Figure 1.4a, the firm itself becomes the core of an extended virtual organization that includes long-term corporate partners who supply goods and services to the core firm. Each of the firms participating in the network organization exercises its **core competencies,** the specific capabilities it has developed that are valued by the marketplace. The ability to deliver goods rapidly anywhere in the world, while maintaining information about their whereabouts at all times, is an example of core competence. Together, a network of small companies can present the appearance of a large corporation. Indeed, an entrepreneur, supported by only a few employees, is frequently at the core of such a virtual organization. This becomes possible when most of the production and services are **outsourced,** that is, provided by specialized suppliers under long-term contracts.

Network organizations are able to exist through the use of computers and wide area telecommunications networks (Tapscott 1996). Thanks to them, for example, product specifications can be developed in an electronic form and then discussed and modified during computerized videoconferences among employees of different companies; product supply can be coordinated using electronic orders as sales take place, replacing time-consuming and error-prone paperwork. Electronic collaboration on many projects, such as planning advertising campaigns or financing a new venture, leads to the rapid deployment of combined and complementary core competencies of several corporations. Wide area networks, and the Internet in particular, help the partnering firms to conquer the limitations imposed by geographic distances.

An organization that wants to sustain its ability to be the core of a virtual organization needs to carefully maintain and hone its capabilities, lest it become superfluous and wither away (Chesbrough and Teece 1996). Typically, the capabilities in designing and marketing new products need to be safeguarded. At the same time, as the use of information technology has become more pervasive, an organization can outsource its functions to outside suppliers. As a result, the average size of the business firm in the United States has decreased (Brynjolfsson 1994). In fact, smaller firms have become vigorous job generators.

The vignette on page 18 presents an excellent example of a virtual organization.

Another hallmark of many virtual organizations is their reliance on teamwork for many of the most important projects. In a **cluster organization** (known also as an *adhocracy,* since the team structures are often created ad hoc or as the need arises), the principal work units are both permanent and temporary teams of people who contribute their distinct knowledge and experience (see Figure 1.4b). These teams may be organized into larger organizational clusters (Mills 1991). Some teams, called business units, have external ("real") customers. Others, called staff units, have customers internal to the company (for example, they may design products to be manufactured by the firm). Project teams are created for the duration of the given project. Alliance teams include the members of the organization and the employees of its business partners. In the alliance teams, two features of virtual organizations (i.e., inter- and intraorganizational partnership) meet. In larger organizations, teams usually coexist with the general functional or divisional structure. In these cases, cross-functional teams, composed of people representing a variety of functional expertise, can be fast problem solvers and innovators.

Teams are greatly assisted in their work by the availability of office information systems such as groupware—software that helps team members to communicate and collaborate.

Figure 1.4

Structures of virtual organizations

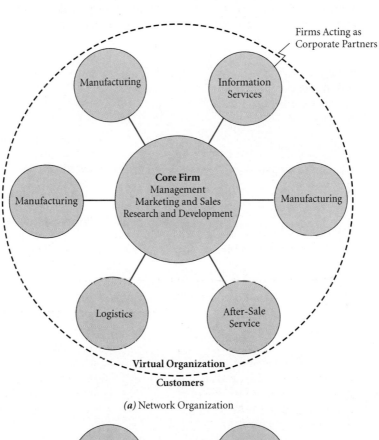

(a) Network Organization

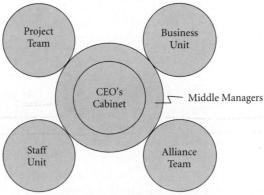

(b) Cluster Organization

A Blooming Business

Calyx and Corolla, of San Francisco, has been created as a network organization. Ruth Owades, the firm's entrepreneurial founder, realized that consumers would welcome guaranteed next-day delivery of flower arrangements fresher than those at the local flower shop. To respond to this perceived need, Owades has devised a network of companies, involving a number of firms other than her own. The overall virtual company is shown in Figure 1.5. It prominently includes the growers and Federal Express (FedEx) as the overnight delivery company.

The very day that Calyx and Corolla receives the order, the grower cuts the flowers and ships them directly to the customer, to arrive at their destination the next day. When a customer orders flowers from Calyx and Corolla, an order-entry system assigns the order a six-digit order number and a ten-digit FedEx airbill number (from a bank of numbers received from FedEx). Each of the 25 flower growers that supply Calyx and Corolla has at least one personal computer running custom order-processing software. The growers' PCs obtain the order information via telephone links from the flower delivery company. Their information systems print out the orders along with a shipping label bearing a FedEx bar code. The grower assembles the flowers, vase, card, and message according to the order, and affixes the label.

By using information systems, the entrepreneur has solved the problem of how to provide a direct link from the growers to the customers, with her company reaping a part of the benefits. The extensive information systems maintained by FedEx permit tracking of orders. To go beyond the operations, all the information needed to manage the company can be obtained from the data that are collected by its information system as the orders are filled.

Based on Joe Panepinto, "Special Delivery," *Computerworld,* March 7, 1994, pp. 79–82; Stephanie Strom, "In the Mailbox, Roses and Profits," *The New York Times,* February 14, 1994, pp. D1 & D4; Lynda M. Applegate and Janis Gogan, "Electronic Commerce: Trends and Opportunities," Harvard Business School note 9–196–006, 1995.

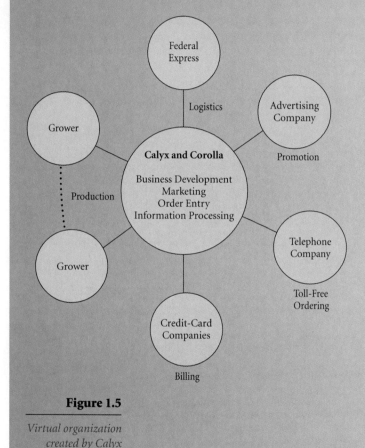

Figure 1.5

Virtual organization created by Calyx and Corolla

Many teams increasingly rely on the use of an **intranet,** an internal corporate network that deploys the Internet facilities, primarily those of the World Wide Web (interorganizational teams may rely on the similar extranets, accessible to the members of the cooperating companies). These networks have emerged as leading computerized tools for information sharing, as users post electronic pages with documents and work-in-progress on their intranet. Discussed in more detail in Chapter 8, groupware and intranets are essential tools for communication and collaboration among team members (Cortese 1996; Wilder 1997).

Telecommuting and Virtual Workplaces

"Work is the thing you do, not the place you go to" has become the slogan of the emerging new workplace. Information systems built around the ever more powerful portable computers, mobile telecommunications, and software that supports individual and group knowledge work, have untethered office workers from "real" offices and enable them to work almost anywhere. Thus a **virtual workplace,** any place outside of the corporate office where a worker can perform his or her tasks with the assistance of information technology and, if desired, in communication and collaboration with other workers, has been born.

Virtual workplaces include home offices, "hoteling"-type offices where a large of employees share a small number of workplaces by reserving an office for a day, regional work centers ("telecenters"), customer's premises, and even mobile offices of people such as insurance adjusters. Professional support systems are provided for the tasks specific to the job, and groupware includes the worker in a larger team.

Employees who work in virtual workplaces, outside of their company's premises, are said to be **telecommuting.** A growing phenomenon, telecommuting is estimated to involve some 12 million workers in the United States (Caldwell and Gambon 1996). Benefits to the organization include reduced costs of providing offices and closer interaction by the telecommuting employees with customers and suppliers. Even more important is the fact that telecommuting, when properly supported, leads to higher employee productivity. Telecommuting employees take responsibility for their work and are often under less stress. Many of them gain a sense of autonomy and control (Jacobs and Van Sell 1996). Their private life can improve and they can use time more efficiently. Telecommuting jobs are open to housebound people. Benefits to society include more equitable geographic distribution of jobs and a reduction of the social costs of traffic.

Chiat/Day, the advertising company, is among those embracing telecommuting wholeheartedly. The company recognized that moving full-time to virtual workplaces is not easy, requiring extensive preparation and attention to people's needs. It is vital to preserve the corporate culture and the sense of belonging and identity that people derive from their corporate affiliation. Team spirit is fostered by providing attractive common spaces and meeting rooms where employees can learn from one another (see Photo 1.3). The company is

Photo 1.3

The design of this meeting room (called the Fish) at Chiat/Day's premises in Venice (California) is expected to stimulate collaboration combined with independent thinking. There are very few private offices at the firm, since many of its employees telecommute. (From Richard Rapaport, "Jay Chiat Tears Down the Walls," *Forbes ASAP,* October 25, 1993, pp. 25–28.)

experimenting with information systems that permit employees to meet in truly virtual offices that exist only on the computer screen. While remotely collaborating on a project, the participants can see on-screen the faces (known as avatars) of their colleagues.

Telecommuting has several significant drawbacks. Obviously, jobs that require frequent personal interaction with co-workers cannot be moved into a virtual workplace. Telecommuting may lead to a feeling of isolation as well as a loss of visibility necessary for a promotion. Security and confidentiality of information widely dispersed outside of the corporate premises are a concern (Tung and Turban 1996).

As you think about the role information systems play in the organizations you have encountered in this chapter, you may notice that—just as we said before—it goes well beyond what we call computing. Let us now look more closely at the actual capabilities of information systems that can be deployed by firms as they compete in the marketplace.

1.5 | CAPABILITIES OF INFORMATION SYSTEMS

Information systems offer a set of capabilities that can be exploited to achieve business results. Drawing on these capabilities by implementing systems that suit specific business needs enables a firm to respond to the demands of its environment. Here are the 10 principal capabilities of information systems.

1. Fast and Accurate Data Processing, with Large-Capacity Storage and Rapid Communication between Sites

This is the fundamental property of computer systems interconnected with telecommunications links. This capability is exploited by operational support systems, which process massive volumes of business transactions, for example, entering incoming orders or maintaining customer records. This capability is also used to derive management reports from the voluminous data kept in computer storage.

Business opportunities are built on this essential capability. Spears Benzak Salomon & Farrell is a small investment management firm in New York. For more than two decades it had been managing either the funds of individuals who could commit at least $10 million to the firm or large institutional portfolios such as pension funds. By computerizing its operations, the firm of 60 people was able to enter into a strategic alliance with a major brokerage house, Merrill Lynch, in order to provide investment services for accounts starting at $100,000. The large brokerage house performs, in effect, marketing for the small investment boutique that can now cost-effectively handle a large volume of individual accounts.

2. Instantaneous Access to Information

In on-line systems, the contents of a computer database are available for queries in subsecond time. Through the telecommunications capability, a query may be directed to a remote site where the data are actually stored without the user's awareness. Ad-hoc (in other words, not predesigned) queries, introduced directly by end users, may in some cases produce extensive reports. Moreover, the presentation of the data may be individualized for a particular user—with various forms of graphics, for example. Through a variety of internal and external on-line information services, knowledge workers can access textual databases in their area of professional interest. As we will see in Chapter 6, many organizations are accumulating their business data into the so-called *data warehouses* in order to make the data accessible to managers and other workers.

3. Means of Coordination

Coordination brings parts of an organization, or several collaborating organizations, together in a common effort. Coordination is rooted in sharing information and communicating. In the most immediate sense, coordination within an enterprise is assisted by office information systems. The work of a team can be coordinated by planning, scheduling of individual tasks, tracking their fulfillment, and keeping track of deliverable documents in electronic form. As we have already discussed, intranets, or corporate networks for internal use that rely on the Internet facilities, are increasingly a means of this coordination (see Photo 1.4). Although portable computing has widened the reach of information systems to create the "portable manager" whose virtual office can be almost anywhere, that manager's work still has to be coordinated with the work of others.

In a deeper sense, coordinate means to harmonize in a common action or effort. Planning serves to establish common goals at all levels, and managerial control aims to ensure that, once goals are established, organization members pursue them with vigor. Information systems assist extensively with planning and control. Combined with the capability of remote communication, this makes information systems a powerful coordination tool. As you have seen in the Chapter Minicase, interorganizational information systems are increasingly used to coordinate efforts of cooperating enterprises.

Let us look at an example. VeriFone is the world's largest supplier of electronic credit-card verification equipment, through which your cards are swept just about every day as you make your purchases. Although the company has its base in Redwood City, California, it is not considered the corporate headquarters. Almost all of the 2,800 employees of the company in 38 countries are expected to work at any location in the world where pursuit of business brings them. The objective is to move fast in order to close deals and to develop ever new products. New employees get laptop computers as soon as they are hired. Work is coordinated through the massive use of the corporate E-mail system and the exchange of electronic documents. The company's financial information system, RevWatch, provides managers with the current status of the worldwide orders and sales. VeriFone has a strong corporate culture of nimbleness and responsiveness to the customer. It is best seen in the

Photo 1.4

The intranet of Morgan Stanley, demonstrated here by chief information officer Kevin Parker, connects 37 offices of the investment bank around the world. Traders in Japan use the intranet to coordinate their work with their American colleagues. (From Alison L. Sprout, "The Internet Inside Your Company," *Fortune,* November 27, 1995, pp. 161–168.)

rapid coming together of project teams that coordinate their work and seek information from others over the telecommunications networks ("VeriFone" 1994; Maglitta 1996).

4. Boundary Spanning

Aside from the internal role played by information systems *within* an organization, information systems increasingly serve to link an organization to the outside world. This can be accomplished in a variety of ways, some of which may be decisive for business success. For example, electronic data interchange (EDI) systems replace the exchange of paper transaction records by computer-to-computer electronic messaging, resulting in economy, speed, and reliability. Interorganizational systems connect suppliers with customers. The Internet is positioned to play a major role in the emergence of electronic commerce, that is, conducting business over wide area telecommunications networks (Zwass 1996).

Through **boundary-spanning** information systems, the organization receives intelligence about the environment, so necessary to compete successfully. Organizations also use boundary-spanning systems to provide computerized information for their customers, suppliers, and the public at large. Internet sites that contain electronic pages presenting a firm's products and services, and often enabling customers to order and discuss them, are becoming ubiquitous.

Dell Computer Corporation, a maker of personal computers and vigorous direct seller of PCs over the Internet, has created a seven-person team whose task is to monitor the Internet and the on-line information services such as America Online, CompuServe, and Prodigy. The objective is to respond to any messages that mention the firm's products in order to help solve customer problems, to try and change any negative perceptions about the firm's products, and to enhance the company's reputation. Competitive intelligence is another objective: The team members monitor the networks for messages about the performance of rival products, delays in product releases, and just good ideas. Dell has, of course, its own electronic site on the Internet. It offers the firm's current and potential customers extensive product information and the ability to order—it is a storefront, as it were. By providing timely and knowledgeable solutions to customers' problems over the Internet, the firm enhances its reputation. It also cuts the costs of responding to telephone calls to its customer support lines (McWilliams 1997).

5. Support for Decision Making

Along with coordination, decision making is another basic aspect of management. By informing managers and permitting them to select from among alternative courses of action, information systems support the decision-making process. However, it is people who remain the ultimate decision makers in the organization.

With the Sales Decision Support system available at Frito-Lay, the Dallas-based snack food company, its divisional sales managers have all the data within their area of responsibility available to them on their desktop or laptop computers. The detailed data include individual accounts (for example, customers, such as A&P supermarkets), brand sales broken down by store and package type, and the performance of each of the sales representatives. The sales managers can use the data to run computer models that help them decide, for example, whether to increase the number of sales representatives in a district or to obtain more shelf space from a given supermarket for a specific product brand. Problems such as flagging sales in a geographic region can be addressed by immediately considering alternative solutions ("Frito-Lay" 1995).

6. Supporting Organizational Memory and Learning

Organizational memory is the means by which knowledge from the past exerts influence on present organizational activities (Stein and Zwass 1995). This memory preserves the experience the firm has accumulated in delivering its products and services to the marketplace. Thanks to this memory, the firm can continue its operations in the face of employee turnover. This is due to the fact that memory is retained not only in the minds of the firm's employees but also in the firm's structure that casts these employees into appropriate roles, in the business processes of the firm (for example, order processing), and in the corporate culture ("this is the way we treat the customer around here"). Increasingly, elements of the organizational memory reside in the software, and in the data and knowledge bases of companies' information systems.

Consider the following examples. Leading automobile manufacturers, such as Ford Motor Company, preserve in an electronic form the designs of its past products so that they may be modified, improved, and customized as needed, rather than designed afresh. This speeds up the time-to-market and lowers development costs. Ritz-Carlton Hotels maintains databases on the particular requirements of its customers so that employees of the luxury chain can delight repeat guests with superior service. Extensive corporate information systems for managing human resources, such as PRISM of FedEx, maintain histories of employees's training, project experience, and benefit use in order to optimize both the deployment of human resources by the firm and the skill development of individuals.

McKinsey & Company, a top-management consulting firm, has created an information system for knowledge management called Firm Practice Information System (Peters 1992). As consulting projects are carried out by the firm, the project leaders are responsible for replenishing this system with extensive information about what has been learned from the project. Brook Manville, bearing the title of Director of Knowledge Management for McKinsey, considers the information system a "marketplace of readily accessible ideas" that will help in other consulting engagements.

As an organization acquires knowledge and modifies its behavior to reflect this, the organization is said to be learning. Organizational memory, increasingly embedded in information systems, perpetuates what has been learned and is a point of departure for further learning. Organizational learning is necessary for the survival of the firm (Senge 1990).

7. Routinizing Organizational Practice

Operational systems handle transactions in a specific way in every organization. E-mail systems and computer conferencing, both components of office information systems, provide a protocol for the interaction of people within an organization. When an expert system approves or refuses credit card transactions, high consistency of response is assured. These are just two instances of how organizational practice may be defined and made routine through information systems. Routinizing does not mean casting in concrete: Properly designed systems should give an organization the capability to evolve its practices as the environment changes.

Let us look at an example. Putting a print advertisement or a television commercial into production used to be a rather haphazard process at the Young & Rubicam advertising agency. The process involves a number of interactions among the account managers, creative people, media buyers, and researchers. In order to streamline the process, the company now employs workflow software, which maps the needed sequence of steps in the process, and the computerized work products automatically flow to the appropriate person. The major steps are the client request for an ad, reaching an agreement between the vendor and the client, completion of the ad by the vendor, and obtaining client satisfaction. All the people involved follow the charts mapped out with the use of the workflow software, Action Workflow System from Action Technologies. The routinization of organizational practice does not take away from the creativity of the advertising people.

8. Differentiation of Products and Services

Firms compete by making their offerings different from those of their competitors. The capability to differentiate, customize, and individualize the product or service with the use of information in a cost-effective fashion may produce a competitive advantage in the marketplace. FedEx gained significant competitive strength by being the first company able to track shipments along with moving them to their destination. By offering its customers information about the present whereabouts of their shipment in transit, FedEx differentiated its service and, in effect, redefined it. To maintain its lead, the company keeps on developing information systems to differentiate its service. It became the first delivery firm to offer its customers the ability to track their shipments through the FedEx electronic site on the Internet's World Wide Web.

Thanks to the electronically entered specifications and an assembly line equipped with information technology, Panasonic bicycles in Japan can be ordered to suit an individual customer—at a premium price. The bicycle is manufactured to the individual's measurements with selected options and painted to his or her specifications. Combining computer-controlled robots with highly skilled workers, the manufacturer (National Bicycle Industrial Company) is able to produce one of the eleven million possible variations of its product to a customer's order within two weeks (Pine 1993). By individualizing its product, the firm has become a strong competitor in the marketplace previously dominated by large global companies.

9. Modeling

Computers are widely used to model future economic conditions, prospective products, and the environments where the products will operate. A **model** is a simplified representation of a real object or phenomenon, be it an automobile, weather, or future sales. Working with a model helps people concentrate on the relevant aspects of the real thing and perform controlled experiments. The use of software models makes relatively inexpensive, fast, and comprehensive experimentation with a model possible. Computer use can be substituted for the use of more expensive physical resources, and time needed to develop a new car or plane can be shrunk.

Owing to all this, knowledge workers increasingly manipulate models of reality in gaining understanding, designing new products, and studying effects of possible changes (see Photo 1.5). Using computer models, corporate chemists design new molecules with desired pharmaceutical properties. Architects work together with structural engineers on a common electronic building structure, to be cast in concrete in the future. In a broader sense, you may think of the real content of the business software as the model of the business whose operations and management this software supports.

10. Automation

Computerized information systems can fully **automate** certain business functions by replacing human labor. However, it happens more frequently that these systems reduce the

Photo 1.5

Ralph Merkle, a scientist at Xerox's Palo Alto Research Center (PARC), is building a molecular machine by laying atom by atom onto its electronic model. This electronic bricklaying builds nanotechnology; such machines may in the future be able to unclog our arteries (From Russell Mitchell, "Fantastic Journeys in Virtual Labs," *Business Week*, September 19, 1994, pp. 76–88.)

need for routine human labor while changing the nature of the labor required. For example, a point-of-sale (POS) system that automatically enters into the system the data about goods sold (by using bar codes and optical scanners) saves a lot of clerical work that would be needed if the data were entered manually. To exploit its potential fully, such a system gives rise to job functions responsible for maintaining the system's operation as well as those that analyze the voluminous information now available for exploitation.

A special case of automation is production control. Information systems are widely used to control production processes in a flexible manner. Today's systems make it possible to produce cost-effectively "batches of one," that is, customized products on an assembly line. This is known as mass customization. We have encountered it already as a means to differentiate Panasonic bicycles in Japan. Another advantage of automation: Computer-controlled production and processing machines can immediately reject defective components, detect variances, and alert operators to faulty processes, leading to high-quality output. The data on product quality, needed to conduct a total quality management (TQM) program, are obtained automatically. The TQM programs, which you will encounter throughout the book, enhance product quality as the result of upgrading the overall management and operational processes of the firm.

Consider an example of automation. Allen-Bradley of Milwaukee, Wisconsin, has become a strong global competitor in producing electrical relays and contactors because it is able to produce different versions of these devices at mass production speeds within twenty-four hours of receiving the customer order and with zero defects—in lots of one. The computer running the assembly line receives orders electronically from headquarters. It produces a bar-code label that is automatically stuck to the plastic casing of the future product. The label tells each station on the line which of the nearly 200 parts to install. All along, computer-controlled sensors ensure quality: Each product passes through 3,500 automatic inspection steps.

We have summarized and illustrated the capabilities that information systems bring to business competition in Table 1.2.

It takes a skillful and persistent management initiative to exploit specific information systems capabilities in order to achieve business results. In particular, these capabilities enable an organizational restructuring known as business process redesign, introduced in the next section.

Table 1.2	Capability	Examples of Use
Ten capabilities of information systems for business competition.	1. Fast and Accurate Data Processing, with Large-Capacity Storage and Rapid Communication Between Sites	Consolidating financial results in a global corporation.
	2. Instantaneous Access to Information	An executive of a supermarket chain checking yesterday's sales in the morning.
	3. Means of Coordination	Planning and controlling the sales for next quarter. Planning, scheduling, and running a workgroup project.
	4. Boundary Spanning	Investigating the competitive opportunities in a new market.
	5. Support for Decision Making	Drawing up the budget for the sales division to support projected sales volume.
	6. Supporting Organizational Memory and Learning	Using electronic descriptions of your previous products to design new products.
	7. Routinizing Organizational Practice	Processing an insurance policy in electronic form with the support of a workflow system.
	8. Differentiation of Products and Services	Thanks to a flexible manufacturing system, customers can order individual versions of your product. Customers can check the status of your international delivery with half-hour accuracy.
	9. Modeling	Your product is engineered and tested electronically until a final physical prototype is made.
	10. Automation	Your assembly line or your data center is run without human participation.

1.6 | BUSINESS PROCESS REDESIGN: USING THE CAPABILITIES OF INFORMATION SYSTEMS FOR BUSINESS RESULTS

The capabilities of information systems can be used to enhance a firm's business processes. A **business process** is a set of related tasks performed to achieve a defined work product (Davenport 1993; Hammer and Champy 1993). Since a business process produces an outcome or a work product, it has customers. These customers may be either "real," paying, external customers, or internal customers within the firm who have to use this product as an input to their own business process. Both types of customer have to be satisfied with the quality of the product. Here are a few examples of business processes: processing customer orders from receipt to the delivery of goods; creating a marketing plan for a geographical area; developing a new product for a market segment; completely handling loan applications; completely processing insurance claims; ordering input materials from suppliers.

Business process redesign aims to rethink and streamline the business processes of a firm in order to produce business results. It is an important avenue to achieve payoff from information technology. The radical redesign of major business processes, sometimes called **business reengineering,** aims at major gains in costs, quality, or time-to-market, and fundamentally changes the way organizations work.

Business processes are often independent of the existing hierarchical organizational structures that had been largely built up along functional lines, such as marketing or production. For example, in order to process a commercial insurance application, people in several departments of an insurance company may have to be involved, including salespeople, actuaries, and experts in the applicant's line of business. Thus, this business process cuts across departmental divisions and that is why such processes are often handled by task-oriented teams. It is also a reason why business process redesign is difficult to implement. Information technology known as a workflow system can route the insurance application in electronic form to the workstations of the appropriate members of the team, ensuring that as many of them as possible work simultaneously. A principal business result (see Table 1.1) is faster processing of insurance applications, reducing the processing time from perhaps two to three weeks to one business day—and thus enhanced quality of service. If the firm's competitors cannot match this speed, the company enjoys a competitive advantage.

As we can see, information technology is an enabler of business process redesign. In other words, this redesign relies on the capabilities of information technology. How can the capabilities of information systems be brought to bear on business processes? Table 1.3

Table 1.3	**How to Redesign a Business Process**	**Exploited Capability of Information Systems**
Using information systems capabilities in business process redesign	Transform unstructured process into a routine transaction.	Routinizing organizational practice.
	Make process independent of geography by rapidly transferring information across large distances.	Rapid communication between sites.
	Fully or partially automate a process by replacing or reducing human labor.	Automation.
	Bring complex analytical methods to bear on a process.	Support for problem solving. Modeling. Supporting organizational memory and learning.
	Speed up a process by altering sequence of tasks and performing multiple tasks in parallel.	Means of coordination.
	Enable collection, storage, and dissemination of knowledge to improve the quality of a process.	Instantaneous access to information. Boundary spanning.
	Allow detailed tracking of the status of a process, and of its inputs and outputs.	Instantaneous access to information.
	Directly connect the parties within a process and thus avoid communication through an intermediary.	Means of coordination.
	Increase the variety of products and services resulting from the process to satisfy the customer.	Differentiation of products and services.

(A part of the table has been adapted from Thomas Davenport and James Short, "The New Industrial Engineering: Information Technology and Business Process Redesign," *Sloan Management Review,* Summer 1990, pp. 11–27.)

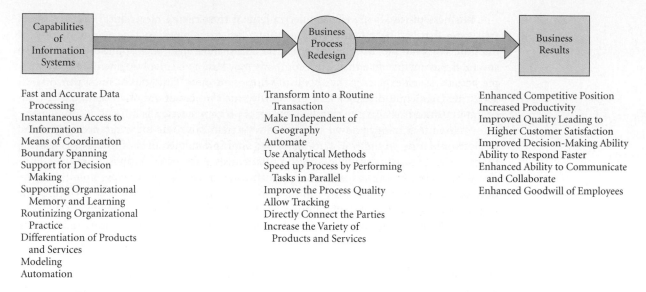

Figure 1.6

How business process redesign helps to exploit the capabilities of information systems in order to produce business results

shows the directions that can be taken in business process redesign. The table also shows which capabilities of information systems these initiatives can rely on.

The direction a redesign effort takes depends, naturally, on the nature of the business process. Consider the product development process. In developing the product, a team of engineers working in different geographic locations may be employed. Rapid communication between sites is a principal capability to be drawn upon. At the same time, complex analytical methods and modeling can be used to avoid developing a physical product prototype until the design matures. By using concurrent engineering, several teams can work in parallel to develop, simultaneously several aspects of the product and the production process. During this work, the designers will be relying on information systems as the means of coordination. Global corporations are working on some products around the clock, moving the work every eight hours to a site where the workday is just starting. In this manner, information systems reduce time-to-market, a crucial competitive advantage in today's marketplace.

We may conclude that business process redesign can be the vital link between the capabilities of information systems and business results. Figure 1.6 summarizes much of our discussion in this chapter.

We will come back to discuss business process redesign in more detail in Chapter 13, after you learn more about the organizational deployment of information systems.

1.7 | AN INITIAL LOOK AT THE HUMAN SIDE OF INFORMATION SYSTEMS IN ORGANIZATIONS AND IN SOCIETY

Organizations do not work with information systems. People do. When implementing information systems in organizations, it is vital to maintain a **sociotechnical perspective** which says that the purely technological approach to achieving higher productivity has to be balanced with the consideration of the social and human aspects of technology. The newest technology has to be forgone if its use might be expected to result in an intolerable workplace. You cannot simply "parachute" an information system into a firm and expect it will be successfully used. Many a failure has resulted from such an approach. One should create workplaces that will provide job satisfaction. Employees should be given an opportunity to contribute to the development of the information systems they will work with, and have to be motivated and trained to use the systems. The information system itself must be designed to fit the needs of its users and the organization at large. It must also evolve as these needs invariably change. Organizational structures are typically altered during process redesign and proper attention has to be paid to the nature of the change as it will affect people, preparing and guiding them through the change. We will return to the issue of the implementation of information systems in Chapter 13.

As the use of information systems has become pervasive in advanced economies and societies at large, the ethical considerations of this use have moved into the forefront. Ethics involve making decisions about right and wrong, rather than about possible and impossible, or about more or less productive. We will discuss the ethical issues involved in the development and use of information systems in Chapter 17. However, as you study the technologies, management techniques, and, in particular, the examples offered in this text, you should think about the ethical issues. Here are the principal ethical issues that may be involved:

Privacy   Does the information system or the way the system is used abridge the right of individuals to control information about themselves? For example, is it all right for the Department of Motor Vehicles to sell your records (or a part of them)—a case that has emerged in New Jersey?[3]

Accuracy   Does the information system contain the necessary safeguards in order to provide accurate information? For example, who is in the wrong if you are denied a mortgage loan based on inaccurate information in the credit record that was used to make the decision? When Ford Motor Company used computer graphics to replace the heads of nonwhite people with white faces in a photographic advertisement scheduled to run in Poland, supposedly the better to enable the intended recipients to identify with the Ford workers pictured in the ad, what ethical issues were involved (Strassel 1996)?

Property   Software embodies intellectual property of considerable value. Is it right to copy a program without permission under certain circumstances? Can you place that magazine article you enjoyed reading (but did not write) on your electronic site on the Internet?

Access   How can we use information systems to break down rather than erect barriers to the enjoyment of benefits that society has to offer? For example, how do we make the Internet truly accessible to all? Is it enough to place access terminals in a public library?

SUMMARY

An information system is an organized set of components for collecting, transmitting, storing, and processing data in order to deliver information. Most organizational information systems today are computer-based. All managers and professionals, as well as most other workers in a corporation, are end users of information systems, since they need to use information delivered by these systems in doing their jobs. This is why information systems literacy is indispensable.

Organizational information systems include systems that support business operations, known as transaction processing systems, as well as systems that support management: management reporting systems, decision support systems, and executive information systems. In addition, professional support systems and office information systems support knowledge work. Information systems rely on a wide range of information technologies, all of them relating to computers or telecommunications, that is, electronic transmission of information over distances.

Organizational information systems are implemented to achieve business results. These outcomes may include enhanced competitive position, higher productivity, improved customer satisfaction, better decision making, faster response in the marketplace, better communication and collaboration, and enhanced employee goodwill.

Traditional organizational structures, which still prevail today, are built along functional or divisional lines. They involve clear, long-term assignment of roles to employees, clear lines of responsibility and command, extensive hierarchy, and clear boundaries between the firm and its environment. Such organizations may be slow to respond to the needs of a highly dynamic marketplace—the objective often better served by virtual organizations. The structures of the emerging virtual organizations are flexible and are created, to a large degree, with information systems. Thus, in a network organization, the core firm surrounds itself with long-term corporate partners, with each company contributing its core competencies. In a cluster organization, the principal work units are teams of varying purpose and lifetime, some of them including the employees of the firm's business partners.

Employees are working more and more frequently in virtual workplaces, outside of their company's premises, and are said to be telecommuting. Telecommuting may lead to higher productivity of the workers, corporate savings, and more even job distribution throughout a country or a region. The drawbacks include lack of visibility for promotion and feelings of isolation.

The principal capabilities of information systems are fast and accurate data processing, with large-capacity storage and rapid communication between sites; instantaneous access to information; means of coordination; boundary spanning; support for decision making; supporting organizational memory and learning; routinizing organizational practice; differentiation of products and services; modeling; and automation. These capabilities can be exploited during a redesign of the firm's business processes in order to reach higher levels of performance. Business process redesign involves rethinking and streamlining the firm's business processes in order to achieve specific business results. The redesign can take several directions, each of them drawing on different capabilities of information systems.

Information systems do not benefit an organization or the society at large by simply being developed and installed. A system appropriate for the firm and its users has to be carefully identified and implemented from the sociotechnical perspective, seeking the technology that would best support the people in the organization. The principal ethical issues involved in the development and use of information systems are privacy, accuracy, property, and access.

KEY TERMS

Information system   *5*

Information systems literacy   *7*

Knowledge work   *7*

Transaction processing system   *8*

Management reporting system   *8*

Decision support system   *8*

Executive information system   *9*

Professional support system   *9*

Office information system   *9*

Interorganizational system   *10*

Strategic information system   *10*

Computer   *12*

Software   *12*

Hardware   *12*

Telecommunications   *13*

Computer network   *13*

Internet   *13*

World Wide Web   *13*

Functional structure   *14*

Organization chart   *14*

Divisional structure   *14*

Virtual organization   *16*

Network organization   *16*

Core competence   *16*

QUESTIONS

1. What is an information system?
2. What business results does the Port of Rotterdam, the organization described in the Focus Minicase, intend to achieve with information systems according to its Plan 2010?
3. How does information systems (IS) literacy differ from computer literacy? What do you consider important for you, as an information-literate student, to succeed in your college work?
4. State six types of information systems and the role of each in organizational computing.
5. What is knowledge work and what types of information systems support it?
6. What is the role of interorganizational information systems in the work of the firms involved?
7. What kind of information system is considered strategic?
8. State and define the two principal technologies that underlie information systems.
9. What do we mean by "virtual" when referring to virtual organizations? How does being a virtual organization relate to information systems? What are the two principal structures of these organizations?
10. What are the advantages and the drawbacks of each of the two structures of virtual organization as compared with the traditional organizational structure?
11. What are virtual workplaces and how do they relate to telecommuting? What is the role of information technology in telecommuting?
12. Which information systems capabilities can be exploited in the systems that are primarily oriented in, toward the company's internal operations and which capabilities have an outward orientation? Select one of each and give two examples of their use (other than the examples in Table 1.2)
13. What capabilities of information systems will the Port of Rotterdam (of the Focus Minicase) be able to exploit with information systems after Plan 2010 has been implemented?
14. What is the objective of coordination? Give an example of an exchange of information in the coordination of activities between a supplier and a customer firm.
15. In what respects can software models of future products be superior to their physical models? Give an example.
16. What is a business process? Give three examples of business processes and describe what information systems can contribute to the performance of these processes.
17. State three possible directions of business process redesign enabled by specific information systems. What capabilities of these systems can be used in each of these initiatives? Give a brief scenario of such a business process redesign with information systems by expanding one of your examples.
18. Why is a sociotechnical perspective important to the success of information systems in organizations?
19. What are the four principal ethical issues of information systems? Give a brief example of each of these issues arising from the use of information systems.

ISSUES FOR DISCUSSION

1. Discuss the limits of automation when it replaces human labor and thinking with computerized information systems. Distinguish what is possible from what you consider desirable. State explicitly your criteria of desirability.
2. Illustrate with examples the variety of levels—from interorganizational to a team—at which information systems can serve as a means of coordination. Do you find that information systems are better coordination tools than the traditional ones (what are they?) in the cases you selected?
3. Discuss the human side of the new organizational environment and new ways to work as described in the chapter. Do you believe any ethical issues emerge as we go virtual? Give examples of situations where the issue can arise and discuss what you consider to be the right course of action and why.

REAL-WORLD MINICASE AND PROBLEM-SOLVING EXERCISES

1. A Virtual Entrepreneur   William O'Malley is a virtual entrepreneur with global reach. His DATA Clearinghouse Corporation offers Pro/Fee Management Service, which automates the issuing and processing of bills for professionals.

With a small 30-person company operating out of South Pasadena, California, O'Malley provides worldwide service and support to customers, 24-hour maintenance of the equipment that runs the customer's business, and local dial access to information from 32 countries.

Yet O'Malley has made no investment in extensive computing facilities of his own or in private telecommunications networks. The computers of AT&T—the same computers that run the public telecommunications network—format the invoices, check them out, ship them between the appropriate parties, and store the data on all transactions in databases for future management use. This is possible thanks to the alliance O'Malley concluded with AT&T. This alliance gives O'Malley's small firm instant credibility. The software application has been built using an off-the-shelf software package, Lotus Notes. It is installed on the computers of DATA Clearinghouse's customers in the legal industry, for example, and on the computers of their clients.

a. Why can we consider DATA Clearinghouse to be a virtual company? What, do you think, is actually supplied by the firm itself?

b. In what respects does O'Malley rely on the information-technology resources available in our developed society? Why can we conclude that computing and telecommunications are converging into a single resource?

c. Compare and contrast DATA Clearinghouse with Calyx and Corolla described in the chapter. Draw a figure similar to Figure 1.4.

Based on Tom Steinert–Therkeld, "Computing in the Public Network: No Escape," *Inter@ctive Week*, December 4, 1995, p.19.

2. Using the Internet's World Wide Web: Find a Job on the Web   You need to find one or more positions corresponding to your selection criteria (taking the job is optional). At this time, you are not posting your resume on the Web but reviewing the posted job openings. Define your criteria first. Using your Web browser, log on to several career services (Online Career Center is one example, but you should use others as well). Investigate the jobs that correspond to your criteria. Using word processing, write a detailed report on your job search. Describe the sites you visited, identifying their uniform resource locators (URL) and stating how helpful each of them proved to be. Write your conclusions on the experience.

3. Read an article in a recent trade periodical, such as *Datamation, InformationWeek,* or *Computerworld* (see also Table 1.4 on p. 34), which discusses how business processes have been redesigned in a specific company. What information systems enabled the redesign? What underlying capabilities of information systems were exploited? What business results were achieved?

TEAM PROJECT

Divide into two- or three-person, teams. Based on personal knowledge, access to a local company (if available), and the use of the Web and current periodicals, each team will select a business process. The process should be relatively simple, involving few inputs and outputs. Each team will analyze the current operation of the process. Then, each team will develop ideas for a redesign of the process, using the directions in Table 1.3. The team will identify specific business results that can be expected from the process redesign. After that, the team will specify the types of information systems that can enable the redesign. Selected teams will make a presentation on the redesign of their business process to the class.

ENDNOTES

1. Management reporting systems are often also referred to as management information systems. Since this usage implies that they satisfy management information needs by themselves, we prefer the first term.

2. The term "virtual" was first used in the context of information technology in the 1960s to name virtual memory. Managed by software, virtual memory is the seemingly expanded main memory of the computer. As we discuss in Section 5.2, the effect is achieved by storing large parts of programs and data on the magnetic disk, with only the needed parts brought into the main memory. The adjective "virtual" has come to mean imitating traditional or physical arrangements with information technology, as in virtual organizations or in virtual reality.

3. A plan by state officials to raise $11 million by selling names and addresses culled from Division of Motor Vehicles records to private companies has drawn criticism from civil liberties lawyers and legislators. "There is an expectation of privacy when you're supplying mandatory information to the government," says one of these lawyers in an article "Sale of D.M.V. Records Assailed," *The New York Times,* February 22, 1996, p. B1.

SELECTED REFERENCES AND A LIST OF PERIODICALS

Brynjolfsson, Erik, and Lorin M. Hitt. "Paradox Lost? Firm-Level Evidence on the Returns to Information Technology Spending." *Management Science,* 42, no. 4 (April 1996), pp. 541–558.

The evidence concerning the business value of information systems.

Brynjolfsson, Erik, and others. "Does Information Technology Lead to Smaller Firms?" *Management Science,* 40, no. 12 (December 1994), pp. 1628–44.

Provides evidence for the "yes" answer.

Caldwell, Bruce, and Jill Gambon. "The Virtual Office Gets Real." *InformationWeek,* January 22, 1996, pp. 31–40.

Chesbrough, Henry W., and David J. Teece. "When Is Virtual Virtuous? Organizing for Innovation." *Harvard Business Review,* January–February 1996, pp. 65–73.

Cortese, Amy. "Here Comes the Intranet." *Business Week,* February 26, 1996, pp. 76–84.

Davenport, Thomas H. *Process Innovation: Reengineering Work through Information Technology,* Boston: Harvard Business School Press, 1993.

An essential and detailed book on business process redesign.

"Frito-Lay, Inc.: A Strategic Transition (1987–1991)," Harvard Business School Case 194–107, 1995.

George, Joey F., and John L. King. "Examining the Computing and Centralization Debate." *Communications of the ACM,* 34, no. 1 (January 1991), pp. 62–72.

Goldman, Steven J.; Roger N. Nagel; and Kenneth Preiss. *Agile Competitors and Virtual Organizations,* New York: Van Nostrand Reinhold, 1995.

Hammer, Michael, and James Champy. *Reengineering the Corporation,* New York: Harper Business, 1993.

Along with Davenport's book, a principal source on business process redesign.

Jacobs, Sheila M., and Mary Van Sell. "Telecommuting: Issues for the IS Manager." *Information Systems Management,* Winter 1996, pp. 18–22.

Jarvenpaa, Sirkka L., and Blake Ives. "The Global Network Organization of the Future: Information Management Opportunities and Challenges." *Journal of Management Information Systems,* 10, no. 4 (Spring 1994), pp. 25–57.

A fascinating scenario of the organizational future, based on specific and realistic assumptions about information technology, organizations, environment, and competition.

McWilliams, Gary. "Whirlwind on the Web." *Business Week,* April 7, 1997, pp. 132–136.

Maglitta, Joseph. "Think Simple." *Computerworld,* May 13, 1996, pp. 77, 80.

Supporting telecommuters with information technology.

Miller, David B.; Eric K. Clemons; and Michael C. Row. "Information Technology and the Global Virtual Corporation," in Bradley, Stephen P.; Hausman, Jerry A.; and Nolan, Richard L., eds. *Globalization, Technology, and Competition: The Fusion of Computers and Telecommunications in the 1990s,* Boston: Harvard Business School Press, 1993, pp. 283–308.

Mills, D. Quinn. *Rebirth of the Corporation,* New York: Wiley, 1991.

An excellent guidebook to cluster organizations.

Peters, Tom. *Liberation Management: Necessary Disorganization for the Nanosecond Nineties,* New York: Knopf, 1992.

Describes how the leading companies support the organizational knowledge work with information systems.

Pine, B. Joseph II; Bart Victor; and Andrew C. Boynton. "Making Mass Customization Work." *Harvard Business Review,* September–October 1993, pp. 108–121.

Senge, Peter M. *The Fifth Discipline: The Art and Practice of the Learning Organization,* New York: Doubleday Currency, 1990.

The fundamental book on organizational learning.

Stein, Eric W. and Vladimir Zwass. "Actualizing Organizational Memory with Information Systems." *Information Systems Research,* 6, no. 6, June 1995, pp. 85–117.

Strassel, Kimberley A. "Ford Turns Red after Putting Blacks, South Asians in Whiteface." *The Wall Street Journal,* February 22, 1996, p. B8.

Tapscott, Don. *The Digital Economy: Promise and Peril in the Age of Networked Intelligence,* New York: McGraw-Hill, 1996.

An accessible review of the organizational effects of information technology.

Tung, Lai-Lai, and Efraim Turban. "Information Technology as an Enabler of Telecommuting." *International Journal of Information Management,* 16, no. 2, April 1996, pp. 103–118.

A thorough review of the tasks performed by telecommuters and information technology that can help in this performance.

"VeriFone: The Transaction Automation Company." Harvard Business School Case 195–088, 1994.

Wilder, Clinton. "Change Is Certain." *InformationWeek,* January 6, 1997, pp. 39–42.

The developments in the business use of the Internet, intranets, extranets, and electronic commerce.

Zwass, Vladimir. "Electronic Commerce: Structure and Issues." *International Journal of Electronic Commerce*, 1,
no.1, Fall 1996, pp. 3–23.

An analytical overview of the entire field of electronic
commerce.

The following table lists some of the periodicals where
good articles about information systems appear most
frequently.

Table 1.4	General Subject of the Periodical	Periodical
Periodicals to follow for articles about information systems	Business	*Business Week* *Forbes* *Fortune*
	Management	*Harvard Business Review* *Sloan Management Review* *Business Horizons* *Long Range Planning*
	Management information systems	*Information Systems Research* *Journal of Management Information Systems* *MIS Quarterly* *Information and Management* *Information Systems Management* *Journal of Systems Management*
	Information technology	*Communications of the ACM* *IEEE Spectrum* *IEEE Software*
	Business computing	*Datamation* *Forbes ASAP* *CIO* *Computerworld* *InformationWeek*
	Personal computing	*PC Computing* *PC Magazine* *PC World* *PC Week* *Byte (technical)* *MacWeek (Macintosh)* *MacWorld (Macintosh)*
	Telecommunications	*Data Communications* *Communications Week* *LAN*
	Internet	*Internet Magazine* *Internet World* *NetGuide* *Web Developer*
	Computing environment	*Wired* *CD-ROM Professional* *Multimedia* *Computer Life* *Connect* *Mobile Office* *Virtual Reality*

CASE STUDY | # Small Vineyard Staying Smart

Winemaking is still an art—you cannot replace a good nose by computers. What you can do with computers is stay in the increasingly competitive and fickle winemaking business.

Take just one—although famous—region: California's Napa Valley. On just 54 square miles of vineyards, there are hundreds of wineries, fiercely competing for awards and name recognition (read *sales*) and dealing with the rising cost of supplies. Of course, the vintners have to compete against the hallowed (by tradition) French wines and the ever new labels coming to the market from, say, Chile, South Africa, or Hungary. Tactical decisions have to be made in projecting next-year sales: For example, in 1993, the sales of fine wines went up 5 percent while the sales of coolers declined 4 percent.

Cakebread Cellars, a family-owned winery in beautiful Rutherford, employs 30 people and produces 45,000 cases annually, with its bottles priced between $13 and $40. Founded in 1973 by Jack and Dolores Cakebread, the company has remained profitable since 1981. The firm is now run by their three sons: Steve (vice president at Silicon Graphics, who doubles as the computer expert at the family firm), Bruce (the winemaker), and Dennis (the chief financial officer). You can see them in Photo 1.6. How does a small company compete in a field dominated by giants such as Mondavi or Gallo Brothers? The answer: Information systems are pervasive at Cakebread Cellars.

To handle accounting, production schedules, and marketing, the winery employs a local area network consisting of seven Hewlett-Packard and two Mitsuba technical workstations (advanced microcomputers with excellent graphical displays) and Dell personal computers, all linked by an Intel communications server (another powerful micro). Novell's NetWare is the communications software. Hard copy output is produced by four Hewlett-Packard (HP) Laserjet printers. Unpredictable rural power outages are the reason for two uninterruptible power supplies (APS SmartUps): When the local power supply goes down, the Cakebread computers stay up.

Photo 1.6

The creators of the smart vineyard: Steve, Bruce, and Dennis Cakebread. (From Michael S. Malone, "Smart Vineyard," *Forbes ASAP,* June 6, 1994, pp. 31–33.)

Based on Michael S. Malone, "Smart Vineyard," *Forbes ASAP,* June 6, 1994, pp. 31–33; William Booth, "Weed-Whacking on Smart Farms," *Wired,* October 1996, pp. 160–164 & 215–216; and http://www.wired.com/4.10/smart-farm/.

Technology in the office is not that unusual. What distinguishes Cakebread Cellars is the pervasiveness of information systems in the firm's growing and production processes. This particular computerization program is run by Bruce's wife, Rosemary. The centerpiece of the system is the database, accessible through the HP network, with machines located not only in the business office but also in the lab and throughout the production and warehouse buildings. With the sensors in giant stainless steel tanks (where the wine is fermenting) and in the barrels (where it is maturing), the system continually pumps data into the database. Software by Vahl, Inc., combines all the data from multiple sources to give Bruce a real-time picture of the fermentation and maturing processes.

But there are other data sources for the database as well. Twice a year, Cakebread buys aerial infrared photographs of its fields, which are used to analyze wine growth. Another aerial service provides photographs of the vineyard soil immediately after it is plowed, used in detecting soil changes. A weather service, California Irrigation Management Information Systems, provides by modem the data on temperature, humidity, and wind speed.

Moisture for the vines has to be controlled very closely: The best wine comes from vines whose growth is limited by tight water supply. To do that, 66 aluminum tubes have been sunk into the vineyard, and once a week its employees drop a probe into each one to measure the moisture at five different levels under the surface. The data are analyzed by the software that determines the data of the next irrigation for the vines. The data also go into the database.

Thanks to the database and the information system relying on it, Bruce Cakebread can bring up on a workstation the complete history of the wine in the barrel he is about to taste, going all the way back to the growing history of the vines the wine came from. This is how Bruce, and the company, learn to make better wine.

Let's listen to Dennis, the chief financial officer: "As I see it, there are really two tasks. The first is to get everybody the right information at the right time to make the right decisions. That's where we are heading now. But just as important, that information needs to be presented in a more intuitive way so that somebody like Bruce can look at the computer screen and get a more dynamic sense of what's going on, and interpret it more effectively. I want him to be able to read the information the same way he 'reads' the wine."

Toward this end, Steve is now investigating three-dimensional visualization of all the soil data. He wants to modify the existing geological and petroleum industry software to be able to accomplish this. Steve's vision is to track each individual vine, from its planting to the sale of each bottle of wine the grapes were used for. Since vines take a long time to develop, Cakebread Cellars has to do all it can to achieve maximum productivity from each vine, without sacrificing quality. According to Dennis, this can be done only by bringing information technology into the task.

Yet, information technology is no crutch for mediocre wine. But, in Dennis's words: "The idea is that if you can use technology to control your costs, you can achieve your profit goals without ever having to compromise the wine. You need technology to be efficient in one area in order to be creative in another."

Cakebread Cellars is part of the larger move to "smart farming"—relying on information technology to dramatically increase the yields, variety, and quality of products in agribusiness. As an example, in precision farming, a computerized map of the farm acreage is created by a specialized company. The salinity, acidity, moisture, and temperature of each square foot of land is measured and combined with the records of past production. The map is then fed into a computer placed on the farmers' tractors when they spray fertilizer and insecticide; it is also used to control the amount of water individual patches of land will get. Here, the newest technologies are dramatically improving the oldest ones—cultivating the land to feed people.

CASE STUDY QUESTIONS

1. Which capabilities of information systems have the Cakebreads used in redesigning the traditional wine-making business? Provide specific examples of its use for each capability you identify.

2. Which information system technology supports each of the capabilities you have identified?

3. Sketch out as best you can the computer network used by Cakebread. Show which computers run which software. Show the location of each machine.

4. Why does the vineyard rely on graphical workstations?

5. Specify three ideas for further expanding the use of information systems capabilities at Cakebread Cellars. What additional information systems resources would be necessary to implement your ideas?

6. What are the limits of what technology can do in winemaking? What about "smart farming" in general?

CHAPTER TWO

Fundamental Concepts of Information Systems

OBJECTIVES

After you complete this chapter, you will be able to:

1. Demonstrate understanding of the relationship between data and information.
2. Specify and explain the attributes of quality information.
3. Explain what systems are and describe their characteristics.
4. Describe the role information systems play in the feedback loop of a firm.
5. Identify the components of information systems.
6. Define the types of organizational information systems and explain their role in the firm.
7. Explain how management support systems support various aspects of management.

OUTLINE

FOCUS   MINICASE

From an Information System to Business Results

The nationwide chain of 77 restaurants, California Pizza Kitchen, deployed a new information system to improve its profit margins, and was able to accomplish more than that.

The company wanted to install a telecommunications network that would let it use a single software package to run the point-of-sale operations, such as placing a customer's order and settling the check, as well as provide management support, such as controlling the food costs and inventory. The firm has installed a server computer and Microsoft's Windows NT Server software to run it, as well as RemoteWare software (from XcelleNet of Atlanta) to provide remote connections to the chain's restaurants. Now, a routine task such as consolidating the biweekly payroll data from all the restaurants, which used to take a week, takes only eight minutes—the time needed to transmit the data from all the restaurants and obtain a summary with the software. As a result, managers spend an "average of 15 percent more time in the restaurant assisting customers," says MIS Director Rick Smith (see Photo 2.1). Daily sales receipts are processed faster, resulting in

Photo 2.1

MIS Director of California Pizza Kitchen Rick Smith does not sell pizza, but his department's efforts account for several percent of the firm's profits (From Laura DiDio, "Pizzeria Eats up Client/Server Pie," *Computerworld,* March 4, 1996, p. 69.)

better cash management.

RemoteWare lets the company's executives and district managers, who often travel among three or four restaurants a day, access the food-cost system from the road. Using the company's information systems, they are well informed about inventory levels, recipes, sales, and personnel schedules. Information on itemized food spending is received quickly throughout the company. Restaurant managers can make informed decisions about labor scheduling and hiring. They also make better decisions about simpler but no less important matters such as when to make all entrées and side dishes.

According to Smith, the new information system has allowed the firm "to trim the fat from the organization and given us better control of the bottom line." And as the new system is used, as much as 5 percent more in profits goes to the bottom line of each restaurant.

Based on Laura DiDio, "Pizzeria Eats up Client/Server Pie," *Computerworld,* March 4, 1996, pp. 69–70.

This chapter will introduce you to the fundamental concepts of information, systems, and management. We will also discuss the components and types of information systems.

2.1 | INFORMATION AND ITS ROLE IN BUSINESS

As we already know from the preceding chapter, information systems transform data into information. Based on the detailed data on the operations of individual restaurants, the information systems used by California Pizza Kitchen, which you encountered in the Focus

Minicase, provide the company's managers with information that helps them make better and faster decisions. This role of information systems is illustrated in Figure 2.1, where a system selects the appropriate data out of a larger database, and computes and presents the needed information. As you can see, to obtain information, we need data.

Distinctions Between Data and Information

How can we distinguish between data and information? Perhaps an illustration will help. If I suddenly throw the word "five" into our discourse at this point, it obviously means nothing to you. It is a data item, but it becomes meaningful information only if it is placed within a context familiar to you. Now, if you had just asked me, "What were the sales of the Packaged Goods division last month?" then I have provided you with information rather than data. I provided information, that is, if you already know that the sales are measured in millions of dollars.

Information, then, is an increment in knowledge: It contributes to the general framework of concepts and facts that we know. Information relies on the context (your question) and the recipient's general knowledge for its significance. To receive really meaningful information in our example, not only would you need to know that "five" means five million

Figure 2.1

Data and information

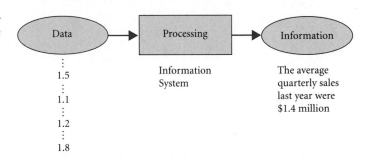

Figure2.2

Transforming data into information

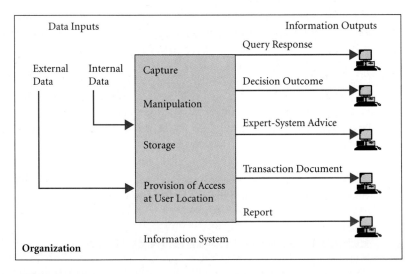

We Are Drowning in Data, but Need Information

Dialog Information Services, belying its corporate name, actually provides access to data, huge quantities of it. It has attempted to serve as a one-stop data megastore. Dialog offers about 3.5 terabytes of data, that is, some 3.5 billion letters and digits, enough to fill more than 2 million floppy disks. The 450 databases to which the company provides access include Toxline (providing data on the adverse effects of various chemicals), the data on coffee production around the world, and airline schedules as well as the full text of the daily *Financial Times*. For a long time, Dialog was able to sell access to these data items at high hourly fees.

But now sales and profits have flattened. There are many alternative cheaper sources of data; for example, the Internet and on-line services such as America Online, CompuServe,

and Prodigy. Moreover, many creators of the data that Dialog sells are increasingly putting their databases at the disposal of their own users.

It is obvious that Dialog cannot maintain its profits by selling raw data. What to do? Dialog needs to facilitate obtaining information from the data, or it must add value to the data, turning it into information. For example, the company could develop new software that will help users navigate through the mass of data. It can also use software known as intelligent agents to provide personalized daily information digests to clients' PCs. The firm has to move from selling data to delivering information.

Based on Jeffrey Young, "Data Is Cheap," *Forbes*, April 11, 1994, p. 126.

dollars, you would also need to know the previous monthly sales of the Packaged Goods division and the projections for the period under discussion.

Data are only the raw facts, the material for obtaining information. Information systems use data stored in computer databases to provide needed information. A **database** is an organized collection of interrelated data reflecting a major aspect of a firm's activities. Examples include customer and inventory databases. If we expand our view of what an information system does (refer back to Figure 2.1), we obtain Figure 2.2.

As you can see, information systems capture data from the organization (internal data) and its environment (external data). They store the data items over an extensive period of time. When specific information is needed, the appropriate data items are manipulated as necessary, and the user receives the resulting information. Depending on the type of information system, the information output may take the form of a response to a database query, an outcome of a decision suggested by a decision support system, advice given by an expert system, a transaction document (say, an invoice), or a report (which may appear on paper or on-screen). As the above vignette tells you, the value of information is much higher than that of data.

In this text, we discuss **formal information systems** that rely on procedures (established and accepted by organizational practice) for collecting, storing, manipulating, and accessing data in order to obtain information. Formal systems do not *have* to be computerized, but today they usually are. Note that much of the information flowing in an organization, and very important information at that, is informal. Indeed, a lot of informal information is gained through interpersonal networking (which relies more and more on the use of electronic mail over physical networks), water cooler gossip, or conversations with the supplier's truckers at the loading dock.

Table 2.1	Attribute	Definition
The attributes of quality information	Timeliness	Available when needed and not outdated when made available.
	Completeness	Includes all the user needs to know about the situation where the information will be used.
	Conciseness	Does not include elements unneeded by the user.
	Relevance	Has direct bearing on the situation.
	Accuracy	Corresponds to the reality it represents; free of errors.
	Precision	Offers quantitative information with a degree of exactness appropriate to the underlying data.
	Appropriateness of Form	The level of detail, tabular versus graphic display, and quantitative versus qualitative form, are selected in accordance with the situation.

Attributes of Quality Information

Today, organizations have recognized that quality is the necessary attribute of products and services. Provision of information is a service. What do we mean when we demand quality information? The attributes we have in mind are summarized in Table 2.1.

As you can conclude from the table, many attributes of information are relative to the problem-solving situation in which the information will be used. Information should be complete yet concise, with only relevant items brought to bear on the problem. Relevance provides the main protection against information overload, a situation that occurs when the decision maker is swamped with too much information and unable to see what is truly important.

Note the distinction between accuracy and precision. **Accuracy** is the degree to which information corresponds to the reality it describes. **Precision** is the degree of exactness with which the reality is described; precision of numerical information is the number of significant digits. Suppose that, on the basis of accurate figures rounded off to the next million dollars, last year's quarterly sales were $505, $610, $408, and $456 million. If we report that average quarterly sales for the year were $494,750,000, our figure is accurate, but the precision we selected is inappropriate. The figure of $495 million better reflects the precision (degree of exactness) of the underlying data.

In general, what is meant by information quality depends on the intended user of the information and should be evaluated with respect to this "customer's" needs (Miller 1996). Many considerations influence the choice of the form to use to present information to a manager. Generally, the higher the management level, the less detailed, and thus more summarized, the information should be. Certain information should not, or cannot, be quantified, that is, expressed in numbers. Much of this largely verbal information is "soft" information, relating general trends or reporting opinions or rumors. These may be gleaned from a news item about a change in your market, a suggestion posted by a customer on your Web site, or from a summary of the weekly competitive information delivered by the salesforce. Such information may be vital to the well-being of your firm.

Internal and External Information

Most of the data captured by information systems relates to the operations of the organization itself, serving to produce internal information. This internal information will tell you, as a manager, how your unit is progressing toward the goals set out for the current month or quarter. But in an increasingly competitive marketplace, a firm needs to access more and more external information. This type of information is partly captured by the information systems of the firm, but a good part of it must be acquired from external sources, such as commercial databases, Web sites, or electronic news wire services.

Examples of external information include the following:

- Sales volume of your firm's primary competitor in a specific sales district.

- Potential customer segments for your company's various product lines.

- Summarized responses to a questionnaire regarding a projected new product, obtained from focus groups.

- Geographical distribution of company stockholders.

- Quality of patient treatment achieved by the best health maintenance organization that competes with the one you are working for. You may use this information for benchmarking (i.e., comparing with the leaders) in your total quality management program.

Much external information is not quantitative; for example, legal, regulatory, tax, and labor union negotiations information is generally difficult to quantify. Since we often lack access to the underlying data, external information is often soft information.

A firm can succeed only by adapting itself to the demands of its external environment. The environment is represented by a number of groups that affect the company's ability to achieve its objectives or that are affected by it. Such groups are called the **stakeholders** of a firm. The internal stakeholders are, of course, a firm's employees, who may be classified in terms of their informational needs, as we will see further on in this chapter. Table 2.2 lists

Table 2.2	**Stakeholder**	**Information Needed**
External stakeholders and the information we need to deal with them	Customers	Marketing and sales information, measures of satisfaction.
	Distributors	Marketing and logistics (distribution) information.
	Competitors	Market penetration, growth trends, innovations, product quality.
	Suppliers	Purchasing terms and quality.
	Labor unions	Compensation, stability of employment.
	Stock- and bondholders	Company performance, performance of securities.
	Financial institutions	Financing terms, investment opportunities.
	Trade associations	Participation benefits, competitive information.
	Governments	Political, regulatory, and legal developments (at local, state, and federal levels, including foreign entities where necessary).
	Special interest groups	Employment of disadvantaged and minority group members, contribution to communities.

principal external stakeholders of organizations, along with the principal information needed to interact with them.

Information systems have to keep our organization continually informed about the activities of these external stakeholders; some of them (for example, stockholders and government agencies) also have to receive information from us. Through a database called EDGAR, the Securities and Exchange Commission of the United States government makes available to the financial and investor community, over the Internet, the financial documents filed by the public U.S. companies. Approximately 15,000 companies whose stock is traded in the securities exchanges are required to file an estimated 12 million pages of documents, such as annual and quarterly reports and shareholder proxy statements. Starting in 1993, an electronic filing program has been gradually phased in, making it possible to abandon the paper filing that has become virtually unmanageable. A wealth of financial data is thus made available for easy and inexpensive access (Kalakota and Whinston 1996).

Many organizations have established a regular program in competitive intelligence, as you will learn from the vignette on page 45.

2.2 | SYSTEMS

Now that you know what the *information* in *information systems* stands for, let us discuss the concepts related to systems.

What Is a System?

We know now what we expect from an information system. But what *is* a system? We will need to know this in order to understand, analyze, and develop organizational information systems. A **system** is a set of components (subsystems or elementary parts) that operate together to achieve a common objective (or multiple objectives). The hallmark of a system, as opposed to an unrelated collection of components, is synergy, an effect best defined by Aristotle: The whole is greater than the sum of its parts. The objectives of a system are realized in its outputs. In particular, the objective of an information system is to provide the appropriate information outputs to the members of the organization.

A system operates in its environment, from which the system is delimited by its boundary. The initial view of a system, known as black box view, since we do not know what's in the box, is shown in Figure 2.3. The black box view is helpful in the initial understanding of the system's function, without becoming swamped in the details of its design.

Figure 2.3

A system: A black box or general view

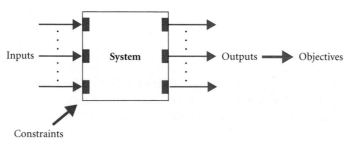

Competitive Intelligence Needed to Compete Intelligently

Competitive intelligence consists in collecting and analyzing information on markets, technologies, customers, competitors, and suppliers. Like its national counterpart, this is a rather secretive world. As you enter it, you realize the vulnerability of your own company. The potential sources are everywhere—an on-line information service, a new employee just hired from the competition, your salespeople, the scuttlebutt at your industry's trade show. Most companies gather competitive intelligence, but few talk about it. If done competently and ethically, competitive intelligence is a potent source of knowledge that can affect your business.

Competitive intelligence serves three purposes: constant monitoring for early warning, tactical field support of your sales force, the support of long-term management strategy. "Intelligence happens in the intersection of the technology and methodology," a competitive intelligence consultant tells us. In other words, technology alone is, as usual, not the answer. Today, however, many answers are obtained with the assistance of information technology.

MassMutual, an insurer in Springfield, Massachusetts, has felt the pressures of shortened product development cycles. Once staid insurers have to rapidly come up with new products and keep an eye on the competition. A corporate program of gathering and disseminating competitor information to executive management was initiated to support long-term planning. Specialized software, Incite from Quest Management Systems, was purchased to assist in the process of information collection and dissemination. The number of users has grown from 10 to 140 in a single year. Another firm, Pacific Enterprises, has published information-gathering guidelines as part of its employee code of conduct.

The company has also set up an intranet to enable its employees to share competitive information and funnel it into a central location.

Many practitioners of competitive intelligence regularly read their competitors' electronic pages on the Internet, as well as the postings on industry-specific Usenet news groups. They also query consumers electronically. By using the World Wide Web search engines, such as Lycos, Yahoo!, or Excite—a media navigation service from Architext that permits concept searches on the Web—sophisticated information can be gleaned. For example, searching for "intellectual property rights" would turn up information on software piracy as well. The Competitive Intelligence Guide (http://www.fuld.com) provides a number of tools for locating competitive data as well as links to many sites containing such data.

Thanks to their extensive databases and knowledge bases, consulting firms have become clearinghouses of competitive intelligence. Searching its own knowledge base, Ernst & Young has uncovered a best-practice firm for its client, a Canadian duck farm. An Asian firm was delivering ducks a week earlier and a pound heavier. Learning that this was possible, the Canadian firm decided it had to match its competitor in order to compete successfully in the future. It did.

Based on E. B. Baatz, "The Quest for Corporate Smarts," *CIO*, September 15, 1994, pp. 48–58; Jenny C. McCune, "Checking out the Competition," *Beyond Computing*, March 1996, pp. 24–29; Ann Monroe and Roy Harris, "Tuning in to Competitive Intelligence," *CFO*, June 1996, pp. 46–52; and Stan Crock, "They Snoop to Conquer," *Business Week*, October 28, 1996, pp. 172–176.

The identification of a system's boundary is often a nontrivial task. Let's say that you have been charged with the task of developing a new on-line system for processing securities (stocks and bonds) held by your bank. One of your first tasks will be to determine exactly what should be included in the system and what its boundary will be. If you make the assumption that the new system should reproduce what people in the bank's

Figure 2.4

A system and its subsystems

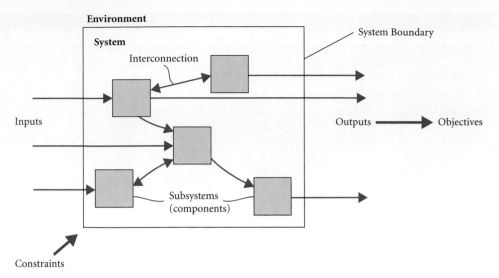

Environment

System

Interconnection

System Boundary

Inputs

Outputs ➝ Objectives

Subsystems
(components)

Constraints

Securities Processing department are doing at present and therefore should be delimited by the department's boundaries, you are almost guaranteed to produce an inferior system. You should, instead, determine the boundaries of the process through which the securities are handled. This method will give you the outlines of the new system.

#5   The entire system and its boundary must be rethought in light of its **objectives** such as the types of transactions it will need to support, and the **constraints** that the system has to conform with, such as the allowed processing time, pertinent government regulations, and interactions with existing systems. As you determine the boundary, you will, in turn, be able to identify the desired *outputs* from the system and the necessary *inputs* to the system. The inputs and outputs should cross the system boundary through well-defined interfaces (shown in Figure 2.3 as small dark rectangles).

A further analysis of a system will identify its *subsystems* and then, in turn, their own subsystems, and so on, in increasing detail (see Figure 2.4). These subsystems produce certain outputs and require certain inputs, both of which provide interconnections between the subsystems.

As you already know, many companies today use information systems in business process redesign: rethinking and streamlining business processes, such as ordering goods from a supplier or developing a new product. Business processes are treated as systems: They are procedural systems. They have objectives (receipt of goods or a new product with specific features); they receive inputs from other parts of the firm or from external entities; and they deliver outputs. Their boundaries contain the individuals or the business units that perform the tasks involved in the newly defined process—these are subsystems of the larger system.

Effectiveness and Efficiency

In this book, we are concerned with **artificial systems,** developed expressly to support certain objectives (Simon 1981), as opposed to the natural system, such as a biological organism. An **organization** is an example of an artificial system: It is a formal social unit devoted to the attainment of specific goals. It does not emerge naturally—it has to be organized. For example, a business firm is a system that has to generate profit. It may also pursue other objectives that include providing employment or contributing to its community in other ways. The principal objective of an information system such as a payroll system is to produce paychecks, subject to all the time constraints.

To measure the value of an artificial system, we use effectiveness and efficiency criteria. **Effectiveness** measures the extent to which a system achieves its objectives. **Efficiency** is a measure of the consumption of resources in producing given system outputs. The fewer resources a system consumes in producing given outputs, the more efficient it is. Since a business process (a procedural system) produces an outcome—a work product—it has customers. The effectiveness of a process is determined by how well it meets its objectives, best defined in terms of customer satisfaction. The efficiency of the process is expressed as the level of resource consumption (say, money) for a given level of effectiveness. We often say that effectiveness is doing the right thing, and efficiency is doing the thing right.

In an information system, the variety and volume of transactions processed, or user satisfaction with the system, are measures of effectiveness. These measures can be evaluated and compared with those achieved by alternative systems. Thus, questionnaires to establish user satisfaction with information systems have been developed and validated (for example, Baroudi and Orlikowski 1988). The use of computer system resources, such as computer processing power measured in millions of instructions per second (MIPS), or the cost of operating a data center where corporate computer systems are located, in achieving a given level of information service is a measure of system efficiency.

Information Systems in the Feedback Loop of an Organization

Where does an information system fit in a larger system, such as the organization that uses it? Many management support systems are employed in controlling the operations of a firm. Such an information (sub)system is a principal component of the feedback loop used to manage the firm, as you can see in Figure 2.5.

Figure 2.5

Information system as a subsystem in an organization (From Vladimir Zwass, *Management Information Systems,* Dubuque, IA: Wm. C. Brown, 1992, p. 400.)

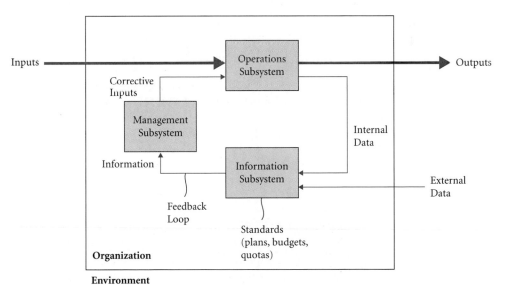

Feedback refers to the outputs of a system that are transformed back into inputs in order to control the system's operation. For example, if our information system tells us that the results we achieved during the last month of operations are worse than planned, we (the management) plan corrective action. As you can see in Figure 2.5, our information system compares the data on the actual performance with the standards developed earlier. Based on the information about the discrepancies, managers can formulate corrective actions, which are then fed back into the firm's operations. For example, information about inventories growing beyond an established level may be fed back to the management in order to slow down production. This is what we mean by "information for action."

The faster the feedback loop, that is, the sooner deviations are identified and action taken, the less likelihood that exceptions will turn into major problems. For example, it is important to obtain information regarding quality problems during the production process rather than wait until the unexpected dip in sales due to inferior product quality.

Systems thinking leads us to consider the system in its entirety and concentrate on the objectives of the whole system before we move to analyze the subsystems (Zwass 1992). By avoiding a worm's eye view of a part of the problem and grasping instead the whole of it, we are able to come up with better and more durable solutions. Total quality management is an excellent example. It replaced dealing with low-quality products by "inspecting out" defective items—an expensive solution that attempted to handle a large problem by dealing with a small part of it. Instead, in total quality management, we address quality as the result of a complete production process. By analyzing and consistently improving this process, we lastingly raise product quality. Indeed, a systems approach helps us solve problems in a disciplined fashion, and information systems are a principal tool in organizational problem solving today.

Many corporations now go beyond the traditional financial standards (such as earnings and profitability) to reach for a richer picture of their performance and to ensure long-term competitive success. A broad and flexible set of performance measures is the balanced scorecard (Kaplan and Norton 1996). In addition to the financial measures, this technique allows a company and its individual units to establish and control performance standards from three perspectives: customers, business processes, and long-term organizational learning and growth. As you can read in the following vignette, some companies go even further by "opening their books" to all their employees.

Now that we have discussed the principal concepts of systems and information, we would like to describe a little more extensively the five components of information systems.

2.3 | COMPONENTS OF INFORMATION SYSTEMS

Components of information systems comprise (1) computer hardware and software, (2) telecommunications, (3) databases, (4) human resources, and (5) procedures. A brief description of each of these components is given in Table 2.3.

Hardware

Today even the smallest firms use computers. These are usually microcomputers, also known as personal computers or PCs. Larger organizations employ multiple computer systems ranging from powerful mainframe machines (sometimes even the most powerful supercomputers), through minicomputers, to widely spread microcomputers.

What Gets Measured, Gets Done

Whole Foods Market, the largest natural-foods grocer in the United States, firmly believes in the old business adage that anything worth doing is worth measuring. With 43 stores spread out from California to New England and with annual revenues of $500 million, the nationwide chain is growing rapidly and shows net profits that are double the industry average. The company also believes in a set of values, such as empowering its employees, fostering employee diversity, and contributing to the communities it operates in. Consistent with these articles of faith, the company shares its performance measurements with everyone in the company. The firm's president and CEO, John Mackey, espouses a "no-secrets" management philosophy, saying: "By sharing information, we stay aligned to the vision of shared fate."

In the Bread & Circus store the company owns in Wellesley, Massachusetts, a sheet posted next to the time clock (yes, there *is* a time clock) lists the previous day's sales broken down by team alongside a sheet listing the sales for the same time last year. Once a week, the sales of every store in New England, broken down by team, are posted, as well as the sales for the same week last year and the year-to-date totals.

Once a month, a detailed report for all 43 stores is available. It includes sales analysis, product costs, salary data, and operating profits. Sensitive information is not posted publicly, but it is available to any employee for the asking. Indeed, since individual teams make decisions about labor spending, ordering, and pricing, these reports are indispensable. To cite Mackey once more, the no-secrets reporting "leads to deeper conversations than you'd have otherwise."

Based on Charles Fishman, "Whole Foods Teams," *Fast Company,* April–May 1996, pp. 102–111.

Table 2.3	Component	Description
Components of information systems	Hardware	Multiple computer systems: microcomputers, minicomputers, mainframes, together with their peripherals. Computer system components are: central processor(s), memory hierarchy, input and output devices.
	Software	Systems programs and applications programs.
	Databases	Organized collections of data used by applications software.
	Telecommunications	Local area networks, metropolitan area networks, and wide area networks.
	Human Resources	Professional cadre of computer specialists; end users when performing tasks involving information systems.
	Procedures	Specifications for the use, operation, and maintenance of information systems, collected in help facilities, user manuals, operator manuals, and similar documents, frequently delivered in an electronic form.

All three principal categories of computers (mainframes, minicomputers, and micro-computers) are similarly organized. The component that controls all units of the system is the **central processor.** The central processor carries out ("executes") the instructions of a program, translated into a simple form. Memories included in a computer system form a hierarchy. They range from the fast electronic units, such as the main memory, to the slower and far more capacious secondary storage (such as magnetic disks) where databases are maintained. Some systems include ultra-high-capacity archival memories. Devices for entering input (for example, a keyboard or a mouse) and producing output (say, a printer and a video display terminal) complete the system. Chapter 4 will discuss computer system hardware in more detail.

Today, the economics of computers has in many applications shifted competitive advantage from mainframes and minicomputers to the use of multiple microcomputers. Over the last three decades, the growth of computing power has been governed by Moore's law[1]: The power of microcomputers doubles every 18 months (see Figure 2.6). In addition, the cost of microcomputers generally decreases at the same time.

Many organizations, as a result, are undergoing a process known as **downsizing,** or transferring some or all of their computing from systems involving mainframes and mini-computers (known as legacy systems) to systems built of networked microcomputers. The advantages of this process are savings in capital expenditures and flexibility in placing system resources directly where they will be used. However, there is no single recipe for computer support; that is why some prefer "rightsizing" to downsizing as the word expressing the use of the best hardware option for organizational computing.

Figure 2.6

Moore's law. The increase in the number of transistors on the chips corresponds to the increase in the microprocessor speed and memory capacity, and thus to the growth of the processing power. The generations of Intel microprocessors around which IBM-compatible PCs are built are shown here. The main memory chip generations are first denominated in thousands (K) and later in millions (M) of bits. (The more exact meaning of K and M will be provided in Chapter 4.) (From Ross, 1996, pp. 116–17.)

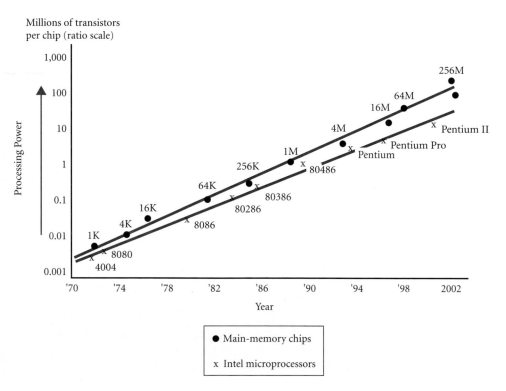

Software

As the costs of hardware decrease, the overall costs of computer systems become driven by software and human resources. Computer software falls into two classes: systems software and applications software. **Systems software** manages the resources of the computer system and simplifies programming. As the principal systems software, an **operating system** manages all the resources of a computer system and provides an interface through which the system's user can deploy these resources. Even if you are just using a personal computer, a complex series of actions takes place when, for example, you start the machine, automatically check out its hardware, and call up a desired program. All of these actions fall under the control of an operating system, such as Windows 95, IBM OS/2, or UNIX. Software translators—**compilers** or **interpreters**—make it possible to program an application in a higher-level language, such as COBOL or C. The translator, another example of systems software, converts program statements into machine instructions ready for execution by the computer's central processor.

Many categories of **applications software** (apps, for short) are purchased as ready-to-use packages. Applications software directly assists end users in doing their work. Examples include general-purpose spreadsheet or word processing programs as well as the so-called vertical applications serving a specific industry segment (for example, accounting packages for small service businesses). In larger firms, much applications software is developed or customized to meet a specific need rather than bought "off-the shelf." We will discuss computer software in more detail in Chapter 5.

Databases

You may cogently argue that many information systems used in business are the delivery vehicles for databases. As we already know, a database is an organized collection of interrelated data. Examples include the human resources database of an organization, or its product database. Particularly valuable to a firm is its customer database that can be "mined" to reach the customers with new products or to develop new products to satisfy the perceived needs of the customers. A database must be organized so that its individual records can be accessed by their attributes ("Give me the names and addresses of all the employees who have been with us over ten years," for example). Databases are managed by systems software known as database management systems (DBMS) and shared by multiple applications. We will discuss databases in Chapter 6.

Telecommunications

Telecommunications are the means of electronic transmission of information over distances. Today, computer systems are usually interconnected into telecommunications networks. Various network configurations are possible, depending upon an organization's need. In a small company, personal computers are connected into local area networks, enabling their users to communicate and share data, work, and equipment. Such fast **local area networks (LAN)** join together machines at a particular organizational site such as a building or a campus. The emerging **metropolitan area networks (MAN)** serve large urban communities, with speeds much higher than those connecting more remote sites. **Wide**

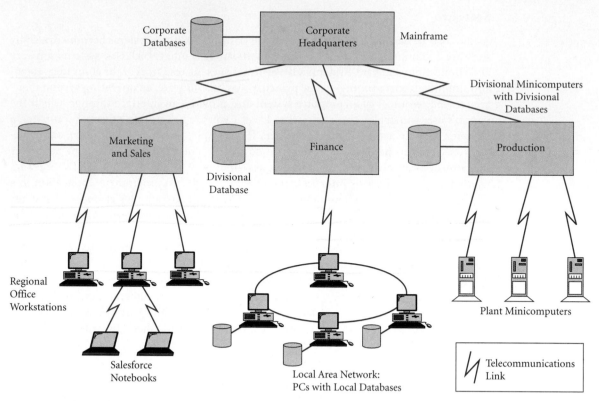

Corporate Databases

Corporate Headquarters

Mainframe

Divisional Minicomputers with Divisional Databases

Marketing and Sales

Finance

Production

Divisional Database

Regional Office Workstations

Salesforce Notebooks

Local Area Network: PCs with Local Databases

Plant Minicomputers

Telecommunications Link

Figure 2.7

A networked information system: three-tier architecture

area networks (**WAN**) connect computers located at remote sites, both within the company and outside of it. The Internet, a network of networks, interconnects a great variety of networks of various scope throughout the world. Through networking, personal computer users gain access to the overall computational resources of the firm, such as large databases, and to people around the globe. This connectivity converts personal computers, today frequently portables, into versatile workstations.

An example of the hardware organization of a three-tier system, including a mainframe computer as the top-level machine, several minicomputers or powerful microcomputers in the middle level, and, as the third tier, the end-user PCs and workstations, is shown in Figure 2.7. An overall design of a computer system (or, far more frequently, networked multiple systems) to satisfy specific organizational requirements is known as **information system architecture.** This architecture serves as the platform for the firm's overall computing efforts.

When computer systems are downsized, the *client/server* configuration is very often employed. In this configuration, illustrated in Figure 2.8, the user's microcomputers, known as *clients,* share the more powerful machines (frequently also microcomputers, but sometimes minis or mainframes), called *servers.* Each server is dedicated to a particular task i.e., it is providing a certain service, such as managing a database, running a fast printer, or providing an interconnection to another network. The client machines provide the user interface that makes it easy to use the facilities of the network. When needed, the software

Figure 2.8

A downsized networked information system: client/server architecture

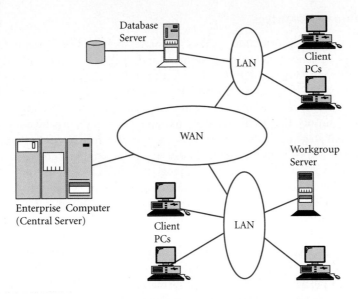

Figure 2.9

System architecture for remote access from virtual offices

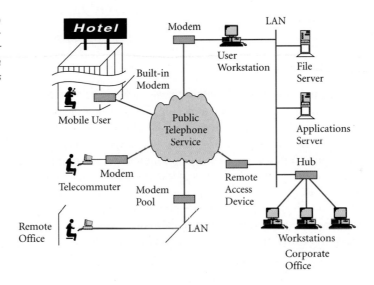

running on the client calls remotely upon the software running on the server to perform its task, to access the specified data from a database, for example.

As we discussed in Chapter 1, today's workplaces are often virtual, located outside of the corporate premises. Moreover, the telecommuting users are frequently mobile, setting up their temporary "office" wherever they happen to be at the moment. Figure 2.9 shows a typical architecture for such remote access (Chae 1996). The public telephone service is employed as the wide area network, to which the user's computer gains access with the use of a modem, as we will discuss in Chapter 7. You will also learn in that chapter about the wireless technologies that can be used for such access.

Human Resources

Professional information systems personnel include development and maintenance managers, systems analysts, programmers, and operators, often with highly specialized skills. Until the 1980s, when personal computing totally changed the landscape, a rather sharp divide existed between the information systems specialists, who acted as systems developers, and the end users. **End users** are the people who use information systems or their information outputs, that is, the majority of people in today's organizations. The hallmark of the present stage in organizational computing is the involvement of end users in the development of information systems. **End-user computing,** or control of their information systems by end users and the development of systems by end users, has become an important contributor to information systems in organizations. Thus, we are witnessing the convergence of end-user computing with general organizational computing (McLean and Kappelman 1992–3).

In many organizations, information systems specialists work for the business units for which they develop and maintain systems, rather than for a central information systems unit. These specialists come to intimately know the business they support and the needs of the people who will be using the information systems. We will further discuss the functions of information systems specialists in Chapter 14.

Procedures

Procedures are the policies and methods to be followed in using, operating, and maintaining an information system. For example, procedures need to be established to run a payroll program, including the times when it is to be run, who is authorized to run it, and who has access to the reports produced and to other outputs (checks, for example). Some procedures are included in the system documentation. Today, many applications include much of this procedural component in the on-line help provided with the software itself. Since many systems are operated directly by their users, support is made available through information centers that employ internal consultants. Increasingly important are help desks for specific systems, which frequently answer questions on-line through electronic mail. As an information system becomes over time an ever more vital component of its user's work, the procedures for its use and the work practices evolve as well (Orlikowski 1996).

The systems resources we have discussed are deployed to deliver several fundamental types of information systems to the users in an organization. We will now describe systems.

2.4 | TYPES OF INFORMATION SYSTEMS

As we know from Chapter 1, information systems in organizations support operations, management, and knowledge work (refer again to Figure 1.1). We will now consider these systems in some detail, before learning about them more fully in Part Three.

Transaction Processing Systems

Transaction processing systems (TPS) support the operations of a firm by processing its business transactions. A **transaction** is an elementary activity conducted during business operations. A merchandise sale, airline reservation, credit card purchase, and inquiry about inventory are all transactions. A TPS makes an appropriate record of the transaction in the database and produces documents relating to the transaction. For example, a sale transaction results in a sale record in the database, a subtraction from the inventory total for the item purchased, and a printout of a sale slip. TPS may also produce detailed reports on transactions. TPS may work either in batch mode, processing accumulated transactions at a single time later on, or in on-line mode, processing incoming transactions immediately. Today, most TPS work in the on-line mode. Considered in terms of the systems concepts we have already discussed, on-line systems provide a tighter feedback loop by giving users more timely information.

Automation of business operations for the sake of efficiency was the earliest objective of computerization. But since TPS accumulate relevant data in databases, these systems are also the foundation for the management support systems that rely on these data. Let us discuss the three types of management-oriented information systems.

Management Reporting Systems

The objective of *management reporting systems (MRS)* is to provide routine information to managers. Managers receive performance reports within their specific areas of responsibility. Generally, these reports provide internal information rather than spanning corporate boundaries. They report on the past and the present, rather than projecting the future.

MRS have acquired a reputation for producing highly voluminous reports that require time to pore over. Since many reports today are produced in electronic form, rather than as printouts, they are somewhat easier to navigate selectively. To prevent information overload, managers may resort to demand or exception reports. Demand reports are requested when needed. Exception reports are produced only when preestablished "out-of-bounds" conditions occur and contain only the information regarding these conditions. MRS may produce reports either directly from databases collected by transaction processing systems, or from specially created extracts from such databases.

A report produced by MRS is shown in Figure 2.10: It is a fragment of a monthly revaluation report for accounts receivable. This report shows a loss or gain on the receivables in foreign currencies. For example, since the French franc went up, any receivable amount due this company in francs also went up in dollar terms. This is an example of a multi-currency report. Note that the globalization of business requires that many companies deal in several currencies: When buying in Japan, you may have to pay in yen while you may be paid in francs when selling in France. With the globalization of operations in many firms, the role of multi-currency systems is increasing.

Decision Support Systems

All information systems support decision making, however indirectly. *Decision support systems (DSS)* are the type of information systems expressly developed to support the decision-making process. These systems facilitate a dialog between the user, who is considering alternative problem solutions, and the system that provides built-in models (for example, sales forecasting) and access to databases. The DSS databases are often extracts from the general databases of the enterprise or from external databases. Recently, data warehouses

Figure 2.10

A monthly revaluation report for accounts receivable

Austin Productions, Ltd.
Accounts Receivable Revaluation for Currency Conversion

Currency: FFR France — French Francs

Invoice Number	Pay Code	Invoice Date	Open Amount	Historical Rate	Historical Value	Current Rate	Current Value	Loss/Gain
006532		06/02/98	784.00 FFR	0.18540	145.35	0.20120	157.75	12.40 USD
098745		06/02/98	8,796.00 FFR	0.18540	1,630.78	0.20120	1,769.76	138.98 USD
000099		04/25/98	1,500.00 FFR	0.17905	268.57	0.20120	301.80	33.23 USD
Totals: USD—U.S. Dollars					$2,044.70		$2,229.31	$184.61 USD

Currency: HFL Benelux — Dutch Guilders

Invoice Number	Pay Code	Invoice Date	Open Amount	Historical Rate	Historical Value	Current Rate	Current Value	Loss/Gain
045632		06/02/98	66,578.50 HFL	0.53524	35,635.48	0.51900	34,554.24	-1,081.24 USD
054236		06/02/98	546.00 HFL	0.53524	292.24	0.51900	283.37	-8.87 USD
564587		06/02/98	45,000.00 HFL	0.54440	24,498.00	0.51900	23,355.00	-1,143.00 USD
Totals: USD—U.S. Dollars					$60,425.72		$58,192.61	$ -2,233.11 USD

Report Total: $ -2,048.50 USD

Previous Month Total: $ -3,111.20 USD

Figure 2.11

*The structure of
decision support
systems*

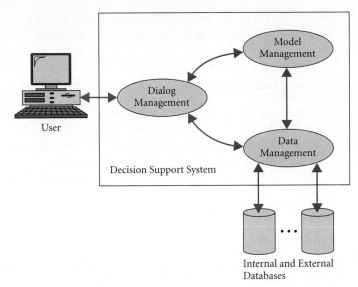

are being used more and more as the integrated source of corporate data (see Chapter 6). The general structure of decision support systems is shown in Figure 2.11.

The systems are interactive. In a typical session, the manager using a DSS will consider a number of possible "what-if" scenarios. For example, a manager attempting to establish a price for a new product may use a marketing decision support system. The system contains a model relating various factors—such as the price of the product, the cost of goods, and the promotion expense—to the projected profit from the product sales over the first five years it will be marketed. By varying the price of the product in the model, the manager can compare predicted results and then select a price.

Unlike management reporting systems, decision support systems are able to help make decisions whose solution procedure cannot be completely programmed into a computer. To do so, some of the dependencies between factors and their consequences are expressed by computerized models, and some judgments are supplied by the manager interacting with the system. The analytical capabilities expressed in DSS models are the reason for the existence of these systems. Spreadsheet programs, which help in manipulating data that can be represented as a table of columns and rows, are often used to develop simpler DSS.

Executive Information Systems

Executive information systems (EIS) provide direct support for top managers by making a variety of internal and external information readily available in a highly summarized and convenient form. We will see such a system in use in the Case Study for this chapter.

Characteristically, senior managers employ a great variety of informal sources of information. Formal, computerized information systems are able to provide only limited assistance. This assistance is important, however, as the chief executive officer, senior and executive vice presidents, and the board of directors monitor the performance of their company, assess the business environment, and develop strategic directions for the company's future. In particular, these executives need a great diversity of external information in order to compare their company's performance to its competition and to investigate general trends in the economies of the many countries where the company may be doing business.

As you will see in the Case Study, EIS present information tersely with colorful graphics and sometimes other media, give the ability to "drill down" on more and more detailed data, and enable the users to control the system in a very easy way. Frequently, top managers equip a special "war room" with large screens onto which the EIS projects color displays. At Smith Barney in New York, for example, the executives of the brokerage house gather in such a room to study demographic data, product lines, and corporate restructuring of their clients and of the companies whose stocks they recommend.

We will now turn our attention to the systems that support knowledge work in organizations.

Office Information Systems

The main objective of *office information systems (OIS)* is to facilitate communication between the members of an organization and between the organization and its environment. OIS help manage documents represented in an electronic format and handle messages, such as electronic mail (E-mail), facsimile (fax), and voice mail. Other types of OIS facilitate teleconferencing and electronic meetings by enabling meeting participants to be dispersed in space and, if desired, in time, since the contributions of conference members can be stored in computer memory. Increasingly, OIS use the facilities of the Internet for communication and access to information, for example, via intranets for corporate use.

Effective work of task-oriented teams has been recognized recently as essential to the health of organizations. A category of OIS, known as groupware, supports this teamwork. Groupware enables the team collaborating on a project to share information, author a document together (for example, a business proposal or a report), or track the progress of a project.

Professional Support Systems

Professional support systems are extended workstations whose resources are specifically designed to support a category of professional work. These workstations generally rely on the facilities delivered by OIS, but go beyond them. As both organizational and individual experience with information systems grow, more and more specialized categories of professional support systems emerge.

With high-resolution graphics workstations and computer-aided design (CAD) software, engineers develop new products—from automobiles to computers. At automobile companies, for example, engineers not only use graphics analysis and visualization to design the car exterior, but also to analyze its crashworthiness and occupant safety. Scientists can access bibliographical databases and thus complete literature on their subject. By using visualization software, they can perform dynamic three-dimensional modeling of molecules and see the components of the new drug they are developing on the workstation screen. Using powerful technical workstations and mathematical software, investment bankers routinely design new financial instruments, known as derivative securities, that can provide the desired features of both stocks and bonds with a given degree of risk and reward. Actuaries rely on the software that helps them calculate risks associated with a group of insured individuals. Designers take advantage of graphics software to come up with more attractive packaging. There are now computerized support systems for all professions.

Expert Systems in Information Systems

Expert systems are a technology that was successfully introduced from the research domain of artificial intelligence into the information systems practice. **Expert systems** suggest a decision based on a computerized process resembling logical reasoning. In doing so, they rely on a knowledge base about the narrow domain of their application, on the facts of the case they need to decide upon, and on the built-in inferencing (reasoning) mechanism. An expert system can also explain how a recommendation was reached. The structure of an expert system is shown in Figure 2.12.

The essential component of the knowledge base is heuristics—informal, judgmental elements of knowledge within the expert system's domain, such as oil exploration or stock valuation. The knowledge base is developed by working with domain specialists. It is further enhanced as the system is used.

Expert systems may be incorporated into all types of organizational information systems or used as stand-alone advisory tools. In particular, they are increasingly combined with conventional programming technologies in transaction processing and decision support systems. In a transaction processing system for order processing, for example, an expert system may determine an order price by considering the customer, order volume, and all the available promotional prices for the items ordered. Because of the multiple promotions offered by companies today—with short duration, regional applicability, and other constraints—this is a nontrivial problem that an order clerk has to handle as the customer is on the phone.

Expert systems may be used to select the cheapest way to mail a package, render a consumer credit decision, diagnose equipment malfunction, plan an investment portfolio, or configure a complicated equipment order. Complexity of these tasks, and of the corresponding expert systems, varies widely. Most frequently, these systems do not replace an expert but rather serve as an assistant to a decision maker.

Figure 2.12

The structure of expert systems

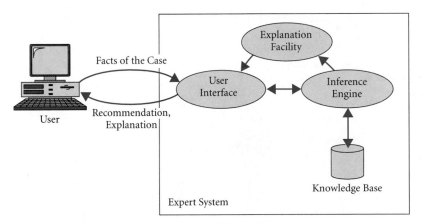

2.5 | SUPPORTING MANAGERS WITH INFORMATION SYSTEMS

As we now know, three types of information systems directly support an organization's managers: management reporting systems, decision support systems, and executive information systems. Other information systems may provide support as well. The better to understand the nature of this additional support, we need to review what managers actually do.

What Managers Do and How Information Systems Can Help

Here are the fundamental functions of management:

- **Planning:** Establishing goals and selecting the actions needed to achieve them over a specific period of time.
- **Controlling:** Measuring performance against the planned objectives and initiating corrective action, if needed.
- **Leading:** Inducing the people in the organization to contribute to its goals.
- **Organizing:** Establishing and staffing an organizational structure for performing business activities.

Managers carry out these functions through a series of varied activities. A realistic behavioral picture of the modern manager has emerged from the work of Henry Mintzberg (1973). He described the daily work of a manager as hundreds of brief activities of great variety, requiring rapid shifts of attention from one issue to another, very often initiated in response to emerging problems. Managers have a "bias for action" (rather than for reflection). They strongly prefer verbal media and spend most of their time in face-to-face meetings, where body language and nuance of expression enhance communication. The distribution of time spent by senior managers (executives) is shown in Figure 2.13.

Mintzberg classified all managerial activities into ten roles falling into three categories, as shown in Table 2.4. The table also shows the information system support available for these roles today.

The interpersonal roles rely largely on face-to-face interaction and the use of information systems here is limited. As a figurehead, a manager (particularly, a high-level executive) represents the organization to his or her subordinates and to the outside world. As leaders, managers influence the subordinates to carry out organizational tasks while they satisfy

Figure 2.13

How executives spend their time

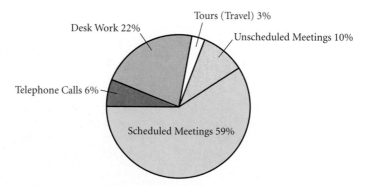

- Desk Work 22%
- Tours (Travel) 3%
- Unscheduled Meetings 10%
- Telephone Calls 6%
- Scheduled Meetings 59%

Table 2.4	Role	Dominant Activity	IS Support
Managerial roles and their information system support	*Interpersonal Roles*	Personal Interaction	*Assistance in Communication:*
	Figurehead		Teleconferencing
	Leader		Teleconferencing
	Liaison		Office Information Systems
	Informational Roles	Information Transfer	*Extensive:*
	Monitor		Management Reporting Systems
			Executive Information Systems
	Disseminator		Office Information Systems
	Spokesperson		Office Information Systems
	Decisional Roles	Decision Making	*Assistance in Decision Making and Communication:*
	Entrepreneur		Decision Support and Executive Information Systems
	Disturbance Handler		Crisis Management Systems
	Resource Allocator		Decision Support Systems
	Negotiator		Group DSS and Negotiation Support Systems

their own goals as well. Teleconferencing systems are increasingly used to project the managers's influence as figureheads and leaders. By developing liaisons throughout the organization, managers build and exercise their own networks of people. Office information systems, and E-mail in particular, have become important to the task, as shown in the brief vignette on the next page.

As we can further see in Table 2.4, managers acting in their informational roles receive (monitor) and spread out information both inside the organization (as disseminators) and outside of it (as spokespersons). Information systems have taken over many of these managerial tasks. Reductions in the ranks of middle managers, whose work consists to a large degree in playing these roles, are partly due to this fact.

Although all managerial roles have an element of decision making, in the decisional roles it is the crucial aspect. An entrepreneur (who may be acting inside an established organization as an "intrapreneur") brings together resources in a novel way to meet a market need. Executive information and decision support systems help identify the need, consider the available options, select an option, and plan appropriate actions. Dealing with exceptional situations, or handling disturbances, belongs to the essence of managerial work. A type of office information systems, known as a crisis management system (Nunamaker 1989) may help in some of these situations. Resource allocation is the content of planning, and decisions support systems have become indispensable in many organizations for this purpose. The activity of any organization can be viewed as a series of negotiated conflicts; mediation between parties is a frequent activity of a manager. Group decision support systems and the emerging negotiation support systems are available to support mediation (discussed in Chapter 10).

The Network Creates the Company

John Gage is the director of the science office of Sun Microsystems, known as one of the most "connected" organizations on the planet. More than one-third of the World Wide Web servers on the Internet are Sun workstations. The Java programming language, developed at Sun, is used to bring Web pages to life by including computer programs (known as applets, for small applications) that enable you to listen to synthesized music or experience walking through a mountain valley. The use of Java is expected to create the market for software-on-demand, distributed from Internet sites.

Sun's 15,000 people generate up to 2 million E-mail messages a day. Here is what John Gage says about the influence of E-mail on the organization:

"Your E-mail flow determines whether you're really part of the organization; the mailing lists you're on say a lot about the power you have. I've been part of the Java group at Sun for four or five years. Recently, by mistake, someone removed my name from the Java E-mail list. My flow of information just stopped, and I stopped being part of the organization, no matter what the org chart said. I got back in a hurry.

The best way to understand what's happening in a company is to get its alias file—the master list of all its E-mail lists. Before the Web, I used the alias file to tell me what was going on at Sun. . . . I didn't need anyone to tell me Java was getting hot. There used to be 35 people on the Java list, then there were 120. Something's happening . . . There's a new, virtual organization taking shape below the CEO."

From the interview with John Gage by Richard Rapaport, *Fast Company,* April–May 1996, pp. 116–121.

Let us now consider how the information systems designed for management support help managers at various corporate levels.

Information Systems for Management Support: General View

Table 2.5 summarizes the features of information systems expressly designed to support managers: management reporting systems (MRS), decision support systems (DSS), and executive information systems (EIS). Note that DSS support the solution of problems characterized by a minimal structure or, in other words, problems requiring the most judgment from the problem solver. It may seem surprising that this is not a characteristic of top-management support systems such as EIS. However, EIS are generally used by executives not to find a solution but to see whether a problem—or an opportunity—exists. A DSS would then typically be employed by staff analysts or middle managers to identify a solution to the problem on behalf of the senior managers.

Expert systems may be used on all levels of management support. They can screen data reported by MRS to minimize output volume, they can indicate trends that require watching in EIS, and they are heavily used in conjunction with traditional DSS in the decision-making process.

The objectives of the three levels of corporate management are listed below:

- **Operations management:** Performed by supervisors of smaller work units concerned with planning and control of short-term (typically, a week to six months) budgets and schedules.

Table 2.5

Information systems for management support

System Type	Target Users	Typical Use Scenario	Dominant Problems	Data Sources	Prevalent Time Horizon
MRS	Lower and middle managers	Study of reports	Operational and management control	Largely internal	Past and present
DSS	Lower and middle managers; staff analysts	Decision-making session	Planning	Internal and external	Future
EIS	Top managers	Quick overview	Top-level control	Internal and external	Past-present-long-term-future

System Type	Problem Variability	Level of Analysis by the System	Level of Detail	Problem Structure
MRS	Recurring problems	Very low	Very high	Very high
DSS	Ad hoc, unique problems	High or very high	Mixed	Relatively low
EIS	Similar problems	Low or medium	Summaries, with detail available	High

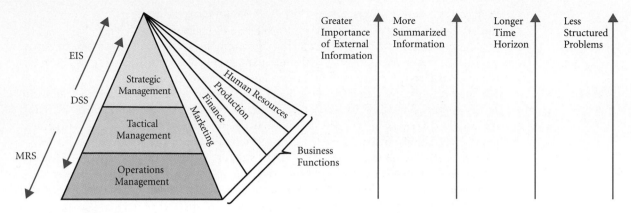

Figure 2.14

A summary of the informational support of management (From Vladimir Zwass, *Management Information Systems*. Dubuque, IA: Wm. C. Brown, 1992 p. 107.)

- **Tactical management:** Performed by middle managers (for example, department heads or plant managers) responsible for acquisition and allocation of resources for projects according to tactical plans, set out for one or two years.
- **Strategic management:** Carried out by top corporate executives and corporate boards responsible for setting and monitoring long-term directions for the firm for three or more years into the future.

A graphic summary of informational support of these management levels is shown in Figure 2.14.

As we can see in Figure 2.14, the higher the management level, the more important is the access to external information. Indeed, higher-level managers need to scan the competitive environment continually. The higher the level, the more highly summarized the information should be in order to protect its users from information overload. The higher we go in the firm, the longer the time horizon of the problems the executives are working with—planning, for example. Also, as we move up in the hierarchy, the problems become less structured and more complex, requiring greater human judgment.

A recent development is the gradual emergence of general management support systems. These combine the EIS capabilities of providing summarized graphical information with the DSS capabilities that support decision making, delivered over office information systems such as enhanced E-mail.

SUMMARY

Information systems transform data, the raw facts, into information that adds to our knowledge. Quality information needs to possess several attributes. Notably, it has to be timely, complete, concise, relevant, accurate, precise, and presented in an appropriate form. Decision makers need both the internal information about their organization and the external information about its environment.

An information system is a specific type of system in general. A system is a set of components (subsystems) that operate together to achieve certain objectives. The quality of the system may be evaluated in terms of its effectiveness and efficiency. Effectiveness measures the extent to which the system meets its objectives. Efficiency is a measure of resources consumed to produce given outputs. If we consider an organization as a larger system, then its information systems assist management by providing feedback on the firm's performance.

Information systems consist of the following general components: hardware, software, databases, telecommunications, human resources, and procedures.

Organizations employ several types of information systems. Transaction processing systems today generally work in on-line mode by immediately processing a firm's business transactions. Management functions are supported by three types of systems. Management reporting systems provide routine information to managers through voluminous reports in the manager's area of responsibility. Decision support systems directly support a decision-making session. Executive information systems support top managers with conveniently displayed summarized information, customized for them. To support general knowledge work, office information systems are used; professional support systems help in tasks specific to various professions. Various types of information systems may employ expert system technology.

A variety of information systems support managers as they play their interpersonal, informational, and decisional roles. The three management-oriented types of systems provide different kinds of support to the three levels of management: strategic, tactical, and operational. The higher the corporate managerial level, the more summarized the provided information; the longer the time horizon, the more important the external information, and the more complex and less structured the problems needing solution.

KEY TERMS

Information   *40*
Data   *41*
Database   *41*
Formal information systems   *41*
Accuracy versus precision   *42*
Stakeholders   *43*
System   *44*
System objectives   *46*
System constraints   *46*
Artificial system   *46*
Organization   *46*
Effectiveness   *47*
Efficiency   *47*
Feedback   *48*
Central processor   *50*
Downsizing   *50*
Systems software   *51*
Operating system   *51*
Compiler or interpreter   *51*

Applications software   *51*
Telecommunications   *51*
Local area network (LAN)   *51*
Metropolitan area network (MAN)   *51*
Wide area network (WAN)   *51*
Information system architecture   *52*
End user   *54*
End-user computing   *54*
Procedures   *54*
Transaction   *54*
Expert system   *59*
Planning   *60*
Controlling   *60*
Leading   *60*
Organizing   *60*
Operations management   *62*
Tactical management   *64*
Strategic management   *64*

QUESTIONS

1. How does information differ from data? Give an example of data and information that are related to each other, using the California Pizza Kitchen of the Focus Minicase. How are the two related?
2. State the attributes of quality information. Select three of these and for each of them give an example of information that does *not* possess this attribute.
3. State three examples of external stakeholders of a business firm and give an example of information each of them receives from the firm or provides to it.
4. Define *system*. Explain the relationship between a system and its subsystem and illustrate this relationship with an information system example.
5. What is the difference between the objectives of a system and the constraints on it? Give an information system-related example.
6. What are the interfaces with the environment (that is, inputs and outputs) that cross the boundary of the following systems:
   a. A student registration system for a university.
   b. An information system for a police patrol car.
   c. A project scheduling system for a business team.
7. What is the difference between efficiency and effectiveness? Give an example of each measure that would be applicable to an information system supporting sales representatives of a company.
8. What is the feedback loop in a system? Why are many information systems considered a part of their owner firm's feedback loop?
9. What feedback information should be provided in each of the following systems:
   a. Deciding on the advertising outlets for your firm for the next budget period.
   b. Selecting suppliers for a new product.
   c. Evaluating the effectiveness of a recent quality improvement program.
10. Why is total quality management an example of systems thinking?
11. Classify the following entities as one of the five components of information systems:
    a. Word processing program
    b. The Internet
    c. Telecommunications specialist
    d. Collection of customer records
    e. Disaster recovery plan
12. What is meant by the downsizing of computer systems and why are many corporations resorting to downsizing?
13. What is the distinction between systems software and applications software?

14. What is a database?
15. What three types of networks are used in telecommunications and how do they relate to the Internet?
16. How has the role of end users and procedures in information systems changed in recent years? Why?
17. What is the function of transaction processing systems (TPS)? Give three examples of TPS.
18. What is the function of management reporting systems (MRS)? Give an example of MRS.
19. What is the function of decision support systems (DSS)? Give three examples of DSS. Who would use each of these systems?
20. What is the function of executive information systems (EIS)?
21. What is the function of office information systems (OIS)? Give three examples of systems in the OIS category.
22. Give three examples of professional support systems. Whom do they assist?
23. What is the function of an expert system? Give three examples of advice such systems can realistically offer. To whom would they offer this advice?
24. What are the three levels of management that management-support systems serve? What are the principal differences in support needs as we move up the managerial hierarchy?

ISSUES FOR DISCUSSION

1. Do computer-based information systems make informal information unnecessary? If not, do you think these systems will *ultimately* make informal information unnecessary? Why or why not?
2. Consider the six types of information systems we have discussed. Which of these systems are primarily directed at efficiency ("doing things right") in the organization and which are directed at effectiveness ("doing the right thing")?
3. Assume you are a chief executive of a firm. What information would you like to receive from your executive information system (EIS)? What features would you like your EIS to have? Do you think this type of system should be available to managers at all levels? What are the pros and cons of such availability?
4. Are there any ethical issues involved as more and more information is being quantified for information system processing? For example, public opinion on a subject is frequently expressed as the average of responses to a few questions within a scale from 1 to 5.

REAL-WORLD MINICASE
AND PROBLEM-SOLVING
EXERCISES

1. Performance Measurement as the Way of Life   The chemicals manufacturer Eastman Chemical of Kingsport, Tennessee, believes in total quality management based on top-to-bottom performance measurement. The company also uses this measurement program to implement its strategic plans.

The process works as follows. The corporate strategic plan is used to develop the measures by which the team of top executives, consisting of 11 members, is evaluated. The performance measures relate to the five principal stockholders of the company: stockholders, customers, employees, suppliers, and the public. Financial measures are only a part of the evaluation program. For example, one top-level measure is customer values, as measured by surveys. Another is employee retention. A third one is community satisfaction: How happy are plant neighbors with Eastman's control of pollution. Four measures trace innovation, including the identification of new product needs and sales of new products as the percentage of total sales. The key financial measure is the company's profit.

Eastman cascades the performance measures down throughout the organization in the following way. Each member of the top-level executive team leads a team that in turn develops its own performance measures, derived from all the relevant top-level measures. Each member of that executive's team runs another lower-level team that creates its own measures, and so on, down the "front lines" of the company. The measures of the lower-level teams "interlock" with those of the higher-level since they are derived from them. For example, while the top-team performance measure is profit, a team on the operating floor might measure the volume of manufacturing-process waste.

Extensive databases of the attained levels of performance are maintained. Key results can be seen on a variety of displays throughout the company. Appropriate incentives are provided to all workers. All this measuring does add up to superior performance: In 1995, Eastman delivered a profit of $346 million, or 13.2 percentage points above the cost of capital.

a. Describe the team organization of Eastman Chemical in terms of system theory.

b. Give several examples of the internal data used in the feedback loop in the operation of the top team in the firm. Where do the standards come from for the operation of that loop?

c. Where do the standards come from for the feedback loops of the lower-level teams? How do the "interlocking"

measures further the execution of the corporate strategic plan?

d. State how each type of the information systems discussed in Section 2.4 can be used to support the performance measurement program at Eastman Chemical.

Based on Bill Birchard, "Eastman Chemical: Quality and Strategy," *CFO*, October 1996, pp. 34–36.

2. Producing a Report and Designing a Cover Page
Using word processing and painting programs, or similar software, produce a report and design the cover page for it. (You will customize the cover page for the other assignments you will hand in during this course.)

The subject of your report is "The Internet as a Source of Business Information." The report should very briefly, but as comprehensively as possible, list and discuss all the categories of business information available on the Internet. You should also use several published sources on the subject (for example, sources on competitive intelligence) and reference them in the footnotes, using the facilities of the word processing program.

The cover page should include the title and number of the assignment, the course information, your name, and the date. The title of the assignment should be formatted in the largest font size and in color, if a color printer is available. The page should include your own drawing to reflect the contents of the assignment. Your objective is to design a page that is both informative and esthetically pleasing. This assignment will be evaluated on its form as well as its content.

3. What Information Would You Need?   Assume you have just become a human resources specialist for a software company, responsible for hiring software developers. List the information you will need to perform the job. List the information systems you are likely to work with.

TEAM PROJECT

Analyze the resources of the enrollment system used by your college or university. Identify and describe in detail the five components of the system, including vendor information where appropriate. Investigate the types of information systems supporting the enrollment; classify each of them in terms of Section 2.4; and categorize the users of each of these systems. Selected reports will be presented to the class.

ENDNOTE

1. Gordon Moore is a founder and chairman of the board of Intel Corporation, the leading maker of microprocessors. He

based his assertion on the continuing and envisaged development of new technologies that allow the number of transistors on a microprocessor chip to quadruple every three years.

SELECTED REFERENCES

Baroudi, Jack J., and Wanda J. Orlikowski. "A Short-Form Measure of User Information Satisfaction." *Journal of Management Information Systems,* 4, no. 4 (Spring 1988), pp. 44–59.

The source of a frequently employed user satisfaction questionnaire.

Chae, Lee. "Battering Down the Hatches." *LAN: The Network Solutions Magazine,* April 1996, pp. 85–90.

Kalakota, Ravi, and Andrew B. Whinston. *Frontiers of Electronic Commerce,* Addison-Wesley: Reading, Mass., 1996.

A thorough sourcebook on its subject.

Kaplan, Robert S., and David P. Norton. "Using the Balanced Scorecard as a Strategic Management System," *Harvard Business Review,* January–February 1996, pp. 75–85.

Describes an extensive technique for measuring corporate performance.

McLean, Ephraim R., and Leon A. Kappelman. "The Convergence of Organizational and End-User Computing." *Journal of Management Information Systems,* 9, no. 3 (Winter 1992–93), pp. 145–156.

Miller, Holmes. "The Multiple Dimensions of Information Quality." *Information Systems Management,* Spring 1996, pp. 79–82.

Mintzberg, Henry. *The Nature of Managerial Work,* New York: Harper & Row, 1973.

Nunamaker, Jay F.; E. Sue Weber; and Minder Chen. "Organizational Crisis Management Systems: Planning for Intelligent Action." *Journal of Management Information Systems,* 5, no. 4 (Spring 1989), pp. 7–32.

Orlikowski, Wanda. "Improvising Organizational Transformation Over Time: A Situated Change Perspective." *Information Systems Research,* 7, no. 1 (March 1996), pp. 63–92.

An accessible description of the evolution of procedures and work practices around a new information system in an organization over a two-year period.

Ross, Philip. "Moore's Second Law," *Forbes,* March 25, 1996, pp. 116–117.

Simon, Herbert A. *Sciences of the Artificial,* 2nd ed. Cambridge, Mass.: MIT Press, 1981.

Zwass, Vladimir. *Management Information Systems,* Dubuque: Wm. C. Brown, 1992.

A more advanced discussion of management information systems.

CASE STUDY | # How Executives Use an Information System

Let's take a look at an actual case that took place in a major North American corporation. The firm employed an executive information system, called RESOLVE, developed by Metapraxis (of Kingston upon Thames, Great Britain, and New York).

As we know, executive information systems (EIS) are used by senior managers and by corporate boards. The principal aim of EIS is to make all the information on the performance of a company available in digestible form, facilitating prompt problem solving. Therefore, information is available in a highly summarized and graphic form. However, the executive users can "drill down" to detailed data during a problem-solving session. Color graphs and data can be projected on a large screen.

The EIS is able to present the performance of the company in four dimensions, as illustrated in Figure 2.15: Even more complex descriptions are possible as well. Thus, finan-

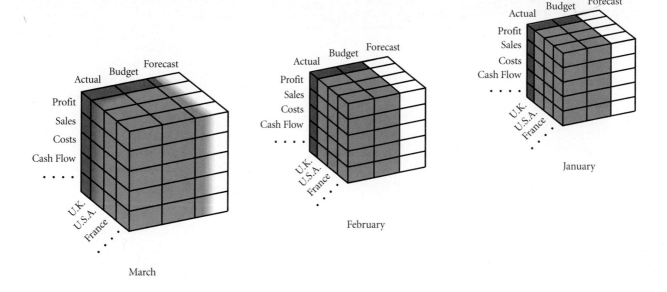

March

February

January

Figure 2.15

An executive informa-tion system can provide a four-dimensional representation of a company's financial performance. You can see here a selection of these dimensions

cial data, such as profits or sales, can be seen as actual results, compared to planned amounts, and projected into the future based on developing trends. The results can be shown for operating units of a company. The multinational company depicted in this case study has geographical divisions, such as the United Kingdom, the United States, and France. Selected time periods for the data are months.

The following series of reports, presented in graphical and tabular form, was obtained during an executive committee meeting of a corporation we will call Diverse Industries. According to the reports, the meeting took place at the end of April 1997. During the meeting, the reports were shown on a central screen. Such reports may indeed be produced during a meeting from corporate databases or, for a faster pace, prepared by the company's financial officers for the session and stored in secondary memory, such as a disk.

Let us follow the sequence of reports used during this very interesting session.

Report 1 (Figure 2.16): This figure, consisting of a graph and a table, is a summary of corporate profit performance for the last five years. The projection (made by management, which is presenting the results to the executive committee) is compared to the long-term corporate plan and to the budget (short-term plan). A problem appears: The management projection for the 1997 year-end shows $73.5 million profit, compared to the budget (annual plan) of $78.1 million. Both figures are well below the strategic (five-year) plan of $91.8 million.

Let us see how the executives tracked the problem to its source.

Report 2 (Figure 2.17): Monthly totals for the company reveal that the problem indeed started in April 1997. This figure shows the capability of the system to make its own projection (preview) of the future. The negative cumulative variance shows a discrepancy between the budgeted and achieved or projected results. The management projection and the EIS forecast (preview) agree that the downturn in profitability will continue at least until the end of 1997.

Report 3 (Figure 2.18): An analysis of divisional results shows that the problems emerged in the Timber and Metals divisions. In fact, the other two operating divisions, Plastics and Glass, have done better than planned.

Figure 2.16

Long-term performance of Diverse Industries, Inc.

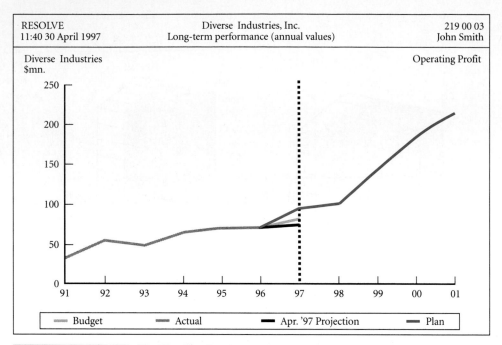

	Budget	Actual	Projection Apr. '97	Plan
1991		32.4		
1992		53.6		
1993		47.8		
1994		61.8		
1995		68.2		
1996		69.2		
1997	78.1		73.5	91.8
1998				97.6
1999				136.5
2000				179.3
2001				210.1

Figure 2.17

Month-by-month performance of Diverse Industries, Inc.

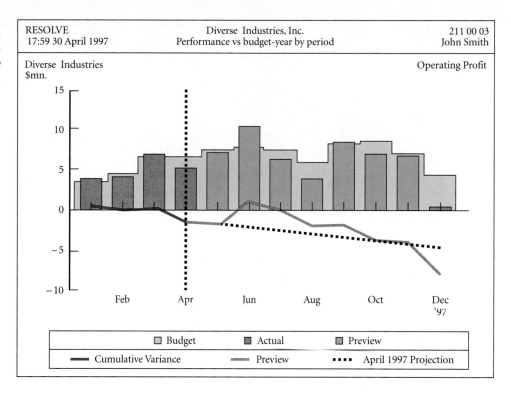

Figure 2.18

Quarterly performance of individual divisions of Diverse Industries, Inc.

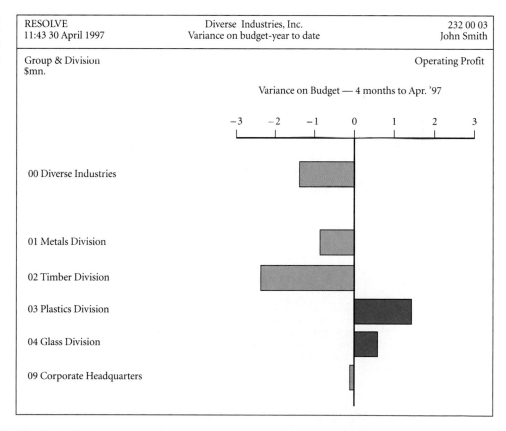

Report 4 (Figure 2.19): Comparison of the monthly profit figures for the four divisions shows that while the Timber division has been underperforming since the beginning of the year, the Metals division shortfall arose suddenly in April. The commentary attached to the report shows the Timber division management already has an action plan. The Metals division needs to be further investigated. The projection made by the management of that division is rather optimistic as compared to the projection (preview) made by the system.

Report 5 (Figure 2.20): This figure reveals that the problem within the Metals division has been caused by the Michigan Steel Company.

Figure 2.19

Month-by-month performance of individual divisions of Diverse Industries, Inc., with a commentary stored in the system

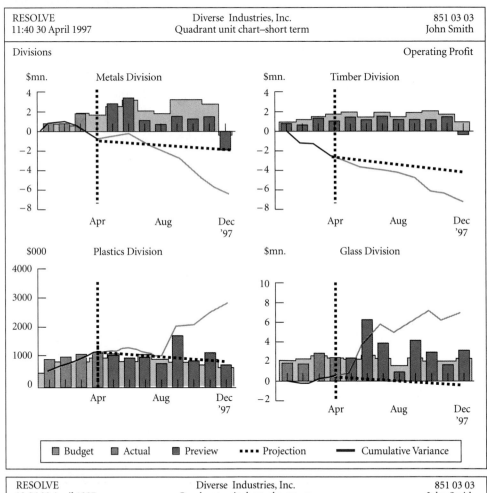

Commentary: The five-stage action plan agreed at the March Executive Committee meeting is currently being implemented and an improvement in results is confidently expected by the end of this quarter. The possibility of increasing marketing spending in order to win back market share from our major competitors in the sector is also being investigated.

Paul Daniels
President, Timber Division

Figure 2.20

*Performance of the
operating companies
that make up the
Metals Division of
Diverse Industries, Inc.*

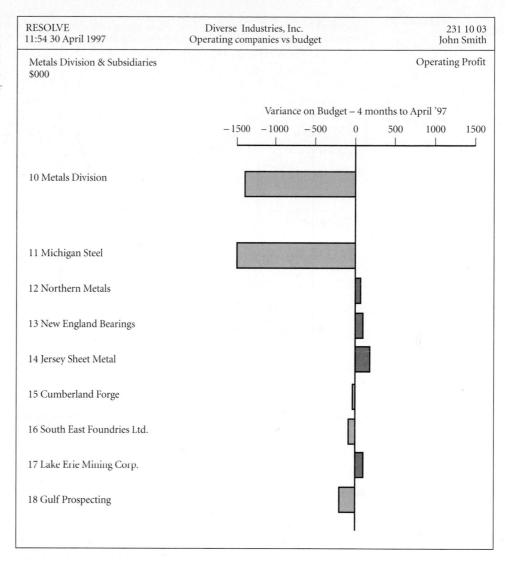

Figure 2.20

Performance of the operating companies that make up the Metals Division of Diverse Industries, Inc.

Report 6 (Figure 2.21): A review of the gross profit margins (percentage of profit in sales before expenses) of Michigan Steel shows a steady decline, with a severe drop in December 1996. It also shows that the projections made by the management of that company, which indicate that the budget goals will be met in December 1997, are wildly optimistic, as compared to the forecast (preview) computed by the system.

Report 7 (Figure 2.22): Is the profitability of the operating companies of the troubled Metals division increasing? Since companies operate within geographical regions, their performance is illustrated on a map of the United States. The graph and the table show the percentage change in profitability over the period for which data are available (shown in the table). It appears that several companies have achieved sustained improvement in

Figure 2.21

A longer view of the monthly performance of Michigan Steel Company—a unit of the Metals Division of Diverse Industries, Inc.

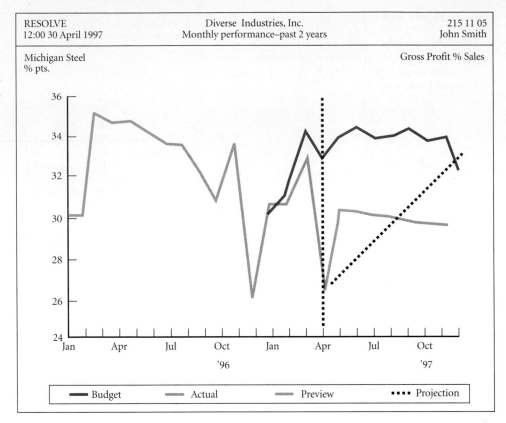

RESOLVE	Diverse Industries, Inc.	215 11 05
12:00 30 April 1997	Monthly performance–past 2 years	John Smith

Michigan Steel % pts.   Gross Profit % Sales

Budget ——   Actual ═══   Preview ═══   Projection ••••

performance. However, one of the regional firms, Lake Erie Mining Company (LEMC) has a severe problem with its profits.

Based on the executive session, a plan was formulated to transfer successful practices of the operating units to the lagging firm. The management of Lake Erie Mining Company was requested to report to the executive committee on a monthly basis regarding the implementation of the plan and the operating results.

CASE STUDY QUESTIONS

1. List five items of information obtained by the executives of Diverse Industries with their EIS. How does the nature of this information relate to their managerial responsibilities (in terms of Table 2.5)?

2. What attributes of information quality can you identify in the information provided by the EIS in the case?

3. Describe how the use of the EIS implements the feedback loop in managing Diverse Industries.

4. Based on the study, do you believe that only the highest level of management can profit from the use of an EIS?

Figure 2.22

Profit margins of the operating companies of the metals division over the last several years

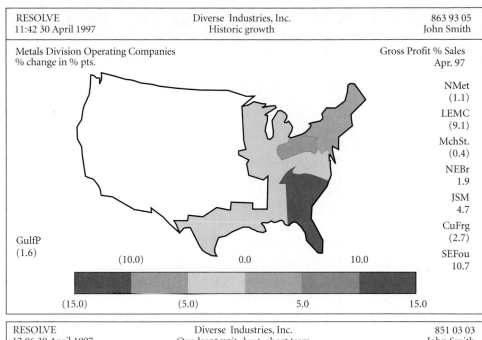

| RESOLVE | Diverse Industries, Inc. | 863 93 05 |
| 11:42 30 April 1997 | Historic growth | John Smith |

Metals Division Operating Companies
% change in % pts.

Gross Profit % Sales
Apr. 97

| RESOLVE | Diverse Industries, Inc. | 851 03 03 |
| 12:06 30 April 1997 | Quadrant unit chart–short term | John Smith |

Metals Division Operating Companies
% pts.

Gross Profit % Sales
Apr. 97

	Annual %	Current Projection	Earliest Actual
Gulf Prospecting	(1.6)	32.3 (Apr)	35.2 (1986)
Northern Metals	(1.1)	23.7 (Apr)	24.8 (1987)
Michigan Steel	(0.4)	33.5 (Apr)	34.4 (1985)
Lake Erie Mining Corp.	(9.1)	30.5 (Apr)	37.6 (1989)
New England Bearings	1.9	34.9 (Apr)	31.1 (1985)
Jersey Sheet Metal	4.7	33.1 (Apr)	25.2 (1985)
South East Foundries Ltd.	10.7	30.0 (Apr)	27.1 (1990)
Cumberland Forge	(2.7)	34.0 (Apr)	41.3 (1985)

5. Which of the following alternatives do you believe is the principal cost component: (a) the personal computer and the executive information system or (b) the acquisition and maintenance of the databases on which the use of the system relies? Based on your answer, consider whether a small company could profitably use an EIS? Why or why not?

6. Draw up an alternative scenario for using an executive information system in a business you are familiar with.

CHAPTER THREE

Competing with Information Systems

OBJECTIVES

After you complete this chapter, you will be able to:

1. Understand what an information society is.
2. Identify the challenges an information society brings to business organizations.
3. Understand how today's information systems have emerged and how their organizational role has expanded over the years.
4. Explain what a strategic information system is.
5. Describe and illustrate three principal thrusts for seeking competitive advantage with information systems.
6. Describe strategies that can be used to compete, forces that operate in competitive markets, and tactics that can be employed.
7. Use a firm's value chain to seek opportunities for developing strategic information systems.

OUTLINE

Weaving the Competitive Web

Les Ottolenghi, director of emerging technologies for Holiday Inn Worldwide, is paid for thinking big thoughts about information systems and for translating these ideas into customer services that will make his company stand out in the hospitality industry.

As the industry first, Holiday Inn's Web site (Figure 3.1) enables customers to book rooms over the Internet. Without additional promotion, the company now averages 700 Internet bookings a week and almost all of them are new business. This is, of course, a tiny percentage of some one million reservations the hotel chain books each week. However, the service pays for itself, since the cost of booking each reservation is 25 percent cheaper than when taken over the phone or through an airline's computerized reservation system. More important, the company is continually learning how to use the Internet for competitive purposes. And as electronic commerce develops, Holiday Inn intends to stay in the front of its industry. This chain of hotels considers its skills in exploiting information technology for business purposes its second core competence.

The company's strategy is, in part, defensive. As Martin Gray, a vice president of marketing, tells us: "On the Net, a company like Microsoft could get into the reservations business and into the distribution channels that are normally operated by the lodging companies and literally take them over. We don't ever want to cede that to any other company." The hotel chain's Holidex reservation system is the only one in the industry that performs real-time bookings on-line 24 hours a day. It deploys several mainframes,

Figure 3.1

The home page of the Holiday Inn World Wide Web site (From World Wide Web—http: //www. holiday-inn. com)

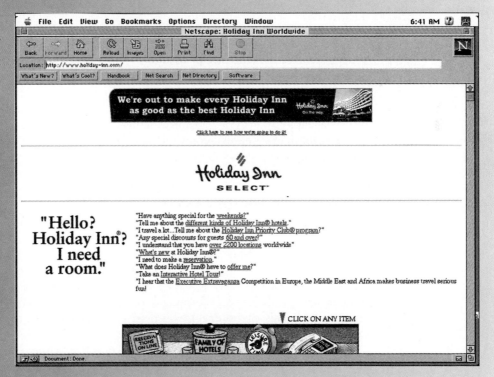

a Hughes aircraft satellite, and a state-of-the-art communications center. In pursuing its aggressive Internet stance, Holiday Inn knows that its more frequent customers are Internet-ready: According to its research, 70 percent of its Priority Club guests have on-line accounts and 80 percent carry portable computers.

Several major applications are being developed. A Web-based tool for meeting and conference planners will enable corporate planners to take virtual reality tours of different properties. An on-line slide rule will be available to compute the costs, based on various combinations of space and meals, and even send faxes and voice messages to others involved in the arrangements. Within 12 months, planners will be able to make all of their arrangements on-line. Another Holiday Inn project is creating an electronic brochure for the Web site to allow visitors to view information in real time.

As a long-range effort, Ottolenghi and his people are planning what they like to call "cyberhotel." Information technology will be ubiquitous in every room in this computerized hotel. Every room will be equipped with a virtual desk, a virtual Rolodex, and a virtual bookshelf—all furnished by information technology. Guests will be able to hold virtual meetings and then go "downstairs" to a virtual (of course) cybercafe. Regardless of whether this is the future you want as a hotel guest, here is the objective: "We want to give people a better experience on the Web," says Ottolenghi, "but it's also about building brand equity."

Based on Leigh Buchanan, "Rooms with a View," *WebMaster,* March/April 1996, pp. 34–44, and the Web site http://www.holiday-inn.com.

Today's organizations compete in an information society. What a firm needs to do to compete successfully depends on the environment in which it has to compete. The environment of an information society presents several serious challenges, and the role of organizational information systems has evolved over time as competing organizations attempt to meet these challenges. By analyzing the forces acting in the marketplace and the chains of activities through which it delivers products or services to that marketplace, a company can identify opportunities for deploying strategic information systems that will help it compete.

3.1 | INFORMATION SOCIETY AND THE CHANGING COMPETITIVE ENVIRONMENT

The technologically advanced nations of the world, the United States among them, are at present in the formative stages of the information society that is emerging from what was formerly an industrial society. Just as energy was the driving force in the industrial society, so information is the key transforming resource in the new social and economic relations. To compete in this environment, you need to understand what it demands from your organization.

In an **information society,** which may be considered either an advanced form of industrial society or a postindustrial society (Bell 1973), most of the people active in the economy are employed in the handling of information. Similarly, most of the goods and

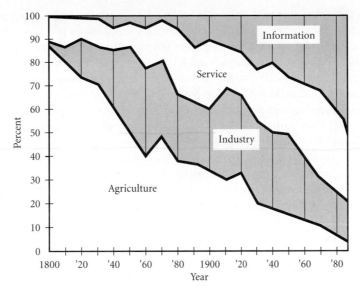

Figure 3.2

Distribution of the U.S. civilian workforce (From James R. Beniger, *The Control Revolution: Technological and Economic Origins of the Information Society.* 1986, p. 23.)

services produced by an information society can be classified as information- (or knowledge-) related. As you can see from Figure 3.2, in the late 1950s the information sector became the largest employer of the U.S. workforce. This sector includes universities, banks, insurance companies, communications companies, and consulting firms. Since the 1980s, more than 50 percent of the U.S. workers have been employed in the information sector. A similar development has occurred in other advanced economies of the world.

As Figure 3.2 also shows, the information sector of the economy had already started to grow during the last century. However, after World War II, the technological push of computers and telecommunications accelerated these developments. Innovations in microelectronics, optics, software development, and other technologies made possible the ever increasing computing speeds, storage of massive quantities of data and information, and the rapidly growing speed and capacity of transmission of an increasingly broader spectrum of information modalities, such as voice, data, text, image, and video. The staggering increase in computing power and telecommunications capacities has been accompanied by steady decreases in costs.

What caused the shift to an information society? James Beniger of the University of Pennsylvania has advanced the influential argument that the origin of the information society may be found in the advancing industrialization of the late nineteenth century (Beniger 1986). As industrial plants increased the speed with which they could process materials, they also had to devote increased resources to control manufacturing and transportation. To exercise this control, through a feedback loop such as the one we discussed in Section 2.2, a firm had to process information ever faster. The demand for more sophisticated information processing equipment ultimately resulted in the development of computers. New technologies, in turn, further push the development of an information society. The continuing cycles of demand pull and supply push account for the progress in the field.

Knowledge work, introduced in Section 1.2, has particular importance in an information society. Peter Drucker, a well-known analyst of management, noted that the ability of a nation's economy to generate knowledge—both theory and technological know-how—and employ it through productive organizations will in the future determine that nation's success in international competition (Drucker 1988). The organizations, in turn, have to be able to generate and skillfully deploy know-how in their area of core competence (Nonaka and Takeuchi 1995). "We are not in the products business—we are in the knowledge business," says the CEO of Johnson & Johnson, a leading producer of pharmaceuticals, showing by this declaration where the firm sees its competitive strength (Lauren 1996).

The performance of its knowledge workers is a key to the firm's success. These workers deal with information, which is an abstraction of reality, rather than with concrete objects. Generating new knowledge is one—and the most creative—aspect of knowledge work. Using and transforming information in your daily work is another. Someone doing knowledge work designs a new product, produces a business plan, makes a decision, writes software or, perhaps, a business letter.

Information systems define the environment in which most knowledge work is done. Each morning, the chief executive officer checks the key indicators of the company's performance as produced by the executive information system. Later the same day, a team of financial analysts consults a group decision support system to recommend the level of prices and promotion needed to shore up a flagging product line. A team of corporate engineers is testing a new design of its earth-moving vehicle by using a computer model of it, a digital prototype. A company salesperson visiting a client connects her laptop computer over the telecommunications network with the inventory database and enters an order with a guaranteed delivery date. At the same moment, office clerks use word processing and electronic document filing, while manufacturing floor supervisors work with an expert system to reschedule production around a failed piece of equipment. As we can see, knowledge work in a modern organization relies on the capabilities of information systems, as discussed in Chapter 1.

3.2 | BUSINESS CHALLENGES OF THE INFORMATION SOCIETY

The competitive environment of the information society presents new and serious challenges that organizations have to meet to prevent their decline (Huber 1984). We can summarize these challenges and the requisite organizational responses as follows:

1. Increasingly keen global competition calls for rapid product and process innovation.

Information society is driven to a large degree by technologies that shrink distances, either computer-based or controlled by computers. These technologies have resulted in the worldwide infrastructure (that is, the facilities necessary for the functioning and growth of economies) of transportation and telecommunications. The availability of this infrastructure, along with political developments, has led to the globalization of business.

Business globalization is the emergence of global markets as the arena of competition and cooperation among firms. Because of this phenomenon, our new competitor can emerge in any area of the world. But so too can we gain a marketplace or locate a production facility in a foreign country. We can also find abroad a firm we can cooperate with: It can become our long-term supplier or distributor, or perhaps our partner in developing new products or services. Business globalization heightens business competition. Unless a firm develops, hones, and maintains a core competence in its operations, something it does better than others, it may lose its business to a competitor located anywhere in the world (Hamel and Prahalad 1994). On the other hand, a successful firm can gain broad access to established and emerging markets.

Continuous product and process innovation are the necessary responses to the ever keener competition. **Product innovation** results in the development of a new product or service. Information systems serve to develop these products and services, and information itself may serve as the product or as part of the product. Let us look at a relatively small company. Its founder, Kevin Clark, has taken advantage of two trends: the growth of the healthcare industry and the growth of the temporary workforce. The 33-year old entrepreneur has built his company, Cross Country Healthcare (of Boca Raton, Florida) around a proprietary database containing data on 1,500 hospitals and over 110,000 nurses, therapists, and other healthcare workers. The company "makes a market" in the services of these workers. Clark also introduced a multimedia information system that allows a nurse to view a video of a hospital and the prospective employers to view an interview with the nurse. The young entrepreneur has already created a marketplace that accrues $70 million in billings to his firm annually (Dumaine 1994). We will encounter similar examples in this chapter.

Information systems are also used for innovation in the ways products are manufactured and services are provided—this is **process innovation.** As you read in the Focus Minicase for the chapter, Holiday Inn employs the resources of the Internet, as well as other information systems, to make its hotel service stand out in the hospitality industry. Many firms have embarked on ambitious business reengineering projects, aiming to radically redesign their business processes by exploiting the capabilities of information technology.

Consider Kodak. A few years ago, it took the company seventy weeks to develop a new camera—too slow to compete with agile rivals such as Fuji of Japan. To regain competitive strength, Kodak drastically cut its time-to-market by reengineering its product development process. Using computer-aided design/computer-aided manufacturing (CAD/CAM) information systems, the firm moved to electronic design on a computer screen instead of on paper. As computers help validate the projected designs, there is no need for multiple physical prototypes. At least equally important, information systems enabled concurrent engineering: Engineers in various specialties work in parallel, with their work integrated into the product design database. Each engineer's work is collected daily into this database. Every morning, design teams inspect the database. If a solution chosen by an optical designer yesterday has created a difficulty in mechanical design, this becomes immediately obvious in the digital prototype and the specialists can resolve the difficulty. Kodak's process innovation consisted in the radical redesign of product development, enabled by the move to a computerized, paperless design process. Thanks to this, Kodak cut the camera development time nearly in half, to thirty-eight weeks (Hammer and Champy 1993).

2. Dramatic increases in knowledge that can affect your business call for organizational knowledge management supported by information technology.

Whether measured in terms of the number of scholarly journals, patents, and copyrights, or in terms of the volume of corporate communications, both the production and the distribution of knowledge have undergone a manifold increase. Information systems have to enable knowledge workers to access the information necessary for their work without being swamped by information overload. Beyond that, knowledge workers have to be empowered to solve problems and make decisions, using their knowledge.

Information systems should be able to perform routine and noncritical decision making, subject to human approval when appropriate. Organizations also need to successfully introduce information technology for both individual and, to an increasing degree, group knowledge work. Information systems must support the units that perform complete tasks in organizations: a group of knowledge workers. The size of a group depends on the task at hand. For example, an electronic mail (E-mail) message broadcast over the corporate network to all managers above a certain level (perhaps a hundred of them), requesting their comments on a new budgeting policy to be implemented during the next quarter, includes a large group in the policy-making process. As we learned in Chapter 1, smaller teams, responsible for a project, are emerging as the basic workforce unit in a firm. Thus, five people developing a new executive information system are a project team. Supported by the appropriate information systems, members of this small, tightly collaborating group may work at several locations, or even partly telecommute by working at home.

The basic support to a knowledge worker is delivered by a personal workstation. Some of the facilities it makes available are shown in Figure 3.3. The workstation is built around a personal computer, with a modem connection to the telephone network. A single workstation has a significant processing capability of its own; but, just as important, it is connected over networks to the workstations of other workers. It also provides access to a number of informational services both within the company (corporate databases, for example) and outside of it (over the Internet, for example). A knowledge worker can also participate in a teleconference from his or her current location.

A number of firms have made the Internet into their vital knowledge resource. Consider the people at Schlumberger, the multinational company that is a leader in oil-field services. The members of the firm use the Internet routinely to monitor technological developments, track standards, exchange electronic mail with colleagues in the company and outside of it (when faced with a problem, you may very quickly get answers from people who have faced it before), and even to conduct business, say to buy software or order parts (Cronin 1995).

Leading corporations have recognized the importance of knowledge accumulated by their members and have instituted processes for knowledge management. **Knowledge management** is the operation of the organizational methods, procedures, and information systems that are used to collect the knowledge and experience of the members of the organization and bring them to bear on problems and opportunities.

Relying on the capability of information technology to support organizational memory and learning (discussed in Chapter 1), corporations are implementing organizational systems that provide integrated performance support for their knowledge workers (Winslow and Bramer 1994). Figure 3.4a shows the screen of a system that supports insurance underwriters as they analyze policies submitted by agents and decide whether to approve them. Figure 3.4b shows the user interface of a system supporting the salespeople of a food company in Japan. Such systems help knowledge workers cope with their workload.

3. Faster pace of business events—the cause and the result of time-based competition.

The pace of events in an information society is set by technologies. The speeds of today's computer and telecommunication technologies have resulted in a dramatic increase in the number of events occurring within a given time. Compare, for example, the volume and speed of trades in the securities and currency markets today with those two decades ago. Widespread use of E-mail and fax, as another example, has removed the

Figure 3.3

*Personal workstation—
a tool of the knowledge
worker*

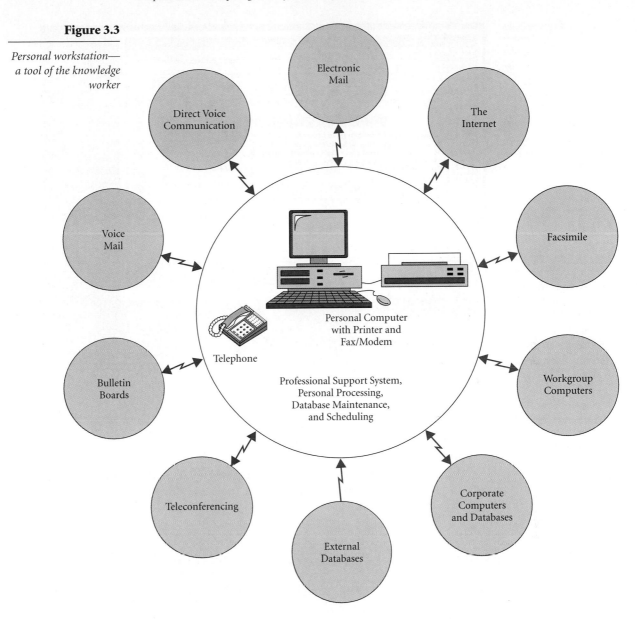

"float", or the lag between sending and receiving, in written communications. This time compression calls for much faster decisions during business problem solving.

Time-based competition takes place where those first to market have a chance to preempt it. To compete, you need to develop a new product faster than your competitors, give a quote on the product price before your rival, develop an agile manufacturing system to instantaneously move the assembly line to a different product, or deliver the product faster than your rival. All of these are the pressures of the new environment.

Figure 3.4a

Integrated performance support for knowledge workers. The screen of a system supporting an insurance underwriter. The underwriter selects a policy for analysis. The system provides an update on this type of policy. Going on, the underwriter will be prompted about a possible resident-student discount. As soon as the underwriter provides the name of the school, the system determines that its distance does qualify and the premium is adjusted. After several similar adjustments, the policy is accepted. The system provides a few details about this long-term customer and helps insert them into a personalized letter (From Winslow and Bramer 1994, p. 111.)

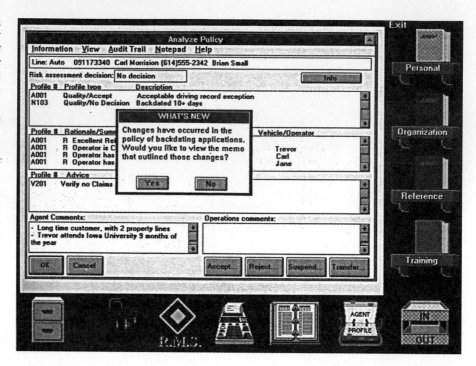

Information systems are based on the technologies that led to the heightened pace of events, but they are also the means to respond to this aspect of the environment, as you may conclude by reviewing their capabilities discussed in Chapter 1. Let us now see how information systems have evolved to respond to the challenges.

3.3   HOW THE ROLE OF INFORMATION SYSTEMS EVOLVED

The role information systems play in organizations has evolved over time. During this evolution, earlier types of systems have not been discarded but rather modified, moved to new hardware and software platforms, and, in many cases, integrated with new systems.

As we have stressed, information systems today are unthinkable (well, perhaps only "thinkable") without computers. The first general-purpose electronic computer, ENIAC, was completed in 1946 at the University of Pennsylvania. Mass production of computers started in 1951 when UNIVAC I was delivered commercially from an assembly line. Organizational computing was born when this computer model was installed in General Electric for data processing in 1954. We can view the development of information systems since then as the four eras shown in Figures 3.5 to 3.8—based in part on the work of Lynda Applegate of the Harvard Business School and her colleagues (Applegate 1996). The consecutive eras expand, rather than replace, the informational support of the prior eras. Let's discuss this development.

Figure 3.4 b

The screen of a prototype system developed by Andersen Consulting's Tokyo office to support the sales force of a large food production company. The system supports planning strategies to expand sales and acquire new customers; developing sales proposals; and reporting and managing productivity. When a salesperson selects an activity from the menu bar, the system displays the flow and description of the tasks to be completed. Boxes across the second line on the screen (the toolbar) show the support tools available, including the "idea box" (the one with the light bulb) that suggests similar real cases from the past (From Charles D. Winslow and William L. Bramer. *FutureWork: Putting Knowledge to Work in the Knowledge Economy.* New York: Free Press, 1994, p. 134.)

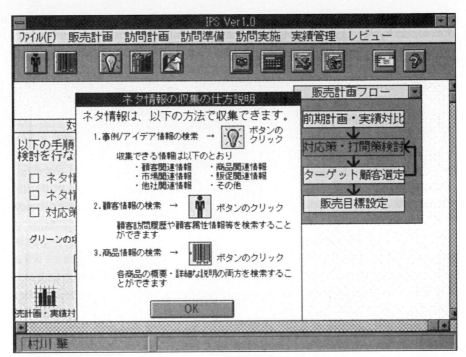

1. Operational Support

From the mid-1950s to the mid-1970s, information systems were used to support business operations (Figure 3.5), in order to raise their efficiency. Management support began to emerge in the form of voluminous reports. The systems were designed to serve the needs of major corporate units rather than individual users.

Companies generally had a single data processing department (later to be renamed information systems department). All applications were developed within this department and largely at its discretion. End users did not have direct access to computer technology: All access to information was through information systems professionals. Applications judged worthy of development often had to wait three or more years until the professionals had time to develop them. Access to computing was thus severely restricted.

2. Support of Management and Knowledge Work

The second era in organizational computing began in the late 1970s when the use of information systems went beyond the support of operations to also support management and knowledge work (Figure 3.6). This was made possible by a number of technological developments. Thanks to more advanced operating systems, users were able to access the computer directly through a terminal. The greatest impact was made by the personal computer, which emerged on an industrial scale in 1977 as Apple II. Propelled by the broadly used spreadsheet programs, IBM and IBM-compatible personal computers and end-user-oriented software empowered the users themselves. End-user computing had begun. Instead of requesting that a system be developed by the information systems department, knowledge workers themselves began using software packages, customizing them for their needs, and even began developing systems of their own. Many information systems were brought under the control of their users.

Figure 3.5

*Era I of organizational
computing: operational
support (mid-1950s
through mid-1970s)*

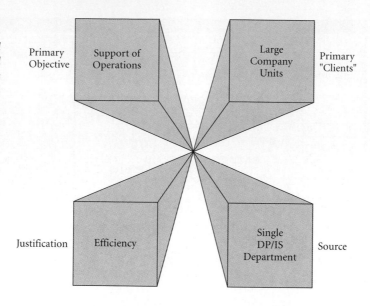

Figure 3.6

*Era II of organizational
computing: support of
management and
knowledge work (mid-
1970s through mid-
1980s)*

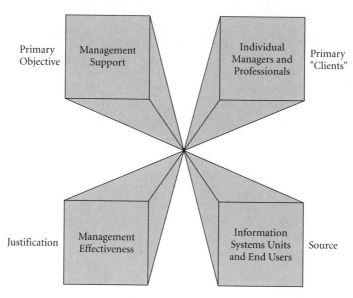

Support of managerial functions became the primary objective, with some informa-tion systems directly supporting the decision-making process, relying on corporate data-bases. Raising management effectiveness replaced operational efficiency as the primary jus-tification for the new systems. To achieve this, systems were designed to support the individual needs of managers and professionals.

3. Support of Business Transformation and Competition

In the mid-1980s, organizations entered a new stage in their reliance on information sys-tems (Figure 3.7). The leading firms wanted their information systems to help them beyond

Figure 3.7

Era III of organizational computing: support of business transformation and competition (mid-1980s through the early 1990s)

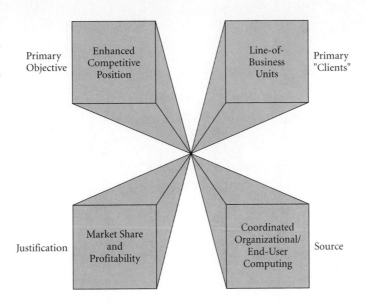

furthering increased operational efficiencies and managerial effectiveness. Strategic information systems gained importance as systems expected to help a company compete. The effects of such systems can be measured in terms of market share and corporate profits. Some strategic information systems are developed to interact with customers, suppliers, or other external stakeholders. Other strategic systems support business transformation through a firm's extensively redesigned internal business processes. These processes are streamlined and extensively supported with information technology.

Information systems support line-of-business units; for example, the units responsible for the development and marketing of individual products. Close interaction between systems developers and users has become mandatory. End users initiate and participate in the development of many systems. They may develop other systems themselves. Line-of-business units control their own information systems. In the leading corporations, end-user computing has become an important part of the overall organizational computing.

4. Ubiquitous Computing

The 1990s brought the recognition that the pursuit of competitive advantage cannot be based on a single information system. Competing with information systems has to be based on a broad and continually enhanced corporate platform of information technology linked to a successful business strategy. The technologies of both client/server computing and the Internet are the hallmarks of these platforms. Networked computers of various power are everywhere in business organizations and virtual workplaces; they are, indeed, ubiquitous.

Electronic integration of the entire organization is the principal objective, and organizational effectiveness is the primary justification for newly introduced systems that join the networked computer infrastructure of the firm (Figure 3.8). Integration with corporate partners is accomplished with interorganizational systems. Collaborating teams, often organized into larger clusters, are the primary "clients" of the information systems function. "Anywhere, anytime" work is enabled. Information systems have to enable collaboration within the team as well as among teams. A sustained process of organizational learning and

Figure 3.8

Era IV of organizational computing: ubiquitous computing (early 1990s–present)

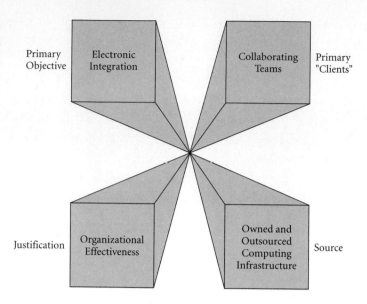

innovation is necessary to continually gain the high ground in competition. Information systems are called upon to enhance core competencies of the owner firms. This is accompanied by outsourcing other functions of corporations to their partners, who supply the materials and services in which the firm does not specialize. In particular, some firms have outsourced a large part of their information processing.

Organizational effectiveness is the result of both competitive initiatives based on new products and services in the marketplace and on redesigned business processes, enabled by the capabilities of information systems. We now rely on information systems to rapidly introduce new products and services, and also to fulfill customer orders, so as to deliver consistently high quality of products and services. We also rely on these systems to help manage increasingly complex interactions within the company and throughout the "extended organization" consisting of our firm, its business partners, customers, and suppliers.

Competitive success remains the touchstone of organizational effectiveness. Individual organizations undergo their own transformation processes in exploiting the capabilities of information technologies (Nolan and Croson 1995). We will devote the rest of this chapter to strategic information systems—the mission-critical systems that help their owner firm compete in the marketplace.

3.4 PRINCIPAL COMPETITIVE THRUSTS WITH STRATEGIC INFORMATION SYSTEMS

An information system is **strategic** if its objective is to improve the competitive position of the organization. Such a system helps the firm attract customers profitably and for an extended period of time. When a strategic information system is deployed, the way the company does business changes significantly. Any type of system supporting operations, management, or knowledge work of the organization may be deployed as a strategic system. The key to the success of a system is to exploit and leverage with information technology an advantage the firm enjoys, such as superior management, access to a market, or brand loyalty. Strategic information systems are distinguished by the following characteristics:

- *External focus,* since they change the way the firm competes in the marketplace.
- *Innovative use of information technology,* rather than the use of the newest technology. It's all about *how* you use the technology, rather than which technology you use.
- High degree of *project risk,* related to the innovative nature and large scale of most of these systems.

Relatively few strategic information systems enable their owner firms to gain lasting competitive advantage over their rivals; that is, to achieve consistently higher profits, expanding market share, or a superior value of the corporate stock. Many strategic systems are competitive necessities: Without them, the companies would be unable to compete effectively.

Let's consider three principal competitive thrusts where strategic information systems can be employed.

Redefining Company Business in Terms of Information

Pursuing a strategic vision, some companies redefine their business: A firm may determine that it is actually in the information business, rather than, for example, in the news or office machine business. By building on its strengths and developing a platform of information technology on which new systems can be developed, the company then changes the way it will compete for years to come. Managers of many financial services companies, such as American Express or the Merrill Lynch brokerage house, realized that their companies are in the information business and acted accordingly.

Aware that they are in the information processing business, a number of banks have created an information technology platform from which they launch ever new competitive products and services. By using information systems strategically, Banc One of Columbus, Ohio, a local bank some twenty years ago, transformed itself into one of the top-performing banks in the United States. The bank offers transaction processing services to a number of credit card consortia and generates a steady and feebased cash flow, which is also not subject to the risks of real estate or other investments. BankAmerica, Citicorp, and J.P. Morgan & Co. are among other notable examples of competitive leadership gained through the deployment of information technology.

Reuters Holdings PLC, a company headquartered in Great Britain, whose roots are in reporting news and quoting currency prices, now sees itself as a supermarket of financial information. Reuters has become the world's leading disseminator of financial data, with over 250,000 terminals in customer offices. In these days of electronic financial markets, a market can be made over a computer network with traders at terminals. Indeed, the London Stock Exchange abandoned its trading floor for such a system in the famous Big Bang of 1986. Reuters has developed a computerized system that allows traders to execute deals at the prices they see on their computer screens. The system is broadly used for trading in currency, gold bullion, and other similar valuables. Further building on its strengths, Reuters intends to move into the consumer finance market by assisting investing from a home computer, and into multimedia by piping in live digital TV coverage to traders' terminals. Reuters intends to provide high-margin intellectual content related to financial decisions, rather than simply the network for others to use.

**What Happens
When You
Reinvent Your
Business with
Information**

United Services Automobile Association (USAA) began as an insurance company. Over time, it has assembled voluminous data about its individual customers as well as information about the various customer segments it serves. This helps in precise risk assessment. Having analyzed the information, USAA's managers invented new lines of insurance business, targeted at specific customer segments such as personal insurance for boat owners.

But then, based on the accumulated information and the corporate expertise in using it, USAA redefined itself as an information company and went beyond the insurance business. For example, the firm designed financing packages for purchasing boats. From there, it went to offering shopping services for items ranging from jewelry to cars; extensive customer databases were built. Now, when a customer calls with a theft claim, the company offers to send a check or to replace the stolen item (the latter is an easy and frequent choice for the customer). By combining the forecasted demand from its buying customers and from theft victims into volume purchases, USAA gets discount prices from its suppliers and can pass the savings on to the customer.

Today, USAA is one of the largest direct merchandisers in the United States. It does not manufacture anything. The central activity of the company is managing information.

Based on Jeffrey F. Rayport and John J. Sviokla, "Exploiting the Virtual Value Chain," *Harvard Business Review,* November–December 1995, pp. 75–85.

Smaller companies also benefit. The chairman of Cadmus Communications Corporation of Richmond, Virginia, a company in the printing and graphic arts business tells us: "Printers traditionally have defined themselves by the process of printing. That's suicide." (Jones 1994). Instead, by defining themselves by the delivery of informational content to customers, printers, (such as Cadmus, R.R. Donnelley & Sons, and others) move into digital services, often using multimedia to deliver information. Once stored in digital form, the informational content can be accessed, modified, and reused many times, generating a stream of revenues.

Another example of a competitive thrust with information systems is provided by the vignette above.

Creating Products and Services Based on Information

Many firms compete by creating new products and services based on information or information systems. In an information society, companies are increasingly conscious of the know-how they accumulate during their operations. A construction company develops superior ways of managing construction projects. A bank may use an ingenious technique for managing a total relationship with its retail customers by analyzing the customer's account dynamics over time. Unless the company prefers to exploit its know-how internally and, therefore, proprietary considerations prevail, it may be packaged as software. The company may sell the software as a product, run it for a one-time charge, or establish an ongoing service business with it.

IN THE SPOTLIGHT

Personalized News in the Information Age: It Is what You Keep Away that Is Important

Donald McLagan has built Desktop Data, Inc., on the premise that keeping informed in the information age means getting the right information—and keeping what is unneeded away. His Burlington, Massachusetts, company (with annual sales of $23 million) sells a software service called NewsEdge and is a "filtered-news" provider. NewsEdge sends an electronic feed culled from over 500 wire services, magazines, and newspapers into a server computer in the customer's office. The Desktop Data software installed on the server selects and distributes headlines and full-text articles to the PCs of the appropriate users at the firm over the local area network (see Photo 3.1).

How does the server software select who gets what news? Each user can enter the codes or keywords for the news categories of interest: Two people working side by side get different news streams. Desktop Data now reaches 81,000 users at 335 companies. The service is not cheap. A basic package of software plus a few news feeds for 100 users runs $55,000 a year. Additional feeds are extra. A major customer, such as Chase Manhattan Bank, spends some $400,000 a year on the filtered-news service. But Craig Goldman, chief information officer for the bank, says: "Without a filter, we can be overwhelmed with quantity." The giant stock brokerage house of Charles Schwab is testing NewsEdge in order to enable the brokers who deal with the most sophisticated investors to have personalized profiles of each client's investment interests. With the service, each broker is kept up-to-date on the companies whose stock is held by the investors.

It was not easy for McLagan to line up his suppliers. The news providers, such as Reuters, Dow Jones, or PR Newswire, were reluctant to appear side by side on the same screen with their competitors. However, the costs of distributing news to NewsEdge are minuscule, while the suppliers receive fixed annual fees for the first 100 users, plus additional royalties for users above this number. For some publications, such as *American Banker,* the exposure given by NewsEdge has actually boosted print sales.

Photo 3.1

NewsEdge screen at a user PC (From John R. Hayes, "Crunching the News," *Forbes,* March 11, 1996, pp. 74–76.)

Based on John R. Hayes, "Crunching the News," *Forbes,* March 11, 1996, pp. 74–76.

Indeed, companies in various industries distinct from the information business itself enter that field by marketing their expertise to others. For example, Bechtel, a company with a worldwide reputation for large-scale construction, markets its line-of-business software for construction management. Mrs. Fields Cookies, known for its skillful use of information systems in running its stores, has built up and sold a small software company. The company sells software that helps manage multiple retail outlets in a strictly prescribed manner, with standard electronic forms sent over a network to and from the stores.

Entrepreneurial opportunities in providing the content (information or entertainment) by exploiting the opportunities afforded by information technologies abound. A characteristic example is provided by the vignette above.

Figure 3.9

The screen of Peapod's on-line grocery shopping service (From Michael Lasky, "The Online Supermarket," *PC World,* September 1996, p. 254.)

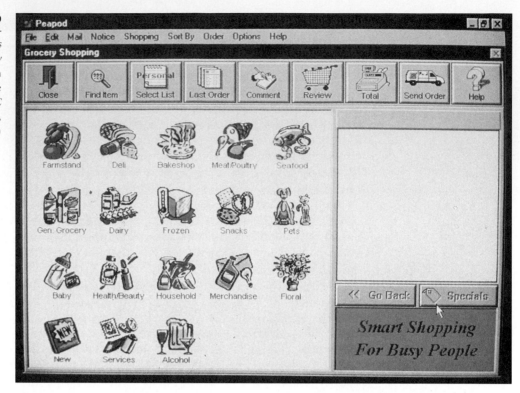

Many companies offer their goods and services exclusively on the Internet's World Wide Web. Here, Amazon.com (see Section 1.1) is the world's largest (and virtual) bookstore and Virtual Vineyards is a purveyor of wine and gourmet foods. Lombard Institutional Brokerage offers its services of buying and selling securities only on the Web. Atlanta Internet Bank provides its services exclusively on the Web and, owing to low costs (start-up costs were below $1 million), is able to offer highly competitive interest rates (Girard 1996). Onsale Inc. is an electronic auction firm that sells overstocked and refurbished PC products and consumer electronics on the Web. Peapod, a national grocery and drugstore shopping and delivery service, has expanded from telephone ordering to receiving orders from a Web site by distributing free access software to its customers (see Figure 3.9).

With information systems, a company can grasp an entrepreneurial opportunity by becoming a one-stop value-adding vendor for a category of products. W. W. Grainger of Skokie, Illinois, has become such a vendor in the prosaic domain of the maintenance, repair, and operation supplies to industrial companies. Grouping 1,000 suppliers and 73,000 products in a single computerized catalog, the company has enabled its customers to dramatically reduce their transaction processing costs. With extensive information systems, Grainger does most of this processing for them. A satellite-based telecommunications network links Grainger's branches and distribution points with the firm's suppliers. Its information-driven business rests on the ability to serve customers at a lower cost than the product suppliers can (Slywotzky 1996).

Transforming Company Products and Processes with Information Systems

Using information systems, companies are able to transform their products and business processes. Thus, a physical product may be combined with service and information and differentiated from the product offered by competitors. Furthermore, by varying the service and information components, the product can be customized for small market segments or even individualized for specific customers. FedEx was the first to realize that its customers would buy not only contracted delivery but also the peace of mind that comes with access to information about the status of their package. FedEx's Cosmos delivery tracking system has brought success to the company and has been widely imitated by its competitors and by firms in other transportation industry segments.

Products can be transformed by customization. The printer R. R. Donnelley & Sons has gained competitive advantage through "narrowcasting," enabled by information technology. As opposed to broadcasting the same edition of its popular *Farm Journal* to all subscribers, the printer maintains a subscriber database and prints up to 9,000 different editions for different groups of subscribers. To do so cost-effectively, R. R. Donnelley uses its computerized Selectronic printing and binding process. Hog breeders receive different editorial and advertising material than the corn planters do. This makes the journal attractive to its readers—and to advertisers. And remember that it is the advertisers who are the actual customers of many publications.

By transforming the processes through which it converts input materials into a product reaching the customers' hands, a company may realize efficiencies that can help it compete. Information systems may be used to tightly control the process, avoiding excessive (or, in some cases, any) inventories. They can also lower the cost of transactions with customers and suppliers. You learned in Chapter 1 (and will see in more detail in Chapter 13) how information systems are used to redesign business processes.

The airline industry's computerized reservation systems, first introduced by American Airlines (Sabre) and United (Apollo), have proven a formidable competitive weapon. These systems handle the flights of the owner company and of other airlines as well. They provide a reliable source of income. The accumulated databases enable the owners to find profitable air links and analyze the needs of the customers who purchase tickets through the system. Computerized reservation systems enable the airlines to run frequent flier programs that aim to increase market share. These systems also make possible **yield management**—maximizing the revenue from each flight. Remember, a seat unsold perishes forever. Therefore, airlines use software to provide a mix of ticket prices that should yield a maximum revenue. This is why there may be 10 or more coach prices on the same flight. Without the requisite information systems, the People Express airline went out of business in the 1980s, unable to compete with airlines that could undercut its prices within minutes. The operational and management processes of airlines have been transformed forever. As you can see in the following vignette, yield management has been imitated in other industries.

We have described the general avenues through which companies may seek competitive edge with information systems. Let us analyze the competitive markets in more detail and discover how to identify opportunities for using strategic information systems.

IN THE SPOTLIGHT

**Developing
Strategic
Systems by
Cloning Ideas**

Photo 3.2

*This dashboard
computer on a
tractor guides
farmers in applying
site-specific amounts
and blends of ferti-
lizer to maximize
their yield* (From
John Bongaards, "Can
the Growing Human
Population Feed
Itself?" *Scientific
American,* March
1994, p. 42.)

The ideas developed in one industry can be used in another. Yield management has been adapted by the hotel industry: An unsold room is as perishable as a seat on a plane. Even more innovative is the use of yield management in agriculture. Indeed, it created a new line of business for the tractor manufacturer Massey Ferguson.

Farmers would traditionally guesstimate the average yield of their entire fields. To assist their customers, Massey Ferguson has developed a yield mapping system that helps a farmer maximize the yield of each square yard in every field. The mapping system makes it possible to record the latitude, longitude, and yield of these small field patches (Photo 3.2). The software on the farmer's PC generates yield maps, showing variations from the targeted yield. Using this information, the farmer can investigate selected areas and determine the reasons for the variations, (for example, excessively compact soil or imbalance of nutrients). The software helps estimate the cost

Figure 3.10

*The satellites of the
Air Force's global
positioning system*
(From John Markoff,
"Finding Profit in
Aiding the Lost," *The
New York Times,*
March 5, 1996,
p. D1.)

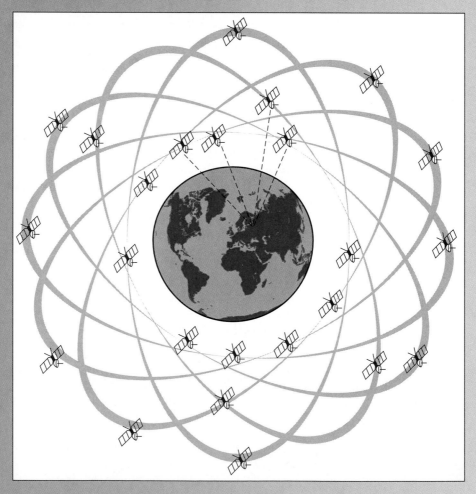

of the lost yield and compare it to the cost of remedies.

The yield management system works by linking the farmer's tractor (sold by Massey Ferguson) to a satellite-based Global Positioning System (GPS). Designed for the military in the 1970s, GPS has 24 satellites equally divided among six orbits in space (see Figure 3.10). Each satellite continuously emits a radio signal that can be received by mobile computers on land, on sea, or in the air. By picking up its signal from four or more satellites, the computer's software can determine its location within 20 to 300 yards of the exact position. GPS has been recently used for civilian navigation, including truck-fleet management, car dashboard guidance, and ambulance dispatch.

The system gives farmers control over the yield of their fields. It gives Massey Ferguson a competitive edge in selling their tractors. In the future, this information system may become a source of revenue for the company that will exceed its profits from tractor manufacturing. After all, many a year American Airlines made more money from its computerized reservation system than from flying its planes!

Based in part on Stan Davis and Jim Botkin, "The Coming of Knowledge-Based Business," *Harvard Business Review,* September–October 1994, pp. 165–170, and John Markoff, "Finding Profit in Aiding the Lost," *The New York Times,* March 5, 1996, p. D1.

3.5 STRATEGIES, FORCES, AND TACTICS IN COMPETITIVE MARKETS

All successful organizations compete. This is obvious in the case of business corporations. Moreover, in the information society, businesses compete globally. Much of U.S. manufacturing has been under acute competitive pressure from abroad. A competitive environment is less obvious, but nevertheless present, in the operation of not-for-profit organizations, such as most hospitals or colleges and universities.

Four fundamental competitive strategies can be employed. These strategies are mustered to combat the competitive forces operating in the marketplace. In pursuing a strategy, a firm can resort to one of the tactics we will describe. We will first discuss the strategies, forces, and tactics of the competitive marketplace, based on the classical work of Michael Porter of the Harvard Business School (Porter 1985, Porter and Millar 1985). We will then summarize them in a framework we call the strategic cube.

Competitive Strategies

To compete in the marketplace, a firm may adopt one of the four competitive strategies shown in Figure 3.11. The first two strategies can be pursued by companies with a broad scope of products, which they market across a number of customer segments. The other two strategies apply to firms that focus on a narrow customer segment. This distinction in competitive scope is best seen when a company with a broad product line in the automobile industry, such as Ford Motor, is compared with a company that specializes in high-performance sport utility vehicles, such as Land Rover.

1. Differentiation

When a company aims to distinguish its product or service from that offered by the competition, it is pursuing the **differentiation** strategy. The distinguishing feature may be the superior attributes of the product itself. However, the blurring of differences between product and service is one of the characteristics of the information society. Thus, ease and

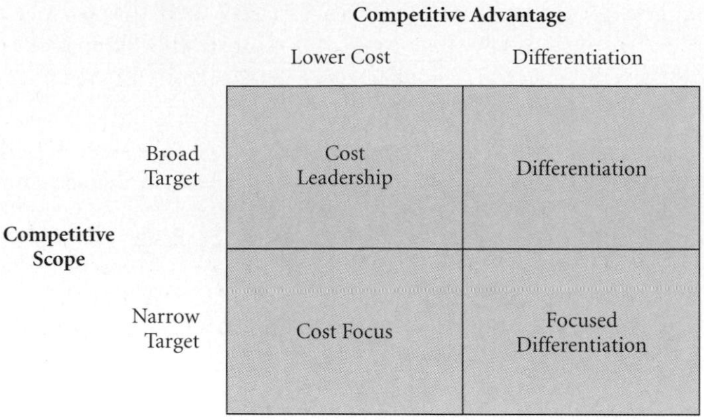

Figure 3.11

Competitive strategies
(From Michael E. Porter,
*The Competitive
Advantage of Nations,*
New York: Free Press,
1990, p. 39.)

Competitive Advantage

	Lower Cost	Differentiation
Broad Target	Cost Leadership	Differentiation
Narrow Target	Cost Focus	Focused Differentiation

Competitive Scope

promptness of product acquisition, better payment terms, and superior maintenance may be equally important to the customer. These are precisely the attributes a firm may be able to impart with information systems.

For example, Pacific Pride Systems, a company providing fueling services for commercial fleets, has been able to obtain a premium price on its fuel, generally a commodity sold at uniform prices, by introducing the Cardlock system based on information technology (Nault and Dexter 1995). Thanks to the system, the firm's customers can obtain access to the fuel at any time and at many locations, with convenient payment terms. Customers can also obtain detailed information on each transaction as well as helpful summaries. The value added by information technology is expressed in the higher prices of the package of good-service-information.

2. Cost Leadership

If a company is able to offer its product or service at a cost significantly lower than its competitors, it is exercising **cost leadership.** This is usually the effect of highly efficient internal operations. If based on economies of scale, this strategy is accessible to a company with a large market share. Its successful application leads to further expansion of the market share. Success feeds on itself. A dramatic reengineering of its business processes by exploiting the capabilities of information systems may enable a company to become a low-cost supplier. Thanks in large part to their employment of information technology large drugstore chains such as Rite Aid and Walgreens have been able to organize their operations so efficiently that they are able to squeeze out many smaller chains and independents in the managed healthcare, cost-conscious environment (Murray 1996). Indeed, the analysis of corporate performance shows that investment in information technologies is a promising avenue to pursuing cost leadership (Hitt and Brynjolfsson 1996).

3. Focused Differentiation

When a company is able to identify a segment of the market (a niche) which it can serve in a superior fashion, it is engaging in **focused differentiation.** Smaller firms in particular compete by specializing a product or a service for a limited-size niche. Information systems may be used to contribute to this goal by helping identify the customers to be served and then customizing the product for their needs.

The niche may be a customer segment, a narrowly defined product, or a geographical region. Information systems relying on extensive customer databases and demographic data are a potent tool in niche identification. This is known as database marketing. The computers of Claridge Hotel and Casino Corporation keep tabs on visitors who use its frequent-gambler's card. The casino sends out discount offers for special events to people who may be interested in them. "We can target our [promotion] dollars directly to customers who justify the costs," says the president of the company (Berry 1994).

4. Cost Focus

If a company serves a narrow market segment with a product or service that it offers at a significantly lower cost than its competitors, that company is employing the **cost focus** strategy. Relatively difficult to pursue for small companies, this strategy may be built on the advantage of geographic proximity combined with the use of information technology to achieve operational efficiencies.

Competitive Forces

Competitive strategies are pressed into service to combat five competitive forces active in the marketplace. The stronger any of these forces acts against your firm, the less power your firm has in the marketplace. Information systems may be used to enact or counteract these forces with respect to customers, existing and potential competitors, or suppliers. These actions are summarized in Figure 3.12. Note that we are competing not just against the existing competitors—that is the richness of this approach, introduced by Michael Porter.

Figure 3.12

Combating competitive forces in the marketplace (From Vladimir Zwass, *Management Information Systems,* Dubuque, IA: Wm. C. Brown, 1992, p. 154.)

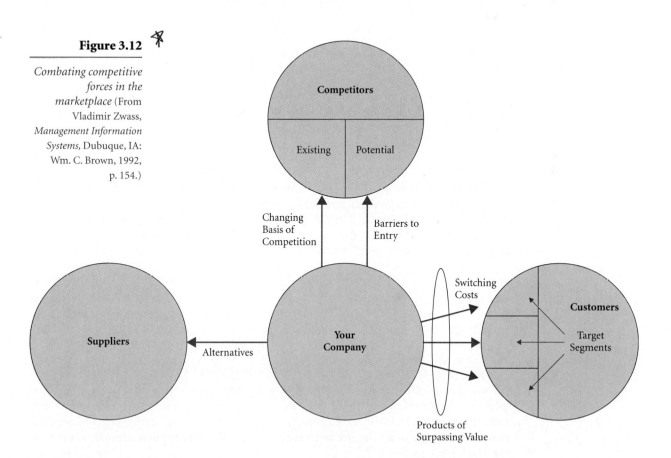

Let us see how information systems can be deployed to our advantage against the five competitive forces.

1. Threat of New Competitors: Erect Barriers to Entry.

As we already know, because of the highly developed infrastructure of an information society, competition may appear from entirely unforeseen quarters. A mail order bookstore with a well-known Web site on the Internet (such as Amazon.com) can become a competitor of your local bookshop—unless you can build on your advantage of proximity to customers. If *barriers to entry* into the marketplace can be erected, this threat is contained. The costs or time needed to enter a business with an information system comparable to those of firms already in the business are potent barriers. Computerized reservation systems have proven to be entry barriers in the airline business, as Donald Burr, the founder of People Express learned when his firm was overmatched by the established competitors.

An automated order-taking system, called ASAP, implemented in the largest hospital distributor in the country, Baxter Healthcare, provides its customers with the means of directly entering their orders into the supplier's computers from PCs placed on the customer's premises. The supplier firm maintains standing order files for each customer and accepts on-line special orders for drugs and supplies, which are fulfilled on the same day. The products bear the stock-keeping numbers of the individual hospital or department and are easy to manage once delivered. The customers, often several individual departments within hospitals, save money by maintaining small purchasing staffs and minimal inventories; they also receive a variety of informational services from Baxter (many services carry an extra charge). The automated order-taking system ASAP has been developed for over two decades and has cost many millions of dollars, but it makes a formidable barrier to entry.

In several industries, notably in insurance and credit card issuing, new entrants have been successful in exploiting information systems to challenge the previously dominant service providers. They accomplished this by identifying the exceptionally profitable market segments with the use of extensive databases and then devising a set of flexible prices to capture these customers (Clemons 1996). Indeed, strategic information systems may be deployed as both a defensive and offensive weapon.

2. Intensifying Rivalry among Existing Competitors: Change the Basis of Competition.

A novel information system can sometimes *change the basis of competition,* helping you offer your customers a product or service with new features. For example, if your delivery service allows the customer to track the delivery process while your competitors' services do not, you have differentiated your offering and no longer have to compete just on a price basis.

3. Pressures from Potential Substitute Products: Deliver Products of Surpassing Value.

A *product of surpassing value,* which offers substantive quality or service advantages, cannot be easily displaced by substitutes. By identifying and continually tracking a market niche with information systems that you can serve better than others, you can prevent such substitution.

4. Bargaining Power of Customers: Introduce Switching Costs.

Switching costs are the costs of switching to your competitor for the product or service you provide. The unwillingness to incur such costs may take bargaining power away from customers. For example, because of contracts and necessary training, travel agents find it difficult to switch to a different airline reservation system. Thus, the first movers become entrenched in the market.

5. Bargaining Power of Suppliers: Develop Alternatives.

A purchasing system that maintains extensive information on the available supply sources confers power on you at the expense of your suppliers. Although you seek stable relationships with your suppliers, ready availability of *alternative sources of supply* may prevent opportunistic behavior on the part of suppliers.

Competitive Tactics

Depending on its current capabilities and long-term plans, an organization may employ any of several tactics to change its products or processes through the use of strategic information systems. *Internal growth* makes it possible to realize economies of scale. Sometimes it is possible to *innovate internally* by generating new knowledge, a notable accomplishment of such firms as Motorola, 3M, or DuPont. Because innovations, including strategic information systems, may take many millions of dollars and several years to develop, companies increasingly employ outward-directed tactics involving *acquisitions* of other companies or *mergers* with them. For example, Merck, a major manufacturer of pharmaceutical brands, has acquired Medco, a leading supplier of generic drugs. The principal attraction of Medco was the enormous database it had amassed on the usage patterns of various drugs by millions of patients. This gives Merck the capability to compete far more keenly in the emerging environment of managed healthcare.

Many firms conclude a *strategic alliance,* a long-term partnership, with another company. Information partnerships, based on sharing of information systems, have become a potent competitive weapon. The advantage of partnership is economy of money and time, and reciprocity of competencies. Each partner needs to contribute only a part of the requisite resources. Moreover, a partner company may contribute an organizational skill, such as the ability to develop and keep enhancing large-scale transaction processing systems, which take years to hone.

Strategic alliances are vital to competing in global markets. By providing a variety of information-based services to their clients, several banks have entered lasting "computer marriages" with them. Fee-based electronic services range from foreign exchange trading, helping customers manage the risks from fluctuating currency values in their global transactions, and automatic payroll deposit. According to an executive of BankAmerica: "When you get wired into a customer's information system and they get wired into you, it becomes [technologically] difficult to lose that business" (King and Lipin 1994).

The Strategic Cube

The combination of competitive strategies, the market forces they target, and the tactics used to implement the strategies can be mapped into a framework we call the strategic cube (Figure 3.13).

Using the strategic cube, a company may review its options for seeking competitive advantage with information systems. For example, to drive off potential new market entrants, a toy company may consider pursuing a strategy of focused differentiation by concentrating on upper-bracket toys for children up to two years of age. To do so, it may conclude an exclusive long-term agreement with a firm distributing baby milk substitutes, which would have a large database of families with newborns. The database permits the toy company to target the desired infant sector. The two companies agree to share the marketing function.

Figure 3.13

The strategic cube
(From Vladimir Zwass,
*Management Information
Systems*, Dubuque, IA:
Wm. C. Brown, 1992,
p. 156.)

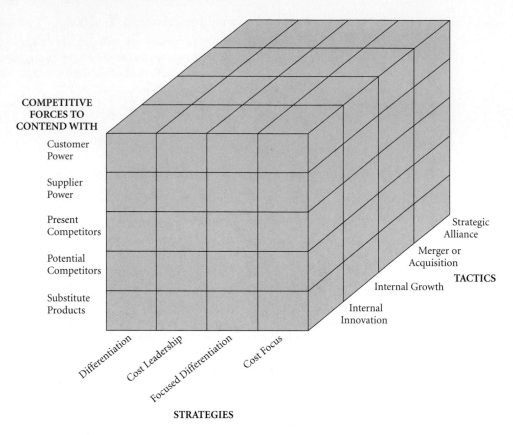

Because a potential competitor would need much time and money to develop the capability to access this market segment, the strategic alliance can create a barrier to entry.

The strategic cube does not tell the company exactly *where* it may apply information systems in its activities in order to seek competitive advantage. We will now proceed to study another tool, designed for more detailed analysis of these opportunities.

3.6   USING VALUE CHAIN TO IDENTIFY OPPORTUNITIES FOR STRATEGIC INFORMATION SYSTEMS

Strategic deployment of information systems is aimed at changing both company operations and its products. To establish targets of opportunity, we need to track the chain of activities through which our company transforms its input resources, such as raw materials, into the products and services it delivers to its customers. This chain of activities during which a firm adds value to its input materials is called **value chain** (see Figure 3.14). The stages of a value chain begin with the inbound logistics that connect the firm to its suppliers, continue with the essential stage of operations—where the actual products are realized—and end with the three stages interacting with the firm's customers: outbound logistics, marketing and sales, and service. As you can see, similar chains of the firm's suppliers provide inputs to the firm's value chain, which in turn feeds the value chains of the customers. The figure also shows some generic strategic information systems mapped onto the appropriate stages of the chain. We will discuss these systems below. The primary activities

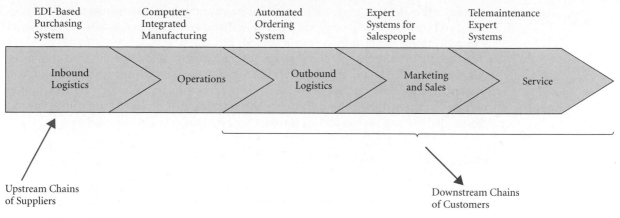

Figure 3.14

Value chain with typical strategic information systems mapped onto it

shown in the value chain are assisted by support activities, such as administration and human resource management.

Let us consider how information systems can be applied strategically at various stages of the company's value chain.

Inbound Logistics

The activities of *inbound logistics* include obtaining raw materials, subassemblies, and other input products from the suppliers, warehousing them, and delivering them to the production site. Inbound logistics is supported by information systems that deal with the company's suppliers.

All companies can apply the old adage that "information is power" to increase their clout in dealings with suppliers. If you have a system that maintains information on alternative suppliers and can evaluate their competing bids, you can get the best buy. Equitable Life Assurance Company has developed an on-line purchasing system for centralized office supply acquisitions. Its database stores information on all contracts. Since the system enables volume buying and offers information on alternative suppliers, the company's bargaining power is high.

Powerful customers are, of course, able to enforce their way of operating things on the supply side. Thus, General Motors, the largest U.S. automobile manufacturer, installed computer-to-computer links with its suppliers. So did Wal-Mart. Known as electronic data interchange (EDI), these systems have replaced the exchange of paper documents, such as orders or invoices.[1] The use of EDI based on the customer's standard is a condition for doing business with GM or Wal-Mart. Suppliers have to modify their transaction processing systems to link in with the ordering systems of these major customers.

Beyond that, a powerful customer company may make the supplier fit its operations and its information systems to the customer's need by requiring the supplier to maintain a just-in-time relationship; that is, to deliver the supplies at the precise time they are needed by the customer. This minimizes the costs of holding inventory. Working on the same principle, the supplier in turn also holds minimal inventory of its own—and becomes, in effect, responsible for managing the customer's inventory. Customers can further require that suppliers become certified by them and take responsibility for quality control; have computer-aided design and manufacturing (CAD/CAM) systems compatible with the customer's information system to introduce engineering and other design changes into the supplier's products under development; use the customer's EDI standards for all transactions; and even wait until the product is sold by the customer for payment to be transferred via an electronic funds transfer system (EFTS).

Grocery chains, using on-line retail tracking data from their computerized point-of-sale scanning systems, can quickly determine a product's sales and profitability. Armed with this information, supermarkets have been able to reverse the traditional power relationship between consumer-goods manufacturers and retailers in their favor: The stores demand fees (called slotting allowances) for introducing new products onto the shelves.

Operations

During *operations*, the input resources are transformed into finished products. The nature of operations depends on the firm's line of business. In manufacturing companies, operations are more clearly defined than in service companies—this is where the goods are made. The operations of service companies are highly information-intensive, however. For example, back-office processing of insurance policies, stock certificates, or charge card receipts constitutes a large part of the operations in financial services and is performed by transaction processing systems.

Information technology has revolutionized manufacturing operations in the leading plants, as will be discussed more fully in Chapter 12. The most powerful, but also most complex—development is called computer-integrated manufacturing. Computer-integrated manufacturing (CIM) is a strategy through which an enterprise takes control of its entire manufacturing process—from computer-aided design (CAD) and computer-aided engineering (CAE) to the factory floor, where robots and numerically controlled machinery are installed and organized into a computer-aided manufacturing (CAM) system. Through the information systems supporting this strategy, the firm melds the existing "islands of automation" into a whole.

A flexible factory automation system can turn out very small batches of a particular product as cost-effectively as a traditional production line can turn out millions of identical products. These systems are enablers for two crucial aspects of today's marketplace: time-based competition and mass customization. Time-based competition requires drastic cuts in the product development cycle. Product development can be done more rapidly with concurrent engineering, by designing the product and its manufacturing process at the same time. Mass customization requires the capability to cost-effectively produce small batches or even individual units of a product.

Service industries offer many opportunities for strategic deployment of information systems. Here, the speed and flexibility made possible by information technology may be exploited to differentiate the service or to pursue low-cost advantages by redesigning service operations around a strategic system. American Color of Phoenix, Arizona, is a color separation company. It produces pictures for various publications and has 14 plants around the United States. The firm established a satellite-based telecommunications network for transmitting very high-quality color artwork and photographs. American Color's competitive advantage comes from its capability to change ad copy or a magazine cover at the last minute—a differentiation of service—and the ability to distribute the workload among its printing sites in order to lower costs.

As we said, in the service-oriented economies of the industrialized countries, financial services are highly information-intensive. Much of this information has traditionally been handled in the form of paper documents such as sales receipts, mortgages, or insurance policies. Several technologies can be exploited to redesign document-based operations around strategic information systems. Thus, electronic data interchange (EDI) helps dispense with much of the paperwork in the interaction between companies. Digital image processing, is used to scan paper documents (say, signed insurance policies) into a computer system, and display and process the resulting electronic documents, which rids companies of the inefficiencies of working with paper. Workflow systems circulate electronic documents within the company and make it possible to organize business processes around this flow.

To obtain a total picture of their relationships with each of their customers, banks found it initially an advantage, and later a necessity, to maintain a central information file (CIF). Actually a customer's record, it lists all of his or her accounts and balances, and makes it possible to calculate each customer's profitability to the bank. A bank can make better credit decisions and initiate targeted marketing of services based on these integrated data.

Outbound Logistics

Outbound logistics involves storing the firm's products and delivering them to customers against orders. Note that the ultimate buyer may actually receive the product from an intermediary, such as a distributor.

Facilitation of customer orders provides an initial and ever-potent opportunity for the strategic use of information systems. Airlines' computerized reservation systems (Sabre and Apollo) and round-the-clock order-entry systems with terminals on the customer premises (ASAP of Baxter Healthcare) have been resounding competitive successes. Dealing with customers through automatic teller machines (ATM) has offered significant savings to many banks and, more promising, created a mechanism for distributing other goods (tickets or coupons) in a labor-saving manner. Universities are beginning to use ATMs for dispensing information about student grades and social welfare agencies are employing them to distribute food stamps through electronic benefit systems. The government of Singapore is using ATMs to distribute shares in companies that are being privatized; Citibank's customers can buy and sell stock via ATM. The vignette on the next page illustrates the need for flexibility in meeting customer's needs.

Small companies can employ a focused strategy. Wright Express of Portland, Maine, has set up a charge card service at gas stations for trucking fleets. It provides fleet owners with information on their fuel, maintenance, and clerical expenses. The company also equips attendant-free gas stations with ATM and its own credit cards. This small company has created 40 jobs and keeps growing by providing ever new services based on the 1.3 million transactions it processes every month.

Information and software are conveniently delivered to customers over computer networks. For example, Indelible Blue of Raleigh, North Carolina, specializes in selling software for IBM PCs and compatibles over the Internet. Cybermedia, based in Santa Monica, California, has been created to automatically deliver over the Internet new releases of software used by a particular PC (Santalesa 1996). As high-capacity telecommunications become available, it will be possible to distribute movies and other image-based material in this fashion.

The ability to track a shipment gives the customer a sense of control. Pacific Intermountain Express, a California-based trucker, can track the status of all shipments from origin to destination. The customer can directly access a trucker's computer. A range of reports on cost allocation is available to customers. When marketing its service to a customer, the firm's representatives discuss not only shipping, but also the customer's information needs. Thus, the firm not only sells the service-information package, but also continually learns from its marketplace and upgrades its information system.

IN THE SPOTLIGHT

Adaptability: the Key to Exporting

Photo 3.3

A customer using an ATM in a Moscow street (Fortune, August 22, 1994, p. 129)

Automatic teller machines are a key to efficient distribution of banking services around the globe. But one needs to respond to the demands of the local market. Here is the lesson from Diebold, a Canton, Ohio, manufacturer of ATMs, and security systems.

When Diebold entered the European markets in 1993 in a joint venture with IBM to install its ATMs, the company was trying to act as a missionary. Some Western European countries encrypt (encode for security) messages sent from the ATM to the central computer. This is supposed to prevent, for example, theft of the customer's personal identification number. The U.S. designers saw this as an unnecessary step, based on the experience in this country. The Europeans insisted on the feature. After wasting 18 months, Diebold redesigned its ATM-based system for the local market and messages are now encrypted.

More recently, Diebold has also sold 30 ATMs to Russia's Polis Insurance and helped install them in the Moscow subways and streets (see Photo 3.3). The demands of that market are different indeed. Since phone lines are few and unreliable, the ATMs are designed to use smart cards with computer chips preloaded with a certain amount of money. However, the company also needed to protect card holders from the inflation of the local currency, the ruble, that is distributed by the ATMs. Therefore, the money is actually stored on the card as German marks until withdrawal.

Based on Rob Norton, "Strategies for the New Export Boom," *Fortune,* August 22, 1994, pp. 124–130.

Marketing and Sales

Establishing customer need for the product and assisting the customer in specifying the assortment and quantities are the tasks of *marketing*. With the assistance of automated ordering and reservation systems, a sales representative can be redefined as a consultant, assisted by laptop computers and information systems, who can help customers define their needs. Computerized ordering systems free the sales force from taking simple orders for the more creative tasks of establishing new products and services and responding to changing customer needs. The better to take more complex orders, the salespeople can be tied in to a database that shows in detail the prospective customer's experience with the company's products.

If sales representatives are equipped with laptop computers tied into an information system, they can access the headquarters' database, reserve stock, and place orders. They can also pick up E-mail, receive leads from the computerized telemarketing system, and check calendars, appointment schedules, and customer lists. Salespeople for many firms can track an order's status right in the customer's office. This informational support leads to increased customer satisfaction and long-term relationships.

Information systems may be designed to play many other roles during the marketing stage, when customers establish their requirements for a product. Owens Corning Fiberglass has developed an expert system that evaluates insulation requirements for new home designs to meet energy efficiency standards. The builders, to whom the service is offered at no charge, must exclusively carry the company's insulation materials. Sales representatives of the drug manufacturer Genentech, calling on physicians and pharmacists with their notebook computers, provide these customers with on-line access to proprietary clinical studies and to a staff of medical specialists who can answer highly technical questions.

Expert systems can select and configure complex equipment to satisfy a customer's needs. Digital Equipment Corporation uses such systems to avoid expensive and time-consuming temporary assembly of ordered computer systems for testing purposes. Several companies in other industries have followed the company's lead.

Electronic kiosks, built around a microcomputer with a touch screen or a similar user-friendly input device, are used in stores, banks, and other customer service centers, most of them for marketing purposes. Newer kiosks employ a multimedia technology of interactive digital video, which gives customers a presentation that combines full-motion video with other media, such as animation and text. Electronic kiosks direct customers to a product—whether, an appliance or a financial instrument—and can facilitate payment or dispense information from a database. Kiosks can process simple transactions and provide fast, accurate, and thorough information; they advise the user to request human assistance when more complex interaction is required. The scope of the application of electronic kiosks is widening beyond marketing. Docunet of San Francisco has started a service providing immediate delivery of airline tickets via electronic kiosks. Several banks have introduced loan processing via these kiosks. The vignette on the next page offers an example of strategic deployment of this information technology by new entrants to an industry.

Service

After-sales continuation of the customer relationship through superior *service* is sometimes a contractual requirement and always a good business practice. Sears, Roebuck has long recognized that being in the service business is also a way to sell replacement products. Sears makes each maintenance contract for a major appliance valid when the appliance is resold, which provides an avenue to a new customer. The company's vast customer databases are used to send reminders to customers whose service contracts are about to expire. American Express has a double-the-warranty program on purchases made with their card. Aside from providing a competitive edge for the card, this practice helps assemble an extensive marketing database. Thanks to its OTISLINE information systems, Otis Elevator has been able to provide high-quality service in the lucrative elevator-service market. The extensive database of the system maintains records of each elevator and every customer, enabling the company to provide proactive maintenance and promptly respond to service calls.

Stratus Computer Corporation, whose market niche is highly reliable, fault-tolerant computing, employs an automatic telemaintenance system. Using its database of customer's computer configurations, the system polls these installations periodically to determine configuration changes and the status of the equipment. Any detected error triggers diagnostic routines. A persistent error leads to automatic notification of Stratus's service-support facility. There, the service people use extended remote diagnostic routines and, usually within an hour, issue an order for a replacement part. The part is delivered overnight, together with replacement instructions, to the customer who may even be unaware of any problem.

Business Migration

Buying a used car has always been a much maligned experience. But now customers can do something about it—and the traditional dealers are threatened.

As Hiram Colon visits a CarMax used car superstore in Duluth, Georgia, he walks over to one of the kiosks with touch-screen computers dotting the showroom floor (similar to the ones in Photo 3.4). He punches in the desired amount of his down payment, the monthly payment he thinks he can afford, and the model and options he is looking for. The system prints out a picture of a gold-colored 1996 Camry, with 7,400 miles and a sticker price of $18,900. There will be no bargaining. The salesclerks' commissions are based on unit volume and not on price. After a test drive, the loan application is completed and approved. The whole process takes two hours. "I felt like I was in control," says Colon. The feeling is not often shared by many visitors to a traditional used car showroom. And CarMax, a four-store division of the major electronics retailer Circuit City Stores, is planning to go national, aiming at 50 dealerships by the year 2000.

But many shoppers prefer not to set foot in a showroom. Auto-By-Tel, in the first 10 months of its activity on the Internet, managed to broker over 25,000 car purchases. From its site on the World Wide Web, the brokerage company runs a referral service with a network of 1,400 dealers who pay $250 to $1,500 a month and agree to sell at low, pre-negotiated prices. Thanks to the service, dealers are able to expand their reach, with new customers coming from much farther away than the traditional ones.

Electronic shopping affects both new and used car buying. Auto retailing is a $500-billion-a-year business. A total of 15 million new and some 28 million used vehicles are sold annually. With the cost of about $6,700 a year for marketing, distributing, and selling, as compared to the cost of $1,175 for assembly, of a typical $20,000 vehicle, the potential for economies in marketing and selling is enormous. The new ways of doing business, enabled by information technology, are radically changing yet another sector of the economy.

Based on Kathleen Kerwin, "Used-Car Fever," *Business Week,* January 22, 1996, pp. 34–35; Keith Naughton, "Revolution in the Showroom," *Business Week,* February 19, 1996, pp. 70–76; Alex Taylor III, "How to Buy a Car on the Internet," *Fortune,* March 4, 1996, pp. 164–168; and Jane J. Kim, "Car Buyers, Dealers Reap the Benefits of Growing Number of Internet Services," *The Wall Street Journal,* September 30, 1996, p. B12A.

Photo 3.4

Computer kiosks at a prototype Chrysler dealership in Dallas (From Keith Naughton, "Revolution in the Showroom," *Business Week,* February 19, 1996, pp. 70–76.)

Expert systems can be used to diagnose malfunctions as a part of telemaintenance. Westinghouse has a number of expert systems running on the mainframe of its Orlando Diagnostics Center. The Center provides service to public utilities: It remotely monitors and diagnoses impending malfunctions of various parts of massive steam turbine generators owned by public utilities all over the United States. The payoff to customers is more generator up-time, thanks to an early diagnosis; each day of uptime is worth between half a million and a million dollars. The cost of service (Westinghouse's revenue) is less than one-tenth of the resulting savings.

Virtual Value Chain and Integration of Value Chains

Support of the individual stages of a firm's value chain with innovative information systems is not enough. A competitive company needs to analyze the entirety of its value chain, in-

Figure 3.15

How a virtual value chain is developed

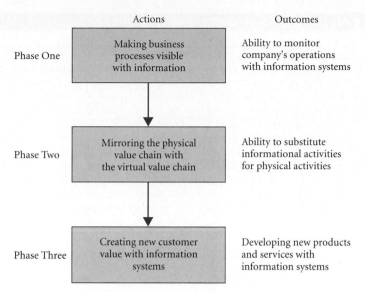

cluding the linkages between the stages. In the process, some firms are able to build an integrated informational value chain—called virtual value chain by Jeffrey Rayport and John Sviokla of the Harvard Business School (Rayport and Sviokla 1995). The virtual value chain mirrors with information the physical value chain. You may note that it is often possible to integrate the information systems mapped onto the physical value chain in Figure 3.14 and thus produce a virtual value chain. Now, the owner company may move some of its activities from the physical value chain into the virtual, informational one (moving from the marketplace into the "marketspace," according to the proponents of the idea). For example, a telemaintenance system vastly reduces the need for service people. Money, time, and energy resources may be saved. The capabilities of information systems (see Table 1.2) are exploited to produce these economies. The stages of development of a virtual value chain are shown in Figure 3.15.

For example, Boeing 777 was the first airplane fully designed electronically, with no paper documentation during the design (see Photo 3.5). Reliance on the modeling capability of information systems enabled electronic prototyping; with the designs in electronic form, it became possible to use information systems as the means of coordination to perform concurrent engineering. Paperless development helped Boeing Company realize significant economies in the development process (that cost $4 billion). The availability of easy-to-manipulate electronic information now enables the company to design and build model 777 to order within 10 months, as opposed to the 18 months required for the earlier

Photo 3.5

This Boeing engineer is testing the "paperless" model 777. (From Andy Reinhardt and Seanna Browder, "Booming Boeing," Business Week, September 30, 1996, pp. 118–125.)

IN THE SPOTLIGHT

From Tailoring to Business Engineering

Ermenegildo Zegna makes some of the finest Italian suits. The 85-year-old family-owned company, based in Trevero at the foot of the Italian Alps, is one of the fastest-growing fashion empires in Europe. The company's idea of marketing includes the glittering regatta that kicks off the yacht racing season in the Italian resort of Portofino each May. But that's not all there is. Zegna maintains a customer database, carefully detailing the tastes and requirements of each client. Several times a year, the best customers are sent fabric swatches for a suit-shirt-tie set, based on their past purchasing patterns, derived from the database. Nearly 2 percent buy the suggested set, a high and profitable percentage.

What makes the company interesting to us is the degree of integration it has achieved throughout its value chain, from making the fabric to the final sale. The house of Zegna spins its own yarn and produces its own fabrics in the mill halfway between Milan and Turin. Finishing the wool, it turns out, re-

quires the purest water, the kind that is available here in Trevero. On the other end of the chain, the company also operates its own retail stores. That is the physical value chain.

It used to take Zegna eight months from the mill to delivery of the suit to the store. By computerizing its manufacturing operations and integrating them with the outbound logistics, Zegna has cut this time in half. To further compress its delivery cycle, the company is working on an inventory-checking system that will anticipate when retail stores will need to restock, a month before they are ready to place an order. This forecast will pull in products from Zegna's value chain. An informational value chain will emerge. "We are moving away from being tailors to being engineers," says Ermenegildo Zegna, and yes, there is such a person.

Based on "Armani's Counterpoint," *Forbes*, July 4, 1994, pp. 122–124; John Rossant, "Is That a Zegna You're Wearing?" *Business Week*, March 4, 1996, pp. 84–85.

("paper-based") Boeing 767. By moving to a virtual value chain, Boeing can deliver more value to its customers. A somewhat more mundane example of establishing an informational, virtual value chain is provided by the vignette above.

Beyond "informating" its own value chain, a firm can link it electronically to the value chains of its suppliers and customers. In this way, an integrated supply chain may emerge for the entire industry. For example, under competitive pressure from discount department stores (Wal-Mart among them) and discount drugstores (such as Walgreens), the grocery industry has developed its Efficient Consumer Response program ("H. E. Butt Grocery" 1994). The program aims to electronically integrate the manufacturers (such as Procter & Gamble), distributors, and grocery chain stores. Driven by the stores' point-of-sale (POS) systems at the registers, just-in-time deliveries into the chain by suppliers and as-needed movement of goods across the chain itself will prevent costly inventory buildups and stockouts. The technological and managerial changes, when fully implemented, are expected to yield total annual savings of $30 billion for the industry.

As another example, car manufacturer Nissan U.S.A. has the supplier of its car seats deliver a shipment every few hours, with the seats transferred straight to the assembly line. How is that for input logistics—no inventory costs and no warehousing of bulky components! Such economies are made possible by Nissan's suppliers delivering on a pre-agreed schedule (yet allowing for rapid modifications) supported by electronic data interchange. Indeed, a purchasing system has to tightly bind the supplier's (so-called upstream) value chains to that of your company (see Figure 3.14). On the outbound (also called downstream) side, a computerized ordering system, such as Baxter's ASAP, tightly links in the customer's operations.

IN THE SPOTLIGHT

Provident Flexibility

Shortly before a recent Christmas, a major competitor of Provident National Bank of Philadelphia announced the availability of free checking for customers meeting certain criteria. Since Provident was not making a similar offer at the time, loss of business was feared. Also, Provident was strategically committed to keep up with any products or services offered by the industry. At the same time, the task of modifying its information systems to offer free checking appeared daunting, particularly in the face of the traditional work inefficiencies during the holidays.

However, upon the preliminary analysis of systems requirements, Provident's information systems managers advised the bank's executives to announce the free checking service immediately. They believed, correctly, that they would be able to implement the unanticipated, unplanned systems change within one billing cycle. Provident was able to sell the product before the insurer had the necessary information system to support it, since the system would be available when actually needed. This was possible because the existing information system was flexible enough to enable a timely modification.

Based on Nancy B. Duncan, "Capturing Flexibility of Information Technology Infrastructure: a Study of Resource Characteristics and Their Measure," *Journal of Management Information Systems*, 12, no. 2 (Fall 1995), pp. 37–57 (and credited by the author to Eric K. Clemons).

3.7 | SUCCESS WITH STRATEGIC INFORMATION SYSTEMS

Identifying opportunities for strategic deployment of information systems is part of the larger process of strategic planning, which we will discuss in Chapter 13. An AT&T-sponsored study of organizations in 11 industries that are reputed to be successful information system strategists has identified these keys to success in strategic use of information systems (Johnston and Carrico 1988):

- Active support of senior company management (and not just of the information systems management) in the discovery of strategic opportunities and in the implementation process.

- Integration of planning for the strategic use of information systems into the overall company strategic planning process.

- Direct reporting by those responsible for strategic use of information systems to the business managers of the area to be affected by the new system.

- Placement of control mechanisms (budgeting and rewards, for example) in the hands of these business managers.

- Readiness for strategic use of information systems, implying successful use of the technological platform already in place and experience with technological innovation.

It needs to be stressed time and time again that you cannot buy competitive edge by acquiring an innovative information system. Such a system can easily be replicated by your competitors. Rather, a strategic information system has to build on the strengths of the company that cannot be easily imitated. It has been determined that lasting, sustainable competitive advantage can be gained with information systems only if an organization possesses other resources as well (Feeny and Ives 1990; Kettinger 1994). Such resources may include a well-developed and flexible information technology platform or a database reflecting the marketplace experience with the firm's products, accumulated over several years. Continual investment is required to maintain the advantage. The brief vignette above shows what "flexible information technology platform" means for a company's ability to compete.

SUMMARY

In an information society, most people active in the economy are employed in the handling of information, and most goods and services are related to processing of information. The work in generating new knowledge and in dealing with information, rather than with physical production or service, is known as knowledge work, which requires extensive support with information systems.

The competition and cooperation among firms takes place today on the global scale. Business globalization heightens the competition but also creates opportunities to seek out new markets and resources, such as labor, abroad. Because of the keen global competition, firms need to innovate continuously. It is necessary to keep developing new products or services (product innovation) and keep coming up with new ways of manufacturing products and delivering services (process innovation).

The amount of knowledge that can affect a business enterprise keeps increasing dramatically. Also, the pace of business events, set by information technology, is rapid and constantly accelerating. It is necessary to organize and deploy information technology for more and faster problem solving by many knowledge workers, frequently organized into teams.

Organizational computing has vastly broadened its scope since the mid-1950s. Information systems initially supported only a firm's operations. Later, their functions were expanded to support management and knowledge work. More recently, organizations began to implement information systems to enhance their competitive position and enable them to cooperate with other firms. At present, electronic integration of an entire organization is the primary objective, including integration with corporate partners.

Strategic information systems are systems whose objective is to improve the competitive position of the organization. The principal competitive thrusts for seeking competitive advantage with strategic systems are redefining a company's business in terms of information; creating products and services based on information; and transforming a company's products and processes with information systems.

Competitive strategies of differentiation, cost leadership, focused differentiation, or cost focus may be deployed. Such a strategy may be used to combat some of the five competitive forces: threats by present or potential competitors or by substitute products, as well as pressures from customers or suppliers. Competitive tactics include internal growth or innovation, mergers or acquisitions, or strategic alliances with other companies.

The value chain through which the firm transforms input materials into its products and services is a powerful means for identifying opportunities for strategic systems. Such systems may be used in any one of the chain's stages of inbound logistics, operations, outbound logistics, marketing and sales, or service. An integrated virtual value chain, realized with information, is the objective of leading companies for the appropriate products and services.

KEY TERMS

Information society   *78*
Business globalization   *80*
Product innovation   *81*
Process innovation   *81*
Knowledge management   *82*
Time-based competition   *83*
Strategic information system   *88*

Yield management   *93*
Differentiation   *95*
Cost leadership   *96*
Focused differentiation   *96*
Cost focus   *97*
Value chain   *100*

QUESTIONS

1. What are the principal challenges our information society poses to organizations? Briefly relate each of them to a possible response with information systems. Illustrate each item with the example of Holiday Inn, described in the Focus Minicase.
2. How is business globalization affected by the use of information systems and how does it, in turn, affect this use?
3. What is knowledge management? How does it relate to knowledge work?
4. What is the difference between the product and the process innovation? Can a given information system be deployed for both purposes? If you think so, give an example.
5. How did the role of information systems expand during the four eras of organizational computing? In other words, what additional areas of corporate activity received support during each era?
6. What are the distinguishing characteristics of strategic information systems?
7. State the three principal competitive thrusts with strategic information systems. Give an example of each of these major initiatives.
8. What is yield management? What industries are the principal users of information systems for yield management? Why?
9. List the four competitive strategies and illustrate how an information system may help in realizing each of them. Why is differentiation preferable to cost-based competition?
10. What kind of barriers to entry can an information system create for your potential competitors? Give at least two examples.
11. You have introduced an interorganizational order entry system that your customers use. The customers' information systems have been modified to work with your system. What kind of switching costs are your customers likely to incur if they move to another supplier?
12. Why have strategic alliances, such as information partnerships, become common? Under what circumstances is this tactic preferable to internal innovation?
13. What is the value chain? Draw the value chain of a restaurant chain (yes, terminology does clash sometimes), such as California Pizza Kitchen, subject of the Focus Minicase in Chapter 2.
14. Map onto the value chain you have produced in the preceding question the strategic information systems that can be deployed by a restaurant chain. For each of the systems you propose, discuss which of the four competitive strategies it is likely to serve.
15. What are the typical strategic information systems deployed in the two Logistics stages of a value chain? What business results do companies pursue with these systems?
16. Describe how the information systems for the operations of manufacturing and service firms differ.
17. Suggest two strategic information systems for the marketing and sales stage of the value chain (other than the ones described in the text).
18. Select a hypothetical company in a service industry. Develop an example to illustrate how this company can progress through the three stages of building and exploiting a virtual value chain.
19. What are the keys to success of a strategic information system?

ISSUES FOR DISCUSSION

1. Describe point by point your ideal personal workstation. Distinguish the features you consider necessary (why?) from the ones that are "good to have."
2. Discuss how information systems have changed the nature of knowledge work and the way this work is organized within firms and across societies. What ethical issues may arise from this change?
3. Discuss this proposition: A strategic information system cannot secure a lasting advantage for a company over its competition. Such a system has to be combined with another asset or resource the company possesses in order to gain a competitive advantage.

REAL-WORLD MINICASE AND PROBLEM-SOLVING EXERCISES

1. Custom-Made Clothes for Everyone: Who Wins and Who Loses? Technology/Clothing Technology Corporation, an apparel industry group in Raleigh, North Carolina, is spending $8.5 million a year to develop a computerized system for the mass production of custom clothes. The system will rely on three-dimensional body scans of individual customers (see Photo 3.6) who will pay a premium for speedy delivery of such a garment. The system is intended to encourage manufacturers to keep factories in the United States, instead of exporting jobs to remote locales from which clothes are delivered after months of waiting.

Installed at retail establishments, the scanner would produce a full-body profile in about two seconds, with measurements going into a database for future orders. To define an individual's shape, six light projectors and six cameras will produce almost 1.4 million data points in three-dimensional space. Computer software will compute the depth dimensions. The scans will be sent over the telecommunications networks to the manufacturing plant, where the measurements will be linked to the pattern of the garment, which will be modified accordingly. The resulting information will be sent to a laser that will cut the cloth for the garment. Agile factories can

Photos 3.6

Making custom clothes at mass-production prices (Based on John Holusha, "Producing Custom-Made Clothes for the Masses," *The New York Times,* February 19, 1996, p. D3.)

Clothes That Are Cut to Fit

Shoppers who are in between sizes or find that their clothes never fit them might have an easier time with a new system that attempts to measure precise body dimensions to produce custom clothes.

1 Scanning

Wearing a body suit or underwear, a person is scanned using ordinary light.

2 Generating a profile

The person stands in front of a banded light source. There are six cameras which read the alternating bands of light and dark from four different angles. The curves provide data on height and width, but not on depth.

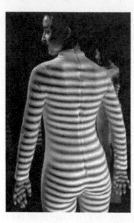

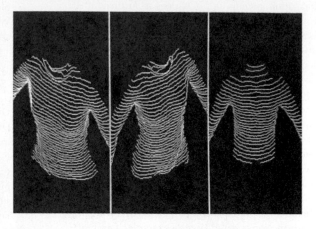

3 Estimating depth

Using software, computers can extrapolate the person's depth, or thickness, using data from the different views.

4 Making clothes

The three-dimensional information is mapped directly onto a cutting pattern that customizes standard patterns for the individual.

deliver the custom garment in a few days. Retail space could be far smaller than it is today, with only samples available for perusal. Everything would be sold before it is made. "The vision is pretty clear and the technology is almost here," says the president of the industry group, "As always, the culture change will be the hardest."

Actually, the Custom Foot shoe store in Westport, Connecticut, is already offering a similar service. After their feet are scanned, customers pick the color, style, and other features of the shoe, using an electronic kiosk placed in the store. At the end of the day, the scans and other data are transferred from the modest-size shop, containing just shoe samples and the computerized equipment, to the nearby offices of its parent company, Measurably Better. Then the data are forwarded to the company's office in Florence, Italy, and from there distributed among seven local factories signed up to produce the shoes. The entire process takes about two weeks.

Based on John Holusha, "Producing Custom-Made Clothes for the Masses," *The New York Times,* February 19, 1996, p. D3; and John Holusha, "Making the Shoe Fit Better: Companies Use Technology to Sell a Market of One," *The New York Times,* March 20, 1996, pp. D1 & D7.

Based on the preceding Minicase, answer the following questions:

a. Describe the value chain of the business of custom-made clothes based on the information provided here. State who is responsible for each of the value-chain stages you have identified.

b. How would the availability of the clothes customization system change the forces in the competitive apparel marketplace?

c. Do you think the system would be able to keep garment manufacturing at home? Why or why not?

d. Relate the mass-customization systems for apparel and for shoes to the idea of a virtual value chain. What additional value can be provided to the customers and how?

2. Supporting University Value Chain with Formation Systems.   Walk through the value chain of a university attracting students, teaching them, assisting in their job placement, and offering further education to and raising funds from the alumni. Suggest the information technology appropriate for various stages of this value chain.

3. Using a Word Processing System Creatively, Write a Report on "Starting a Mail-Order Company."   Suppose you are planning to start a mail-order company. How can you use strategic information systems to gain competitive edge? What do you expect will be the competitive position of your company with respect to the capabilities offered by the Internet? What do you think you will need to do in the future to sustain your advantage?

Your report should include several fonts of different size and italic, underlined, and boldface text. It should also include at least one table as well as footnotes and references in the back.

TEAM   PROJECT

Each two- or three-person team should select an industry segment and research the use of information systems for strategic ends in this segment. What stages of the value chain are generally supported by strategic information systems in your selected industry segment? Do you see other opportunities for strategic uses of information technology?

After selected teams make a presentation to the class, opportunities for importing ideas from one industry segment to others may be identified and discussed in class.

ENDNOTE

1. A fascinating story of the technology of EDI emerging from the Berlin airlift of 1948 is told in Tony Seideman's, "What Sam Walton Learned from the Berlin Airlift,"

Audacity: The Magazine of Business Experience, Spring 1996, pp. 52–61.

SELECTED   REFERENCES

Applegate, Lynda M.; F. Warren McFarlan; and James L. McKenney eds. *Corporate Information Systems Management: Text and Cases,* 4th ed. Burr Ridge, Ill.: Irwin, 1996.

An extensive discussion of a managerial approach to information technology.

Bell, Daniel. *The Coming of Post-Industrial Society,* New York: Basic Books, 1973.

This book is basic to understanding the societal change that has been called the "information society."

Beniger, James R. *The Control Revolution: Technological and Economic Origins of the Information Society,* Cambridge, Mass.: Harvard University Press, 1986.

How the Industrial Revolution led to the emergence of the information society two centuries later.

Berry, Jonathan. "Database Marketing: A Potent New Tool in Selling." *Business Week,* September 1994, pp. 56–62.

Clemons, Eric K.; David C. Croson; and Bruce W. Weber. "Market Dominance as a Precursor of a Firm's Failure: Emerging Technologies and the Competitive Advantage of New Entrants." *Journal of Management Information Systems,* 13, no. 2 (Fall 1996), pp. 59–75.

Cronin, Mary J. *Doing More Business on the Internet: How the Electronic Highway Is Transforming American Companies,* New York: Van Nostrand Reinhold, 1995.

A sourcebook of ideas for using the Internet in electronic commerce.

Drucker, Peter F. "The Coming of the New Organization." *Harvard Business Review,* January–February 1988, pp. 45–53.

An important article, setting out the premises of knowledge-based organizations.

Dumaine, Brian. "America's Smart Young Entrepreneurs." *Fortune,* March 21, 1994, pp. 34–41.

Feeny, David F., and Blake Ives. "In Search of Sustainability: Reaping Long-Term Advantage from Investments in Information Technology." *Journal of Management Information Systems,* 7, no. 1 (Summer 1990), pp. 27–46.

Once you gain a competitive advantage with information systems, how do you keep it? How do you deploy the systems so as to sustain the advantage?

Girard, Kim. "Browser Interface Sets Atlanta Bank Apart." *Computerworld,* November 4, 1996, pp. 67–70.

Hamel, Gary, and C. K. Prahalad. *Competing for the Future,* Boston: Harvard Business School Press, 1994.

How to compete by honing and exploiting the core competencies of your corporation.

Hammer, Michael, and James Champy. *Reengineering the Corporation,* New York: Harper Business, 1993.

"H. E. Butt Grocery Company: A Leader in ECR Implementation." Harvard Business School Case 196–061, 1994.

Hitt, Lorin M., and Erik Brynjolfsson. "Productivity, Business Profitability, and Consumer Surplus: Three *Different* Measures of Information Technology Value." *MIS Quarterly,* 20, no. 2 (June 1996), pp. 121–142.

Huber, George P. "The Nature and Design of Post-Industrial Organizations." *Management Science,* 30, no. 8 (August 1984), pp. 928–951.

A classical paper on its subject.

Johnston, H. Russell, and Shelley R. Carrico. "Developing Capabilities to Use Information Systems Strategically." *MIS Quarterly,* 12, no. 2 (March 1988), pp. 37–48.

What organizational measures are needed to be able to develop and deploy strategic information systems?

Jones, Kathryn. "Seeing a Digital Future, Printers Rush to Get Beyond Ink and Paper." *The New York Times,* September 2, 1994, p. D5.

Kettinger, William J., and others. "Strategic Information Systems Revisited: A Study in Sustainability and Performance." *MIS Quarterly,* 18, no. 1 (March 1994), pp. 31–58.

It is easier to gain sustainable competitive edge with information systems in the industries with fewer competitors and a relatively stable marketplace.

King, Ralph T., Jr., and Steven Lipin. "Corporate Banking, Given Up for Dead, Is Reinventing Itself." *The Wall Street Journal,* January 31, 1994, pp. A1, A6.

Lauren, Ralph S. Interview in *Forbes,* February 26, 1996, p. 56.

Malone, Thomas W.; Joanne Yates; and Robert I. Benjamin. "Electronic Markets and Electronic Hierarchies." *Communications of the ACM,* 30, no. 16 (June 1987), pp. 484–497.

An important paper, arguing that the increasing use of information technology will lead to buying more products and services in the marketplace rather than producing them internally in a firm.

Murray, Matt. "Rx for Pharmacies: Bigger Line of Products and Services." *The Wall Street Journal,* September 12, 1996, p. B4.

Nault, Barrie R., and Albert S. Dexter. "Added Value and Pricing with Information Technology." *MIS Quarterly,* 19, no. 4 (December 1995), pp. 449–463.

Nolan, Richard L., and David C. Croson. *Creative Destruction: A Six-Stage Process of Organizational Transformation,* Boston: Harvard Business School Press, 1995.

How to transform your organization using the capabilities of information technology.

Nonaka, Ikujiro, and Hirotaka Takeuchi. *The Knowledge-Creating Company,* New York: Oxford University Press, 1995.

How to convert the tacit knowledge in the minds of the organization's workers into a lasting organizational memory.

Porter, Michael E. *Competitive Advantage,* New York: Free Press, 1985.

A fundamental work that defined much of the current thinking on competitive strategy.

Porter, Michael E. *The Competitive Advantage of Nations,* New York: Free Press, 1990.

What determines the competitiveness of national industries?

Porter, Michael E., and Victor E. Millar. "How Information Gives You Competitive Advantage." *Harvard Business Review,* July–August 1985, pp. 149–190.

Rayport, Jeffrey F., and John J. Sviokla. "Exploiting the Virtual Value Chain." *Harvard Business Review,* November–December 1995, pp. 75–85.

How to move your company's operations from the physical marketplace into a "marketspace" created with information systems.

Santalesa, Rich. "Getting the Latest Version of Software Via the Internet." *The New York Times,* July 1, 1996, p. D5.

Slywotzky, Adrian J. *Value Migration,* Boston: Harvard Business School Press, 1996.

How to ensure that your company is where the value is migrating.

Winslow, Charles D., and William L. Bramer. *FutureWork: Putting Knowledge to Work in the Knowledge Economy,* New York: Free Press, 1994.

Describes information systems that can provide specialized assistance to various categories of knowledge workers.

CASE STUDY | # The Molson Way to Competitive Success

Molson Breweries is the largest beer manufacturer in Canada and the oldest in North America, with roots dating back to 1786. Headquartered in Toronto, Ontario, Molson operates eight highly automated breweries across Canada, producing Molson Canadian, Molson Ice, and several other well-known brands. With just under 50 percent of the Canadian market, Molson also brews beers under its licensing agreements with companies in several other countries, beers known as Kirin, Lowenbrau, Fosters, and Miller.

Molson has a very clear strategy: It wants to become the domestic low-cost provider of beer. One of the driving forces behind the strategy is the impact of the North American Free Trade Agreement (NAFTA). Previously, Canada's markets were sheltered by extensive government regulation. With NAFTA, these markets have become wider open to competition from the U.S. brewers, who introduced discount pricing as part of their strategy aimed at expanding their market share.

Molson does not intend to attain low costs by lowering the quality of the hops it uses for the beer or by accelerating the brewing process. Instead, it is building an integrated supply chain of suppliers, breweries, warehouses, distributors, and retailers, who become partners in meeting the actual demand, not a more speculative forecast. "Companies can't operate by themselves in today's market," says Brent Galardo, director of corporate systems for Molson. "You've got to think globally and use information to build partnerships within your supply chain. Without communications and information-sharing, everyone in a supply chain is just building to forecasts from different crystal balls, which leads to great waste and inefficiencies."

Molson has turned to information systems to help in seeking efficiencies. "We must have complete visibility [provided with information] of supply and demand on a daily basis, where possible, and be able to share this with our suppliers," says Galardo. "It's quite a challenge to ensure that all brands are available in the right quantities at all locations in Canada, while dealing with multiple supply and sourcing, and keeping production steady in each of our eight breweries."

The company uses a proprietary PC-based network to provide forecasts of manufacturing requirements and raw-material inventory levels to all its suppliers, who will deliver hops, malt, cartons, and bottles as needed. After receiving this information, Molson's suppliers transmit back the manufacturing plans and projected shipping dates. The company uses E-mail (under X.400 communications standard) for the information exchange.

"We've looked closely at electronic data interchange for several years now. But, truthfully, we don't have the transaction volume among our relatively few suppliers and distributors to cost-justify the move from our current network with customized interfaces that have evolved over 15 years," says Galardo. Molson has also investigated the possibility of using the Internet for exchanging information with its business partners, but did not pursue it because of security concerns. However, Molson uses the Internet for general E-mail and has established its site (see Figure 3.16) on the Web, allowing the Net users to ask questions of the Molson Brewmaster.

While the supply picture is relatively simple, distribution is far more complicated, since it varies among Canada's ten provinces and two territories. Only in Quebec does Molson rely on its own three-tier distribution network, consisting of direct delivery, distribution centers, and agencies. Elsewhere, the provincial distributors are owned by the local government or co-owned by all the major breweries. "On our network, we share daily inventory

Figure 3.16

Molson's home page on the World Wide Web.
(From http://www.molson.com)

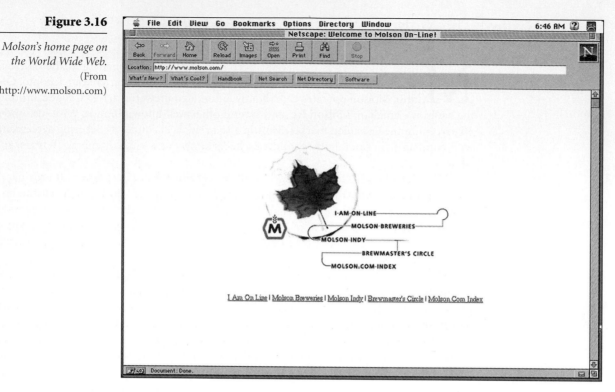

levels among all distributors and receive daily sales information from most distributors," says Galardo. The sales and inventory information is fed into a central IBM AS/400 mid-size computer at the Toronto headquarters, which is linked with other AS/400s acting as servers within four regions—Western, Eastern, Ontario, and Quebec—within a client/server network Molson calls LINK. The central computer runs the information systems for forecasting, purchasing, manufacturing resource planning, and distribution resource planning. The regional AS/400s handle information systems that support customer-order processing and accounts receivable, local manufacturing, inventory status and control, and local purchasing. The firm uses applications software from American Software of Atlanta, Georgia. The bilingual software accommodates the needs of both English- and French-speaking employees.

Each plant has several customized PC-based applications for manufacturing, inventory control, and purchasing, with PCs connected into local area networks. Wide-area connectivity among the plants, regional servers, and headquarters is accomplished with a 56 Kbps (thousands of bits per second) network, whose traffic is directed by Cisco routers. Since the network traffic is growing rapidly, Molson has installed a fiber optic cable in all of its campus-like locations and plans to increase the capacity of the network.

Using the information based on existing inventory as well as on the distributor and retail sales, Molson draws up its supply, inventory, and production requirements, generally on a weekly basis. The information is sent out to the regions and plants over the company's network, which is also used for the interchange of order receipts and shipment confirmations. "The software gives us complete visibility of supply and demand," says Galardo.

Once the manufacturing plan has been developed, it is shared with the appropriate suppliers, who can align their production with Molson's requirements, achieving close to just-in-time relationship for major raw materials. "This information sharing via electronic exchange has helped smooth out production planning and greatly reduced the requirement of rescheduling production in a reactionary mode due to a lack of materials," says Galardo.

The detailed production information has enabled Molson to tighten its business processes in order to eliminate the necessary costs. "After analyzing the data, we found that we were shifting production too much to accommodate low-margin, low-volume products . . . We were also putting too much effort into time-limited offers such as Christmas or other promotional runs. Our time was being spent attempting to meet the forecasts, instead of concentrating on our demand signals from our business partners," says Galardo. As the result of this realization, the company has enhanced its communication with its distributors in an effort to concentrate on high-margin items.

The challenge of NAFTA brings opportunities as well. Now Molson wants to expand its presence in the United States. Owing in part to its enhanced information interchange via the LINK system, Molson has become the second largest beer importer to this country. Molson USA is integrated into the overall Molson information network.

The investment in information technology and the integration of its supply chain bring well-defined business results for Molson. Because of more accurate supply planning, the relationships with suppliers have improved and inventory levels have decreased. By following customer demand more closely, Molson is able to avoid both stock-outs and inventory obsolescence (beer has, of course, a limited shelf life). In fact, the costs went down 6 percent during the first year after the business initiative surrounding the LINK system and the system itself were implemented. Most important, however, is that integrating its supply chain has helped Molson meet its principal objective and become the domestic low-cost producer.

Based on Nick Wreden, "Something's Brewing," *EDI World*, February 1996, pp. 20–24; John H. Mayer, "Supply-Chain Tools Cut Inventory Fat," *Software Magazine*, May 1996, pp. 77–80; and the Web site http://www.molson.com .

CASE STUDY QUESTIONS

1. What is the principal competitive strategy of Molson Breweries?

2. What are the principal competitive forces Molson has to contend with?

3. What capabilities of information systems does Molson exploit in the pursuit of its competitive objective?

4. Sketch out the information system network of Molson, including its business partners.

5. How can you evaluate the nature of the information technologies deployed by Molson? Is it the leading edge technology?

6. Compare and contrast Molson's use of information technology with that of Holiday Inn, discussed in the Focus Minicase for the chapter. Discuss the reasons for the differences.

7. Sketch out Molson's value chain and the supply chain that Molson Breweries is a part of.

8. What is the principal reason for Molson's success in achieving its competitive results with information systems?

PART TWO

Information Technology

Information technology (IT) is a principal means for creating information systems. This part of the text will present the IT resources that may be used to raise the operational efficiency of an enterprise, increase the effectiveness of its management, and enhance the competitive position of the firm.

Chapter Four will discuss the hardware resources of information systems and show how their proper selection can contribute to business success.

Chapter Five will present information systems software. Both systems software, such as operating systems, and applications software will be discussed. Particular attention will be devoted to personal productivity software that defines the working environment of each of us. Fourth-generation languages and object-oriented programming, the software facilities that have changed the programming landscape, will also be presented.

Chapter Six will show how the data of an enterprise can become a potent resource when organized into databases that are exploited throughout the firm. You will see the technological as well as the organizational components of managing organizational data resources.

Chapter Seven will present telecommunications networks, another major IT resource of today's enterprises. You will see how some of these nets may be used to support a group of collaborating knowledge workers, while others span an entire global corporation and connect it to other companies around the globe. The Internet, a global network of networks, and in particular its World Wide Web facility, is changing world commerce and affects virtually all organizations. Developing an information system architecture is important in gaining full advantage of the competitive opportunities offered by telecommunications.

Throughout this part of the text, we will aim to understand how information technology may be used to produce business results. Using advanced information technology for technology's sake (known as the "bleeding edge" syndrome) can adversely affect the performance of your firm. New and appropriate information systems have to be justified as part of the solution to business problems or as tools in the pursuit of new business opportunities.

CHAPTER FOUR

Information Systems Hardware

OBJECTIVES

After you complete this chapter, you will be able to:

1. Understand the structure of a computer system.
2. Distinguish and understand the applications of four categories of computers.
3. Understand what the system's processor (the central processing unit) does.
4. Understand why there is a need for a hierarchy of memories in a computer system.
5. Specify and explain the use of secondary storage, input, and output devices.
6. Understand how multimedia computing can contribute to business success.

OUTLINE

Creativity and Information Technology Go Together

Malone Advertising of Akron, Ohio, is a 50-year-old agency with 60 employees and annual billings of some $50 million, whose clients include Goodyear Tire & Rubber and Kimberly-Clark. When Fred Bidwell became the agency's president four years ago, he turned to information technology to help the agency weather the difficult times of the recession that began in the late 1980s.

By today, information technology has touched almost every task and employee at Malone Advertising. The hand-drawn storyboards that the agencies have traditionally used to help clients imagine how their expensive television commercials will look on the air are gone. Using his Apple Macintosh PowerBook laptop computer running the graphics package from Avid Technology, Bidwell can show the clients what looks like an actual ready-to-air TV commercial—before a single dollar is spent on the video production.

Graphics workstations liberally sprinkled around the agency create layouts that look as professional as full color magazine ads. Thanks to E-mail, Malone is able to continue servicing accounts handled by the offices in several cities that were closed by the firm due to the recession. Actually, the firm does more business today outside Ohio than it did when it had all its branch offices. Voice mail has replaced the receptionist, and the PCs running personal productivity software have replaced the secretaries. Indeed, all employees, including the mail clerk, have their own PCs. Bidwell himself uses his laptop as a portable office. He stores in it the agency's financial records, all the client proposals, and his calendar for the past three years and into the future.

Bidwell estimates that the pre-computerized Malone Advertising of five years ago would have needed 10 additional full-time employees to manage the current increased workload. "Technology eliminates steps in the process and keeps you close to the product," says Bidwell. "We thought we were in a creative business," he adds, but "I don't think anyone saw what technology can bring to an ad agency."

Another entrepreneur, Dominick Segrete, believes that his small New York architectural design firm owes much of its success to information technology. The firm, Tucci, Segrete, and Rosen, brings in $6 million in billings a year designing retail space for large department stores. "High technology is no longer optional," says Segrete. Over the last 10 years, he has spent some $350,000 on information technology, including 30 networked PCs. Like many designers these days, the firm uses the computer-aided design and drawing software AutoCAD. But particularly effective is the combination of AutoCAD with ProShare, a videoconferencing software for personal computers. Working with the resulting information system, the designers work not only more efficiently, but smarter.

When the firm's designers were creating, for example, the retail space for the huge Printemps department store in Paris, they would send off the AutoCAD file of the proposed design to the client's PC via telecommunications networks and then discuss the design using ProShare. Either party can mark up the electronic blueprint with a pen-like stylus right on the screen. If the client wants to move the Ralph Lauren boutique from the second floor to the fourth, the designer can do this in New York while the client watches in Paris.

When the right technology gives his firm a competitive edge, it pays for itself in no time, according to Segrete. Recently, he beat a competitor to an $800,000 contract by sending a proposed floor plan to a remote client via ProShare before the competitor's plane touched down at the site. Segrete says that the use of information technology has opened up a wellspring of creativity and collaboration in his firm. Designers can discuss ideas with each other and with clients more easily, by trying them out right then and there with the software. "Once all of [our information technology] is in place, you really start to see the creative process take over," says Segrete. "It enhances the way you think, the rooms you have to create. We can now include perspectives on drawings, as well as take clients on virtual walkthroughs with video. When designers actually think in 3D, it opens up worlds like never before."

Based on "Techno Convert: Never Met a Computer I Didn't Like," *Business Week,* October 17, 1994, pp. 100–102; and Rivka Tadjer, "Better by Design," *Success,* October 1996, pp. 55–56.

As we have seen in the above Focus Minicase, information technology may determine the realm of the possible in today's work. This chapter will introduce you to the hardware components of information systems and show how firms seek competitive edge by exploiting the properties of these components.

4.1 | ORGANIZATION OF COMPUTER SYSTEMS

Almost all computer systems have a similar, rather simple, structure consisting of a processor, main memory, and peripheral devices, such as secondary storage, and input and output devices. The speeds and memory capacities of computer systems have been expanding ever more rapidly over the last decades. This translates into more and more potent business applications.

What Is the Structure of a Computer System?

A **computer system** is a set of devices that can accept and store programs and data, execute programs by applying their instructions to the data, and report the results. As I write this book on my personal computer, I interact with my input device (a keyboard). Under the processor's control, the input device transmits encoded symbols, which represent letters, numbers, and special symbols (a $ or a blank), into memory, and the output device (a monitor screen) displays them. The program that my computer is executing is a word processing program. Indeed, what a computer does at any given time depends on the instructions of the program it is executing. This is why the computer is called a general-purpose information processor. The same machine, when executing an expert system program, can render advice on a complex financial deal or, running yet another software program, can produce the best routes for thousands of an airline's planes. This flexibility accounts for the pervasive presence of computers in the business landscape.

It is rather amazing that the general organization of computer system hardware is as simple as it is. As you can see in Figure 4.1, the principal components of a computer system are the processor, main memory, input and output devices, and secondary storage. The same organization is used to build a microcomputer for your desktop and a mainframe computer that fills a large room and costs perhaps a thousand times more. The devices

Figure 4.1

*The organization of
computer systems*

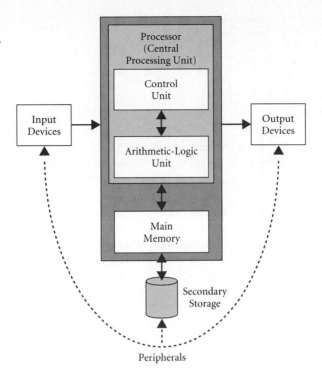

actually included in these configurations, their speeds, and their processing capabilities will, of course, be different.

We will now briefly discuss the components of the computer system shown in Figure 4.1. Later on in this chapter, we will come back to them for a closer look. Let us begin with the processor—the central unit of the computer system.

The Processor (CPU)

At the heart of the computer is its processor. Also called the **central processing unit (CPU)** of the computer, the **processor** executes machine instructions. These instructions are encoded in binary form, that is, as 1s and 0s, corresponding to the two possible states of digital circuitry: on or off. To "execute machine instructions" means that the control unit of the CPU fetches these instructions one by one from the main memory, retrieves the data for each instruction from the main memory as needed, carries out the instruction, and stores the results back in the main memory. Depending on the instruction it executes, the control unit sends signals that tell all other units of the computer system what to do; it indeed controls them.

A machine instruction does very detailed work. For example, an instruction may specify any of the following:

- An arithmetic operation, such as the addition of two numbers.
- Movement of data from one location to another, including input from or output to a peripheral device.
- Selection of which program instruction to execute next, depending on a certain condition. This ability to carry out sequences of instructions conditionally or repeatedly accounts for much of the computer's power.

Figure 4.2

A schematic view of memory

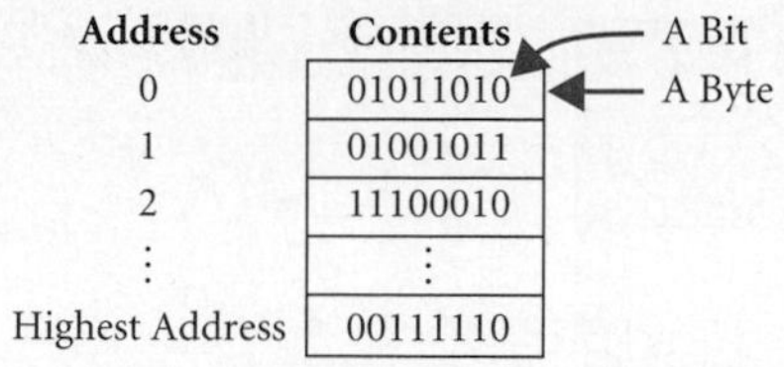

Address	Contents	
0	01011010	◀── A Bit / A Byte
1	01001011	
2	11100010	
⋮	⋮	
Highest Address	00111110	

When arithmetic or logical operations are to be carried out, the arithmetic-logic unit (ALU) of the CPU is used. This circuitry can, for example, add or multiply operands as well as perform logical operations, such as comparisons. The ability to perform millions of arithmetic operations per second underlies the computer's capability to display high-resolution graphics, among other uses.

Computer programs are actually written using programming languages that offer instructions far more convenient for humans than the machine instructions consisting of 0s and 1s. Programs written in these programming languages need to be translated into machine language by software, as we will see in the next chapter. Then, when the time comes to have the program carried out (that is, executed) by the processor, a machine-language program is placed in the main memory.

Main Memory

To be ready for execution, the programs and their data must be transferred into the main memory. The **main memory** is a fast electronic component of the computer system that serves to store programs to be executed by the CPU and the data these programs require. A main memory consists of a large number of locations, identified by their addresses, as shown in Figure 4.2.

The elementary unit of digital representation is a **bit** (short for *b*inary digi*t*), whose value can be either 0 or 1. Character representations are built out of combinations of bits, with each character represented by a sequence of eight bits, called a **byte.** Processors can generally fetch and manipulate several bytes at one time from the main memory. The largest number of consecutive bytes that can be accessed at one time in the main memory is called a **word.** For example, a 32-bit machine has a word that equals 4 bytes. Main memories have capacities measured in megabytes, units somewhat larger than millions of bytes.

Each memory, identified by its own address, can store one letter, digit, or special symbol encoded in the binary code used by the machine. The cell whose address is 0 in Figure 4.2 stores the letter Z in the ASCII-8 code, used in most machines (ASCII, pronounced "askee", stands for American Standard Code for Information Interchange). Another character code, used by the IBM mainframes, is also an 8-bit code, called EBCDIC (pronounced "ebsidik" and standing for Extended Binary Coded Decimal Interchange Code). As the following vignette will tell you, a more powerful code has been developed to represent the characters of the world's languages.

Of course, text is only one of the data types stored in computer memories. Numbers, for example, have a variety of representations of their own. **Multimedia computing** that integrates various media, such as text, graphics, sound, and video, is becoming more popular and, therefore, images are often stored as well. A memory representation of an image is the equivalent of a grid of dots, called **pixels** (for picture elements); we will encounter them again in Section 4.5, when discussing video displays.

Today's main memories are made of semiconductor chips, referred to as **RAM,** for **random access memory,** since it takes the same amount of time to access any randomly chosen

**Unicode: A
Universal
Character
Code**

Have you ever thought what happens in our age of globalization when we want to write software that can interact with users in different countries? The ASCII-8 and EBCDIC codes can represent only 256 different characters. This does not accommodate the accented characters of French, and certainly not Chinese ideographs (also used in Korean and Japanese), not to mention Arabic, Bengali, or Hebrew.

To solve this problem, 12 top computer companies formed a consortium, that has developed a worldwide standard called Unicode. Using a sequence of 16 bits to represent a single character, it allows for 65,536 representable symbols. And that is enough to give each char-

acter used in a living language its own representation (and to leave some for cuneiform used in ancient languages as well). Of course, new and sweeping standards are notoriously slow to be accepted, but the need for internationalized software is very real.

Based on Jurgen Bettels and F. Avery Bishop, "Unicode: A Universal Character Code," *Digital Technical Journal*, 5, no. 3 (Summer 1993), pp. 21–31; M.E. Davis, J.D. Grimes, and D.J. Knoles, "Creating Global Software," *IBM Systems Journal*, 35, no. 2 (1996), pp. 227–243; and the Unicode electronic site http://www.stonehand.com/unicode.html.

memory location. A RAM chip of the current generation has a capacity of 16 megabits (more than 16 million bits!)[1]. If you use eight such chips, you have a main memory with the capacity of 16 megabytes. The next generation, which is already in fabrication (see Photo 4.1), will store 64 megabits per chip—the equivalent of about 4,000 pages of double-spaced typewritten text (about four times the size of this book's text). A prototype chip with four-gigabit capacity has already been developed (Pollack 1997).

Even though a computer's main memory contains a number of RAM chips, its capacity is still limited as compared to the total requirements for the storage of data and programs. Moreover, semiconductor RAMs are volatile—when power is removed, their contents disappear. To extend memory capacity in a cost-effective manner and to provide more permanent memories, secondary storage devices are employed.

Photo 4.1

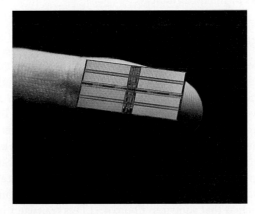

A 64-megabit memory chip. The narrowest circuit line on such a chip has the width of 0.35 micron, or about one-thousandth the diameter of a human hair. Manufacturers that take the lead in memory chips gain immense competitive advantage in semiconductor manufacturing by being able to apply their know-how and equipment to making other devices.

Peripherals

Secondary storage devices (such as disks and tape drives), along with input and output devices are called **peripherals.** Input and output devices transfer programs and data between the outside world and the main memory. Some of these devices connect the computer systems to a network and will be discussed in Chapter 7. The peripherals of a computer system are selected to satisfy the needs for permanent storage of programs and data and for communication with the system's environment.

In a microcomputer (a micro, as we commonly call it), the processor and the main memory are packaged into the system unit together with such peripheral equipment as disk drives. Recently, many peripherals for microcomputers, such as modems and storage devices, have become available as credit card-size PCMCIA[2] cards that can be easily plugged into the slots on the back or side of a computer. System configurations for larger computers generally include several cabinets, housing additional processors and peripherals. We will return to a more detailed discussion of peripherals after we review the capabilities of various categories of computers.

4.2 COMPUTER CATEGORIES: MICROCOMPUTERS, MINICOMPUTERS, MAINFRAMES, AND SUPERCOMPUTERS

Computer system hardware is now available in a spectacular variety of capabilities and costs. The relative cost of hardware as compared to software has declined no less impressively. The challenge consists in using information technology to increase operational efficiency and managerial effectiveness, and, ultimately, to deploy it to seek competitive advantage. To do this, it is necessary to select the most appropriate technologies to meet a business objective within the context of the given enterprise and its already existing information systems capabilities.

Here, we will discuss the different categories of computers and the principal capabilities they offer a firm. The general technological trend is downsizing. As we described in Section 2.3, this means moving applications from larger machines, such as mainframes and minis, to the networks of microcomputers.

What Are the Categories of Computers?

Computers initially emerged in the 1940s as daunting machines that filled entire rooms with equipment; today, far more powerful computers than those early models can be held in the palm of your hand. A capsule history of computing is shown in Figure 4.3, which illustrates when the ever smaller machines put in their appearance. In organizational computing, stand-alone computers have been supplanted by networks, connecting machines of various categories. Throughout their development, computers have undergone several generational changes. The principal characteristic of a computer generation is the fundamental technology employed to build computer circuits. **Very large-scale integration** (VLSI) made it feasible to place millions of semiconductor devices (for example, transistors) on a single silicon chip, such as that shown in Photo 4.1. This translates into the high speeds of processor chips and the high capacities of memory chips.

Four categories of computers—microcomputers, minicomputers, mainframes, and supercomputers—are in production and use. Before we discuss the four computer categories in some detail, let's look at Table 4.1, which shows their typical capabilities. A warning: It is difficult to make direct speed comparisons among machines across categories (and from

Figure 4.3

How computer categories emerged

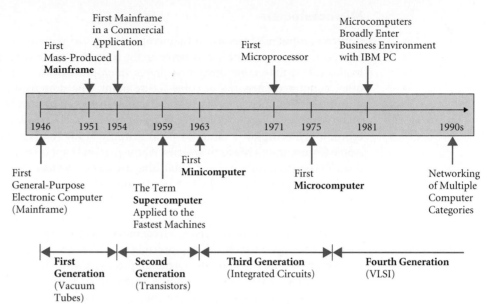

Category	Microcomputer	Minicomputer	Mainframe	Supercomputer
		These are usually multiprocessors		
Instruction execution rates	100–200 MIPS	200–800 MIPS	300–2,000 MIPS	2–20 GFLOPS
Main memory (Mbytes)	16–64	64–256	128–3,048	256–8,096
Price (in thousands of dollars)	3–5	150–500	1,000–15,000	5,000–25,000

Table 4.1

Characteristics of various categories of computers

different vendors). Minicomputers and mainframes can support more plentiful and more powerful peripherals than a micro. Generally, uniform benchmark programs are run on various machines to make such comparisons.

Computer speed is roughly determined by two measures: instruction execution rate and machine clock rate (the speed of the circuitry). The instruction execution rate is measured in millions of instructions per second (MIPS), but since different machines have instructions of different power, this measure can serve only as a tentative means of comparison. In supercomputers, this measure is replaced by the count of billions of floating-point operations, that is, arithmetic operations on real numbers, performed per second (GFLOPS, or gigaflops). Thus, a machine whose speed is 1 GFLOPS can add or multiply a billion pairs of numbers in a single second! The speed of microprocessors, on the other hand, is frequently measured by their clock rate and expressed in megahertz (MHz), or millions of cycles per second. Typical speeds are 166, 200, 233, and 266 MHz. It may take several clock cycles to execute an instruction; a 200 MHz machine may have an instruction execution rate of 100 MIPS.

Microcomputers

A **microcomputer** is built around a microprocessor—a processor on a single chip. Although microcomputers were the last to arrive on the computer scene, they redefined it completely, to the extent that some observers foresee microprocessor-based machines replacing all other computer categories at some future point. The dominant microcomputers in the business environment are the IBM PC series and IBM-compatible machines offered by many vendors, such as Compaq, Dell, or Gateway 2000. The newer IBM and compatible microcomputers employ Pentium Pro and Pentium II microprocessors. Microcomputers in Apple Corporation's Macintosh series, whose market share is far smaller, are popular in industries such as advertising and publishing because they work easily with graphics.

The cost of a microcomputer system depends on the processor chip, memory capacity, and the peripherals configured. Microcomputers are frequently called personal computers (PCs), in reference to their most common application. Indeed, unlike other machine classes, microcomputer systems are frequently selected, configured, and installed by end users for their personal use. More powerful than PCs are **technical workstations,** which typically support a variety of industrial design processes with high-resolution graphic processing (Sun Microsystems is a well-known vendor of such workstations). These workstations are often used as Web servers by the companies that want to establish electronic sites for public access (Mysore and Melson 1996).

Some microcomputers and almost all technical workstations are now built around microprocessors called **reduced instruction set computers (RISC)**. These microprocessors have a limited set of simple machine instructions, which results in very high processor speeds. They are particularly well suited to graphics processing and other applications that require extensive computation. The concept of streamlining the instruction set of a processor has also influenced the design of the traditional chips, such as Pentium, which are called, by contrast, complex instruction set computers (CISC). In spite of the RISC's speed advantage in many applications, Pentium and similar CISC microprocessors from Intel Corporation dominate the microcomputing market. A large body of software available for CISCs is a principal reason.

The hardware of a microcomputer is generally built around a bus, or set of lines that interconnect all the other hardware components (see Figure 4.4). Input and output devices communicate with the microprocessor (CPU) and the main memory via this bus, which they share with other devices. The microprocessor chip, a part of the main memory (RAM) chip set, and the read only memory (ROM) chips are placed directly on the system (mother) board of the machine. The contents of **read only memory (ROM)** cannot be changed and, therefore, ROM stores a number of permanent service routines. The vital one is the bootstrap program, which is activated when you turn on the computer: This program performs the diagnostics to check out the machine's circuitry and then loads the operating system (actually, its memory-resident part) from a disk into RAM. Once the operating system is loaded, you can run an application by specifying its name to the operating system.

The input and output devices, as well as secondary memories, are connected to the bus with adapter circuits. This makes it possible to connect a variety of peripherals made by different vendors. In addition, add-in cards may be placed in the expansion slots of the system board to enhance the performance of the microcomputer or to connect any needed devices. Table 4.2 will give you an idea of the variety of such devices and enhancements. In particular, it is necessary to back up the contents of the hard disk periodically by copying these contents onto another storage device. In many cases, floppy disks are used for backup. However, a tape backup device provides greater convenience. The need to connect into a local area network (see Chapter 7) calls for the installation of an appropriate adapter card. Multifunction cards are available. By handling several functions, these boards maximize the use of expansion slots.

Figure 4.4

How a microcomputer is organized

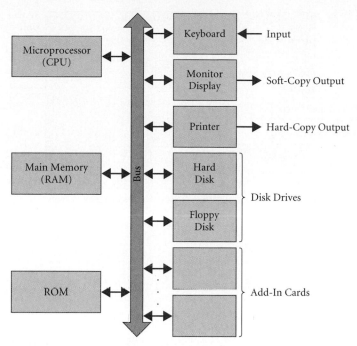

Table 4.2	**Card**	**Function**
Popular add-in cards for microcomputers	Accelerator	Boosts the processing speed; often used to upgrade an older machine. Graphics accelerators speed up the display of graphics.
	Adapter	Connects a peripheral to the system. Disk adapter boards may actually contain a hard disk. Mouse, CD-ROM, or backup tape adapters connect specific devices.
	Emulator	Enables the microcomputer to operate as a terminal connected to a larger host computer.
	Fax	Enables the micro to function as a facsimile (fax) machine. Includes a modem.
	Local Area Network (LAN) Interface	Connects the microcomputer to a LAN.
	Modem	Provides a modem for telecommunications purposes.
	Sound	Provides audio recording and playback capability in multimedia systems.
	Video	Provides the capability to display (sometimes to capture as well) video images in multimedia systems.

Figure 4.5

A microcomputer in a small business: A dental office system handles patient billing

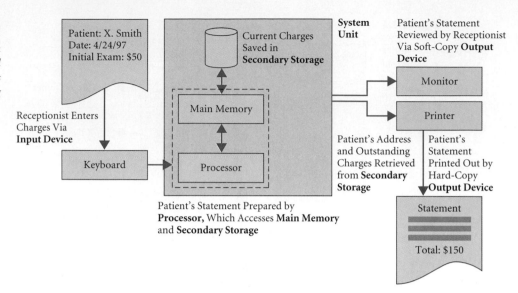

A microcomputer is frequently a sole information processor in a small business. Figure 4.5 illustrates how a small business, a dentist's office, can be equipped with a microcomputer system that handles all its computational needs. To review the role of various system components, we illustrate one of the functions handled by the system—patient billing. Specialized software packages are on the market for virtually all business segments, however small, from auto repair shops to beauty salons.

Desktop machines (even though in many cases the system unit, called the tower, goes under the desk) are only a part of personal computing today. The needs of organizations and individuals for mobile computing have given rise to the following portable machines:

Notebook computers (also known as laptops) combine all computer components, including peripherals other than the printer, in a single package that weighs between four and seven pounds (see Figure 4.6). Because they are battery powered, notebooks can operate for several hours without external power sources. Some notebook computers provide processing power equal to that of midrange desktops. By moving processing power out of the office and at the same time enabling the notebook carrier to communicate with the office via the telephone or wireless media, these portable computers are used, for example, to support salespeople in the field. Known as field-force automation, the equipping of personnel working in the field with notebooks or other portable computers has changed many business processes in some corporations. For example, Citibank conducts its internal field auditing with the help of notebooks.

Palmtop (or **handheld**) **computers** weigh around one pound. This computer category includes general-purpose machines (which, however, do not use disks) as well as specialized devices for data collection. Handheld computers may have only an eight-line display, but they can be used to great advantage in retail shops or in warehouses to store data about available products; the data can be regularly transmitted to a company's data center.

Pen-based notepads have a liquid crystal display (LCD) screen built into the top panel. Instead of a keyboard or a mouse, the user employs a pen-like stylus to fill out a form that appears on the screen, to edit text, to enter or modify a drawing, or to take notes that are stored as an image. The notepad also accepts tapping and flicking gestures of the stylus against the screen in order to launch a program, for example.

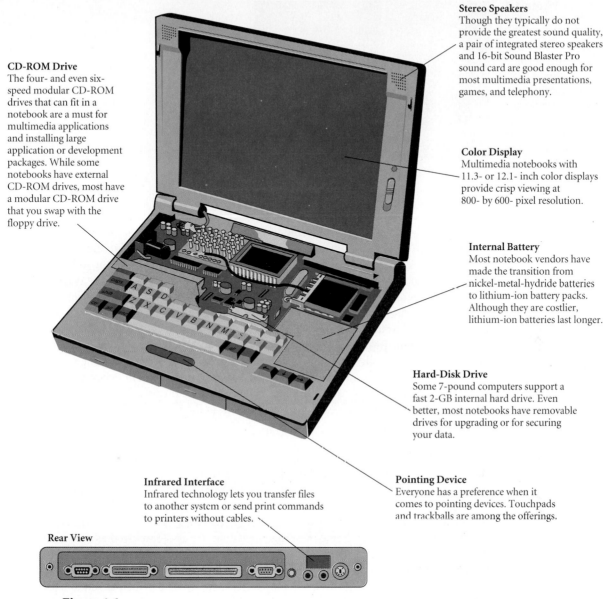

Stereo Speakers
Though they typically do not provide the greatest sound quality, a pair of integrated stereo speakers and 16-bit Sound Blaster Pro sound card are good enough for most multimedia presentations, games, and telephony.

CD-ROM Drive
The four- and even six-speed modular CD-ROM drives that can fit in a notebook are a must for multimedia applications and installing large application or development packages. While some notebooks have external CD-ROM drives, most have a modular CD-ROM drive that you swap with the floppy drive.

Color Display
Multimedia notebooks with 11.3- or 12.1- inch color displays provide crisp viewing at 800- by 600- pixel resolution.

Internal Battery
Most notebook vendors have made the transition from nickel-metal-hydride batteries to lithium-ion battery packs. Although they are costlier, lithium-ion batteries last longer.

Hard-Disk Drive
Some 7-pound computers support a fast 2-GB internal hard drive. Even better, most notebooks have removable drives for upgrading or for securing your data.

Infrared Interface
Infrared technology lets you transfer files to another system or send print commands to printers without cables.

Pointing Device
Everyone has a preference when it comes to pointing devices. Touchpads and trackballs are among the offerings.

Rear View

Figure 4.6

A notebook computer (the hardware will be discussed in this chapter)
(Adapted from Maggi Bender and others, "19 Pentium Portables Do Multimedia," *Byte,* October 1996, pp. 114–125.)

Personal digital assistants (PDA), somewhat similar to pen-based notepads, weigh less than a pound and enable their users to input data into or retrieve data from computers anywhere in the world, using wireless telecommunications. Exemplified by Apple Computer's Newton, they are expected ultimately to become as easy to use as portable telephones. As initially introduced, PDAs have been somewhat a solution in search of a problem. It is expected, however, that PDAs such as Pilot from US Robotics or Sony's Magic Link will be used to send and receive E-mail and launch software agents into telecommunications networks, for example, to access World Wide Web sites. By launching such an agent, a user may buy theater tickets or seek information about a recent stock offering. We will come back to PDAs and other information devices in the Case Study for this chapter.

Photo 4.2

A JavaStation network computer from Sun Microsystems, built around a RISC microprocessor (From Michael Moeller and others, "Thin Clients, Server Frameworks Face Interoperability Obstacles," *PC Week,* November 4, 1996, p. 1.)

A more recent development than the portables is the **network computer** (Photo 4.2), a microcomputer designed for accessing the Internet. It includes a microprocessor, a screen, a network connection, a pointing device, and provisions for text input and audio output. Local storage, such as a disk, is optional, since this computer will rely on the software downloaded from the Internet and coded in Java, as described in the next chapter (Wayner 1996).

A user interacts with the computer system through a combination of means called the **user interface.** As we further discuss in the next chapter, most systems today have moved away from the character-based user interfaces, that is, from keyboarding instructions to the computer system. Instead, in **graphical user interfaces (GUI),** commands are issued by pointing an arrow (called the cursor) at little pictures (called icons) or at menu selections, followed by clicking a mouse on them. In pen-based notepads and in personal digital assistants, the interface is designed to imitate pen-and-notepad operation: The user writes or marks with a stylus-like pen on the screen located on the top of the lightweight computer.

Minicomputers

Before the development of microcomputers, the smallest category of computers had been the **minicomputers (minis).** They entered the business scene from scientific and engineering applications, and they are still often used as dedicated processors for computer-assisted design (CAD) or on-line transaction processing (OLTP), where real-time demands of fast response have to be met. These midrange machines are also employed as corporate computers in midsized organizations or as departmental computers in larger firms, where they communicate with personal computers on the one hand and with the corporate mainframe on the other (see Figure 2.7 for such a three-tier system). The principal vendors are DEC, IBM, Hewlett-Packard, and Data General. A midrange system is shown in Photo 4.3.

In recent years, a perceptible squeeze has taken place in this midrange market. Microcomputers connected into client/server networks and technical workstations have taken over the lower end, and the applications that require management of very large databases have migrated to mainframes, now redefined as servers.

Mainframes

Although it is difficult at this time to say where the mini category ends and mainframes begin, the largest computers in general use are considered **mainframes.** Located in specially designed data centers (illustrated in Photo 4.4), mainframes require extensive professional support. The cost of building and equipping a data center whose mainframe

Photo 4.3

IBM's AS/400 midrange computers are frequently used as servers in client/server configurations. Owing to the availability of several models in the series, the enterprise can scale up as it grows (Courtesy IBM Corporation.)

Photo 4.4

A mainframe-based data center. In the middle of the photograph you can see an IBM's mainframe in the series Enterprise System/9000 (ES/9000) Operator's console, memory units, and other peripherals surround the mainframe (which is actually a multiprocessor, comprising up to six CPUs).

costs $5 million may run as high as $25 million, not including personnel or other running costs. This is the reason many corporations are consolidating their mainframes in as few data centers as possible, or even outsourcing their data centers to outside vendors (as we discuss in Chapter 13).

Mainframe systems are often leased, at a cost of $100,000 to $250,000 a month. Here, IBM with its ES/9000 series is the undisputed world leader. Unisys, Control Data, Amdahl, and DEC are its major U.S. competitors, while Fujitsu and Hitachi are important Japanese contenders.

Many powerful peripherals may be managed by a mainframe or, actually, by dedicated input/output processors called channels that are included in the mainframe system. Mainframe systems may also include thousands of on-line terminals that access organizational databases of huge capacity. Major organizational applications, such as transaction

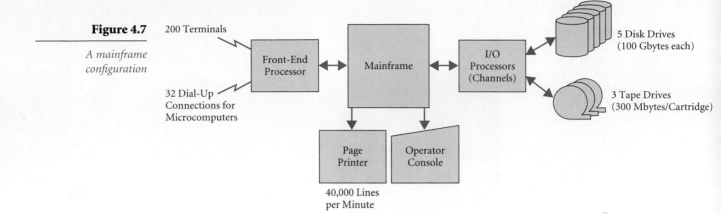

Figure 4.7

A mainframe configuration

processing or management reporting systems, are often run on a mainframe, which integrates information processing in the firm. In such organizations a mainframe plays the role of the central server of information processing services in a large network. An example of a mainframe-based configuration is shown in Figure 4.7. This configuration is the central computer of a midsized distributor company with $200 million in sales.

Mainframes (as well as other categories of computers) are often configured with two or more processors sharing the same memory in a so-called **multiprocessor** configuration. Aside from the obvious advantage of higher processing speed, a multiprocessor offers the additional benefit of higher reliability: Should one of the processors fail, the others keep running.

Supercomputers

The most powerful computers, able to carry out billions of arithmetic operations per second, are called **supercomputers.** Supercomputers exploit several design approaches, all based on **parallel processing** at some level of computer design. In this type of processing, impressive speeds are achieved by performing a large number of operations simultaneously. Thus, many pairs of operands may be processed in parallel in a vector processor that contains a pipelined arithmetic-logic unit, something like an assembly line for arithmetic operations. Some machines contain an array of multiple arithmetic-logic units, all applying the same operation to a different operand pair. Yet other designs comprise a large number of processors carrying out their tasks in parallel.

Supercomputers may be used to model any phenomenon that can be described by a set of equations. These machines have traditionally been used to solve mathematical problems in physics, to forecast weather, and to design rockets. More recently, with the availability of new software and with the increased sophistication of organizational computing, supercomputers have moved from the scientific laboratories into business organizations. Some firms use them in a more traditional fashion—to help design cars or telecommunications networks—while others employ them to determine the degree of risk in an investment or to find a trading opportunity.

Traditional supercomputing is being successfully challenged by **massively parallel computing**—systems that lash together hundreds, or even thousands, of microprocessors. The idea is rather simple from the economic point of view: If a thousand microprocessors

IN THE SPOTLIGHT

**Super-
computing and
Multi-
processing for
Competitive
Advantage**

The investment firm of Goldman, Sachs of New York sells mortgage-backed securities: The firm combines outstanding mortgages into a pool and offers investors shares in it. As the mortgages are paid off, the investors receive the principal and interest payments. However, if interest rates fall, many mortgages are paid off prematurely and the yield on the investment goes down.

Goldman, Sachs has developed a mathematical model that predicts the prepayment rate depending on a number of variables, such as interest rates and the age of the mortgages. Based on this model, the firm decides to include or not include a particular mortgage in an investment pool. When the model was run on minicomputers, it took two days, and the firm had to forego many investment opportunities because decisions could not be made fast enough. Now, a more sophisticated model is run by buying time on a Cray supercomputer at the Minnesota Supercomputing Center in Minneapolis (one of several such machines run by consortia of major universities). Goldman, Sachs obtains the answer within an hour. The timely information is now a useful competitive tool.

The pharmaceutical firm Rhone-Poulenc Rorer, based in Collegeville, Pennsylvania, uses a Digital Equipment Alpha-Server 8400 multiprocessor to support marketing queries against its database. Before installing the powerful machine, the company had to rely on a set of canned (pre-designed) queries, available from the vendor that supplied the firm's marketing data. The lack of flexibility, combined with the inability to get a sameday response (!) from its mainframe, pushed the firm to search for a better solution. With the new system in place, the company's business and marketing analysts can run arbitrarily complex queries against the firm's own marketing database to relate drug sales to specific regions, salespeople, and many other factors. The company is able to respond almost immediately to an emerging trend that can be perceived by analyzing the data. The detailed data helps the pharmaceutical company become proactive.

Based on Charles Babcock, "Parallel Processing Mines Retail Data," *Computerworld,* September 26, 1994, p. 6; and Christopher Rauen, "Parallel Processing Means Business," *Beyond Computing,* April 1996, pp. 30–33.

costing $50 each can be put together to work in parallel, the processor obtained will be much cheaper and much faster than a traditional supercomputer. For this to be feasible, a program must be broken down into many tasks, each of them running simultaneously with others on a different processor. This presents many problems to solve, including dividing the work among the processors (many classes of programs are difficult to make parallel), ensuring efficient communication among the processors, and building up a software base for this new technology.

You can read about the competitive value of supercomputers and multiprocessors in the vignette above.

Now that you are familiar with the four categories of computers, let us discuss the peripherals—secondary storage and input and output devices—that are combined with the central processor and the main memory to make up a computer system.

4.3 | SECONDARY STORAGE

The variety of available memory technologies, combined with the fact that only a small fraction of the programs and data stored in memory are actually used by the processor within an immediate time frame, make it possible to organize computer memories into a

Figure 4.8

The memory hierarchy

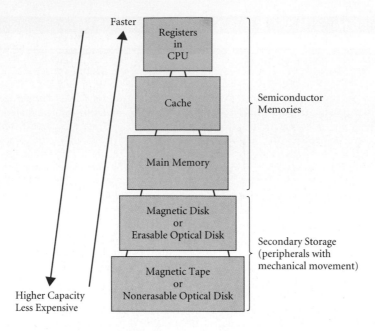

hierarchy. Secondary storage devices provide the high capacity and relatively inexpensive back end of this hierarchy. Programs and data stored on these devices are brought into the main memory as required by the processor. Magnetic technologies (disks and tapes) are now being challenged by optical disks for use as secondary storage devices.

Memory Hierarchy

Throughout the history of computers, the demand for memory has grown steadily. A variety of memory technologies offers a trade-off between high speed on the one hand and low cost and high capacity on the other. Computer memories are therefore organized into a hierarchy, shown in Figure 4.8. At the top of this hierarchy, the fastest memory units are actually registers included in the CPU, where data are brought in to be manipulated by the arithmetic-logic unit. Most machines also include a fast semiconductor **cache memory** in their processors, where blocks of data and instructions may be transferred from the main memory prior to their use by the processor. As we know, semiconductor main memory is used to store the programs currently being processed (or their active parts), as well as the data they currently need or produce. All these memories are electronic and therefore fast. Since they contain no moving parts, they are highly reliable. But electronic memories are volatile: Their contents are lost when power is turned off.

Secondary storage devices form the lower stages of the memory hierarchy. These devices offer nonvolatile, permanent means of storing large volumes of programs and data. To be used by the processor, these programs and data items must first be transferred to the main memory. The principal device for on-line storage today is the magnetic disk. The medium used for archival storage is magnetic tape. Optical disks suffer from the disadvantage of slower speeds, but their higher storage capacities make them a competitor of the magnetic media as a means for secondary storage.

Since the speeds and memory capacities of computer equipment play a vital role in understanding a system's operation and in selecting the needed system components, we have

	Speed Unit	Relationship to a Second	Abbreviation	What It Means
Table 4.3	Second	1	sec	Time to mount a tape in a drive: 120 sec.
Speeds and memory capacities in computer systems	Millisecond	.001	msec	Time to get a record from a disk: 10 msec.
	Microsecond	.000001	μsec	A typical microcomputer executes 20 instructions in 1 μsec.
	Nanosecond	.000000001	nsec	Many main memories take 50 nsec to fetch a data item.

Memory Capacity Unit	Relationship to a Byte	Abbreviation	What It Means
Byte	1	—	Stores the representation of one character (8 bits).
Kilobyte	$20^{10} = 1,024 \approx 1,000$	Kbyte (K)	A fast cache memory in the CPU: 256 Kbytes.
Megabyte	$20^{20} \approx 1,000,000$	Mbyte (M)	Typical main memory in a microcomputer: 16 Mbytes.
Gigabyte	$20^{30} \approx 1,000,000,000$	Gbyte (G)	Magnetic disk units: several Gbytes.
Terabyte	$20^{40} \approx 1,000,000,000,000$	Tbyte (T)	Optical disk "jukeboxes" for document storage: several Tbytes.

compiled Table 4.3 to explain the different units of measurement. You will note the wide range of speeds and capacities of the available memory devices.

As we have already described the fast, fully electronic members of the hierarchy, we will now proceed to discuss the peripherals known as secondary storage.

Magnetic Disks

Generally, secondary storage devices are used to store data records, be they records of customer orders, a firm's employees, or airline flights. We will further discuss the organization of these records into files and databases in Chapter 6. **Magnetic disks** are secondary storage devices that afford the capability of both direct (random) and sequential access to records. **Sequential access** means that all records must be accessed in the sequence in which they are stored until the desired record is reached. **Direct access** to a record means that the record can be accessed by its disk address, without the need to access any intermediate records. A good analogy is the sequential access you have with a cassette tape as opposed to the direct access with a music compact disk. On-line systems require direct access to records. It is this capability of direct access that has made the magnetic disk (known as the DASD, for direct access storage device) a ubiquitous secondary storage device.

Figure 4.9

A hard disk drive
(Adapted from Vincent P.
Heuring and Harry F.
Jordan, *Computer Systems
Design and Architecture*,
Menlo Park, CA:
Addison-Wesley, 1997,
p. 416.)

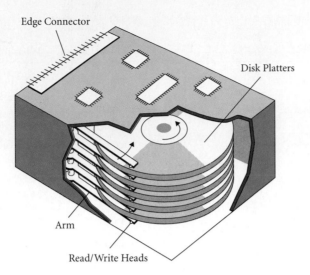

The principal varieties of magnetic disk are hard disks, employed in computers of all categories, and floppy disks, employed in microcomputers. A floppy disk is actually a distribution medium, serving to distribute programs and data. The floppies with a diameter of 3 1/2 inches have all but replaced the ones that are 5 1/4 inches in diameter. Common storage capacities of floppies are 1.44 and 2.88 Mbytes.

The design of a hard disk is shown in Figure 4.9. The disk pack, which is the storage medium, consists of a stack of platters and spins continually. The platters are coated with a thin magnetic film, and data are stored in concentric circles, called tracks, on each of the two surfaces of the platter. Data are accessed by a comblike assembly of read/write heads, one of which flies over or under each surface without touching it. If a head touches the surface, a disk crash is said to occur and the disk needs to be replaced.

Read/write heads move together as a group horizontally, as shown in Figure 4.9. Thus, the same track on each surface can be accessed when the read/write heads move to a given position. Such a set of tracks is called a **cylinder.** For faster access, consecutive records are laid out vertically in cylinders (rather than across a platter's surface); when a cylinder is filled, the following records are placed on the next cylinder.

To access a particular disk address, the disk unit performs the following steps:

1. Electronically selects the head which flies over or under the appropriate surface (this takes place in a negligible amount of time).

2. Moves the access mechanism to the desired track (this seek time may take, for example, 7 msec).

3. Continues rotating until the proper address is under the head and the data can be accessed (this results in the rotational delay of some 3 msec).

In total, hard disk access time is typically close to 10 milliseconds. As soon as a disk address has been accessed, data are transferred from the disk at a very fast rate of up to 10 Mbytes per second. Disk capacity typically ranges from 1 to many Gbytes. For example, a 1-Gbyte drive may consist of 11 platters, which provide 20 surfaces (the top and bottom surfaces are generally not used for storage), 2000 tracks, and 25,000 bytes per track. Many disks, in particular the hard disks used in microcomputers, are *sectored*. Each surface is then

**Translating
Superior
Hardware into
Business
Results**

It is sometimes difficult to see how replacing one "disk farm" with another can have a meaningful effect on a company's business. Let's take a look.

The brokerage firm of Edward D. Jones & Co. of Maryland Heights, Montana, has replaced its traditional disks with a total capacity of 120 Gbytes with a new 180 Gbyte disk array. The disks are configured in the IBM 3090 600J mainframe computer system. The new RAID is the Symmetrix 5500 array from EMC Corporation, a firm that has captured over 40 percent of the storage marketplace. A 17-square-foot refrigerator-size unit occupies one-fifth of the floor space the traditional DASDs used to take up, with room to add more array elements within the cabinet and expand the total secondary storage capacity to 1 terabyte.

Thanks to the new fast secondary storage, the brokerage has expanded its capability for on-line transaction processing. The firm will now "insource," that is, bring in-house, during the current year, all the key transaction processing necessary to support its 2,900 branches, such as processing the money market funds. The processing had previously been outsourced to third-party vendors such as Automatic Data Processing. Savings and better control of operations are the expected business results.

The installation of the disk array has already helped the brokerage house to be more responsive to customers. For example, during a particularly turbulent season on the stock markets, the company broke its record by logging 6.5 million online transactions in a single day. With the disk array, the transaction response time of the computer system has been made faster by nearly half a second. The fastest possible response is crucial in processing brokerage transactions. The customer goodwill accumulated due to the improved transaction processing is another business value obtained with the new hardware.

Based on Thomas Hoffman, "Brokerage Replaces DASD Storage with Disk Arrays," *Computerworld*, May 2, 1994, p. 73; and Josh McHugh, "When It Will Be Smart to Be Dumb," *Forbes*, May 6, 1996, pp. 118–119.

divided into pieshaped sectors (which typically contain 256 bytes). These sectors are the smallest individually addressable elements in such disks.

Larger systems most often use hard disks with interchangeable media: A disk pack may be removed and stored off-line. On the other hand, in microcomputers (and sometimes in larger systems), nonremovable and hermetically sealed disks are employed. In microcomputers, hard disk capacities commonly range from 1 to 4 Gbytes, and the devices are usually internal—they are packaged into the system unit.

As the performance of electronic components of computer systems continues to advance, it is necessary for the storage to keep pace. The amount of data corporations generate is estimated to grow 60 percent a year (Barney 1995). An important development is, therefore, the increasing use of disk arrays, known as **RAID** (for **redundant array of inexpensive disks**), which package a number of smaller disks into a single unit. By distributing the stripes of data over several disks (data striping), it is possible to achieve high speed of data transfer through parallel access. By replicating data on redundant disks (disk mirroring), it is possible to boost reliability, since a failure of a disk merely causes a switchover to another containing the same data. Combinations of the two techniques gave rise to several types of RAIDs. The vignette above shows how these disks can play an important role in pursuit of business objectives.

Figure 4.10

A fragment of magnetic tape

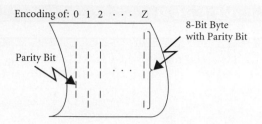

Encoding of: 0 1 2 · · · Z

Parity Bit

8-Bit Byte with Parity Bit

Magnetic Tape

Magnetic tape has an obvious limitation—it permits only sequential access. However, it is the least expensive of the commonly used storage media and is widely used to back up magnetic disks, although it has also been employed for on-line secondary storage in the batch applications of many legacy systems.

Systems other than microcomputers have traditionally used detachable tape reels. The tape is coated with a magnetic film, across which data bytes are stored in nine tracks: 8 bits plus 1 parity bit added for error detection, so that the number of 1s in all nine tracks is odd (see Figure 4.10). A standard 2,400-foot reel stores 50 Mbytes of data, which may be transferred to the main memory at a rate of some 2 Mbytes per second. As the tape moves from the supply reel to the take-up reel in a tape drive, the read/write head of the drive reads or writes the consecutive bytes, as desired.

Tape cartridges, commonly used to back up hard disks in microcomputer systems, are now replacing reels in larger systems. They are much easier to handle and take up less storage space. Cartridge capacity is generally above 200 Mbytes, with a data transfer rate of 3 Mbytes per second. Digital data storage cartridges (or DAT for digital audio tape) intended only for backup purposes, are able to back up 1.3 Gbytes of data; helical scan tape cartridges can hold 5 Gbytes of data. Since this equals 26 reels of tape and 100 reels, respectively, these high-density technologies may enable system managers to place unattended minicomputers at user sites without fear that data backup will be neglected.

To facilitate the management of large numbers of reels or cartridges at mainframe sites, automated tape libraries are available. Robotic arms are used to mount the reels in the drives. However, some installations are moving away from tapes to the more convenient optical storage technologies.

Optical Disks

Optical technologies, which offer far higher storage densities and thus far higher capacities than magnetic devices, are revolutionizing secondary storage. Most exciting is the expansion of computer capabilities in the direction of multimedia: Data, text, audio, and video information can be cost-effectively stored on **optical disks.** Like magnetic disks, these devices offer direct access to information. The information is written with high-intensity laser beams and read with lower-intensity beams. Precise beam focusing by the laser makes high storage density possible. The main disadvantage is slower access as compared to magnetic disks. Nevertheless, several varieties of optical disks are playing greater roles: In fact, CD-ROM devices are now commonly installed in personal computers.

1. CD-ROM   The most common type of optical disk is **CD-ROM (Compact Disk–Read Only Memory).** Such disks are used to distribute prerecorded information: Once written ("mastered"), the contents of the disk cannot be changed. A CD-ROM disk is read by an optical disk unit, which is a computer peripheral with an access time of 100 to 200 msec. It is thus a slower medium than magnetic disk. However, this optical medium is much cheaper per byte, thanks to its huge capacity. A single 4 3/4-inch CD-ROM disk has a capacity of up to 680 Mbytes and may thus hold either of the following:

- The text of 180,000 printed pages (that is, enough text to fill 300 thick books).

- Sharp images of 18,000 pages of business documents (enough to fill two tall filing cabinets).

- The contents of about 480 3 1/2-inch diskettes of 1.44 Mbyte capacity.

- A crisp color picture and 10 seconds of narration for each of the 3,500 segments of an educational or training program (almost eight hours of content).

- Any multimedia information that can be represented digitally, although some of the storage requirements in this area are daunting. Even though a single disk can store about 74 minutes of high-quality sound, it may hold only about 30 seconds of uncompressed video. This is why video is usually compressed by removing redundant pixels and then restoring them before displaying the image. For example, you can compress a picture whose upper half shows a clear sky by simply storing the dimensions of the field of blue color. By applying techniques of image compression, the Indeo technology from Intel makes it possible to store on a single CD-ROM disk 72 minutes of motion video which can be played at 30 frames per second for a full-motion effect.

We will further discuss the use of CD-ROM in multimedia computing in the last section of this chapter.

2. WORM Optical Disks   WORM (write-once, read-many) optical disk drives enable users both to read and append information until a cartridge is full. However, the information written on the disk cannot be altered. By contrast, without specialized and rather expensive equipment, users cannot write onto a blank CD-ROM disk, which limits these disks to the role of a distribution medium. WORM disks, on the other hand, are used as a means of archival storage for the users' own information.

Photo 4.5

A "jukebox" of write-once-read-many-times (WORM) optical disks may be used to store very high volumes of data. You see here the Optical Jukebox from Digital Equipment Corporation (DEC).

Over time, WORM disks have advanced from the province of microcomputers to larger machines. A typical disk has 150 to 250 msec access time and 262 Kbytes per second data transfer time—slower than magnetic disks. A single larger WORM disk may have a capacity of 2 Gbytes, and this medium is now cheaper than most tapes (but more expensive than CD-ROM).

WORM systems play a major role in office information systems, since they are used as a document storage medium. Particularly useful in this regard are WORM "jukeboxes," which may contain 16 to 2,000 optical disk platters (see Photo 4.5). An addressed platter is loaded into the drive by an auto-loader and spun to speed. This makes terabytes (trillions of bytes) of storage available for access in as short a time as 10 seconds.

Uses of WORM disks multiply. The Department of Motor Vehicles of the State of California uses a WORM-based system for storing the pictures, signatures, and fingerprints of the holders of drivers' licenses. The Veterans Administration employs a similar system to handle benefit claims, with large savings over paper-based systems. We will see further uses of such image management systems in Chapter 8.

3. Erasable Optical Disks   Both the CD-ROM and WORM disks suffer from a significant limitation: The information cannot be changed once it has been written on a disk. **Erasable optical** (or, actually, magneto-optical) **disks** are full-fledged competitors of magnetic disks. Their access time is slower (48 msec for fast ones, with a 1 Mbyte-per-second transfer rate) because of their large read/write heads, which contain both a laser and a magnetic coil. However, their capacities are high for a microcomputer configuration (several Gbytes per cartridge). Erasable optical disks show great promise: Not only do the individual cartridges have a high capacity but the device offers, in effect, an unlimited capacity because the cartridge is removable (as opposed to fixed magnetic disks). The removable cartridge may also be securely stored away from the computer.

4.4   INPUT DEVICES

The traditional input device—the keyboard—is not an efficient means for entering large amounts of data. Also, in some countries, much more so than in the United States, managers and professionals resist using it. Pointing devices, such as the mouse, are a partial solution to the second problem. A large and growing number of technologies have been developed to avoid keyboarding data, resulting in the efficiencies of direct data entry from the source.

Keyboards

The keyboard is the principal input device in virtually all microcomputers. It is also a component of the video display terminals employed for remote access to larger machines. A variety of special-purpose keyboards are used for data input in various applications, such as securities trading or fast-food outlets.

When employed as a principal method of data entry, keyboarding by data entry personnel is highly inefficient. At data entry stations, keyboarded data need to be transcribed onto a disk volume (key-to-disk entry). The disk pack is then mounted in the drive when needed. Data entry clerks generally have to enter all the data twice for verification purposes; the process is labor-intensive and error-prone. Many corporations use cheaper offshore labor for this function. However, the general trend is away from keyboarding and toward direct capture of data at the source with devices for **source data automation:** the use of input technologies that capture data in a computer-readable form as the data are created. We will see these devices for direct data entry below.

Pointing Devices

Pointing devices are used to identify a position on a computer screen. A **mouse** is used to control the cursor that appears on a video display. By rolling the mouse on a flat surface, we move the cursor in a corresponding manner. Graphical user interfaces of desktops are typically mouse-driven. Various functions (for example, file opening or deleting) may be performed by clicking a button on the mouse while the cursor points to the corresponding icon. The mouse, joystick, trackball, touchpad, and a special pen-like stylus applied to the screen are all examples of devices commonly employed in various multimedia applications. Computer kiosks typically use touch screens, whose transparent surface sends a signal to the computer system, indicating the position that was touched. A touch screen specially designed for securities trading is pictured in Photo 4.6.

Devices for Direct Data Entry

Many advantages are gained by entering data directly into a database (after an appropriate validation) from the source of its capture, avoiding the keyboard. Among the advantages of such source data automation are labor economies, timely availability of information in databases, and far greater data accuracy. We discuss the use of these devices in a variety of transaction processing systems in Chapter 9 (see Table 9.1). Electronic data interchange (EDI), also discussed there, with its computer-to-computer exchange of data, is another way to avoid keyboarding. Frequently, the burden of data entry is shifted onto the customer, as it is done, for example, with automatic teller machines (ATM). Let us review the more important technologies for direct data entry.

Image scanners are used to digitize and enter into computer memory figures, photographs, and signed documents. Scanners enter into memory a digitized image of a document, which may then be stored on an optical disk. An image scanner may be combined with optical character recognition software to make an **optical character recognition (OCR) scanner.** An OCR scanner can recognize printed or typed text and various codes and enter the corresponding characters into computer memory. For example, both the illustrations and the text of a book can be entered into a microcomputer system with an OCR

Photo 4.6

This Tradeboard Touch Screen from Siemens Rolm is designed for securities trading rooms. It can be used to connect to a telecommunications network (Courtesy Siemens Rolm.)

Photo 4.7

This portable bar code reader can scan, display, and store thousands of bar codes, which may then be transmitted to a computer through a telecommunications port built into the reader (Time Wand from Videx, Inc., of Carvallis, Oregon.)

scanner, ready for modification. Once entered with an OCR scanner, the text may be indexed for future retrieval. A warning is necessary here: Text produced with OCR may contain errors (and usually does). It needs to be reviewed!

Bar-code scanners, or wands that read bar codes, have been put to significant use in a variety of manufacturing systems that firms use to seek competitive advantage, as we discuss in Chapter 12. Among the many bar codes used in various industries, the best known is the universal product code (UPC) read by supermarket point-of-sale scanners. In banking, the characteristic fonts for magnetic character recognition (MICR) that appear on the bottom of checks are also read by optical scanners. Photo 4.7 shows a compact bar-code reader.

Smart cards, which carry voluminous data on chips, or on laser-optic or magnetic strips, can serve as a key to many services (see Figure 4.11). For example, Lufthansa passengers in Germany can check into the airline's flights using a smart card: They can select a seat, change a flight, and get a boarding pass—all using an electronic kiosk with a card reader. Thanks to the identifying information stored in them, smart cards provide higher security than the popular magnetic-strip cards, such as credit cards. For example, the state of Texas is transferring its food stamp system onto such a system for electronic benefits administration. The major credit card corporations, Visa International, MasterCard International, and Europay International, are developing a global standard for smart cards, envisaging broad use of electronic cash stored on such cards over the Internet (Lavin 1996). Smart cards holding a complete medical history of the bearer are expected to become common in healthcare within a few years ("Connect" 1997).

Voice data entry devices that can accept input from any speaker are able to enter reliably and cost-effectively limited kinds of data, such as spoken digits or letters. If we combine such a device with one that produces spoken output, we obtain systems which enable users (telephone users, for example) to access databases without any need for a conventional terminal. A voice response system is shown in Figure 4.12. Several technologies are employed in the system. Speech (or voice) recognition of a limited number of words (digits and "yes" and "no") uttered by any speaker into a microphone is performed by an input device. Input may also be received from a touch-tone phone. The system may respond either through a voice synthesizer that transforms a text represented in a character code (such as ASCII) into a spoken utterance, or with a voice digitizer that retrieves pre-stored speech fragments and other sounds. The entire system offers the user easy access to information (Fried 1996).

Voice data entry is particularly advantageous in manufacturing environments, where workers' hands and eyes are busy. This technology permits them to continue what they are

Figure 4.11

Services that can be made accessible through a smart card (Updated and adapted from James G. Kobielus, *Smart Cards: A New Perspective* (Washington, DC: The International Center for Information Technologies, 1987.)

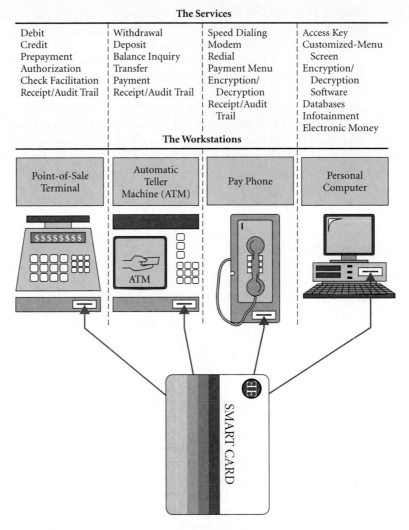

The Services			
Debit	Withdrawal	Speed Dialing	Access Key
Credit	Deposit	Modem	Customized-Menu
Prepayment	Balance Inquiry	Redial	Screen
Authorization	Transfer	Payment Menu	Encryption/
Check Facilitation	Payment	Encryption/	Decryption
Receipt/Audit Trail	Receipt/Audit Trail	Decryption	Software
		Receipt/Audit	Databases
		Trail	Infotainment
			Electronic Money

The Workstations

Point-of-Sale Terminal	Automatic Teller Machine (ATM)	Pay Phone	Personal Computer

Figure 4.12

A voice response system makes voice-oriented database access possible

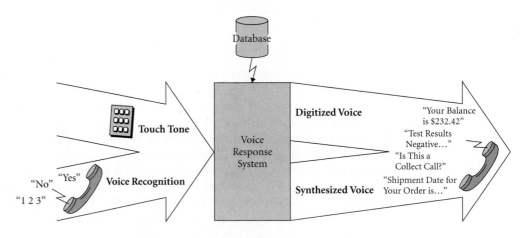

doing while interacting with the information system. As the vignette on the next page illustrates, in applications that permit training by an individual user, there are many other opportunities for speech recognition systems.

Touch-tone telephone entry is increasingly employed to provide access to a bank account or insurance claim information, sometimes in a rather annoying fashion. By removing the human intermediary, such systems push a large part of the inquiry cost onto the consumer.

Entry of handwritten characters (block-printed only) is possible with an electronic "pen" through a special screen located on top of pen-based notebooks and personal digital assistants (PDA). Pen-based notebooks from Sony recognize the Kanji characters of Japanese writing along with the standard character set. Devices that recognize general cursive writing are not foreseeable in the near future.

4.5 | OUTPUT DEVICES

The principal output devices are video displays for soft-copy and printers for hard-copy output. As we already know, devices that produce voice (speech) output are also entering the market.

Video Displays

Computer displays have become one of the most common artifacts of our age. They display computer output on a screen and serve as the monitors in microcomputer systems and, when combined with a keyboard, as the **video display terminals** (VDT) that connect users to a computer system. Much of the soft copy output in transaction processing, decision support, and executive information systems is never printed. Progress in this area has been driven by the development of more sophisticated monitors, particularly for technical workstations. Experts expect the common cathode ray tube (CRT) monitors of today to be gradually replaced by flat panel displays. Today these displays, typically based on liquid crystal technology, can be seen in various portable computers. They take up less space, use the screen surface more fully, consume much less energy, and give out less radiation than CRTs.

Simpler monitors can display only alphanumeric characters: They typically display 25 lines of 80 characters each. More sophisticated are the now generally used graphics monitors, which may display high-resolution images formed from pixels. The smaller the pixels, the greater the screen resolution and the sharper the image. The displays of graphics monitors are bit-mapped, which means that each dot can be individually controlled as to intensity and color. Images often resemble a fine photograph. For example, a standard VGA (video graphics array) standard for displays, has in its graphics mode a resolution of 640 by 480 pixels and the ability to employ 256 colors at one time; higher-resolution displays are in general use. The size of monitors in business use is growing: Monitors with 14 inches measured along their diagonal are giving way to 17-inch and even 21-inch ones. The larger the screen size and the finer the resolution, the more data can be displayed on the screen.

When deployed in the so-called X terminals, VDTs also give users access to a variety of machines, some much larger than micros. An **X terminal,** which has a limited processing capability, is used to access services provided by other computers to which it is connected. Such a terminal includes a keyboard and a mouse, but no disk drive, and gives its user a

IN THE SPOTLIGHT

Voice-Driven Systems Eliminate Drudgery

Speech recognition systems have much to offer. While the speaker-independent recognition systems recognize only a few words, in many applications this requirement can be relaxed. Systems that have to be trained to recognize the voice of a specific individual can recognize up to 60,000 words. These systems include a microphone, a sound card that converts the sound waves into a digital sequence of 0s and 1s, and the software that compares the words with those stored in the system's vocabulary.

You can see in Figure 4.13 how this happens in a limited vocabulary speech interface that is now available as command-and-control devices for many personal productivity systems, such as Lotus SmartSuite or WordPerfect. You can open your files or save them just by saying so.

The more elaborate speech-to-text systems rely on a large pre-stored vocabulary. Physicians have been among the earliest adopters of speech recognition technology. They can create a medical record for a patient by talking into a telephone attached to a PC that is running, for example, VoiceMed and ChartChecker software from Kurzweil Applied Intelligence of Waltham, Massachusetts. To create a record, known as the chart, the physician responds by voice to queries that appear on the screen. The queries are generated from a database describing more than 100 common medical symptoms. Using a similar system, the radiologists at Community General Hospital in Syracuse, New York, are able to handle up to 50 percent more cases. Instead of waiting up to four days for a hand-typed transcription of the report, as in the past, the reports are now available in 75 minutes. Each Kurzweil system can support up to seven radiologists, paying for itself in less than a year.

Another field of knowledge work where speech recognition is being adopted are legal services. In particular, DragonDictate from Dragon Systems of Newton, Massachusetts, is often the system of choice. As Darcy Readman, a partner in the law firm Duncan & Craig in Edmonton, Canada, dictates a letter, his speech-recognition system responds to standard abbreviations by converting "re" to "regarding," and offers about 10 choices of words on the screen for each spoken word. The system presents the right word as its first choice about 94 percent of the time, and Readman confirms the choice or selects an alternate. At Duncan & Craig, the system paid for itself in six months as the secretarial staff was cut in half. With the price of a DragonDictate with a 30,000-word vocabulary now dropping below $1,000 (a 60,000-word vocabulary is also available), the payoff would have been almost immediate.

At Lenox China, the DragonDictate system is used as part of the total quality management program. As workers inspect products coming out of manufacturing, they report results by voice into a computer system. These voice commands invoke software routines that control production. When the slightest flaw is reported, production is halted and the adjustment specified by the information system is made. It is expected that similar systems will be widely used in manufacturing.

Indeed, Kurzweil Voice for Windows is now available as a low-cost solution for corporate environments. "I started using the product right out of the box without training," says Philip Terry of Moody's Investment Service in New York. Neither does the system need to be trained for the user's voice. Although the system still requires discrete rather than continuous speech, the time between words has been reduced.

Yes, all these systems are still far from the ideal of the ability to recognize continuous speech by any speaker. But already on the horizon are laptops with built-in speech recognition.

Continued

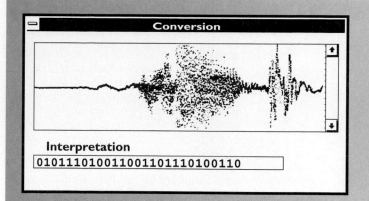

You speak into the microphone connected to your sound card. The chip on the card converts the analog wave of your command into a digital form.

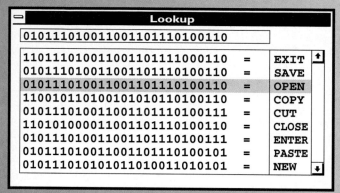

The speech recognition software compares the digital command to those in its vocabulary. It recognizes "OPEN."

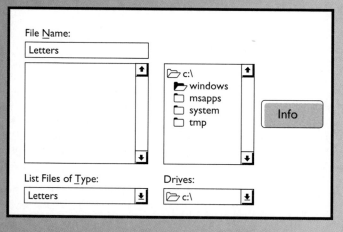

The translated command is passed to your application—just as if you used your keyboard or mouse.

Figure 4.13

A command-and-control use of speech recognition. Adapted from Ron White, "Voice Recognition," *PC Computing,* September 1994, pp. 252–253.

Based on Mary E. Thyfault, "The Power of Voice," *InformationWeek,* May 9, 1994, pp. 39–46, DragonSystems press releases, 1996; and Lisa Nadile, "Voice Recognition Could Strike Cord with Users," *PC Week,* May 6, 1996, pp. 31–34.

Figure 4.14

An X terminal displays in its windows outputs produced by applications running on a variety of computers in the network it is connected to (Modified from John Markoff, "New Rival for Personal Computer," *The New York Times*, January 3, 1990, pp. D1, D6.)

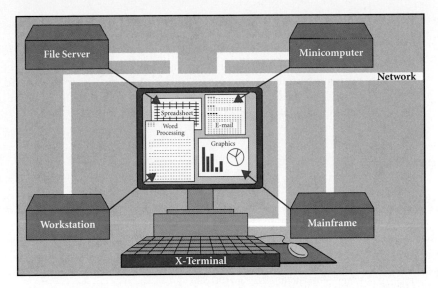

window-type interface (Figure 4.14). An X terminal displays outputs from several programs in different windows, just as a microcomputer monitor does. However, in the terminal's case, the actual programs that "run in the windows" are executed on other processors in the network to which the X terminal is connected. When compared to personal computers, this terminal is often a cost-effective vehicle for the delivery of computing power to a certain class of users, since an X terminal itself costs less than a typical business microcomputer.

Printers and Other Hard-Copy Output Devices

A variety of technologies has been pressed into printing service—a paperless environment is definitely not in the cards. The printer is the most popular device for producing hard copy output. Printers can be classified into two categories: impact and nonimpact. In **impact printers,** the printing element strikes the paper to produce the impression. The most frequently used impact printers in microcomputer systems are dot-matrix printers equipped with a print head with tiny pins that are pushed out to form a character. As the pins strike a ribbon, the character is printed. A dot-matrix printer can produce draft-quality copy of a document or, by striking the paper more than once, most such printers can also produce at lower speeds near-letter-quality documents. Larger computer systems employ either chain or band impact printers that produce letter-quality output rather than forming letters from a series of dots.

Nonimpact printers do not rely on striking the paper for printing an image. Two important types of nonimpact printers are laser printers and ink-jet printers. Laser printers produce high-quality output by using heat to burn the image into the paper, in a process similar to that used in copiers (Knorr 1995). Ink-jet printers spray ink on paper to form images. Ink-jet or laser printers can print graphics or text, with some of these devices printing in color. In particular, ink-jet technology is used in inexpensive color printers. Current trends favor the use of nonimpact printers.

Plotters are output devices used to produce engineering drawings and similar designs. Ink-jet technology is also employed in plotters that produce graphical output and in output devices that produce transparencies for presentations.

4.6 | ENRICHING BUSINESS SYSTEMS WITH MULTIMEDIA

As computing power and storage capacities are matched by the growing telecommunications capacities, multimedia computing increasingly enters business life. **Multimedia computing** integrates various media, such as text, data, graphics, sound, still images, and motion video, and enables the user to interact with such a system. A personal computer equipped for multimedia is shown in Figure 4.15.

Figure 4.15

A personal computer configured for multimedia (Adapted and updated from Ziff-Davis, *Personal Computing*, Supplement to *The New York Times*, Spring 1994, p. 22.)

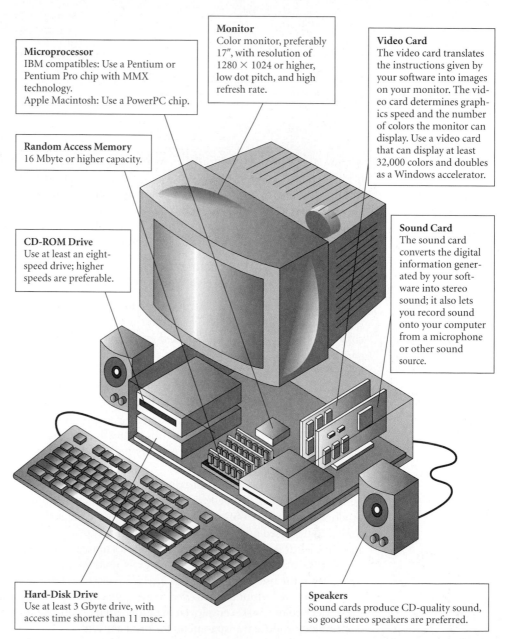

Microprocessor
IBM compatibles: Use a Pentium or Pentium Pro chip with MMX technology.
Apple Macintosh: Use a PowerPC chip.

Random Access Memory
16 Mbyte or higher capacity.

CD-ROM Drive
Use at least an eight-speed drive; higher speeds are preferable.

Monitor
Color monitor, preferably 17″, with resolution of 1280 × 1024 or higher, low dot pitch, and high refresh rate.

Video Card
The video card translates the instructions given by your software into images on your monitor. The video card determines graphics speed and the number of colors the monitor can display. Use a video card that can display at least 32,000 colors and doubles as a Windows accelerator.

Sound Card
The sound card converts the digital information generated by your software into stereo sound; it also lets you record sound onto your computer from a microphone or other sound source.

Hard-Disk Drive
Use at least 3 Gbyte drive, with access time shorter than 11 msec.

Speakers
Sound cards produce CD-quality sound, so good stereo speakers are preferred.

IN THE SPOTLIGHT

Virtual Reality Is for Real

Virtual reality (VR) systems have moved from a fantasy world into the real one. By using interactive multimedia software and specialized hardware, these systems create worlds that exist only in a computer.

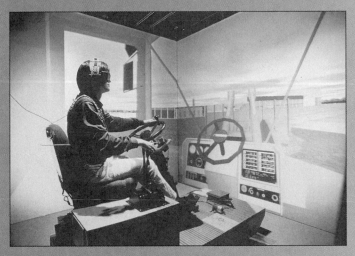

Photo 4.8

A Caterpillar engineer is testing an earth mover at the National Center for Supercomputing Applications in Urbana-Champaign, Illinois, using a virtual reality test track. He can maneuver the machine to lifelike sounds and scoop up virtual gravel (From Gene Bylinsky, "The Digital Factory," *Fortune*, November 14, 1994, pp. 92–110.)

Depending on the application, such systems include a head-mounted display, gloves, or other clothing that sense a user's movements, and the software that simulates the desired three-dimensional environment on a technical workstation or more powerful computer. The user is able to interact with the environment by moving parts of his or her body. Users feel as if they are part of the environment.

The applications of this futuristic technology are often very down to earth. Indeed, at Caterpillar of Peoria, Illinois, virtual reality is used to test as yet nonexisting earth-moving equipment (Photo 4.8). The test driver sitting in a very simple mock-up cab is actually testing the new design that is simulated with a VR system. Matsushita Electric Works of Osaka, Japan, has placed a VR system in department stores that customers use to select kitchen cabinets and appliances. The customer can open a virtual cabinet and store a virtual microwave oven in it. With a system developed at the University of North Carolina, a researcher can virtually be present within a scanning, tunneling microscope to enter the molecular structure of graphite. Some entertainment systems allow you to assume a new body form, say that of a fish.

The financial industry is intensely investigating the potential of VR. Data visualization with these systems can help you overcome information overload. It may help beat the competition in making a market-related decision. A striking display of financial data, produced with such a system, is shown in Photo 4.9.

SGS-Thomson Microelectronics, a semiconductor manufacturer in Phoenix, uses Superscape VR software (from the company of the same name in Palo Alto, California) for training. "We've found that multimedia training is best for giving trainee information," says the company's training specialist. "For learning a process, the virtual reality simulation is more realistic, and it allows the activity to be more in-depth and interactive." Indeed, VR lets the trainee "experience" the action. Running on PCs under Windows, Superscape is estimated to save the firm some $500,000 a year in training costs and results in more thorough training as well.

As the processing power and the speed and capacity of storage devices keep on increasing, ever more striking—and useful—VR systems are becoming possible.

Based in part on Howard Rheingold, *Virtual Reality*, New York: Simon & Schuster, 1991; John A. Adam, "Virtual Reality Is for Real," *IEEE Spectrum*, October 1993, pp. 22–29; (Singh 1996); and Andy Patrizio, "VR Training Gets Real," *InformationWeek*, October 28, 1996, p. 94.

The most advanced applications of multimedia computing are the **virtual reality** (**VR**) systems that immerse users in three-dimensional artificial worlds, creating an illusion of an alternative reality (Singh 1996). The above vignette will tell you more about these systems.

Multimedia computing is increasingly enabling innovative systems in various business domains. Consider the following uses of multimedia:

Photo 4.9

A display produced by a virtual reality system for the visualization of financial data. Geometric surfaces represent the value of financial instruments, such as stocks or bonds. The user (e.g., a securities trader) searches for the best trading strategies using a special glove that detects the position of the hand (reproduced on the upper right). By picking up surfaces and moving, or scaling them, the user performs "what-if" analyses on large volumes of data (Courtesy of Clifford Beshers and Steven Feiner, Columbia University.)

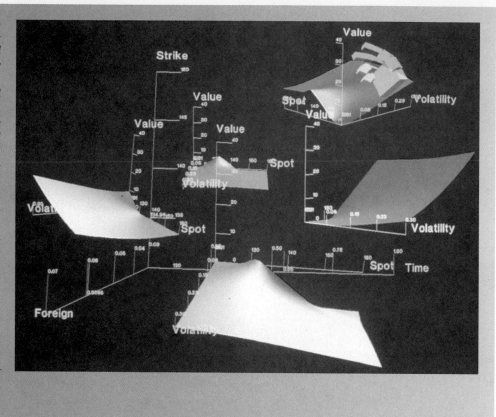

1. Marketing

Using multimedia authoring software (discussed in the next chapter), you can create a sales presentation that combines traditional bulleted text with spoken narrative and sound effects, color images of your product, and video clips that show the product in actual use. Sales representatives of Reebok International of Stoughton, Massachusetts, bring to the desk of their customers customized presentations that include previews of commercials showing sky divers and similar sneaker-clad achievers. Stored on a multimedia server, this presentation can be accessed on demand by the salespeople for training purposes or for a session with customers. Downloaded to a notebook computer with multimedia capabilities, it can be taken on the road and shown at customer sites. If warranted by the volume, the presentation may be distributed to customers on CD-ROM disks as well. Alternatively, the multimedia presentation can be stored in a computer in an electronic kiosk, installed on a trade show floor, with prospective customers interacting with it through a touch screen.

2. Engineering and Manufacturing

Engineering departments for some time now have used three-dimensional graphics during the process of product prototyping to minimize the need for time-consuming and expensive physical mock-ups. Multimedia assist in concurrent engineering, or simultaneous development of a product by engineers from different disciplines. Using the computer-

Photo 4.10

Sample output from the computer-aided design software used in developing Boeing 777. The software can be used simultaneously on thousands of workstations, under the control of four mainframes (From Peter Cassidy, "Multimedia Comes of Age," *CIO*, May l, 1994, p. 60.)

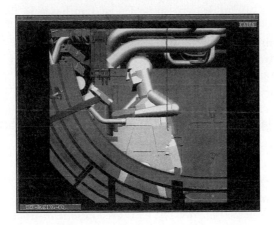

aided design (CAD) software developed by Dassault Systemes of France (see Photo 4.10), Boeing engineers developed their model 777—the first jet designed entirely via computer screens, without physical prototypes. Multimedia virtual reality systems have been developed, which some firms use to simulate the actual experience of product use. United Technologies is developing a virtual drafting table that the company's global corps of engineers can share. Using videoconferencing, the engineers around the world will be able to discuss their designs, mark up blueprints, and annotate photographs. The bottom line is faster time-to-market for the company's new products.

Following the design, engineers can prepare and send to the plant floor an electronic work packet that includes step-by-step assembly instructions, illustrated with images and video clips and accompanied by a sound narrative. When a problem emerges on the plant floor, workers can initiate a multimedia videoconference with the engineers. By sharing his or her screen with the engineer and using "digital chalk" (a stylus) for drawing on the screen, the worker can show the engineer where problems are occurring, leading to immediate problem resolution and a future redesign.

3. Human Resource Management

A multimedia employee database includes the traditional data and text about each employee. But it also contains their color images and a regularly updated multimedia portfolio. Within the portfolio, you may find a video of an interview, during which the individual outlines his or her accomplishments and career goals. A system of this type is part of FedEx's human resource management system, which we discuss in Chapter 12.

4. Training

Multimedia training facilities have been installed at a number of firms to support education and training programs that are necessary to keep up with the rapid change in business conditions. Andersen Consulting, for example, has converted its business practices course to interactive multimedia. The course, taken by all new consultants, used to require 60 hours of self-study and 40 hours of instructor-led sessions at the firm's facility in St. Charles, Illinois. The new multimedia course allows a consultant to "wander" on-screen through a simulated company, learning about its problems and attempting to solve them. The system is delivered on a personal computer with Intel's Indeo technology. Andersen consultants are now able to complete the course in as little as 35 hours, instead of the former 100, with equal or better results. The multimedia course saves $2 million a year in consultant payroll and $8.5 million a year in delivery costs. The system has paid for itself in less than six months.

Interactive multimedia is a fundamental technology that fuels the development of the new media expected to drive the Internet's World Wide Web. By providing the information content with various applications of this technology—sophisticated educational programs, open-ended games, electronic newspapers, movies combining actual film clips with computer-generated graphics, interactive advertisements—new industries are being created and the existing entertainment and publishing industries are being redefined.

SUMMARY

A computer system consists of the processor (the central processing unit, or CPU), the main memory, and the peripherals. The CPU executes the instructions that it fetches from the main memory and, by executing them, controls other units of the computer system. The peripherals include secondary memories, and input and output devices.

The four categories of computers are microcomputers, minicomputers, mainframes, and supercomputers. The most common of these are the microcomputers, built around a microprocessor, a processor on a chip. Most microcomputers are used as personal computers. More powerful are technical workstations, often employed in the industrial design. A range of portable microcomputers, such as laptops and notebooks, is available.

Minicomputers are midrange computers, often used as the main information processor in a midsized organization or as a departmental computer in a larger one. Mainframes, the largest computers in general use, are located in expensive data centers. They are deployed as the main computer in large corporations, often to manage large databases. To expand their computing power, computers of any category can be used in a multiprocessor configuration, with several processors sharing a common memory.

The most powerful computers available at any time are called supercomputers. They rely on the parallel processing concept, performing a number of operations at the same time.

The memory of computers is organized in a hierarchy to balance the need for high capacities with keeping down the cost of the system. In particular, secondary storage expands the capacity available in the main memory at a reasonable cost.

The principal secondary storage devices are magnetic disks and magnetic tape, as well as optical disks. The disk media provide direct access to the information stored on them, while the use of magnetic tape is limited to sequential access to items stored. Among the optical disks, CD-ROM disks are used to distribute pre-recorded information, and WORM disks enable the users to write once and then read the information many times, without being able to change the written information. The most general are the facilities of erasable optical disks, which permit both reading and writing. Although they offer higher capacity than magnetic disks, erasable optical disks are slower.

The principal input devices are the keyboard and the pointing devices, such as the mouse. Many types of input devices serve to enter the data directly into the database from the point of capture. They include, for example, image scanners, bar-code scanners, smart cards, and voice data entry devices. The principal output devices are video display for soft copy output and printers for hard-copy output.

Multimedia computing that integrates various media, such as text, data, graphics, sound, and video, is an enabler for many new and important applications in organizational computing. In particular, the capability to visualize information is important in sales, engineering and manufacturing, and training. More advanced multimedia systems provide virtual reality by immersing their users in artificial, computer-generated worlds.

KEY TERMS

Computer system   *122*

Processor (central processing unit or CPU)   *123*

Main memory   *124*

Bit   *124*

Byte   *124*

Word   *124*

Multimedia computing   *124*

Pixel   *124*

Random access memory (RAM)   *124*

Peripheral   *126*

Very large-scale integration (VLSI)   *126*

Microcomputer   *128*

Technical workstation   *128*

Reduced instruction set computer (RISC)   *128*

Read only memory (ROM)   *128*

Notebook computer   *130*

Palmtop (handheld) computer   *130*

Pen-based notepad   *130*

Personal digital assistant (PDA)   *131*

Network computer   *132*

User interface   *132*

Graphical user interface (GUI)   *132*

Minicomputer (mini)   *132*

Mainframe   *132*

Multiprocessor   *134*

Supercomputer   *134*

Parallel processing   *134*

Massively parallel computing   *134*

Cache memory   *136*

Magnetic disk   *137*

Sequential access   *137*

Direct access   *137*

Cylinder   *138*

RAID (redundant array of inexpensive disks)   *139*

Magnetic tape   *140*

Optical disk   *140*

CD-ROM (Compact Disk–Read Only Memory)   *140*

WORM (write-once, read-many) optical disk   *141*

Erasable optical disk   *142*

Source data automation   *142*

Pointing device   *143*

Mouse   *143*

Image scanner   *143*

Optical character recognition (OCR) scanner   *143*

Bar-code scanner   *144*

Smart card   *144*

Voice data entry   *144*

Video display terminal (VDT)   *146*

X terminal   *146*

Impact printer   *149*

Nonimpact printer   *149*

Plotter   *149*

Virtual reality (VR)   *151*

QUESTIONS

1. What is a computer system? What are its principal components?
2. What does the processor (CPU) do in a computer system?
3. What is the role of the main memory, and how does it relate to the processor?
4. What does a byte correspond to? How does it relate to a bit?
5. What devices are referred to as peripherals? What is the principal difference between the input and output devices on the one hand and secondary storage on the other?
6. What are the four categories of computers? What are the principal distinctions among them?
7. Using Table 4.1, compute the approximate price/performance ratios for microcomputers, minicomputers, and mainframes (that is, $/MIPS). Compare the results and state your conclusions.
8. What are RISCs and what are their advantages?
9. Describe the function of each of the computer system components in the dental office systems shown in Figure 4.5.
10. What types of microcomputers were introduced to you in this chapter? Give an example of an application for each of them.
11. Name the principal areas of business application for the following:
   a. Minicomputers
   b. Mainframes
   c. Supercomputers
12. Why do computer systems rely on a hierarchy of memories? What are the principal differences between the main memory and the secondary storage?
13. Describe how a magnetic disk accesses its contents. What is the reason why we access hundreds of bytes (such as a sector) on a disk, as opposed to a single byte or a word in the main memory?
14. Compare the uses of magnetic disks and magnetic tapes.
15. What are the advantages and drawbacks of optical storage technologies as compared to the magnetic ones? What are the three categories of optical disks and what are their uses?
16. List the input devices you know and state their application.
17. List the output devices you know, together with their areas of application. In your opinion, why is there a greater variety of input than output devices?
18. Define multimedia computing and give three examples of its use.
19. What is virtual reality? What are the advantages of virtual reality representations as compared to the more traditional multimedia?

ISSUES FOR DISCUSSION

1. Based on your reading of periodical literature, discuss the proposition that microcomputers will ultimately replace the larger computers, such as minis and mainframes.
2. Many larger firms establish an "emerging technologies" group, responsible for tracking new technologies that might contribute to the firm's business objectives. What are the advantages and drawbacks of establishing such a unit? How can the drawbacks be avoided?
3. Do you believe a firm can gain long-term competitive advantage by purchasing superior information technology?
4. A well-known manufacturer developed a new microprocessor chip, sold a significant quantity of the chips, and subsequently discovered a flaw in the design. Since the manufacturer decided that the flaw would not surface in the applications running on the PCs using the microprocessor, the decision was made not to inform the public. What are the ethical concerns here?

REAL-WORLD MINICASE AND PROBLEM-SOLVING EXERCISES

1. The Golden Wok of Silicon Valley   Roger Kao, the owner of Golden Wok, a chain of four Chinese restaurants in Mountain View, California, with annual sales of $3 million, is a believer in using information technology. Kao did not set out to be an IT pioneer among the Chinese eateries—he simply wanted to stay in business. Then a prolonged street beautification project made his restaurant hard to reach. The alternatives were to expand to other locations and deliver the food to customers, or close shop. His inspiration became the delivery system of Domino's Pizza. Kao acquired 20 PCs, which he networked via a leased phone line. The PCs run a real-time order- and inventory-management package, called the Hospitality Management System (HMS) 3000 from ISSL of Deerfield Beach, Florida. The cost of hardware and software was about $70,000, and the system took about a year to implement.

Now, Kao's customers are identified in the database by their phone number, with the delivery address and directions a part of each customer's record. Standing orders are stored as well, so that new orders can be compared with them ("No egg rolls tonight?"). The customer may call any of the four Golden Wok locations and the information system will automatically route the incoming order to the location closest to the customer's address. The system then sends the order to the right person in the restaurant: the fry cook, the prep cook, or the dispatcher, if the order calls for an already prepared dish. All these people have PCs at their workstations. Kao can monitor all four Golden Wok outlets from any PC.

He can also generate hourly sales reports as well as bar graphs that help him identify dishes that need to be prepared in advance to meet customer demand. Since the restaurants are a few miles apart, he can move cooks and delivery drivers as the volume dictates. Thanks to the system, "I can tell you exactly how much money is in each register," says Kao. Any time an order is prepared, the inventory is updated, so there is no danger of running out of beef or walnuts. The system also contains a "modifier" database and can calculate the price of a special order based on its ingredients.

The trouble is, "there's not much for me to do here anymore," says Kao. So he is planning to open five more outlets in the next five years.

a. What specific business benefits does the restaurant management system deliver at the Golden Wok?

b. Show with a diagram, similar to Figure 4.5, the functions of the information system components (as presented in the Minicase) at the Golden Wok.

Based on Hal Plotkin, "Dining á la Carte," *Inc. Technology,* December 1995, pp. 85–86.

2. Opening the Workplace to People with Disabilities Personal computer systems and, in particular, certain types of input and output devices, have opened the workplace to many people with disabilities. Research several categories of such systems and discuss how they enable their users to function at work.

3. Direct Data Entry for a Midsized Publisher   As an IS manager for a midsized publishing company, you were asked to introduce direct data entry into as many aspects of its operations as possible. Write a memo to your superior, the vice president for operations, outlining the operations you intend to automate and the devices you wish to use.

TEAM PROJECT

Each two- or three-person team will recommend a microcomputer system for a small business, such as a florist shop, a restaurant, an architect's office, or a beauty salon. The team will specify the functions the system will perform, select all the equipment, and determine the price of the system. Do not forget to visit a local computer store as you research the system. The team will produce a report containing a narrative, a diagram similar to that in Figure 4.5, and the cost breakdown of the system.

ENDNOTES

1. Note that the capacity of memory chips is expressed in bits, while the capacity of memories is expressed in bytes. This is due to the way the chips are designed.

2. The abbreviation PCMCIA stands for Personal Computer Memory Card International Association, which developed the standard to which these easily interchangeable devices conform.

SELECTED REFERENCES

Barney, Lee. "RAID to the Rescue." *Wall Street and Technology,* December 1995, pp. 28–31.

Cassidy, Peter. "Multimedia Comes of Age." *CIO*, May 1, 1994, 58–64.

Chen, Peter M., and others. "RAID: High-Performance, Reliable Secondary Storage." *ACM Computing Surveys,* 26, no. 2 (June 1994), pp. 145–185.

A thorough tutorial survey of the contemporary disk technology.

"Connect the Docs," *The Wall Street Journal,* February 6, 1997, p. A1.

Fried, Louis. "Automatic Speech Recognition." *Information Systems Management,* Winter 1996, pp. 29–37.

Grimes, Brad. "Top 100: The Ultimate Hardware Guide." *PC World,* September 1996, pp. 195–243.

An annual review of the recommended hardware components.

Hennessy, John L., and David A. Patterson. *Computer Organization and Design: The Hardware/Software Interface.* San Francisco: Morgan Kaufmann, 1994.

An excellent text on computer organization.

Heuring, Vincent P., and Harry F. Jordan. *Computer Systems Design and Architecture,* Menlo Park, Calif.: Addison Wesley, 1997.

A reasonably accessible text on the way computers are designed.

Lavin, Douglas. "French Smart Card Proves a Bright Idea." *The Wall Street Journal,* April 22, 1996, p. A18.

McCracken, Harry. "Personal Printers." *PC World,* December 1996, pp. 161–175.

A good periodical review of printers for PCs.

Moore, John. "Speed Limit : 133." *Mobile Computing Communications,* January 1997, pp. 91–112.

A good periodical survey of notebook computers.

The Multimedia Company. *Multimedia,* 2, no. 1 (1994), pp. 32a–33a.

Mysore, Chandrika, and Brent Melson. "6 Servers Tangle on the Web." *Byte,* March 1996, pp. 124–133.

Peleg, Alex; Sam Wilkie; and Uri Weiser. "Intel MMX for Multimedia PC." *Communications of the ACM*, 40, no. 1, January 1997, pp. 25–38.

How the Pentium technology has been modified for multimedia processing.

Pollack, Andrew. "Japan Chip Maker Unveils Next-Generation Prototype." *The New York Times*, February 7, 1997, p. D5.

Singh, Gurminder; Steven K. Feiner; and Daniel Thalmann, eds. "Special Section: Virtual Reality Software and Technology." *Communications of the ACM*, 39, no. 5 (May 1996), pp. 35–76.

Several articles presenting the state of the art in virtual reality.

"Technology 1997." *IEEE Spectrum*, 34, no. 1 (January 1997).

A survey of the state of the art in computers and telecommunications. Such a survey is published by this journal every year in January.

Tredennik, Nick. "Microprocessor-Based Computers." *Computer*, October 1996, pp. 27–37.

An accessible description of the past and expected future developments in microcomputing.

Tucker, Michael J. "The Workstation Warriors." *Computer Graphics World*, January 1995, pp. 25–43.

A review of technical workstations and their uses in 3D graphics.

Ullah, Nasr, and Philip K. Brownfield, eds. "The Making of the PowerPC." *Communications of the ACM*, June 1994, pp. 22–69.

A series of articles describing a modern microprocessor.

Wayner, Peter. "Inside the NC." *Byte*, November 1996, pp. 105–110.

Provides the most general specification for network computers.

Weiser, Mark. "The Computer for the 21st Century." *Scientific American*, September 1991, pp. 94–104.

An interesting vision of future computers becoming vital to our work and our lives by disappearing into the everyday artifacts.

General note on references: Consult the recent issues of PC-oriented periodicals.

CASE STUDY | # Information Devices on the Move

Computers and their peripherals are getting smaller, diversify into many shapes and forms, and can be seen in unusual places. We start realizing that the principal thing about these devices is not what's in them, but what they connect us to—a little like the telephone, but much smarter. Like the telephone, these devices are no longer stationary—they are on the move. The possibilities for business applications using these devices can capture your imagination. Here are a few examples.

Personal digital assistants (PDA) are special types of handheld, pen-based electronic notepads, calendars, and, perhaps first of all, wireless communications devices. A PDA enables you to receive (and in the future, send) E-mail and fax messages. Lightweight (a pound or less) and costing from $300 to $1,000, they are supposed to capture much of the notebook computer market.

Seemingly an ideal field device, where the keyboard has been replaced by a screen on which you write with a stylus or electronic "pen," a PDA offers mobility while keeping you in touch with your office and the world at all times. The best known PDAs are Apple's Newton and Pilot from US Robotics. But be forewarned. Here is what Julie Stephen, who oversees the efforts of DHL Airways to integrate PDAs into the company's operations, has to say about the devices: "We wanted to roll them out this year, but nothing met our specifications." Indeed, PDAs have a great future but, as yet, a modest present. Let us see what they offer and where they can be used—a PDA is definitely a device whose time is coming.

Photo 4.11

A custom-designed PDA is used by traders at Chicago commodities exchange (From Greg Burns, "A Handheld Computer That's Combat-Hardened," *Business Week,* April 18, 1994, p. 94.)

Pen-based input promises ease of use to people who shun keyboards (say, executives) or who cannot conveniently work with a keyboard, say meter readers who need to fill out forms. A restaurant waiter can transmit an order directly from your table to the kitchen and then use the PDA to get your signature for a credit card charge. Truck drivers can have their area maps prestored in their PDA's memory and use it to plan routes. PDAs can replace a hospital patient's bedside chart or a warehouse worker's inventory book. Equipped with a PDA, the "road warriors", or salespeople on the move, can gain wireless connection to their headquarters, home, or the Internet and other information services such as Dow Jones News Retrieval.

We like to say that these notepads recognize handwriting. A dictionary of words, stored in the PDA's memory, helps in the recognition task. We have to be very careful here. What the devices usually recognize is text written in unconnected block printing, with each character printed separately in uppercase with the electronic stylus on the screen. Even with block printing, the recognition is only 90–95 percent correct. In many uses, this makes this form of input intolerable. However, with some PDAs you can store notes in your usual cursive writing as images (known as "power ink").

Because of the problems with entering text with the use of the stylus, alternative modes of entry have been designed. Instead of commands, so-called gestures are used. For example, you can delete a word by crossing it out on the screen. Tapping the "pen" on the name of a stored document will bring it onto the screen. Text can also be entered by tapping with the stylus on the appropriate letters from an on-screen virtual keyboard.

There are great expectations for combining PDAs with the power of intelligent agents that would be sent into the network to complete a task for the user. At one time, Motorola and Sony released a PDA run by the MagicCap operating system from General Magic (of Mountain View, California), which offered the Telescript, a telecommunications language for specifying the agents to be sent into cyberspace. A Telescript agent sent from a PDA could negotiate the best meeting time with people across the world or get you the best travel itinerary and ticket prices in the electronic marketplace. The PDA effort failed. It has not met with the expected customer response. Now, Telescript is being retargeted for use on the Internet's World Wide Web.

The salespeople of F. D. Titus & Sons, a medical supplier in City of Industry in California, travel today with a cellular phone, electronic organizer, a 600-page binder of prices and customer information, and a remote order entry device. "Every bit of these functions will fit into a PDA," says a company salesperson. This is why the company is evaluating PDAs for distribution to its 140 sales representatives.

There are many variations on the PDA theme. Chicago's futures exchange, where commodities (pork bellies, say) are traded, uses a specially designed PDA, Audit by Synerdyne (of Santa Monica, California), shown in Photo 4.11. Rugged enough for the rough-and-tumble of the exchange's pit, the device replaced the paper cards the traders used that lent themselves to fraud. The PDA provides instant matching of a seller with a buyer as well as a crucial audit trail to make sure that the customers's trades are properly executed. Easy to hold, it includes a radio transmitter that instantly broadcasts the data on each trade to the exchange's computers. Audit has to recognize only digits and a very limited vocabulary. To break in their machines, traders train them to recognize their handwriting by writing each digit and letter several times.

Wearable computers free their users' movements. The Long Island Lighting Company (Lilco), an electric utility, and AIL Systems of Deer Park (both of New York State) have developed a wearable computer to free the utility's technicians from having to carry paper manuals. The seven-pound device, including an Intel microprocessor, is strapped to a belt. The display unit is positioned close to the eye. A microphone can receive verbal commands directed at the unit or at a remote server and transmit them by wireless telecommunications. A few years ago, I attended the first computer fashion show, staged by GRiD Systems Corporation to introduce their wearable computers, strapped to a wrist or a shin.

Wearable computers developed at Carnegie Mellon University include a position-sensing facility that continually determines the user's location within a geographic area. Knowing this, the computer can provide the user with information relating to his or her current position. Applications in utilities maintenance are envisaged.

Media Lab at MIT, the leader in human-computer interaction, runs a smart-clothes project. If microprocessors, cameras, microphones, and sensors, run by the appropriate software are built into your clothing, the system can "know" your environment and help you as an intelligent assistant. For example, it can supply the names of the people you meet or give you directions to your next appointment. Whenever someone mentions the Omega merger to you, the systems will "hear" and its software can project the details of Omega finances onto the display in your glasses. Two of the Media Lab's graduate students already wear their computer systems all day every day.

Active badges have been introduced by Xerox to be worn as ID cards by employees who wish to stay in touch at all times while moving around the corporate premises. The clip-on badge contains a microprocessor that transmits its (and its wearer's) location to the building's sensors, which send it to a computer. When someone wants to contact the badge wearer, the phone closest to the person is identified automatically. When badge-wearers enter their offices, their badge identifies them and their PCs turn on automatically. Active badges are a part of "ubiquitous computing," systems of tiny embedded computers being developed at Xerox Palo Alto Research Center to spread the computing power around the office environment.

Yet another device related to mobility is the memory button. Made by Dallas Semiconductor, this nickel-sized device stores a small database relating to whatever it is attached to. You may think of it as a bar code, but with far greater informational content and, moreover, a content that is subject to change. Using handheld peripherals, data can be uploaded from the button to the computer, or downloaded from it to the button.

The U.S. Postal Service is placing memory buttons on thousands of mailboxes to improve collection schedules. A button-based system to track the productivity of farm workers has been developed by Agricultural Data Systems of Laguna Niguel in California. At Ryder Systems in Miami, the buttons are affixed to trucks leased to customers in order to improve vehicle maintenance. The buttons collect data on vehicle performance, maintenance, and safety. Ryder shares the data with the customers who lease the trucks, assisting the customers in cost management.

These are only some information devices that are entering the business world. Many similar devices will come into everyday use as information appliances.

And here is a demo that Todd Chaffee, senior vice president of new technologies at Visa International, watched carefully at MIT in Cambridge, Massachusetts. Two men approach each other, shake hands, and trade business cards. What's fascinating is how it happens. As their hands touch, the electrical circuitry of the men's own bodies is used to transmit the digitized cards to the wristwatch displays of the wearable computers. (Oh yes, they also wear portable hard drives in their sneakers.) The equipment needs no batteries—it is powered by the energy generated as the wearers move. Visa International is interested and perhaps, sometime in the future, its customers will use similar devices for their business transactions.

Based on Evan I. Schwartz, "Software Valets That Will Do Your Bidding in Cyberspace," *The New York Times,* January 9, 1994, p. B11; Michael Fitzgerald, "Agent Technology Stirs Hope of Magical Future," *Computerworld,* January 31, 1994, pp. 37, 43; Greg Burns, "A Handheld Computer That's Combat-Hardened," *Business Week,* April 18, 1994, pp. 94–96; Bruce Caldwell, "The Latest in Fashion," *InformationWeek,* April 25, 1994, p. 20; Scott Leibs, "Data? Look for the Button," *InformationWeek,* August 1, 1994, p. 68; Kim S. Nash, "See Me, Feel Me, Touch Me, Heal Me," *Computerworld,* February 5, 1996, pp. 83–84; Alex P. Pentland, "Smart Clothes," *Scientific American,* April 1996, p. 73; Steve Mann, "Wearable Computing: A First Step toward Personal Imaging," *Computer,* February 1997, pp. 25–32; and http://wearcam.org.

CASE STUDY QUESTIONS

1. What are the advantages and disadvantages of the pen-based input employed in PDAs?

2. What is the role of the components discussed in Section 4.1 in the systems employing each of the devices discussed in the Case Study?

3. Think of two new applications for each of the information devices discussed in the case.

4. By consulting the current trade literature, find technical and application information about an information device that untethers people or objects, enabling them to move around. Be careful to distinguish what is actually available in the marketplace from what is projected (and may turn into *vaporware*).

CHAPTER FIVE

Information Systems Software

OBJECTIVES

After you complete this chapter, you will be able to:

1. Understand the role of system software and applications software in information systems.
2. Describe the functions of an operating system and the modes of computer operations these systems enable.
3. Classify personal productivity software and describe what it does.
4. Understand the capabilities of programming-language generations.
5. Explain the distinction between the procedural high-level languages and the nonprocedural fourth-generation languages (4GL).
6. Discuss the capabilities of the three classes of 4GLs.
7. Understand the concept of object-oriented programming.

OUTLINE

Focus Minicase. Working Smart with Software

5.1 Software Overview

5.2 Operating Systems

5.3 Personal Productivity Software

5.4 Programming Languages and Their Translators

5.5 Fourth-Generation Languages

5.6 Object-Oriented Programming

Case Study. A Multimedia System for Jewelry Appraisal

Working Smart with Software

Nordstrom Valves of Sulphur Springs, Texas, is considered the Cadillac of its industry, both in terms of the features of the valves it manufactures for the oil and gas industries, and in terms of their price. However, a valve's features that would justify its price cannot be demonstrated in a test drive. Therefore, Nordstrom Valve implemented an interactive application to demonstrate the value of its products. The software program that shows the products' features and benefits to customers is loaded on the salespeople's PCs.

The salespeople use the software to compare the life-cycle cost of the valves with those made by the firm's competitors. Although Nordstrom valves cost 15 to 25 percent more than those made by other firms, their high quality helps save money in the long run. The software shows the customer how the costs of maintenance and the costs associated with not being able to produce oil or gas when the pipeline goes down because of a faulty valve accumulate over time. The demonstration makes the benefits of quality tangible.

A recent addition to the successful software application helps to configure the valves for the customer's needs. Previously, a customer would specify such requirements as the pressure and the flow the valve would have to withstand, and the salesperson would use manuals and a calculator to recommend a product. The new application draws on a database of product specifications and helps the salesperson to select one of the over 500 valves the firm manufactures. The product database is updated online, providing the current data. The results are presented in a graphical, easy-to-understand format.

The salespeople are now more productive. The decisions the customers make are based on more detailed data and higher-quality information. The sales-support program has been translated into Spanish for use throughout Nordstrom Valve's sizable Latin American market. The application software is often left behind so that customers can configure products themselves—and continue to rely on Nordstrom Valve's products.

Based on Megan Santosus, "New Value Systems," *CIO*, October 1, 1994, p. 80.

Software may be called the gasoline of the information age. It gives flexibility to products and business processes; under its guidance products move across the landmasses and oceans; and it can help service the products as they are used. Information systems software is now necessary to run a business or virtually any other organization. You have read in the Focus Minicase how a salesperson supported with appropriate software can demonstrate the value of an expensive product to the customer, increasing the likelihood of receiving an order. This chapter will help you understand the capabilities of software.

5.1 SOFTWARE OVERVIEW

The hardware of a computer system cannot directly process payroll, produce a sales report for the last quarter, or maintain the customer database. To make hardware useful, we need **software**: the programs that control the operation of a computer system. The trends in information systems have shifted cost concerns from hardware to software. Indeed, most of the hardware employed in personal computing, while not always inexpensive, has reached a commodity status, with the producers of hardware with similar features competing largely on price and service. Since software actually customizes the hardware for specific needs, the development and maintenance of software are highly labor-intensive, as reflected in the ultimate costs of a customized package or of an application developed in-house by a user firm. Only mass-distributed packages, such as word processing or spreadsheets, are low-priced.

Systems Software

Systems software manages the resources of a computer system and enables people to program in more expressive languages than the machine language of the computer. At the heart of systems software is the operating system—it runs everything. Other systems software includes database management systems (see Chapter 6) and the networking software that manages a system's communications with other computers (see Chapter 7). Systems software also includes translators, such as compilers, that translate programs written in programming languages into the machine language whose instructions can be executed by the computer.

Another category of systems software is utilities, which perform generalized resource-management tasks in computer systems. Examples include sort/merge programs that process data files, programs that transfer data from one peripheral device to another (for example, from disk to tape for backup), and text editors that allow the user to create and modify text files that contain programs and data. Utility software also includes a variety of programs that assist the user in developing other software. The general trend is to blend operating systems with these software development environments.

Applications Software

Applications software assists a system's end users in performing various functions, be they word processing, making decisions regarding quarterly budgets, or answering customer queries by accessing a product database. Some of this software is of a more general nature and can be purchased as a package (word processing packages are an example), while other software is developed internally or externally to meet the specific needs of an organization. Decision support systems are an example of applications software that is often developed to meet specific needs. Applications programming can be done in a variety of languages, which we shall discuss below.

The trend in recent years has been away from the expensive development of custom-made applications software and toward the use of packages. Two types of packages are available: vertical and horizontal. **Vertical packages** assist users within a specific industry segment. There are on the market vertical packages that help to manage construction projects, keep track of the inventory of hospitals, or run fast-food outlets. **Horizontal packages** can perform a certain general function, such as accounting, or office automation, for a range of businesses. All of these packages may be customized to meet some of the specific needs of a firm. We will further discuss software development and other avenues of software acquisition in Part Four of this book.

Relationship between Hardware and Software Components

The relationship between computer systems hardware, systems software, and application software is illustrated in Figure 5.1. This "onion-skin" model indicates that the outer layers rely on the facilities furnished by the inner ones. The figure also summarizes systems and applications software used in computer systems. We shall now proceed to discuss the software layers from inside out.

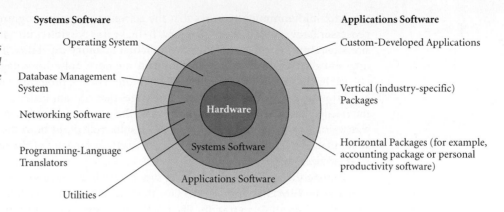

Figure 5.1

*The principal categories
of systems and
applications software*

5.2 | OPERATING SYSTEMS

Every computer system runs under the control of an operating system. Operating systems for computers that are shared by many users are considerably more complex than operating systems for personal computers. Shared systems have to ensure that the programs of all users progress to completion within a reasonable time and in secure separation from one another. Operating systems can manage a computer system in various modes: batch, time-sharing, or real-time. They can also manage multiple processors in a system and ensure communication with other systems across a network. The drive toward creating open systems, systems that can employ the hardware or software of any vendor, includes a search for a common operating system.

What Does an Operating System Do?

The **operating system** is the software that controls all the resources of a computer system. It assigns the needed hardware to programs: It schedules programs for execution on the processor, and it allocates the memory they need, as well as assigns the necessary input and output devices. Operating systems also manage the data and program files stored in secondary storage, maintaining file directories and providing access to the data in the files. In addition, operating systems interact with users. Operating systems are among the most complex software in common use.

We can view an operating system as a traffic cop in the computer system: The operating system sequences programs for the processor, giving the programs the resources they need to progress to completion. Another way to view an operating system is to see it as the provider of a user interface. For example, when a PC user works with Windows the user's perception of the entire computer system is furnished by that operating system.

We know that a mainframe frequently supports hundreds of users working at remote terminals; indeed, even larger micros can support several users working at the same time. How can a single processor accomplish this? This capability to run a number of programs at the same time on a single processor, called **multiprogramming,** is furnished by the operating system. Because processors are much faster than input- and output devices, many programs can run seemingly simultaneously. However, only one of them is actually using the CPU while the others are doing input- or output-related tasks, or simply waiting for a needed resource for an imperceptible millisecond. After all, a 100 MIPS processor can execute 100,000 instructions in a single millisecond!

Multiprogramming requires that the active parts of the programs competing for the processor be available in main memory. To make this possible with a limited main memory size, operating systems generally have a **virtual memory** capability. They divide programs into so-called pages and keep in the main memory only those pages that appear to be needed by the processor in the immediate future. The full programs are kept on disk. As the execution of the program progresses, the pages that contain instructions to be executed or the needed data are rolled in from the disk; the pages no longer needed for execution are overwritten or, if they contain computed results, rolled out onto the disk. This operating system facility vastly expands the apparent (virtual) capacity of the main memory over its physical size.

Among the well-known operating systems for larger machines are MVS and VM running on the IBM mainframes and OpenVMS running on the Alpha-based computers of Digital Equipment Corporation. The UNIX operating system runs on machines of all categories. We shall discuss operating systems for personal computers in more detail below.

Modes of Computer System Operation

Operating systems can make the system they manage operate in various modes. In **batch processing,** the job (or program), once submitted to the system, is run without a user's interaction. The principal objective in batch processing is to maximize throughput: the number of jobs processed per unit of time. A payroll or a weekly set of reports may be run off in this mode. By contrast, **time-sharing systems** are designed to provide fast service by allowing multiple users of a large server computer to simultaneously interact with it via their workstations, such as a terminal or a personal computer. Each workstation is allocated a time slice for the use of the server (say, 10 milliseconds), which is generally more than necessary to handle an interaction. If not, the workstation will get another time slice after others have been served. If the processing capacity of the system is adequate, most users get the impression that a dedicated computer is working exclusively for them. The best measure of effectiveness for such an interactive system is the response time experienced by its users. Many commercial information services are provided on time-sharing systems.

Real-time operating systems are able to handle tasks that require **real-time processing** as they occur, such as process control in a manufacturing plant, data collection from several pieces of equipment in a laboratory, or control of a space shuttle. In these systems, a hard constraint is imposed upon the response time of the system. If the processing of the incoming data is not completed during the allotted interval, with the system taking action as necessary, data are lost and, in some cases, considerable harm may ensue. An acceptable response time is guaranteed by ensuring high processing capacity of the hardware.

With the move toward multiprocessors, in which several (or even many) processors are configured in a single computer system, **multiprocessing operating systems** have been designed to allocate the work to the multiple processors. These systems also support multiprogramming, which allows many programs to compete for the processors. As computing becomes distributed among systems included in networks, the operating system running on a given machine must support access to the variety of computer systems connected to the net. System security, an important concern of all operating systems, is of particular concern here (we shall discuss this subject in Chapter 14).

Operating Systems for Personal Computers

The operating systems of personal computers dedicated to a single user are vastly simpler than the operating systems running larger machines, to which hundreds or thousands of users may have simultaneous access. One important capability an operating system can offer in a personal computing environment is **multitasking:** the ability to run several tasks at once on behalf of a user. This goes beyond multiprogramming which, as you remember, makes it possible to execute virtually simultaneously programs of several users. A multitasking operating system enables the user, for example, to run a spreadsheet program while a database is being accessed and a previously word-processed letter is being printed out. Each task can run in its own window.

The most important operating systems for personal computing are:

Windows 95 from Microsoft is the most popular environment for personal computers. It is a multitasking operating system that enables you to work with a great variety of personal productivity packages. Each application can run in its own window on the screen.

DOS (for Disk Operating System), distributed as MS-DOS or PC-DOS, is an older operating system for the IBM and IBM-compatible PCs. This system, distributed by Microsoft (that's what MS stands for), laid the foundation for that firm's good fortune. The system itself does not support multitasking and provides only a command-driven interface. Today, this system is most often used with Windows software running "on top" of it, which means that the user actually interacts with the Windows graphical user interface, which supports multitasking. To a large extent, the DOS Windows combination has been replaced with Windows 95 as a complete operating system in network environments.

OS/2 Warp is a powerful operating system from IBM, competing (rather unsuccessfully) with Windows in IBM environments. The system supports multitasking and local area networking.

Windows NT (for New Technology) is an operating system from Microsoft that competes with OS/2 in organizational (rather than home) settings. The system is often used to manage network servers. It is a robust program that rarely crashes and has strong security-oriented features. This system is not limited to the IBM and IBM-compatible PCs and thus supports the movement toward open systems in network environments.

UNIX is a popular operating system that is used across micro (with the exception of the less powerful ones), mini, and mainframe platforms. UNIX supports multiprogramming and multitasking, as well as networking. The system provides a collection of tools for program development and extensive utilities. Since the system itself is not very user-friendly, frequently a graphical user interface, such as Open View, is run on top of it.

System 7 is an operating system for Macintosh computers produced by Apple Computer. System 7 features multitasking and networking capabilities. It also supports multimedia and globalization of information systems, the latter by providing non-Latin character sets.

User Interface

A **user interface** is a combination of means by which a user interacts with the computer system. When the business world came to be dominated by IBM-compatible personal computers, command-driven, character-based user interfaces were prevalent for a period of time: We simply keyboarded an instruction to the ubiquitous MS-DOS in response to a C> prompt. Today, character-based interfaces have been largely replaced by graphical user interfaces, such as that in Figure 5.2.

As mentioned in the previous chapter, in a **graphical user interface** (GUI—pronounced "goo-ey"), computer actions are caused by a user's moving and clicking a pointing device. Several windows on the screen enable the user to work with several programs, either simultaneously (in a multitasking system) or by suspending all but one.

The most popular graphical user interface is that provided by Windows 95. All other popular microcomputer operating systems offer GUIs similar to Windows. Since virtually all popular personal computing programs run under Windows, this environment has

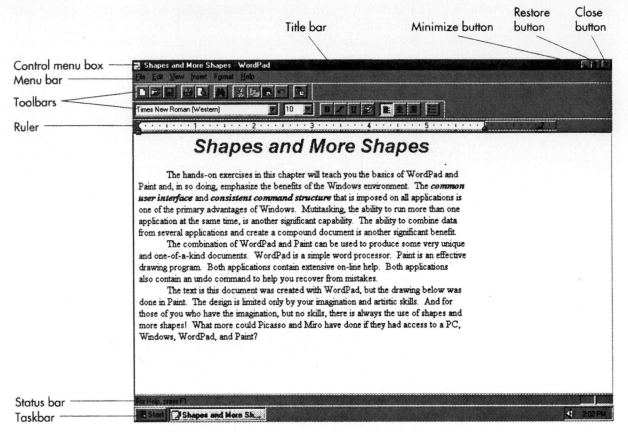

Figure 5.2

A graphical user interface in Windows 95 (From Robert T. Grauer and Maryann Barber. *Exploring Windows 95 and Essential Computing Concepts,* Englewood Cliffs, NJ: Prentice Hall, 1996.)

become a standard platform. Such systems software as Visual Basic (from Microsoft), PowerBuilder (from Powersoft), or Delphi (from Borland International) provide development environments for building graphical user interfaces and complete applications running on Windows (Drips 1996).

The Goal of Open Systems

A drive to use **open systems** in organizational computing, so that the software and hardware of any vendor can operate with those of any other, calls for an operating system that would run on any hardware platform. The technical specifications for an open system are made public by its vendor. The term "open systems" is used as the opposite of proprietary systems of a specific manufacturer. Although the ideal of fully open systems is still remote, in general computing systems are far more open today than they were a decade ago.

When they say they want open systems, organizations want portability, scalability, and interoperability of applications software. A *portable* application can be moved from one computer system to another. As shown in Figure 5.1, if a standard operating system is used in the systems software layer, then an application in the outer layer can easily be placed on any computer where this operating system runs. A *scalable* application program is one that can be moved, for example, from a smaller machine to a larger one without significant reprogramming. *Interoperability* means that machines of various vendors and capabilities can work together to produce needed information. Altogether, the use of open systems should provide a flexible informational platform for an evolving organization. The drive to open systems often centers on the UNIX operating system as the possible universal operating system.

UNIX Unity Is Difficult to Reach

The UNIX operating system has become a system of record and of considerable contention. The initial version of UNIX was developed between 1969 and 1973 in a classical "bootlegging" manner by two computer scientists, Ken Thompson and Dennis Ritchie, at Bell Laboratories. Thompson worked largely after hours to develop an operating system that would be much simpler conceptually than the huge resource hogs of the day. As Dennis Ritchie explained later, "It began in 1969 when Ken Thompson discovered a little-used PDP-7 minicomputer and set out to fashion a computing environment that he liked."

UNIX soon acquired extraordinary popularity in academic settings owing to its simple design, the great variety of facilities it offered for the development of applications, and its close connection with the increasingly used C language (in which it was rewritten in 1973). The elegant facilities UNIX provides for development of programs make it, in effect, an applications development environment. UNIX has never been known for its user-friendliness, however.

The fact that UNIX is written in a higher-level language rather than an assembly language specific to a particular machine makes it transportable across various computer platforms. UNIX works on larger computer systems as well as a variety of microprocessors, including more powerful portables. This makes the operating system attractive as a standard software platform.

Everyone agrees on the need to have a standard UNIX. It is simply that no agreement can be reached on *whose* UNIX is to be the standard. Several UNIX versions are competing for the mantle of an open-systems standard at this time. They include AIX from IBM, Solaris from Sun Microsystems, and Open DeskTop from Santa Cruz Operation. A UNIX clone called Linux, written by a college student Linus Torvalds, is available free over the Internet and is used at many college campuses. A standard was proposed by a Standards Board of the Institute of Electrical and Electronics Engineers (IEEE) as POSIX. Novell has acquired UNIX System Laboratories from AT&T in order to promote yet another standard UNIX version. Alas, the real standard is not yet in sight.

Based in part on Mike Ricciuti, "UNIX Takes to the Road," *Datamation*, April 1, 1994, pp. 59–64; Tom R. Halfhill, "UNIX vs Windows NT," *Byte*, May 1996, pp. 42–52; and Laurent Lachal, "UNIX Leads the 64-Bit Charge," *Byte*, November 1996, pp. 139–144.

5.3 | PERSONAL PRODUCTIVITY SOFTWARE

Personal productivity software is the most common applications software. Run on personal computers, these programs assist the user in a certain range of tasks. Taken together with professional support systems and systems supporting groupwork, both of which we discuss in Chapter 8, personal productivity software is a potent enabler of today's knowledge work.

Functions of Personal Productivity Software

Personal productivity software enhances its user's performance on a specific range of common tasks. Managers using spreadsheets are able to make higher-quality decisions by performing data analyses; secretaries are more effective with word processing, spreadsheets, and other programs; corporate communications specialists produce better work with desktop publishing systems. Several functional categories of personal productivity software have emerged. Figure 5.3 shows the general functions supported by this software: data management and analysis, authoring and presentation, activity and notes tracking, and communications and cooperative work. The figure also shows particular categories of software to support these functions. We shall return to a broader discussion of systems that support message handling, conferencing, and cooperative work in Chapter 8. Indeed, work in a group is an important aspect of personal productivity.

Figure 5.3

*Functions and
categories of personal
productivity software*

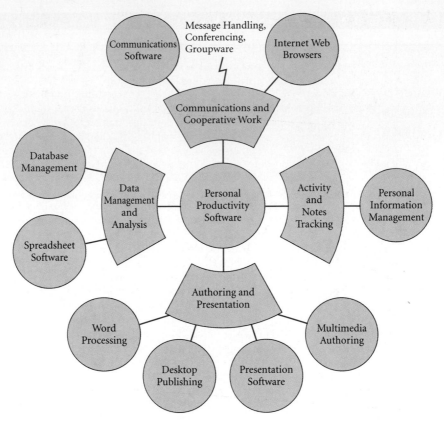

The capabilities of individual software packages vary widely, and a thorough selection process is necessary to ensure proper support for the functions of an individual user or a group of users (see Section 13.10). At the same time, firms must standardize much of the personal productivity software used by their workers. More extensive capabilities come at the price of more extensive hardware requirements, longer learning time, and the need to maintain the acquired proficiency. A casual user who must once in a while prepare several slides for a business presentation will be well served by a rudimentary presentation software. On the other hand, a specialist in developing software for computer-based training (called courseware) should investigate the newer field of multimedia authoring packages.

Several general trends are currently discernible. Most personal productivity packages have been expanded to a local area network (LAN) version and thus support the functioning of a workgroup; they are Internet-capable; and they may be used as part of a groupware package, or they may work with such a package. Another trend is blurring the lines between these offerings. The functionalities of various packages are overlapping more and more: Database management packages offer the analytical capabilities of spreadsheets as well as data presentation capabilities; word processing and desktop publishing share more functions. At the same time, a user who wants several packages to work together will encounter many difficulties and should very carefully investigate all aspects of their compatibility.

Suites of relatively compatible packages are offered by software vendors. They generally include a package for every personal productivity need. Examples are Microsoft's Office, Lotus Development's SmartSuite, and Corel Corporation's Corel Office. The acquisition of a suite prevents some of the problems of incompatibility and makes it possible, for example, to include a worksheet in a report that is being written (as in Figure 5.4), and then send the report by E-mail.

Figure 5.4

Using a suite of personal productivity packages, you can include a worksheet in a word-processed electronic document
(From Gary B. Shelly, Thomas J. Cashman, and Misty E. Vermaat, *Microsoft Office 95: Introductory Concepts and Techniques,* Danvers, MA: Boyd and Fraser, 1996, p. EI 1.2.)

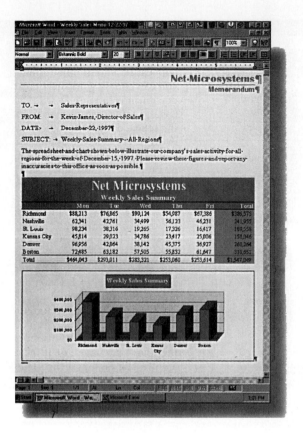

We will now review the principal categories of personal productivity software shown in Figure 5.3, paying particular attention to the newer technologies. We will begin with the tools for data management and analysis.

Spreadsheets

Running a spreadsheet program is the most common business use of a personal computer after word processing. **Spreadsheet** programs enable the user to manipulate any data that can be represented in rows and columns: The data may be sorted, summarized, and aggregated into categories. The principal business strength of spreadsheets (a term that, in the vernacular, refers to both the programs and the worksheets they produce) lies in manipulating numerical data for financial analysis. Spreadsheet programs are most commonly used as a planning tool relying on rather simple business models. As spreadsheet programs become more sophisticated, more complex modeling is becoming possible, approaching the power of decision support system (DSS) generators, which we shall discuss in more detail in Chapter 10.

A worksheet displayed on a screen by a spreadsheet program is shown in Figure 5.5.

The contents of a *cell*, the intersection of a numbered row and a column identified by a letter, may be a number (for example, cell B5 in Figure 5.5 contains 254.76). However, the power of spreadsheets derives from the fact that a cell's contents may also be given as a formula. For example, in our worksheet, the contents of cell B6 are a formula that computes the sum of the contents of cells B3 through B5. Should the contents of any cell change, the contents of all the cells whose values depend on that first cell are automatically recomputed. This feature permits the user to consider various "what-if" alternatives during problem-

Figure 5.5

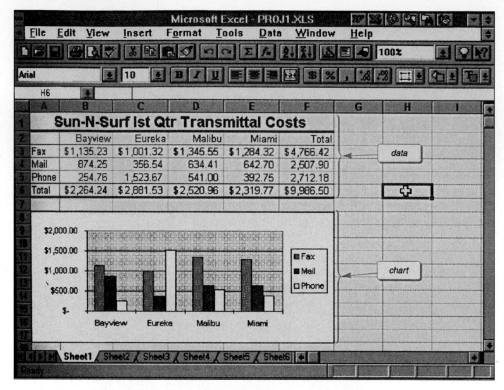

A worksheet displayed by the Microsoft Excel spreadsheet program. The worksheet contains the data on the transmittal costs for four locations of the Sun-N-Turf company. The spreadsheet calculates all the totals and displays the column chart. (From Gary B. Shelly, Thomas J. Cashman, and Misty E. Vermaat, *Microsoft Office: Introductory Concepts and Techniques,* Danvers, MA: Boyd and Fraser, 1995, p. E3.)

solving. The ease of spreadsheet use fosters an analytical approach to managerial decision making.

A number of mathematical, statistical, financial (such as the present value of a series of cash flows), text-handling, and other functions are available in spreadsheet programs. Sets of commands may be stored as macros and reused. Templates are available from independent vendors for various business situations. A template contains only the description of a worksheet and its formulas; the data are supplied by the user.

Spreadsheet programs can handle thousands of rows and hundreds of columns, which are scrolled on the monitor screen. Leading packages handle three- and multidimensional worksheets. They also offer excellent presentation-quality output, including a variety of three-dimensional color graphics. Several popular spreadsheets are listed in Table 5.1.

Table 5.1

A selection of spreadsheet software

Product	Vendor
Excel	Microsoft
Lotus 1-2-3	Lotus Development
PlanPerfect	Corel
Quattro Pro	Corel
VP-Planner	Paperback Software International

Table 5.2	Product	Vendor
	Access	Microsoft
A selection of	Approach	Lotus Development
database	dBASE IV	Borland International
management	FoxPro	Microsoft
systems for personal	Oracle	Oracle
computers	Paradox	Borland International

Database Management

Database management systems (DBMS) are systems software that provides assistance in managing large databases to be shared by many users. The DBMSs for personal computing are a powerful tool for managing collections of records, such as human resources records, records of sales made by each salesperson, or inventory records. Microcomputer DBMSs enable the users to:

- Create and maintain a database.
- Query a database with a query language.
- Prepare formatted reports.

In addition, packages offer security features, network connectivity, and the ability to present graphical output, as well as to perform spreadsheet-type computations. A number of full-featured DBMS packages are listed in Table 5.2. These packages are relational, with data represented as tables, as we will learn in Chapter 6, where we discuss database management at length. Database management is the foundation of many business information systems. This is why DBMS packages generally offer easy to use languages for accessing data and developing systems. Whenever large volumes of interrelated data records have to be maintained and accessed, a DBMS is the more appropriate tool for the task than a spreadsheet.

Multimedia databases, containing interlinked informational items represented in a variety of media, are emerging. They may be built with the use of hypermedia technology, which we describe when discussing authoring systems below.

Word Processing

Word processing is the most popular authoring and presentation activity. In fact, it is the most common personal computing application. **Word processing** packages facilitate text entry, storage, manipulation, and printing. Memos, letters, internal reports, and product documentation can be created using a word processing package with an ease that has made typewriters obsolete.

General capabilities of word processing include text editing with moving, deleting, or replacing blocks of text, and formatting a text on printed pages. Other features include indexing, preparation of a table of contents, and use of a spelling checker or a thesaurus of word synonyms. Some packages are integrated with database management systems (which help to produce a mailing, for example) or spreadsheet programs (which help, say, to include a table in the text). The mailmerge feature of a word processing package enables the user to store a boilerplate letter and then customize it, with names and addresses from a client's file. (Not all of us mail readers are happy about that.)

Table 5.3	Product	Vendor
A selection of word processing software	Ami Pro	Lotus Development
	MultiMate	Borland International
	Volkswriter	Lifetree Software
	Word	Microsoft
	WordPerfect	Corel
	WordStar	WordStar International

To enhance the quality of produced documents, one may use text-revision features of the word-processing software to proofread text for potential hitches in writing style or word usage. The packages point out faulty grammar, wordy expressions, use of slang, weak paragraphs, and similar failings. Word processing packages for virtually all the world's languages are available from a number of vendors in the U.S. marketplace.

Some of the popular word processing packages are listed in Table 5.3; Microsoft Word is the most popular of them.

As a general trend, word processing software is increasingly acquiring some of the features of desktop publishing systems—our next topic of discussion.

Desktop Publishing

When instead of writing an internal memo, we have to produce a report for a customer, a catalog, or a high-quality business newsletter, we can turn to **desktop publishing.** As word processing software assists a writer with the tools for editing a text, so does desktop publishing software assist a designer of a publication for broader distribution (see Figure 5.6). The cost of the hardware necessary to run desktop publishing systems has become rather modest: a high-resolution display, a laser printer, and perhaps a scanner may be configured to create a functional desktop publishing system. Desktop publishing has become accessible to even small businesses. At the same time, sophisticated desktop publishing may require expensive hardware and software, as well as considerable skill on the part of the user. Image-processing technology is very powerful at its high end.

Figure 5.6

Using a desktop publishing package, you can lay out the page, include and touch up photographs, and draw graphical objects (Canvas 5 from Deneba Software; From Reviews, *Publish,* December 1996, p. 44.)

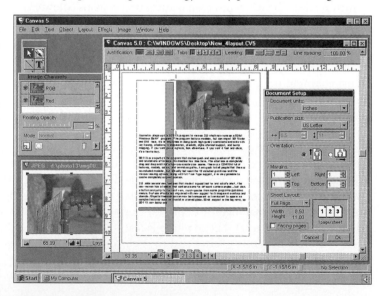

Table 5.4	Product	Vendor
A selection of desktop publishing packages	Adobe PageMaker	Adobe
	Interleaf Publisher	Interleaf
	Quark XPress	Quark
	Ready, Set, Go	Letraset USA
	Xerox Ventura Publisher	Xerox Desktop Software

Desktop publishing packages offer flexible layouts, with the ability to wrap the text around graphics as desired; the ability to create, size, and manipulate the graphics; and extensive typographic controls over the typefaces and fonts. These publishing packages enable the user to print word-processed text in a great variety of typefaces (for example, Times Roman) and fonts (sets of characters in a particular size and style in the typeface, for example, 12-point Times Italic), combining the text with line artwork, such as figures, and photographs. It is possible to import the text and graphics from the programs with which they were originally created. Color may be used if the appropriate equipment is available. Many packages provide extensive assistance with automatic layouts of the printed material.

Some well-known desktop publishing packages are listed in Table 5.4.

Here is a typical example of the steps required to publish a document on a desktop:

1. *Prepare text and illustrations.* The text copy is produced with a word processing program, with the word processing component of a publishing package, or scanned in with an optical character recognition (OCR) scanner. Line art may be created with a graphics program and imported into the publishing package, or clip art (prepackaged sets of images) may be used. Alternatively, artwork (including photographs) may be imported with a scanner.

2. *Format pages.* A page-format template is created, together with a style sheet that specifies the typefaces for all the components of the page. The appearance of the document can then be changed by simply modifying the style sheet. Scalable fonts permit you to select the precise type you desire for all segments of the page.

3. *Place illustrations in the text.* Text and illustrations are placed on the appropriate pages; the system automatically "flows" the text through the publication, laying it out in columns and wrapping it around illustrations. Illustrations may be scaled to fit the allotted space. What-you-see-is-what-you-get (WYSIWYG) graphics software enable you to see the output on your monitor in its final form.

4. *Print the document.* The inspected pages may be printed camera-ready copy. This means that it may now be reproduced in a variety of ways: by running off multiple copies on a high-quality printer, by duplicating the original on copy machines, or by photographing the copy to produce traditional printing plates. Many systems also support slide- and transparency-makers for presentation purposes.

Presentation Software

The availability of high-quality presentation software has significantly raised the expectations of an organization for a professional presentation. Desktop presentation packages emphasize full-color images rather than the text that desktop publishing concentrates on. Desktop **presentation software** will help you to:

Table 5.5	Product	Vendor
A selection of presentation software	Compel	Asymetrix
	Corel Presentations	Corel
	Freelance Graphics	Lotus Development
	Harvard Graphics	Software Publishing
	Persuasion	Adobe Systems
	PowerPoint	Microsoft

- Create graphs automatically from a database or from a spreadsheet.
- Produce your own graphics, edit scanned-in images, or edit images from a library of clip art.
- Include text in a variety of typefaces and formats such as bulleted text, for example.

Although the output may be included in paper-based reports, the most frequent use of presentation software is in the production of transparencies or slides. Most presentation packages include arrangements with service bureaus to generate slides or photos from the produced files, which may be transferred to the service bureaus via a modem. Many products also have the capability to run a slide show from a desktop or portable computer.

Popular presentation packages are listed in Table 5.5.

Multimedia Authoring Software

The extension of presentation software into the world of multimedia is becoming possible with **multimedia authoring software,** which enables its users to design multimedia presentations (Salamone 1996). Using these packages, you can develop attractive computer-based training (CBT) courseware or customer presentations. We learned about many uses of multimedia in Section 4.6. This technology, or, rather, conglomerate of technologies, is intended to deliver what is often called infotainment. Superior graphic imagery, computer animation, and motion video may be combined with high-fidelity sound as well as with the text. This software helps its user collect pieces of the presentation from a variety of equipment, such as voice recorders, scanners, videotape and videodisk players, and other sources. If desired and if the specialized equipment is available, one may produce a CD-ROM disk, which can serve as a master for duplication. Multimedia packages are listed in Table 5.6 (Seachrist 1996).

Some of the packages listed in Table 5.6 support the **hypermedia** method of information delivery, in which linkages may be established among various items in a large multimedia document. These linkages enable the user to move from one topic directly to a related one, instead of scanning the information sequentially (see Section 8.3 for further discussion and illustration of hypertext and hypermedia).

Hypermedia databases may include graphics, video, voice messages, or other units of information such as worksheets. Imagine how you could create a complete history of your management of a customer account, including product specifications, scanned-in photos of your contacts and handwritten notes from the customer, E-mail messages, and voice memos. As another example, a law enforcement database might include witness sketches, fingerprints, voice recordings, and photos. Indeed, these systems blur the distinction between a database and a document. The technology was launched into personal computing with the Macintosh HyperCard software. Some of the packages that specifically support the hypermedia concept are Hyperties from Cognetics and PLUS from Spinnaker Software.

Table 5.6	Product	Vendor
A selection of multimedia authoring software	Authorware	Macromedia
	Corel Click and Create	Corel
	IconAuthor	AimTech
	Innovus Multimedia	Innovus
	mTropolis	mFactory
	Oracle Media Objects	Oracle
	PowerMedia	RadMedia
	ToolBook	Asymetrix

Today, many hypermedia presentations are made on the Internet's Web sites, using such packages as 3D Studio Max from Kinetix or Cosmos Worlds from SGI; a much less-expensive package for the task is Internet 3D Space Builder from Paragraph (Sweet 1997).

Personal Information Management

In the course of their daily activities, knowledge workers deal only occasionally with data that may be represented as database records. Beyond that, we all need to organize such scraps of information as names of business contacts, reminders, telephone messages, ideas, or other short textual items. We need to access this information to track projects, write memos, or develop financial projections.

Personal information management (PIM) packages are tools that help knowledge workers track tasks, people, projects, commitments, and ideas. These packages assist users in several ways, including the following:

- Allow users to enter short notes and assign them to categories they define (for example, "Accomplishments for this Quarter"). These categories may also be organized into a hierarchy (for example, a higher-level category might be "Accomplishments for the Next Performance Appraisal").

- Enable users to browse through the categories and the items they contain, helping them to examine the information from several points of view.

- Support time management in scheduling events; for example, by discovering time conflicts, maintaining a "tickler" file to remind the user about things to do, and showing time commitments in graphical form.

- Handling various chores, such as automatic telephone dialing.

Some of these packages are listed in Table 5.7.

Table 5.7	Product	Vendor
A selection of packages for personal information management	Act!	Symantec
	Agenda	Lotus Development
	Primetime Personal	Primetime Software
	Totall Manager	Bartel Software
	Who-What-When	Chronos Software

IN THE SPOTLIGHT

How One Manager Uses a Personal Productivity Package to Manage Better

Roger Corea is the vice president of IDS Financial Services in charge of the Northeast region. He oversees 15 division vice presidents, each of whom supervises several dozen financial planners. Corea uses ManagePro for Windows from Avantos Performance Systems of Emeryville, California, to help him supervise his subordinates. Corea says that ManagePro is always on his screen (see Photo 5.1), whether he is on the road with his Toshiba notebook computer or in his office, with the notebook mounted in the docking station and connected to the local area network. Thanks to the software, he spends less time writing plans and more time taking action.

Corea found that personal information management (PIM) packages did not give him enough support in his job of managing. With ManagePro, Corea can establish goals for his subordinates (see Figure 5.7), monitor their progress toward these goals, and conduct performance reviews. The package can also be used by managers who do not have people reporting to them but who need to monitor the progress of several projects they are involved in.

We shall let Roger Corea walk us through his software-enabled management style:

"Each fall I list all the managers in my region. Then I click on each name using a mouse and enter that person's goals for the next year, such as financial planner productivity and number of new clients. Under each goal, I list strategies that the manager and I have agreed on to reach it.

After my database is ready, I use ManagePro to monitor my managers' progress. I keep

Photo 5.1

Roger Corea always has on his PC screen a display from ManagePro that helps him do his managing job (From Sprout 1994.)

Figure 5.7

The Goal Planner window of ManagePro (From ManagePro documentation.)

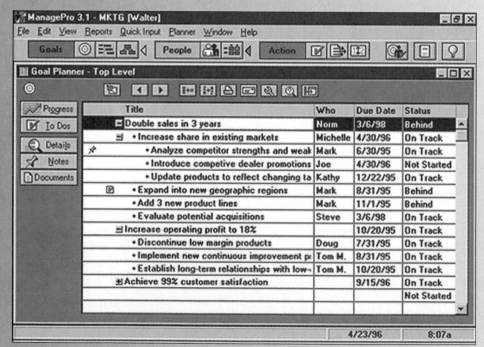

a running record of phone conversations and meetings in the Progress section [of the ManagePro package] under each person's name and take notes on how they are doing. My administrative assistants enter numbers taken from standard performance reports we have for each division and pipe them into my machine via the office network.

The Feedback and Coaching section lets me record the advice I'm giving as well as the manager's response. Whenever I talk to that manager, I can call up what we talked about before and see whether the things have improved. I can also program ManagePro to re-

mind me when it's time to check in with different managers. . .

I have cut the time I need to prepare a performance review by at least 70 percent, and my reviews are more comprehensive and relevant. I used to do only semiannual reviews; now I do them every quarter."

And also: "My anxiety level is a lot lower! That's because I'm much better organized and more efficient."

Based on Alison L. Sprout, "Using a PC to Be a Better Boss," *Fortune*, March 7, 1994, p. 197; and Reviewer's Guide, ManagePro 3.0 for Windows, 1995.

Various PIMs offer special features; for example, the packages for mobile computing have small program size and are easy to use. Yet, a PIM is not always an appropriate tool for handling personal information. When information similar to that maintained with PIMs has to be managed for a team of knowledge workers, groupware should be employed, as we shall see in Chapter 8. As the vignette above illustrates, certain personal productivity packages provide more extensive support for management functions than PIMs.

Communications Software and Web Browsers

Communications software enables the user to connect to a telecommunications network in order to send or receive messages. The software provides the following capabilities:

- Sending and receiving electronic mail (E-mail).
- Connecting to an external information service or the Internet.
- File transfer. You can *download* a program or a data file from a remote computer to your own workstation or *upload* a file to the remote computer.
- Terminal emulation—enabling the personal computer to act as a terminal when required in a particular application.
- Sending and receiving a fax (with many software packages).

The communications software includes text editors for creating messages. It is also possible to import a document created with a word processing or a spreadsheet program. The communications packages include Crosstalk of Attachmate, Delrina Communications Suite from Delrina, and Procomm Plus from Datastorm Technologies.

More and more frequently, the reason for connecting to a telecommunications network is to gain access to the resources of the Internet (see Chapter 7). You may wish to browse the information available at millions of the World Wide Web sites around the globe. Web browsers are rapidly becoming one of the most ubiquitous categories of software packages. A **browser** is a program that enables its user to access electronic documents included in the Internet's World Wide Web, a collection of interlinked hypermedia databases distributed among remote sites. An electronic document placed on a Web server with the use of the appropriate software is represented in a standard format and contains embedded links to related documents. You can access any one of them by identifying its URL (Uniform

Resource Locator). By clicking on your mouse, you select a link in that document and your browser will cause the new document on a remote site to be fetched and displayed on your screen. The most popular browsers are Navigator from Netscape Communications Corporation and Internet Explorer from Microsoft.

5.4 | PROGRAMMING LANGUAGES AND THEIR TRANSLATORS

Off-the-shelf packages satisfy only a part of the need for applications software. The software for more powerful organizational systems has to be developed or customized to match a specific need. Since computers cannot process instructions specified in a natural language such as English (with the exception of carefully chosen phrases), they are programmed using specially designed programming languages.

Programming languages have progressed from the first-generation, binary machine languages to the fourth-generation nonprocedural languages that help us specify what needs to be done by the computer rather than how to do it in detail. As this progression occurred, the languages helped in using the human resources of the systems developers more efficiently at the expense of less efficient use of computer time. This is appropriate, since during the same period the costs of human resources have gone up, and the costs of computing resources have dramatically decreased. Many of the fourth-generation languages are specifically designed for the end users, as we shall see in the next section.

Generations of Programming Languages

Programming languages developed over four generations. Figure 5.8 traces this development, starting with the machine languages in the mid-1940s and proceeding with a full-fledged take-off into high-level languages in the mid-1950s. Very high-level, nonprocedural languages came into use during the 1970s. As the level of the language increases, the programmer needs to specify less and less detail of the task to be carried out by the computer. The third- and fourth-generation languages gave birth to important new directions in programming in the 1980s and 1990s. We shall now proceed to discuss the four **programming-language generations**.

The first computers were programmed in the machine language of each specific machine. Due to the binary (on-off) nature of computer hardware, instructions or statements in these early languages were simply strings of 1s and 0s, as shown in Figure 5.9. A glance at this figure is all you will need in order to appreciate why machine languages have not been used to program computers for long.

Figure 5.8

Generations of programming languages

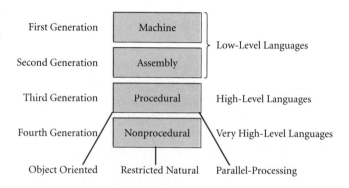

Figure 5.9

*An instruction in a
machine language*

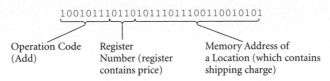

| Operation Code (Add) | Register Number (register contains price) | Memory Address of a Location (which contains shipping charge) |

The Instruction Adds the Shipping Charge to the Price.

Figure 5.10

*An instruction in an
assembly language*

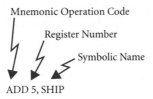

Mnemonic Operation Code

Register Number

Symbolic Name

ADD 5, SHIP

The first real programming languages to emerge were assembly languages. Since an **assembly language** is also a low-level language (that is, it refers to machine resources, such as registers and memory addresses), it is also specific to a computer model or a series of models. Therefore, programs written in an assembly language are not portable. As Figure 5.10 shows, an assembly language permits the use of relatively easy-to-remember operation codes and of symbolic names for memory locations.

An assembly language program is translated into a machine language by a simple translator called an **assembler.** Assembly languages are used today only when tight control over computer hardware resources is required, such as in certain systems programs, particularly those for real-time computing. The advantage of efficient use of computer resources by these languages is outweighed by the high costs of very tedious systems development and by lack of program portability.

Today, the bulk of programming is done in **high-level programming (procedural) languages** that provide statements, each of which is translated into several machine-language instructions. These languages are far more expressive than low-level languages: Fewer instructions are needed to develop a program. Moreover, the nature of these instructions permits the programmer to concentrate on the problem at hand rather than on the use of machine resources. These languages facilitate program development and maintenance, resulting in much higher productivity than assembly languages.

The language in which most business applications were written until not long ago is COBOL (for *Common Business-Oriented Language*), developed in 1960. The language was specifically designed for processing large data files residing in secondary storage and for relatively easy coding. Although highly readable, COBOL programs are very lengthy and the language is hardly suitable for the increasingly used object-oriented development. As we will further discuss in Chapter 16, maintenance of a large legacy of COBOL programs requires much effort on the part of today's information systems departments.

High-Level Languages

A great variety of high-level languages is in use. Table 5.8 summarizes the features of the high-level languages you are most likely to encounter. In particular, C, C++, and Visual Basic are becoming more and more widely used.

In general, most of these third-generation languages are procedure-oriented: They specify the procedure for obtaining the desired result, which is known as an **algorithm**. Detailed specification of such a procedure requires a significant effort. Since much of the

Table 5.8

Important high-level languages

Ada	Developed as the standard language for real-time applications by the U.S. Department of Defense (for example, aircraft control), Ada is used in IS applications as well. Its powerful facilities support parallel processing and object-oriented programming.
APL	APL is a language for very terse programming, relying on Greek characters and thus requiring a special keyboard. APL is used for scientific programming, but also in other applications where large arrays of data are to be processed—such as DSS modeling. Programs are interactive and the language is interpretive.
Basic	Basic is a language for novice programmers, though powerful versions are available for the PC environment. Programs are interactive and the language is interpretive.
C	C is a powerful language that combines the facilities of high-level and assembly languages. C is now widely used for systems and applications software development, particularly in the UNIX environment.
C++	This extension of C is used for object-oriented programming.
COBOL	Once the preeminent language of data processing (particularly for the development of transaction processing and management reporting systems); today few new programs are developed in COBOL, but many COBOL programs are maintained.
FORTRAN	FORTRAN is used for scientific applications; the new versions offer facilities for developing programs for parallel-processing environments.
Java	Object-oriented language for programming applets, i.e., executable applications that can be distributed on the Internet's World Wide Web.
LISP	The original language of artificial intelligence, it manipulates lists of words, numbers, sentences, or other items. The language is usually interpretive. Special-purpose hardware may be needed to ensure efficient program execution.
Pascal	Pascal is a good language for learning disciplined programming; the Turbo version is common in the PC environment.
PL/I	PL/I is an elaborate language designed for both business and scientific computing. It is used largely in the IBM mainframe environment.
Prolog	A contraction for "programming in logic," Prolog is used in artificial intelligence, particularly in Japan. The program is essentially a specification of facts about objects and relationships among objects, as well as rules about the "world" described by this knowledge base. The program answers questions about the "world" by inferring answers from this knowledge base.
RPG	RPG is a report generation language. It permits the programmer to specify *what* the report should contain and *what* it should look like, rather than detailing the steps of *how* it should be produced (as in COBOL). RPG is a precursor of very high-level (4GL) languages.
Smalltalk	A language specifically developed for object-oriented programming.
Visual Basic	A popular form of Basic for visual programming.

processing in the information systems environment is fairly repetitive and revolves around accessing databases, many specialists and end-users moved toward programming in very high-level, fourth-generation languages.

Beyond High-Level Programming Languages

The low productivity of programmers using high-level languages and the resulting backlogs of applications awaiting development have led to the **fourth-generation languages (4GLs)**, which specify what needs to be done rather than detailing steps for doing it. Therefore, in contrast to the procedure-oriented high-level languages, the 4GLs are known as nonprocedural languages. The approach was derived from the RPG (for *Report Program Generator*) language. Some of the fourth-generation languages are designed primarily for professional programmers, others for the end user. Many languages combine end-user facilities with facilities for applications programmers. We shall discuss this very important category of languages in the next section.

A number of languages could lay claim to belonging to a fifth generation. The following types of programming languages are likely to influence the development of such a new paradigm:

- Languages for object-oriented programming (such as Smalltalk and C++), further described in Section 5.6, which are particularly apt for handling multimedia programming. Visual programming languages, such as Visual Basic, enable the user to assemble a part of the program from visual objects displayed on the screen (as discussed further in Section 5.6).

    A special type of object-oriented language is Java, designed at Sun Microsystems for developing executable content for the Internet's Web pages. With Java, programs (called "applets") can be developed and translated into a bytecode. When surfing the Web with a Java-enabled browser (such as HotJava or Navigator), the user can obtain a page of information together with the applet that will make it possible to manipulate this information. For example, a spreadsheet can be obtained together with a modeling applet that will manipulate it as desired and graph the results. Java software ensures portability of the applets' bytecode among a variety of computers: All Java-enabled browsers can cause the code to be executed (see Figure 5.11). Since Java programming requires specialized skill, a so-called scripting language (consider it a form of shorthand), JavaScript, has been developed to simplify the programming of applets. Java's popularity is increasing.

- Languages that facilitate parallel processing in systems with a large number of processors.

- Functional languages (such as LISP), based on the mathematical concept of computation as an application of functions.

- Limited subsets of natural languages which can be processed thanks to the progress in artificial intelligence, which we shall discuss in Chapter 11.

Figure 5.11

How Java applets work
(Adapted from Jason Levitt, "Java Makes the Web Perform," *InformationWeek,* January 1, 1996, pp. 54–57.)

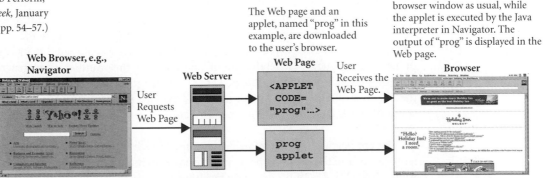

The Web page and an applet, named "prog" in this example, are downloaded to the user's browser.

The Web page is displayed in the browser window as usual, while the applet is executed by the Java interpreter in Navigator. The output of "prog" is displayed in the Web page.

Web Browser, e.g., Navigator

User Requests Web Page

Web Server

Web Page

User Receives the Web Page.

Browser

Translators: Compilers and Interpreters

A program in a high-level language must be translated into a machine language before execution. Most languages are translated by systems programs known as **compilers,** which translate the program—written in a higher-level language known as the source program—in its entirety into the binary machine language of the computer. The compiler produces the so-called *object code* of the program that can be run repeatedly without a need for another translation, unless the source program has to be modified.

Some languages, such as Basic, APL, or LISP are interpretive: they are translated statement-by-statement by a systems program called an **interpreter.** Each statement is executed immediately following its translation and no object code is produced. Interpretive translation is of advantage when users are expected to interact with the program as it is running. However, programs written in interpreted languages are generally slower in running than compiled programs.

5.5 | FOURTH-GENERATION LANGUAGES

The use of fourth-generation languages permits a severalfold increase in productivity in information systems development. Some of these tools, such as query languages, actually make it possible to avoid developing applications. These languages enable end users to access databases directly. Others, such as report generators, simplify the arduous tasks of output presentation. The most powerful of the 4GL tools, application generators, permit substitution of a single, relatively simple instruction for the 10 or more instructions necessary in a procedural language such as COBOL. Query languages and some report generators are largely end-user tools, while many application generators require the expertise of information systems professionals.

However, programs written in 4GLs are generally far less efficient during program execution than programs in high-level languages. Therefore, their use is limited to projects that do not call for such efficiency. For example, 4GLs are generally not used to develop transaction processing systems.

Categories of Fourth-Generation Languages and Their Role in End-User Computing

Much of business information processing consists of accessing data in databases, relatively routine data processing (such as sorting, classification, and summarization), and presenting information on a display screen or in a report. In response to the needs of this environment, fourth-generation languages provide direct access to the database or make it possible to develop applications without specifying copious processing details.

The distinguishing feature of 4GLs is that they specify *what is to be done* rather than *how to do it.* In other words, the languages are nonprocedural: They do not specify the complete procedure for accomplishing the task. These details are filled in by the software translator for the 4GL. The program developed in 4GL is terse as compared to its equivalent in a procedural language. Generally, about one-tenth of the number of instructions are required. A good illustration of the power of these languages is furnished by a comparison of the length and complexity of a procedural-language program (do not attempt to actually study it!) with the simplicity of an equivalent 4GL program, both of which are shown in Figure 5.12.

An application may therefore be developed much more rapidly. The languages are easier to learn, and the resulting programs are easier to maintain than in procedural languages. All in all, high levels of productivity result from the appropriate use of a 4GL.

Figure 5.12

A comparison of programs in a procedural language and in 4GL to accomplish the same task (Courtesy of Harvey Lowy)

COBOL Program to List Employees of Department B by Name:

```
IDENTIFICATION DIVISION.
PROGRAM-ID.
    EMPLOYEE-LIST.
AUTHOR.
    TOM SMITH.
ENVIRONMENT DIVISION.
CONFIGURATION SECTION.
SOURCE-COMPUTER.
    VAX-750.
OBJECT-COMPUTER.
    VAX-750.
INPUT-OUTPUT SECTION.
FILE-CONTROL.
     SELECT EMPLOYEE-FILE ASSIGN TO "EMPLOYEE.INP".
     SELECT PRT-FILE      ASSIGN TO "EMPLOYEE.DAT".
DATA DIVISION.
FILE SECTION.
FD EMPLOYEE-FILE
    RECORD CONTAINS 50 CHARACTERS
    LABEL RECORDS ARE STANDARD
    DATA RECORD IS EMP-REC.
01   EMP-REC.
     02    DEPT-CODE          PIC     X.
     02    EMP-NAME           PIC     X(20).
     02    EMP-ADDRESS        PIC     X(20).
     02    FILLER             PIC     X(9).
FD   PRT-FILE.
     RECORD CONTAINS 132 CHARACTERS
     LABEL RECORDS ARE OMITTED
     DATA RECORD IS PRT-REC.
01   PRT-REC.
     02    FILLER             PIC     X(20).
     02    PRT-EMP-NAME       PIC     X(20).
     02    FILLER             PIC     X(20).
     02    PRT-EMP-ADDRESS    PIC     X(20).
     02    FILLER             PIC     X(52).
WORKING-STORAGE SECTION.
01       NO-MORE-DATE         PIC     X(1) VALUE 'N'.
PROCEDURE DIVISION.
     OPEN INPUT EMPLOYEE-FILE
        OUTPUT PRT-FILE.
     PERFORM READ-EMPLOYEE.
     PERFORM PROCESS-EMPLOYEE UNTIL NO-MORE-DATA = 'Y'.
     CLOSE   EMPLOYEE-FILE PRT-FILE.
     STOP RUN.
READ-EMPLOYEE.
    READ EMPLOYEE-FILE AT END MOVE 'Y' TO NO-MORE-DATA.
PROCESS-EMPLOYEE.
    IF DEPT-CODE = 'B'
         MOVE EMP.NAME      TO PRT-EMP.NAME
         MOVE EMP-ADDRESS   TO PRT-EMP-ADDRESS
         WRITE PRT-REC.
    PERFORM READ-EMPLOYEE.
```

4GL Program to Accomplish the Same Task:

```
DATABASE EMPLOYEES
LIST
     BY EMPLOYEE__NAME EMPLOYEE__ADDRESS
     IF DEPARTMENT__CODE = 'B'
```

Figure 5.13

Categories of fourth-generation languages

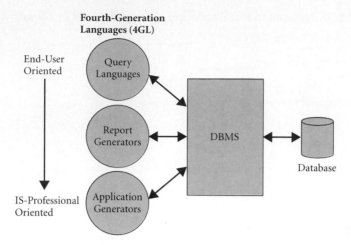

The principal categories of 4GLs are query languages, report generators, and application generators, many of which include screen generators. The 4GLs, in their essence, facilitate access to corporate databases and work with the database management systems (see Figure 5.13). Thus, query languages and report generators make it unnecessary to develop certain applications by providing direct access to a database, while application generators make it relatively easy to specify in nonprocedural terms a system for such access. Indeed, many 4GLs are provided as a part of a DBMS package.

One may also include among 4GLs the software generators for producing decision support and executive information systems, which we will discuss in Chapter 10. Some 4GLs are therefore also provided by spreadsheet packages used to produce simpler decision support systems.

Many 4GLs are used in **end-user computing,** or the development of their own applications by the end users, which has become an important part of organizational computing. Some of the packages providing these languages are specifically designed for end users; others contain end-user facilities together with the procedural facilities used by professional developers. However, the demands that 4GL tools, and particularly applications generators, impose on the skills of the people who use them differ significantly. If end-user development is desired, both ease of use and the power of the tool to accomplish the task should be carefully evaluated. Table 5.9 lists some popular 4GL tools. Of these, application generators such as IDEAL, MANTIS, and Natural should be considered tools for information systems professionals rather than for the end users.

Another frequent use of 4GLs is prototyping, that is, developing an initial working model of an application in order to establish the requirements of its users, with the final system then often developed in a procedural language.

We shall now discuss the three categories of 4GLs.

Query Languages

Query languages are employed to retrieve data from databases. Here are two examples of queries, expressed in a query language close to the natural (English) language:

```
PRINT CUSTOMER NAMES IN MAINE
PRINT EMPLOYEE NAME AND EMPLOYEE SKILL IF SALARY > 50,000
```

Query languages are used online for ad-hoc queries, that is, queries are not predefined. Interaction is usually simple, only very simple computations are involved, and the result is

Table 5.9	Category	Product	Vendor
Popular 4GL tools	Query languages	SQL	IBM and many others
		Query-by-Example	IBM and others
		INTELLECT	AlCorp (licensed to many others)
	Report generators	Easytrieve Plus	Pansophic Systems
		Datatrieve	Digital Equipment Corporation
		Mark V	Answer Systems
	Application generators	FOCUS	Information Builders
		IDEAL	Applied Data Research
		MANTIS	Cincom Systems
		MAPPER	Unisys
		Natural	Software AG
		NOMAD2	MUST Software International
		Ramis II	Computer Associates International
	Generators of decision support and executive information systems		See Chapter 10

generally not formatted since it is displayed in a default format selected by the system itself. Most query languages also make it possible to update databases. With many query languages, it is possible to request a graphical output to a query.

There are six primary styles for querying a database:

- Form fill-in, in which the user enters the query by filling in fields on the display screen.
- Menu selection, that is, choosing from a set of options displayed on the screen. A hierarchy of menus is often employed in graphical user interfaces.
- A command-type query language, such as SQL, which we discuss in Chapter 6.
- Query by example, illustrated below.
- Direct manipulation by moving the cursor on the screen to manipulate the representation of an object or an action.
- Restricted natural language, as we have seen above.

All of these languages, with the exception of SQL, a powerful and standardized query language, may be appropriate for direct access to data by end users. SQL queries are frequently "hidden" from end users by more user-friendly interfaces. Very simple query languages, based on a system that prompts the user or the user selects an option from a limited menu, are appropriate for such applications as automatic teller machines or electronic kiosks. But such languages do not have sufficient power and may be quite annoying to the more advanced users in an organizational setting.

A query language that is available commercially as an interface to a number of systems is Query-by-Example (QBE). Most users find this style much simpler than SQL. Figure 5.14 shows the formulation of a reasonably complex query: "List all salespeople who sell sheets in District 3."

Figure 5.14

*Query expressed in a
query-by-example
(QBE) system*

SALESPEOPLE	NAME	DISTRICT	SALESTARGET
	P.	3	

PRODUCTS	PRODUCTNAME	DISTRICT	SALESVOLUME
	SHEETS	3	

Assuming that we have in our database a SALESPEOPLE file and a PRODUCTS file that lists our products, the figure shows the names of the fields (attributes) displayed by the system. The user then gives the system an example of what he or she wants by underlining the "3" (district numbers have to match). The "P." specifies the field that is to be printed (or displayed). QBE is available in such DBMSs as Microsoft Access and dBASE IV.

Direct manipulation query languages enable the user to manipulate the objects that represent what the user wants. For example, by selecting with a mouse an icon (picture) of a diary, the user may read the list of appointments for the coming week. Some systems allow the user to issue commands with voice, gesture, and even eye movement (research is being done on these systems at the Media Lab at MIT, for example).

Restricted natural languages may be used to formulate a more complex query than those that opened this section, such as:

```
REPORT SALES AND COMMISSIONS, BROKEN DOWN BY REGION, FOR SALESPEOPLE IN
CALIFORNIA, TEXAS, AND UTAH
```

Natural-language systems rely on a lexicon of words likely to be used in queries, including the terminology of the subject area. Some of these systems engage in dialog with the user to clarify an ambiguity, others restate the query for the user to check and respond. Natural language queries are used in voice input systems and are expected to become common in the future.

Report Generators

A **report generator** enables an end user or an information systems professional to produce a report without detailing all the necessary steps, such as formatting the document. A report generator offers users greater control over the content and appearance of the output than a query language. Thus, the specified data may be retrieved from the specified files or databases, grouped, ordered, and summarized in a specified way, and formatted for printing as desired. The report title, headings, and other text may be included. A sample report, produced with a nonprocedural program of fewer than twenty lines, is shown in Figure 5.15. A program in a procedural language required to produce this report would be far longer, and the detailed specification would be far more subject to the programmer's error.

If more complex processing is needed, many report generators permit the inclusion of procedural statements (say, in COBOL or C). This is generally done by an information systems professional. Indeed, some report generators (including the RPG III report generation language) are designed to be used by these professionals.

Application Generators

An **application generator** makes it possible to specify an entire application, consisting of several programs, without much detailed coding. Based on this specification, most generators produce (generate) code in a procedural language. This code may then be modified (or supplemented by additional routines) to meet the precise needs of the application.

Figure 5.15

*A report produced with
the use of a report
generator* (Information
Builders, Inc.)

Report Across Cities

		NOVEMBER SALARY PAYMENTS			
CITY		NEW YORK		LOS ANGELES	
PAY_DATE	DEPARTMENT	SOC_SEC	GROSS	SOC_SEC	GROSS
97/11/30	MIS	047-49-6523	$2,400.36	212-43-2319	$2,343.20
		113-50-3420	$2,101.30	350-88-6500	$2,450.00
		351-78-1183	$1,904.22	360-91-4301	$2,451.10
		376-11-3213	$2,001.00	400-19-6520	$3,000.21
		661-44-3210	$2,450.22	512-69-1234	$1,891.50
		961-31-5632	$2,600.00	.	.
		990-32-1290	$2,913.50	.	.
	MIS DEPT. TOTAL		$16,360.60		$12,136.01
	MARKETING	042-41-6733	$1,341.94	061-21-4922	$1,530.20
		047-91-5420	$2,010.45	101-45-6720	$1,872.40
		050-79-1234	$2,179.60	212-55-3401	$2,781.00
		111-56-8721	$2,594.00	.	.
		661-32-5981	$2,439.10	.	.
		990-44-4982	$3,020.50	.	.
	MARKETING DEPT. TOTAL		$13,585.59		$6,183.60
	SALES	002-34-1529	$2,789.00	150-31-5762	$2,451.10
		050-78-4987	$2,569.20	152-66-8271	$2,872.50
		350-10-3962	$2,884.50	251-10-6341	$3,001.50
		350-29-4500	$3,253.66	350-10-8727	$2,910.00
		410-30-6590	$2,520.10	410-20-7621	$2,391.50
		555-91-1001	$2,580.00	501-31-6290	$3,001.00
		.	.	678-33-5525	$3,909.44
		.	.	679-40-1101	$2,594.20
		.	.	990-30-1290	$3,103.10
		.	.	991-73-2690	$2,104.42
	SALES DEPT. TOTAL		$16,596.46		$28,338.76
	TOTALS BY CITY 97/11/30		$46,542.65		$46.658.37
	TOTAL PAY DATE 97/11/30		$93,201.02		

Total by Department (annotation pointing to MARKETING DEPT. TOTAL)

Embedded Parameters   Total Across Cities

Generators targeted toward end users are simple to employ. They produce the code mostly from a specification of the structure of files and databases and from the given layouts of screens and reports. The requisite processing is specified in terms natural to the end users. A screen-painting facility makes it possible to specify the graphical user interface for the system under development. For example, EASEL (by Interactive Images) is a development environment for rapid building of graphical user interfaces. It runs on microcomputers and permits the creation of colorful, windowed interfaces for executive information systems, shop floors, or information kiosks.

More powerful application generators are meant for use by information systems professionals. They often may run on mainframes and minicomputers. Some of the tools may be considered very high-level languages which permit a very concise procedural specification of the task. End-user 4GLs are generally targeted to a limited application domain, while those for IS professionals are general-purpose tools. Application generators are increasingly integrated into computer-aided software engineering (CASE) environments, which we shall discuss in Section 16.8.

5.6 | OBJECT-ORIENTED PROGRAMMING

A new way of looking at the world drives much of the computing developments in the 1990s. This new paradigm is called object orientation. Object-oriented languages and extensions of traditional languages support this paradigm. The idea of **object-oriented programming (OOP)** is to build programs of software objects, with these objects communicating—and accomplishing their task—by sending messages to each other. The software objects contain data and instructions that work with these data: they are said to *encapsulate* their instructions and data. A software object represents a real-world object. By building programs of such objects, we actually model the part of our world that the program supports, whether it's the way we manage our human resources or the way we process an insurance policy. Since the objects in our organizational domain are relatively permanent, object-oriented programming extends the promise of software reuse. We can build up libraries of object code and use them as needed in the future.

Three fundamental concepts of object-oriented programming are objects, classes, and inheritance. **Objects** are the basic components of which programs are built; you may think of them as variables that know how to manipulate themselves. Such an object may represent an employee or an insurance policy. This is because an object includes not only its attributes, but also the applicable operations (called methods). Actually, most of the programming is done by specifying the classes of objects to be used in a system. A **class** is a template from which objects are created. Much of the power of OOP rests in **inheritance.** Classes can be defined in a hierarchy, with classes lower in the hierarchy inheriting properties (attributes and methods) of those higher in it. This property saves much programming since, in effect, inheriting properties means reusing the code that implements them.

You may see a class hierarchy shown in Figure 5.16a. Here, subclasses Salesperson and Engineer inherit from their superclass Employee all the attributes (such as Name or Skills) and methods (such as Give_Raise or Assign_To_Team). However, in addition, the class Salesperson also has an attribute Quota and method Assign_Territory, and Engineer has an attribute Licenses. The subclass Salesperson is a subclass of Sales_Manager, since a sales manager is a specialization of a salesperson: Note that this hierarchy is different from the organizational one! This subclass inherits both from Employee and Salesperson and, in addition, includes the method Summarize_Accounts. The actual properties of the class Sales_Manager, obtained in large part through inheritance, are shown in Figure 5.16b.

Inheritance is not limited to simple identity. A subclass definition may override and redefine various features of its superclass (for example, Assign_Territory may be defined differently for Salesperson and for Sales_Manager). The inheritance relation is known as an "is-a" relation: A Sales manager is a Salesperson but, in addition, has other properties.

Having defined, or reused from a prior definition, the above classes in our program, we can define objects (e.g., John Lee) as instances of these classes (e.g., an Engineer), and use the objects by sending messages that activate their methods (e.g., Assign_To_Team).

Traditional programming separates the data from the operations that act on them. In object-oriented programming, objects combine (encapsulate) the data with the operations that act on the data. Consider a list of items. In traditional programming, the list is passive: Any program that works with the list contains the procedures (operations) for maintaining it, such as accessing an item, inserting, deleting, or changing a value of an item. In OOP, the object list is implemented by encapsulating the operations (methods) for manipulating the list together with the list. A program working with the list asks the list, by sending a message to it, to perform an appropriate operation on itself. The integrity of an object is preserved by the fact that its representation and applicable operations, once implemented, are not changed and are used uniformly by other objects.

Figure 5.16

A class hierarchy and inheritance

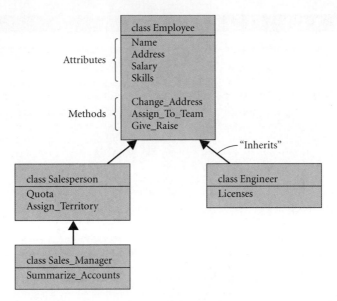

(a) A class Hierarchy

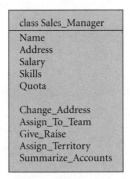

(b) The Properties of the class Sales_Manager, as the Result of Inheritance

Under OOP, we accumulate in a software library the code for higher-level classes (e.g., Employee, Account, Inventory_Item) and reuse this code by deriving (specializing) subclasses we need. Then, we build an application by connecting instances of these classes, which are our objects.

Object-oriented technology includes specialized programming languages such as Smalltalk, C++, or Java; object-oriented usage of more traditional languages such as Ada; object-oriented analysis and design of systems (which we discuss in Section 16.8); and object-oriented databases (discussed in Section 6.11). Object-oriented languages support class definition and inheritance, creating objects as instance of classes, sending messages to the methods in these objects during program execution, and other features of OOP. Object-oriented programming simplifies design of multimedia systems and of graphical user interfaces (GUI). GUI, in turn, make it simpler to develop object-oriented systems by using **visual programming**—rapidly building applications that are themselves GUI-oriented with drag-and-drop programming. By using (dragging with the mouse and dropping into the appropriate place in the program) software objects provided with packages and, if desired, adding one's own, the user can rapidly build up a program from prefabricated components. You will see some of the uses of visual programming in the following vignette.

Uses for Visual Programming

The tool you choose for visual programming depends on what you want to do. Simple applications can be developed with a visual programming product such as ProdeaSynergy from Prodea of Eden Prairie, Minnesota. This software package lets you automate the flow of information between off-the-shelf personal productivity packages, without going into the details of how they work.

For example, by moving icons on the screen for about an hour, you can create an application that (1) downloads the quotes for your company stock from the CompuServe online information service, (2) downloads your corporate sales data from your Microsoft Access database, (3) flows both sets of data to a Novell Quattro Pro spreadsheet to correlate the stock swings with the variations in sales by territory, (4) represents the correlated data as graphs with Lotus Freelance, and (5) uses Delrina WINFax to fax the results to your board of directors.

More complicated applications may be built with two Microsoft products, Visual Basic or Visual C++. Actually, working with Visual C++ involves a lot of traditional code-writing. You can create objects with Visual C++ and then use Visual Basic to interconnect them in a drag-and-drop fashion in your application.

For example, Bankers Trust is using Visual Basic to interconnect existing software objects for an application that manages large investment portfolios. The bank finds that a large new application can be developed in a few weeks. Sun Hydraulics has to create an application that tracks the inventory of machinery and navigates the parts catalog. By selecting a visual-programming tool for the job, the company wanted not only to shorten development time but also give the end users an ability to modify the application. Harley-Davidson is creating a trademark tracking program to track licensed products, such as leather jackets or T-shirts with the firm's logo. Built with the use of Visual Basic and a user-friendly database management system called Q&E from Pioneer Software, the application will enable the company to file and locate data and documents, such as contracts.

An ambitious project at Intrust Bank, N.A. has been initiated with Visual AppBuilder from Novell. With ever new services provided by banks, Intrust finds it difficult to give a customer the total status of his or her account. The bank intends to integrate all the accounts of a given customer, including holdings in mutual funds and securities. According to a consultant, the project can be placed "somewhere between the leading and the bleeding edge so far as object technology is concerned." The bank is aware of the risk, but considers the project a worthwhile learning experience.

Based on Andy Kessler, "Fire Your Software Programmers—Again," *Forbes ASAP,* September 1994, p. 23; and Joseph C. Panettieri, "Putting Trust in AppWare," *InformationWeek,* July 4, 1994, pp. 70–73.

SUMMARY

Software controls the operation of computer systems and makes hardware useful. There are two large categories of software: systems software and applications software. Systems software manages the resources of a computer system and facilitates translation of programs written in programming languages. Applications software directly assists end users in their work.

The operating system is the principal instance of systems software. It controls all of the resources of a computer system and provides the user–system interface. The operating system enables multiple programs to run at the same time. Most operating systems also provide virtual memory by storing the currently unused parts of programs and their data in secondary storage and calling them in as required for execution. As required for the given installation, operating systems make possible batch processing, time sharing, and real-time processing.

Personal productivity software supports data management and analysis, authoring and presentation, and activity and notes tracking. All these are software applications. Data management is supported by database management systems, while spreadsheet software assists in data analysis. For the needs of authoring and presentation, users employ the applications software for word processing, desktop publishing, presentation, and multimedia authoring. Personal information management software is used to track activities and personal notes. Communications software enables the user to connect to a telecommunications network in order to exchange information with other users or systems. Web browsers are used to access the resources of the Internet's World Wide Web.

Much of the applications software used in an organization needs to be programmed or customized. Programming languages for the task have evolved over four generations. The first generation, that of machine languages, is no longer used for programming. The languages of the second generation, known as assembly languages, are sometimes used for systems programming. Most programming is done, however, in the procedural high-level languages of the third generation and in the nonprocedural fourth-generation languages (4GLs).

A variety of procedural high-level languages permit the programmer to specify in detail the procedure for obtaining the desired results. This detailed specification is the program. Such a program has to be translated in its entirety by a compiler, or translated and executed statement by statement by an interpreter. The nonprocedural 4GLs, whose domain of applications is more limited than that of the procedural languages, make it possible to specify what is to be done by the computer system, rather than how to do it. This saves human resources and enables faster applications development.

Fourth-generation languages include query languages, report generators, and application generators. Query languages make it possible to retrieve data directly from databases, without a need for programming. Most of these languages are simple enough for an end user to employ. Report generators enable end users or information systems professionals to produce reports with very brief programs. Application generators, many of which are designed for use by IS professionals, make it possible to specify an entire application consisting of several programs without much detailed coding.

Object-oriented programming, a very important direction in today's software development, consists in building programs of software objects that communicate with each other. Classes of objects are created and accumulated in a software library of an organization. These classes may be reused in future systems, to economize programming effort and to enhance the quality of information systems, built of field-tested components.

KEY TERMS

QUESTIONS

1. What is the relationship between the information system software and its hardware?

2. What is the difference between systems software and applications software? What is the difference between vertical and horizontal applications packages? How would you classify with respect to these two characteristics the software marketed as:

   a. computer-virus detection software

   b. sales-management software for dog-grooming parlors

3. What is an operating system? What is the multiprogramming capability in these systems?

4. What is virtual memory? Why is it called "virtual"? What capabilities does it offer in a computer system?

5. Compare and contrast the objectives of batch processing, time sharing, and real-time processing.

6. What are the differences among multitasking, multiprogramming, and multiprocessing?

7. What is a graphical user interface (GUI)?

8. Why are open systems important to most users?

9. State the four general functions supported by personal productivity software. For each function, state the categories of packages that help their users carry out the function. Describe in one sentence what each of the package categories does.

10. What are the comparative strengths of spreadsheet and database management software?

11. How do packages for personal information management compare with database management packages? Describe a scenario in which each would be used.

12. Describe a scenario for using each of the categories of authoring and presentation packages.

13. What are the principal features of each of the four generations of programming languages? What is the advance over the previous generation?

14. What are the differences between the compiler, the interpreter, and the assembler?

15. What are the advantages and disadvantages of 4GLs as compared to high-level languages? Give two examples of projects that should *not* be programmed in 4GL.

16. What are the three categories of fourth-generation languages? How does each of these categories support end-user computing (if at all)?

17. What is the principal idea of object-oriented programming (OOP)? How does this technology relate to software reuse?

18. Which high-level languages support object-oriented programming?

19. What is an object and a class in OOP?

20. What is visual programming? What are its advantages and drawbacks?

ISSUES FOR DISCUSSION

1. Over time, the cost of software in organizational computing has become much higher than the cost of hardware, reversing their original relationship. What trends do you believe have contributed to this? What do you think will happen in the future to the relative costs of hardware and software and why?

2. What do you believe the role of end-user computing will be in the future organizational computing?

3. What general trends can you discern in the evolution of programming languages from the first generation onward?

4. Should the vendor be able to own the "look and feel" of the software it developed?

PROBLEM-SOLVING EXERCISES

1. What you see in Figure 5.17 is an "infoimage," an executable program file that can be sent by fax. Infoimaging Technologies in Palo Alto, California, markets 3D Fax

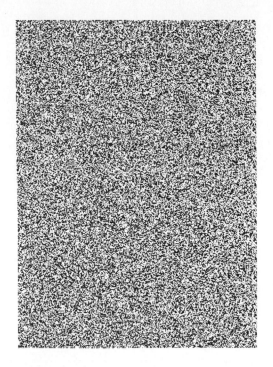

Figure 5.17

This encoded "infoimage" of an executable program file can be faxed to a remote site (From "This Isn't a Test Pattern," *Computerworld*, February 26, 1996, p. 4.)

Software, which compresses executable files and encodes them into a two-dimensional black-and-white pattern (the technology is proprietary).

The image can be then sent from one PC fax modem to a remote one, or it can be printed and sent to another fax machine, with the recipient scanning it into a PC. The recipient's software restores the file to its original format, including color pictures and multimedia clips, if contained in the original file.

a. How can the "infoimage" idea be deployed to produce business results? Produce two scenarios and state the potential advantages of the approach over the traditional methods.

b. What other uses than sending executable files over fax can "infoimage" be put to?

Based on "This Isn't a Test Pattern," *Computerworld*, February 26, 1996, p. 4.

2. Investigate the differences between the object-oriented languages available in the marketplace. Consider their generality, the intended user (the IS professional versus the end user), ease of use, efficiency in terms of consumption of the computer system resources (such as the main memory and secondary storage) and in terms of the running speed of programs, availability of software supporting applications development, acquisition cost, and other variables you care to define. Describe how widely a given object-oriented language is used and, for specialized languages, identify their application niche. Business and personal computing periodicals listed in Table 1.4, as well as a number of Web sites (which you should identify) will be of help.

3. Several programming teams in your firm have been using object-oriented programming (OOP) for some time. You have been asked to organize a software reuse initiative for your company, based on the principles of OOP. Write an extensive memo, outlining the specific actions that will need to be undertaken to start this program. Precede your memo with an executive summary that summarizes your findings in about half a page.

TEAM PROJECT

Each two- or three-person team should select a category of personal productivity software and read a review of these packages in a recent periodical. The teams should summarize and present the features of this category to the class. The teams should discuss how the category is evolving, that is, what features are being added by the vendors. They should also make a projection for further evolution. The class should decide which categories of personal productivity software seem to be blending together.

SELECTED REFERENCES

Avison, D. E., and H. U. Shah. "From Third Generation to Fourth Generation Applications Development: A Case Study." *Information Technology and People*, 6, no. 4, 1994, pp. 233–248.

Moving to the development of information systems in a 4GL.

Booch, Grady. *Object-Oriented Analysis and Design with Applications,* 2nd ed. Redwood City, Calif.: Benjamin/Cummings, 1994.

Contains an excellent explanation of the concepts of object-oriented programming.

Drips, Michael. "Windows Development Tools That Work," *Datamation,* May 1, 1996, pp. 36–39.

Korson, Tim, and John D. McGregor. "Understanding Object-Oriented: A Unifying Paradigm." *Communications of the ACM,* 33, no. 9 (September 1990), pp. 40–60.

Explains what object orientation is about.

Nutt, Gary J. *Open Systems,* Englewood Cliffs, N. J.: Prentice Hall, 1992.

Pratt, Terrence W., and Marvin V. Zelkowitz. *Programming Languages: Design and Implementation,* 3rd ed., Upper Saddle River, N.J.: Prentice Hall, 1996.

A textbook on programming languages and their translators.

Regan, Elizabeth A., and Bridget N. O'Connor. *End-User Information Systems: Perspectives for Managers and Information Systems Professionals,* New York: Macmillan, 1994.

Contains a thorough review of personal productivity software.

Salamone, Salvatore, ed. "Making Multimedia Happen." Special Section, *Byte,* March 1996, pp. 65–90.

Seachrist, David. "How Multimedia Multitools Compare." *Byte,* November 1996, pp. 122–126.

A good comparison of tools for multimedia development.

Sweet, Lisa L. "Creating the Perfect World." *ZD Internet Magazine,* March 1997, pp. 47–56.

Tanenbaum, Andrew S., and Albert S. Woodhull. *Operating Systems: Design and Implementation,* 2nd. ed., Upper Saddle River, N.J.: Prentice Hall, 1997.

A modern textbook that offers a listing of a complete operating system.

Wojtkowski, W. Gregory, and Wita Wojtkowski. *Applications Software Programming with Fourth-Generation Languages,* Boston: Boyd & Fraser, 1990.

A thorough practical text on using 4GLs.

Zwass, Vladimir. "Computer Science." *Encyclopaedia Britannica,* Macropaedia, Vol. XVI, pp. 629–637.

Provides a concise overview of the subject.

General note on references: consult the recent issues of PC-oriented periodicals.

CASE STUDY | A Multimedia System for Jewelry Appraisal

A piece of jewelry has relatively high market value—but so do its components. When a piece is unsalable, should the jeweler try to lower the price or break it up? This is, in a nutshell, the problem that Zale Corporation faced. Actually, for the world's largest jewelry retailer, with annual revenues of over $1 billion and 568 stores, the problem was magnified manyfold.

Each year, the jewelry processing center at the firm's headquarters in Irving, Texas, receives about 300,000 unsalable pieces of discontinued, damaged, or repossessed jewelry from its 1,500 stores. In the past, Zale would periodically ship these goods to a local smelter, to be melted down in acid baths. The smelter would return to Zale a payment for the gold it recovered and the glass bottles containing the gem stones retrieved from the jewelry. A bottle may contain some two million dollars worth of diamonds. The gems were then sold in large batches through brokers, without regard for their individual value.

The firm perceived an opportunity (a problem in disguise). Since the value of melted-down jewelry is far lower than its original cost and the damage was frequently very minor, significant losses were taking place. Zale had to take the smelter's recovered value at that firm's word; the retailer had no way to control the recovery. Also, Zale frequently needed specific stones for customer repairs and to satisfy insurance claims. The firm would buy the stones and pay finder's fees to brokers. Recovered gemstones could be used instead. Pieces with slight damage could be refurbished.

One solution to the problem would be to have each piece appraised by a gemologist. However, a careful gemologist can appraise only 25 pieces a day. Therefore, the traditional appraisal would not be cost-effective for a high-volume operation.

The adopted solution was to develop a software application for jewelry appraisal, named MEDUSA. The system was supposed to significantly increase the productivity of gemologists. Three design criteria were identified: (1) allow the gemologist's hands and eyes to be used only for evaluating jewelry; (2) eliminate the need to evaluate every item as much as possible; (3) provide as much automated support as possible for the appraiser's decision making.

The requirements naturally led the implementers to a multimedia system. The system was implemented on a local area network (LAN) of personal computers. Here is how the application works.

The personnel at the store that is sending an item to Zale headquarters enters the transaction through its point-of-sale system, which is reflected in the central database maintained in Irving. When the piece is received in the processing center, an identifying bar code is affixed to it. For multiple items of the same kind, the quantity is verified. Items are sorted into common categories by an auditor (e.g., watches, gold jewelry with stones, etc.) to await the evaluation by the MEDUSA-supported gemologist.

The jewelry evaluation subsystem of MEDUSA is the most interesting one (see Figure 5.18). To satisfy the requirement of keeping the gemologist's hands and eyes only on jewelry, voice recognition technology is deployed. The appraiser uses a lightweight microphone headset plugged into a voice processing card of the PC. Digital calipers and a sensitive digital scale, used to measure and weigh the jewelry, are also connected to the PC via serial ports. The item is identified by its bar-code label, scanned in by an appraiser with a laser scanner. A bar-code label printer can create a label for the repair that the appraiser prescribes.

To meet the second requirement, eliminating the need to evaluate every item, the gemologist can access over the LAN the previously installed MIDAS information system, which contains the specification for all items that originated as Zale's own inventory. A complete specification comes on screen for such items, and the gemologist can modify it if, for example, one of the stones is missing. To confirm the evaluation, the gemologist retrieves from MIDAS and displays a full-color image of the item.

Figure 5.18

An overview of the jewelry appraisal system MEDUSA (Adapted from Julie Newman and Kenneth A. Kozar, "A Multimedia Solution to Productivity Gridlock: A Re-Engineered Jewelry Appraisal System at Zale Corporation," *MIS Quarterly,* March 1994, pp. 21–30.)

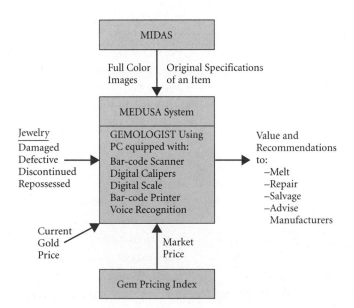

If the item did not originate at Zale, a complete evaluation is necessary. The script for the evaluation of a pendant with a single diamond is shown in Figure 5.19. The software approximates the depth of the stone from its shape, length, and width; it also approximates the weight of the mounted stone from its dimensions. The application uses the quality of the diamond (note the codes for color and quality entered by the appraiser) to estimate its current market price, employing a gem pricing index, downloaded to the system weekly. To calculate the value of gold, the current market price is provided.

The appraiser either accepts the values calculated by the application by saying "End," or speaks out a new value, digit by digit, followed by "End." The total melt, or salvage, value is displayed for the appraiser's approval. An experienced user can turn off the audio prompts and reduce the time during which the recognizer is listening for a valid vocabulary word.

The application not only supports the appraiser's decision making during the evaluation, but also helps with the disposition by displaying the cost of necessary repairs and a possible retail price.

Figure 5.19

A script of a voice-supported appraisal system (From Julie Newman and Kenneth A. Kozar, "A Multimedia Solution to Productivity Gridlock: A Re-Engineered Jewelry Appraisal System at Zale Corporation," *MIS Quarterly*, March 1994, pp. 21–30.)

MEDUSA PROMPTS:	USER SAYS:	SCREEN DISPLAYS:
Type?	"Pendant"	Pendant
Metal?	"Gold"	
Karat?	"Fourteen"	14K
Weight?	(Puts pendant on scale) and says, "Read."	2.32 gm
Stones?	"Yes"	
Type?	"Diamond"	Diamond
Shape?	"Oval"	Oval
Quantity?	"One"	1
Color	"H"	H
Clarity?	"SI2"	SI2
Length?	User measures length with caliper and says, "Read."	10.5mm
Width?	User measures width with caliper and says, "Read."	6.60mm
Depth?	"End," to accept the system calculated value.*	3.79mm
Carat?	"End," to accept the system calculated value.*	1.55ct
Value?	"End," to accept the system calculated value.*	$4,050.00
Type?	"Continue," to indicate that there are no more stones.	
Melt Value?	"End," to accept the system calculated value.*	$4,051.26
Disposition?	"Liquidation"	Liquidation

*The application now returns to the "Enter bar code" prompt.

Speaker-independent voice recognition, with a vocabulary of 127 words, was used. To create the vocabulary, 40 male and female volunteers recorded each of the words. The voice-recognition software was run in the training mode, based on the composite of all the 40 samples of each word. Moreover, the software is adaptive—it learns from its mistakes, with performance improving over time. Accuracy rate of over 99 percent was reached.

After two years of use, the system has accumulated data about Zale's inventory of unsalable jewelry. Asset management is vastly improved. The managers now know the value of each commodity (such as gold or diamonds) in each of the disposition categories. They can respond to market conditions by changing the disposition of a certain category. For example, if the price of gold goes up, the items designated for repair can be designated for meltdown, and, moreover, Zale can verify that the smelter pays for the correct amount of the commodity. When specific gems (say, 0.25 carat diamonds) are needed, they can be drawn from the maintained inventory.

The corporation is now in a position to improve the quality of its merchandise by identifying chronically defective products and notifying the manufacturers about the defects.

The application has been very well received by its end users, the gemologists. The user-system interface was found easy and flexible. The system frees the users to concentrate on the creative aspects of their work, without the need for computations and other routine activities done by the computers. The users found they could increase both the productivity (it went up 600 percent) and the quality of their work. Moreover, "driving" a multimedia system that is unique in the industry contributes to the level of user satisfaction. The direct financial benefit to the firm is measured in several millions of dollars per year, with more gains accruing to the improved control and asset management.

Based on Julie Newman and Kenneth A. Kozar, "A Multimedia Solution to Productivity Gridlock: A Re-Engineered Jewelry Appraisal System at Zale Corporation," *MIS Quarterly,* March 1994, pp. 21–30; and Robert Hurtado, "Market Place," *The New York Times,* May 2, 1996, p. D12.

CASE STUDY QUESTIONS

1. State all aspects of the problem to be solved at Zale Corporation.
2. Why was the development of a computerized application the adopted solution?
3. What were the principal requirements for the application system?
4. How did these principal requirements lead to the system features?
5. What were the benefits realized with MEDUSA?
6. This is an application used to compete and, naturally, certain details are not available. Do you believe the application could be developed with an end-user oriented 4GL? Why or why not?
7. How would you classify the MEDUSA system using the categories of information systems shown in Figure 1.1?

CHAPTER SIX

Database Management

OBJECTIVES

After you complete this chapter, you will be able to:

1. Specify the elements of the data hierarchy.
2. Understand what can be accomplished with files and what the limitations of a file-based environment are.
3. Understand the advantages of a database environment and the role of a database management system (DBMS).
4. Specify the three levels at which data are defined in databases.
5. Compare the three data models.
6. Understand the operation of relational databases and their query language SQL.
7. Understand the role of the data dictionary.
8. Explain the components of information resource management.
9. Describe the developmental trends in database management, including distributed databases, data warehouses, and object-oriented and other rich databases.

OUTLINE

Focus Minicase. Database Marketing

6.1 Hierarchy of Data

6.2 File Environment and Its Limitations

6.3 Database Environment

6.4 Levels of Data Definition in Databases

6.5 Data Models or How To Represent Relationships between Data

6.6 Relational Databases

6.7 SQL—A Relational Query Language

6.8 Designing a Relational Database

6.9 The Data Dictionary

6.10 Managing the Data Resource of an Organization

6.11 Developmental Trends in Database Management

Case Study. Database for Global Customer Service at the Shipper's Core

Database Marketing

There are several names for the new technology of persuasion: database marketing, relationship marketing, one-to-one marketing, or precision marketing. The meaning is the same. In their databases, companies are collecting huge volumes of detailed data about your buying behavior. These data can be combined with the personal data about you available from public records. By processing the resulting database, marketers can gain information about the likelihood of your buying a specific product. Moreover, the database will help its owners craft a marketing message precisely worded to get you to do so. How about this: "It may not be celebrated as a national holiday, but it's a pretty big deal around here. Happy birthday from the Claridge Casino Hotel, Atlantic City!" Yes, the casino does send such messages.

Actually, many companies assemble two kinds of marketing databases. Along with assembling the databases of prospective consumers, these firms establish databases of the actual purchasers of their products. Marketing software draws on the purchaser databases to identify the model consumer for each product, based on the common characteristics of high-volume buyers. Next, using the large databases of prospective consumers, clusters of people who share the purchasers' characteristics are identified as targets for marketing efforts and for the development of new products. The purchaser databases are continually updated with the data coming from point-of-sale scanners, product-oriented clubs, Internet Web sites, responses to coupons, and sweepstakes entries.

Coopers & Lybrand, the accounting firm, estimates that it costs three to five times as much to acquire a new customer than to keep a present one. Therefore, purchaser databases are used to cement relationships with the existing customers. For example, Kraft General Foods has accumulated a database of more than 30 million users of its products who have sent in their coupons or responded to other promotions. The company regularly sends them nutrition tips and coupons for specific brands. The marketers at Kraft believe that the more the consumers know about the product, the likelier they are to use more of it. Harley-Davidson wants to urge its customers to use their motorcycles and so mails a bimonthly magazine to 256,000 "hog" owners showcasing events they can attend. Seagram uses its 10-million-name database to create loyalty-building programs for existing products; Philip Morris has a 26-million-name database of smokers the company can reach directly—an advantage to the firm, considering the existing restrictions on tobacco advertising. Marketers recognize that past customer behavior, reflected in customer databases, is the best predictor of future buying patterns. This is why marketers wish to move from expensive and low-yielding broadcasting of their advertising message to a dialogue with carefully selected consumers, now often conducted over the Internet. Indeed, some database marketers garner a double-digit response rate to their promotions—compare that with the typical 2 to 4 percent response to mass marketing.

Privacy concerns accompany database marketing, and there are horror stories. Nynex, a regional telephone company, mailed several million circulars to customers, urging them to use their calling cards. Customers' personal identification numbers, or PINs, were printed on the mailers, which lacked envelopes. Such relationship marketing results in eroded relationships. But change has already occurred: Instead of your local salespeople, it is the growing databases that seem to know what you need.

As database computing proliferates, the need for secondary storage devices is skyrocketing. The growth of the storage market outstrips severalfold the growth of the sales of PCs and other computers. "Computers are becoming a sidelight to the data ware-houses," says Jerry Higgins, who manages a database of 21 trillion bytes at Nynex.

Based on Jonathan Berry, "Database Marketing: A Potent New Tool for Selling," *Business Week,* September 2, 1994; Regis McKenna, "Real-Time Marketing," *Harvard Business Review,* July–August 1995, pp. 87–95; Audrey Choi, "Storage Devices Take Spotlight in Computer Industry," *The Wall Street Journal,* April 22, 1996, p. B4; Sarah Varney, "Database Marketing Predicts Customer Loyalty," *Datamation,* September 1996, pp. 50–68.

Data are a principal asset of a modern organization. You have read how databases have become a potent tool in competing for customers' attention and holding it for a long time. Most business decisions are based on information from corporate databases; therefore, management of data as a resource from which operational efficiency, management effectiveness, and competitive advantage flow is an important organizational objective. The essential technological tool for accomplishing this is a database management system (DBMS) that maintains data in integrated databases and provides controlled access to the data.

6.1 | HIERARCHY OF DATA

Data are a principal resource of an organization. By storing organized collections of corporate data, you can answer customers' questions about their orders; you can identify your most reliable suppliers; and you can derive information to make decisions regarding the volume of future purchasing. Data stored in computer systems form a hierarchy extending from a single bit to a database, the major record-keeping entity of a firm. Each higher rung of this hierarchy, as shown in Figure 6.1, is organized from the components below it.

The smallest unit of data representation in a computer system is a **bit,** whose value may be 0 or 1. Eights bits make a **byte** which can represent a character or a special symbol in a character code, as we discussed in Chapter 4. Bits and bytes are *physical* units of data representation: They reflect the way computer storage is designed. The higher rungs of the data hierarchy are *logical:* They deal with the real-world objects the data represent.

The smallest named unit of data is a **field.** For example, the name of a supplier company in a supplier database is a single field, since we will never break that supplier's name down into smaller parts. On the other hand, a supplier's address may be broken down in the database into four fields: street address, town, state, and zip code. Such separation may be useful. Thus, in some applications we would like to identify all suppliers in a certain city; in other applications we may want to sort the suppliers by zip code. We may then conclude that data organization depends on what use we want to put the data to.

A **record** describes a real-world entity. This entity may be tangible, such as a supplier, or intangible, such as a shipment. A record consists of fields, with each field describing an attribute of the entity. This is why we sometimes refer to fields as attributes. For example, the name of a supplier could be an attribute.

Records of the same type, that is, describing the same type of entities, are aggregated into a **file.** (We deal largely with data files in this chapter; a file is, of course, also a broader term for any named unit of information stored in secondary storage; thus, we may have a text file or a program file.) A supplier file would contain records of all of our suppliers. Generally, a field in the file identifies a record so that we can access a needed record by presenting this identifier. This identifier field is called the **primary key** of the file. For example, supplier number may be the primary key of the supplier file. Sometimes, the key must consist of more than one field to ensure a unique identification. In certain applications, files remain the highest organizational component of persistent, that is, continually maintained, data.

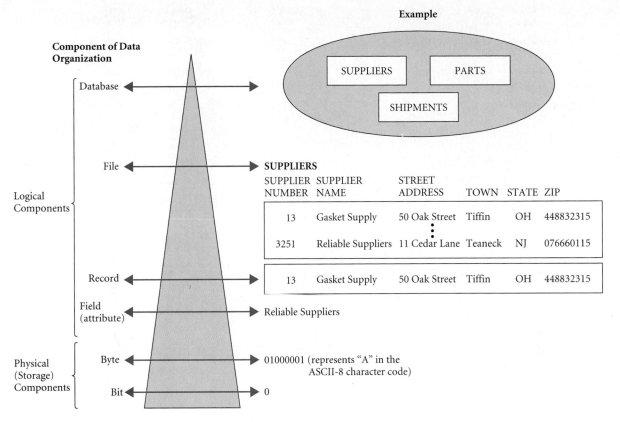

Example

Component of Data Organization

Database

SUPPLIERS   PARTS

SHIPMENTS

File   **SUPPLIERS**

SUPPLIER NUMBER	SUPPLIER NAME	STREET ADDRESS	TOWN	STATE	ZIP
13	Gasket Supply	50 Oak Street	Tiffin	OH	448832315
3251	Reliable Suppliers	11 Cedar Lane	Teaneck	NJ	076660115

Logical Components

Record

| 13 | Gasket Supply | 50 Oak Street | Tiffin | OH | 448832315 |

Field (attribute)   Reliable Suppliers

Physical (Storage) Components

Byte   01000001 (represents "A" in the ASCII-8 character code)

Bit   0

Figure 6.1

Hierarchy of data organization in computer storage (From Vladimir Zwass, *Management Information Systems,* Dubuque IA: Wm. C. Brown, 1992, p. 287.)

In today's information systems, files most often exist as parts of **databases,** or organized collections of interrelated data, managed by systems software called database management systems (DBMS). In Figure 6.1, we show a database that maintains records of suppliers, the parts they supply, and part shipments in progress. The crucial advantage of databases as compared with a collection of files is that, aside from storing the records of individual files, databases also store relationships among these records. In the next section we will describe the broader advantages of the database environment as opposed to a file-oriented environment.

Files and databases are maintained in secondary storage. Database management requires direct access to records, and databases are therefore stored on disks (with tapes often used for backup). We will first discuss rather briefly the organization of data files and then focus on the database environment. The concepts of file organization apply to the physical storage of data in databases; that is, the way data are actually stored on a disk.

6.2 | FILE ENVIRONMENT AND ITS LIMITATIONS

There are three principal methods of organizing files, of which only two provide the direct access necessary in on-line systems. File management systems are used to access records in a file environment. The file-oriented approach may be cheaper for simple applications than managing a database. However, we will see that a file-oriented environment suffers from very significant limitations that make it unsuitable as an organizing principle for an enterprise's data.

	File Organization	Access Method	Environment of Application	Advantages	Disadvantages
Table 6.1 *File organization methods and their applications*	Sequential	Sequential	Batch	Simplicity of management; efficient use of storage; may be placed on cheap storage (tape).	Insertions and updates usually impossible without creating a new file; general disadvantages of batch processing.
	Indexed-sequential	Sequential or direct (random)	Batch or on-line	Relatively good storage utilization; both access modes are possible.	Space for indexes and time for their maintenance; slow direct access to large files. Periodic file reorganization is necessary.
	Direct (random)	Direct (random)	On-line	Fast direct access.	Relatively poor space utilization; difficult to use when records are needed in sequence.

File Organization

Data files are organized so as to facilitate access to records and to ensure their efficient storage. A trade-off between these two requirements generally exists: If rapid access is required, more storage must be expended to make it possible (for example, by providing indexes to the data records).

Access to a record for reading it (and sometimes updating it) is the essential operation on data. As we mentioned in Chapter 4 when discussing the secondary storage devices where files are kept, there are two types of access: sequential and direct. **Sequential access** is performed when records are accessed in the order they are stored. Sequential access is the main access mode only in batch systems, where files are used and updated at regular intervals (for example, every night or every week). A payroll file may serve as an example of a file that can be processed sequentially. Such a file is updated periodically, to reflect, for example, hirings and separations of employees. In the interim, the contents of the master file, that is, the main data file used for transaction processing, do not reflect changes that have taken place since the last update. The records that reflect these changes are kept in a transaction file, used to update the master file.

On-line processing requires **direct access** (also called random access), whereby a record can be accessed without accessing the records stored between it and the beginning of the file. The primary key serves to identify the needed record. A direct access storage device, such as a magnetic disk, is required for direct access.

Three methods of file organization are in predominant use and are supported by operating systems with so-called access method routines. These methods—sequential, indexed-sequential, and direct organization—are summarized in Table 6.1. We will now proceed to discuss them in more detail.

Figure 6.2

A sequential file

SOCIAL SECURITY NUMBER	NAME	WEEKLY SALARY	DEPARTMENT
011731391	John A. Weeks	525	Manufacturing
231426182	Gilbert Lee	650	Personnel
452398651	Andrew L. Boyd	550	Manufacturing
•			
•			
•			

Figure 6.3

Indexes of an indexed sequential file

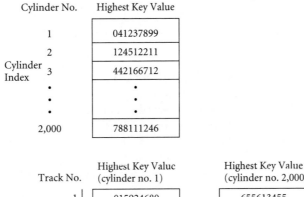

The disk has 2,000 cylinders and 20 surfaces (40,000 tracks).

1. Sequential Organization

Sequential file organization is the simplest: File records are stored in the sequence of the values of their primary keys. Thus, in Figure 6.2, human-resource records are stored in ascending order of employees' Social Security numbers.

Efficient use of sequential files requires that a large number of records be accessed during a run, which is typical in a batch system. All update transactions, such as deletions, insertions, and modifications of field values, are accumulated over a period of time in a transaction file. Then, the transaction file is sorted in the same primary key sequence as the master file, and finally run off against the master to create a new master file. You will see the use of such a file in a transaction processing system in Chapter 9 (Figure 9.2).

2. Indexed-Sequential Organization

In **indexed-sequential files,** records are also stored in their primary key sequence, which makes possible efficient sequential access. This type of access may be needed, for example, for detailed reporting from the file. In addition, to provide direct access, indexes to the file are maintained. We may, for example, organize a human resources file to ensure sequential access in order to run off the payroll and yet to be able to access an employee's record directly to see his or her salary.

File *indexes* are tables, generally also stored as files, that show where the file records are located in secondary storage. One way to organize such indexes is illustrated in Figure 6.3.

Figure 6.4

A hashing procedure

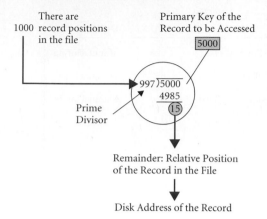

This is the way indexes are organized in the popular Indexed Sequential Access Method (ISAM) provided by IBM software.

As we discussed in Chapter 4, records are placed on a disk, cylinder by cylinder, in their key sequence. They are located on consecutive tracks of a given cylinder, that is, on consecutive disk surfaces. The index of Figure 6.3 has, therefore, a hierarchical structure, with the highest values of the key on a given track or cylinder placed in the index. When a record is being accessed, first the cylinder index is used to find the record's cylinder. Then, the track index for that cylinder is consulted, and the track itself is searched for the record.

Insertions are usually made into a special overflow area of the disk, with a pointer to that record placed in the track where the record belongs. Periodically, the file is reorganized in order to merge the records from the overflow area into the main (prime) area of the file.

3. Direct Organization

Direct file organization provides the fastest direct access to records. No indexes are maintained in this case. Instead, the primary key of a record is transformed directly into its disk address. A *hashing* algorithm computes the address where the record is to be stored directly from the primary key of the record. When the record is accessed in the future, the same hashing procedure will be used to find it. The intent of hashing is to spread records uniformly over the space allocated for the file.

A popular hashing procedure is the division–remainder method illustrated in Figure 6.4. In this hashing technique, the key is divided by the prime number closest to (but smaller than) the number of record positions available in the file. The remainder of the division gives us the relative position of the record in the file and is translated into its disk address.

You may note that more than one key may hash into the same storage position on the disk. Thus, in our example, a record with the key 3006 will collide with the record having the key 5000. The number of such collisions is limited, however, because significantly more space is allocated to a direct file than will actually be taken up by the records, and we must remember that hashing spreads records rather uniformly over this space. Still, we need to handle this limited number of collisions. To do so, a pointer to a colliding record, placed elsewhere on the disk, may be placed in a position where it would have been found, had that position not already been taken up by another record.

Limitations of a File-Oriented Environment

Let us step back and take a more general look at the file environment, illustrated by the example in Figure 6.5. As we can see, in this environment each application system relies on its

Figure 6.5

A file-oriented environment

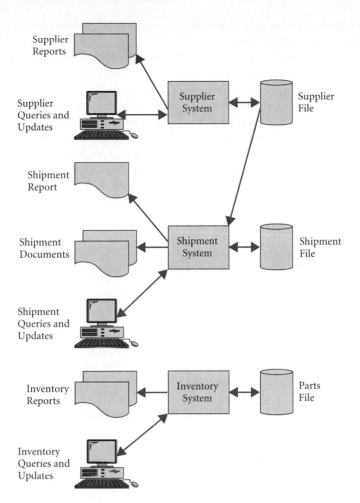

Supplier Reports

Supplier Queries and Updates

Supplier System

Supplier File

Shipment Report

Shipment Documents

Shipment Queries and Updates

Shipment System

Shipment File

Inventory Reports

Inventory Queries and Updates

Inventory System

Parts File

own files. In other words, files are "owned," as it were, by a given application and are specifically designed for the needs of the application. In a scenario that goes with our example, a supplier system was designed to maintain the file of suppliers, while the parts file is maintained by the inventory system to reflect the parts inventory stored in our warehouses in various cities. The shipment system handles shipments in progress of parts by suppliers. Because of the sequence in which the three systems were designed, the shipment program does not have access to the parts file, although it is able to access the supplier file.

If we need a report that would list all suppliers who are currently shipping items whose inventories are below a certain level, additional programming will be necessary. In particular, the shipment system will have to access the parts file. It may turn out that parts are identified in different ways in the parts file and in the shipment file. Therefore, to produce the desired report we would have to modify programs and files. Worse yet, it may turn out that although the shipment file is maintained on-line, the inventory file is updated only every other day. Therefore, the data in the two files are inconsistent.

As we can see, numerous negative consequences result from the file-based approach, particularly when it is used for larger systems. Overall management of the data resource is all but impossible: There is no single source for these data, since files go with individual applications. Sharing data is, therefore, very difficult. Redundant data are maintained for various applications. In our example, the shipment file probably replicates some of the data stored in the parts file, such as current inventory levels. Beyond the high costs of redundancy, the file-based approach results in inconsistencies when file updates are made by one application but not by another.

Files are related to one another by programs rather than by the data themselves. For example, to answer the question, "Has a given supplier delivered all outstanding shipments?" we need to incorporate appropriate programming into either the shipment or the supplier system. Any change in the way the data are represented (for example, when using a longer zip code) will call for program changes. A degree of file sharing among applications further complicates the change process. If the supplier file has to be changed because of the requirements of the supplier system, we will have to change the shipment system accordingly.

As data proliferate in applications-owned files, it becomes ever more difficult to maintain existing applications because of the ripple effect on other systems that would need changing if the specifications of data files change. It also becomes more difficult to develop new applications, because some data must be extracted from the existing files and data redundancy problems will increase further.

Limitations of the file-oriented environment are the reasons why a database environment has to be created to gain organizational control of data.

6.3 | DATABASE ENVIRONMENT

A **database** is an organized collection of interrelated data that supports multiple applications of an enterprise's business process or functional unit. The database stores not only the values of the attributes of various entities but also the relationships between these entities. A database is managed by a **database management system (DBMS),** a systems software that provides assistance in managing databases shared by many users. A DBMS helps organize data for effective access by a variety of users with different access needs and for efficient storage. A DBMS makes it possible to create, access, maintain, and control databases. Thanks to DBMS, data can be integrated and presented on demand.

A database environment is illustrated in Figure 6.6. You may contrast this illustration with Figure 6.5, which illustrates a file-oriented environment.

Figure 6.6

A database environment

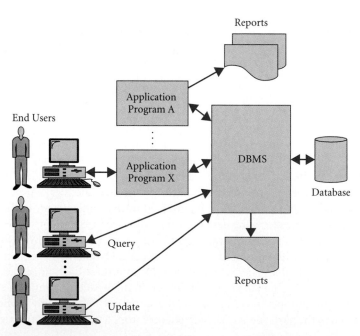

Application programs access the database through the facilities provided by the DBMS, which we discuss in this chapter. End users may access a database either through these application programs or directly, using a query facility. Let us continue with our suppliers–parts–shipments example. A DBMS would control all the data stored in the three files and, by using the relationships between the entities defined in the database itself, could provide information that the individual file-based applications were unable to offer. For example, the management query regarding suppliers shipping parts with current inventories below a certain level could be answered without the need for programming, if the data were managed by a DBMS.

DBMSs for larger machines permit a number of users to work simultaneously on the same database by temporarily locking records being updated by one of the users or applications. A DBMS generally relies on the access methods of an operating system to read and write actual disk records.

The following features of integrating data into databases and controlling them with a DBMS show up the advantages of database management:

1. Avoiding Uncontrolled Data Redundancy and Preventing Inconsistency

Applications share the data stored in a database rather than owning private files that would often store redundant data. This reduces storage costs and there is no need to update multiple copies of the same data. Most important, this prevents the possibility that inconsistent data will reside in multiple files.

2. Program–Data Independence

When the database is managed by a DBMS, programs can be written independently of the actual physical layout of the data or even of the overall logical structure of the data (this is **program-data independence**). DBMS "knows" these structures and can provide the mapping from the data named in a given application to the actual physical items located on the storage device, as discussed later in this chapter. Applications will remain unaffected if the physical layout of the data is changed.

An applications programmer thus deals with relatively simple logical descriptions of data, without having to be concerned with their physical representations. This simplifies the development and maintenance of applications that rely on the database. Overall programming productivity is thus enhanced.

3. Flexible Access to Shared Data

The database approach opens data for access to users and applications. Query languages enable end users to access data directly. Applications can be written to use any data stored in corporate databases, rather than relying only on the files specially created for them. A variety of relationships between data entities may be rather easily defined within the database itself by using a DBMS. Thus, a variety of queries can be answered without the need for programming.

4. Advantages of Centralized Control of Data

The fact that a database may be centrally defined and controlled with the use of a DBMS leads to several vital benefits enabling us to treat the data as a corporate resource. Among these benefits are:

- The data resource can be planned to support the needs of the organization.
- Security can be maintained by specifying with the DBMS who is authorized to access or modify the data. The DBMS, which serves as the means of access to the data (see Figure 6.6), enforces these constraints. These security measures may be employed to protect the privacy of individuals the stored data concern.

• Integrity constraints may be imposed to promote the accuracy of the data in the database. Thus, certain rules may be specified to insure that inaccurate data cannot be entered. Examples of such data validation rules are: "No employee may work more than 80 hours a week" or "Weekly salary of an employee in Purchasing never exceeds $1,000." The rules are stated when the database is created, using the DBMS facilities. It is, of course, virtually impossible to make sure that no incorrect data are ever entered, and a set of information system controls has to be instituted and enforced (see Chapter 14).

• Corporate-wide standards in naming and representing the data can be enforced by the DBMS.

While a small firm may maintain a single database, large organizations typically have a number of databases. Sometimes an organization may even deploy several DBMSs, either because of the history of the installation or owing to the trade-offs between performance, functionality, and costs that exist among various DBMSs. In general, it is best if a single database serves a major process or a functional aspect of your company's operations.

The features of a database environment come at a cost. While a single-user DBMS for personal computing may cost $400 or less, a mainframe DBMS could cost $300,000 or more. This software also consumes extensive hardware resources. An existing computer system may need to be upgraded to a more powerful one to accommodate a DBMS. The process of establishing an organizational database is also costly. Organizational databases may confer competitive advantages on their owners. Examples include customer databases of credit card companies, equipment performance databases of manufacturers, and design databases allowing reuse of engineering designs in computer-aided design and engineering systems. Since such databases contain data accumulated over many years of corporate experience, competing companies find it impossible to imitate this strategic database use rapidly. The databases thus create potent barriers to entry into the marketplace.

Owing to this, for example, the databases accumulated by firms that have supplied drugs to patients in managed healthcare have made these firms attractive acquisition targets for large pharmaceutical companies. Using these enormous databases, reflecting the experience with drugs prescribed to millions of patients over a number of years, the pharmaceutical companies can perform sophisticated studies to compare the cost-effectiveness of various drugs. In a striking comment, a leading analyst of the pharmaceutical industry tells us: "The name of the game in the future is going to be information." Referring to Martin Wygod, who sold his Medco Containment Services, a distributor of prescription drugs to managed-care patients, to Merck & Company, a major pharmaceutical company, the analyst says: "Marty Wygod made himself $6 billion because he developed a database" (Freudenheim 1994).

Corporations maintain ever growing volumes of data. Kaiser Permanente, the nation's largest health maintenance organization, headquartered in Walnut Creek, California, has about 2 terabytes (trillions of bytes) of data in its databases. The vignette on the next page will show you how one company is using databases for superior performance in its industry.

6.4   LEVELS OF DATA DEFINITION IN DATABASES

We have seen that in a file environment, the data and the programs that use them are highly interdependent. We will now look more closely at how a DBMS ensures independence between the simplified view of the database offered to an individual user or an application and the actual, complex organization of the database.

To do so, a DBMS enables us to define a database on three levels, as shown in Figure 6.7.

**A Database
and
Empowered
Knowledge
Workers**

PanCanadian Petroleum of Calgary, Alberta, drills through more earth than any other Canadian oil company–1,500 wells a year. Having doubled its oil production since 1990, it has also lowered its cost per barrel and raised its revenues and profits during the period when the price of crude oil has dropped. When asked to account for the recent success of the firm he leads, David O'Brien, who took over as chief executive of PanCanadian in 1990 says: "It may sound funny, but this is a knowledge business."

Much of the success can be accounted for by more selective drilling, and the more selective drilling is accounted for by the integrated and accessible exploration database the company has accumulated. The problem PanCanadian faced was this. There are no more undiscovered large oil deposits in Western Canada, where the company operates. The goal of the exploration is to find small oil pools or to intensify the use of the already exploited large pools. Since the payoff from both methods is modest, it is necessary to select drilling sites very carefully. Seismic data are the key to this selection. Seismic data are largely obtained by setting off explosives, monitoring the resulting mini-earthquakes, and logging the data at several points. These data, when processed by a supercomputer, can give a picture of the rocks below the surface, including pockets of oil.

The company has indeed been accumulating such data for years—but the data were dispersed in paper-based files and separate computer files. It was difficult or impossible to answer questions such as these: What prospective sites are competing with the given one for the drilling resources? Does the company own drilling rights at all applicable depths? How close is the nearest pipeline? As a result, the choices of drilling sites had not been the best.

Now, all the data concerning existing and potential drilling sites has been placed in a single database. Thanks to the cross-referencing provided by the DBMS, it is possible to do research on any specific location by specifying its name and selecting the kind of data desired. The desirability of a location for drilling can be evaluated in an on-line session. Exploration professionals were given Sun technical workstations and PCs, connected both to the database located on a dedicated server machine and to each other in order to enable collaboration.

However, technology is not everything. The field geologists and engineers responsible for selecting the sites were also given authority to make decisions—without waiting to get their choices okayed by managers. Since the decisions are based on solid and multifaceted data, they can be trusted.

Based on David Freedman, "Savvy IT Lets PanCan Dance," *Forbes ASAP,* October 10, 1994, pp. 45–47.

Figure 6.7

Levels of database definition

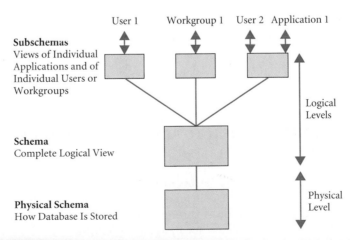

Subschemas
Views of Individual
Applications and of
Individual Users or
Workgroups

User 1   Workgroup 1   User 2   Application 1

Logical
Levels

Schema
Complete Logical View

Physical Schema
How Database Is Stored

Physical
Level

The complete structure of the entire database is defined as its **schema.** The schema shows all the record types stored in the database, along with the relationships among them. The way the schema is designed depends on the data model adopted by the DBMS, as we will see in the next section. However, an individual user, a specific application, or a user workgroup need to access only a fraction of data stored in the database. Take a marketing and sales database. A sales manager may need to access only the records of salespeople in her territory and the records of their customers. A sales representative may need to access only the records of his customers. They each need a partial view of the schema. A **subschema** is a portion of the schema defined for the needs of specific users or applications. The subschema simplifies the database for a user or for a programmer developing an application. Of course, the schema has to be defined so that all the necessary subschemas can be derived from it. Defining subschemas as partial views of a database is also a technique for handling security and privacy in databases, since users can access only the data defined in their subschema.

The schema and the subschemas are *logical* definitions of the database. That is, they define the data as the applications or the users see them, rather than describing how the data are actually stored. The *physical* layout of data in secondary storage is specified by the **physical schema.** This can be done to a great degree independently of the logical layout. Of course, the data actually exist only on the physical level; the two logical levels are the vital abstractions furnished by the DBMS.

The concept of the three levels of a database is illustrated with our suppliers–parts–shipments database in Figure 6.8.

As we can see, the schema defines the complete database in logical terms. Two different subschemas are provided based on this overall definition. One of the subschemas has been defined for an application program that processes supplier invoices for payment. The other has been defined for a user who checks the availability of parts in the company's warehouses. The physical schema of the database defines the actual layout of the files, with all the indexes and links that are necessary to relate the data entities to one another, thereby ensuring efficient access to data.

We now realize that we actually have two levels of data independence in databases. If we change the logical representation of a database in the schema, an application does not have to be changed so long as its own subschema remains unchanged. On another level, if the physical layout of data is changed (for example, if the data are reorganized on a disk because of file growth), both logical levels remain unaffected. The mappings between the three levels are provided by the DBMS.

A DBMS provides the language, called **data definition language (DDL),** for defining the database objects on the three levels. It also provides a language for manipulating the data, called the **data manipulation language (DML),** which makes it possible to access records, change values of attributes, and delete or insert records. An example of a database language that contains both a DDL for the logical levels of databases and a DML is SQL, which we will discuss further on in this chapter.

6.5 | DATA MODELS OR HOW TO REPRESENT RELATIONSHIPS AMONG THE DATA

A **data model** is a method for organizing databases on the logical level, the level of the schema and subschemas. The main concern in such a model is how to represent relationships among database records. Three principal data models—hierarchical, network, and relational—are in use by commercially available DBMSs.

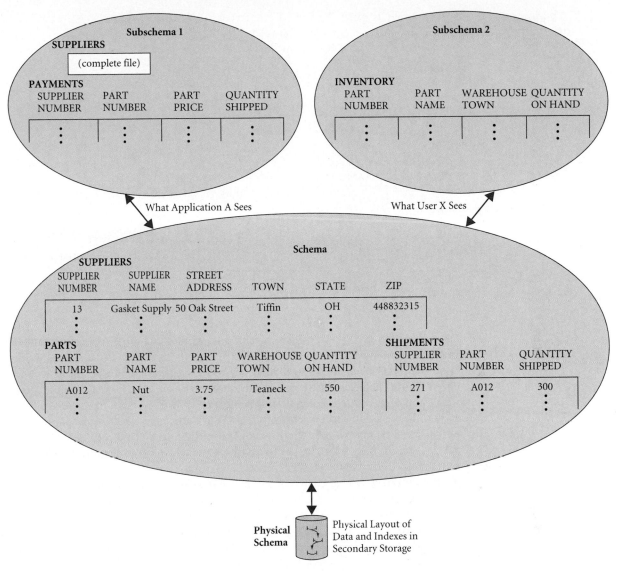

Figure 6.8

Three levels of definition in a suppliers–parts–shipments database

Two older models—the hierarchical and the network models—rely on explicit linking of related records. As we will see, these two models are inflexible in answering ad hoc queries, but they offer superior performance in transaction processing systems. These models still remain a mainstay of the airlines' computerized reservation systems and similar operational-level systems that process routine transactions at very high rates. The design of these databases is optimized for the specific transaction mix. With these two models, providing the data access paths that the database was not designed for generally requires stopping the processing to perform the needed modifications.

The third model, relational, has become the most popular owing to its flexibility in relating data entities. The relationships among data entities in this model are established by field values, with no need to preestablish data access paths by linking the appropriate records. The relational model supports well the organization's need to provide managers and other knowledge workers with broad access to information.

Figure 6.9

A hierarchical database

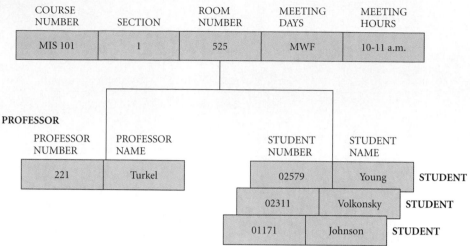

Hierarchical Model

Database representation with the **hierarchical model** will look familiar to anyone who has seen an organization chart, which looks like a tree with its root on top. Let us look at the very simple database in Figure 6.9, which we will use as a running example in this section.

A hierarchical database consists of a number of trees of the same kind. Each of the trees has a single top-level root record and a number of lower-level records. In our example in Figure 6.9, we have a database of scheduled classes at a university, each with its professor and students. In a hierarchy, each "child" record (for example, **STUDENT**) may have only one "parent" record (here, **CLASS**). The database contains links (record addresses) to specify these parent–child relationships. An access to a "child" record begins at the root. Thus, we can answer a query: "What are the names of the students taking MIS 101?"

Few real-world situations are strictly hierarchical. For example, most students take more than one course, and each professor generally teaches more than one class. To maintain strict hierarchy, we may have to reproduce the professor's and student's records for each class. Alternatively, we may have to depart from the hierarchy and introduce multiple links to the records that are shared among several trees. Also, what happens to a student's record when the student has completed the course? We certainly do not want to delete the student's record, but it no longer has a parent (the course record) to link it to. These and similar problems are dealt with in commercial hierarchical databases at the expense of replicating records or introducing special links that depart from the tree-like structure.

However, for data that can be mapped into a tree-like structure, performance is excellent. The hierarchical model is still important due to the fact that IBM's IMS (for Information Management System) DBMS remains the workhorse in many firms for the older (so-called *legacy*) transaction processing systems running on mainframes.

Network Model

The **network model** is more general than the hierarchical, since each record in a network can have more than one parent. Thus, the records in such a database are connected by a network of links that identify relationships among them. Figure 6.10 shows a network model

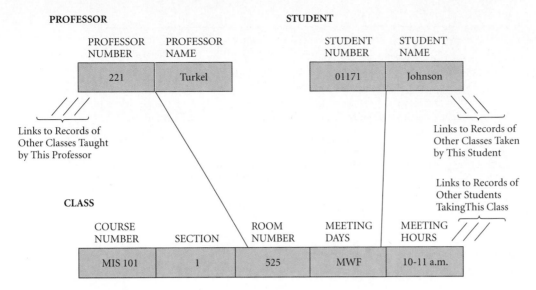

Figure 6.10

A network database

for our small sample database. We can see that the record replication needed with the hierarchical model can now be avoided: A professor's or a student's record can be linked to several class records.

The network database model is most prominently represented by the IDMS (for Integrated Database Management System) DBMS of Computer Associates International. Network systems are complex, and the maintenance of a large number of links consumes hardware resources.

Both hierarchical and network databases lack flexibility because the available access paths to records are preestablished through links at the time the database is designed. Accesses that were not provided for when the database was designed usually cannot be accommodated without redesign. This is why most new databases are designed with the relational model.

Relational Model

In the **relational model,** which we will discuss in more detail in the following sections, relationships among records are established without recourse to links. Rather, these relationships emerge as correspondences between field values. Data files are represented as tables, as we can see in Figure 6.11, which continues our running example.

Our database is represented by four tables. The data tables used in the relational model are called **relations,** hence the name of the model. The relationships among the data entities, which were established with links in the other two models, are provided by the common fields shared by the tables. For example, we can establish the name of the professor teaching the first section of MIS 101, since the tables **CLASSES** and **PROFESSORS** have a common field PROFESSOR NUMBER.

We can also answer more complex queries. For example, we can establish who teaches the classes taken by a given student from the tables **CLASSES** and **ENROLLMENT.** For a

CLASSES

COURSE NUMBER	SECTION	ROOM NUMBER	MEETING DAYS	MEETING HOURS	PROFESSOR NUMBER
MIS 101	1	525	MWF	10-11 a.m.	221
MIS 101	2	715	M	5-8 p.m.	413

STUDENTS

STUDENT NUMBER	STUDENT NAME
01171	Johnson
02311	Volkonsky
02579	Young

PROFESSORS

PROFESSOR NUMBER	PROFESSOR NAME
221	Turkel
315	Smythe

ENROLLMENT

COURSE NUMBER	SECTION	STUDENT NUMBER	STUDENT STATUS
MIS 101	1	01171	Auditor
MIS 101	1	02311	Regular
MIS 101	2	02579	Regular

Figure 6.11

A relational database

given STUDENT NUMBER in the **ENROLLMENT** table, the corresponding values of the attributes COURSE NUMBER and SECTION in both tables will give us PROFESSOR NUMBER from the **CLASSES** table, which in turn allows us to look up the professor's name in the **PROFESSORS** table. As we can see, relational databases do not need links to navigate the database. Since there is no need to preestablish the links, it is much easier to modify the database as the needs of the organization change.

Once entered into a table of a relational database, the data can be used in a variety of applications, as illustrated by another example in Figure 6.12.

Most of the databases currently being built are represented according to the relational model. Relational databases demand more extensive processing power than the two link-based models, but they offer flexible access for end users to the databases. While many organizations still maintain existing transactional databases with the hierarchical IMS database management system, its use is gradually being supplanted by the relational DBMSs. Popular relational DBMSs include DB2 (IBM), Ingres (Computer Associates International), Oracle (Oracle Corporation), and dBASE IV and Paradox (both from Borland International). A standard language, called SQL (for Structured Query Language—pronounced sequel) is used to define the tables in these DBMSs and to access the data.

Because of the importance of the relational model, we will now take a closer look at it.

Figure 6.12

The database management system automatically supplies detailed data from the database. As the clerk fills out the order-form display shown on top, the DBMS automatically supplies the details on the customer and the product from the existing tables. (From John Moore, "Road-Ready and Relational," *Mobile Office,* April 1996, pp. 58–64.)

6.6 | RELATIONAL DATABASES

As we have seen, the relational model represents all the database files as tables. Table rows are records for individual entities; table columns are fields of the records, which describe the attributes of the entities. Thanks to this familiar form of representation, relational databases are easy to understand. Our class database shown in Figure 6.11 consisted of four tables. Another example of a relational database is the suppliers–parts–shipments database shown in Figure 6.13.

The tables in Figure 6.13 are actually well-defined mathematical constructs known as relations. Two tables may be interrelated by their columns, whose values are drawn from the common domain. Thus, in the suppliers–parts–shipments database in Figure 6.13, we can get a list of suppliers located in the same town where parts are warehoused, since the values of the TOWN attribute in the **SUPPLIERS** table are drawn from the same domain as the values of the warehouse town (WHSETOWN) attribute in the **PARTS** table. Likewise, the relationships between the **PARTS** and the **SHIPMENTS** tables are established by the values of the PARTNO (part number) attribute. As we can see, the relationships are defined by the attribute values themselves, without any need for links.

All records in the table of a relational database must have a unique primary key, which means that all records must be distinct. A primary key may be composite; for example, the

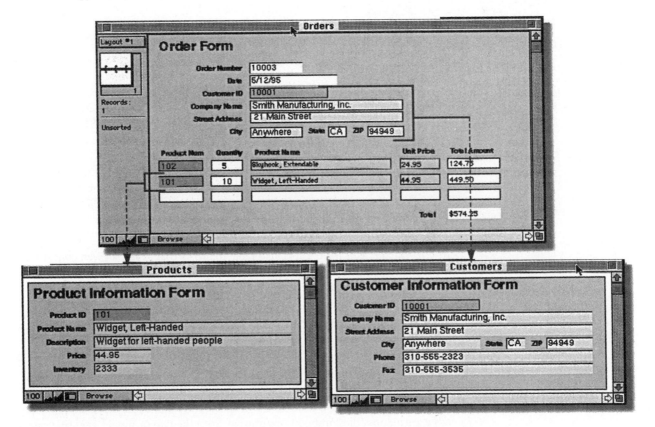

SUPPLIERS

SUPPLIERNO	SUPPLIERNAME	STREETADDRESS	TOWN	STATE	ZIP
13	Gasket Supply	50 Oak Street	Tiffin	OH	448832315
271	Parts for You	231 Market Square	Boston	MA	021153516
2274	Speedy Express	1 Shady Avenue	Tiffin	OH	448830123
3251	Reliable Suppliers	11 Cedar Lane	Teaneck	NJ	076660115

PARTS

PARTNO	PARTNAME	PARTPRICE	WHSETOWN	ONHAND
A012	Nut	3.75	Teaneck	550
D242	Pad	14.20	Boston	1200
Z971	Bolt	7.95	Columbus	325

SHIPMENTS

SUPPLIERNO	PARTNO	QUANTITY
271	A012	300
271	D242	100
3251	A012	250

Figure 6.13

Relational database of suppliers, parts, and shipments

key to the **ENROLLMENT** table in Figure 6.11 consists of three attributes: COURSE NUMBER, SECTION, and STUDENT NUMBER. The fourth field, STUDENT STATUS in the given course section, depends on this key. (A student may wish to audit some courses, while being a regular participant in others.)

An access to attribute values stored in tables is composed of one or more strictly defined operations. These operations do not have to be specified by the user; their complexity may be hidden in a simpler language. Each operation produces a new table. Relational systems support at least three principal operations on tables, without any predefined access paths (see Figure 6.14):

1. *Select,* which selects from a specified table the rows that satisfy a given condition. For example, a select operation could be used on the **SUPPLIERS** table in Figure 6.13 if we want to locate the records of all the suppliers located in Tiffin.

2. *Project,* which selects from a given table the specified attribute values; for example, by projecting the **PARTS** table in Figure 6.13, we can print out the numbers, names, and prices of all the parts being supplied.

   Note that select and project together can select given attributes from given rows. For example, we could display only the names of all the suppliers located in Tiffin.

3. *Join,* which builds a new table from two specified tables. The rows in that new table are all possible combinations of rows from the two original tables that sat-

Figure 6.14

Relational operators

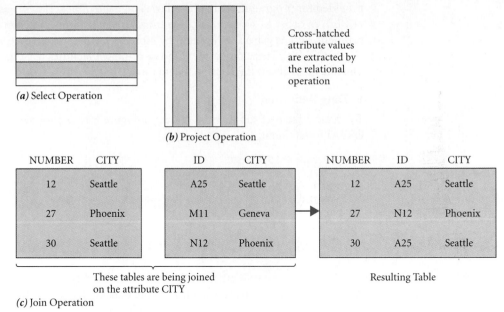

(a) Select Operation

(b) Project Operation

Cross-hatched attribute values are extracted by the relational operation

NUMBER	CITY
12	Seattle
27	Phoenix
30	Seattle

ID	CITY
A25	Seattle
M11	Geneva
N12	Phoenix

NUMBER	ID	CITY
12	A25	Seattle
27	N12	Phoenix
30	A25	Seattle

These tables are being joined on the attribute CITY

Resulting Table

(c) Join Operation

isfy a given condition. Thus, in Figure 6.14c, the join condition is that the values of the CITY attribute of the rows be the same. Of course, tables can be joined only on the attributes whose values are compatible. For example, using the database in Figure 6.13, we can answer the query: "Who are the suppliers located in the same town as one of our warehouses?" by joining the tables **SUPPLIERS** and **PARTS.** The query will identify Parts for You and Reliable Suppliers.

The power of the relational model derives from the join operation. It is precisely because records are related to one another through a join operation, rather than through links, that we do not need a predefined access path. The join operation is also highly time-consuming, requiring access to many records stored on disk in order to find the needed records.

A variety of language types is available for accessing a database, that is, for querying it. Some of these languages, designed for direct access by end users, were discussed in Section 5.5. More general query languages offer extensive data definition and manipulation facilities for use primarily by information systems professionals. Foremost among the latter languages is SQL (for Structured Query Language), the language for defining and accessing relational databases, which we describe in the next section.

6.7   SQL—A RELATIONAL QUERY LANGUAGE

SQL (the acronym stands for **Structured Query Language** and is usually pronounced "sequel") is a data-definition-and-management language of relational databases. SQL is now an international standard and is provided by most well-known DBMSs, including some nonrelational ones. SQL may be used as an independent query language to define the objects in a database, enter the data into the database, and access the data (we illustrated these direct interactions with DBMS in Figure 6.6). The so-called embedded SQL is also provided for programming in procedural languages ("host" languages), such as C, COBOL, or PL/I, in order to access a database from an applications program. In the end-user environment, SQL is generally "hidden" by more user-friendly interfaces.

Let us familiarize ourselves with the principal facilities of SQL, which will further refine our ideas about the relational data model.

1. Data Definition

To create a table of suppliers, as shown in Figure 6.13, all we have to do in SQL is use the CREATE statement:

```
CREATE TABLE SUPPLIERS
   (SUPPLIERNO INTEGER NOT NULL,
    SUPPLIERNAME CHAR (20) NOT NULL,
    STREET ADDRESS CHAR (20) NOT NULL,
    TOWN CHAR (10) NOT NULL,
    STATE (CHAR) (2) NOT NULL,
    ZIP CHAR (9) NOT NULL,
    PRIMARY KEY (SUPPLIERNO));
```

As we can see, most attributes (fields) are defined as consisting of characters, and all the attribute values must be specified when the data are loaded into the table (that is what the NOT NULL clause does). The other two tables in the database in Figure 6.13 may be created in the same way.

A new database table may be created at any time with CREATE TABLE. Additional columns may be added to an existing table with the ALTER TABLE statement. An entire table may be deleted with the DROP TABLE statement. These are the three principal statements of SQL's data definition language.

SQL makes it possible to define user views with the CREATE VIEW statement, which relies on the SELECT statement we will discuss below. In this case, SELECT defines which attributes are to be included in the view, which is again a table. (Since in SQL a user view is a single table, several statements may be necessary to provide a complete subschema, such as shown in Figure 6.8.)

To improve access performance for often-executed queries, an index may be provided for a particular attribute with the CREATE INDEX statement. An index or a view may be DROPped at any time.

2. Data Manipulation

SQL enables a user to retrieve data from a database with the SELECT statement: Each retrieval produces another table (even if it consists of a single row).

Here is a query to obtain the names and full addresses of all the suppliers located in Tiffin:

```
SELECT SUPPLIERNAME, STREETADDRESS, TOWN, STATE, ZIP
FROM SUPPLIERS
WHERE TOWN = 'Tiffin';
```

As a result, we obtain this table:

SUPPLIERNAME	STREETADDRESS	TOWN	STATE	ZIP
Gasket Supply	50 Oak Street	Tiffin	OH	448832315
Speedy Express	1 Shady Avenue	Tiffin	OH	448830123

As we already know, the power of the relational model derives from its capability to join tables using columns whose values are drawn from the same domain. Here is the query that gives us the numbers and names of the suppliers and the numbers and names of parts only if the supplier is located in the same town where the part is warehoused:

```
SELECT SUPPLIERNO, SUPPLIERNAME, PARTNO, PARTNAME, TOWN
FROM SUPPLIERS, PARTS
WHERE TOWN = WHSETOWN;
```

Considering the data shown in Figure 6.13, we obtain the following table. (Trace it to the original tables in the figure!)

SUPPLIERNO	SUPPLIERNAME	PARTNO	PARTNAME	TOWN
271	Parts for You	D242	Pad	Boston
3251	Reliable Suppliers	A012	Nut	Teaneck

The SELECT statement has additional features that enable the user, for example, to obtain a sum or an average value for all of the entries in a column.

The data manipulation language of SQL also includes three statements for changing the contents of tables:

- INSERT is used to populate the table initially and to subsequently insert additional records.

- DELETE makes it possible to delete one record or a category of records from a table.

- UPDATE makes it possible to change values of one or several attributes in one or more records in a table.

As we can see, SQL furnishes the user with both data definition and data manipulation facilities.

6.8 | DESIGNING A RELATIONAL DATABASE

Database design progresses from the design of the logical levels of the schema and the subschemas to the design of the physical level.

The aim of **logical design,** also known as **data modeling,** is to design the schema of the database and all the necessary subschemas. A relational database will consist of tables (relations), each of which describes only the attributes of a particular class of entities. Logical design begins with identifying the entity classes to be represented in the database and establishing relationships between pairs of these entities. For example, in a database of students and classes, the relationship between the attributes is that of enrollment of a student in a class. A relationship is simply an interaction between the entities represented by the data. This relationship will be important for accessing the data. Frequently, **entity–relationship (E–R) diagrams,** are used to perform data modeling (Sanders 1995). In such a diagram, rectangles show entities and diamonds show relationships between two entities. A very simple entity–relationship diagram is shown in Figure 6.15 on the next page.

Entity–relationship diagrams for larger systems contain scores of rectangles and diamonds. We may further refine an entity–relationship diagram to show the attributes of the entities and of the relationships. We may also indicate the number of times an entity occurs. This has been done in Figure 6.16 on the next page.

The primary key of each entity or relationship is underlined. In some cases, this key is composite; that is, we need several fields to identify a record. Thus, for example, the key of the ENROLLMENT relationship must consist of three fields. Our figure indicates the most general relationship: Each student may take more than one class and each class may enroll more than one student, which is indicated as an N-to-M (or N:M) relationship. Such a relationship must be represented by a separate table, as shown in Figure 6.11. On the other hand, the relationship between a professor and the classes he or she teaches is one-to-many

Figure 6.15

An entity–relationship (E–R) diagram

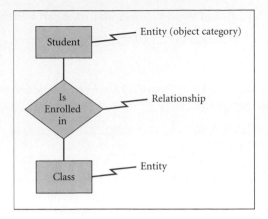

Figure 6.16

An E–R diagram with attributes and occurrence counts

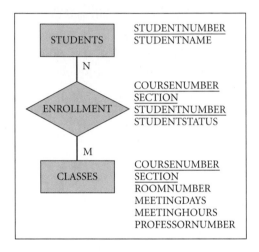

(1:M) and can be reflected by stating the professor's number in the record of each class taught.

Following the modeling with E–R diagrams, we arrive at a set of tables that represent entities and relationships between them. To complete the logical database design, this set of tables is simplified through a process known as **normalization.** Each table is normalized, which means that all its fields will contain single data elements, all its records will be distinct (we thus always have a primary key), and each table will describe only a single class of entities. The objective of normalization is to prevent replication of data, with all its negative consequences. For example, if in our table **CLASSES,** shown in Figure 6.11, we had included the name of the course, we would have to repeat the course name for each section of the course offered. Indeed, a course name does not describe a class, it describes the course.

Database modeling is assisted by computer-aided software engineering (CASE) tools, which we will discuss in Section 16.8. Following the design of the schema of the database, subschemas based on it are also defined during the logical design.

After the logical design comes the **physical design** of the database. All fields are specified as to their length and the nature of the data (numeric, characters, and so on). A principal objective of physical design is to minimize the number of time-consuming disk accesses that will be necessary in order to answer typical database queries. Frequently, indexes are provided to ensure fast accesses for such queries. For example, if we know that many queries will request a printout of the utilization of particular classrooms, we may provide an index to the **CLASSES** table in Figure 6.11 on the ROOM NUMBER attribute. The outcome of the physical design is the physical schema of the database.

Following their design, all the schemas are stored in the data dictionary, which we will now discuss.

6.9   THE DATA DICTIONARY

We gain control of data with database systems. A principal tool for maintaining this control is the data dictionary (directory). A **data dictionary** contains "data about data"—it is a sophisticated inventory of the database contents. Data dictionaries describe the enormous number of data elements whose values are stored in a database.

Data dictionaries store the following information about the data maintained in databases:

- Schema, subschemas, and physical schema – and, thus, which entities are represented in the databases, what their attributes are, and how the entities are interrelated and stored.

- Which applications and users may retrieve the specific data and which applications and users are able to modify the data. This information is used to establish security and privacy controls (as discussed further in Chapter 14).

- Cross-reference information, such as which programs use what data and which users receive what reports. This information is necessary to assess the impact of any future modifications of the applications and databases.

- Where individual data elements originate, and who is responsible for maintaining the data.

- What the standard naming conventions are for database entities. These conventions are necessary to ensure that all units of the organization speak the same language.

- What the integrity rules are for the data (for example, a salary field cannot contain a negative value or a value over 100,000).

- Where the data are stored in geographically distributed databases.

Thus, a data dictionary contains all the data definitions, and the information necessary to identify data ownership and to ensure security and privacy of the data, as well as the information used during the development and maintenance of applications which rely on the database.

Larger DBMSs include active data dictionaries, which directly interact with the operation of the DBMS. The use of an active data dictionary ensures that all the rules regarding the data are enforced as the contents of the database are being defined and used. In contrast, passive data dictionaries play only an informational role and lack the ability to enforce the rules they store.

As we will further discuss in Section 15.5, data dictionaries may be used to store not only data about data, but also a variety of information about systems under development and, in general, about the firm's information systems (data description in such a dictionary is shown in Figure 15.18). Data dictionaries are a powerful tool on which more elaborate computer-aided software engineering (CASE) tools are based. They play a vital role in system documentation.

6.10 | MANAGING THE DATA RESOURCE OF AN ORGANIZATION

Database technology enables organizations to control their data as a resource. However, as with any technology, establishment of databases does not automatically produce desired organizational results. Broader organizational processes and functions are necessary to effectively manage organizational data resources.

Components of Information Resource Management

Both organizational actions and technological means are necessary to ensure that a firm systematically accumulates data in its databases, maintains the data over time, and provides the appropriate access to the data to the appropriate employees. The principal components of this information resource management are shown in Figure 6.17.

A DBMS and a data dictionary are the principal technologies in this approach. However, as with any sophisticated technology, their proper use does not happen automatically. This is especially obvious in the case of data dictionaries: Some firms treat them in a rather perfunctory fashion; after all, they do not contain the real "working" data. Such neglect can lead to a loss of control over the data resource. The data that are not properly catalogued in the dictionary are at best nonexistent.

Planning of the data resource is a key component of an organization's information systems planning. A planning methodology known as enterprise analysis aims to establish the principal business processes, the classes of data these processes require, and the individual data entities within these broad classes. We will discuss Business Systems Planning (BSP), an enterprise analysis methodology, in Chapter 13. After the planners identify the principal data classes and entities for an enterprise or one of its units during the planning process, they do data modeling. Such modeling is often based on the entity–relationship approach we have outlined.

Introducing or changing a database environment and making major changes in data ownership is a process of organizational change. It should not be treated casually. Data ownership is often jealously guarded and defended through political ploys. Conflicts among the affected individuals, stemming from data integration in databases, must often be resolved during database implementation. We will discuss how to conduct organizational change in Chapter 13 as well. In the meantime, the following vignette will tell you about a notable failure.

Figure 6.17

Organizational and technological components in information resource management

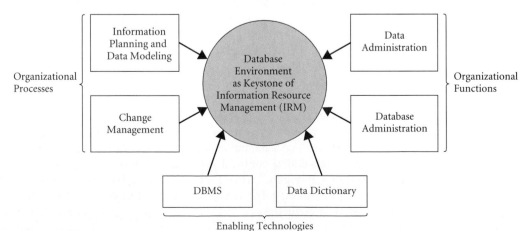

IN THE SPOTLIGHT

Do We Learn from Failures?

California's Department of Motor Vehicles (DMV) has been trying since the late 1980s to replace a mainframe database system that it was using since the 60's to store vehicle registration and drivers' records. The two databases are separate. The intent behind the new system was admirable: to combine both databases into a single one and to gain better control of the information resource. Moreover, the database was to be moved onto a distributed system running on smaller machines, with the consequent savings.

The system development project became one of the class known as "runaways," going far beyond the original schedule and way over the budget. The original developer, Ernst & Young, dropped out four years ago. Finally, after several years of development, the system appeared functional.

However, according to the Department's director, Frank Zolin, the system did not meet the needs of its users. The records were difficult to access, since the applications could not be successfully moved from the original hierarchical model into a relational database. Although intended to be faster than the mainframe system, the distributed system was actually much slower. After six years and $49 million in expenditures, the California DMV had to abandon the system and is starting over. California is not unique. Just about any state or federal agency has a similar story to tell—but they usually resist the temptation.

Based on Robert X. Cringely, "When Disaster Strikes IS," *Forbes ASAP*, August 29, 1994, pp. 60–64; and Christine White, "DMV Hits a Pothole," *Byte*, February 1996, pp. 72NA 2–6.

As the above vignette shows, database projects are complex enterprises that require careful planning, projecting the necessary computing capacity, and implementation involving the intended end users. Data administration and database administration are the organizational functions necessary to manage the data resource and avoid similar failures. We will proceed to discuss these functions.

Data Administration and Database Administration

The functional units responsible for managing the data are the data administrator and the database administrator. Their responsibilities are shown in Figure 6.18.

The person who has the central responsibility for an organization's data is the **data administrator (DA)**. The data administrator establishes the policies and specific procedures for collecting, validating, sharing, and inventorying data to be stored in databases and for making information accessible to the members of the organization and, possibly, to persons outside of it. Data administration is a policy-making function and the DA should have access to senior corporate management. For example, Director of Data Administration at MetLife Canada, Bill Post, reports to the chief information officer of the insurance company. "Data administration reduces costs through standardization," he says (Hammer 1996). His department is responsible for building the logical data models of the corporate databases, a function that may also be performed by a database administrator.

In contrast, the **database administrator (DBA)** is a database professional who creates the database and carries out the policies laid down by the data administrator. The management skills of a DA are thus combined with the technical skills of a DBA. In a larger organization, the DBA function is actually performed by a group of professionals. In a small firm, a programmer/analyst may perform the DBA function, while one of the managers acts as the DA. The DA and DBA functions give an organization the capability to maintain an overall perspective on its data resource.

Figure 6.18

*The responsibilities of
the data administrator
(DA) and the database
administrator (DBA)*
(From Vladimir Zwass,
*Management Information
Systems,* Dubuque, IA:
Wm. C. Brown, 1992,
p. 320.)

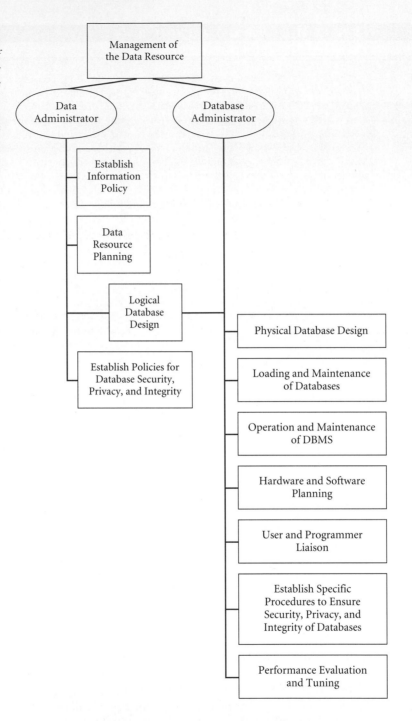

The DA is a key person (or unit) involved in the strategic planning of the data resource, a task which may be accomplished through an enterprise analysis. The DA often goes on to define the principal data entities, their attributes, and the relationships among them. The schema and the subschemas of the database are most often defined in the data definition language of the specific DBMS by the DBA, who has the requisite technical knowledge. The DBA goes on to define the physical layout of the database, with a view toward optimizing system performance for the expected pattern of database usage. A variety of utilities furnished by DBMSs support the work of the DBA. We must note that only some organizations perform enterprise analysis; logical and physical database design, on the other hand, is a must for all firms.

In addition to their responsibilities during the development of databases, the DA and the DBA, respectively, determine policies and implement these policies for the following aspects of database operation:

- Maintaining the data dictionary.
- Standardizing names and other aspects of data definition (for example, zip code lengths).
- Providing backup; that is, making sure that duplicates exist of the data stored in a database and that these duplicates can be entered into the database if all or a portion of it is damaged.
- Providing security for the data stored in a database and, further, ensuring privacy based on this security.
- Establishing a disaster recovery plan for the databases, discussed in Chapter 14.

As we will see in the following section, the organizational database support is expanding, and this expansion keeps redefining the DA and DBA roles.

6.11 | DEVELOPMENTAL TRENDS IN DATABASE MANAGEMENT

Three important trends in database management may be discerned in today's computing. In the environment where geographically distributed computer systems are interconnected with telecommunications, the databases of the enterprise are often distributed as well. The operational data of some organizations are being selectively transferred from these sites into data warehouses to support informed decision making throughout the firm. The contents of databases themselves can be richer, going far beyond numerical data. We will now review these three vital trends: distributed databases, data warehousing, and rich databases that include object-oriented databases.

Along with these three trends, the use of databases external to the organization is increasing rapidly. Access to commercial databases over the Internet or proprietary networks is vital in searching out business opportunities and in everyday decision making. Increasingly, organizations gain access to parts of the databases of their customers, suppliers, and business partners. Thus, database management underpins strategic business relationships.

Distributed Databases

As we will further discuss in the next chapter, today's information systems are often composed of a number of computer systems placed in different locations and interconnected with telecommunications networks. Such systems may rely on **distributed databases;** that is, databases that are spread across several physical locations. In distributed databases, the data are placed where they are used most often, but the entire database is available to each authorized user, as shown in Figure 6.19. Each site runs the DBMS software. The sites may be halfway across the world, connected by a wide area network (WAN), or they may be in the same building and connected by a local area network (LAN). The data are frequently placed on server computers dedicated to database management.

Figure 6.19

*A system with a
distributed database*

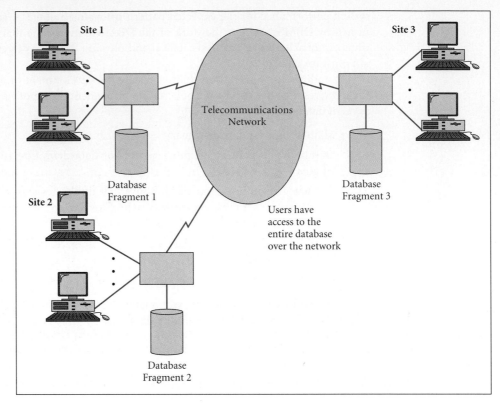

Distributed database systems enable the structure of the database to mirror the structure of the firm. The traffic on the network may be minimized by maintaining the local data where they are used most. At the same time, all of the organizational data may be made accessible to any site. Indeed, many managers of business units today insist on maintaining their data on their unit's site. The basic principle of distributed databases is that a distributed system ought to look to a user as though the data were *not* distributed. In other words, data distribution ought to be transparent to database users. Distributed database management is supported by all broadly used DBMSs.

Management of distributed databases poses several major technical problems. The primary question is how to distribute the data. Frequently, parts of the data are replicated on several sites to ensure fast access (Watterson 1996). But then an update propagation problem emerges: When data are modified, an update has to be made on all sites where the copies of the data are stored. The other alternative is to partition the data among the sites, but then the users face all the disadvantages of remote access, such as transmission delay.

The data dictionary, which describes all of the data stored in a database, must contain information on where the particular data are stored. But where is the dictionary itself stored? It may be centralized, replicated on all sites, or partitioned among the sites. To locate a data item, a DBMS has to first of all locate the part of the data dictionary that specifies the location of the appropriate database fragment.

The dispersion of data across many sites has brought its own problem: It is now more difficult for the end users to access the needed data at will in order to analyze them and make informed decisions. Here, the use of a data warehouse, to which we now turn, will help.

Data Warehouses

Operational databases of corporations are usually unsuitable for supporting managerial analysis and decision making. These databases are designed to support specific business processes or functions and contain only the more recent data. They are also built to provide rapid response to on-line transactions; the analytical work, which usually calls for massive data access, would interfere with this response-time objective. This why some 70 percent of the Fortune 1000 largest U.S. corporations have implemented or are considering building data warehouses (McWilliams 1996). A **data warehouse** is a subject-oriented, integrated collection of data, both internal and external, accumulated over time and maintained in support of managerial decision making. The objective of a corporate data warehouse is to continually select data from the operational databases, transform the data into a uniform format, and open the warehouse to the end users through a friendly and consistent interface. Some companies transfer subsets of data relevant to specific business processes or corporate functions from the central data warehouse to the so-called data marts located on workgroup servers, in order to cut down on the query traffic on corporate networks.

The performance of data warehouses is optimized for ad hoc accesses, increasingly possible over the World Wide Web (Gardner 1997). The users may employ end user-oriented query languages, such as those we discussed in Section 5.4. However, the real power of data warehouses consists in offering to the users analytical tools, such as decision support systems (DSS), which we describe in more detail in Chapter 10 and, in particular, tools for On-Line Analytical Processing (OLAP), and for data mining, which we discuss below. Indeed, the availability of data warehouses can enable the use of large organizational decision support systems as an important complement to the small-size DSSs developed and deployed by individuals or teams.

For example, a data warehouse built to support Marketing and Sales may contain several years' worth of data, reflecting sales to all of the firm's customers. All the records have a time stamp and new data are continually added to the warehouse from the operational information systems. The warehouse differs from the sales database that contains current data, needed to support the on-going sales. Thanks to the availability of the warehouse, the operational data are not deleted with time and lost forever, but archived in the warehouse, to be accessed in order to, for example, forecast future sales for specific regions or individual outlets.

OLAP software assists in fast analysis across multiple dimensions of data shared among many users (Greenfeld 1996). For example, if a company wants to determine which of its products are selling better over the years, when, and where, the firm will need the data for the past years accumulated in the warehouse as well as the analytical OLAP tools to discover the trends. Data warehouses are also used for **data mining**: automated discovery of potentially significant relationships among various categories of data (Inmon 1996). Using specialized software for data mining, an insurance company, for example, may deploy its data warehouse to discover what attributes of the insured are the best predictors of the frequency of different kinds of claims. A telephone company may mine its data to discover what kind of customers are most likely to drop a particular kind of service—and perhaps try to make its offering more attractive to these customers.

The system supporting a data warehouse consists of three components, shown in Figure 6.20. The first subsystem extracts the data from the operational systems, many of them

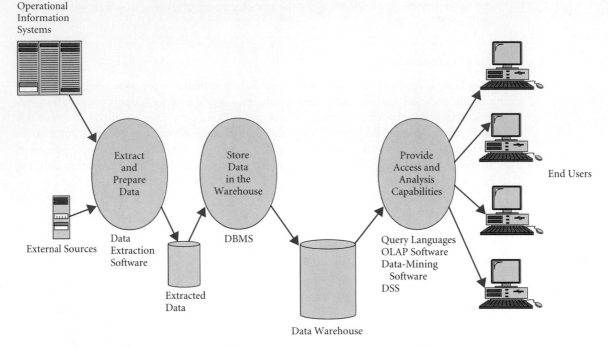

Operational
Information
Systems

External Sources

Data
Extraction
Software

Extract
and
Prepare
Data

Extracted
Data

Store
Data
in the
Warehouse

DBMS

Data Warehouse

Provide
Access and
Analysis
Capabilities

Query Languages
OLAP Software
Data-Mining
Software
DSS

End Users

Figure 6.20

Support for a data warehouse

older legacy systems and "scrubs" it by removing errors and inconsistencies. The second support component is actually the DBMS that will manage the warehouse data. The third subsystem is made up of the query tools that help users access the data and includes the OLAP and other DSS tools supporting data analysis.

Companies that introduce a data warehouse are able to gain considerable business insight from the accumulated data. When Victoria's Secret Stores, a lingerie chain with annual sales of $1.3 billion, used a trial set of queries on its pilot data warehouse, it found that its established concept of allocating the merchandise to each of its 678 stores based on a mathematical "store average" was wrong. In the analysis of the warehouse data, geographic demand patterns emerged, with stores in certain areas outselling the "average" store tenfold on certain categories of products. Analytical use of the data warehouse enabled the store chain to stock geographically appropriate merchandise (Goldberg and Vijayan 1996).

Object-Oriented and Other Rich Databases

With the vastly expanded capabilities of information technology, the content of the databases is becoming richer. Traditional databases have been oriented toward largely numerical data or short fragments of text, organized into well-structured records. As the processing and storage capabilities of computer systems expand and as the telecommunications capacities grow, it is possible to support knowledge work more fully with rich data. To do this, we need to store and interrelate for access such components of information as longer, unstructured text (e.g., salespersons' notes or competitive intelligence); documents' images (e.g., insurance policies); engineering drawings (such as those used in computer-aided design); and photographs, voice, and motion video (for example, in multimedia-based marketing presentations or training materials).

The following vignette will show you how the use of geographical data in combination with other databases gives companies important new capabilities. The vignette illustrates

IN THE SPOTLIGHT

Geographic Information Systems or Business Geographics

Let us think a little more broadly about the capabilities of databases. If we do, we may come up with the idea of combining geographic data with the data about the subject we want to see on a map, combine this with mapping software—and we have a geographic information system (GIS). Using such a system, we can develop sales territories, select areas for real estate investment, or compare ourselves to our competitors with respect to market penetration. Indeed, geography plays an important role in many business decisions.

Consider this problem: A retailer is developing a plan to open a new store in a major city. The real-estate department of the firm will be able to use a GIS to seek a good property, close to residences and other stores and reasonably priced. Marketing will use the sys-

tem to analyze the demographic distribution of the people living in the area, both to select the merchandise mix and to target the promotions. The logistics department will analyze how to fit the new store in the merchandise distribution plan, represented on the area map. As all these departments share a common database, a common GIS-based solution is developed.

Indeed, the problems that can be solved by using GISs are so frequent that the field has acquired the name of business geographics and attracted several hundred vendors selling GIS software and related databases. The level of detail can vary from a city block to the entire globe. You can see a map produced by one of the GISs in Figure 6.21. A great variety of databases can be acquired from the vendors, either
Continued

Figure 6.21

Sales managers rely on geographic information systems for the analysis of sales territories. This map with the associated demographic information was obtained with GIS software by MapInfo of Troy, New York. (Courtesy of MapInfo.)

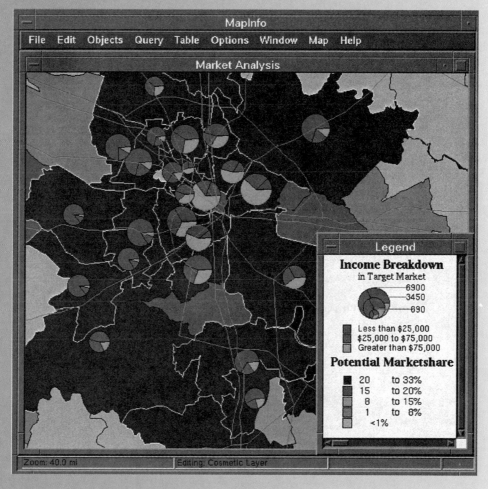

the suppliers of GIS or independent database suppliers. As a leading example of database suppliers, Claritas of Alexandria, Virginia, has developed a PRIZM database that segments the entire U.S. population by lifestyle related to the zip code. The database classifies neighborhoods into 62 segments depending on their buying patterns. People living in one area are likely to purchase imported cars, tennis weekends, and designer jeans, just as those living in another would go for trucks, fishing trips, and Shake 'n Bake.

Chicago Tribune, the newspaper publisher, uses a business–geographic analysis to develop new sales territories. Arby's does a site selection for its fast-food outlets with a GIS. Boise Cascade, a leading producer of timber products in North America, uses a GIS to manage timberlands. Conrail manages quite a few aspects of its railroad business with a GIS, from track maintenance and real-estate operations to coordinating response to emergency situations. Chase Manhattan Bank uses mapping software to analyze the effectiveness of its automatic teller machine (ATM) deployment as compared to its competitors. Insurers analyze the risks of insuring particular clients based on their proximity to hazards, such as flood zones and hurricane-prone areas.

Here is one example where seeing the distribution of the target items on a map may be highly persuasive: The Community Redevelopment Act requires banks to show that their lending practices meet the needs of the areas where they do business. The intent of the Act is to prevent redlining, a practice of restricting mortgage lending in the areas with racial minority populations. Using a GIS, a bank can compare, by area, the volume of deposits with the volume of mortgages and show, if this is the case, that it is indeed approving numerous loans in the areas where it does significant deposit business.

Take another example. Synthes, USA, a manufacturer of orthopedic instruments and implants uses the MapInfo desktop mapping software from MapInfo in Troy, New York, to optimize its sales effort. Synthes's sales manager, Michael Ward, says: "Take, for example, hip screws, which are frequently needed by people over 50. We can view an area, then overlay demographic census data for the area, overlay the locations of the hospitals, and finally product-sales area. If the sales are not proportional to the percentage of people over 50, then we know where to push."

MapInfo's software for managing geographic data is also available for client/server configurations (and called SpatialWare), to enable users to store and analyze large databases on powerful servers.

Based on Nora Sherwood Bryan, "A Sense of Place," *CIO,* February 1, 1994, pp. 54–58; Christina Del Valle, "They Know Where You Live—and How You Buy," *Business Week,* February 7, 1994, p. 89; Arun Vaidya, "When Information Is Everyone's Business," *Business Geographics,* March/April 1994, pp. 24–26; and Juan C. Perez, "Back Offices Are Target of MapInfo Server Suites," *PC Week,* November 21, 1996, p. 36.

the use of **geographic information systems (GIS)**—systems that support presentation of geographically distributed data on maps.

The following are other technologies that combine to enrich the database support for information systems.

1. Object-Oriented Databases

Relying on the concepts adapted from the software domain, which we discussed in Section 5.6, object-oriented databases go beyond the relational model (Barry 1997). These databases help in managing objects that belong to various classes. The objects include (encapsulate) both the data and the procedures that manipulate the data. An object can be a traditional record, but also a spreadsheet, a voice-annotated text, or a video clip. At this time, object-oriented databases focuses are deployed primarily in computer-aided design (CAD) and in publishing, although their use is spreading to other areas. Although the major relational databases, such as Oracle and Ingres, have been extended to handle complex objects, smaller database vendors are releasing DBMSs that were designed as object-oriented from

Figure 6.22

A collection of data objects organized with links in a hypermedia database (From Parsaye and Chignell, 1993, p. 243.)

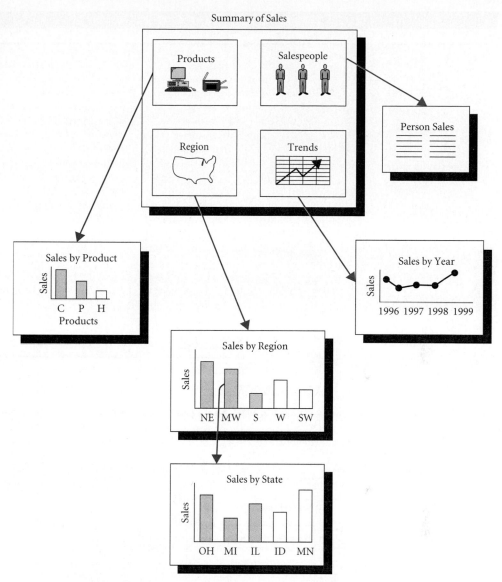

the outset. Such DBMSs are, for example, GemStone from Gemstone Systems of Beaverton, Oregon, and Objectivity/DB from Objectivity of Mountain View, California.

2. Hypertext and Hypermedia Databases

Systems that interlink the fragments of text (hypertext) or units of multimedia information (hypermedia) and allow the user to navigate this information at will provide extensive support for knowledge work, battling information overload (Parsaye and Chignell 1993). During a decision-making session, you can follow the links as you wish (see Figure 6.22). The World Wide Web is a distributed hypermedia database.

3. Image Databases and Text Databases

Collections of insurance policies, maps, design solutions, or fingerprints require fast access to an image by its selected attributes. An image database with extensive indexing is a repository for such information. Experiences with clients, competitive intelligence, and

IN THE SPOTLIGHT

A Database Enables Electronic Commerce in Photographic Images

Based in Seattle, PhotoDisc is a 120-employee company with annual sales of $25 million, which sells digital photographs from its voluminous archive to designers, media, and other individuals and corporations. Such firms are known as stock–photography houses. The company has recently entered the field of electronic commerce by selling its images over the Internet. To do so, PhotoDisc has established an image database of 25,000 pictures on the World Wide Web (you can visit the site at http://www.photodisc.com). The key to success is the potential customer's ability to search for the exact image that is needed.

The image database is stored on a Netra server from Sun Microsystems. It is managed by Visual Information Retrieval software from Virage, combined with the Oracle DBMS that runs on a SPARC multiprocessor. The combined software enables the potential customer to search the image database indexes either by keyword or image number. However, the high-resolution images can also be searched by the desired picture components or textures, broadening the appeal of the offering. The search-and-purchase system enables customers to find the desired image, pay for it, and download it to their own site—all over the Internet.

Mary Jo Foley, "Hot New Database Technologies," *Datamation*, September 1996, pp. 44–49.

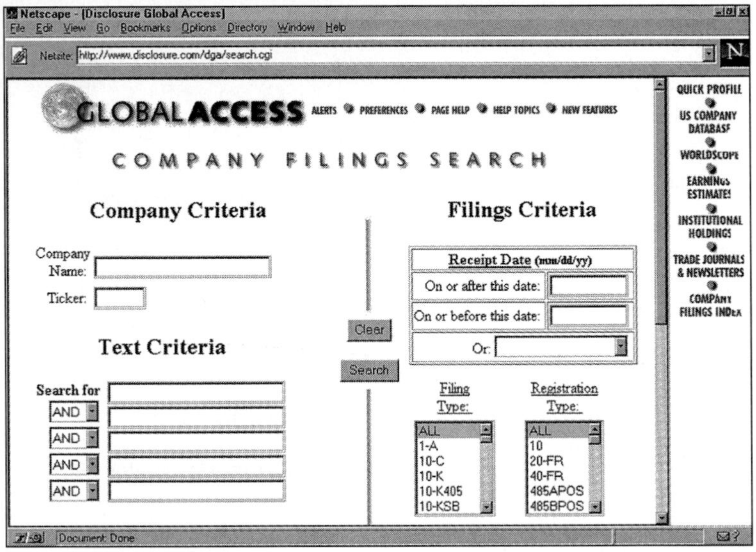

Figure 6.23

The screen for full-text searching of the EDGAR database of corporate filings with the Securities and Exchange Commission, offered by Disclosure, Inc. (Courtesy of Disclosure, Inc., Bethesda, MD.)

protocols of decision-making sessions, all stored in text databases, can become a vital part of organizational memory (Stein and Zwass 1995). By accessing these databases, future managers can learn from this accumulated and recorded experience.

The vignette above shows an example of a firm using an image database at the core of its business.

Text databases of business information are offered for searches by commercial on-line services. Figure 6.23 shows the screen of the EDGAR (for Electronic Data Gathering Analysis and Retrieval) database that offers the corporate reports filed with the Securities and Exchange Commission (SEC).

We will further discuss the hypertext, hypermedia, text, image, and external databases in the context of their use for knowledge work in Chapter 8.

SUMMARY

Data stored in computer systems form a hierarchy, the smallest element of which is a bit and the two largest—a file and a database. Data stored in secondary storage over extended periods of time may be collected in these files or databases. Data files may be organized as sequential files, which permit only batch processing, or as indexed—sequential or direct files, which allow direct access and thus support on-line processing. The file-oriented approach to data suffers from severe limitations. Redundant data are stored in files that belong to different applications, which leads to inconsistencies. Also, data sharing among applications is difficult to achieve with these application-owned files.

It is common today to organize data into databases. A database is an organized collection of interrelated data. A database serves a major aspect of a firm's operations, and its data may be shared among many users and applications. A database management system (DBMS), the systems software that manages databases, affords broad and controlled access to data. To simplify applications development and maintenance, a DBMS makes it possible to define a database at three levels. With the two logical levels of the schema and the subschemas, we can define the entire database and provide separate views of it for individual applications. With the physical schema, we specify how the data are to be physically stored. This separation between levels supports program–data independence.

There are three data models for representing databases on the logical levels. While hierarchical and network data models remain in use for high-volume transaction processing, they are limited in their representational abilities and inflexible with respect to change. Most of the new databases are implemented with relational DBMSs. A relational database is a collection of tables. Such a database is relatively easy for end users to understand. Relational databases afford flexible access to data and are easy to modify. Structured Query Language (SQL) has become a standard access language for defining and manipulating data in databases.

All the data definitions are stored in a data dictionary which, like a DBMS, is a major technological tool for controlling organizational data. The use of database technology does not automatically produce organizational control of data. Rather, the organizational processes of information planning and data modeling, as well as change management, and the organizational functions of data and database administration are necessary for effective information resource management.

Several developmental trends are discernible in the database environment. Databases are increasingly distributed among several sites in an organization. Many companies organize data warehouses that contain corporate data accumulated over a long time in order to support managerial decision making. The contents of databases are becoming richer, going beyond well-structured records to store geographic information, indexed text, and collections of multimedia objects, sometimes interlinked to form hypermedia documents.

KEY TERMS

Bit   *202*

Byte   *202*

Field   *202*

Record   *202*

File   *202*

Primary key   *202*

Database   *202*

Access (to a record)   *204*

Sequential access   *204*

Direct access   *204*

Sequential file   *204*

Indexed-sequential file   *205*

Direct file   *206*

Database management system (DBMS)   *208*

Program-data independence   *209*

Schema   *212*

QUESTIONS

1. What is the relationship between a field, a record, and a file? Give an example including all three.

2. What two file organization methods support on-line processing, and what is the basic distinction between these two methods? Describe one application for which each of the methods would be suitable.

3. What is the purpose of hashing?

4. What is a database? How does it relate to a database management system (DBMS)?

5. What are the advantages of database management, as compared to file management?

6. What are the three levels at which data are defined in databases? Why do we need each of these levels?

7. What is the difference between the logical and the physical organization of data? Why is it good to separate the two?

8. What are the advantages of the relational data model as compared to the hierarchical and network models?

9. How are the data about different entities interrelated with the relational data model?

10. What is SQL and how does it relate to such DBMSs as DB2?

11. What do we use entity–relationship diagrams for?

12. What is a data dictionary? Give three examples of the information stored there.

13. State three distinctions between the functions of a data administrator and a database administrator.

14. How do distributed databases relate to the client/server environment of computing?

15. Define data warehouse.

16. What is the principal objective a corporation pursues when establishing a data warehouse? What is the relationship between a data warehouse and On-Line Analytical Processing (OLAP)? What is data mining?

17. What directions can be taken in database management to go beyond numerical databases?

18. What is a geographic information system and how does it relate to databases?

ISSUES FOR DISCUSSION

1. How has the availability of databases influenced the operations and management of organizations? What is the effect of data warehousing?

2. Database management technology enables huge quantities of personal records to be kept for ready access by various governmental agencies and corporations. Discuss the effect of this on personal privacy. What other ethical issues can emerge in connection with the use of databases? (See Section 1.7.)

3. Most traditional databases store numeric data or short strings of characters, such as addresses. Does this limit their usefulness and, if so, how? How does the move toward rich databases relieve these constraints? Be specific in discussing which constraints are removed by the given type of databases.

4. One may claim that each of the four ethical issues mentioned in Section 1.7 can arise from the use of databases. Discuss this proposition and provide examples for your claims.

REAL-WORLD MINICASE AND PROBLEM-SOLVING EXERCISES

1. Another Kind of Warehouse at Sears   Every night, shortly after 9 p.m. EST, when Sears, Roebuck and Co. retail stores on the East Coast lock their doors, the data gathering begins. During the next six hours, the record of every one of 1.5 million daily point-of-sale transactions from the Sears stores across the country will flow over leased network lines into three mainframe computer systems—in Illinois, Ohio, and Texas. From there, the preprocessed data will be sent to the NCR 3600 massively parallel processor located in Columbus, Ohio. That system, with 250 processors and 864 magnetic disks, stores one of the world's largest commercial data warehouses. In 1.8 terabytes (trillion bytes), it stores every sales transaction concluded at one of Sears' 3,000 domestic retail locations, going back to December 1, 1993. This is, of course, only part of the task.

Next morning, carefully selected items of these sales data will begin flowing out, in much smaller bursts, to the PCs on a local area network in Sears' store support office in Hoffman Estates, Illinois. Here, some 1,500 buyers, merchandisers, inventory managers, and marketing analysts use custom-developed software that enables them to extract the needed data from the warehouse and analyze them. If it's Monday, for example, a merchandiser can see how many of the Trader Bay polo shirts advertised in Sunday's newspaper circular were sold—where, in what color, and in what sizes. Fresh shipments can be immediately dispatched as necessary. By comparing the information with the previous Sunday's sales, the effectiveness of the advertisement can be ascertained.

The warehouse serves only the decision support purposes—no transaction processing systems access it. This is one reason why every one of 1,500 users gets an almost immediate response to a query. Of course, a warehouse costs money, some $3 million a year, all things considered. This does not include the query and OLAP tools installed on the users' PCs and generally priced at $500 to $1,000 a desktop.

In the future, many companies are expected to give suppliers access to their data warehouses in order to track inventories and shipments. Indeed, vendors of the OLAP software are marketing systems that are able to work with web browsers.

a. What operational, tactical, and strategic decisions can be assisted by the availability of the data warehouse at Sears? Give two examples of each.

b. What is the role of a data warehouse in resolving the inconsistencies among the data stored in the older, so-called legacy, systems?

c. Sears is reportedly considering using the data warehouse in the future as the main database for its operational systems. Is this a good idea? Why or why not?

Based on Edward Teach, "Tapping Your Hidden Assets," *CFO,* May 1996, pp. 47–56.

2. Creating and Updating a Database   Using a DBMS available to you, define the four tables of the university database shown in Figure 6.11. You may use your own class section to populate the **STUDENTS** table with about 20 records. Also, populate the **CLASSES, PROFESSORS,** and **ENROLLMENT** tables with about seven records each.

- Add the column "OFFICE" to the **PROFESSORS** table and enter office numbers in it. Print out all the tables.

- Write a query to list the course numbers and the sections of all classes meeting in a specific room. Print out the query and the resulting table.

- Write a query to list all professors who teach in a specific room and include their office numbers in the list. Print out the query and the resulting table.

- Three students joined the class late. Open the **STUDENTS** table and add their records. Print out the new table.

3. Using SQL.   Do the following with SQL:

a. Define **SHIPMENTS** and **PARTS** tables in Figure 6.13.

b. Query the database in Figure 6.13 for all the towns where bolts are warehoused.

c. Query the database in Figure 6.13 for the names of all the suppliers who have shipments on the way, together with the numbers of parts and quantities being shipped.

TEAM PROJECT

Each two- or three-person team should study an object-oriented DBMS or a system that offers the capability to store hypermedia, images, or richly indexed text. At least one of the teams should investigate systems that enable Web browsers to provide links to databases (e.g., those of Electric Press of Reston, Virginia). The teams should then present the capabilities of the system to the class. The class should discuss the differences and similarities among these technologies.

SELECTED REFERENCES

Barry, Douglas K. (Editor). "The Current State of Object-Oriented Database Management Systems: Special Section." *Object Magazine,* February 1997, pp. 27–60.

Several articles describing the features and current capabilities of object-oriented database management.

"Database Technologies." Special Report, *Datamation,* September 1996, pp. 44–73.

The new technologies used to get information out of databases.

Fayyad, Usama, and Ramasamy Uthurusamy, eds. "Data Mining and Knowledge Discovery in Databases." *Communications of the ACM,* 39, no. 11 (November 1996), pp. 24–68.

Several articles that describe how to discover patterns in the data stored in databases and data warehouses.

Freudenheim, Milt. "A Shift of Power in Pharmaceuticals." *The New York Times,* May 9, 1994, pp. D1 & D3.

Gardner, Dana. "Cashing in with Data Warehouses and the Web." *Databased Advisor,* February 1997, pp. 60–63.

Goldberg, Michael, and Jaikumar Vijayan. "Data 'Wearhouse' Gains." *Computerworld,* April 8, 1996, pp. 1, 16.

Greenfeld, Norton. "OLAP." *Unix Review,* April 1996, pp. 15–20.

Gray, Jim. "Evolution of Data Management." *Computer,* 29, no. 10 (October 1996), pp. 38–46.

An accessible and concise overview of the development of and recent trends in database management.

Hammer, Signe. "Taming the Data Monster." *Perspectives on Technology,* 9, no. 1 (July 1996), pp. 8–11.

Inmon, W. H. "The Data Warehouse and Data Mining." *Communications of the ACM,* 39, no. 11 (November 1996), pp. 49–50.

Kahn, Beverly K., and Linda R. Garceau. "A Developmental Model of the Database Administration Function." *Journal of Management Information Systems,* 1, no. 4 (Spring 1985), pp. 87–101.

A good description of database administration.

Khoshafian, Setrag, and Razmik Abnous. *Object Orientation: Concepts, Languages, Databases, User Interfaces,* New York: John Wiley & Sons, 1990.

Contains a good introduction to object-oriented databases.

Kroenke, David M. *Database Processing: Fundamentals, Design, and Implementation,* 5th ed. Englewood Cliffs, N.J.: Prentice Hall, 1995.

A popular introductory textbook.

McWilliams, Brian. "Seeing through the Hype." *Computerworld Client/Server Journal,* April 1996, pp. 24–27.

How to build a data warehouse.

Melton, Jim, and Alan R. Simon. *Understanding SQL: A Complete Guide,* San Francisco: Morgan Kaufmann, 1993.

An accessible tutorial.

Parsaye, Kamran, and Mark Chignell. *Intelligent Database Tools and Applications: Hyperinformation Access, Data Quality, Visualization, Automatic Discovery,* New York: Wiley, 1993.

Redman, Thomas C. "Improve Data Quality for Competitive Advantage." *Sloan Management Review,* Winter 1995, pp. 99–107.

Shows how to implement a quality management program for corporate data.

Sanders, G. Lawrence. *Data Modeling,* Danvers, MA: Boyd & Fraser, 1995.

A terse yet thorough introduction to data modeling, with excellent examples.

Stein, Eric W., and Vladimir Zwass. "Actualizing Organizational Memory with Information Systems." *Information Systems Research,* 6, no. 6 (June 1995), pp. 85–117.

Watterson, Karen. "Database Replication Explained." *Datamation,* September 1996, pp. 62–68.

General note on references: Consult recent issues of PC-oriented periodicals.

CASE STUDY | Database for Global Customer Service at the Shipper's Core

How the shipping industry has changed! Freight forwarders, customer brokers, distributors—all have now become integrated logistics providers. Global markets, offshore manufacturing, and the rigors of just-in-time delivery replacing large inventories have transformed the shipping business. To be more accurate, those who could not respond to the opportunities (or demands?) of the information age have disappeared.

Harper Group has thrived. The customers of the firm include Digital Equipment Corporation, The Limited, and Procter & Gamble. If, say, a customer needs to ship goods from a factory in China to an assembly plant in Frankfurt, Harper arranges the transport by air, ocean carriers, and trucks so that the shipment arrives on time and within specified cost. To meet the customers' needs, the firm also warehouses goods, manages the customers' inventory, and should be able at all times to inform the customer about the whereabouts of the shipment.

A shipping company with $430 million in annual sales and based in San Francisco, a few years ago Harper Group established electronic data interchange (EDI) links between more than 500 of its customers and its IBM 3090–300E mainframe and IBM AS/400 minicomputer, situated at its headquarters. The links, based on the EDIFACT global EDI standard are used to transmit paperless bills of lading, waybills, invoices, and other documents. But this is no longer enough to keep a customer. Customers now need far *more information.*

The business challenge was to create a global database to integrate data generated by a variety of information systems located around the world.

To respond to the challenge, Harper Group has outsourced its data centers built around the IBM hardware, previously located in its headquarters, to Affiliated Computer Systems of Dallas. The contract with the outsourcer is expected to cut costs and provide superior disaster recovery. The outsourcing contractor may, in the future, transfer these information systems to downsized hardware platforms. The main objective of outsourcing, however, was to free the company's information systems developers to concentrate on what was strategically important to the firm: to develop a unified database that will assist the firm's customers in buying, shipping, and tracking their freight worldwide.

The problem to be solved is that each of Harper's subsidiaries in 45 countries functions independently. All of the data that the firm's customers need is somewhere in these subsidiaries' information systems—but the data are very difficult to access. Each subsidiary has different account codes for the same customer and has implemented the account handling programs corresponding to the national business practices. A customer representative tracking a shipment from Bombay to Sao Paulo would have to deal with the incompatible systems of at least these two countries to track the shipment. The chief financial officer of the firm speaks about the "pig's breakfast" of technology deployed around the world.

All freight forwarders can help customers select the most suitable method of transportation these days. But here is a typical problem that a competitive forwarder is expected to help a customer with. The cost of buying and transporting a line of blouses from Taiwan was generally lower than doing so in Bombay. However, a recent expiration of export quotas reversed this relationship. If the forwarder can become an informed advisor to the customer, the forwarder gains a competitive advantage. Harper Group's database is expected to include these external, environmental data as well. Moreover, the firm's information systems, grounded in the database, are expected to be specific to customers' need, thus increasing the customers' switching costs. For example, the information about each customer's shipping patterns will be maintained, such as the specific events that are supposed to trigger sending the electronic documentation to the customer.

In the words of Patrick Morrison, the company's chief information officer: "We are determined to be an information company. We don't own ships or trucks. Information is the asset we have to market."

A relational database management system will be used. At this time, nine months have been spent on the design of the database, and it is estimated that 18 months will be needed to complete the project.

Based on Rochelle Garner, "Harper's Freight Is Data," *InformationWeek*, June 20, 1994, pp. 32–33.

CASE STUDY QUESTIONS

1. What principal business problem did Harper Group set out to solve?

2. Why did Harper Group consider the unified database project a strategic system? Specify which competitive advantages the firm expected to reach for.

3. Note that, at the time the case was written, Harper Group made no decision as to the location, or locations, of its unified database. What factors would you consider in making this decision and other related ones, whether to go with the partitioned or replicated database?

4. Why did the firm decide to outsource its data centers?

5. How would you explain what the firm is doing with respect to its database in terms of systems theory? (See Chapter 2.) What results can be expected based on the systems approach?

CHAPTER SEVEN

Telecommunications, the Internet, and Information System Architecture

OBJECTIVES

After you complete this chapter, you will be able to:

1. Specify the components of a telecommunications network.
2. Understand the functions of local area networks and of wide area networks.
3. Specify the communications media.
4. Understand how communication costs may be reduced by multiplexing and signal compression.
5. Specify network topologies.
6. Explain how interconnections in a network can be established with network switching.
7. Understand the role of protocols in telecommunications networks.
8. Explain the difference between peer-to-peer and server-based local area networks.
9. Explain how client/server computing is accomplished.
10. Specify the telecommunications equipment used in wide area networks.
11. Explain how the Internet and its World Wide Web assist communication and information access in organizations.
12. Specify the possible uses of the Internet in electronic commerce.
13. Define information system architecture.
14. Explain how telecommunications help business firms compete.

OUTLINE

The Internet's World Wide Web Helps Small Manufacturers Compete

Most big manufacturers have computer-to-computer connections with their suppliers via electronic data interchange (EDI) systems and can have their products ordered or their own orders filled at the push of a button or click of a mouse. Most small manufacturers don't and can't. But thanks to Industry.Net, accessible on the Internet via the World Wide Web, the playing field is much more even. The electronic marketplace for manufacturers offers message boards, new product announcements, advertisements, electronic mailboxes, and other facilities (see Figure 7.1). The main objective is the facilitation of buying and selling, rather than simply providing information.

Access to the network costs little and having a PC is enough to enter this marketplace. The cost of the service is largely borne by the big companies that act as national advertisers and by the smaller regional advertisers aiming to reach a limited audience at a lower price. Today, some 4,500 manufacturers pay from $3,000 to $20,000 a year to maintain their electronic storefronts on Industry.Net's Web site. For now, customers only shop but, in the near future, will be able to complete buying transactions by ordering the product. Part of Industry.Net's appeal is its international reach, achieved with the worldwide Internet.

The network has limitations. Obviously, you are not able to deal with firms that are not connected to it. However, for a typical small manufacturer, the use of Industry. Net is far better than the alternative—scouring catalogs and calling dozens of potential suppliers. Another advantage of having a presence on a network is pointed out by Jon Pentz of

Figure 7.1

The home page of Industry.Net on the World Wide Web.

Livingston Products, a diversified manufacturer in Wheeling, Illinois. On Industry. Net, few know that he works for a small, six-engineer firm. When he used to contact possible suppliers over the telephone, "a lot of places didn't have time to mess with you because you weren't talking in tens of thousands" of dollars in orders. When Jon requests information or supplies through Industry.Net, he finds that the response is rapid. "It allows us to be able to act like a big guy," says the engineer.

Behind Industry.Net is a company of the same name. Building on the success of its manufacturers' network, the company is already looking forward to creating similar "nets" for such products as hospital services and office supplies.

Based on Stephanie N. Mehta, "On-Line Network Offers Fast Lane to Small Businesses," *The Wall Street Journal,* October 11, 1994, p. B2; Donald H. Jones and D. Navin-Chandra, "Industry.Net: A Model for Commerce in the World Wide Web," *IEEE Expert,* October 1995, pp. 54–59; Stephen Baker, "This Is My Last Startup, Honest," *Business Week,* March 25, 1996, pp. 81–82; John W. Verity, "Invoice? What's an Invoice?" *Business Week,* June 10, 1996, pp. 110–112; and Henry Goldblatt, "Industry.Net," *Fortune,* July 8, 1996, p. 90.

The electronic transmission of information over distances, called telecommunications, has become virtually inseparable from computers: Computers and telecommunications create value together. Telecommunications networks, consisting of user workstations and computers that act as servers of computing resources interconnected by telecommunications links, have become vital for integrating organizations. As you have seen in the Focus Minicase, a telecommunications network can also become a marketplace. The Internet, a worldwide network of networks, has become a global means of communications, information access, and electronic commerce.

7.1 TELECOMMUNICATIONS NETWORKS AND THEIR SCOPE

Components of a Telecommunications Network

As you travel, an automated teller machine (ATM) gives you access to the account in your bank located across the ocean. By accessing the Internet from your desktop computer, you can read the research results posted at a computer in a remote university or review the product update of your favorite software vendor. Your engineers working on a team that is developing a new product with the use of a computer-aided design system remain in constant communication through their personal computers to review each other's work; it does not much matter that some of them work in Wichita, Kansas, and others in Yokohama, Japan. Your salespeople check the status of the customer's order right from the customer's premises, using a notebook computer with a wireless connection. The work on distant sites of your corporation is coordinated with the help of a worldwide information system that includes multiple computers on each location. Your firm's computer automatically processes electronic orders sent in by your customers' computers and sends orders to your suppliers' computers.

All of these very different needs are satisfied by a common enabler: telecommunications. **Telecommunications** are the means of electronic transmission of information over distances. The information may be in the form of voice telephone calls, data, text, images, or video. Today, telecommunications are used to organize more or less remote computer systems into telecommunications networks. These networks themselves are run by computers. A **telecommunications network** is an arrangement of computing and telecommunications resources for communication of information between distant locations. As

Figure 7.2

Components of a telecommunications network

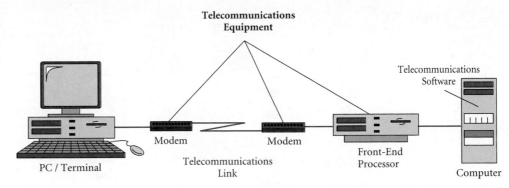

telecommunications networks pervade business life, the solution of many business problems requires the understanding of options in the use and design of these nets.

The telecommunications networks include the following components, shown in Figure 7.2, which we will discuss in detail in this chapter:

1. *Terminals* for accessing the network. A terminal may be a personal computer, a telephone, an automatic teller machine, or a point-of-sale terminal.

2. *Computers* that process information and are interconnected by the network. Many networks include *servers,* that is, computers dedicated to making a specific resource available to other computers and terminals. For example, database servers manage a database and deliver specific data in response to queries.

3. *Telecommunications links* that form a channel through which information is transmitted from a sending device to a receiving device. At various times, terminals and computers play the role of these devices. Telecommunications links are implemented with various media, such as fiber optic cable or satellite transmission.

4. *Telecommunications equipment* that facilitates the transmission of information. **Telecommunications equipment** ranges from modems that facilitate the transmission of data over telephone lines to front-end processors; that is, computers that perform all telecommunications chores for large computers that serve as information processors, called hosts. Telecommunications equipment also includes computer-based switches that store messages or their parts temporarily and then forward them to their destination.

5. *Telecommunications software* that controls message transmission over the network. For example, host computers run telecommunications monitors and microcomputers run network operating systems.

Scope of Telecommunications Networks

Two principal types of telecommunications networks can be distinguished from the point of view of their geographical scope. They are local area networks and wide area networks.

A **local area network (LAN)** is a privately owned network that interconnects processors, usually microcomputers, within a building or on a campus site that includes several buildings. LANs are the principal tool of workgroup computing. A LAN ensures high-speed communication within a limited area and enables the users to share facilities connected to it. These facilities usually include a large-capacity secondary storage device, where database and applications software are maintained, managed by a microcomputer acting as a file server that delivers data or program files to other computers. Other facilities may include a jukebox optical memory and a fast printer (see Figure 7.3). More and more frequently, one of the facilities in a LAN is the gateway hardware and software that give the network users

Figure 7.3

A local area network for workgroup support

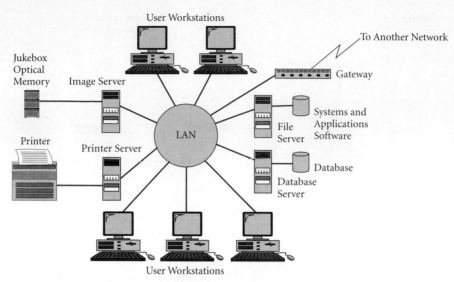

Figure 7.4

A wide area network

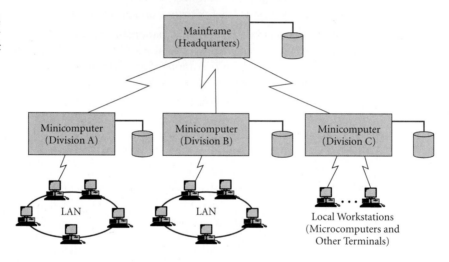

access to other networks. Also, more and more often, group members may connect to the network from remote sites using wireless telecommunications.

Large firms rely on wide area networks for interconnecting their sometimes far-flung computer systems. A **wide area network (WAN)** is a telecommunications network that covers a large geographical area. For example, the information system of an entire organization may be structured as a hierarchy. This matches the traditional structure of many organizations. The system's architecture, that is, its overall design, looks very much like an organization chart, as you can see in Figure 7.4. A wide area network (WAN) connects all the divisional minicomputers to the headquarters mainframe, with a variety of local microcomputers and terminals located at remote sites connected, in turn, to the minicomputers. A firm's wide area network provides the backbone through which all other nodes (computers and terminals) communicate. As shown in Figure 7.4, in most cases the local micros are organized into a LAN. A classic hierarchical network is the corporate network of Dow Corning Corporation. Dow's main data center is located in its Midland, Michigan, corporate headquarters, with regional processors in plants in such cities as Chicago and Elizabethtown, Kentucky, but also in the area headquarters around the globe; for example, in Brussels, Hong Kong, Sydney, and Tokyo (Rowe 1995).

Figure 7.5

Interorganizational links cross corporate boundaries

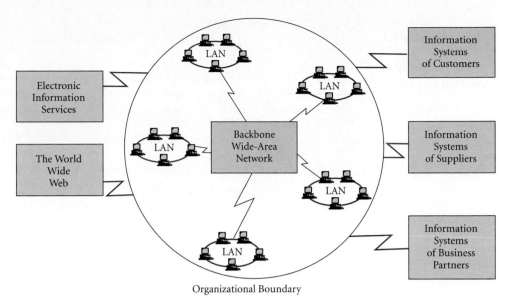

Organizational Boundary

WANs often use telecommunications links and equipment provided by specialized vendors, called common carriers. The links and equipment of LANs are owned by the user company, and these networks are generally much faster. Broadly speaking, WANs serve to interconnect multiple LANs and can make specific resources (such as the computational and data-accessing power of the bigger machines) available to a large number of workstations. LANs, on the other hand, are generally networks of microcomputers.

A more recent development is the emergence of **metropolitan area networks (MAN)**. The purpose of MANs is to interconnect various LANs within a metropolitan area, that is, within approximately a 50-mile range. Cities compete for business by offering fast MANs—their speed approaches that of LANs and they use a similar technology.

Telecommunications networks enable creation of information systems that go beyond the boundary of an organization. Such **interorganizational information systems** are shared by two or more companies (see Figure 7.5). The Internet, which we will further discuss in this chapter, has emerged as a global public network of networks. Some of the interorganizational systems, such as those accessing electronic information services or the Internet's World Wide Web, are employed in knowledge work. Other interorganizational systems, which connect the firm's computers to the information systems of its customers, suppliers, and business partners, are also used to execute business transactions.

We will now turn to the technologies of telecommunications and the networks they enable. We will then see how these technologies may be deployed to redesign business processes for greater effectiveness and efficiency and also to seek competitive advantage.

7.2 | TELECOMMUNICATIONS LINKS

Communications Media

Telecommunications links may be implemented with various communication media, with a corresponding variety of characteristics. The main feature of a medium is its potential transmission speed, also known as **channel capacity,** which for data transmission purposes is expressed in bits per second (bps). An alternative measure of transmission channel capacity is bandwidth—the range of signal frequencies that can be transmitted over the channel.

Table 7.1

Characteristics of transmission media

Characteristics	Transmission Medium					
	Guided			Wireless		
	Twisted Pair	Coaxial Cable	Fiber Optics	Terrestrial Microwave	Satellite	Radio
Potential Transmission Speed	4 Mbps	500 Mbps	30 Gbps	100 Mbps	100 Mbps	2 Mbps
Ease of Installation	Easy	Moderate	Difficult	Moderate	Difficult	Moderate
Cost	Low	Moderate	High	High	High	Moderate
Maintenance Difficulty	Low	Moderate	Low	Low	Low	Low

Note: 1 Gbps = 1,000 Mbps = 1,000,000 Kbps = 1,000,000,000 bits per second.

Six principal media are employed to implement telecommunication links. Three (twisted pair, coaxial cable, and fiber optic cable) are guided media, in which the signal moves along an enclosed path. Guided media require wiring. To use wireless media—terrestrial and satellite microwave transmission or radio transmission—the signal is broadcast (radiated in many directions) over the air or space and received through an antenna. Table 7.1 compares the attributes of the transmission media.

Here are the principal communications media:

1. Twisted Pair

A **twisted pair** of wires is familiar to us all: It is employed as the local loop that connects our telephones to the central office. As they approach the office, these wires are bunched together into cables. Each pair connects to a single telephone or data circuit. The capacity of a twisted pair is limited, but it may be significantly expanded by using wires shielded in aluminum foil or woven copper and by installing additional equipment. This is indeed done when using twisted pair connections in local area networks.

2. Coaxial Cable

A **coaxial cable,** introduced by the cable television industry, consists of a relatively thick central conductor shielded by several layers of insulation and a second conductor just under the cable's shell. Several coaxes may be packed together into a very thick cable.

3. Fiber Optics

A medium of very high capacity, which increasingly replaces other guided media, is **fiber optic cable.** Each optical fiber is a thin strand of pure glass with a data-carrying core in the middle, surrounded by a reflective coating and a protective sheath. The total diameter of the fiber is less than that of a human hair (see Photo 7.1). Data are sent over the fiber in the form of light-beam pulses emitted by a laser or a light-emitting diode. This medium is also quite secure: It is virtually impossible to tap and it does not emit radiation that may be intercepted.

4. Terrestrial Microwave

Terrestrial microwave transmission employs microwave signals for long-distance telecommunications on the surface of the earth. As these signals travel in straight lines, the transmitter and the receiver must be in a direct line of sight. To extend the distances, transmit-

Photo 7.1

The very high data transmission speeds offered by fiber optics are revolutionizing computer networking. This will be the fundamental guided communications medium of the coming fully digital global networks

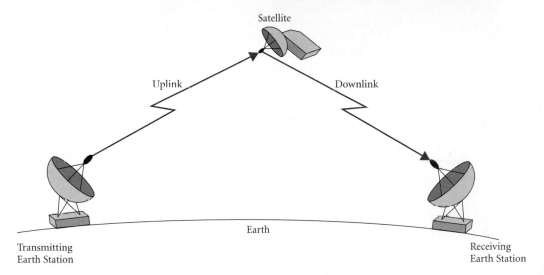

Satellite

Uplink   Downlink

Earth

Transmitting
Earth Station

Receiving
Earth Station

Figure 7.6

Satellite communication

ters and receivers are placed on towers or high buildings, ensuring a range of up to 30 miles. Organizations sometimes establish private microwave links for such limited distances, bypassing local telephone companies. Encryption—encoding the communicating data in a cipher—is needed for secure microwave transmission of any kind.

5. Satellite Transmission

Satellite transmission is a form of microwave transmission, but it can span the globe. A microwave signal is transmitted by an earth station to a satellite orbiting the earth at the equator at an altitude of 22,300 miles. The satellite appears stationary, since its speed matches that of the earth's rotation. The microwave signal is sent to the satellite on the uplink frequency, amplified by the satellite, and rebroadcast to the dish antenna of the receiving station (see Figure 7.6). A single satellite can transmit over more than one-third of the earth.

Satellite communication is burdened by significant propagation delays. Because of the distances involved, the total delay on the uplink and the downlink is about a quarter of a second. This delay must be taken into account in the design of on-line systems, where the average response time for many transactions should be no greater than two seconds.

Satellite Dishes Are No Big Deal Anymore—and Companies Profit

Many earth stations for satellite communication are 10 meters tall and cost over $100,000. But much smaller and less expensive antennas have opened new strategic opportunities for companies involved in the distribution of goods.

Roberts Express of Akron, Ohio, is the world's largest surface expediter of "hot" freight; that is, freight that someone must have right away. Roberts dispatches 975 trucks operated by independent contractors. On the cab of each truck, the firm has mounted a satellite antenna only 11 1/2 inches in diameter and 6 3/4 inches high. Each cab is also equipped with a laptop computer and a communications unit that uses a global positioning system to pinpoint the location of the truck within 300 yards, anywhere in the United States. The cost of equipment, about $4,500 per truck, is split between the company and the truckers.

A system (called Omnitracks) developed by Qualcomm of San Diego, California, enables company dispatchers to know the location of any truck, its cargo, and its proximity to its destination at all times. Dispatchers track the trucks with an on-screen mapping program that allows them to see the vehicles moving on a map. A message sent by a dispatcher travels by telephone lines to Qualcomm's network management facility, which bounces it off a satellite to the cab of the appropriate trucker. Truckers can either send free-form messages, which they type into their terminals, or use predefined fill-in-the-blank message skeletons (which increases their efficiency). Customers can dial in and track their shipments. The system helps avoid "deadheading"—traveling without a cargo because the dispatcher was unable to contact the trucker in time to make a pickup.

Customers use Roberts Express for emergencies. Therefore, the firm competes not with other truckers but with air-freight companies. The firm's management believes that the satellite-based system gives Roberts Express a competitive advantage by raising entry barriers for potential entrants into its niche business; it plans to keep upgrading this system.

Consider another trucker, Schneider National of Green Bay, Wisconsin. The company has doubled its business over the last few years. If you glance behind the cab of its tractor–trailers, you may notice a low-cost satellite antenna. Inside the cab, there is a laptop computer that gives the driver information on road conditions and loads to be picked up. Each truck has become a node in the company's nationwide network. The company's CEO, Don Schneider, has joined many others in perceiving that his real business is managing information rather than just running trucks. Based on this recognition and the constantly introduced new strategic information systems that deploy satellite-based telecommunications, Schneider National has been able to transform itself from a trucking company into a full-service logistics outsourcing firm.

Based on Agis Salpukas, "Satellite System Helps Trucks Stay in Touch," *The New York Times,* June 5, 1991, p. D7; Cheryl Currid, "The CEO's New Clothes," *InformationWeek,* May 9, 1994, p. 96; Todd Lappin, "Trucking," *Wired,* January 1995, pp. 118–123, 166; and Jeanne W. Ross, Cynthia M. Beath, and Dale L. Goodhue, "Develop Long-Term Competitiveness through IT Access," *Sloan Management Review,* Fall 1996, pp. 31–42.

Relatively inexpensive and unobtrusive satellite antennas, known as **very small aperture terminals (VSAT),** have become widely available. A number of companies have replaced their leased-line telecommunications networks with VSAT satellite nets (see Photo 7.2). Such nets are of particular advantage to freight carriers and distributors. Equipped with VSAT, each moving vehicle can be in constant communication with the dispatchers. You may see two examples in the vignette above.

6. Radio Transmission

Radio transmission is a wireless technology that transmits voice or data over the air using a lower frequency band than microwaves. This technology offers lower transmission capac-

Photo 7.2

This is an example of a very small aperture terminal (VSAT) for satellite telecommunications, used by leading automobile dealers. The network-based system broadcasts messages to dealers, performs credit card processing and check authorization, provides access to a database to obtain price information, and supports inventory, parts, and warranty processing.

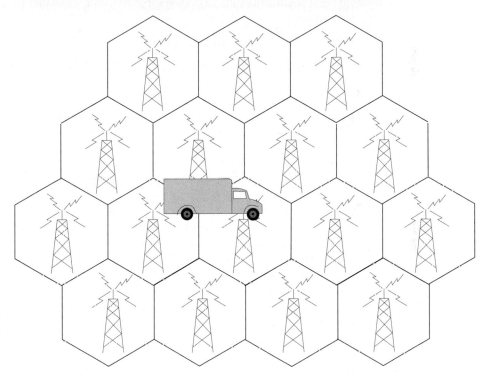

Figure 7.7

The layout of a cellular radio system (From Rowe, 1995, p. 202.)

ity than microwaves but has fewer limitations. It requires neither line-of-sight transmission nor dish antennas. The principal radio transmission technology is cellular radio, with other traditional radio technologies used less frequently for data communications.

Cellular radio systems, used for mobile telephones, are being adapted to the needs of data communication. A cellular service district is subdivided into geographical areas, called cells, each with its own antenna (see Figure 7.7). The user is connected to the antenna closest to his or her current location. As the user moves away from this antenna, the service's computer switches the transmission to the one that is currently closest. The user's device, such as a pager or a personal digital assistant, communicates through the cellular network with the public telephone net. FedEx uses cellular radio terminals in its ubiquitous delivery vans to provide information on request about the status of package delivery. There is a significant interest in remote troubleshooting systems based on cellular radio. Europe has taken the lead in digital cellular service, thanks largely to the single cellular standard spanning the continent. The standard was prompted, of course, by the business needs of so many smaller countries that share the continent.

Table 7.1 showed the potential speeds of communication media. We should note that the transmission speeds actually achieved in a system depend on the equipment employed in it and on how the medium's potential speed is shared among the channels using the medium. Transmission speeds keep on rising, particularly in the fiber optics area. We are now moving toward a global infrastructure of gigabit-speed fiber optic links relying on digital transmission. In this multimedia environment, data, text, voice, images, and video will travel at speeds of billions of bits per second. Wireless media will help people on the move connect to this global network.

As the vignette on the next page illustrates, new telecommunications media offer new competitive opportunities. They also present new problems. Some of these problems come from the immaturity of the technologies, others from resistance to new technologies.

Analog and Digital Communications

Most of the lines in the telephone systems of the world at present are **analog:** Signals are transmitted as continuous waves. This is a satisfactory way to transmit voice, but digital data sent by computers, that is, a sequence of pulses representing 0s and 1s, must be converted into an analog signal for transmission over an analog line. The analog data must then be converted back into digital before entering the memory of the receiving computer. The conversion of data from digital form into analog for transmission and then back into digital at the receiving end is done by a pair of interface devices called **modems** (for modulator-demodulator). Figure 7.8 shows the simple use of a modem in computer telecommunications. Faster modems operate at speeds of 28.8 Kbps or 33.6 Kbps, with 56 Kbps modems becoming available for downloading the information from the Web. To give you an idea of modem speeds, 100 pages of double-spaced text may be sent from New York to San Francisco in about 45 seconds using a 28.8 Kbps modem.

Modem-based telecommunications have created a significant bottleneck in an environment where computer and peripheral speeds have increased dramatically. The wait for the images accessed over the World Wide Web with the use of modems can be excruciating. The solution is end-to-end **digital** communications, in which signals are sent as streams of on/off pulses. Digital lines are capable of much faster communication and digital circuitry is now cheaper than analog. All the new equipment now installed in telephone networks is indeed digital. An analog line can be converted to digital by changing the telecommunications equipment. Thus, the analog/digital property is not a characteristic of the medium but rather of the electronic equipment which ensures undistorted transmission of the signal from one end to another. Repeaters installed in a line at certain intervals to restore the quality of the signal, which deteriorates as it is transmitted, are an example of this equipment.

To remove the bottleneck, a shift toward digital telecommunications is taking place throughout the world. In the United States and in Europe, a digital system for telecommunications, called **T1 carrier,** is in wide use in parts of the telephone network. With its capacity of 1.544 Mbps, it can carry 24 voice channels by multiplexing them (as discussed below). T1 facilities may also be leased by firms or individuals for high-speed data

Is Wireless Ready for Prime Time? It Depends on What You Wish To Do

The golf division of Wilson Sporting Goods of Chicago introduced wireless telecommunications for its sales force in July 1993. Using radio-frequency modems attached to their laptops, the 50-odd salespeople of the company connect over the cellular ARDIS network to the corporate mainframe. They can check inventory and customer credit, place orders, and get immediate confirmation right in the field.

Before the wireless system was established, the salespeople had to download inventory and customer files as they set out on the road. Since the inventory fluctuates continually, this meant that by the end of a week-long sales trip, they were relying on inaccurate data. Sales rep Mike Auger says that his access to on-line information is a big selling point: "My customers can see the inventory numbers changing right on my laptop; it makes them feel more confident in the information I'm giving them." On-the-spot ordering also cuts several days out of the order cycle, speeds up invoicing and shipping, and thus increases customer satisfaction.

The national sales manager of the golf division feels that the wireless application gives the company a competitive edge. But he also sees the limitation of the system. In more remote areas of the country, the cellular coverage is poor. In addition, some salespeople feel they are inconvenienced by carrying around the radio-frequency modem, which is about the size of a small portable telephone. There is also some reluctance among the salespeople to try out new technology. Therefore, they revert to dialing headquarters for information. The information systems supervisor of the golf division is reevaluating its commitment to the technology. Indeed, Wilson's other two divisions have already dropped their wireless projects.

On the other hand, Sara Lee Knit Products, a knit-clothing manufacturer located in Winston-Salem, is a satisfied user of wireless local area networks. Installed in the shipping departments of the company's eight cutting plants in the United States and Puerto Rico, the LANs are used to track the contents of the containers being prepared for shipping. These contents are the pre-cut garment parts destined for any one of the 35 apparel plants Sara Lee owns in Latin America. Portable computers (IBM 2484) with built-in bar-code scanners and adapters for wireless communication are placed on forklifts. The computers exchange radio signals with LAN access points (radio transmitters-receivers) located on the facility's floor. The access points are connected to the wired LAN and, through a WAN, to the central minicomputer that generates work orders sent via the network to the forklifts. The work orders tell the operators what goods to pick and where to send them.

Thanks to the wireless system, the efficiency of picking and moving goods at Sara Lee has increased significantly. Beyond that, the firm now pays a fraction of up to the $60,000 a month it used to pay to U.S. Customs in penalties for wrong goods placed in containers. After the total investment of $450,000 for the eight plants where the wireless LANs have been installed, Sara Lee saves about one-half million dollars a year, thanks to the use of this system.

Based on Carol Hildebrand, "Getting Unwired," *CIO*, October 1, 1994, pp. 37–43; and Sam Dickey, "Wireless to the Rescue," *Beyond Computing*, October 1996, pp. 50–53.

Figure 7.8

Telecommunication over a telephone line

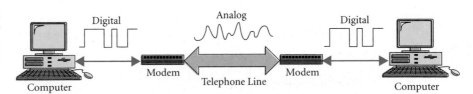

communication, in particular, for accessing the Internet. Carriers of much higher speed (T2 through T4) are being introduced as well. While T1 carrier can rely on a twisted-pair connection, the higher-speed versions must employ higher-speed media.

The future of global telecommunications is linked to the gradual introduction of the advanced form of an **Integrated Services Digital Network (ISDN)**—a completely digital telecommunications network standardized by an international committee (CCITT[1]). Although ISDN services are already available in some areas, including most of the United States, worldwide ISDN is not expected to become operational until after the year 2000. The countries of the European Union are more advanced than the United States in the deployment of ISDN. Any digital equipment conforming to ISDN standards will be able to connect directly to the global network and to communicate with any appropriate device at the other end. The network will automatically furnish the channel required by a terminal, fax machine, or telephone. The channels supplied by ISDN today have speeds of 64 or 144 Kbps—a significant speed-up from today's analog environment, but not sufficient for fully capable multimedia transmission. This is why the interest of telecommunications providers and users has shifted to broadband ISDN (B-ISDN) for future computer-to-computer communications and for carrying video information. This digital service is expected to provide transmission speeds between 155 and 622 Mbps—some 2,500 faster than plain ISDN! The users of broadband ISDN will be able to carry on a conversation and simultaneously exchange images and data over a single line of the telephone network. High-quality television images could be transmitted over the fiber optics transmission lines relying on B-ISDN.

How to Reduce the Costs of Telecommunications: Multiplexing and Signal Compression

With the geographical distribution of information systems, increased volumes of transmissions, and the move to multimedia, the costs of telecommunications are a significant business concern. Two principal methods of reducing these costs are multiplexing—the sharing of a high-capacity link by a number of transmissions, and signal compression—using the link more efficiently by removing redundancies from the signal. Let us discuss them.

1. Multiplexing

There are economies of scale in telecommunications systems: the higher the system capacity, the lower the unit cost of transmission. For example, the cost of laying a cable or launching a satellite is, up to a point, independent of the transmission capacity, and so it pays to provide high-capacity media. Many individual transmissions can share a physical channel through a variety of techniques collectively called **multiplexing.** Multiplexing combines several lower-capacity transmissions into a single transmission, which is split at the receiving end. Thanks to multiplexing, a single coaxial cable can carry up to 10,800 conversations and a fiber optic cable—over 20,000.

2. Signal Compression

Most data to be transmitted have elements that can be removed without information loss. **Signal compression** is the reduction of the need for channel capacity by removing redundancies from the signal. To reduce the transmission needs, we can remove the redundancies at the sender site, transmit the compressed signal, and then restore the signal at the receiving end.

Consider video transmission that is used, for example, in videoconferencing (discussed further in Chapter 8). To get a full-motion video effect, we need to transmit 30 frames (individual screen images) a second. Each frame is transmitted as a series of color specifications for consecutive pixels (picture elements). We can compress each frame by specifying in a code that, for example, "the next 50 pixels are of color with code 215." We can also compress across frames, by specifying only the distinctions between a given frame and the preceding one. Thus, we transmit only the "moving parts," reusing the background from a previous frame when possible.

Compression has an impressive effect on multimedia transmission needs. A television signal without compression requires a 45 Mbps link as contrasted with videoconferencing systems that use 1.544 Mbps channels, or even 64 Kbps channels if some jerky movements or blurring can be forgiven. Compression techniques have been devised to bring video-on-demand to individual residences without the need to replace twisted pair connections "from the curb" by fiber optic links, which would be prohibitively expensive.

7.3 | COMPUTER NETWORKS

As we know, computer networks differ in scope from relatively slow wide area networks, employed to transmit messages across vast geographic distances, to very fast local area networks that may connect computers located in the same building. System designers may select one of several arrangements for interconnecting network nodes, depending on an organization's requirements. There are also several ways to establish a connection between the sender and the receiver of a message.

Network Topologies

Computers, switches, and terminals interconnected by network links are collectively called *nodes*. The purpose of network control is to provide a connection between nodes that need to communicate. The arrangement of nodes and links in a network is called its **topology.** A variety of arrangements is possible, each with its own advantages and drawbacks. Network topology has to fit the structure of the organizational unit that will use the network, and this topology should also be adapted to the unit's communication traffic patterns and to the way the databases will be stored in order to facilitate access to them.

The following topologies are the most widely used:

1. Hierarchical Network

A hierarchical network with a corporate host computer (often a mainframe), divisional minicomputers or powerful workstations, and workgroup support via micros was shown in Figure 7.4. This topology matches the organizational structure of many firms and is still frequently used in wide area networks. The user workstations may be, in turn, interconnected using one of the LAN topologies. Failure of the host does not disable divisional processing, which is a fail-safe feature. Cost-effectiveness of micros and the growing importance of groupwork leads some downsizing firms to move away from hierarchical networks to client/server computing, discussed in Section 6 of this chapter.

2. Star Network

In a star network, shown in Figure 7.9a, a hub computer or switch (such as a PBX, which we will discuss later) interconnects a number of workstations. The computer at the hub acts as the network server, providing access to the shared database and software. All communications between the workstations must go through this central node. The star network is rather easy to manage and expand, since in both cases it is largely the single central node that is affected in an expansion of a processing capacity. But this central node is also a locus of vulnerability: It may be overloaded or it may fail, disabling the entire network.

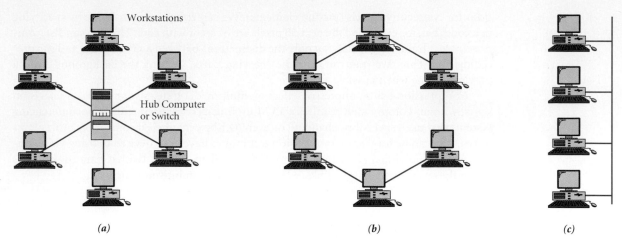

Workstations

Hub Computer
or Switch

(a)   *(b)*   *(c)*

Figure 7.9

*Network topologies
a. Star; b. Ring; c. Bus*

Computerized airline reservation system and automatic teller machine (ATM) nets are generally configured in a star: A large mainframe computer (usually a multiprocessor) in the hub serves many terminals.

3. Ring Network

Each node in a ring network is connected to two of its neighbors, as shown in Figure 7.9b. The nodes are usually close to one another; this topology is frequently used in LANs. When one node sends a message to another, the message passes through each intermediate node, which restores the signal, as signals deteriorate in transmission. If a node fails, the ring is out of service, unless the ring contains two channels transmitting in opposite directions.

4. Bus Network

The nodes on a bus network (see Figure 7.9c) are connected to a common link such as coaxial cable. As is true of the ring, this arrangement is used in LANs. A failing device does not affect the rest of the network; failure of the bus itself, of course, brings the network down.

Switching in Networks

Many users can be connected at the same time to a network of communication channels. How is the connection between two nodes established so that communication can take place? Establishing this interconnection is called **switching** and it is done by computer-based switches. Here are the principal techniques for switching:

1. Circuit Switching

The circuit switching technique is employed in a telephone network. Communication links are connected to switching centers, which connect one node to another on demand. The circuit is established for the entire duration of the communication. Circuit switching is suitable for file transfers and similar longer transmissions.

2. Packet Switching

Packet switching is of particular importance for data communication owing to its speed and its superior utilization of communication links when handling "bursty," intermittent, traffic. Indeed, data transmission involves short bursts of activity by a computer or a termi-

Figure 7.10

Packet switching

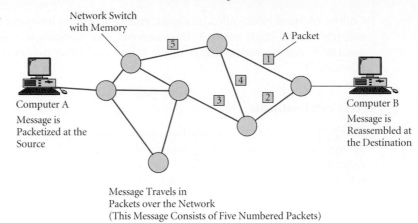

Packet-Switching Network

Network Switch with Memory

A Packet

Computer A

Message is Packetized at the Source

Computer B

Message is Reassembled at the Destination

Message Travels in Packets over the Network
(This Message Consists of Five Numbered Packets)

nal when the data are sent, followed by long periods when there is no transmission. Packet switching also offers flexibility in connecting to a network. It is used by most of the public data networks provided by value-added carriers.

In packet switching, messages are divided at the source into fixed-length chunks, called packets, that also include bits identifying the receiver. Typically, a packet contains 128 bytes of data. Each packet can be transmitted independently, with routing determined at each node the packet passes through (as opposed to circuit switching, where the route is predetermined). Packet switching using this technique is illustrated in Figure 7.10.

Each intermediate node may store and then forward a packet. The destination node reassembles the packets into a complete message. Packet switching, in which each packet of a message follows the same route, is standardized in the CCITT Recommendation X.25. Thanks to this international standard, national public packet-switching networks may be interconnected into a global network. Indeed, the Internet relies on packet switching.

3. Fast Packet Switching

Traditional packet switching under X.25 standard checks each packet for errors at every node the packet passes through. Yet, modern telecommunications equipment is far more noise-free than that for which packet switching was originally designed. To take advantage of this fact, two fast packet-switching technologies are being introduced.

Frame relay checks a packet for errors only at the entry and exit nodes of the network, thus reducing transmission delay. Frame relay systems can take packets from various LANs, enclose them into variable-length frames, and transmit them over a WAN backbone network at speeds ranging between 56 Kbps and 2.048 Mbps.

Cell relay, also known as the **asynchronous transfer mode,** or **ATM** (do not confuse it with banks' ATM!) is an even newer technology, which transfers very short fixed-length packets, called cells, over fast LANs or WANs. A cell is 53-bytes long and comprises 5 bytes of address and 48 bytes of data. Such short packets sent over high-speed networks (from 45 Mbps to 1.2 Gbps—that's over a billion bits per second!) enable superior transmission of video information. Because of high speeds, this technology may be used to combine transmissions of packets from several LANs at the same time. ATM is becoming the principal technology of broadband integrated services digital network (B-ISDN), discussed earlier, and thus a technology of choice for multimedia transmissions.

7.4 | COMMUNICATIONS PROTOCOLS IN COMPUTER NETWORKS

Communication rules, called protocols, enable dissimilar hardware and software to communicate over a single network. Inter-network communication is also a frequent requirement of businesses today; that is why it is important that networks conform to standard protocols.

Network Protocols

Computer networks exist to provide connectivity among a variety of computers and access devices, such as point-of-sale terminals or automatic teller machines. To ensure orderly communication over a network, all the nodes in the network must follow a set of rules called **protocol**. These rules are complex. They extend from the electric connection to the network and the format of the message, all the way to the interaction between application programs that run on different nodes. With the globalization of telecommunications, protocol design is best handled by international bodies. In fact, the International Standards Organization has developed the Open Systems Interconnection (OSI) model—a seven-layer structure for organizing protocols. This *open system* approach opens the field to a broad array of competing vendors, a situation that benefits users, who need not be locked into the closed, proprietary protocol structure of a specific manufacturer.

The OSI model gives both users and vendors flexibility in conforming to a standard. They can select a protocol for any layer of the model, as long as the protocol performs the necessary services and provides the same interface to the adjacent layers. If a layer has to be changed, only the hardware or software implementing that layer need be modified. The OSI model is illustrated in Figure 7.11. A protocol layer in one node interacts with the corresponding layer in another one. It is useful to study the OSI model to understand the functions that computer networks must handle.

Table 7.2 explains the function of each of the seven layers of protocol. It is best to start your reading with the functions of the highest, or seventh, layer. Network architecture such as OSI involves three levels of connectivity: physical (between hardware devices and communication channels), systems (between various levels of systems programs), and applications (between application programs).

To understand how the OSI architecture operates, let us consider a PC user on node A who wants to send a file to another computer (node B). The application layer on both nodes

Figure 7.11

The Open Systems Interconnection (OSI) model

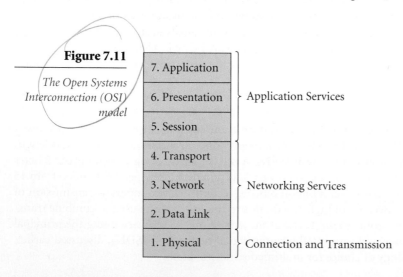

Table 7.2	Layer	Function
Layers of the OSI model and their functions	1. Physical	Provides access to the telecommunications medium and ensures transmission of the bit stream over it.
	2. Data link	Ensures error-free transmission of frames (blocks) of data over a network link.
	3. Network	Routes message (or packets) from source to destination by selecting connecting links.
	4. Transport	Provides reliable end-to-end connection between two communicating nodes. When packet switching is used (according to the X.25 standard), this layer breaks a message into packets.
	5. Session	Establishes, maintains, and terminates a connection (session) between two applications running on communicating nodes. A session lasts, for example, from a log-on to a specific application to a log-off.
	6. Presentation	Provides any necessary conversions of the characters being sent (encryption/decryption, compression/decompression, or character code conversions). Issues requests for establishing and terminating a session to the session layer.
	7. Application	Provides services to communicating application programs; examples include file transfer, running a remote program, allocating a remote peripheral, and ensuring integrity of remote databases.

receives the user's instructions and identifies the file. The presentation layer ensures that the file, when transferred, is in the format appropriate for node B. The session layer initiates the transfer session. The transport layer breaks up the file into packets (assuming that ours is a packet-switching net) that the network layer routes to node B. The data link layer transmits packets over individual links, checking for errors, and the physical layer makes sure that the bits reach node B.

Note that the overhead encountered in implementing the OSI model is significant. In a sending node, the "protocol stack" is descended as the message is sent, while in the receiving node, the stack is ascended as the message is received.

Two protocol sets have gained importance. A widely used proprietary protocol set, which by now has many characteristics of an open system, is IBM's Systems Network Architecture (SNA). Its functions are broken down into layers, just as in the OSI model. There are five layers in SNA, basically performing the functions of the five middle OSI levels. The Internet, which we discuss in the next section, relies on a set of packet-switching protocols known as TCP/IP (for Transmission Control Protocol/Internet Protocol). In this five-layer protocol suite, TCP provides the higher-level services in connecting the communicating applications (for example, establishing a connection for E-mail programs), while IP ensures the lower-level functions of routing and addressing, guiding the packets over the Internet.

Interconnections among Networks

As communication needs increase, network connectivity becomes a major issue: A user at a terminal wants to be able to access a computer resource located virtually anywhere or to send a message to another, remote, user. To gain access to a remote resource, such as a database or a mass storage device with a document base, the user must not only be placed on a network but that net must be connected to the one where the resource is. The ideal is a "seamless" system, in which users are not aware that the resource is not directly a part of their system. In a multivendor environment, connectivity is difficult and costly to achieve. Gateways such as routers and bridges help solve the problem.

Interconnection between two networks of the same type is accomplished by a relatively simple **bridge,** implemented in hardware and software. Interconnection between dissimilar networks, for example, a LAN and a WAN, is achieved through a more complex **router,** as it is done in the Internet. A router is a device that accepts messages in the format produced by one of the networks and translates them into the format used by the other. For example, in networks providing an integrated environment for an office information system, routers are available to connect the workgroup LANs to the company's backbone WAN as well as to connect this backbone to other wide area nets. Specialized software is available to control traffic in these interconnected networks. Interconnecting multiple LANs, operating under different protocols, is now frequently done through an *intelligent hub*—a single box into which an adapter for each of the nets is inserted.

7.5 | LOCAL AREA NETWORKS

Organizations small and large use fast local area networks (LANs) to interconnect personal computers and thus make them a basic workgroup tool. Instead of wiring local computers together through communication links, some firms elect to interconnect them with a private branch exchange (PBX), an upgraded telephone switchboard.

Local Area Network: Workplace for a Workgroup

A local area network (LAN) interconnects computers within a single site, such as an office building, a manufacturing plant, or a corporate or university campus. With the use of additional equipment, a LAN can cover distances of a few miles, but commonly its scope is measured in feet. Communication speeds are very high, in some cases up to 100 Mbps. This makes network transmission almost transparent to the users.

Today, local area networks are the principal nets of smaller businesses and are used as local means of computing and communication among users in larger firms. LANs are owned by the organization, and, in another sense, "owned" by the workgroup that uses them. This affords a sense of control and the flexibility to meet the demands of the end users. Indeed, LANs are the principal building blocks of today's office information systems, which we will further discuss in Chapter 8.

A LAN gives its users the following capabilities:

1. Users can share resources, such as a fast printer or a database.
2. Users can collaborate by communicating over their LAN. This collaboration may be facilitated by groupware that runs on a LAN, as we will see in Chapter 8.
3. Users can access other networks within a firm or outside of it via bridges and routers.

There are two principal LAN designs: peer-to-peer and server-based networks. In peer-to-peer networks, which are generally simpler, the peripherals are located at terminals and system administration is largely left up to the users. The more powerful server-based LAN architectures place shared resources at dedicated servers—high-speed micros (and some-

Photo 7.3

This server makes up to 14 CD-ROM optical disk drives accessible to workstations over a local area network (This is CD Net from Meridian Data, Inc., of Scotts Valley, California.)

times larger machines) that manage a given resource on behalf of user workstations sharing the resource. Thus, a network may include a file server, which manages a disk on which the database and application programs are stored, a printer server, and a gateway that connects the LAN to other dissimilar networks (see Figure 7.3). An optical-disk server is shown in Photo 7.3. Most of the servers are dedicated to their task; using them as workstations degrades the performance of the net. Server-based networks facilitate centralized administration and professional support of the net. An especially important type of server-based network is client/server nets, discussed in the next section.

The most frequently used LAN topologies are bus and ring. Bus or star topology is used in networks based on the Ethernet technology, pioneered by Xerox and offered by many vendors. When using this technology, a workstation broadcasts its message over the network, indicating the address of the receiver, which detects when it is being addressed. While Ethernet LANs generally operate at the speed of 10 Mbps, new fast Ethernet LANs run at 100 Mbps. Other networks, notably IBM's PCNET, are token rings. The nodes in such a ring communicate by token passing. In a token-passing network, an "envelope" message, called a token, is passed from one node to the next. When a node receives the token, it may place its message on the ring, addressing it to an appropriate receiver, or simply pass the token to the next node. A LAN is controlled by a network operating system, which can be placed on every workstation or on a dedicated file server. The leader in this software market is Novell Corporation's NetWare, which offers a number of protocols and configurations, including client/server. Some versions of NetWare replace single-machine operating systems, others run under these systems.

Twisted pair is the most frequent communication medium in LANs. Coaxial cable and fiber-optic cables are also used. To avoid the cost and inflexibility of wiring, wireless LANs are increasingly installed. The wireless media include infrared light, which permits only line-of-sight connections with a speed of up to 1 Mbps, and radio transmissions that do not have these limitations (see Photo 7.4).

Local Networks Based on Private Branch Exchanges

A company with a large number of telephones (from 50 to over 10,000) often elects to own a computer-based **private branch exchange (PBX)**, an electronic switchboard that interconnects its telephones and provides connections to the public network. A PBX gives a

Photo 7.4

*This device is a part of
a local area network in
the Wireless Warehouse
of Peak Technologies
Group. The wireless
network uses high-
frequency radio signals
for communication. The
computers, terminals,
and communications
devices may be placed
hundreds of feet apart,
some of them on fork-
lift trucks, and they
may communicate over
obstructing walls*
(Courtesy of Peak
Technologies Group,
Columbia, Maryland.)

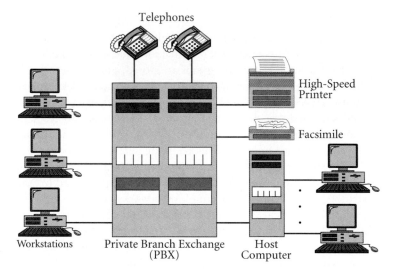

Figure 7.12

*A local network based
on PBX*

company control over the usage of its telephone system and offers a variety of features, such as call forwarding or voice messaging.

A PBX may be employed as a switch for data communications as well (see Figure 7.12). For example, with a PBX we may connect user workstations to one another, to a larger host computer, and other shared equipment. Many newer PBXs are expressly designed to support data communication. They use digital technology, eliminating the need for modems, and perform conversions needed to ensure connectivity between various equipment and telecommunications links.

Among the advantages of PBX use for local networking is the ease of connecting a new workstation to the net: All one needs to do is plug it into a telephone outlet. However, speeds of PBX-based networks are limited.

7.6 | CLIENT/SERVER COMPUTING

An important current development in organizational computing is **downsizing:** moving from platforms based on mainframes and minicomputers to a microcomputing environment. We need not conclude that the larger machines will no longer be used in information systems. When drawing up an organizational information system architecture, we need to consider, however, the opportunities offered by networks organized from micros. Increasingly, these architectures are based on the client/server model. In this model, personal computers share the work on a given application with more powerful machines, acting as servers. Servers may, indeed, be mainframes, but usually they are powerful microcomputers (such as IBM's RS/6000 workstations) or, in some cases, minis.

In **client/server computing,** the processing of a given application (such as handling a spare-parts inventory, for example) is split up among a number of clients—serving individual users—and one or more servers—providing access to databases and doing most of the computing. The main objective of a client, usually a personal computer, is to provide a graphical user interface (GUI) to a user. The main objective of a server is to provide shared services (such as access to a database or generation of a report) to clients. Client/server computing goes beyond allocating a specific service, such as managing a printer or a database, to a server. In this environment, *individual applications* are actually written to run on several computer platforms to take advantage of their capabilities. This also makes client/server computing difficult to implement.

The most frequently used models of client/server computing are shown in Figure 7.13. In the two-tier architecture, shown in Figure 7.13a, the client (user's workstation) performs presentation services: It displays the graphical interface and runs the program that determines what happens when the user selects a menu option. The application logic—for example, the calculation of the average sale per store in a specific region in the second quarter—is either done completely, or largely, on the server. The server manages completely the accesses to the database, which are necessary to obtain the sales data for the computation.

Figure 7.13

Client/server configurations

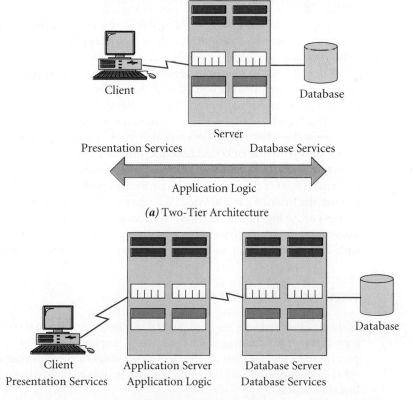

Client
Presentation Services

Server
Database Services

Application Logic

(a) Two-Tier Architecture

Client
Presentation Services

Application Server
Application Logic

Database Server
Database Services

Database

(b) Three-Tier Architecture

Figure 7.14

An enterprise-wide client/server network

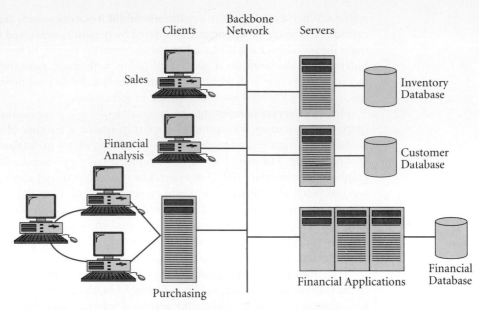

Clients send *remote procedure calls* to activate specific applications logic on a server. For example, a client may send a request for a server to compute and send over the average sale amount without sending the detailed data.

In the three-tier architecture, shown in Figure 7.13b, the application server runs most of the application logic, with the user workstation responsible for the display at the front end and the database server providing database services at the back end. The objective is to distribute an application so as to reduce the overall hardware costs while minimizing the network traffic.

Client/server architectures are attractive both in terms of their acquisition price as related to their performance and because they move computing control out of the data centers and into the end-user areas. This is achieved through the considerable complexity of the software, which is expensive to maintain and, in many cases, bears the costs of migration from the older legacy systems. Also, these architectures tend to generate significant traffic on the firm's backbone network, that connects clients and servers, for example, as shown in Figure 7.14. It is wise to invest in an expandable backbone net.

Client/server computing can be performed both in a LAN and in a WAN environment. Indeed, the Internet's World Wide Web relies on this model for connecting the workstations of users accessing the information resources of the Web to the remote servers that make this information available to them (as we will discuss below). We will now turn our attention to wide area networks that undergird long-distance telecommunications.

7.7 WIDE AREA NETWORKS

Wide area networks are the fundamental infrastructure of organizational computing. These long-distance telecommunications networks employ a variety of equipment so that the expensive links may be used efficiently. The offerings of common carriers and of providers of value-added services may be combined with private networks to create an overall organizational network.

Telecommunications Equipment for Wide Area Networks

Aside from telecommunication links, wide area networks also include the equipment that controls message transfers and makes it possible to share the links among a number of transfers. A configuration comprised of the principal equipment is shown in Figure 7.15, although a variety of topologies is, of course, possible. In addition, user workstations may be connected into a LAN that communicates with the WAN via a gateway.

The configuration in Figure 7.15 includes a powerful computer, called the *host* of the network. The host runs a systems program, called a **telecommunications monitor,** which processes incoming messages, passing them to the appropriate application programs, and accepts outgoing messages from the applications in order to transmit them into the network. To relieve the host of most of the tasks involved in network control, these tasks are allocated to the **front-end processor** which, under the control of its own software, accepts messages coming from the network and routes outgoing messages to their destinations. The front-end processor performs the necessary code conversions, encrypts and decrypts secure messages, and performs error checking so that the host deals only with "clean" messages.

On remote locations of the network in Figure 7.15 are three types of devices that may be used to control access terminals. All of them may be implemented using minicomputers or powerful micros. A **cluster controller** manages several terminals, connecting them to a single telecommunications link, and performs communication tasks for them, such as screen formatting, code conversion, and error checking. A cluster controller may also allow

Figure 7.15

Telecommunications equipment in a wide area network

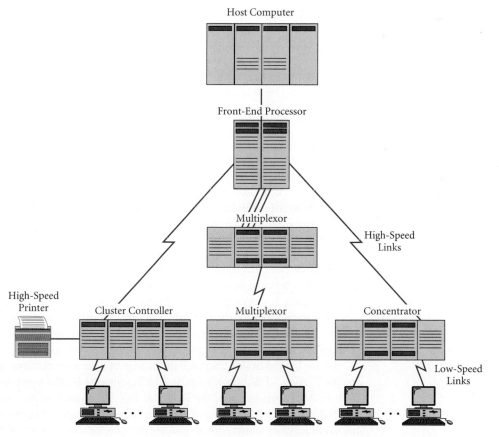

the terminals to share a high-speed printer and may handle electronic mail among the cluster terminals. Such a controller may be installed, for example, in a bank's branch office for a cluster of tellers' terminals.

Multiplexors and concentrators are used to utilize communication lines more efficiently: The lines are an expensive item in network operation. A **multiplexor** combines the data that terminals send to it over local low-speed links into a single stream. This stream is then transmitted over a high-speed telecommunications channel and is split by another multiplexor on the opposite end of the channel. For example, the data from four terminals transmitting at 14.4 Kbps bps over a short cable to the local multiplexor may be combined into one 57.6 Kbps bps transmission over a transoceanic cable, at significant savings.

A **concentrator** combines transmissions from several slower terminals that operate in a burst mode (such as data queries sent to a host) into a single transmission stream that requires a link of lower speed than the sum of the speeds of all the terminals combined. A concentrator does this by storing messages from the terminals and forwarding them when warranted, thus squeezing out idle terminal time and helping to use the available link capacity more efficiently. The use of concentrators (which are more expensive than multiplexors) produces further economies in the utilization of telecommunication links.

Another type of equipment used in computer communication networks is a switch, generally computer-based. A network *switch* establishes connections between nodes that need to communicate, since relatively few nodes are connected point-to-point for economy's sake. We saw such switches in the packet-switching network pictured in Figure 7.10.

Access terminals include a variety of dumb terminals, with no processing capacity (e.g., some automatic teller machines or bar-code readers) and intelligent terminals with processing capacity, such as personal computers. When intelligent terminals are employed, some message handling tasks may be off-loaded to them. The overall distribution of "intelligence"—or processing capability—among the hosts, the various telecommunications equipment, and the workstations depends on the network's overall topology and the nature of the applications to be handled by the network. It is established at the time of network design.

Where Do Facilities for Wide Area Networks Come From?

Some network facilities are owned by user organizations; others can be leased by them, or simply used on a pay-as-you-go basis. Among the typical facilities owned by user firms are workstations, host computers, and front-end processors. The essential providers of telecommunications links and services are common carriers and the vendors of enhanced services on value-added networks.

1. Common Carriers

Common carriers are companies licensed by a country's government to provide telecommunications services to the public. The vast majority of common carriers provide telephone service. These carriers offer the use of a wide-area telecommunications infrastructure; that is, facilities for the transmission of voice and data messages. Many countries of the world have a single common carrier owned by the government, since this service is considered there a natural monopoly. In other countries, common carriers compete.

In the United States, there are thousands of common carriers, with only a few of them "major players." The best-known is AT&T, followed by the seven companies that resulted from its break-up in 1983, the Regional Bell Operating Companies (RBOCs). These regional companies provide services in the non-overlapping regions of the country. For example, Bell Atlantic owns the operating companies that provide telephone service to all of the northeastern seaboard of the United States. Other larger common carriers include GTE (which operates US Sprint) and MCI Communications. Most of the remaining companies are small independents. Specialized common carriers are also emerging. Of particular importance are the satellite common carriers, which operate satellites and sell the communication capacities that they provide. The earth stations may be owned by the user firms. The telecommunications links provided by common carriers are shared by their users, be it an individual making a telephone call or a retail store sending its daily operating data to corporate headquarters. Wide area corporate networks often rely on public telephone links. Linkage between communicating agents in the public telephone system is established by circuit switching.

A new service offered by common carriers is a **virtual private network:** A user firm can purchase guaranteed access to facilities with specified capabilities, such as transmission speed and access points. However, the user does not lease an actual set of links: The configuration is defined in software, and links are shared with other users. Virtual private networks offer lower prices and greater flexibility for reconfiguration as compared to private networks. It is expected that companies will increasingly establish virtual private networks over the Internet for multimedia telecommunications (Heath 1996).

2. Providers of Value-Added Networks

Value-added vendors lease facilities from the common carriers and provide telecommunications services to their own customers. These vendors add value to the basic infrastructure furnished by the common carrier. The **value-added networks** (VAN) provided by the vendors furnish services over and above those provided by common carriers. The sophistication of the service varies widely. A value-added carrier may simply provide a packet-switching network. For example, Telenet (owned by GTE) offers packet-switched communication services as well as electronic mail. Subscribers pay for the actual number of packets transmitted, which proves economical if they send only moderate amounts of data over long distances.

Table 7.3 lists the principal value-added services available over telecommunications networks. We discuss these services in Chapters 8 and 9, according to their use in organizational computing. The Internet offerings are discussed in the next section.

There are many value-added networks that serve specific industries, such as the SWIFT network, owned cooperatively by the member banks of the Society for Worldwide Interbank Financial Telecommunications. The network connects over 2,000 banks around the globe and performs electronic funds transfers. More than a trillion dollars a day are transferred over this network. As another example, GEISCO, a subsidiary of General Electric, is the largest "enhanced communications" supplier in the world. It uses its telecommunications infrastructure to offer a great variety of value-added services, from processing electronic payments to furnishing communications and information services for "smart buildings."

Of particular importance are the VANs providing wireless data telecommunications. By untethering users from their offices, wires, and wall jacks, they offer new business opportunities. United Parcel Service, for example, has equipped its entire fleet of delivery trucks with cellular equipment using the services of McCaw Cellular Communications.

3. Private Lines and Private Networks

Instead of using a service that has to be shared with others, a firm may lease its own private lines or entire networks from carriers. This can have economic advantages as compared with VAN use, as well as provide faster and more secure communications. The U.S. common carriers, including the satellite carriers, offer a number of tariffs (that is, prices with corresponding services) for leased communication channels. Leasing links can result in savings for high-volume point-to-point communications. The links may also be upgraded to meet the specific requirements of a particular user firm.

Table 7.3

Services available over value-added telecommunications networks

Internet Access	Access to the Internet and through it to the World Wide Web and many other facilities.
Audiotex	Information and entertainment ("infotainment") services furnished over the telephone (800 and 900 numbers).
Videotex	Information and entertainment delivered via a personal computer (for example, Prodigy).
Electronic Mail	See Chapter 8 for a discussion of E-mail and related services.
Videoconferencing	People at different sites can see and hear each other, but also are able to exchange documents and graphics.
Electronic Data Interchange (EDI)	Computer-to-computer interchange of electronic transaction documents (see Chapter 9).
Facsimile	Fax transmission of documents has become ubiquitous.
Transaction Processing	Banks' automatic teller machine (ATM) networks, merchants' point-of-sale (POS) services, credit verification services for credit-card companies.
Electronic Information Services	Vital for corporate environmental scanning—see the listing in Chapter 8.
Time-sharing	On-line access to computing facilities.

7.8 | THE INTERNET AND ELECTRONIC COMMERCE

It is difficult to exaggerate the importance of the Internet, a global network of networks, in the way people in organizations access information, communicate with others, and do business with people in other firms or within their own company. In particular, the World Wide Web, a distributed software facility that organizes the information on the Internet into a network of interrelated electronic documents, has changed the face of individual and organizational computing. Driven by the possibilities offered by the Internet and the Web, electronic commerce is expanding its reach.

Present and Future of the Internet

The Internet is the global network of computer networks without a centralized control that has become the contemporary "information superhighway." To connect to the Internet, a member network has to send and receive data packets using the TCP/IP protocol suite. A series of routers forwards the packets to their destination. In 1995 this explosively growing network interconnected over 44,000 networks in 160 countries, with 40 to 50 million computers connected to them (Spar and Bussgang 1996). The number of Internet host computers doubled in 1995 from the previous year both in North America and in Europe (Lavin 1996) and the number of networks interconnected by it surpassed 100,000 by the end of 1996. In the United States alone, between 30 and 40 million people are estimated to use the World Wide Web or other Internet facilities (Cortese 1997). The explosive growth continues.

The Internet has evolved from a small research network started in 1969, as related in the following vignette. The network is run in a decentralized fashion by a number of

IN THE SPOTLIGHT

We Give You a Brief History and We Give You the Father of the Internet, Vinton Cerf

In the late 1960s, the Advanced Research Projects Agency (ARPA) of the U.S. Department of Defense started funding research in computer networks. The agency wished to support the development of a computer network without central control, which has led some people to believe that ARPA's interest was in developing a computing resource that could withstand a nuclear attack. The research led to the creation of the ARPANET, which began as an experimental four-node computer network. On November 21, 1969, Leonard Kleinrock, a computer science professor at the University of California, Los Angeles, and a few graduate students were present at the birth of computer networking. As they typed the message "are you receiving this?" into a typewriter keyboard wired to a telecommunications processor, they received a reply from Stanford University in Palo Alto, "Yes."

This small network evolved into the Internet—a network of networks, spanning the globe. For a long time, the backbone of the network was funded by the National Science Foundation. More recently, the U.S. government has moved toward shifting the supervision of the Internet into the private sector. Vinton Cerf (Photo 7.5), creator of the TCP/IP telecommunications protocol suite, founder of the Internet Society, and chairman of many boards that coordinate the activities of the voluntary network, is considered the father of the Internet. In 1973, Cerf sketched the simple protocol that now unifies the global Internet on the back of an envelope in a San Francisco hotel. He then had to work for years to have it adopted as standard. Cerf once compared the task of keeping the network working to "holding a tiger by the tail." Let's see how he answers a few interesting questions.

Photo 7.5

Vinton Cerf, father of the Internet (From Gary Anthes, *Computerworld,* February 7, 1994, pp. 121, 122.)

Question: The Internet is doubling in size every year. Can it continue to scale up indefinitely?

Cerf: I think we have a reasonable handle on how to get the system to scale up into the billion-network range. That's the target that is inescapable. There are 600 million telephones in the world, and in seven years there could be twice that number. My ultimate either dream or nightmare is that in every place there is a telephone, there will be a switching instrument connected to a LAN for the office or household.

One can easily imagine 600 million networks, and that doesn't count all the mobile platforms in automobiles, airplanes, and so forth. So it's not hard to terrify yourself with the possibility that there could be a billion networks.

Question: Are the Internet and its hosts as vulnerable today in terms of security as they were in 1988, the year of the Internet Worm [when a Cornell student released into the network a rogue program that rapidly spread itself, jamming the memories of many computers and bringing them to a standstill]?

Cerf: I'd say yes.

Question: The Internet is pretty hard to navigate for the non-technical user. Will that improve?

Cerf:. . . Romping around the Internet is a challenge because it's not easy to find things. I think what will happen is that some people will make a living out of cataloging and indexing the informal material.

It's not enough to provide bit carrying capacity. If we're creating an information infrastructure, it needs to be a business infrastructure. Certain business-related functions such as advertising, registration, billing, collections, and establishment of contracts must be embedded in the system.

Cerf is now a senior vice president of MCI Communications, one of the largest suppliers of the Internet backbone—the high-capacity links that carry most of the Internet traffic.

Based on an interview with Vinton Cerf, conducted by Gary Anthes, *Computerworld,* February 7, 1994, pp. 121–122; and Amy Barrett, "The 'Father of the Net' Has a Problem Child," *Business Week,* September 30, 1996, pp. 76–78.

voluntary organizations, the principal of which is the Internet Society. The Internet is a medium of communication, a source of information (or infotainment, that is, information mixed with entertainment), and a developing means of electronic commerce. As more and more organizations and individuals are joining the Internet and as information content moves into multimedia, a major obstacle to its development has become the limited capacity of the links interconnecting the networks.

As an individual, you can connect to the Internet via an Internet service provider (such as Netcom On-Line Communication Services or MCI) or by using an electronic information service (such as America Online, CompuServe, or Prodigy). Organizations join the Internet by implementing the TCP/IP protocol suite, establishing the desired servers and clients and acquiring dedicated network access via a router placed on their location by a service provider.

Facilities for Communication and Information Access

The Internet provides several essential facilities that organizations can use for internal as well as interorganizational information sharing and communication. Individuals use these facilities avidly. The facilities available over the Internet are summarized in Table 7.4.

Large and small corporations, as well as individuals, increasingly use the network to access information, communicate, collaborate, and do business. The principal categories of Internet use include communication and information access. We will proceed to review them here, and return to electronic commerce later in the section.

1. Communication

Electronic mail (E-mail) facilitates quick exchange of information and ideas, and is the Internet facility in widest use. We will discuss further the organizational role of E-mail in Section 8.4 of the text. You can use E-mail for one-to-one communication; you can send messages to a larger mailing list; you can send and receive multimedia files; or subscribe to electronic magazines distributed via E-mail.

You may also participate in larger communication forums. A newsgroup can be used to post your message for all interested people to read. *Usenet,* short for Users Network, is a collection of thousands of bulletin boards, or **newsgroups,** accessible via the Internet. There are now well over 13,000 newsgroups on the most specialized of topics, some attracting people with rare expertise. With Usenet, you can ask a question of a worldwide forum of experts (some of them, alas, self-declared). In fact, newspeople often use the newsgroups to check their facts before publication. Many newsgroups have a Frequently Asked Questions (FAQ) document that itemizes the "netiquette," that is, the etiquette guiding this particular network of users.

Frequently, software, such as shareware (you try it out and then keep it for a small fee) or freeware, is distributed via a bulletin board. You can *upload* your file to a remote bulletin board for others to access, or you can *download* a file posted there to your own computer. In order to do that, you can use the file transfer protocol, known simply as *ftp.*

For those who prefer an on-line discussion, the Internet Relay Chat (IRC) facility will help you join a chat group for a real-time electronic conversation. In one of thousands of virtual chat "areas," called channels, you can meet someone with a nickname that appeals to you, and perhaps see the conversation go into a very unexpected channel indeed. Internet software will also enable you to make telephone calls or send a fax.

2. Information Access

The Internet provides access to the largest organized (loosely) repository of information on earth: the collection of electronic documents stored on sites all over the world. The quality of the electronic documents you can access varies widely, but there is no better way to

Table 7.4	Facility	Description
Facilities of the Internet	E-mail	Sent to an address, such as asmith@alpha.mit.edu individual account — host computer — institution code — type of institution (.edu for educational .com for commercial .gov for government)
	Searching the **World Wide Web** (**WWW**) with a browser, such as Netscape **Navigator**	**WWW** (The Web) is a collection of distributed hypermedia databases. As you read a document, you can click with a mouse on a highlighted text or an icon. This will automatically deliver to you a related document, usually located on a different server. You can set up your own electronic site on the Web and have it linked to other sites.
	Participating in a **Usenet** newsgroup or an on-line discussion	You can read and post messages in your area of interest. Read the FAQ (frequently asked questions) file before you post!
	Remote log-in (**telnet**)	You can log onto a remote computer while working on your own machine. You can now work on the remote computer, e.g., access a database or use software residing there.
	File transfer (**ftp,** for file transfer protocol)	After a remote log-in, as above, you can transfer (**get**) a file from the remote computer to your own site, or send (**put**) your file over to that computer. With **anonymous ftp** facility, you do not need to have a password to log on and can browse a directory of files set up for such access.
	Browsing with **Veronica** to find the **Gopher** with the file you need	**Gopher** servers are computers on the Internet which store files that you can access through a series of menus. In order to find the **Gopher** with the file you need, you may use the **Veronica** index.
	Searching a file directory (**Archie,** for archives)	You can search worldwide catalogs of files. This includes catalogs of major libraries, but also catalogs of films, recordings, and archives. Keyword search is available for many files, which may then be transferred with **ftp.**
	Searching **WAIS** (Wide Area Information Service)	You can search **WAIS** databases with keywords. Many articles and unpublished papers can be accessed and displayed on your workstation. Located documents will be scored for relevance.

quickly research a topic than a skillful use of the Internet facilities in general, and the World Wide Web, which we discuss next, in particular.

The main problem is finding what is there. The use of the Web's search engines has overshadowed the services for information access available earlier. These services include Gopher sites, servers that contain hierarchical menus of their contents and will refer you, in turn, to other Gopher sites. To find a Gopher server of interest to you, you can use the global Veronica index, or you can get there with a Web browser. Less popular is Archie, a worldwide file catalog, with objectives similar to Veronica. Once you find your file, you can download it to your client site, using ftp. If you can specify a site to WAIS (Wide Area

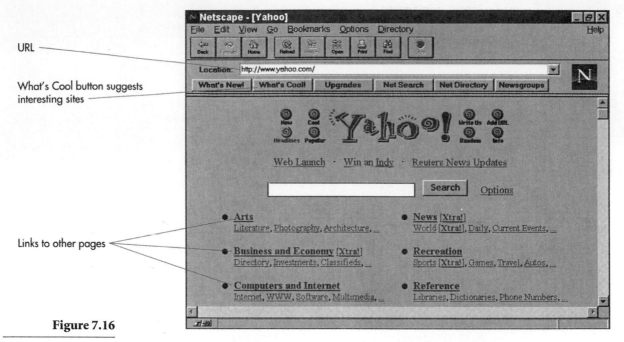

URL

What's Cool button suggests
interesting sites

Links to other pages

Figure 7.16

*You have just accessed
the home page of the
Yahoo! search engine by
using the Web browser
called Netscape
Navigator* (From
Gretchen Marx and
Robert T. Grauer,
Exploring the Internet,
Upper Saddle River, NJ:
Prentice Hall, 1996,
p. 89.)

Information Service), this facility will help you search the site via keywords. In this way, you can search document contents.

All of these resources are accessible from the World Wide Web, which has become the principal medium for information sharing—and much more than that as discussed below.

The World Wide Web

The **World Wide Web** (or, simply, the Web) is an information service available over the Internet, providing access to distributed electronic documents via hyperlinks. The Web grew out of the need of scientists affiliated with CERN, the European center for nuclear research, to share information and to collaborate from geographically dispersed locations. Indeed, this is the capability the Web offers to all organizations and individuals.

The Web is a client/server system. From a user's point of view, the Web is a collection of electronic sites stored on many thousands of servers all over the world. Each site consists of a home page and often other pages stored with it. Pages contain hyperlinks (see Section 8.3) to related pages, usually stored on other sites. We thus have a mammoth distributed hypertext database, or hypermedia when non-textual information is included as well. To navigate ("surf") the Web, you follow the link by clicking the mouse button on it. Electronic documents are transferred between Web sites by a protocol called HyperText Transfer Protocol (HTTP), which runs "on top of" the TCP/IP protocol suite of the Internet.

A user accesses the Web through a client program, known as a **browser**. Netscape Navigator (see Figure 7.16) is the most popular browser program; others include Microsoft's Internet Explorer and Quarterdeck Mosaic. The browser sends out the request for the needed page into the Internet, interprets the formatting directions on the retrieved page, and displays the page accordingly on the screen. As we discussed in Section 5.3, more powerful browsers are Java-enabled; that is, they can interpret and execute programs (applets) written in the Java language. A super-browser that includes the Navigator, along with various tools for communication and collaboration, is the Internet Communicator (Udell 1997).

To access a Web site, you provide the browser with the site's identifier, known as a URL (for Uniform Resource Locator). For example, *http://www.yahoo.com* identifies the site of the Yahoo! search engine. To seek out unknown URLs, you run a search engine (frequently, you can substitute the name of the company whose site you wish to visit in the example URL given above). Or, you connect to a site through a hyperlink on the electronic document you are examining, which automatically provides the locator of the related site.

To find the desired information, the user can deploy one of several search engines available on the Web, such as Yahoo!, Lycos, Alta Vista, or InfoSeek. A **search engine** maintains its own collection of information about the documents available on the Web. To perform a search, you run the engine via the browser and enter a topic or keywords. If you find an interesting document, you can create a bookmark for it; that is, you can add it to your Bookmarks menu for easy access in the future. As we said earlier, you can use Gophers or WAIS from the Web as well.

You can create your own home page—your own calling card posted in cyberspace. For this, you use HTML (HyperText Markup Language) with an editor, such as HTML Assistant or Internet Assistant. The HTML tags (markings) specify how the page is to be displayed on the screen. Graphical information is most frequently specified in the so-called GIF format; video and audio information is also increasingly provided on the Web. To make your site available to others, you need to place it on a Web server, which may be owned by your Internet service provider or by your organization.

Webcasting software enables you to avoid repeatedly seeking out the sites you are interested in ("pulling" the information). Instead, you download the Webcasting software, such as PointCast, register your interests, and have the information you need regularly supplied to you. The use of this so-called *push technology* is growing apace. For example, Ford Motor uses push technology to distribute the information about the firm's car models and availability, as well as promotions, financing, and repair techniques, to its 15,000 dealers worldwide (Wagner 1997).

Electronic Commerce

Electronic commerce is sharing business information, maintaining business relationships, and conducting business transactions by means of telecommunications networks (Zwass 1996). In simple words, electronic commerce is doing business electronically, replacing most of the paper and telephone work with computer-mediated information and transaction exchange. The Internet, and the Web in particular, are emerging as the principal means for this new way of doing business. In the process, business relationships are changing, as we will further discuss in the last section of this chapter.

The process of conducting business generally includes seeking out the best offering from a seller, negotiating the terms, coordinating the provision of the contracted goods or services, and a settlement to pay for them. Let us review how these activities can be assisted by the Internet and its Web.

Thanks to its capability to make information available around the globe almost instantaneously at a limited cost, the Internet has become a major factor in presenting a seller's offerings to potential buyers. Some of the possibilities include:

- Establishing an electronic site on the Web to promote your business, now common practice (it needs to be noted that sites do require maintenance, and the more elaborate ones at considerable expense). Indeed, some of the firms do not just rely on a "virtual storefront"—they are virtual themselves and sell only over the Internet, reducing their operating costs. For example, Virtual Vineyards sells wines and gourmet foods 24 hours a day exclusively through a Web site that provides interesting and entertaining product information.

- "On-line marketplaces," that is, business-to-business or business-to-consumer electronic directories, such as the one provided by Industry.Net featured in the Focus Minicase for this chapter.

- Advertising at frequented Web sites. To attract advertisers, companies obtain and analyze the number of hits (that is, visits) to their sites. Considering that Web surfing may lead to a large number of rather accidental hits, it is difficult to establish meaningful advertising rates. In accepting ads, site owners need to respect the sensibilities of their audience; many segments of the Internet community are opposed to any form of overt advertising. A less explicit form of advertising is establishing links from other sites to your own.

- Establishing newsgroups with useful and regularly updated product information to attract knowledgeable users.

- Job classifieds, with individuals posting their resumes, and companies and agencies seeking out potential employees with their "wanted" ads.

The activities of commercial negotiation and coordination involve interorganizational commerce as well as internal corporate business processes. These activities rely on the use of E-mail, and other communication and information-sharing facilities discussed above. For example, FedEx has established a Web site for its customers in order to give them access to the company's package-tracking database. As 12,000 customers per day use the site to track one of the 2.4 million pieces scheduled for delivery on that day, FedEx saves some $2 million a year by reducing the labor of human operators (Cortese 1996).

The last of the activities in the electronic commerce chain, financial settlement, is largely handled outside the Internet at this time, because of security considerations. In particular, the perception of insufficient security is a barrier to consumer-oriented electronic commerce. However, much work is being done on developing Internet payment schemes, including the development of electronic cash (E-cash), to be issued by intermediaries and honored on the Internet (Kalakota and Whinston 1996, "Electronic Money" 1997). The major credit card companies have developed the Secure Electronic Transaction (SET) protocol, likely to become the standard for credit card payments over the Internet (Bruno 1996).

The Internet has become an active marketplace for selling information-based products such as hotel reservations, airline tickets, and software. Corporate stock is also beginning to be sold over the Internet, giving smaller firms greater access to capital. Spring Street Brewing Company, a small brewery in New York, was the first firm to complete the initial public offering of its stock on the Internet. In the future, information will be sold over the Internet as well, with "micropayments" as small as a few cents charged to your account as you access the information.

The overall framework of electronic commerce is shown in Table 7.5. The higher levels of the framework rely on the lower ones to support them.

Table 7.5	Level	Function	Examples
The framework of electronic commerce		**Products and Structures**	
	7	Electronic marketplaces and supply chains	• Electronic auctions, brokerages, dealerships, and direct search markets • Interorganizational supply chain management
	6	Products and systems	• Remote consumer services (shopping, banking, stock brokerage) • Infotainment-on-demand (fee-based content sites, educational offerings) • Supplier-consumer linkages • On-line marketing • Electronic benefit systems • Intranet-based collaboration
		Services	
	5	Enabling services	• Electronic catalogs/directories, smart agents • Electronic money • Digital libraries, copyright-protection services • Traffic auditing • Smart card systems
	4	Secure messaging	• EDI, E-mail, electronic funds transfer (EFT)
		Infrastructure	
	3	Hypermedia/multimedia object management	• World Wide Web with Java
	2	Public and private communication utilities	• Internet and value-added networks (VANs)
	1	Wide area telecommunications infrastructure	• Guided- and wireless-media networks

The framework recognizes that the enterprise of electronic commerce consists of three major layers:

- *Infrastructure.* The hardware, software, databases, and telecommunications that together deliver such functionality as the World Wide Web over the Internet, and support EDI and other forms of messaging over the Internet or over value-added networks.

- *Services.* Messaging and a variety of services enabling the finding and delivery (on business terms, if desired) of information, as well as negotiation, transacting business, and settlement.

- *Products and structures.* Direct provision of commercial services to consumers and business partners, intraorganizational information sharing and collaboration, and organization of electronic markets and supply chains. We have seen in the text how automobiles are sold by electronic dealerships and how Industry. Net provides a direct search market where the buyer searches out the supplier of the needed manufacturing goods. Onsale Inc. runs highly successful weekly auctions of equipment for personal computing over the Internet (Roberts 1996). As multiple suppliers and their customers perform their ordering and related functions over the Internet, supply chains joining the value chains of multiple firms emerge.

Intranets

Using the Internet resources, many firms have implemented internal networks of Web sites, known as **intranets.** Intranets are set up on corporate LANs and WANs. Hardware and software facilities that manage and access the intranets (such as servers and browsers), as well as protocols and standards, are the same as those on the Internet. However, an intranet is separated from the public Internet by a facility called *firewall.* The firewall program runs on the server computer, preventing access to the intranet from the public Internet, but allowing access *to* the Internet. Intranet is, in effect, the owner company's private Internet.

Intranets have become an important tool for sharing information and knowledge among a company's employees, accessing databases and data warehouses, organizing the corporate workflow around electronic documents, and enabling collaboration. For instance, Ford Motor Company has linked its design centers in the United States, Asia, and Europe with an intranet, enabling the engineers to develop on-line electronic prototypes of automobiles and their components. Intranets are generally less expensive and more reliable than the alternative means for accomplishing the tasks they support ("Getting" 1996). You can see an example in the vignette on the next page.

With the explosion of the business use of the Internet, interorganizational systems as well as the intranets implemented with the use of the Internet's facilities have all become a part of organizational system architecture, which we will now proceed to discuss.

7.9 INFORMATION SYSTEM ARCHITECTURE

The high-level design of a blueprint for the organizational information system is known as the **information system architecture.** The importance of developing a coherent architectural plan to support the present and future computing and communications needs of a business cannot be overestimated. Decisions must be made on where to locate the processing power and the databases and how to interconnect the nodes of the network, such as host computers and workstations. Today, the architectural blueprint of many organizations rests on internetworking: interconnecting a number of local area networks with a corporate wide area backbone net, or using the Internet connectivity.

There are many options in developing a system architecture for a firm. Actually, it is extremely rare to design such a system afresh. Developers work with a holdover of the existing legacy systems, which in some cases include over a dozen functioning networks. The developers need to provide a master plan for a new system architecture and an evolutionary path from the system presently in place to the planned new one.

The plan has to be based on the analysis of the applications that will be run on the network, such as inquiry/response, transaction processing, or decision support systems. The

Dreaming the Possible Dream

The high-profile trio of entertainment moguls, David Geffen, Jeffrey Katzenberg, and Steven Spielberg, have created a high-profile (of course) new movie studio. Called DreamWorks SKG, its objective is to become *the* digital entertainment studio of the 21st century. The first project is an animated feature film, "Prince of Egypt," to be released for the 1998 holiday season.

To coordinate the many facets of the project, a computerized production-management system had to be created. A principal objective was to do it quickly. Here, the less well-known trio of the company's technology co-heads considered themselves lucky: They had no legacy system and were working in what's known as green field—everything had to be done anew. The IT specialists decided against designing their own conventional client/server network, estimating that too much time would be spent in program development. Instead, they implemented an intranet and placed a Netscape Navigator browser on each desktop. The system, called Nile, connects 100 production managers and animation artists. It will be used to check on the daily status of the individual projects, track animation objects, and coordinate scenes. NeXT Computer's WebObjects will handle database management and queries.

The intranet will become a pilot for a larger system, to be used eventually throughout the company in the production of live-action films, music, and new media. Best of all, the company expects to deploy the ever expanding facilities of the Web: "It is an evolving architecture. And that's what DreamWorks is all about," says Rob Hummel, one of the technology trio.

Based on Arny Cortese, "Here Comes the Intranet," *Business Week,* February 26, 1996, pp. 76–84.

points of access to the network need to be established and the kinds of services provided at various points defined. Based on this, the traffic over the network can be estimated. The fundamental components of an architectural plan are shown in Figure 7.17. According to this framework, the following concerns must be addressed in developing such systems:

1. How will the *processing power* be distributed? In other words, where will the computers be located, and what categories of computers will be used? What operating systems and telecommunications software will be installed?

The principal objective of networking is to move processors under the user's control by distributing the computing power out of the corporate data centers. It is important to minimize the number of vendors and platforms, both in order to ensure interoperability of hardware and software and to secure quantity discounts.

2. Where will the *databases* be located? The database, or multiple databases, can be maintained on a central site, with the appropriate parts made available to other processors

Figure 7.17

A framework for the architecture of a distributed system

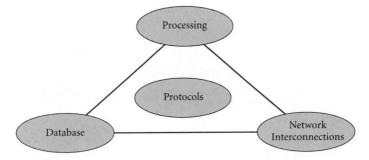

as needed. With a centralized database, the advantages of excellent database control may be outweighed by excessive message traffic on the network due to the high volume of data accesses. Therefore, databases are often distributed to the local server computers. The placement of databases frequently determines the location and speed requirements of processors.

3. *Network interconnections* must be provided for user communication over the network, for Internet access, for access to processors, as well as for processor-to-processor telecommunications.

The interconnections include links over a variety of media as well as the telecommunications equipment to manage the traffic on the network. Wireless links need to be provided to support a mobile sales force or delivery vehicles. Decisions as to sourcing (leased, furnished by a value-added network supplier, or via the Internet), and to management (in-house or outsourced) of the WAN links have to be made.

Links of appropriate capacity must be provided. Thus, the screens of workstations connected to a host computer have to be refreshed in a second or two; the average time of transaction processing should not surpass two seconds, even if the data are bounced off a satellite; and if we want a feeling of immediacy and good image quality in a videoconference, high-capacity links are needed. Reliable communications require at least two paths between any two nodes in the network. The links must be used in an efficient manner, since telecommunications are costly.

4. *Protocols* have to be selected for each of the networks. To provide for communications between networks, the appropriate equipment, such as bridges and routers, have to be specified.

Figure 7.18

Information system architecture of Ryder System (From David C. Churbuck, "Data Dial Tone," *Forbes*, March 14, 1994, pp. 114–115.)

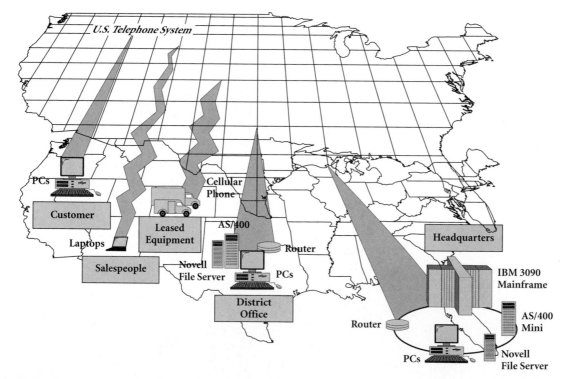

An organization may choose not to own some of the three components of the triangle in the framework shown in Figure 7.17. Many resources are available via the Internet. Remote access to various external databases may be provided by information-services firms. Outsourcing firms may furnish processing capacity. As we discuss in Chapter 13, these firms can even run a firm's entire information systems function on its behalf. Long-haul wide area network links can be leased from a common carrier or from a firm that has excess communication capacity. To pay for the capacity actually used, many firms use value-added networks instead of leasing dedicated links. The multiple sourcing of the components of information system architecture compounds the difficulty of drawing up its plan, but provides competitive opportunities for those who do it successfully.

The resulting architectural blueprint is, of course, highly technical. The information system architecture supporting the long-term plans of Ryder System, the truck lessor and provider of contract logistics to other companies, is shown in less technical terms in Figure 7.18.

The goal of Ryder's information system is to link together its own Miami headquarters, 89 district offices, salespeople in the field, and the 170,000 vehicles available for leasing or renting. At the same time, the system has to be open to the firm's corporate customers, who should be able to access the data on vehicle availability, billing, and maintenance schedules. For now, Ryder decided to keep two IBM 3090 mainframes in headquarters and 77 IBM AS/400 minis in district offices—perhaps subject to downsizing later on. The connectivity will be provided by the telephone network, but the firm will use frame relay equipment to move data at the speed of 45 megabits per second. Its stated objective is to have a WAN that feels like a LAN.

By developing an information system architecture, an organization can leverage the impacts of telecommunications, which we will now proceed to discuss.

7.10 | USING TELECOMMUNICATIONS FOR BUSINESS PROCESS REDESIGN AND TO SEEK COMPETITIVE ADVANTAGE

Telecommunications give an organization the capability to move information rapidly between distant locations and to provide the ability for the employees, customers, and suppliers to collaborate from anywhere, combined with the capability to bring processing power to the point of application. All this offers a firm important opportunities to restructure its business processes and to capture high competitive ground in the marketplace.

A value-chain analysis of a company's activities, as discussed in Chapter 3, is a good method for seeking these opportunities. If we consider just some of the business examples presented in that chapter, it becomes clear that, in many cases, telecommunications are indeed the crucial element. Many immensely successful strategic systems originated when remote terminals were placed at customer sites (as in the case of order-taking systems) or distributor sites (as in the case of airline reservations systems).

An excellent framework, which managers may use as they strive to reshape business processes and seek competitive advantage in the marketplace, is offered by Michael Hammer and Glenn Mangurian (1987). Somewhat adapted, this framework is shown in Table 7.6. It helps a manager seek out applications that can create a business value for the firm. This value might be an increase in the efficiency of operations, improvement in the effectiveness of management, or innovation in the marketplace. The use of telecommunications can provide these values through the following impacts:

Impacts \ Values	Operational Efficiency	Management Effectiveness	Innovation for Competitive Advantage
Compressed Time	Accelerate business process	Reduce information float	Create service excellence
Geography Conquered	Recapture scale and scope	Ensure global management control	Penetrate new markets
Restructured Relationships	Bypass intermediaries	Distribute scarce knowledge	Build umbilical cords

Table 7.6

How impacts of telecommunications may be translated into organizational values

(Adapted from "The Changing Value of Communications Technology" by Michael Hammer and Glenn Mangurian in *Sloan Management Review,* Winter 1987, pp. 65–71 by permission of the publisher. Copyright © 1987 by Sloan Management Review Association. All rights reserved.)

1. Time Compression

Telecommunications enable a firm to transmit raw data and information quickly and accurately between remote sites. As a consequence, any number of business processes that would otherwise rely on other media, such as mail or telephone, can be rethought and accelerated. Order filling, for example, can be done rapidly if the order is transmitted from a notebook computer in the field directly to the warehouse. Citibank's WorldLink foreign currency payment system permits companies worldwide to make payments electronically in over 90 currencies from the convenience of their own office. The system is used by more than 4,000 customers the world over, whose objective is to keep their money invested at all times.

By reducing the information float, that is, the time it takes for a data item to reach the decision maker in the form of information, we can raise the quality of decision making. For example, as point-of-sale data become available on a daily basis to retailers' executives in the form of analytical reports, the merchandising function is vastly improved.

Service excellence has been recognized as the prime source of competitive advantage. By tracking deliveries and selling the ability to access this information as a part of service, FedEx and United Parcel Service raised the quality of their services and used information systems strategically.

2. Overcoming Geographical Dispersion

Telecommunications enable an organization with geographically remote sites to function, to a degree, as though these sites were a single unit. The firm can then reap benefits of scale and scope which would otherwise be unobtainable. For example, Chrysler has an inventory management system that allows it to efficiently share parts located in a number of dispersed warehouses, with huge cost savings. Back-office functions may also be performed in locales where an inexpensive labor force is available, often through outsourcing to foreign countries.

Consistent management is possible throughout dispersed, perhaps globally dispersed, corporate sub-units. The ability to exercise effective centralized control with the help of information systems enables corporations to decentralize decision making to local managers.

Being close to the customer is time-hallowed business wisdom. But in the age of telecommunications, "closeness" does not require the physical presence of a large corporate entity. It may mean communicating with the customers via the firm's Web site on the Internet. Or, it may mean merely a quickly established field office with a skeleton staff, supported with telecommunications links to other parts of the firm. Merrill Corporation, a financial printer, maintains only sales offices in the field, close to its clients, with its production facility located at headquarters in St. Paul, Minnesota. A wide area network connects sales offices to the plant in St. Paul, where an inexpensive and well-trained labor pool is on hand. This has given the firm a competitive advantage over its competitors, who are saddled with high costs of multiple production facilities maintained at sales offices across the country.

3. Restructuring Business Relationships

Telecommunications make it possible to create systems which restructure the interactions of people within a firm as well as a firm's relationships with its customers. Operational efficiency may be raised by eliminating intermediaries from various business processes. Such intermediaries include people who handle paperwork now being replaced by electronic data interchange (EDI), middle managers whose primary role is providing information, and brokers whose services are no longer needed since the firm can replace them with its own telecommunications-based sales and service network. In this manner, telecommunications are a vital technological foundation for business reengineering.

An expert's knowledge may be distributed by providing access to him or to her via teleconferencing facilities. A site of collective knowledge may be created by setting up a teleconference on a topic of interest, or by installing a remotely accessible expert system. In more general terms, opening databases to broad remote access or establishing E-mail links distributes knowledge throughout a firm. Several consulting companies, for example, McKinsey & Company and Price Waterhouse, have created an organizational memory built with groupware, such as Lotus Notes (see Chapter 8). This memory contains a detailed directory of the expertise and experience of the firm's members, as well as instructive records of client engagements. The memory assists future projects.

The most widely known strategic systems tie customers to a firm with telecommunications links. Once such a link is established, additional services may be provided to the customer, increasing revenue as well as raising the costs of switching to another supplier. Such links become umbilical cords, and they may be used in many contexts. Order-taking systems placed on the customers' premises in the health industry, pioneered by Baxter Healthcare and McKesson, are well known as sustaining their owners' competitive position (as we discussed in Chapter 3). There are many ways the idea can be adapted. For example, a hospital may upgrade its relationship with its affiliated physicians by giving them access to its information system and being granted access to their information bases.

Successfully architected organizational information systems provide a flexible infrastructure for developing applications that can combine some of the impacts we have described.

SUMMARY

Telecommunications are the means of electronic transmission of information over distances. A telecommunications network is an arrangement of computing and telecommunications resources that enables telecommunications. These networks consist of the following components: terminals, computers, telecommunications links and equipment, and telecommunications software.

Local area networks are fast networks that interconnect computers within a limited area, such as a building or a campus. They are used to support a workgroup and share resources, such as a database or a secondary storage device. Wide area networks cover a large geographical area. Such a network can interconnect the worldwide computer systems of a large organization.

Communications media include the guided media, in which the signal moves along an enclosed path: twisted pair, coaxial cable, and fiber optics. They also include wireless media through which the signal may be broadcast: terrestrial microwave, satellite transmission, and radio transmission. Communications costs may be reduced by multiplexing and signal compression. Multiplexing combines several lower-capacity transmissions into a single transmission over a higher-capacity link. Signal compression removes redundant elements from the signal and thus lowers its need for channel capacity.

The principal network topologies are hierarchical, star, ring, and bus. The interconnections within a network may be established by circuit, packet, or fast packet switching. The rules for establishing the connection and performing the transmission in a network are called protocols.

Local area networks, which are owned by the user organization, may be configured as peer-to-peer or server-based networks. In a peer-to-peer network, all workstations manage their own facilities. In server-based networks, dedicated server computers run the facilities for the benefit of the user workstations. A special type of server-based network is the client/server network, in which a given application may be split among several computers. The client computers (user workstations) are responsible for managing graphical user interfaces and call upon more powerful server computers to do most of the application processing and access the databases. Client/server technology can be applied in local or wide area networks.

Wide area networks may include such equipment as the host computers, front-end processors, cluster controllers, multiplexors, concentrators, and terminals. Some of the facilities for these networks may be used on the pay-as-you-go basis; others may be leased from common carriers or value-added vendors.

The Internet, the global network of networks, is now widely employed for interpersonal communication via E-mail, newsgroups, or on-line discussions. Access to information distributed over the sites around the world can be performed via Gopher sites, using indexes such as Veronica, or via a WAIS keyword search. However, by far the most widely used information facility on the Internet is the World Wide Web that enables users to navigate its global databases via hyperlinks, moving from one electronic site to another related one by using a browser and, if desired, a search engine.

The Internet is becoming the primary vehicle for electronic commerce. It assists marketing goods and services via Web sites, some of which carry advertisements. It helps to negotiate deals and coordinate the provision of goods and services with E-mail, workflow tools, and intranets. Electronic means for payments, such as E-cash, are emerging.

To gain maximum benefit from its telecommunications networks, an organization should develop an information system architecture, or overall plan of its computing resources. By using telecommunications strategically, an organization can compress the time necessary for its business processes, overcome geographic dispersal, and restructure its business relationships.

KEY TERMS

Telecommunications   *242*

Telecommunications network   *242*

Telecommunications equipment   *243*

Local area network (LAN)   *243*

Wide area network (WAN)   *244*

Metropolitan area network (MAN)   *245*

Interorganizational information system   *245*

Channel capacity   *245*

Twisted pair   *246*

Coaxial cable   *246*

Fiber optic cable   *246*

Terrestrial microwave   *246*

Satellite transmission   *247*

Very small aperture terminal (VSAT)   *248*

Radio transmission   *248*

Cellular radio   *249*

Analog vs. digital communication   *250*

Modem   *250*

Tl carrier   *250*

QUESTIONS

1. Define telecommunications and telecommunications network. How do telecommunications networks relate to computers?
2. What are the five components of a telecommunications network?
3. What is the organizational role of local area networks (LANs)?
4. What are the organizational and interorganizational roles of wide area networks (WANs)?
5. List and briefly describe the guided and the wireless communications media.
6. Assume that a book page contains 2,400 characters (each character is an 8-bit byte). How long will it take to transmit a 200-page book over each of the following:
   a. a voice-grade twisted pair, with the speed of 28,800 bits per second.
   b. a T1 digital circuit at 1.544 megabits per second (Mbps).
   c. a broadband ISDN service at 155 Mbps.
7. What is the purpose of a modem?
8. What are the advantages of digital communications? What is ISDN?
9. By what means are the costs of telecommunications reduced with:
   a. multiplexing
   b. signal compression
10. Describe the four principal network topologies and discuss their reliability.
11. What does "switching" mean in telecommunications networks? What are the principal switching methods? Why are switching methods relying on packets particularly important in telecommunications networks?
12. What is a network protocol? Why do we need protocols? What is the OSI model?
13. What are the means of interconnecting different computer networks?
14. Compare and contrast peer-to-peer and server-based local area networks.
15. What is client/server computing and what are its principal advantages? What are the disadvantages? What is the role of the client? What is the role of the server?
16. What is the purpose of front-end processor, cluster controller, and multiplexor in a wide area telecommunications network?
17. What is the principal difference between a common carrier and a value-added carrier?
18. Name five services available over value-added telecommunications networks.
19. What are the principal uses of the Internet?
20. How can the Internet be used for interpersonal communication?
21. What is the World Wide Web and how does it relate to the Internet?
22. What software is necessary to access the resources of the Web?
23. What are the principal activities in the process of electronic commerce and how can each of them be supported by the resources of the Internet?
24. What is an intranet and to what uses can it be put in a firm?
25. Why do the managers of many firms believe that their company needs an information system architecture? What principal decisions have to be made in devising such an architecture?
26. Present a scenario of using telecommunications to compress time in order to increase managerial effectiveness in a firm.

ISSUES FOR DISCUSSION

1. The Internet has become a medium of access to knowledge and information for many knowledge workers and members of the general public. At the same time, business uses of the Internet are growing. Discuss how an "information superhighway," such as the Internet, can reconcile the interests of its business users with the interests of the citizenry at large. What ethical issues can emerge and what is your position on each of these issues?

2. Telecommunications networks serve as workplaces for workgroups as well as organizational backbone nets. Contrast the factors that should be considered in setting up a local area network for a workgroup with the factors the management of a multinational company needs to take into account in planning an organizational wide area network.

3. Discuss the possible influence of the increasing use of multimedia in computing on the future evolution of telecommunications networks.

4. A statement has been made that the Internet "subtly degrades the privacy of the home life" (cited in Shellenbarger 1996). Discuss.

REAL-WORLD MINICASES AND PROBLEM-SOLVING EXERCISES

1. How to Get Paid for Information A pay-for-information delivery system has been developed by IBM for use on the Internet. It is being marketed as part of IBM's infoMarket search-engine service. The service provides cryptolope (for *crypto*graphic enve*lope*) containers to "wrap" information or E-mail messages into. The contents of cryptolopes are encrypted, that is, encoded with the use of a secret key. Cryptolopes are designed to prevent people from reading files sent over the Internet, unless they have paid for the information.

First, the user finds the needed information with the infoMarket search engine (see Figure 7.19). If the information is provided on a commercial basis, the user will have to pay to get more than just an abstract. There will be a separate decoding key, and perhaps a separate payment, for each service the user wants—for viewing, printing, excerpting, etc. Cryptolopes are readable only in the browser that downloaded them. Encrypted cryptolopes can be passed on, and the new user will have to pay again in order to get the decoding key. Micropayments are involved here; many services will cost pennies.

Figure 7.19

How information can be purchased on the Internet with the cryptolope technology (Adapted from Whit Andrews, "Content Providers See Dollar Signs," *WebWeek,* April 29, 1996, pp. 21, 24.)

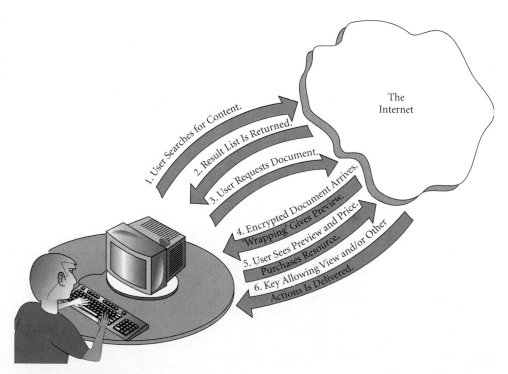

One interested company is Gale Research of Detroit. Gale makes a number of databases available on a subscription basis via its Web site. Now, the company is also considering "retailing" on a pay-per-access principle. The firm particularly likes the fact that as cryptolopes are passed from one user to another, payments will keep accruing for new keys. Of course, you can put anything into a cryptolope, for example, E-mail. Indeed, some companies intend to use cryptolopes for confidential conversations, attaining privacy that is not available with ordinary E-mail.

a. What obstacles have to be overcome before the cryptolope technology finds broad use as a means of "retailing" information?

b. How can the technology be used to seek competitive advantage? Think of two uses aiming to do so. What capabilities of information systems (see Chapter 1) do these uses draw upon?

(Based on Whit Andrews, "Content Providers See Dollar Signs," *WebWeek,* April 29, 1996, pp. 21 & 24.)

2. Suppose that you are considering going into business as a distributor of software packages. Your target market will be small businesses, some of them home businesses. Specify the ways you expect to use telecommunications networks to organize your business processes and to seek competitive advantage in the marketplace.

3. As the telecommunications manager for a large law firm, you need to select a local area network. The firm employs 75 professionals and a support staff of 100. The present environment is entirely unsuitable and you need to take a "green field" approach, that is, start from scratch. Before conducting a full analysis of the firm's requirements, you have been asked to prepare a memo for the managing partner outlining the most obvious options available to the firm. Use periodical literature to investigate these options.

TEAM PROJECT

Each two- or three-person team will define and investigate an aspect of electronic commerce (E-commerce) over the Internet. Some teams will research an electronic marketplace, such as Industry.Net or CommerceNet. Others will study marketing and advertising on the Web, consumer-oriented commerce, intranets, marketplaces for information, use of multimedia and virtual reality in E-commerce, the state of security, legal issues surrounding E-commerce, electronic data interchange (EDI), and electronic payment systems. It is vital to use the latest information, some of it available in periodicals, but much of it accessible only on Web sites. All the sources are to be scrupulously cited and dated.

Each team will report on the maturity (or immaturity) of the information technologies underlying its aspect of E-commerce, the degree to which this aspect is used, and then assess the future prospects. The class will draw conclusions on the most likely directions of the commercial use of the Internet.

ENDNOTE

1. CCITT is the acronym of an international body whose name in the English translation is International Telegraph & Telephone Consultative Committee. The committee sponsors a number of recommendations, or standards, in the area of telecommunications networks, which are widely followed. The specifications of the standards are republished every four years in a series of books that take up over two feet of shelf space.

SELECTED REFERENCES

Bruno, Charles. "Ready, SET, Go." *Network World,* May 13, 1996, pp. 45–47.

The SET secure credit card payment protocol over the Internet.

"Communications, Computers and Networks." *Scientific American,* Special Issue, September 1991, pp. 62–164.

The issue contains a series of important, fascinating, and accessible articles on the present and future roles of telecommunications and network-based computing in organizations and in the society at large.

Cortese, Amy. "A Way Out of the Web Maze." *Business Week,* February 24, 1997, pp. 94–104.

Cortese, Amy. "A Census in Cyberspace." *Business Week,* May 5, 1997, p. 84.

"Electronic Money: Toward a Virtual Wallet." *IEEE Spectrum,* February 1997, pp. 18–80.

An excellent review of the payment options available (or soon to be available) on the Internet.

"Getting Your Company's Internet Strategy Right." *Fortune,* March 18, 1996, pp. 72–78.

Hammer, Michael, and Glenn E. Mangurian. "The Changing Value of Communications Technology." *Sloan Management Review,* Winter 1987, pp. 65–71.

How to obtain business value from telecommunications.

Heath, Donald M. "Business Will Put More Multimedia on 'Net." *Computerworld,* April 22, 1996, p. 58.

An interview with the president of the Internet Society.

Kalakota, Ravi, and Andrew B. Whinston. *Frontiers of Electronic Commerce,* Reading, MA: Addison-Wesley, 1996.

Keen, Peter G.W., and J. Michael Cummins. *Networks in Action: Business Choices and Telecommunications Decisions,* Belmont, CA: Wadsworth, 1994.

An extensive text that teaches you how to produce business value with telecommunications and information systems architectures.

Lavin, Douglas. "Internet Is Assuming Global Proportions." *The Wall Street Journal,* March 15, 1996, p. A6.

Loshin, Pete. *Electronic Commerce: On-Line Ordering and Digital Money,* Rockland, MA: Charles River Media, 1995.

Murphy, Kathleen. "Professors Release Estimates on Internet Use." *WebWeek,* April 29, 1996, p. 5.

PC Novice Guide to the Internet, 1996.

A readable guide to the Internet, the World Wide Web, their facilities, and commercial uses.

Roberts, B. "Online Auction House Finds Growth with Second-Hand Merchandising." *WebWeek,* June 17, 1996, pp. 23, 26.

Rowe, Stanford H., II. *Telecommunications for Managers,* 3rd ed., Englewood Cliffs, NJ: Prentice Hall, 1995.

Shellenbarger, Sue. "Growing Web Use Alters the Dynamics of Life at Home." *The Wall Street Journal,* November 20, 1996, p. B1.

Sinha, Alok. "Client-Server Computing." *Communications of the ACM,* 35, no. 7, July 1992, pp. 77–98.

A technical explanation and illustrations of client-server computing.

Smith, Patrick, and Steve Guengerich. *Client/Server Computing,* 2nd ed., Indianapolis: Sams Publishing, 1994.

Spar, Deborah, and Jeffrey J. Bussgang. "Ruling the Net." *Harvard Business Review,* May–June 1996, pp. 125–133.

Stallings, William. *Data and Computer Telecommunications,* 5th ed., Upper Saddle River, NJ, 1997.

A comprehensive textbook.

Stewart, Thomas A. "Managing in A Wired Company." *Fortune,* July 11, 1994, pp. 44–59.

How telecommunications networks lead to changes in the way companies are managed and operated.

Udell, Jon. "Will Netscape Set the Standard?" *Byte,* March 1997, pp. 66–84.

Vetter, Ronald J., and David H.C. Du. "Issues and Challenges in ATM Networks." *Communications of the ACM,* 38, no. 2, February 1995, pp. 28–109.

A collection of papers presenting the advances in asynchronous transfer mode networks, an important technology of the future multimedia networks.

Wagner, Mitch. "Ford Pushes 'Net Data." *Computerworld,* February 24, 1997, pp. 71, 73.

Zwass, Vladimir. "Electronic Commerce: Structure and Issues." *International Journal of Electronic Commerce,* 1, no. 1, Fall 1996, pp. 3–23.

An analytical overview of the entire field of electronic commerce.

General note on references: consult recent issues of PC-oriented periodicals.

CASE STUDY | # Telecommunications for Global Electronic Commerce at Benetton

Benetton has become known to many of us for its colorful clothing and for its purposely outrageous advertising. Some of us also know it as a firm that has managed to exploit information technology to excellent competitive advantage while providing employment to over 500 small subcontractors in the scenic Veneto region in northern Italy. Over the last three decades, Benetton has grown from a small family-run clothing company to a global family-run operation with 6,500 retail outlets in over 100 countries and revenues reaching two billion dollars. Here is a look at the global web of commerce spun by the firm, whose headquarters you can see in Ponzano Veneto in Photo 7.6. The company believes in combining the advantages of centralized management with those of decentralization. Bruno Zuccaro, vice president of information systems, handles centrally only the purchasing negotiations for IS contracts over 100 million lira (about $60,000). But for the rest of the deals, "our divisions are very autonomous—entrepreneurs," says Zuccaro. "Centrally, we manage the infrastructure, but certain things should be done locally."

Photo 7.6

The Italian clothier Benetton Group SpA has its headquarters in this 17th-century villa in Ponzano Veneto, a village located 30 kilometers north of Venice.

Actually, we are dealing here just with the ordering network of the firm. Employing other capabilities of information systems, Benetton is well known for its ability to respond rapidly to its market, thanks to its fast retailer reporting system and its practice of dyeing at the last moment garments produced with neutral yarn, according to the market demand for particular colors.

Fideta is the company that manages 300 Benetton clothing stores (actually, franchises) throughout France, one of 28 country agents the firm has around the world. When Asuncion Henry, Fideta's office manager, arrives at the firm's quarters in Paris's garment district in the morning, she invariably boots the network connection to Benetton headquarters on her PC. Depending on the day, she either forwards a batch of electronic orders to Benetton or downloads information from the firm. To the country agents such as Fideta, Benetton electronically provides the item master file and price lists.

The intermediary between the two companies is GEIS (General Electric Information Service), headquartered in Rockville, Maryland, provider for a value-added network that spans 110 countries. GEIS's technology comprises the network and three data centers (one in Amsterdam and two in the New York City area). To provide cost-effective access to local users, GEIS has concluded multiple contracts with local telecommunications carriers. Thanks to this, the cost of network access in many localities is that of a local call. To provide reliable and accessible operation, GEIS ensures that network capacity is twice that of the average traffic. The data centers track the traffic and, if average traffic between countries is growing, capacity is increased.

Benetton's use of GEIS VAN goes beyond electronic data interchange (EDI). Aside from this computer-to-computer exchange of business documents in a standard format, the firm uses the VAN for E-mail with its partner firms, customers, and suppliers, and to access the appropriate databases of these trading partners or to provide access to its own databases.

The agents can connect directly over the network to Benetton's IBM 3090 mainframe in Ponzano Veneto to obtain on-line information on order or shipment status, or on customer credit. To facilitate routing of orders, the VAN service also includes connecting the country agents to Benetton's separate production agencies in Italy (say, Divarese for shoes or Azimut for shirts) and to factories in Argentina, Brazil, and other countries.

Let us track the orders Fideta's Asuncion Henry sends. Before she actually sends the batch of orders, the order management program (developed by Benetton and GEIS) checks it out. The program compares the client and item codes to her frequently updated database. All the flagged items (e.g., the client did not order the specified minimum number of units) need to be corrected before the orders are sent. It takes three minutes for the orders to reach the GEIS data center. ("It's an old modem," says Henry.)

The French Bull DPS 9000 mainframe at GEIS's data center receives the orders from all Benetton's agencies worldwide and uses the codes to order them, for example, by country of destination. As a part of the value-adding, GEIS "cleans up" the data by performing error checking, removing inconsistencies, and inserting missing data items, whenever possible. The various Benetton production agencies connect three times a day to get the orders.

It is a part of the Italian business culture to cultivate personal relationships. Largely for this reason, the reps for smaller subcontractors show up in person at Benetton, where they receive floppies with orders to run on their PCs. Only the subcontractors who handle packaging of orders connect to Benetton over the network. At headquarters, a token-ring network is run over a fiber-optic backbone to carry the office traffic that includes digitized clothing designs that are sent to larger manufacturing plants over telecommunications networks.

Benetton ships packaged garments to the customers' agents in the appropriate country using one of 13 transportation firms in 11 countries. The company sends electronic documentation to those firms over the GEIS network, and they forward the documentation electronically to customs agents. By the time the garment boxes arrive, the importation documentation is completed.

Benetton used to manage its business with leased lines. However, dealing with multiple leased line suppliers became unwieldy. Dealing with a VAN is much simpler for the company. "With GEIS, it is just like a telephone network. We don't know what technology they use and we just pay monthly for the service," says Bruno Zuccaro, Benetton's information systems head. There is one place to call in case of a problem.

With 30 country agents, the GEIS network handles 8 million transactions annually for Benetton, with 100 characters per transaction on the average. Zuccaro is planning to grow this volume by 30 to 40 percent by adding an application that would connect individual stores to the network. The company would send the data on the items being sent to the store and receive data on sales. Bigger stores are interested in being able to track the incoming shipments in real time. The pilot for the application will be run in the Benetton chains in Italy and Germany.

Bruno Zuccaro considers Benetton, together with its worldwide sales agents and manufacturing subcontractors, to be a virtual company. "In a virtual company," he says, "information systems and communications are the real organization. Communication enables us to manage all the world from this little village near Venice. We don't have to be in New York or Tokyo."

Based on Marsha Johnston, "Electronic Commerce Speeds Benetton Business Dealings," *Software Magazine*, January 1994, pp. 93–95; Marsha W. Johnston, "Buy Global, Skip Local," *CIO*, April 1, 1996, pp. 30–38; and Elisabeth Horwitt and Ron Condon, "Right Here, Right Now," *Computerworld/NetworkWorld*, September 9, 1996, pp. 20–24.

CASE STUDY QUESTIONS

1. What are the interrelationships between the categories of firms mentioned in the case? Provide a rough graphical sketch.

2. What is the value added by GEIS to the plain telecommunications service? How does Benetton perceive the advantage of a VAN over leased lines? What are the possible advantages of leased lines, on the other hand?

3. In what ways does electronic commerce speed up commercial transactions? What are the advantages to the participants?

4. How does Benetton blend high-tech commerce with sensitivity to the local business culture?

PART THREE

Business Information Systems

The third part of the text will discuss in detail the types of information systems that support operations, management, and knowledge work in an enterprise.

Chapter Eight will describe the contemporary information systems that support knowledge work of individuals and groups. You will learn about the range of professional support systems that aid their users in performing the tasks specific to their profession. You will study how office information systems support document management and message handling, as well as teleconferencing and electronic meetings. Support for group work with groupware will also be discussed. Today, many of these information systems are available over corporate intranets.

Chapter Nine will describe transaction processing systems and management reporting systems. You will see how the transaction processing systems represent a model of the enterprise they serve and how they underlie the emerging electronic commerce. You will also learn about the vital strategic potential of these systems.

Chapter Ten will discuss decision support systems and executive information systems. You will see what kind of problems lend themselves to solutions based on the decision support approach. You will read how these types of systems are built. You will also learn about group decision support systems that help teams solve problems. You will realize that the approach to information delivery taken by executive information systems can be used more broadly to serve the needs of managers other than top executives.

Chapter Eleven will present the subject of expert systems and other areas of applied artificial intelligence. You will see how the research field of artificial intelligence is contributing practical solutions to business problems. You will read about the areas of expert systems applications and study how these systems work. Other areas of applied artificial intelligence, such as natural language processing, robotics, computer vision, computerized speech recognition, and machine learning, will be described as well. You will also learn about a different approach to producing artificial intelligence, the neural network approach.

Chapter Twelve will show how information systems can support the principal functional areas of business: marketing, manufacturing, accounting and finance, and human resource management.

CHAPTER EIGHT

Support of Individual and Group Knowledge Work

OBJECTIVES

After you complete this chapter, you will be able to:

1. Identify and evaluate the features of professional support systems (PSS) that support individual knowledge work.
2. Specify the principal functions of office information systems (OIS).
3. Discuss the components of electronic document management.
4. Define the function of workflow systems and discuss their role in business process redesign.
5. Specify the message-handling services and evaluate their applicability.
6. Identify the capabilities of teleconferencing and electronic meeting systems.
7. Specify and evaluate the support for workgroups provided with groupware.

OUTLINE

A Clear Workflow Makes Responsibilities Clear

Bankers Trust (of New York) manages assets for major financial institutions. With large amounts of money spread among various types of investments, clients may occasionally detect an error, or may think they do.

When such questions arose in the past, clerks in New York City would haul out boxes of paper documents, consult other departments by telephone, and then mail or fax all the documents to a servicing and records center (now located in Nashville, Tennessee) for double checking and more research. The center would then fax back a reply, perhaps an annotated copy of the original fax. The entire history of the case was kept in a manila file folder. It usually took three to five days to complete an inquiry, but it could get worse.

The process cried out for automation. Now, an electronic case folder is stored using the Notes groupware product from Lotus Development. In this form, the folder is accessible to all authorized individuals over the Bankers Trust's telecommunications network.

But it is not only that the paper folder was replaced by its electronic equivalent. The entire process of handling the inquiry was redesigned by a team that spent two weeks analyzing all the necessary steps. Bankers Trust employed workflow software from Action Technologies of Emeryville, California, to redesign the work and implement the new process. The team created a workflow analysis diagram that detailed the steps and the roles of the people researching the inquiry. The team participants included account administrators who receive the query and manage the process, money managers who invest the portfolios, the staff of the records and servicing center, and supervisors who approve the final response to the inquiry.

Only the necessary people were included in the redesigned workflow. It was possible to reduce both the number of people involved in responding to an inquiry and, perhaps consequently, the time it took to respond. The inquiry-handling system that supports the redesigned process was implemented by five developers within seven months. It now supports 125 users, in Nashville and at two locations in New York.

Now the bank guarantees a response to client inquiries within three days, with most inquiries completed within one day. The workflow software automatically routes the cases to the workstations of the responsible people. If someone is out, all the facts of the case can be easily picked up by another worker. Several people no longer needed in the more efficient process were reassigned to other jobs at the bank. As a technology project manager at Bankers Trust tells us: "There used to be a black hole: 'It went to Nashville.' Now people take responsibility." It is now indeed clear who is responsible for an inquiry and where each inquiry stands.

The use of workflow software in the financial industry has been found to increase the quality of business processes that employ it by increasing the accuracy of information, prevention of information loss that frequently takes place in a paper-based environment, and the elimination of superfluous processing by software-assisted analysis of the electronic documents.

Based on David Kirkpatrick, "Groupware Goes Boom," *Fortune,* December 27, 1993, pp. 99–106; and Christy Tauhert, "Reworking Workflow," *Insurance & Technology,* September 1996, pp. 46–48.

Figure 8.1

*General structure of
professional support
systems*

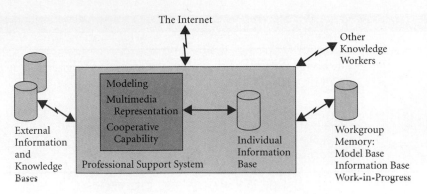

Knowledge work drives an information society. Developing new knowledge, processing information, and using knowledge and information to provide new products and services generate growth and jobs, shape workplaces and lives. Most jobs today may be either defined wholly as knowledge work, or contain tasks that involve knowledge work as their component. Knowledge work is increasingly supported by information systems. This chapter will introduce you to the support that information systems provide for the more prosaic, information-driven aspects of knowledge work (as you read about in the Focus Minicase) and to the support of the professional aspects of knowledge work.

8.1 | PROFESSIONAL SUPPORT SYSTEMS

Professional support systems (PSS) aid users in performing the tasks specific to their profession. In this assistance PSSs go beyond the support of essentially clerical tasks offered by personal productivity software, which we discussed in Chapter 5. Professional support systems convert a PC into a professional workstation. Using professional support systems, knowledge workers are in a better position to expand the firm's intellectual capital. This capital consists of the intangible assets of the knowledge and skills of the firm's people, who are supported by information systems, as well as of the capital embodied in the proprietary technologies, patents, knowledge bases, and databases.

Since the tasks specific to a profession differentiate it from others, the specifics of various PSSs also differ. At the same time, PSSs have a common general structure, presented in Figure 8.1. We will discuss these general features and illustrate them with characteristic examples.

Here are the important general features of PSS:

- Modeling capability—support for producing, maintaining, and using the abstractions of reality, specific to the professional domain. Using these simplified representations of reality, knowledge workers can rapidly and relatively inexpensively conduct experiments. For example, an automotive engineer can produce an engine design using a specialized computer-aided design (CAD) package. The system helps the engineer evaluate the performance of a series of "virtual" prototypes, that is, electronic models of the engine. Since fewer physical prototypes have to be produced and tested, the cost of product development and the development time are significantly cut. Thanks to the PSS, the new car model will reach the market sooner. Using a PSS with a financial model, a financial analyst in a bank can rapidly design a new derivative financial instrument, perhaps a mixture of a stock and a bond, with the desired levels of potential gain and risk, and with the desired tax aspect. Using another PSS, a corporate chemist can model a series of molecules she believes will be useful in a new pharmaceutical and evaluate their properties.

- Multimedia representation—the ability to visualize the models, and, if needed, to affect other senses, such as hearing. Automobile designers and graphic artists designing packaging, for example, need to perceive the quality of the product they are modeling in three dimensions. Beyond this, the model may be incorporated by the PSS into a film clip of the scenery characteristic to the target use, be it rough terrain for a jeep or a crowded urban street for a small car. Movie designers may be equipped with workstations, often driven by supercomputers, that help them combine artificial and real images and sounds. As the use of virtual reality expands, giving the user the feeling of being part of the modeled environment, the illusion of actually using the modeled product can be created.

- Connectivity with other knowledge workers—from corporate colleagues to professionals across the world. As knowledge work spans the globe, it is necessary to maintain working contacts with contributors located continents away. The Internet has become a primary means of worldwide collaboration and information sharing; intranets serve the same objective within firms. E-mail and teleconferencing facilities are in day-to-day use, augmenting periodic meetings in person.

- Cooperative capability—the ability to work together with other knowledge workers while developing a new product or idea. Effective knowledge work is rarely conducted in isolation. Rather, product-development and other task-oriented teams have to find support in information systems that help them exchange ideas and partial designs, perhaps represented as multimedia (also called compound) documents. These systems permit the developers to comment on one another's work and combine the individually developed work products, as well as support the more mundane tasks of scheduling and project management. Concurrent engineering in manufacturing is done with a cross-disciplinary team of knowledge workers, or several such teams, working in parallel on several aspects of the product under development. Cooperative capability may be achieved by combining these information systems with groupware, discussed further on in this chapter.

- Group memory—the ability to store in an electronic form and access rapidly the ideas in progress, partial designs, test results, literature, and news pertaining to the group's work. Such group memories constitute a part of the larger organizational memory.

- Access to external information and knowledge bases—the ability to access on-line library catalogs, periodicals, software, expert system knowledge bases, and specialized information bases such as Lexis, in the case of lawyers. Digital libraries are being created for such access. Of course, access to many information and knowledge bases around the world is available over the Internet.

The vignette on the next page illustrates the capabilities of a professional support system used in automobile engineering.

Professional support systems are becoming integrated with office information systems that support communication and collaboration throughout a company. We will now turn to these systems.

8.2 | OBJECTIVES AND FUNCTIONS OF OFFICE INFORMATION SYSTEMS

Objectives of Office Information Systems

Office information systems (OIS) support office tasks with information technology. The primary goal of these systems, which are sometimes rather threateningly called "office

Before You Build a Car

The Visual Engineering Lab at Ford Motor Company provides professional support systems for the company's engineers. The lab employs a specialist, Richard Pawlicki, to develop these systems with the use of off-the-shelf software packages. Working under the direction of an experienced designer, Pawlicki creates realistic presentations of cars from computer-added design (CAD) databases, simulates manufacturing processes, and develops pilot design processes that engineers can then adapt to their own needs.

Using these tools, the engineers can simulate vehicle crashes, perform group design reviews with exploded views of car components, carry out packaging studies, and develop complex surfaces of engine components or stylized surfaces of the car body.

To take one example, Pawlicki developed a fluid dynamics model with a visualization subsystem that can be used to optimize the car's air conditioning. The entire interior of a future car is visualized. A design analyst uses the model to apply different forces and physical properties of materials in order to study what happens when particles are released from the air conditioner in the car interior with ducts pointing in different directions and under different fan speed settings. When data from a temperature database were added to the model, it became possible to know the exact temperature anywhere in the car when the simulated air conditioner was operated in different ways.

Now Ford Motor is cloning the visualization lab in various areas of the company. The goal is to give professional support systems to as many designers as possible.

Based on Caren D. Potter, "Ford Motor Company: The Visualization Lab Uses a Range of Software," *Computer Graphics World,* November 1994, pp. 25–26.

automation," is to increase the productivity of office work. While the productivity of agricultural and industrial workers has been leveraged manyfold by industrial and information-age machinery, until recently office work has been very scantily supported by information technology. Now, firms using integrated OISs are beginning to harvest the fruit of greater productivity and higher quality of office work.

An **office** is an environment where the management and administration of an organization take place, but it is also an arena of social action where people play out work roles, make decisions, and exchange information. Managers, other professionals (for example, financial analysts, engineers, or salespeople), and clerical and secretarial personnel work in an office setting, or in virtual offices when they telecommute (as we discussed in Chapter 1). The nature of the work these categories of personnel perform varies. A distinction is sometimes drawn between the more creative knowledge work performed by professionals and based on formal education, and clerical information work—however difficult it is to draw a line between the two. As we will see, all these work roles are affected by OIS.

The decision-making aspects of knowledge work are supported by management reporting and decision support systems (MRS and DSS). Executive information systems (EIS) primarily facilitate executive monitoring and control. Transaction processing systems (TPS) handle routine business transactions, mostly customer-driven, such as processing an order, but also internal, such as hiring a new employee. What is left to OIS?

The primary purpose of OIS is to facilitate communication between members of an organization and between the organization and its environment. An ideal (and expensive) system would allow people to communicate in the medium of their choice: data, document, image, voice, or video. This ideal OIS would support the creation, storage, and transfer of such messages. Access to the system would be available anywhere in the organization. It also

Figure 8.2

Electronically integrated office

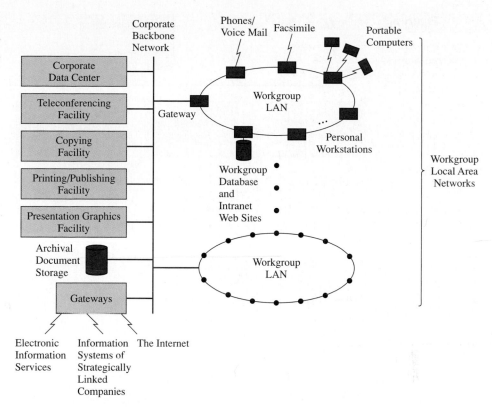

has become increasingly apparent that an ideal OIS should support team collaboration in working on a project. What we are talking about is an electronically integrated office, shown in Figure 8.2. Note that all elements of such a system are already in place—what remains is their integration into a seamless whole. Thanks to the movement toward open systems, the equipment and software made by different manufacturers and covering various aspects of office operations are becoming interconnected.

You will note that the principal unit of an OIS is a workgroup local area network (LAN), which permits coordinated teamwork. Workgroup members communicate within their local area network, as well as with other workgroups and, as needed, with the firm's environment. Communication between workgroups takes place along a high-speed backbone network. Many companies have established intranets that permit them to establish and access internal Web sites using Internet facilities. Through the gateways, the workgroup can also access the corporate servers in the data center (which may be mainframes, divisional minicomputers, or powerful micros), and a number of facilities for office work, as well as the outside world, including the Internet.

Functions of Office Information Systems

The functions offered by OIS, which we will discuss in this chapter, are summarized in Figure 8.3. Office information systems leverage personal computing; they do not replace it. The personal productivity software we described in Chapter 5 and the professional support systems we described earlier in this chapter are vehicles for personal knowledge work. OISs

Figure 8.3

Office information systems (Adapted and updated from Vladimir Zwass, *Management Information Systems*, Dubuque, IA: Wm. C. Brown, 1992, p. 612.)

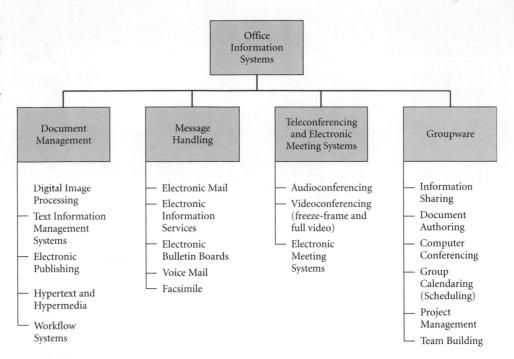

Table 8.1

Augmentation or replacement of traditional office functions and equipment by OIS

OIS Function	What It Augments/Replaces
Document Management	Typewriter/Word processor File cabinet Manual typesetting/Commercial printing
Message Handling	POTS ("plain old telephone service") Memos
Teleconferencing and Electronic Meeting Systems	Travel and physical presence at meetings
Groupware	"Sneakernet" (collaboration by exchanging diskettes) Manual scheduling and tracking of projects

help organize work in the office by providing a smooth flow of documents and messages, assisting groupwork through support for meetings of various kinds, and enabling cooperative work on a project.

To understand OIS functions, it is a good idea to look at their heritage. Table 8.1 shows these functions and the artifacts each of them either replaces or augments. Storing documents on optical disks definitely rids us of file cabinets, but teleconferencing is a substitute for only some meetings: It augments rather than replaces this customary mode of communication among several people. Indeed, there is no electronic substitute for establishing rapport in person.

A broad array of noncomputer devices remains, of course, as part of the office landscape: copiers, facsimile machines, dictation equipment, micrographics that store document images on microfilm or microfiche, and, not to be forgotten, telephones and, ever so rarely, typewriters. Now, however, many of these have built-in microprocessors.

The arrival of portable computing has broadened our very idea of what an office is. Equipped with a computer notebook and connected to a telecommunications network, you can conduct business from your home, car, or boat. Any of these can become your virtual office from which you can access your corporate OIS.

8.3   DOCUMENT MANAGEMENT AND WORKFLOW SYSTEMS

When an office worker refers to "information," it is as likely as not that he or she has in mind a document. Depending on the nature of a business, a document may be a customer's order on a paper form, a policyholder's claim against an insurance company, or a three-inch-thick user manual that accompanies a firm's equipment. Do all of these documents have to be kept on paper? In other words, is paper the necessary medium for a document, with the attendant file cabinets and "slow fires" of destruction caused by the acids contained in the paper? Most of us know the answer is no, but many of us also mistakenly believe that office automation implies a paperless office. Paper documents are not about to disappear—they are a fine presentation medium. But paper is not an appropriate medium for long-term document storage or for most office communications.

Elimination of paper from many internal corporate functions means the elimination of many unnecessary time delays, as we saw in the Focus Minicase. OIS must limit the flow of paper documentation within a firm, facilitate prompt access to stored document images, and make it possible to produce documents in a streamlined fashion. Moreover, multimedia documents may contain components that are never presented on paper, such as voice or moving image sequences.

The document-management functions of OIS include creation, storage, and retrieval of documents. Certain documents, such as corporate policy manuals, must also be updated as needed. Indeed, all documents are not created equal. A copy or an image of a policyholder's application has to be available, signatures and all, for the company's reviewers. Legal and regulatory requirements make it necessary to preserve such documents or their images. A piece of equipment manufactured by a firm is usually accompanied by the manufacturer's documentation, although the latter is also maintained as a text file that will be updated in the future.

Document management relies on several major technologies, which we proceed to describe.

Electronic Document Management

Some documents are stored as images whose content will not be changed; others can be stored as text files that may be updated as needed. Thus, **electronic document management** relies on **digital image processing** technology, which stores the document image in an archival computer storage where it will not be changed, or on managing text documents in writable secondary storage, where changes are possible. The elements of electronic document management and the supporting equipment are shown in Table 8.2. Note that many applications involve only the entry–storage–retrieval components of this process, without paper-based presentation.

Table 8.2	Away from Paper	Paperless			Onto Paper
Elements of electronic document management	**Entry (Input)**	**Storage**	**Retrieval**	**Updating**	**Printing/ Publishing**
	Scanner	Optical disks	Computer-assisted retrieval via indexing	Requires writable storage	Laser printer
	OCR equipment and software	Magnetic disks			Color printer (ink-jet or laser)
	Fax machine		High-resolution monitor or large-screen workstation for image viewing		

Figure 8.4

Electronic document management: document archiving and text management systems

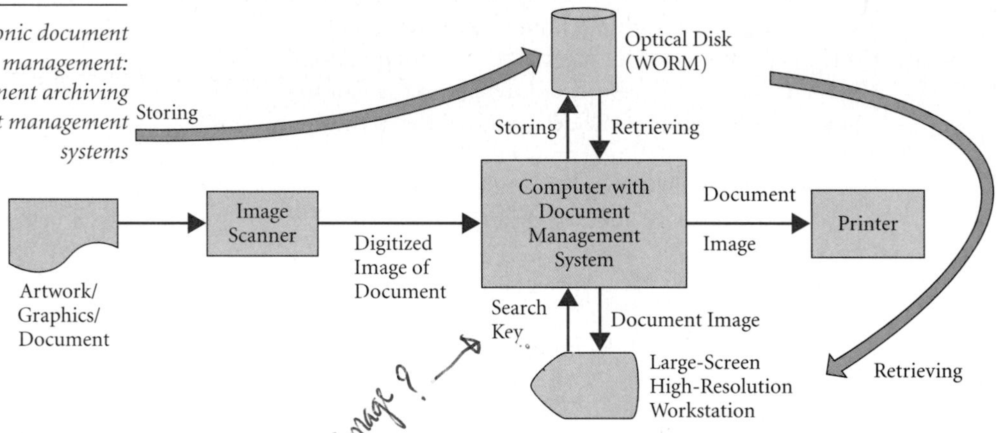

(a) Document Storing and Retrieving with Digital Image Processing

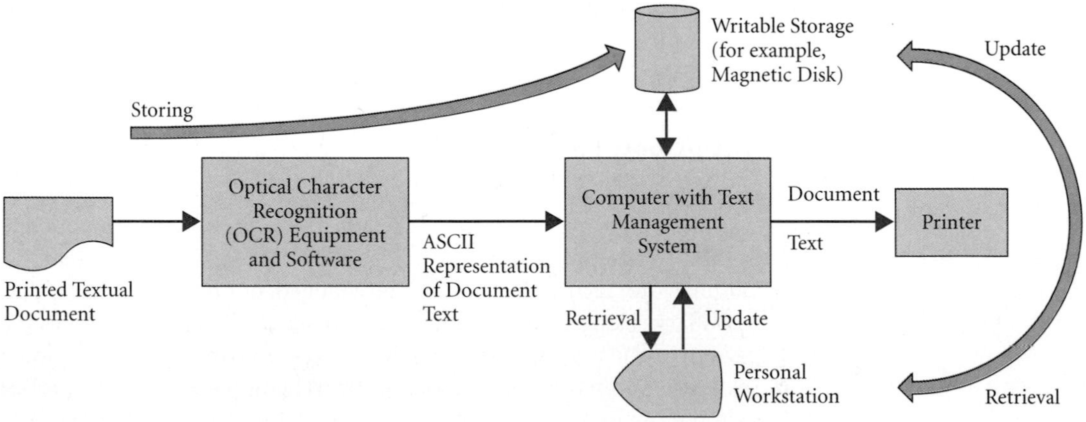

(b) Text Management

Electronic Document Management Enhances Customer Service

The regional service center of Canon USA in Irving, Texas, employs only 15 workers. It is the smallest service center of the electronics manufacturer in the United States. The employees not only repair consumer products, but also have answer calls for help from the purchasers of any of the more than 6,000 electronic goods sold by Canon in this country. To find answers to customers' questions, service reps previously had to look up technical specifications for the products in a massive wall-to-wall library of paper reference binders. Productivity was suffering, and so was the level of customer service. "If you can't answer customers' questions when you have them on the phone, it'll take you on average three more calls to finish the transaction," says Larry Snider, manager of the service center. Due to telephone tag, several back-and-forth phone calls would result.

Electronic document management was the solution to the problem. PaperLess Filer document management system (from PaperLess Corporation of Richardson, Texas) has been installed on the NetWare local area network that links the employees' desktop PCs. When a customer phones in a question, the service rep retrieves the answer or the manual with a few clicks of the mouse. Document images appear on the screen. If needed, the rep can fax installation instructions or a diagram to the customer right from the PC.

Now, scanning in the manuals for the new products has become the bottleneck. Snider is trying to champion broader use of imaging at Canon. He hopes that his service center will be linked to other Canon service centers, with their electronic document bases, within a year. Then manuals will be scanned in centrally and made available to all service centers.

Based on Alice LaPlante, "Imaging Your Sea of Data," *Forbes ASAP*, August 29, 1994, pp. 36–41.

The vignette above illustrates how electronic document management can be translated into better customer service.

We will now discuss the elements of electronic document management. Since some applications require storage and management of a document image, and other applications rely on storage and management of a document's text, we have contrasted the two methods of electronic document management in Figure 8.4.

1. Input

Digital image technology employs scanners to enter digitized images of documents, artwork, maps, and so forth into the computer where the image is preserved and may even be enhanced. The document—check or credit card receipt—is stored as an image and may be accessed within seconds. It can be reproduced in reduced form if desired. To lower memory requirements, images are stored in a highly compressed format (a ratio of 1:15 between the respective storage requirements of compressed and original images is typical).

If we wish to store the document's text or data rather than its image, a scanner and the **optical character recognition (OCR)** software may be employed as an alternative to manual keyboarding. With OCR, letters, numbers, or bar codes are converted into their equivalent representations in a computer character code (usually ASCII) and stored as database records or records in a text management system. Once scanned in via OCR, the text can be searched and updated.

2. Storage

Documents are stored in a computer-managed archiving system. The dominant storage technology of digital image processing is optical disks, in particular, write-once-read-many (WORM) optical disk cartridges, which are frequently combined into high-capacity multi-cartridge jukeboxes. Optical disks of the WORM type, discussed in Chapter 4, permit the user to store and retrieve but not to update a document. Optical technology is rapidly replacing micrographic recording on microfilm or microfiche.

Documents processed as text rather than image are most often stored on magnetic disks, which permits the current contents to be overwritten. Rewritable optical storage is only now becoming available.

3. Retrieval

The main advantage of computerized document management systems is that the documents can be indexed. A user can retrieve a given document within seconds by employing a variety of attributes; for example, the account number or customer name, or a topic under which the document has been filed. **Text information management systems** are the equivalent of a DBMS in the realm of words instead of numbers. They support access to documents based on the keywords assigned to them. One frequently used system called TOPIC (by Verity of Mountain View, California) retrieves documents based on the probability of correspondence of the document to the query topic, which enables the knowledge worker to browse the document base.

Multiple technologies are often used for document management. Some systems permit not only storage of text, graphics, and signatures, but also phone conversations or dictated memos. Such multimedia documents are an emerging trend. When a client calls an account officer at U.S. Trust, for example, the bank's officer can access the original documents, memos, and even voice files regarding the client's account at a moment's notice. They are stored in a 150-gigabyte optical disk jukebox. Large-screen workstations permit the viewing of several documents side by side.

Systems that allow access to the stored documents with spoken commands begin to enter organizational practice. By integrating digital image processing with optical character recognition and expert system technologies, new retrieval capabilities may be created. For example, Sun Microsystems relies on such an integrated system for processing the 400 to 500 resumes the company receives daily. Both the scanned-in text and the image of the resume are stored. An expert system, containing a knowledge base of resume structures and job descriptions, assembles an abstract of the resume from the text and files it in the database, ready for access by any specified characteristic of the applicants. The original document's image is available for retrieval as well, whenever a detailed study is desired.

4. Updating

Transaction documents and other items stored as images are not updated. We can simply add another item to a customer's "electronic file." Indeed, the entire area of document processing has traditionally concentrated on simply archiving the information in accessible form. This application still dominates.

But you may want to enter text material with OCR equipment or simply by keyboarding, index the material, and then modify it at will. For example, engineering documentation must not only be retrieved, but also continually updated. Moreover, it is desirable to create a trail of such updates by preserving the older versions. Of course, you must use a rewritable form of storage. Since the content of a text document can be "understood" by software, as opposed to the document's image, which cannot, you can perform content-dependent queries and updates. Text information management systems support keyword access to and editing of text documents. Edited material is ready for printing or publishing.

5. Printing and Publishing

Remember, office automation does not imply a paperless office. It means, rather, the provision of appropriate technology for various office tasks. Frequently, a professionally published document has to be prepared.

Corporate electronic publishing is growing rapidly. It is based on powerful servers, since large volumes of text require the management of extensive storage. In the perception of some executives, "If you and I submit similar bids, but mine looks professionally published and yours does not, I have an advantage." Departments of a typical corporation may use electronic publishing for a variety of projects. The marketing department may produce sales brochures; the engineering department—user manuals; and the finance department—quarterly reports. For example, at GTE Corporation, corporate electronic publishing produces 8,000 different forms as well as display ads, public relations material, and so forth. The latest version of a document can be printed on demand; there is no need to order any warehouse large runs from a commercial printer.

Reprographics, reproduction of multiple copies of documents, is now beginning to integrate photocopiers into information systems. Recognizing the importance of corporate publishing, Xerox Corporation first introduced its powerful DocuTech Production Publisher that can print 68 double-sided copies a minute (see Photo 8.1), and then began to offer the DocuColor printer, able to transform electronic files into full-color pages at a rate of 40 pages a minute (Holusha 1996). These versatile machines can be used to change business processes related to producing bid proposals, advertising brochures, contracts, and similar documents. They integrate copying with document processing by creating an electronic image of a document to be printed, rather than producing a photographic image as traditional copiers do. These printers, built around powerful computers, can manipulate the image (for example, by changing typefaces or combining several documents) and communicate with other computers by sending or receiving images. Instead of storing multiple copies produced with traditional reprographics, users can rapidly print on demand.

Hypertext and Hypermedia: Electronic Documents of the Future

A novel form of electronic document is used with increased frequency. Called **hypertext,** this approach to information management stores "chunks" of information in units, called nodes, connected by meaningful links, known as hyperlinks. A node may contain a

Photo 8.1

DocuTech Production Publisher from Xerox Corporation—a vast corporate publishing engine, which may be used as a server in a network

Figure 8.5

*Display of a node from
a hypertext database*

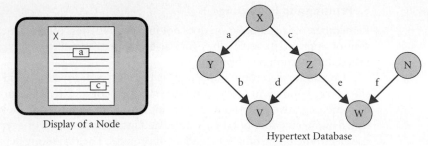

Display of a Node

Hypertext Database

well-defined fragment of textual knowledge. In a broader implementation of this concept, called **hypermedia,** a node may also contain graphics, an audio message, a video image, or an executable spreadsheet. A document is built by creating nodes with information chunks and linking them to other related chunks. A user reads, or actually, navigates, the document by selecting links of interest. It is easy to follow a thread of thought and skip parts that are of no interest at the moment.

Let's say I am writing a book (or a company's procedures manual). I start with a node containing a brief statement of purpose and the titles of the book's parts. Each part title will be linked to the chapter outline for that part, which in turn will be linked to the chapters themselves. A hierarchy of linked nodes will result. My nodes may also contain notes to myself; for example, at some point I might insert a note saying that "a figure or drawing would help here." Most important, I could provide links to related information. For example, in the paragraph preceding this one, I could insert a link to a discussion of spreadsheets.

When you navigate a hypertext or hypermedia document with a mouse, you can, for example, click on it to call up on the screen the node containing information about spreadsheet programs. For each node, the screen displays the "from" link pointing to the node you just read, and "to" links, which lead you to related nodes, one of which you might select to read next. When you read an electronic document, you no longer have to read a linear, book-like text. Instead, you can pursue issues of interest to you through the links; you impose your own structure on the document (of course, within the limits of the link structure provided by the document's designer). Notable hypermedia software called NoteCards has been developed at the Xerox Palo Alto Research Center.

Figure 8.5 presents a screen display showing node X, which has been selected from the hypertext database, whose structure is also illustrated in the figure. The node X contains links to two other nodes. In a windowing environment, each window may display one node, or a part of it. A hypertext database may contain a single document, such as an extensive user manual, with all the cross-referencing done by links. On the other hand, such a database may contain the organized knowledge of an individual or a workgroup.

The World Wide Web on the Internet is built around the concept of hypermedia, with the document databases distributed over many computer sites all over the world. Figure 8.6 presents a home page from the Web; such a page is actually a node in the vast hypermedia database (as we learned in Section 7.8).

Workflow Systems

Electronic documents are the foundation of workflow systems that enable an organization to redesign its business processes in the office. Processing of paper documents by multiple workers is difficult to control: The location of the document, the status of its processing,

Figure 8.6

Home page of a World Wide Web document, with four links (From Gretchen Marx and Robert T. Grauer, *Exploring the Internet*, Upper Saddle River, NJ: Prentice Hall, 1996, p. 87.)

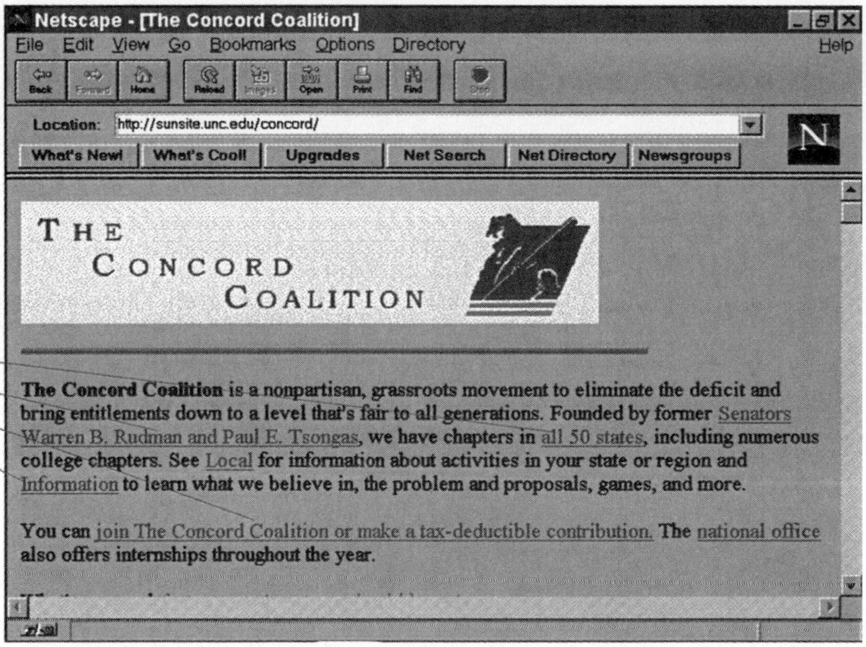

Links

and the backlog of work are all difficult to determine. **Workflow systems** support document-based organizational processes by automatically routing electronic documents over the computer network to the appropriate workers for their contribution. Since they route document images to the appropriate people, workflow systems combine the features of electronic mail with those of image processing systems. We have seen a workflow system in action in the Focus Minicase for the chapter.

As their name suggests, workflow systems are used to organize the entire flow of various work processes in the office. They are a frequent tool in business process redesign. For example, a process to underwrite an insurance policy can be restructured with a workflow system to secure the appropriate evaluations, approvals, and issuance of policies. Workflow systems can automatically assign insurance claims to a proper adjuster based on the type of claim or can route a credit application to the appropriate loan officer based on the amount of the loan. The systems can check whether documentation is complete before it is presented at a given location. Thus, workflow systems get the work and the necessary information to the right people at the right time. An example of a computer-supported workflow is shown in Figure 8.7.

As the process is being defined with a workflow system, the process is redesigned to avoid redundancies, to ensure that all steps are completed in the shortest proper sequence and to track and report the status of work. This leads to savings and enhanced quality control. Thanks to workflow automation, several financial companies have been able to reduce the time necessary to process a loan application or insurance policy five- or even tenfold. Recent releases of workflow software enable users to guide the flow of work over intranets (Nadile 1996).

Figure 8.7

Workflow management: a system for expense approvals (Modified from John Verity, "Getting Work to Go with the Flow," *Business Week,* June 21, 1993, pp. 156–161.)

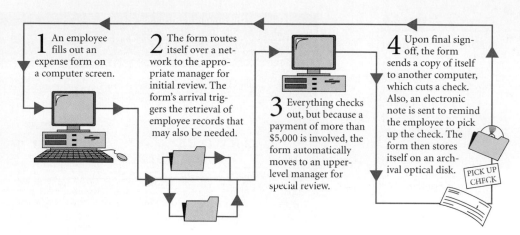

1 An employee fills out an expense form on a computer screen.

2 The form routes itself over a network to the appropriate manager for initial review. The form's arrival triggers the retrieval of employee records that may also be needed.

3 Everything checks out, but because a payment of more than $5,000 is involved, the form automatically moves to an upper-level manager for special review.

4 Upon final sign-off, the form sends a copy of itself to another computer, which cuts a check. Also, an electronic note is sent to remind the employee to pick up the check. The form then stores itself on an archival optical disk.

PICK UP CHECK

8.4 MESSAGE HANDLING

Electronic mail has brought with it immense capabilities for organizational communications. By uncoupling both the sender and the recipient of a message in time as well as in space, it offers a cost-effective medium for global communication. As more and more people are telecommuting, that is, working at locations other than their company's office (see Chapter 1), electronic mail offers a convenient way for a telecommuter to "plug in." It also gives executives a powerful means of control.

Other messaging technologies have also become available. Thus, electronic mail enables you to communicate from your personal workstation by means of textual messages; through voice mail, you can send or receive voice messages by telephone; a facsimile device lets you send a handwritten message or printed document.

Electronic Mail and Its Effects on Work in Organizations

Electronic mail, or **E-mail,** is generally used to exchange written messages sent and retrieved from personal workstations over telecommunications networks. An E-mail user is assigned an electronic mailbox with an address. A message is frequently a note or a memo, but it can also be a working document, such as a spreadsheet, graph, or technical proposal, sent for comment. Voice annotations are possible in some E-mail systems. By obtaining an electronic mailbox on the Internet, you can join a vast cyberspace of people and information. A window used to compose an electronic mail message in the Eudora E-mail package from Qualcomm is shown in Figure 8.8.

The key capability of an E-mail system is storing and forwarding messages. Many other E-mail capabilities derive from it. You can send your message when it is convenient for you, and the recipient can read it when it is convenient for him or her. Moreover, the recipient can read the message wherever convenient, since it is sent to a person identified by an E-mail address and not to a specific telephone number. "Telephone tag," the annoying calls back and forth to absent parties, is avoided. You get the benefit of the "VCR effect," so desirable in television viewing, of shifting time and structuring your work as you want it, rather than being at the mercy of callers. You learn how to screen out messages of no interest to you. You can work at home or sell in the field and be always in touch via E-mail.

E-mail systems generally allow you to store incoming messages in labeled files so that you can use the system as a private file cabinet. Some meetings can be avoided, while others

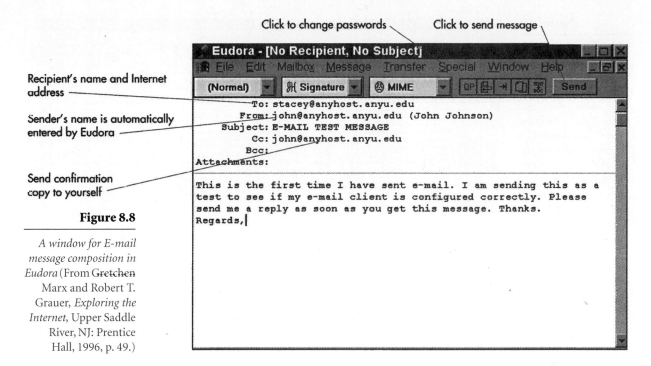

Click to change passwords

Click to send message

Recipient's name and Internet address

Sender's name is automatically entered by Eudora

Send confirmation copy to yourself

Figure 8.8

A window for E-mail message composition in Eudora (From Gretchen Marx and Robert T. Grauer, *Exploring the Internet,* Upper Saddle River, NJ: Prentice Hall, 1996, p. 49.)

may become shorter because the participants have discussed the issues over E-mail beforehand. E-mail systems can provide greater security than many alternative ways of communicating, since users have passwords for accessing their messages. E-mail systems save money in many areas, particularly as an alternative to overnight international mail.

E-mail has affected structure and corporate culture in organizations where it has become a principal means of communication. It has made it possible to expand a manager's span of control in an organization, and it has enabled communications across managerial levels. Philippe Kahn, founder of the software vendor Borland International, ascribed the flattening of his organization to the way its members use E-mail. Opinions from any level of his organization could be sent to the CEO directly—and the chief executive "cannot write louder than anyone else." When combined with executive information systems, E-mail gives executives a powerful means of control.

The proliferation of E-mail brings its own problems, among others, unwanted messages. It is very easy to broadcast a message to everyone's mailbox. Information overload may result. Some E-mail systems include software that acts as a user's personal agent, automatically assisting him or her with a task, according to the rules defined by the user. Such software is known as **intelligent agents.** In E-mail systems, an intelligent agent can dispose of unwanted messages and classify other messages into the categories the user desires. You can see the recommendations made by an intelligent agent in Figure 8.9.

Many corporations have extended the reach of their internal E-mail systems to their customers and to their peers in the industry. To do so, they have to scale the barrier created by incompatible systems. Therefore, many firms choose to follow the X.400 international standard of the International Organization for Standards (ISO). As one example, Chase Manhattan Bank has adopted this standard to communicate with its large business clients. The bank perceives the convenience of E-mail communications as a marketing tool which

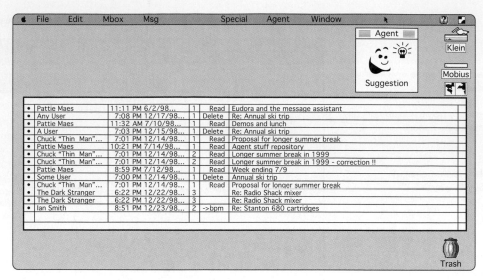

would bind client corporations and trust funds more closely to it. The use of E-mail in pursuit of competitive advantage is seen as follows by a manager of Anchor Glass of Tampa, Florida: "By getting through the doors with E-mail, you can give customers other services."

Electronic Information Services and Bulletin Boards

Service providers such as America Online, CompuServe, and Prodigy combine E-mail facilities with access to **electronic information services**. These services are also available over the Internet. The most expensive category of these services includes access to databases with information on specialized subjects: patents, technical documents, legal precedents, or legislation. Another class of information services makes available a variety of general databases, such as the Official Airline Guide, wire service news, or financial databases for investors. Thousands of electronic databases are available at present. As opposed to the freewheeling world of the Internet, electronic information services provide excellent directories. Several frequently used business databases are listed in Table 8.3. To cope with the thousands of new articles available every day over on-line news services, managers can employ filtering software, such as First! from Individual, Inc., of Cambridge, Massachusetts. This software uses a list of topics specified by the user to deliver only relevant news.

E-mail systems usually offer **electronic bulletin boards** as the simplest form of computer-supported, many-to-many communication. An open mailbox is established, and users can post messages to it or scan messages posted there by others. A bulletin board can be set up where informal feedback from the company's distribution channels (distributors, wholesalers, and retailers) is posted. Internal bulletin boards are commonly used within organizations for posting company announcements. Boards for external communications may show job openings available in a company.

Voice Mail

A **voice mail** system stores and forwards voice messages converted to digital form. Voice mail systems, like E-mail, are computer-based, athough this fact is transparent to users who

Table 8.3	Database	Subject	Providers
Major business databases	ABI/Inform	Business literature	BRS, Dialog, Mead
	Business Dataline	Regional business news	BRS, Dialog, Dow Jones
	Dun's Financial Records	Corporate financial information on U.S. businesses	Dialog
	Dow Jones News/ Retrieval	News and analysis	Dow Jones
	Lexis Financial Information Service	Financial analysis of firms	Reed Elsevier
	Moody's Corporate News	News on U.S. firms	Dialog
	Nexis	Newsletters and wire services	Reed Elsevier
	Standard & Poor's	Corporate information and news	CompuServe Dialog

send and retrieve messages with a telephone. A sender dictates a voice message into the recipient's phone mailbox. The voice message is digitized and stored on a secondary storage device, such as a magnetic disk. When the recipient retrieves the message from the mailbox, the message is converted back to its original voice form. Voice messaging is controlled by pressing a sequence of telephone buttons. Users are guided through a sometimes elaborate (or annoying?) sequence by a recorded voice. The message recipient can replay or skip messages or can route them to another mailbox. Messages may be circulated as voice memos, with each recipient appending an oral comment.

Voice mail can replace many real-time conversations by message-type communications. At the Travelers Companies, a Hartford, Connecticut, insurance concern where 10,000 employees use voice mail, it is estimated that 60 percent of internal telephone calls do not require two-way communication. Secretaries, receptionists, and other office workers are relieved of many chores related to handling "while you were out" slips.

A word of caution is necessary. Voice mail ought to be employed judiciously in relationships with present or potential customers. It may degrade the perceived quality of service and you may lose clients.

Facsimile

The technology that has profoundly changed the way people communicate today is **facsimile (fax)**—a long-distance copying technology. It is a premier tool in a portable office. A relatively inexpensive fax machine or a PC board is used to send a copy of a document or any other written message. Text, graphs, signatures, and handwritten marginalia are transmitted as they appear on the original. As shown in Figure 8.10, the sender's fax machine scans the document or any handwritten message and sends the digitized image over the telephone line to the recipient's fax machine, which produces a copy of the document. A fax machine

Figure 8.10

Facsimile (fax) transmission

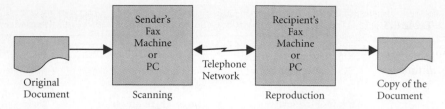

or add-in board has both sending and receiving capabilities, since it has a built-in modem. Some machines have a memory for storing messages. Transmission speeds, copy resolution, and the available extra features depend on the sophistication and the price of the fax machine or PC board. In general, several pages can be sent per minute.

8.5   TELECONFERENCING AND ELECTRONIC MEETING SYSTEMS

About two thirds of a manager's time is spent in meetings of various kinds. This much maligned method of many-to-many communication has always played a crucial role in coordinating organizational work, as well as in collaborating with other firms, including customers and suppliers. People develop working relationships in a meeting; they share information, negotiate common objectives, and stimulate each other's thinking. An organization's culture evolves in large measure through meetings.

The advent of computer and communications technologies has broadened the possibilities of many-to-many communications. A meeting can now be distributed with regard to place and time, in accordance with the situation. Several technologies are combined in different ways to provide alternatives. The participants can be situated at remote locations and supported by audio- or videoconferencing, or by electronic meeting facilities. Along with providing a teleconferencing capability, electronic meeting systems allow meetings to be distributed over time and offer support for group decision making. Electronic meeting systems can also be used to support same-time-same-place meetings.

Audio and Video Teleconferencing

Teleconferencing facilities enable people at remote locations to hold a meeting in which they can communicate by voice, text, or images—depending on the conferencing facility. There are three principal ways to hold a teleconference: audioconferencing, videoconferencing, and computer conferencing. We will hold off our discussion of computer teleconferencing, which is possible with an electronic meeting system. Audio and video teleconferencing do not require that participants use computers; yet, personal computers are now used for personal videoconferencing (for example, using Intel's ProShare system).

Audioconferencing is an extension of the conference call without the need for an operator to establish the connection between remote conference sites. Typically, managers located in a conference room at one of the organization's sites hold a face-to-face meeting and, at some point, establish an audio teleconference connection with a similar meeting being held at another company site. With speaker phones installed in both conference rooms, all the participants can hear one another but, of course, the remote participants cannot be seen. Specialized portable systems for audioconferencing are available.

Making Money with Video-conferencing

What happens when you marry an automatic teller machine with videoconferencing? Huntington Bancshares did just that in creating its Personal Touch video banking service (see Photo 8.2). The Columbus, Ohio, bank invested more than $10 million in developing electronic banking services that have replaced face-to-face banking in 15 of its branches. The bank intends to cut its branch banking costs by a quarter by closing as many as 40 percent of its traditional, staffed branches in the Ohio area.

Photo 8.2

Video banking at Huntington Bancshares combines videoconferencing with an automated teller machine in this small office (From Connie Guglielmo, "Here Come the Super-ATMs, *Fortune*, October 14, 1996, pp. 232–234.)

The Personal Touch video banking machine lets the customer interact with remote bank personnel from a small office that is open 24 hours a day, and contains only automated teller machines, the new video-banking machines, and perhaps a human concierge. There are three or four tiny glass-walled offices, each with a video-banking machine and a desk. Customers can obtain a wide range of banking services. Thanks to the videoconferencing facility, the customer sees a banker on the screen and the banker sees the customer. Customers can fax the banker the images of appropriate documents, including their identification.

The bank promises a 10-minute loan decision. As soon as the "phone banker" receives the information through the video-banking machine, she types the brief identifying details of the application into her workstation and an information system places the customer's record on the screen and orders a credit-bureau record on the customer. The "phone banker" then pages one of the loan officers who roam the telephone banking center. Using the print-outs of the customer's records from the bank and the credit bureau, together with the loan application analyzed by an expert system, the loan officer can generally make a decision in less than a minute. If the loan is approved, the printer at the video-banking machine prints out the loan document, the customer signs it, and faxes it back. The money is deposited in the customer's account.

Video-banking lowers banking costs and provides service at a time and place convenient to customers. In the first year of the system's operation, Huntington received 1.1 million phone calls and opened 75,000 new accounts, nearly triple the rate of the year before. Credit problems are no greater than at the traditional branches. In the second year, the bank expects over 2 million phone calls as it is planning to accept home-mortgage applications and to sell mutual funds on the video line. The effects of the system on the morale of traditional bankers are not discussed by the bank.

Based on Saul Hansell, "Into Banking's Future, Electronically," *The New York Times*, March 31, 1994, pp. D1, D13; Paul Strauss, "Beyond Talking Heads: Videoconferencing Makes Money," *Datamation*, October 1, 1994, pp. 38–41; and Connie Guglielmo, "Here Come the Super-ATMs," *Fortune*, October 14, 1996, pp. 232–234.

Videoconferencing extends the well-established one-way closed-circuit TV concept. In a two-way video teleconference, the participants can see and hear one another at a distance. Although audio teleconferencing is less expensive, participants in a video teleconference can see the body language that accompanies verbal utterances. Full-motion video is

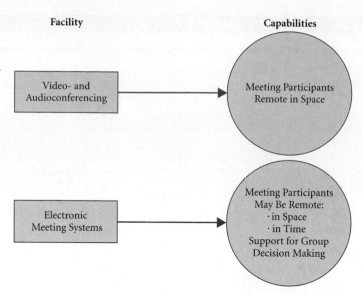

Figure 8.11

*Capabilities of video-
and audioconferencing
compared with those of
electronic meeting
systems*

significantly more expensive than freeze-frame video, where periodic snapshots are sent over the telecommunications channel. Freeze-frame videoconferencing limits the ability to establish eye contact but certainly makes it possible to present a graph, a report, or an image of a computer screen.

Video images are captured by one of several cameras located in the conferencing room and are viewed at the remote site on a TV monitor screen, a special large-size screen (the kind we see on TV when a correspondent at a remote site is being interviewed), or on a videoconferencing workstation. Two PC users whose computers are equipped with cameras can conduct a videoconference on their screens using, for example, ProShare (DeVoney 1997). Videoconferencing has been used for instruction, to introduce a new car model to the sales force (by Ford and General Motors), or to brief brokers on new financial instruments. The vignette on the preceding page shows how videoconferencing can be used directly in the core business of a company.

Electronic Meeting Systems

Electronic meeting systems support meetings, which may be distributed in space and time, with information technology. As we have seen in audio- and videoconferencing, the telecommunications media provide connectivity. Electronic meeting systems provide not only connectivity but also memory: The capabilities of computer storage enable participants to be at remote locations and their participation in a meeting to be spread over time. We will see that decision-room computer conferencing facilities are also valuable, even though all the participants may be in the same place at the same time. The distinctions between electronic meeting systems and audio and videoconferencing are summarized in Figure 8.11.

The most-often-used settings for electronic meetings are shown in Figure 8.12. Two notable settings are the decision room for same-place-same-time conferences and the computer teleconference for meetings distributed both in space and time. A videoconference with computer support combines the decision-room facilities with those of videoconfer-

Figure 8.12

Settings for electronic meetings (From Detmar W. Straub, Jr. and Renee A. Beauclair, "Current and Future Uses of GDSS Technology: Report on a Recent Empirical Study," *Journal of Management Information Systems,* 5, no. 1, Summer 1988, pp. 101–116.)

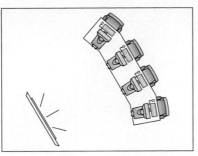

(a) Decision room: all participants are in the same place at the same time

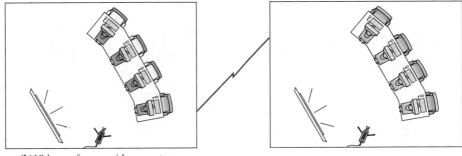

(b) Videoconference with computer support: distribution in space

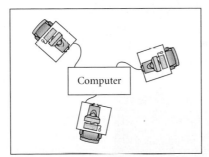

(c) Computer teleconference: distribution in space and time

encing, discussed above. In all of these settings, it is possible to use group decision support systems (GDSS), which we will discuss in Chapter 10. A GDSS includes software that assists group processes such as brainstorming in the search for creative ideas; reaching consensus via voting or the Delphi method; or negotiating, defined as a form of group decision making in which the parties communicate in an effort to resolve conflicting interests.

1. Decision Rooms

A **decision room** is an electronic meeting system facility for same-time-same-place meetings. A room installed at an IBM location is shown schematically in Figure 8.13 and the facility available at the University of Arizona is shown in Photo 8.3. A semicircle of tiered

Figure 8.13

Schematic of a U-shaped electronic meeting room (decision room)

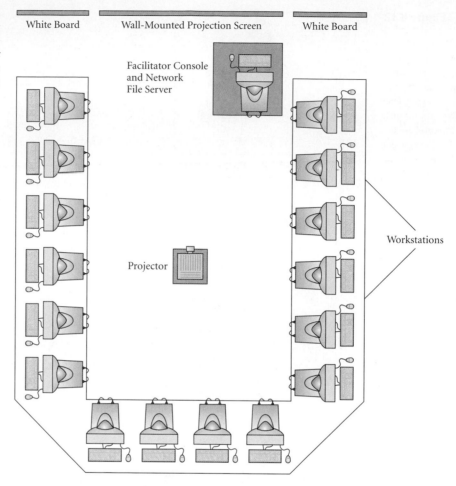

White Board   Wall-Mounted Projection Screen   White Board

Facilitator Console and Network File Server

Projector

Workstations

Photo 8.3

A meeting room for the use of an electronic meeting system at the University of Arizona in Tucson. Such installations are provided by Ventana Corporation of Tucson, Arizona

tables (for a large group) or a U-shaped table is equipped with personal workstations connected into a local area network. An additional workstation controls the central display on a large central screen. The meeting is generally conducted by a facilitator who is in charge of this workstation, where all the input that the participants provide is stored. Participants' work, which may be displayed on the projection screen, is anonymous. Participants have access to personal productivity software and may also communicate by E-mail. The facilitator activates various software tools from the GDSS suite (to be discussed in Chapter 10), as planned before the meeting.

In several corporate settings, computer-supported meetings have been found to be more productive than traditional ones; in some cases, they also proved more effective by resulting in higher-quality decisions. However, the overall effects of these systems are still being assessed, since they depend on the task at hand, the nature of the group, the process adopted for the meeting, and other variables (Nunamaker 1996–1997).

2. Computer Teleconferencing

Computer teleconferencing systems support meetings distributed in time as well as in space. Only in rare cases are group decision support tools employed. A "meeting" takes place over an extended period of time. The conference chairperson opens the "meeting" with a statement defining its purpose and the key topics. This is then broadcast to all participants. Within the prescribed "meeting" time, perhaps a week or two, the participants read the chairperson's message and the contributions of other conference participants and then broadcast their own messages. Conference members may contribute their statements at any time during the "meeting." At the prescribed completion time, or at some time deemed appropriate, the chairperson summarizes the results of the meeting, broadcasts them, and closes the meeting. The records of the meeting are available at all times in full detail.

Computer teleconferencing is supported by some of the public E-mail services. For example, CompuServe offers a service called Participate, and some organizations use this system to set up internal computer conference facilities. The software package offers a branching option: A user can create a branch to any existing conference, asking some of the parent conference participants to join. A "greenhouse effect" conference may thus branch off to a "customer reaction" subconference.

8.6   WORKGROUP SUPPORT AND GROUPWARE

The variety of technologies available for exchanging messages and holding meetings, combined with a recognition of the importance of teamwork, has led to the emergence of groupware. Groupware supports communication and collaboration of a group of coworkers over an extended period of time. Group size depends on the project and on the organization. In general, it ranges between 2 and 45 members.

The Organizational Role of Workgroups

As the information society shapes new organizational forms, team-based horizontal organizations emerge as a replacement for vertical, hierarchical structures in order to respond to the fast-paced competitive marketplace. The realization has also occurred that much of organizational effectiveness stems from the effective work of groups, equipped with autonomy and proper tools, more than from actions of isolated individuals. The well-known analyst of management, Peter Drucker, sees task-focused teams as the principal working units (Drucker 1988), and the importance of teamwork both in manufacturing and in the business office has been recognized by several leading organizations.

Back-office work, such as processing securities in a bank, lease applications in a credit corporation, or insurance policies of a certain type in an insurance company, is now increasingly assigned to a team, as opposed to being divided into meaningless segments to be

IN THE SPOTLIGHT

Sharing Information Does Not Come Naturally

The main advantage of groupware is that it enables the sharing of information. Yet, information is the currency of organizational power—sharing it does not come easily. In fact, a more natural reaction is resistance to the sharing of information. In other words, companies wishing to exploit groupware to its highest potential should give employees incentives for sharing their information.

Diagraph, a St. Louis manufacturer of equipment for bar coding and ink-jet printing, decided to use groupware as a vehicle for moving to a centralized sales program. In the past, the company salespeople would handle their own customer leads. Now, customer information is shared by all the reps, who are collectively responsible for selling. Diagraph employs groupware for customer management, called Telemar, from Information Management Associates of Trumbull, Connecticut. Telemar provides a central database of current and prospective customers that can be tapped throughout the firm.

The beginnings were tricky. "We had a hard time getting sales reps to let their [customer] data be centrally deposited," says the director of information systems for the company, Susan Ittner. "But we told them it was the company's data and it belonged to everyone." Now, every Diagraph department, from sales to product support, has access to customer information. Any employee who talks to a customer is required to file a note on the contact in the customer's file. This leads to faster and more consistent customer service. Now a customer is served by the entire firm, rather than by an individual.

The sales rep who initiated the lead still gets credit if the sale is closed. In fact, Diagraph ranks its reps' performance in large part based on the number of customer leads they provide to co-workers. The incentives for sharing the information are part of the corporate human-resources policy.

Based on Stephanie Stahl, "Groupware's Culture Problem," *InformationWeek,* May 23, 1994, pp. 52–56.

turned over to workers on an "electronic assembly line." Effective team organization and motivation result in job enrichment and a sense of responsibility. Indeed, in some firms, such teams are largely self-managed.

A team can be a highly responsive and flexible structure in responding to the uncertainties of the shifting business environment. As we know from Chapter 1, clusters of such teams are the principal structural components of some organizations. Various teams serve different purposes. Project teams, task forces, brand teams, sales teams, account teams, new-product teams, and crisis-response teams are the workgroups that have emerged in today's organizations (Johansen 1988). Some of these groups are relatively permanent, others are organized and disbanded as needed. In some teams, members are doing similar jobs, other teams consist of members with different specialties. Group members may work in the same building or be separated by oceans. A workgroup has a functional goal; its members take on roles in the overall task set for the group; and a set of norms develops in the operation of a group.

Groupware and Its Functions

Groupware is the software that supports a business group whose members work on interconnected personal workstations. Groupware offers support for *communication* and *collaboration* among group members, and for *coordination* of group work. The function of groupware reaches beyond the personal productivity software and professional support systems of individual members. The principal emphasis of groupware is on the use of computers to facilitate human interaction. Groupware generally runs on personal computers that provide connectivity to other members of the organization and to the external world. Today, many functions of groupware are implemented using intranets, internal corporate networks relying on the Internet facilities (see Section 7.8). Let's discuss the principal functions of groupware.

1. Information Sharing

Group members must share information and knowledge bases in order to work both in their "private" computer workspaces and in a group workspace. Thus, the leading groupware package, Lotus Notes from IBM makes it possible to share an information base consisting of multimedia documents, which combine text with graphics, sound, image, and video. Each Notes application is built around such an information base, with group members entering new information, using forms, and retrieving the information by keywords, using views. The most significant feature of Notes is replication: automatic updating of remote information bases with information entered into all of them. Using Notes, group members are able to accumulate information pertaining to a topic, comment on one another's work, and assemble a group memory. As you read in the vignette, information sharing requires motivation.

2. Document Authoring

An authoring group needs to collaborate in producing technical documentation, reports, or business proposals. Many groupware products enable a group to produce a multimedia document, combining text, graphs, and images. Workgroup members may append text comments and voice annotations. When a loudspeaker icon appears on the screen, the reader knows that a voice comment has been appended to the text and listens to the comment by invoking the playback command. A screen containing a sample multimedia document is shown in Figure 8.14.

Figure 8.14

A screen with a multimedia document

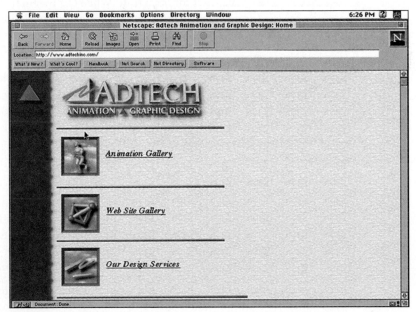

A variety of presentation subsystems that display the graphical information on workstation screens, transparencies, or slides may be combined with an authoring system. Hypertext and hypermedia technologies are employed in some systems. Care has to be exercised in group authoring. When a person other than the original author of a document can change it, controversy about authorship and document integrity may arise.

3. Messaging Systems

Much of groupware is built as an extension of E-mail facilities. The internal and external messaging capability of groupware is used extensively to support group communication between meetings. Management of distribution lists, notification of arriving E-mail, confirmation of receipts, and message-history tracking are some of the available facilities.

Some groupware systems permit users to impose a structure on message communication. For example, certain messages may impose obligations and commitments, such as deadlines. The system may automatically remind group members about these. Many organizations do not desire that the messaging system structure their teamwork and use only the messaging facilities of the system. This is one example of the importance of selecting groupware to match an organization's culture.

4. Computer Conferencing

Depending on the task and the makeup of a group, various computer conferencing options may be desirable. A groupware conferencing program may assist in exchanging progress reports and discussing problems by exchanging messages. The complete text is saved and may be searched by any team member. Several users may view the same document on their workstations and exchange messages, while the participant who has the "floor" can modify the draft in full view of everyone.

5. Group Calendaring

Groupware systems maintain individual calendars to keep track of time commitments. This simplifies the scheduling of a meeting. For example, if you were planning a meeting with a groupware product, you would provide the system with a list of people you want to meet. It would then scan their calendars for open time. When the system finds an open slot, it "pencils in" the meeting and requests confirmation from all parties. Note that one has to be very careful about systems appearing to automatically manage someone's time.

6. Project Management

The progress of group projects must be tracked. Some groupware systems offer such project management tools as activity lists and Gantt charts that specify timelines for the activities (see Figure 8.15). Gantt charts visualize workgroup activities on a project as bars and indicate the overall status of a project (completed, on schedule, overdue). The best, most likely, and worst-case scenarios of project completion and the associated costs can be computed as well.

7. Support for Team Building

A team-building tool, such as SuperSync of SwixTech USA (of Irvine, California), can "administer" questionnaires to team members in order to identify patterns of interpersonal communication, establish the presence of harmful alliances, and find leadership potential. A graphic output shows alignments around leaders. Since much of teamwork depends on good interpersonal relations, a tool of this kind assists human resources policy.

We have summarized the functions of groupware in Figure 8.16 in terms of its support for coordination, communication, and collaboration. It is crucial to adapt the capabilities of a groupware package to the needs and work styles of a specific group and the individuals

Figure 8.15

*Project management
tools for a group*

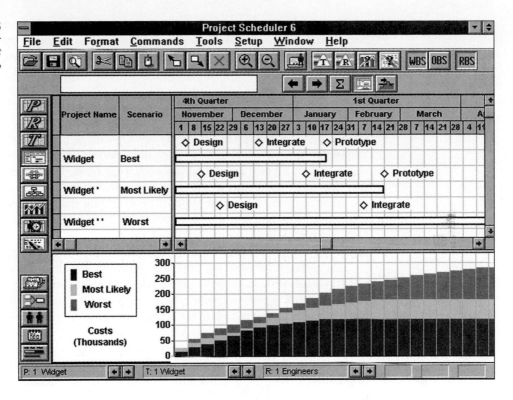

Figure 8.16

*Workgroup support
offered by groupware*

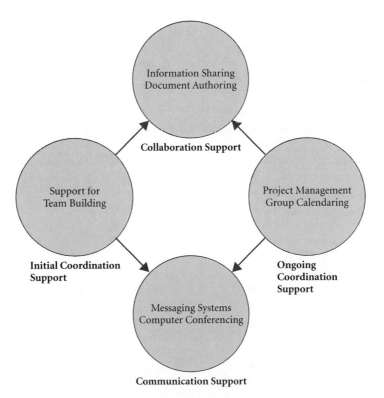

within the group. New group norms emerge during groupware work. For example, having begun to use a group authoring system, members of the law department in a real estate firm cut their customary five-page memos to one page. While groupware is in use, the security and privacy of individual information bases should be safeguarded.

SUMMARY

Knowledge work consists in developing new knowledge, processing information, and using knowledge and information to provide new products and services. Professional support systems (PSS) support an individual's knowledge work. The specifics of the PSS a person uses depend on the nature of the work he or she performs. At the same time, a PSS offers the following general features: support for modeling the objects to be developed; multimedia representation of the objects; the ability to connect with other knowledge workers over telecommunications networks and to cooperate with some of them on a project; group memory; and access to external information and knowledge bases.

The principal functions of organizational office information systems (OIS) are: document management; message handling; teleconferencing and electronic meeting systems; and support of groupwork with groupware. Many of these OIS facilities are being integrated with the Internet and, in particular, internal corporate networks relying on the Internet software, known as intranets.

Electronic document management supports creation, storage, and retrieval of electronic documents. In some applications, these documents can also be updated and printed or published. New forms of documents, such as hypertext and hypermedia, which enable the user (or reader) to move through a longer document by pursuing only the issues of interest, have become possible with electronic document management.

Workflow systems support document-based organizational processes by automatically routing electronic documents to the appropriate workers for their contribution. With these systems, it is possible to define and track the entire business process as a sequence of actions by various members of the organization.

Message-handling services of office information systems include forwarding electronic mail, providing access to electronic information services, and handling voice mail and facsimile.

Teleconferencing facilities of OIS enable people at remote locations to hold a meeting. In audio- and videoconferencing, the meeting participants are all present at the same time. Using an audioconferencing facility, all participants can hear each other; during a videoconference, they can both see and hear each other. Electronic meeting systems support a meeting with computer–resident facilities, such as group decision support systems. Participants can work all at the same time at their workstations in a decision room, or be dispersed in space and time during a computer teleconference.

Workgroups, such as project teams or task forces, play a vital role in today's organizations. Groupware supports communication and collaboration among group members, and helps coordinate their work together. Groupware can assist its users with information sharing, document authoring, sending and receiving messages, computer conferencing, maintaining a common calendar, project management, and team building.

KEY TERMS

Professional support system (PSS)   *290*

Office information system (OIS)   *291*

Office   *292*

Electronic document management   *295*

Digital image processing   *295*

Optical character recognition (OCR)   *297*

Text information management system   *298*

Reprographics   *299*

Hypertext   *299*

Hypermedia   *300*

Workflow system   *301*

Electronic mail (E-mail)   *302*

Intelligent agent   *303*

Electronic information services   *304*

Electronic bulletin boards   *304*

Voice mail   *304*

Facsimile (fax)   *305*

Teleconferencing   *306*

Audioconferencing   *306*

Videoconferencing   *307*

Electronic meeting system   *308*

Decision room   *309*

Computer teleconferencing   *311*

Groupware   *312*

QUESTIONS

1. What features should a professional support system for the following professions offer and why?
   a. lawyers
   b. architects
   c. accountants

2. What is an office and what are office information systems (OIS)? Which aspects of the office require the physical presence of the employees in it and which can be virtualized with OIS?

3. What is the primary objective of OIS? How does this objective relate to the electronic integration of the office?

4. Does office automation mean that offices are becoming paperless? What changes are taking place in this regard thanks to electronic document management?

5. What are the steps in processing an electronic document stored as an image?

6. What are the steps in processing an electronic document stored as a text file? What are the principal advantages and drawbacks of text representation as compared to image representation?

7. What is the principal distinction between hypertext and the traditional document from the user's (reader's) point of view? Is the reader entirely free in "navigating" the hypertext? How does hypermedia relate to hypertext?

8. What is a workflow system? How does such a system relate to business process redesign? Why is the World Wide Web considered an excellent means of workflow support?

9. List the capabilities E-mail can offer to an organization and to its individual members. Relate these to the fol-lowing words of Andrew S. Grove, CEO of Intel: "The informed use of E-mail has two simple but startling implications: It turns days into minutes, and allows each person to reach hundreds of co-workers with the same effort it takes to reach just one" (Grove 1995).

10. What are intelligent agents and how can they be used in an E-mail system?

11. Present three scenarios of the use of electronic information services in the everyday work of a manager to address specific problems.

12. Name three ways to hold a teleconference. What are the principal differences between audioconferencing and videoconferencing on the one hand, and computer conferencing conducted with an electronic meeting system on the other? What capabilities of information systems does computer conferencing rely on?

13. What are the three possible settings for an electronic meeting and what are the differences among them? Present a scenario for the use of each setting in a problem-solving situation.

14. What could be the advantages of supporting a same-time-same-place conference with an electronic meeting system (after all, everyone is there anyway)?

15. What is groupware? What is the basic distinction between the role of groupware and the role of electronic meeting systems?

16. Compare and contrast groupware with workflow systems.

17. What are the principal uses of groupware? Give a scenario for three such uses by a team developing a new marketing campaign.

ISSUES FOR DISCUSSION

1. How does the use of information systems supporting knowledge work change the nature of this work? Include in your discussion the change in the way the work is being done (for example, travel, telecommuting) and in the content of the work (for example, computer modeling of car crashes during the automobile design process instead of crashing physical prototypes).

2. Discuss the influence of E-mail on the way organizations operate and are managed. Consider also the symbolic role of E-mail in such phenomena as power, influence, or recognition as an expert (read for example, what John Gage of Sun Microsystems says on the subject, as cited in Section 2.5 of the text). What ethical issues can arise in the organizational use of E-mail?

3. Throughout the book, we discuss networks of organizations, telecommunications networks, and the representation of information by networks of hyperlinks in hypertext or hypermedia. What are the relationships among these three kinds of networks? Do you believe that these relationships are significant or accidental?

REAL-WORLD MINICASE AND PROBLEM-SOLVING EXERCISES

1. Groupware and Intranets   With the growing popularity of the Internet, enterprises have a wider range of alternative ways to support communications and collaboration among their members. Besides using the World Wide Web to communicate with the world at large and access information outside the corporate walls, many organizations are developing intranets. Discussed in Section 7.8, intranets provide the look, feel, and functionality of the Web, but offer access only to authorized users (intranets are protected from Internet access by firewalls).

A number of firms are finding that the ideal solution is to combine an intranet with traditional (already!) groupware, such as Lotus Notes. Such is the case at Xerox (of Stamford, Connecticut). Malcolm Kirby, manager of applied collaborative technology (note the title), observes that "neither environment does everything." Xerox has introduced its own intranet, known as Webboard, which is now available to 20,000 employees of the firm. Groupware can be used over the intranet. In this way, a common groupware backbone can be created for the firm. "Webboard serves as a knowledge base," says Cynthia Casselman, manager of interactive employee communications (note this title, too). "Ultimately, we want to create an interactive community, a virtual Xerox world." Employees use the intranet to retrieve news items from in-

ternal and external sources, to exchange ideas, and to collaborate. "It's a relatively inexpensive way to make information available to employees and to create a sense of belonging," says Casselman. "We want to make this environment available across all of Xerox."

a. What capabilities of Webboard do you think are provided by the Internet facilities (such as Web browsers and others), and which are furnished by traditional groupware, such as Lotus Notes?

b. What is the symbolic role of Webboard (as identified by Casselman)? Do you think other information systems may also have a symbolic role? If so, give examples.

c. What other office information systems can be integrated with intranets in the future and what could be the principal means and ends of doing so?

Based on Jenny C. McCune, "All Together Now," *Beyond Computing,* May 1996, pp. 26–31.

2. Designing a Presentation   Using presentation software, such as Microsoft PowerPoint, design the following on-screen presentation:

You are a sales manager presenting your groupware product to a potential customer firm. Select an actual product available on the market and evaluate its features—this is what you will be presenting. Your audience will include sophisticated users and your presentation should be highly objective.

The presentation is to consist of at least 10 slides. You will need to create a template for all slides, containing your company name, the date of the presentation, and the slide number. Your first slide will present your company name and its logo. The second slide will introduce you in the manner you select. The third slide should name the product and associate it with an attractive graphical image, which you will then carry over to the following slides. Six or more subsequent slides will present the features of your product (i.e., groupware) in a bulleted form. The last slide should contain an attractive message that will be certain to clinch the deal.

The presentation should be appealing graphically, contain the appropriate information in concise form, and be carefully spell-checked. The slides should be printed out and presented in a report form as well.

3. You have been placed in charge of selecting a workflow package to support teams of insurance claims adjusters who work on client claims. Research the available workflow packages. Draw up a memo that outlines the specific aspects of work that will be supported by the package you suggest be acquired. Specify what business results are to be expected from the package and what the costs of its acquisition and implementation will be (such as training, for example).

TEAM PROJECT

Each two- or three-person team will interview several people who may be considered to form a workgroup in the college or university (including the president's cabinet, for example), or in a local organization, to find out how they conduct various meetings today. It is desirable to include groups that participate in interorganizational meetings. Each team will identify different types of meetings in terms of their frequency, number of participants, diversity of participants, and their geographic dispersion. The team will also include in its interviews questions about the communications that are not presently conducted as meetings (such as several telephone calls on a subject). Each team will suggest how the workgroup it studied can best be supported with information systems.

After the selected teams present their conclusions to the class, all the participants will attempt to draw general conclusions on electronic meeting support, relying on the material presented in this chapter.

SELECTED REFERENCES

Bender, Eric. "Workgroup Computing." Special Section, *PC World*, January 1995, pp. 225–244.

DeVoney, Chris. "Desktop Videoconferencing." *Computerworld*, February 24, 1997, pp. 81–84.

A guide to personal videoconferencing systems.

Drucker, Peter F. "The Coming of New Organization." *Harvard Business Review*, January–February 1988, pp. 45–53.

Grove, Andrew S. "A High-Tech CEO Updates His Views on Managing and Careers." *Fortune*, September 18, 1995, p. 229.

Holusha, John. "Xerox Is Offering a New Category of Color Printer." *The New York Times*, April 29, 1996, p. D23.

Horton, Marjorie, and Kevin Biolsi. "Coordination Challenges in a Computer-Supported Meeting Environment." *Journal of Management Information Systems*, 10, no. 3, Winter 1993–94, pp. 7–24.

Johansen, Robert. *Groupware: Computer Support for Business Teams*, New York: Free Press, 1988.

Contains a large number of scenarios for using groupware.

Kay, Roger. "Paper Chase." *Computerworld*, February 6, 1995, pp. 87–89.

A move from paper to electronic forms throughout industries.

Leinfuss, Emily. "Suppliers Reposition to Go with the Flow." *Software Magazine*, February 1995, pp. 69–73.

A review of workflow systems and how to use them.

Maes, Pattie. "Agents That Reduce Work and Information Overload." *Communications of the ACM*, 37, no. 7, July 1994, pp. 31–146.

Marca, David, and Geoffrey Brock, eds. *Groupware: Software for Computer-Supported Cooperative Work*, Los Alamitos, CA: IEEE Computer Society Press, 1992.

A comprehensive collection of articles on groupware.

Nadile, Lisa. "Action, Ultimus Build Apps on Workflow Standards." *PC Week*, April 15, 1996, pp. 36–37.

Nunamaker, Jay F., Jr.; Alan R.Dennis; Joseph S.Valacich; Doglas R.Vogel; and Joey F. George. "Electronic Meeting Systems to Support Group Work." *Communications of the ACM*, 34, no. 7, July 1991, pp. 40–61.

An excellent survey of electronic meeting systems.

Nunamaker, Jay F., Jr., and others. "Lessons from a Dozen Years on Group Support Systems Research: A Discussion of Lab and Field Findings." *Journal of Management Information Systems*, 13, no. 3, Winter 1996–97.

Powell, David, ed. "Group Communication." Special Section, *Communications of the ACM*, 39, no. 4, April 1996, pp. 50–97.

Several information systems designed to support group communication and collaboration.

"Publish Without Paper." Special Section, *PC Magazine*, February 7, 1995, pp. 110–169.

A detailed discussion of PC-based electronic publishing.

Riecken, Doug, ed. "Intelligent Agents." Special Issue, *Communications of the ACM*, 37, no. 7, 1994, pp. 18–147.

Sixteen readable papers that will give you the overall view of this fascinating field.

Thornton, Caroline, and Erik Lockhart. "Groupware or Electronic Brainstorming." *Journal of Systems Management*, October 1994, pp. 10–12.

Tyran, Craig K.; Alan R. Dennis; Douglas R. Vogel; and Jay F. Nunamaker. "The Application of Electronic Meeting Technology to Support Strategic Management." *MIS Quarterly*, 16, no. 3, September 1992, pp. 313–334.

Can Information Systems Help Contain the Expense of Legal Work?

Managing the litigation caseload for a large corporation in the United States is a little like managing a small war, and almost as expensive. DuPont, the country's leading manufacturer of chemicals, decided to do something about it. And information systems were seen as an obvious weapon.

DuPont has every reason to pay attention. The company is sued more than five times a day. From 1990 to 1994, the number of lawsuits on file against DuPont grew from 1,200 to 4,500. The firm's legal expenses grew correspondingly, to $160 million a year. Of this amount, $75 million was spent annually on the services of nearly 400 outside law firms. In addition, DuPont employs 150 in-house attorneys.

The explosion in legal spending coincided with the corporate austerity program, initiated in response to the shrinking profits during a recession. Under the program, $1 billion had to be cut out of the $11 billion annual budget for corporate services. Although the legal department was not specifically targeted, it was clear that major savings were necessary.

In late 1991, a task force was created to study how to apply computerization in order to cut legal expenses radically. After 10 months, the task force, led by an in-house lawyer, Daniel Mahoney, delivered the recommendation that is being implemented by the firm. The ties with more than 300 of the law firms traditionally servicing the DuPont account were to be severed. Some 50 legal firms were selected as the "primary firms" that will do almost all the outside legal work for the company. These firms are being linked with DuPont via a wide area network (WAN). Thanks to the network, all the in-house and outside lawyers will be able to use a common library of research material, trial documents, and strategy notes.

To motivate the primary firms to computerize their operations in a manner compatible with DuPont's system, the company will channel 90 percent of its legal work to these firms. In many cases, DuPont will be their largest client. Each primary firm will also discount its stated billing rates by an average of 15 percent. The costs of litigating individual cases are expected to drop by at least 20 percent.

But acquisition of information technology is less important than the cultural change the primary firms must undergo. First, technophobia has prevented many legal professionals from acquiring information systems literacy. Second, the law firms will have to submit to the cost-monitoring techniques that become possible with the information systems that are being implemented. Now DuPont will have an ability to monitor the costs of individual lawsuits as they proceed and to compare the rates charged by different law firms for similar tasks. By selecting 50 primary firms, DuPont is creating a network of firms committed to its purposes and committed to learning how to employ information technology to increase the efficiency of their work. "We could not have set up the network with a loose amalgam of 400 firms, all of which are competing with one another," says Mahoney.

Let's see where the saving will come from. The corporation is now defending itself against four major families of lawsuits. One group of approximately 450 cases stems from DuPont's having supplied five cents' worth of raw Teflon that went into joint implants in people's mouths. Many of them shattered during use. The manufacturer of the implants, Vitek Inc., went into bankruptcy and DuPont is being sued as a "deep-pocket" defendant (that is, an entity with the ability to pay). Suits against DuPont have been launched in 40 states. Because product liability laws vary somewhat among the states, DuPont had to hire

40 local firms to defend its cases. Yet the cases differ little: The facts in each case are similar, as are the legal arguments. As a result, approximately 90 percent of the motion for summary judgment (that is, an attempt to close the case before trial as being without merit) made by DuPont is the same in each state. Indeed, DuPont has already won more than 230 cases in 19 states, with a single lost case being appealed. The attorneys in different states shared little of their legal documents. Indeed, without computerization, such sharing would have entailed a flurry of phoning and faxing. All of that took place at more than $200 an hour.

With access to the WAN, all lawyers gain access to one another's work. An attorney will open the case folder in the central case database, open the subfolder of motions in the case, download to her workstation the model summary judgment motion, and customize it. DuPont will pay only once for the complete model summary motion in such a case. Once the model motion is placed in the database, the lawyers will bill the company only for adjusting the motion to comply with state laws. Other legal documents will be similarly reused and customized.

DuPont also expects to raise the effectiveness of its in-house counsel. By using E-mail and groupware over the network, lawyers will be able to discuss their arguments and compare notes on expert witnesses, for example. Indeed, jury verdicts frequently depend on an expert's testimony. Total judgments to individual plaintiffs in a family of suits can reach hundreds of millions of dollars. Winning an additional case thanks to improved legal work can result in major gains for DuPont. "We started off with this whole program thinking in terms of attorney's hourly rates. We've since realized that that's peanuts compared to the cost of [mishandling] a case," says DuPont's Associate General Counsel Marjorie Doyle.

In addition to creating the WAN, DuPont is purchasing an extensive software package for case management from CompInfo in New York City. Led by Yiorgos Athanassatos, the firm is the leading software supplier to captive (i.e., in-house) legal departments. The Corporate LawPack for Windows package costs about $400,000, which includes minor customization and training for 200 users. Using the package, DuPont's in-house lawyers will determine how much money is at stake whenever a new suit is filed against the company. Then, the screens will guide them in drawing up budgets for each step of the litigation, from the initial filing through the trial. As outside firms submit their bills, the package will be used to check for cost overruns. The firm wants to prevent spending excessive amounts on relatively minor suits. Figure 8.17 shows the principal window of Corporate LawPack being used to manage a specific legal matter, whose costs can be managed with the package.

Starting in 1995, the firm will be compiling comparative data on performance of the prime firms. Mahoney's team is now devising a standard invoice form that divides what outside lawyers do into a small number of standard tasks, such as drafting a summary judgment motion, as one example. Cost comparisons across the primary law firms will be possible.

It is estimated that DuPont's up-front costs of the central data server, networking equipment, and networking software will run about $800,000, with monthly telecommunications costs of $30,000 to $50,000. A 13-lawyer primary firm selected by DuPont, Dillingham & Murphy of San Francisco aims to meet DuPont's requirements. It has hired a systems integrator to build its local area network with more than three dozen desktop computers based on Intel microcomputers and a central file server with 1.1 gigabyte secondary storage. The system will cost nearly $200,000, quite a lot for a firm grossing $4 million annually. However, "if we want to continue living well, we are going to have to learn to be more productive," says partner Bill Dillingham. But then the status as primary firm for DuPont can be used as a marketing tool. "Other clients want to capture the benefits of what we are learning from DuPont," says Dillingham.

Figure 8.17

The Matter Management window of Corporate LawPack (Courtesy of CompInfo, New York.)

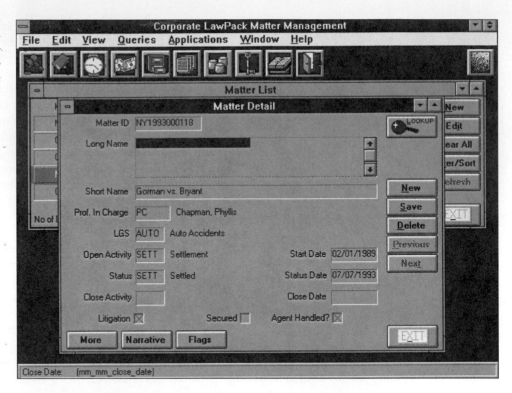

And then there are legal firms that thrive on information technology. Hale and Dorr, a 275-attorney establishment with a highly prestigious background, is considered by some the country's most technologically sophisticated law firm. Annual technology spending of $2 to $3 million is justified by expanded client relationships and savings in other areas. The culture of embracing technology is by now entrenched. The managing partner runs the firm using a Sun workstation; indeed all lawyers here use technical workstations under UNIX rather than PCs. The firm's Boston headquarters are becoming paperless. The internal correspondence is done only via E-mail. The firm applies electronic imaging to prepare major lawsuits: By replacing the usual mountains of paper with electronic documents, Hale and Dorr can save clients' money and speed up the preparation of their case. An electronic site has been on the Internet's Web since January 1995, and over 200 of the firm's attorneys have their own Web sites. The site averages 15,000 hits a week—it's http://www.haledorr.com, if you're interested.

Based on Mike France, "Reengineer Your Lawyers," *Forbes ASAP,* June 6, 1994, pp. 54–61; author's conversations with Yiorgos Athanassatos, November 1994 and December 1995; and Mike France, "Law.com," *Forbes ASAP,* April 8, 1996, pp. 28–34.

CASE STUDY QUESTIONS

1. Why can knowledge work such as legal work be highly affected by computerization? What capabilities of information systems will have the greatest effect on this work and what do you expect this effect to be?

2. What is the interaction between the organizational network created by DuPont and the wide area network it is developing?

3. Discuss how the information systems being placed in operation at DuPont are expected to affect the effectiveness and efficiency of the legal services.

4. What problems do you foresee in placing DuPont's system into operation?

5. What can DuPont do next, after the described system is implemented?

6. What business results can justify the information-technology expenditures made by legal firms such as Hale and Dorr?

CHAPTER NINE

Transaction Processing and Management Reporting Systems

OBJECTIVES

After you complete this chapter, you will be able to:

1. Define what a transaction is and what transaction processing systems (TPS) do.
2. Distinguish between on-line and batch transaction processing and determine where each is appropriate.
3. Identify the principal transaction processing subsystems in a firm.
4. Specify the general transaction processing activities.
5. Specify the outputs produced by TPS.
6. Define electronic data interchange (EDI) and describe its role in organizations.
7. Specify the characteristics of management reporting systems (MRS) and the types of reports these systems produce.
8. Discuss the strategic potential of TPS.

OUTLINE

How to Break into Motion Pictures

A fast-growing breed of firms that intensively use information technology is logistics providers. They provide complete warehousing, distribution, and transportation services to their client firms. In simple words, logistics providers take products off their clients' hands as soon as the products are finished. Typically, these service companies are subsidiaries of leading transportation firms that have over a long time developed their transaction processing systems for competitive purposes. These information systems include package tracking and inventory management systems, relying on bar coding and electronic data interchange (EDI). Thanks to EDI, systems of the logistics providers can be linked to the clients' internal transaction processing systems.

Here is how a logistics provider has become a hit in Hollywood. Actually, this subsidiary of Airborne Express, Advanced Logistics Services (based in Seattle), had failed when it first approached several major movie studios seeking to manage their film-distribution business. Using EDI, Airborne had proposed to link its own transportation and billing systems with the studios' information systems that process their distribution transactions. It took Technicolor Inc., a company that duplicates films for the studios and has extensive connections throughout the industry, to bring Airborne into the picture as its business partner.

Owing to its extensive experience in logistics-oriented transaction processing, Advanced Logistics found it relatively easy to respond to the specialized demands of film distribution. At every step from Technicolor's Burbank, California, facility to the movie theaters and back, Airborne employees scan in bar codes on the film cans. Film studios and their distributors are especially sensitive to any possible theft of movie prints by videotape counterfeiters. To respond to these concerns, Airborne has initiated what it calls "proactive monitoring" of movie packages. The firm's information system automatically alerts a customer service representative if a package does not arrive at its destination on time and immediately helps to track its whereabouts. Since the can's bar code is scanned into a mainframe–resident database at each change of venue, a complete audit trail is available. According to Tom Schwaninger, the chief information officer at Technicolor, this is "a continuous history of who touched the print along the route."

The computer systems at Technicolor and Airborne communicate using the standard X.12 EDI protocol. However, Airborne keeps its main database private. Indeed, the transaction processing systems and their databases are a source of competitive strength to the company.

Based on Julia King, "Logistics Providers Enable 'Virtual Firms,'" *Computerworld*, July 18, 1994, p. 28; and Eric R. Chabrow, "An Up and Coming Star," *InformationWeek*, August 29, 1994, pp. 44–45.

Transaction processing systems (TPS) are the bedrock of business operations today. Most businesses could not be run without these systems. Conversely, advanced transaction processing systems that leverage a strength of the company can give it a competitive advantage in the marketplace. You can read in the Focus Minicase how Advanced Logistics Services was able to start a new line of business with such systems. As business operations proceed, TPSs acquire, process, and maintain data reflecting business transactions—sales, purchases, payments, and so forth. Based on the data collected by TPS, management-

Transaction Processing Systems are Vital to a Business

When a software supplier involved in a contract dispute with New York-based Revlon disabled Revlon's on-line TPS responsible for inventory management, the cosmetics company had to close two of its main distribution centers for three days. As much as $20 million in product deliveries was halted and hundreds of workers were idled.

The software supplier had planted a so-called logic bomb in the TPS code it delivered to Revlon. As we will see in Chapter 14, this method of attacking a software system involves inserting in it a code that may be activated by the attacker. The code (program instructions) can cause a shutdown of the system, for example. When Revlon failed to pay the supplier for the inventory management system that, according to the cosmetics giant, did not perform as promised, the supplier activated the code by accessing the system over a telephone line.

A legal action by Revlon ensued. The supplier claimed that it simply "repossessed" the software system; Revlon alleged that the supplier had committed "commercial terrorism." Thorny legal issues, as well as technical issues of system protection, arose. The case was settled out of court, with a payment by the software supplier.

Take another case. FedEx has built its business on the promise to deliver packages on time and the ability to keep customers informed of package whereabouts in transit. Yet when a software problem forced the company to suspend its "on-call pickups" of packages for most of a single day, FedEx could not keep its promise of dependability. The suspension of pickups was ordered when a computer system at corporate headquarters could not be placed back in service after maintenance. The TPS running on this system sends pickup instructions from the PCs of the order-takers who take orders over the phone to the company's trucks via satellite.

The problem was limited to about 15 percent of the two million packages handled daily by FedEx, since relatively few customers use the pickup service. The cost of the failure to the company could not be easily determined. Yet its reputation was affected. "Someone who was inconvenienced today, will remember it tomorrow," said one technology analyst. "You live by technology, you die by technology," said another. Indeed, the operation of many businesses today is wholly dependent on their transaction processing systems.

Based on Andrew Pollack, "Revlon Accuses a Supplier of Sabotaging Its Software," *The New York Times,* October 29, 1990, pp. D1, D4; and Andrea Adelson, "Computer Glitch Stalls Federal Express," *The New York Times,* November 9, 1994, p. D5.

oriented information systems assist managers in running the business. The oldest of these are management reporting systems that assist lower- and middle-level managers in controlling the operations of the enterprise.

9.1 FUNCTIONS OF TRANSACTION PROCESSING SYSTEMS

Transaction Processing Systems Undergird Business Operations

A **transaction** is an elementary activity conducted during business operations. A merchandise sale, airline reservation, credit card purchase, and inquiry about inventory are all transactions. **Transaction processing systems (TPS)** process the company's business transactions and thus support the operations of an enterprise. A TPS records a non-inquiry transaction itself, as well as all of its effects, in the database and produces documents relating to the transaction. For example, a sale transaction is accompanied by the sale record in the database, a subtraction from the inventory totals for the items purchased, and the printing of a sales slip. Today, many transaction documents, such as purchase orders or invoices, are produced in an electronic form and never appear on paper. By accessing databases, TPSs also process inquiry transactions and thus provide information, for example, about the status of product inventory or the credit rating of a customer.

TPSs are necessary to conduct business in almost any organization today. Since TPSs bring data into the organizational databases, these systems are also a foundation on which management-oriented information systems rest. Transaction processing systems for accounting and payroll were the first information system applications, introduced in the mid-fifties. According to our developmental model of information systems presented in Chapter 3, automation of business operations for the sake of efficiency was the earliest objective of computerization. The vignette on the preceding page vividly illustrates how today's companies rely on TPS for conducting their primary business processes.

System Charts

To describe TPS, as well as other information systems, in an accessible manner, we need to use graphic tools. System charts are a well-established tool for such high-level representations. These charts show the sources of input into the system, major processing steps, data storage, and system outputs. System charts rely on a set of established graphic symbols. Figure 9.1 reproduces a useful subset of these symbols.

Transaction Processing Modes

Transaction processing may be accomplished in one of two modes, on-line or batch, depending on the need for immediate outputs and database update.

On-line processing means that each transaction is completely processed immediately upon entry. "Immediately" means that processing occurs within the response time expected by the individual waiting for the transaction to be completed. In a properly designed system, most transactions should be processed within one or two seconds. On-line transaction processing (with its own acronym, OLTP) is the most common mode used today. This is particularly true in customer-driven applications, such as those supporting point-of-sale terminals, automatic teller machines, or computerized airline reservation systems.

Figure 9.1

System chart symbols

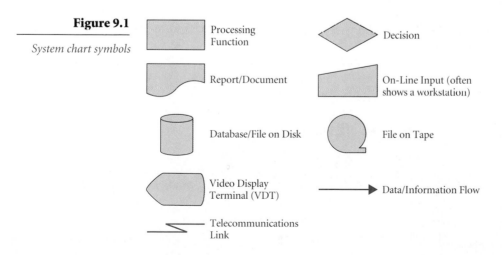

Processing Function

Decision

Report/Document

On-Line Input (often shows a workstation)

Database/File on Disk

File on Tape

Video Display Terminal (VDT)

Data/Information Flow

Telecommunications Link

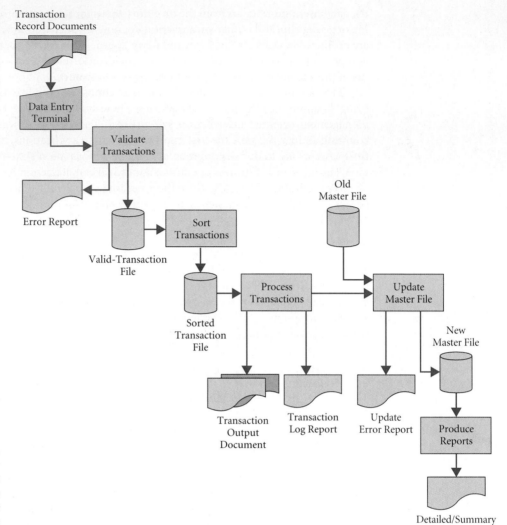

Figure 9.2

Transaction processing—batch mode. Note that many reports and documents are produced in an electronic form only

Figure 9.3

Transaction processing—on-line mode. Note that many reports and documents are produced in an electronic form only

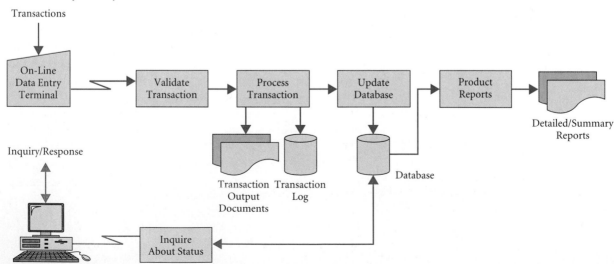

Certain kinds of transactions do not call for such an immediate and, in general, relatively costly, response. The alternative processing mode, **batch processing,** relies on accumulating transaction data over a period of time and then processing the entire batch at once. Batch processing is usually cyclic: A daily, weekly, or monthly run cycle is established, depending on the nature of the transactions. Aside from the advantage of lower costs, batch processing is also easier to control than on-line processing, as we will see in Chapter 14.

A typical batch application is payroll: It is run periodically and requires a special set-up for check printing, as well as calling for certain security precautions. Order transactions transmitted to a distributor daily over telephone lines or other telecommunications media by customers such as pharmacies or supermarkets may be processed on a daily cycle. It is possible to provide on-line access to the data entered in batch mode.

A system chart for batch transaction processing is shown in Figure 9.2 and a chart for OLTP in Figure 9.3. Note a very important distinction between these two modes: The database is always up-to-date in the case of on-line transaction processing as opposed to batch processing. For example, when the state government of New Hampshire wanted tighter financial controls, the batch financial system was converted to OLTP. It is now possible to track revenues and expenditures in the state's $1.3 billion budget as they occur.

Although magnetic tape *can* support batch processing as the means of secondary storage, batch systems today are usually built around disk files, as shown in Figure 9.2. On-line systems, on the other hand, *require* the use of fast secondary storage such as magnetic disks (as we learned in Chapter 4).

9.2 | TRANSACTION PROCESSING SUBSYSTEMS IN A FIRM

Let us review the principal data flows that transaction processing subsystems produce in an organization. Overall transaction processing, also known as data processing, reflects the principal business activities of a firm. Figure 9.4 shows the principal transaction processing subsystems, which correspond to a companys principal operational units, as well as the fundamental documents that flow between them. Note that in many cases a hard copy document is not actually issued, with the information instead produced on a display screen or stored in secondary storage. Also, a number of documents are sent electronically via EDI. As you study these transaction processing subsystems, you get a picture of a company's operations. This is why we can say that information systems can be considered a model of the firm they support.

The system chart in Figure 9.4 is, of course, simplified. Each business is different to at least some degree and, of necessity, a number of assumptions have been built into the chart. The figure does not show databases or workstations. We have omitted any exceptions, such as backorders for out-of-stock products or customer returns. We have also shown transaction processing exclusively, omitting the reporting usually included in these systems.

We will now describe the subsystems (shown as rectangles) and the flows of information between them. As we have pointed out, much of this data flow today occurs electronically, without the need for paper-based documents and reports. This results in significant operational efficiencies. We will learn more about the information systems serving the principal functions of a firm in Chapter 12.

Here Are the Principal Transaction Processing Subsystems:

1. *Sales* receives a customer *order* and prepares a *sales notice* based on it, to be sent to Production and to Billing. A *shipping order* notifies Shipping about the need to send out the order. When the order is sent, Sales will receive a *shipping notice* from Shipping. Based on current sales levels and past experience, Sales produces a *sales forecast* for Production. Sales

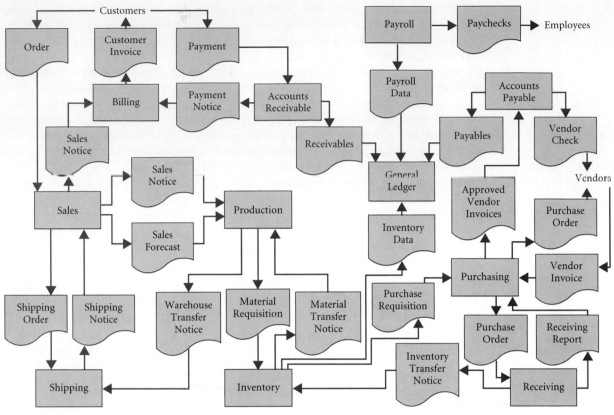

Figure 9.4

Transaction processing subsystems of a firm. Note that many reports and documents are produced in an electronic form only and transmitted via EDI

also usually handles credit authorization and backorders regarding out-of-stock products. It needs to notify customers about these conditions and it has to respond to customer inquiries.

2. *Production* bases its output levels on the *sales notices* as well as on a *sales forecast*, both furnished by Sales. Materials needed for production are requested with a *material requisition* from Inventory. Finished goods are transferred to a warehouse run by Shipping, accompanied by a *warehouse transfer* notice.

3. *Inventory* transfers needed materials to Production, accompanied by a *material transfer notice*. When the inventory needs replenishment, Inventory requests materials needed for Production from Purchasing with a *purchase requisition*. Many manufacturing firms today minimize their inventory holding costs by operating in a just-in-time (JIT) mode, with supplies delivered shortly before they are to be used. Suppliers deliver many materials on a pre-agreed schedule, without requisitions and orders.

4. *Purchasing* sends a *purchase order* to the vendor and approves vendor invoices for the delivered goods. A copy of the *purchase order* is sent to Receiving. When Receiving notifies Purchasing with a *receiving report* about the delivery of the goods, an approved vendor invoice will be forwarded to Accounts Payable. In many leading firms, the Purchasing function is tied in electronically via EDI to the suppliers' Sales functions, to enable rapid response.

5. *Shipping* receives the goods from Production, accompanied by a *warehouse transfer notice*. Shipping dispatches the products to the customer according to the *shipping order*

it received from Sales and also sends a *shipping notice* to Sales. The best shipment method and, sometimes, the appropriate insurance are selected.

6. *Receiving* reports on the goods received from vendors to Purchasing with a *receiving report* (so that the vendors can be paid) and to Inventory with an *inventory transfer notice* (so that production can be continued).

7. *Accounts Payable* sends out *vendor checks* against *approved vendor invoices* received from Purchasing.

8. *Billing* sends out *invoices* to customers, with a copy sent to Accounts Receivable. Many customers receive bills periodically, rather than following every shipment of goods. Accounts Receivable will notify Billing with a *payment notice* when the payment has been received.

9. *Accounts Receivable* processes customer *payments* and notifies Billing with *payment notices.* Proper handling of receivables is vital to the financial health of an enterprise—outstanding balances must not be allowed to linger.

10. *Payroll* issues paychecks on an appropriate schedule. The subsystem applies appropriate withholdings, such as Social Security payments and taxes, and produces information for tax authorities.

11. *General Ledger* subsystem maintains the consolidated records of all of the financial transactions of the organization. It thus receives data on the transactions from the subsystems that deal with these transactions, such as accounts payable, accounts receivable, payroll, and inventory. General Ledger system produces periodically the balance sheet of the firm, which shows its assets and liabilities, and the firm's profit-and-loss statement that relates its income to its expenses over a period of time. Because of its integrative role, General Ledger is usually an elaborate subsystem.

When a transaction processing subsystem is developed for a business function in a firm, this should be considered an opportunity to rationalize the business function. To automate what is done manually or to move to a higher level of automation without a redesign of the business function itself usually means missing an opportunity. For example, by paying their suppliers on receipt of goods and thus eliminating invoices, Ford Motor Company was able to cut its accounts payable staff from 500 to 125. Business process redesign, as we said in Chapter 1, often cuts through the boundaries between individual business functions, whose roles nevertheless have to be understood.

Now that we have reviewed what a transaction processing system does, let's consider more analytically the activities necessary to process an individual transaction.

9.3 | TRANSACTION PROCESSING ACTIVITIES

The processing of individual transactions, of course, depends to a degree on their nature. Here, however, we will discuss the general elements of transaction processing: data capture and validation, transaction-dependent processing steps, and database maintenance.

Data Capture

Early methods of recording a transaction relied largely on manual capture. Fewer and fewer systems now employ such techniques as keyboarding data from documents, for example. Today, **direct data entry** is commonly employed through *source data automation*. Popular examples of direct entry are summarized in Table 9.1. The alphabet soup of acronyms featured in the table has wide currency—but you do not need to remember all of them. This table depicts a major component of today's informational environment.

Table 9.1	Transaction	Data Entry Device	How Entered
Sources of direct data entry	Inventory taking in packaged-foods warehouse	Bar-code reader (OCR scanner)	Optical character recognition (OCR) scanner reads the Universal Product Code (UPC) for the grocery product.
	Order entry by sales representative	Laptop computer	Salespeople transmit orders from customer locations into headquarters' computer.
	Retail sale in supermarket	POS terminal	Point-of-sale (POS) terminal registers the sale with a bar-code scanner and transmits the data to a computer.
	Retail sale in department store	Touch-sensitive VDT screen	Sales clerk touches video display terminal (VDT) screen with a wand and identifies the product through keyboard or bar-code scanner.
	Checking account deposit	ATM	Automatic teller machine (ATM) enters the deposit; magnetic ink character recognition (MICR) unit reads in account identifications from deposit slip and checks.
	Airline reservation	CRS terminal	Terminal of airline's computerized reservation system (CRS) is on-line to the computer.
	Spoken inventory request	Voice recognition device	Item must be identified by numeric code with speaker-independent technology.
	Gasoline purchase	Smart-card reader in POS terminal	POS terminal accepts smart credit cards or debit cards; card contains a microprocessor chip or storage strip with customer information.
	Insurance claim entry by adjuster	Pen-based notepad computer	Working at the damage site, the adjuster fills the form appearing on the screen with the electronic "pen" and transmits the claim to the office via cellular phone modem.

Increasingly, transaction processing systems rely on electronic data interchange (EDI), which warrants a section of its own further on in this chapter. By replacing paper documents with formatted transaction data sent over telecommunications networks, these systems provide for computer-to-computer communication without repeated data entry. Although used internally by some firms, EDI primarily serves the needs of intercompany communication, as we have seen in the Focus Minicase for the chapter.

Data Validation

Let us assume that a customer calls a mail-order company with an order. The transaction is entered by a sales clerk through a series of VDT screens. Typical validation tests include checking for missing data items, valid codes (size, alphabetic and/or numeric composition), and valid values (is the amount or the code within the proper range?). More extensive validation may entail authorization of the transaction based on the customer's record and available inventory. We discuss validation at length among other systems controls in Chapter 14.

Processing Steps Dependent on the Transaction and on Processing Mode

Depending on the nature of the transaction and on whether the system operates in on-line or batch mode, the following processing steps may be performed.

1. Classification

The system classifies incoming transactions to select further processing steps. For example, transactions coming from an ATM terminal may be classified as withdrawal, deposit, or balance inquiry.

2. Sorting

Transaction records are arranged in order of the value of the data item(s) that uniquely identifies each of them. Called the key, this value may be, for example, the identification number assigned to each transaction or the employee's Social Security number. This step is almost always included in batch systems.

3. Data Retrieval

The purpose of an inquiry transaction is, of course, retrieval of data from the database. Other transactions may involve data retrieval as well. For example, when a product bar code is scanned by a supermarket point-of-sale scanner, the price for the product is looked up in the database. This provides flexibility in changing prices. However, if a fast response to a transaction is needed, the number of database accesses has to be limited.

A screen for retrieving checking account information in a banking application produced by Citicorp is shown in Figure 9.5. Several other screens are available to bank tellers in order to track deposits and withdrawals in an account.

Figure 9.5

Status screen for checking accounts

```
INQUIRY DATE: 12/31/98    TRANSACTION SYSTEM ACCOUNT INQUIRY        20-700
REQUESTING OFFICER:
                                  *--------ACCOUNT NAME/ADDRESS-------*
ACCOUNT NUMBER:     039 260 36    ODB   1: KAREN ZIEGENHORN
SHORT NAME:    ZIEGENHORN KAREN         2: C/O IVEYS
DATE OPENED:       6/01/90              3: 228 EAST LAKE BLVD
O.D. LIMIT:          1                  4: WINTER PARK, FL 32789
STATEMENT CYCLE:    020                 5:
*-----------BALANCE DATA-----------*
CURRENT BALANCE:                  11,209.93
AVAILABLE BALANCE:                11,209.93 STOPS-HOLDS ACTIVE              Y
AVAILABLE TOMORROW:               11,209.93 DATE LAST ACTIVE        11/02/98
MEMO BALANCE:                     11,209.93 DATE LAST DEPOSIT       11/02/98
ACCOUNT TYPE:                           002 AMOUNT LAST DEPOSIT      2418.34
PROCESSED THRU                      1/04/98 CHECK CREDIT BAL      100,000.00
                  *-----------PREVIOUS STATEMENT DATA---------*
                  LAST STATEMENT DATE                  1/05/98
                  LAST STATEMENT BALANCE               7,976.63
                  CHECKS SINCE
                  DEPOSITS SINCE                             4
                  SERVICE CHARGE CODE                     A 03
                  STATEMENT CONTROL CODES                 D 0
                  INTEREST PAID LAST YEAR                  .00
  PRESS CMD 1 FOR ANOTHER INQUIRY/CMD 2 FOR ACTIVE STOPS/CMD 3 FOR CREDIT
```

4. Calculation

The calculations required depend, of course, on the nature of the transaction. A credit card authorization would entail calculating the total credit extended so far and comparing it to the customer's credit limit. An ATM withdrawal from a bank lowers the account balance through a simple calculation.

5. Summarization

Usually performed to obtain simple reports offered by TPS, this step computes summaries across all or some of the transactions. For example, we may need to know the number of accounts delinquent over 30 days.

Database Maintenance

After transactions other than inquiries, system files or databases must be updated. The data accumulated by TPSs thus serve as a source of detail for management-oriented components of information systems. For example, hiring a new employee may call only for the insertion of his or her record into a simple, file-oriented system. A more elaborate human resources database would be updated by also modifying the skills inventory, open positions data, and so forth.

Individual transactions may result in insertions and deletions of records or updates of record fields. Let's consider an airline reservation system, for example. A reservation causes the insertion of a passenger record into the database and an update of the "seats available" field in the proper flight record. On completion of a flight, the flight closing transaction causes deletion of a number of passenger records. These entries may be written into a marketing database for future promotional campaigns.

On-line transaction processing systems have to process a large number of transactions per second, with the transactions sometimes arriving from thousands of remote terminals. To measure the volume of this so-called throughput that a given system can handle, system designers can enter benchmarks (that is, standardized transactions) from multiple simulated terminals. Depending on the hardware and software platforms, some systems have a throughput of hundreds or even thousands of transactions per second while maintaining a response time of less than a second. For example, the peak rate of transaction processing for the NASDAQ stock market is 1,430 transactions per second[1]. Fault-tolerant computer systems (see Chapter 4) are employed to support TPSs that have to be available virtually at all times, for example, airline reservation systems. In such systems the failure of one of the computers or other devices included in it causes the workload to be taken over by another.

9.4   OUTPUTS PROVIDED BY TRANSACTION PROCESSING SYSTEMS

The outputs provided by TPSs may be classified as transaction documents, query responses, and reports.

Transaction Documents

Many TPSs produce transaction documents, such as invoices, purchase orders, or payroll checks. These transaction documents produced by TPSs may be divided into two classes: action documents and information documents.

1. Action Documents

Action documents direct that an action take place. For example, an airline ticket calls for granting a flight seat, a picking slip directs a warehouse worker to pull an inventory item,

**Do We Really
Need Airline
Tickets?**

Nearly 10 percent of an airline's labor costs are tied to managing tickets. The costs of paper ticketing can eat up the entire slim 3-percent profit margin of a travel agent who books the flight. Both the airlines and the agents would be glad to see tickets disappear.

Airlines are beginning to do something about it. For example, Southwest Airlines and United Air Lines inaugurated new ticketless travel systems in California. Instead of issuing a ticket, the airlines are issuing a reservation number. Both American Airlines and Continental offer electronic ticketing as well. The scope of the initiative is still limited, since standards need to be introduced before travelers will be able to journey on more than one airline during a given trip. The Air Transport Association, an airline industry group, has already established a committee to develop such industry-wide standards.

Another avenue for getting rid of tickets is being tested by Delta Air Lines. On its Boston–New York–Washington shuttle, the passengers use smart cards. Preloaded with a certain amount of cash, the cards are debited through a terminal at the airport as their owner takes the flight. After all, if we are replacing the green paper with E-cash in electronic commerce, are airline tickets really necessary?

Based on Bruce Caldwell, "Paperless Air Travel," *InformationWeek*, November 14, 1994, p. 22; and "Techno-Travel," Special Advertising Section, *Fortune*, November 11, 1996.

and a bank has to pay against a check drawn on it. Some of these are turnaround documents, such as the portion of the credit card statement you are asked to return with the payment. Turn-around documents initiate action and are returned after their completion to the requesting agency. They therefore also serve as input documents for another transaction, in our example, payment recording.

2. Information Documents

Information documents confirm that a transaction has taken place or inform about one or several transactions. A voucher sent with a payment to explain it, or a list of credit card charges arriving with the bill, are examples of information documents.

Transaction documents require manual handling and, in some cases, distribution of multiple copies. The process is costly and may lead to inconsistencies if one of the copies fails to reach its destination. The advances of EDI, which we discuss in the next section, will ultimately eliminate much of this documentation, replacing it with the electronic exchange of transaction records. Many of these records will travel over the Internet. Already, electronic deposits made by many employers into employee bank accounts have made payroll checks unnecessary. The vignette above presents other initiatives.

Query Responses and Reports

Through the use of DBMS facilities and end-user-oriented fourth-generation languages, the users of OLTP systems may garner a variety of information from the database. However, as we discussed in Chapter 6, today the transaction data are often selectively transferred into data warehouses for analytical access. TPSs themselves offer certain querying and simple reporting capabilities, albeit much less elaborate than those of management reporting systems. Most queries produce a screenful of information. However, reports (on multiple screens or on paper) are also often produced as a result of inquiries. A range of preprogrammed screens is available in certain systems for preprogrammed queries (as shown in Figure 9.5).

Unlike management reporting systems, TPSs typically provide a limited range of pre-planned reports. The content and format of such reports are programmed into the TPS software, and the reports are produced on schedule. The TPS reports are often quite long. The status of various organizational resources, such as funds and equipment, may be specified in detail. Transactions may be tracked using TPS reports. For example, employee movement—into the company, within it, through educational experiences, and, perhaps, into retirement status—may be traced step by step.

The following report types are produced by TPS:

1. Transaction Logs

Transaction logs are listings of all transactions processed during a system run and include purchase order manifests or sales registers.

2. Error (Edit) Reports

Error reports (also known as edit reports) list transactions found to be in error during the processing. They identify the error and sometimes also list the corresponding master file or database records.

3. Detail Reports

Detail reports are extracts from the database that list records satisfying particular criteria. For example, a detail report lists inventory items with expiring shelf warranties or describes all copy machines in the inventory of an office equipment distributor.

4. Summary Reports

Financial statements—balance sheets and profit-and-loss statements—are typical reports produced by TPS. A variety of other **summary reports** may be programmed, depending on the application.

9.5 | FROM ELECTRONIC DATA INTERCHANGE (EDI) TO ELECTRONIC COMMERCE

A prominent means of source data automation is electronic data interchange. **Electronic data interchange (EDI)** is the computer-to-computer interchange of electronic transaction documents, involving at least two trading partners. With EDI, paper transaction docu-

Figure 9.6

Interorganizational data flows in electronic data interchange (EDI)

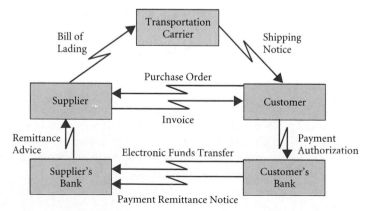

Figure 9.7

*A payment message
(transaction set)
expressed with the two
common EDI standards.
The message indicates
that company A is
paying company B's
bank account 98765432
the sum of US$59,400
for three invoices in the
amounts, $10,000,
$20,000, and $30,000.
Each invoice amount is
discounted by 1 percent.*
(From Kalakota and
Whinston 1996, p. 374.)

```
EDIFACT PAYORD, version 91.2 UNH+1+PAYEXT:2:912:UN'
  BGM+451+0101+137:920515:101+9' NAD+OY+COMPANY A'
  FII+BF+98765432+COMPANY
  B+BANKXX:25:5'DTM+203+920515:101'MOA+7+9:59400:USD'UNS+S'
  DOC+380+101'
  MOA+7+9:10000+52:100+12:9900 DOC+380+102'MOA+7+9:20000+52:200+12:19800
  DOC+380+103'+MOA+7+9:30000+52:300+12:29700+MOA+3+128:59400:USD'
  UNT+15+0101'


ANSI X12 820, version 003.020 ST*820*0101
  BPR*C*59400*C*SWT********02*BANKXX*DA*98765432 TRN*1*0101
  DTM*007*920515
  ENT**0101 N1*PR*COMPANY A N1*PE*COMPANY B
  RMR*IV*101*PO*9900*10000*100
  RMR*IV*102*PO*19800*20000*200 RMR*IV*103*PO*29700*30000*300 SE*11*0101
```

ments, such as purchase orders or invoices are eliminated and replaced with standardized electronic communications involving, for example, the computer systems of the customers and suppliers. As we already know from Chapter 7, EDI underlies much of electronic commerce by enabling companies to conclude commercial transactions over telecommunications networks, and the Internet in particular (Sokol 1995). Figure 9.6 shows an example of EDI exchanges by parties involved in transactions relating to a purchase. One of the data flows in the figure shows electronic funds transfer (EFT), which an organization usually implements prior to EDI.

EDI components include the following:

1. Transaction Standards

The messages are exchanged in a standard form, agreed on by the participating partners. The X.12 data interchange protocol is widely used in the United States, although some U.S. industries have developed their own standards. Thus, the pharmaceutical industry uses ORDERNET, while the grocery industry uses UCS; however, the electrical and chemical industries adopted X.12. Some large firms, such as General Motors and Sears, developed their own proprietary standards, which their suppliers need to follow. The international EDIFACT[2] standard is broader than X.12 and this compounds the problems of standards incompatibility in a global business environment. Figure 9.7 shows a sample payment message (or transaction set, in the EDI terminology) in X.12 and EDIFACT.

2. Industry Standard for Product Identification

Partners have to agree on the standard way to identify (and mark, if needed) their products. For example, the universal product code (UPC) used in the grocery industry has become a principal factor for the widespread use of EDI in that business sector.

3. Translation Software

Translation software converts the incoming EDI messages into a format that can be used by the owner firm's applications. It also converts outgoing messages into the standard EDI format for transmission.

4. Telecommunications System

EDI can be carried out via direct telecommunications links between the partners, using a value-added network (VAN) from a third-party supplier (see Chapter 7), or over the

IN THE SPOTLIGHT

Expanding EDI, While Moving to Electronic Commerce

As part of a corporate reorganization aimed at saving more than $1 billion a year, Mobil Corporation has asked its information services (IS) department to lead a broad venture into electronic commerce, while reducing the ranks of the department nearly by half. The second-largest oil company in the U.S. has recentralized its IS department and plans to cut its staffing from 2,900 to 1,600. The company has reorganized its EDI, Internet, groupware, and E-mail groups into a single unit responsible for electronic commerce. Corporate business processes, such as purchasing, will be reengineered to move them away from paperwork and to get better deals with suppliers. Projected savings amount to $320 million a year.

Some of the components of the electronic commerce initiative are:

- Signing up nearly 500 new EDI partners, mostly service suppliers.

- Installing an intranet that would bring news of buying agreements and contracts to purchasing agents. Users in 120 countries will be able to access the information using Mobil's site on the World Wide Web.

- Expanding an intranet/EDI system to 230 North American distributors of Mobil's heavy lubricants. Data on the availability of products, such as 55-gallon oil drums, will be sent from the corporate mainframe to a Web server. After the distributors log on to Mobil's Web site, the data will be automatically downloaded to their PCs. They will be able to order the product via EDI.

- Letting Mobil credit card users pay their bills via the firm's Web page, with the payments automatically transferred to the company's bank.

With the consolidated global purchasing data, Mobil will be able to leverage its buying power worldwide. Until now, each of the corporation's five product groups has struck its own deals. Now, there will be global contracts on expected better terms. EDI invoices will be automatically routed to the appropriate applications and paid within authorized ranges. The cost of processing an invoice will be cut from $15 to less than $5. The biggest challenge is to get a buy-in from suppliers. But, Mobil has already mandated that all of them have to use EDI.

In this fashion, Mobil plans to build its global electronic commerce strategy using the mix of traditional EDI and Internet technologies. "It's not an either/or choice," says the corporate webmaster Sandy Massey. "We're looking at ways to marry the two."

Based on Joseph Maglitta, "Mobil Revamp Devastates IS," *Computerworld*, April 29, 1996, pp. 1, 70.

Internet. Among other services, VANs supply electronic mailboxes that can hold messages for the addressee.

EDI eliminates processing of paper documents, thus resulting in significant savings by avoiding multiple data entry from paper forms, paper processing, and mailing. Thanks to EDI, some firms have been able to reduce clerical staff in their purchasing department by a factor of ten. Aside from the direct saving of money, EDI saves time, which further enhances its financial effect.

Beyond direct savings, electronic data interchange has significant potential in competitive and strategic applications of information technology. Among the principal effects are:

- Compressing the business cycle by speeding up communications.

- Supporting time-based competitive moves, such as the just-in-time (JIT) manufacturing strategy that drastically reduces or even removes inventories, and quick-response retail strategy that permits a rapid response to customer buying patterns by "pulling in" the products in demand from the point-of-sale terminals.

- Intensified relationship between trading partners. This is due to the cost of switching to another EDI system after the given one is in place and to the avoidance of misunderstandings because of errors, common in the exchanges of paper documents.

The strategic effects are often combined. Design, Inc., a retailer selling Levi Strauss jeans, has been able to minimize its inventories by cutting the replenishment cycle for the merchandise from 14 to 3 days by using the manufacturer's LeviLink system. The retailer has become a significant business partner for the manufacturer.

As the use of the Internet proliferates, many companies are moving from specialized value-added networks (VANs) to the Internet as the carrier for EDI messages. Internet usage generally costs less and the cost is largely independent of the number of messages transferred. In doing so, these companies forgo the services and support provided by VANs. Since many organizations throughout the world are Internet users, it is easier to establish new connections in the open environment of the Internet than when using the proprietary networks of the VAN vendors. It is also possible to integrate EDI with other Internet services and facilities. Thus, a seamless network of electronic commerce is beginning to emerge (we discussed it in Section 7.8). The vignette on the previous page shows how a large corporation is broadly expanding its EDI system as part of a broad electronic commerce initiative.

9.6 | MANAGEMENT REPORTING SYSTEMS

Characteristics of Management Reporting Systems

Management reporting systems are the most elaborate of the management-oriented information systems. The main objective of **management reporting systems (MRS)** is to provide lower and middle management with printed or electronic reports and with inquiry capabilities to help maintain operational and management control of the enterprise. Management-oriented systems such as MRS are based on the data collected by transaction processing systems, as illustrated in Figure 9.8.

Management Reporting Systems Have the Following Characteristics:

1. They are usually developed by information systems professionals, rather than by end users, over an extensive period of time, with the use of life cycle-oriented development methodologies (analyze–design–code–and–test), as opposed to a rapid development by first building a simpler prototype system and then refining it in response to user experience. Great care is exercised in developing such systems because MRSs are large and complex in terms of the number of system interfaces with various users and databases.

2. These systems are built for situations in which information requirements are reasonably well known and expected to remain relatively stable. Modification of such systems, like their development, is a rather elaborate process. This limits the informational flexibility of MRS but ensures a stable informational environment.

3. MRSs do not *directly* support the decision-making process as a search for alternative solutions to problems and the selection of the solution to be implemented. Naturally, information gained through MRSs is used in the manager's decision-making process. These systems are used in the feedback loop we discussed in Chapter 2 to compare the actual results with standards and expectations. Such standards as, for example, economic order quantities for ordering inventory or accounting formulas for computing various forms of return on equity, are built into the MRS itself. Consequently MRSs often present information in a comparative manner and highlight exceptions.

4. MRSs are oriented toward reporting on the past and the present, rather than projecting the future.

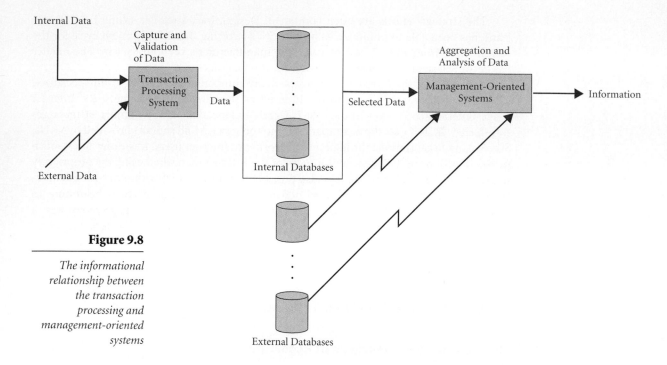

Figure 9.8

The informational relationship between the transaction processing and management-oriented systems

5. MRSs generally have limited analytical capabilities. They are not built around elaborate models, but rather rely on extraction of data from databases according to given criteria, and on summarization of the data. Based on simple processing of the data extracts and summaries, report information is obtained and may be printed in a prespecified format. Characteristically, today's MRSs have moved to electronic reports, which are generated and stored but not printed, unless specified by the user. Such reports may be reviewed on-line.

6. MRSs largely report on internal company operations rather than spanning the company's boundaries by reporting external information.

Reporting by Management Reporting Systems

MRSs may produce reports either directly from a database collected and maintained by a transaction processing system, or from databases spun off from the central database for the purpose (for example, a data warehouse). Separate spin-off databases may be created for several reasons, such as avoiding interference and delays in transaction processing, maintaining the security of central databases, or economizing by using local databases accessible to local managers to counter the heavy telecommunications costs of working with a central database.

MRSs provide the following types of reports:

1. Scheduled (Periodic) Reports

Scheduled (periodic) reports are furnished on a daily, weekly, biweekly, or other regular basis depending on the decision-making need. A weekly sales analysis report may be used by a sales manager to assess the performance of sales districts or individual salespeople. A brand manager responsible for a particular product might obtain a weekly sales report containing information useful in his or her decision making, by showing regional sales and

Figure 9.9

A hierarchy of performance reports (From Barry Cushing and Marshall B. Romney, *Accounting Information Systems and Business Organizations*, Reading, MA: Addison-Wesley 1987, p. 51.)

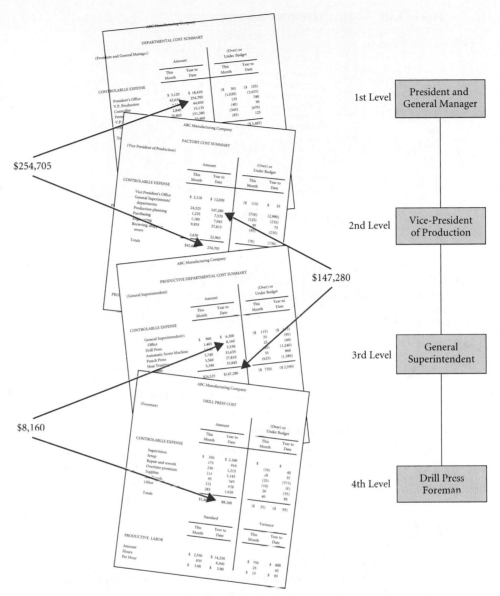

sales to various market segments, for example. We have seen a fragment of a monthly accounts receivable revaluation report in Figure 2.10.

The format and the informational content of scheduled reports is fixed in advance. However, it is crucial to identify the essential informational needs of various managers to facilitate each manager's decision making and to prevent information overload. The concept of *responsibility reporting* is generally applied: Managers receive reports within their specific areas of responsibility. A performance report states the financial results achieved by the manager and compares them with the planned results by stating variances, that is, differences between planned (budgeted) and actual results. A hierarchy of performance reports arises, with each report including only the items that the manager can control. Such a report hierarchy is shown in Figure 9.9: It includes the performance reports of a top manager, two middle-level managers, and a lower-level manager.

Figure 9.10

Exception reporting

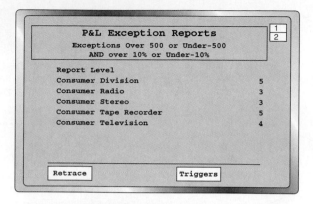

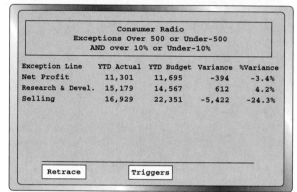

2. Exception Reports

Another means of preventing information overload is resorting to **exception reports,** produced only when preestablished "out-of-bounds" conditions occur and containing only the information regarding these conditions. For example, purchasing managers may need an exception report when suppliers are a week late in deliveries. Such a report may be triggered automatically by the delay of an individual supplier or produced on a scheduled basis, but only if there are late suppliers. The report might include a list of late suppliers, the extent to which each is late, and the supplies ordered from each. Two related electronic exception reports are shown in Figure 9.10. Exception reporting helps managers avoid perusal of incidental figures and concentrate on deviations from the norm and on unusual events.

3. Demand (Ad Hoc) Reports

The ability of a manager to request a **demand (ad hoc)** report or screen output as needed enhances the flexibility of MRS use and gives the end user (the individual manager) the capability to request the information and format that best suit his or her needs. Query languages provided by DBMSs make data accessible for demand reporting.

9.7   STRATEGIC POTENTIAL OF TRANSACTION PROCESSING AND MANAGEMENT REPORTING SYSTEMS

Transaction processing is often written off as an efficiency-oriented area that calls for no more than, perhaps, technical ingenuity. However, TPSs can be enablers of major process innovations. Redesigned business processes, supported by TPS, cut through functional business lines and can ensure rapid and high-quality customer service. Strategic TPSs may become a source of competitive advantage or competitive parity by focusing on the internal or customer-oriented processes.

Several highly successful strategic information systems are actually transaction processing systems. Computerized reservation systems developed by major airlines first radically simplified internal reservation processes and then changed the interorganizational processes involving travel agents and customers (Davenport 1993). The ordering system for pharmacies, introduced by the drug distributor McKesson, changed the firm's processes for managing customers' inventories and changed the customers' ordering processes as well. Electronic data interchange (EDI) plays a significant competitive role by strengthening relationships between trading partners, by enabling business process redesign in back offices, and by quickening the pace of business.

The customer-driven nature of many TPSs affords some firms the opportunity to gain a competitive advantage by providing unique systems. There are many ways a customer's order can be entered and processed. Systems that provide convenience, the ability to customize or individualize a product, and prompt and flexible service are likely to bind customers to the company. A wealth of data on the environment of the firm can be collected by TPS. Using these data, management-oriented information systems can help analyze customer behavior (who buys what, how much, and when), identify profitable customer segments, and track supplier and subcontractor performance.

We have outlined the capabilities of information technology that address various aspects of business process redesign in Section 1.6. The following are some of the types of information systems based on these capabilities which can be exploited for competitive effect:

- *Tracking systems*—management reporting systems that continuously track the status of a project or a product under development.

- *Locational systems*—transaction processing systems that monitor the geographic location of materials or vehicles. These systems are becoming a necessity in corporate logistics. They underlie the success of FedEx, UPS, and a number of other global megacarriers. For example, Schneider National, the largest North American full-truckload carrier, monitors the location of each of its 6,700 trucks via satellite-based communication networks so that trucks en route can be deployed to the best advantage. Within 15 to 30 minutes of sending an order to Schneider National, the customer knows when the truck will arrive (Lappin 1995).

- *Asset management systems*—transaction processing and management reporting systems that maintain and report on-line the status of financial, inventory, and human resources assets. The deployment of these systems is particularly vital with perishable resources, such as hospital beds, hotel rooms, or airline seats. Both airlines and hotels now routinely use yield management systems that allow them to vary the price of a seat or a room depending on demand and the available inventory.

A potent and growing application of transaction processing systems is the creation of an electronic marketplace for securities, software, ideas or, ultimately, any goods or services. Such marketplaces are developing, for example, on the Internet.

SUMMARY

A transaction is an elementary activity conducted during business operations, such as a merchandise sale. Transaction processing systems (TPS) process data that reflect a company's business transactions. In on-line transaction processing, transactions are processed immediately upon entry. In batch processing, the transaction data are accumulated over a period of time and then processed at once. As opposed to batch processing, on-line transaction processing results in up-to-date database contents.

The principal transaction processing subsystems in a firm are those supporting sales, production, inventory maintenance, purchasing, shipping, receiving, accounts payable, billing, accounts receivable, payroll, and general ledger.

The general transaction processing activities include data capture, data validation, database maintenance, and, depending on the application, classification, sorting, calculation, and summarization of data necessary to produce the appropriate reports. TPSs may produce action and information documents. Among the reports produced by TPSs are: transaction logs, error (edit) reports, detail reports, and summary reports.

Electronic data interchange (EDI) is the computer-to-computer interchange of electronic transaction documents, involving at least two trading partners. These interorganizational systems play an important role in speeding up commercial processes and in producing savings owing to elimination of paper-based documents. They are becoming one of the foundations of electronic commerce.

Management reporting systems (MRS) provide lower and middle management with reports and inquiry capabilities that help them control the operations in their enterprise. MRSs are elaborate organizational systems that change relatively little over time and report on the past and the present, supporting decision making only indirectly by providing the necessary information. MRSs can produce scheduled (periodic), exception, and demand (ad hoc) reports.

TPS and MRS can be deployed in seeking competitive advantage. By exploiting the capabilities of information systems, tracking, locational, and asset-management systems can be used to provide exceptional levels of customer service as well as exceptional operational efficiencies.

KEY TERMS

Transaction *326*	Error (edit) report *336*
Transaction processing system (TPS) *326*	Detail report *336*
	Summary report *336*
On-line processing *327*	Electronic data interchange (EDI) *336*
Batch processing *329*	Management reporting system (MRS) *339*
Direct data entry *331*	Scheduled (periodic) report *340*
Action document *334*	Exception report *342*
Information document *335*	Demand (ad hoc) report *342*
Transaction log *336*	

QUESTIONS

1. What is a transaction? Give three examples of transactions (other than those mentioned in Section 9.1).

2. What do transaction processing systems do? Be precise. Why are these systems generally more critical to the functioning of most firms than management reporting systems?

3. Present in a table the comparative advantages and disadvantages of on-line versus batch processing.

4. Why can we say that a firm's transaction processing systems are a model of the firm?

5. Consider the *Sales* subsystem in Figure 9.4 in more detail. Present a system chart for that subsystem alone.

6. How does the development of a transaction processing system for a firm relate to business process redesign?

7. List three data entry devices that can be used for source data automation in a large and well-equipped fast food outlet. State the objective of each use.

8. What validation steps would you perform for a "Ship Order" transaction? Consider using various databases of the firm.

9. Consider a transaction "Produce Vendor Check," which is performed by the Accounts Payable subsystem in Figure 4.9 (detailed transactions are not shown in the fig-

ure). What specific activities are needed to process this transaction?

10. What is electronic data interchange (EDI)? What are the necessary components of EDI implementation?
11. How does EDI relate to electronic commerce?
12. What are management reporting systems (MRS)? How do they relate to transaction processing systems?
13. What are the principal characteristics of MRS?
14. What is responsibility reporting? What would be the typical information a district sales manager would get in a performance report?
15. What are exception reports? How do they relate to the possibility of information overload?
16. Give one example each of how a transaction processing system can be deployed as a locational system and an asset management system in the retail industry.

ISSUES FOR DISCUSSION

1. Discuss how the total set of a business's transactions can be represented with an information system as a set of business rules that specify the way business is done. What could be the business results of having such a model of your business?
2. Why are transaction processing systems frequently deployed as strategic systems? Review the material in Chapter 3 and relate the TPS and MRS named in Section 9.6 to the five forces active in the competitive marketplace. Suggest other categories of these systems that can be deployed in the marketplace and relate them to the competitive forces.
3. Discuss the effects of electronic data interchange (EDI) on the industries that use it broadly. Discuss how these systems can become the foundation for electronic commerce for the companies concerned.
4. As many accounts payable clerks have been replaced in various companies by transaction-processing systems, it has been found that the incidence of errors and fraud has gone up (Berton 1996). What would have been noticed by an experienced clerk is no longer "noticed" by the information system. Are there any ethical issues involved here?

REAL-WORLD MINICASE AND PROBLEM-SOLVING EXERCISES

1. EDI Is Moving to the Internet   Tom St. Peter, the manager of worldwide electronic commerce at Texas Instrument's (TI's) semiconductor group in Austin, Texas, has begun to move the EDI messaging of his company to the Internet. He tells us that this move lets him speed up the mes-

saging, reach new markets, and move more fully into electronic commerce — while cutting costs at the same time. "Granted, you're talking about pennies [per message]," says St. Peter, "but these add up over time."

TI's semiconductor group processes nearly 180,000 EDI messages a month. Most still travel through the nets of the seven value-added network (VAN) service providers, including IBM's Advantis unit and General Electric Information Services (GEIS). Without the Internet, EDI use is expensive. EDI users pay their VAN service providers twice. First, they pay rental fees for electronic mailboxes; then they are charged for each message, typically about 25 cents per electronic page. A corporation that handles 125,000 messages (transaction sets) a month pays $50,000 to $100,000, depending on the VAN and on how much traffic is transmitted during prime time. Generally, the service providers offer a 20 percent discount for off-peak use. The same volume of traffic sent over the Internet could cost no more than $10,000, and there is no prime time on the Net.

St. Peter of TI has seen savings of "four orders of magnitude" (that is, shaving four zeros off the cost!) through EDI over the Internet during a four-month pilot project. Responses came back in 7 to 10 minutes after a message was sent. This can be compared to waiting several hours for a response to a message sent over a VAN, mainly because the company sends messages at night in batches to hold down costs. The semiconductor group is about to go live over the Internet with its first trading partner, a North American multinational company. By running EDI over the Internet, TI expects to take advantage of other electronic commerce tools. These will include multimedia capabilities offered by the World Wide Web and the interactive EDI that lets both parties interact in real time, rather than in a batch style, as is the case with VAN-based EDI. Of course, working over the Internet, TI's semiconductor group cannot count on the training and support offered by the VAN service providers.

a. Where do the business results from moving EDI to the Internet, mentioned by St. Peter, come from (other than being a godsend, as puns the author of the article)?
b. What capabilities can be gained from the availability of multimedia for EDI use?
c. What could be the drawbacks of using a public network such as the Internet for EDI?
d. What will be the likely response of the VAN service providers to the move the EDI over the Internet?
e. Some believe that the next logical step will be unsolicited EDI (or "open EDI"): You may simply send out an open order over the Internet and see who will fulfill it. Do you find this a promising idea? Why or why not?

Based on Richard Adhikari, "EDI Heads for the Net," *InformationWeek*, May 6, 1996, pp. 59–60; and Tony Baer, "Don't Try This @Home," *Computerworld Electronic Commerce Journal*, April 29, 1996, pp. 34–36.

2. Familiarize yourself with the operation of a small local firm and represent its transaction processing subsystems in a manner similar to Figure 9.4. If you see possibilities for re-designing some of these operations, show the redesigned subsystem in a separate system chart.

3. As a consultant, you have been asked to explore the possibilities for the use of electronic data interchange (EDI) by a small supermarket chain. You need to investigate the use of EDI by the grocery industry and describe the pros and cons of the move in a report to the chain's president. If possible, you should include the approximate costs of moving to EDI, as well as the annual costs of its use.

TEAM PROJECT

Each two- or three-person team will select an industry segment and investigate the use of source data automation in it. Grocery and railroad industries are good candidates. The teams will report to the class on the data entry devices deployed in their selected segment and describe how they are used. They will also report on the integration of source data automation with other information systems.

ENDNOTES

1. From the speech of Alfred Berkeley III, President of NASDAQ, at the First Financial Technology World Conference, New York, September 17, 1996.

2. EDIFACT stands for Electronic Data Interchange for Administration, Commerce, and Trade.

SELECTED REFERENCES

Berton, Lee. "Many Firms Cut Staff in Accounts Payable and Pay a Steep Price." *The Wall Street Journal*, September 5, 1996, pp. A1, A6.

Davenport, Thomas. *Process Innovation: Reengineering Work through Information Technology*, Boston: Harvard Business School Press, 1993.

DeLottinville, Paul. "Open OLTP: To Monitor or Not to Monitor." *Datamation*, November 1, 1994, pp. 59–61.

Placing on-line transaction processing systems in the open-system environment.

Eliason, Alan L. *Online Business Computer Applications*, 3rd ed., New York: Macmillan, 1991.

A detailed description of on-line transaction processing systems.

Kalakota, Ravi, and Andrew W. Whinston. *Frontiers of Electronic Commerce*, Reading, MA: Addison-Wesley, 1996.

Kimberley, Paul. *Electronic Data Interchange*, New York: McGraw-Hill, 1991.

Lappin, Todd. "Trucking." *Wired*, January 1995, pp. 118–23, 166.

Describes the superb use of information technology by a leading trucking company.

Premkumar, G.; K. Ramamurthy; and Sree Nilakanta. "Implementation of Electronic Data Interchange: An Information Diffusion Perspective." *Journal of Management Information Systems*, 11, no. 2, Fall 1994, pp. 157–186.

Salemi, Joseph N. "Just-in-Time EDI Hot-Wires Electronics Industry." *EDI World*, January 1995, pp. 20–23.

Describes how EDI is used at Motorola to support just-in-time manufacturing and logistics.

Sokol, Phyllis K. *From EDI to Electronic Commerce: A Business Initiative*, New York: McGraw-Hill, 1995.

Business approach to EDI, with the discussion of application in several industries.

Zack, Michael H. "The State of EDI in the U.S. Housewares Manufacturing Industry," *Journal of Systems Management*, December 1994, pp. 6–10.

A good example of EDI penetration in an industry segment.

Zwass, Vladimir. "Electronic Commerce: Structures and Issues." *International Journal of Electronic Commerce*, 1, no.1, Fall 1996, pp. 3–23.

CASE STUDY | # Were the Transporters of Gamblers Gambling Themselves?

S hun Tak Ferries transports millions of passengers annually between Hong Kong and Macao, an island forty miles west in the South China Sea. The principal interest of the passengers is gambling in Macao's world-renowned casinos. Helping them in this pursuit, the ferry company sends out ferries, helicopters, and jetfoils (see Photo 9.1) from Hong Kong every 15 minutes, 23 hours a day, seven days a week. Ticketing these passengers is the

Photo 9.1

A Hong Kong jetfoil
(Photo by Vladimir
Zwass.)

principal on-line transaction processing (OLTP) application of Shun Tak; in fact, it is *the* mission-critical system for the firm.

A few years ago, in 1989, Shun Tak faced a problem. It was using a centralized transaction processing system, running 50 ticketing terminals off an aging PDP minicomputer (from Digital Equipment Corporation). The hardware needed a major upgrade. However, to run the system that would support the firm's rapidly growing operation, it would need a powerful mainframe—expensive both to acquire and to operate. Advised by the systems integrator Information Systems Management (ISM), headquartered in Regina, Canada, the ferry company decided to move its ticketing and reservation system, JetTix, to a client/server system. At that time and, particularly, in a region where midsized computers running centralized systems were considered the machines of choice, the move could have been considered a major gamble.

The challenge was to develop a system that would accommodate the current workload of some 13 million tickets sold annually as well as provide for the rapid growth to transport some 650,000 more passengers annually. Uninterrupted system operation was necessary. The peak Sunday traffic had to be handled. The service was to be delivered at a much lower cost than that associated with the alternative of mainframe processing. Because of the high employee turnover (employment in Hong Kong was booming), the system had to be easy to learn.

As designed by the system integrator, the client/server system was to include servers from Stratus Computer, a firm that offers fault-tolerant computer systems, linked to a network of PCs. Since fault-tolerant systems contain redundant hardware and software, failure of a processor or other components does not prevent the system from operating. Three Stratus systems were placed in the firm's headquarters in Hong Kong's Central district. A relational database management system from Sybase was employed to maintain the reservations database. Considering the need to maintain a single central seat inventory, a centralized database was implemented.

Called JetTix, the on-line transaction processing system can handle both telephone ticket reservations and the walk-up traffic at the Hong Kong and Macao terminals, subway stations, hotels, and travel agencies. Placement of IBM-compatible PCs at the ticket stations permitted the system to offload much processing from the servers, including the power needed to drive the numerous ticket printers. Bar-code readers are also connected to the PCs.

The Stratus computers at company headquarters and the PCs are interconnected in a local area network (LAN); however, the Stratus computers also act as servers for the distributed ticketing PCs, connected with headquarters by a wide-area network (WAN), provided by the telephone circuits. Packet switching is used for the WAN traffic. A dial-up capability is used at hotels and travel agencies, where the system is accessed with PC Anywhere software from Symantec. Currently, about 100 PCs are running in the system. From the printers connected to them, customers receive a multilingual ticket with bit-mapped Chinese characters as well as text in English and Portuguese (Macao is a Portuguese territory until 1998). The ticket also bears a bar code, handy for cancellations (particularly during the typhoon-prone late summer).

A software development tool supporting development of client/server systems, JAM (for Jyacc Application Manager) from Jyacc, was used during the development. The system helped to express the business rules that went into JetTix in a concise manner, but some programming in C was also done. The JAM and the attached C code invokes Sybase procedures for accessing the database on the servers. The data entered into the PCs are validated right there, to minimize the network traffic and the response time.

To provide for simple operation, the PC operators need only one keystroke to issue most tickets. This is possible by programming hot keys with JAM. The graphical user interface relies on few screens, carefully designed with ample use of vivid color. The operators' training time was dramatically reduced as compared with the old system.

Careful selection of the system development software enabled ISM, the system integrator, to work on the project with a lean team of no more than 12 people, and yet to deliver the initial prototype of the system in less than two months. After the prototype was presented to Shun Tak, the system design was changed considerably. While the system continued to be developed by the ISM team, an integrator's operations manager stayed on at Shun Tak to train the staff and install the Stratus fault-tolerant servers, working with that firm's Hong Kong office.

Two months later, the jetfoil part of the system (which accounts for 80 percent of Shun Tak's business) was functional. However, the firm waited until the end of the high season in September to cut over to the new system. Five months later, in February 1991, the entire system was up and running. In February 1992, Shun Tak requested additional training so that it could become self-sufficient in maintaining the system and training its own employees. Because JetTix was a pioneering application in Hong Kong, Shun Tak experienced a high turnover of its information system specialists; such is the way of technology diffusion.

The estimated cost of system development and subsequent enhancements, as well as of employee training, was $2.5 million, not including the hardware acquisition.

It appears that Shun Tak and the systems integrators responded to the challenge. Perhaps, they have actually risked too much by their pioneering development. Let us see what the opinion in the firm itself is. David Hill, executive director of Shun Tak's parent company, has this to say: "I will state that this fault-tolerant system is less reliable than the system built on more conventional hardware," meaning the monolithic minicomputer systems.

Moreover, Shun Tak is an organization that does not believe in outsourcing its information system or other operations (it repairs its own vessel fleet, for example). "We have been able to make great cost savings and efficiencies [in running our business]," says Hill. "We deviated from this in developing this ticketing system. We're going to bring it in-house. I intend to build up our own computer staff so we can handle our own software needs."

Based on Connie Winkler, "Hong Kong Transport Firm Risks C/S OLTP for Ticketing," *Software Magazine,* August 1993, pp. 91–95.

CASE STUDY QUESTIONS

1. What was the problem to be solved with the transaction processing system in this Case Study?

2. What principal solution was adopted and how risky was it?

3. Describe the five components of the JetTix transaction processing system (hardware, software, database, telecommunications, human resources, and procedures).

4. What enabled the systems integrator ISM to develop the system rapidly?

5. The system works. Speculate on the following topics: Why is the executive director of Shun Tak's parent company less than satisfied? Do you believe this dissatisfaction is in part related to the culture of the company and why? Do you believe the very idea of a distributed client/server system differs from Shun Tak's corporate culture? What could make a fault-tolerant system *less* reliable than the more conventional one?

Decision Support and Executive Information Systems

OBJECTIVES

After you complete this chapter, you will be able to:

1. Discuss the types of problems that can be solved with the assistance of decision support systems (DSS).

2. Explain what are the models used in DSS.

3. Compare and contrast the "what-if" and goal-seeking modes of DSS use.

4. Explain the relationship among the three principal components of a DSS.

5. Relate the principal classes of DSS to the problems that call for DSS assistance.

6. Specify three levels of DSS technology.

7. Identify and compare the three approaches to building a DSS.

8. Define group decision support systems (GDSS) and specify their main features.

9. Define executive information systems (EIS) and describe what can be accomplished using them.

10. Specify the main features of EIS.

OUTLINE

Making Decisions Together with a Computer

A clothing merchant with 1,400 stores and thousands of items of different colors and sizes needs to make daily decisions about stock replenishment. You don't want to run out of stock with fast-moving items, and yet you can't afford to get stuck with the slow-moving ones. Sure, you have billions of bytes of sales data coming in daily from your store registers. But how do you convert them into information? Some store chains, selling a fairly stable merchandise mix, can go on automatic pilot: They use inventory replenishment software. This application uses past sales data to forecast future sales for each store and automatically generates orders for an appropriate item quantity to suppliers.

This cannot be done at The Gap, where "decisions are creative—you have to factor in fashion along with historical sales and weekly sales rates," says Bruce Watson, director of information administration for the San Francisco-based casual clothing retailer. That is why The Gap has turned to decision support: a collaboration between people and computers. The sales data and data from other sources are funneled into the data warehouse, implemented as the mainframe-based relational database. The purpose is to accumulate data for access by decision makers. Here, the data can be accessed by more than 2,000 merchandisers, planners, analysts, and store managers. Using a decision support system, acquired from a specialized vendor, they can decide which items to buy and when to bring them in. In other words, they are planning the store inventory.

The merchandising specialists can look at the data showing the effects of special promotions in the past. They can ask a question: "What if we run a similar promotion next month?" and see how it would affect sales of the promoted items. They can change their assumptions and again see what the outcome will be. They can investigate several scenarios introducing a new line of casual wear by drawing on the experience with the introduction of a similar line last year, as reflected by the data. The system does not make decisions for these experienced workers. It gives them the tools needed to access and manipulate data and to consider various scenarios for the future. The decision support system helps people arrive at an informed judgment. And the data warehouse helps shrink the expensive warehousing of slow-moving clothes.

Based on Richard Pastore, "Minding Your Business," *CIO*, July 1994, pp. 54–66.

Decision support systems (DSS) are a type of information system whose principal objective is to support a human decision maker during the process of arriving at a decision. You have read in the Focus Minicase how the merchandisers at The Gap are able to project the effects of their decisions with such a system. The strength of DSS lies in supporting decision making in situations where both human judgment and the power of the computer are required. While decision support systems primarily support planning, executive information systems (EIS) are powerful tools for monitoring and control. An executive using an EIS gains the ability to track all aspects of the company's operation, and to locate problems and opportunities.

	Type of Problem	Examples of Problem Areas	Characteristics	How Decisions Are Made
Table 10.1 *The degree to which a problem is structured*	Structured	Order validation Inventory reorder	Availability of an algorithm (standard operating procedure)	Fully computerized (transaction processing systems)
	Semistructured	Sales forecasting Budgeting Risk analysis	Programmable aspects present	Human decision maker supported by computer
	Unstructured	Promotion of personnel Introducing new technology	No standard procedures or aspects available	Principally by a human, with some computer support

10.1 | WHEN SHOULD YOU USE THE DECISION SUPPORT APPROACH?

The Problems that Decision Support Systems Help Solve

Decision support systems (DSS) are interactive information systems that assist a decision maker in approaching ill-structured problems by offering analytical models and access to databases. These systems are designed to support the decision-making process, rather than to render a decision. The hallmark of these systems is (or should be) flexibility. Personal DSSs should be easy to develop: End-user-oriented tools are available for the purpose. On the other hand, an organizational DSS, used throughout an enterprise, should be developed in a well-planned, disciplined process. All DSSs should be easy to use. We can think of a DSS as a set of capabilities. Within its area of application, such a system should give its user a way to use models and databases in an interactive session that best supports his or her way of thinking about the problem at hand.

What, then, is the essence of DSS? In what business situations should we think about using the DSS approach? We will discuss these issues in the opening sections. Later in the chapter, we will see what tools we need to implement a DSS and how we can go about developing such a system.

Problems that people in organizations face differ in terms of how structured the problems are; that is, the extent to which a solution procedure can be stated for them. Table 10.1 shows the classification of problems in terms of the degree to which such a solution procedure can be explicitly presented.

As we can conclude, the principal domain of DSS is support of decision making for semistructured problems, where parts of the decision process itself often require very significant computer support. This is so because a model, in some cases containing hundreds of equations, has to be applied against a database often comprising many millions of data items, with human judgment injected at critical junctures. We have seen how the decision makers in the Focus Minicase for this chapter use a DSS to help them make merchandising decisions. DSSs are also employed to assist a decision maker facing an unstructured problem, often injecting the necessary factual grounding through access to data.

Decision making to solve unstructured problems is now also supported by expert systems, but within narrow domains, such as, for example, a decision regarding loan approval (we will discuss expert systems in the next chapter). When tackling **ill-structured**—both semistructured and unstructured—**problems,** the exploration of alternative solutions cannot be completed before a choice must be made. When we say that one of a manager's principal tasks is to deal with ambiguity, we mean that he or she will be called upon to solve many ill-structured problems.

To make all this more tangible to you, let us consider a few brief examples of DSS application.

Examples of Problem Solving with DSS

Let us consider five different scenarios of DSS application. These examples should give us insight into what a DSS can do for us.

1. Firestone Rubber & Tire Company of Akron, Ohio, built a DSS to assess the best strategy for rolling out a new brand of tires. The system permits analysts to look for relationships between past financial results and external variables, such as total car production and gross domestic product, and thus build sales forecasting models.

Using the system containing these models, the Firestone analysts were able to rapidly build for the corporate vice-president of technology a database on all 200 competitive brands of tires, including data on their construction, tread, volume, and sales estimates. The executive used this database to assist him in defining a competitive strategy. The system enabled the organization to integrate the technological and financial aspects of a product decision and thus create a basis for joint decision making by the company's various functional areas.

2. Houston Minerals Corporation was considering a joint venture with a petrochemicals company to build a chemical plant. Using a DSS generator (a software system for building DSS), the planning staff of the company built—in a few days—a DSS projecting the risks of the venture, taking prices, supply, and demand into consideration. The results suggested that the project would have a positive outcome.

However, the executive vice-president responsible for the decision requested an answer to the question: "What is the chance that this project will result in a disastrous outcome?" In the words of the company's chief planner: "Within twenty minutes, there in the executive boardroom, we were reviewing the results of his 'what-if' questions. Those results led to the eventual dismissal of the project, which we otherwise would probably have accepted."

Thus, a DSS enabled the decision maker to bring his judgment to bear on the problem. This judgment was fully supported by the information made available by the DSS and by the knowledge of the planners, which went into the construction of the model.

3. A portfolio manager of a large pension fund is responsible for investing billions of dollars in assets. A huge variety of investment vehicles with varying degrees of risk and reward are available at all times, and the funds are at all times placed in a complex array of investments. The manager needs to make constant investment decisions consistent with the objectives of the fund, with a variety of environmental factors, and with her or his experience and informal information. Certain aspects of this work can be handled by expert systems that suggest decisions. However, overall risk analysis with the use of a DSS permits the manager to balance various forms of investment to achieve the desired ratio of reward to risk and to spread the funds over a variety of investments.

4. A DSS for police-beat allocation was built for the city of San Jose, California. An officer could display a map on a screen and display the data showing police calls in each zone: the nature of service needed, service times, and activity levels. The officer could experiment with various alternatives involving the assignment of police patrols by interacting with the system. The system became a tool that helped its users exercise their judgment. An experiment was run to compare an assignment made by an officer using the DSS with an assignment made by a linear programming model that did not rely on human judgment (a management science model). The officer–DSS team arrived at a superior solution.

5. As the utilization of a DSS assisting the navigators of vessels on the lower Mississippi River increased, the number of accidents on this once extremely dangerous waterway decreased precipitously. The system simulates the traffic of the vessels in the area by dead-reckoning. That is, the system updates the vessels' positions from their original locations by considering the direction and speed of their movement—with all the initial information radioed in by the ships' navigators. The Coast Guard personnel use the system by watching blips on their consoles, resembling air traffic control displays. They alert navigators to any developing situations of undue proximity to other vessels by radio communication, and accidents are thus prevented.

Now that we have reviewed these examples, let us consider in more general terms the capabilities offered by DSS.

10.2 | CAPABILITIES OF DECISION SUPPORT SYSTEMS

What Are Models?

A **model** is a representation of something else, developed for a specific purpose. It is usually an abstraction or a simplification of the phenomenon being modeled. A model represents the relationships among the salient aspects of the phenomenon. Let us consider simple plan modeling as an example.

Financial plans rely on planning models, which show the dependence of projected financial results on the values of input variables. These planned financial results generally represent such measures of performance as profit and market share, expressed through a variety of indicators. A typical input variable, projected by forecasting, is sales volume.

Financial plans obtained with these models include a statement of projected profit or loss for a given time period (which is called an income statement) and a projection of company assets and liabilities at the end of that period (called a balance sheet). These projections are prepared in the same fashion as accounting reports on actual performance. The projections are called *pro forma* statements to distinguish them from actual results. Figure 10.1 shows a model you could use for a DSS that helps you obtain a pro forma annual income statement. In this model, sales volume is the only input variable; that is, a projected sales volume has to be supplied to run the model.

The pro forma income statement shown in Figure 10.2 was obtained with this model under the assumption that the sales volume will be 100,000 units. The selling price during the previous year was $10.

Figure 10.1

A DSS model for a pro forma income statement

sales volume = input variable
selling price = 1.10 * previous year selling price
sales = sales volume * selling price
unit cost = 0.50 * selling price
variable cost = sales volume * unit cost
overhead = 0.20 * variable cost
cost of goods sold = variable cost + overhead
gross margin = sales − cost of goods sold
operating expense = 0.25 * sales
net income before tax = gross margin − operating expense
tax = 0.42 * net income before tax
net income = net income before tax − tax

Figure 10.2	**Consolidated Small Company Pro Forma Income Statement for Year 2000**

A pro forma income statement obtained with the DSS model

Sales	$1,100,000
Cost of goods sold	660,000
Gross margin	440,000
Operating expense	275,000
Net income before tax	165,000
Tax	69,300
Net income	$ 95,700

As we can see, a model is built using a variety of assumptions (premises) about the dependence between its variables. By considering various alternatives (what if's), we can vary these premises and compare the outcomes. For example, what if we choose a higher selling price? What if the tax rate increases? We may also wish to ask a different type of question: What value of a variable do we need in order to achieve a certain result? For example, what sales volume do we need to achieve a given net income?

Let us see how a DSS supports asking these two types of questions.

Scenario Generation and Goal Seeking with a DSS

Projecting possible futures during a planning process is a particular strength of DSS. Two principal modes of analysis are available. In the **"what-if"** mode, the user considers alternative scenarios and their results. For example, "What if we increase advertising expenditures by 5 percent?" The use of a simple marketing DSS is shown in Figure 10.3. Both this and the following example were produced with the fourth-generation language NOMAD2 from Must Software International. The language commands are shown in the upper part of each figure. The lower part shows the impact of the projections.

In the **goal-seeking** mode, the user asks, "What would it take in terms of input factors to achieve a particular performance?" This mode of interaction is illustrated in Figure 10.4.

Let us now see how the DSS capabilities can be deployed in the decision-making process.

Using DSS in the Decision-Making Process

The general **decision-making process** consists of four steps, shown in Figure 10.5 (expanded from Simon 1960).

During the first step, known as intelligence, a search of the environment is made to find and define the problem or an opportunity. During the next stage, called design, several alternative solutions are developed, to be compared to one another during the following stage of "choice." The solution is then implemented and tracked, in order to be improved upon. As you may note in Figure 10.5, each of the steps may require backing up to a preceding one, in order to redefine the problem or select a better solution, for example.

DSSs support various stages of this decision-making process. Let us walk you through the use of such a system. Say, you are a marketing manager for a pharmaceutical company, using a marketing DSS. This DSS is designed to help you establish customer response to

Figure 10.3

"What-if" analysis with a marketing DSS (From Efraim Turban, *Decision Support and Expert Systems: Management Support Systems,* 4th ed., Englewood Cliffs, NJ: Prentice Hall, 1995, p. 65.)

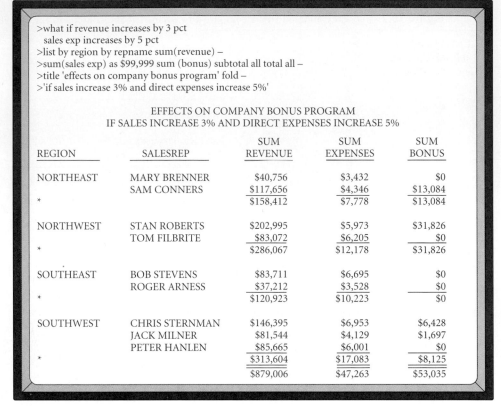

```
>what if revenue increases by 3 pct
  sales exp increases by 5 pct
>list by region by repname sum(revenue) –
>sum(sales exp) as $99,999 sum (bonus) subtotal all total all –
>title 'effects on company bonus program' fold –
>'if sales increase 3% and direct expenses increase 5%'
```

EFFECTS ON COMPANY BONUS PROGRAM
IF SALES INCREASE 3% AND DIRECT EXPENSES INCREASE 5%

REGION	SALESREP	SUM REVENUE	SUM EXPENSES	SUM BONUS
NORTHEAST	MARY BRENNER	$40,756	$3,432	$0
	SAM CONNERS	$117,656	$4,346	$13,084
*		$158,412	$7,778	$13,084
NORTHWEST	STAN ROBERTS	$202,995	$5,973	$31,826
	TOM FILBRITE	$83,072	$6,205	$0
*		$286,067	$12,178	$31,826
SOUTHEAST	BOB STEVENS	$83,711	$6,695	$0
	ROGER ARNESS	$37,212	$3,528	$0
*		$120,923	$10,223	$0
SOUTHWEST	CHRIS STERNMAN	$146,395	$6,953	$6,428
	JACK MILNER	$81,544	$4,129	$1,697
	PETER HANLEN	$85,665	$6,001	$0
*		$313,604	$17,083	$8,125
		$879,006	$47,263	$53,035

various forms of product advertising, specific promotion campaigns, and salespeople. It will enable you to compare the product volume your firm is shipping to various types of distribution outlets (such as drugstores, distributors, and hospitals) with the volumes shipped by your competitors. Through the DSS, you will have access to both internal and external databases. By analyzing the results, you will sharpen your future marketing campaigns.

A DSS can help you find a problem. During a session with your system, you request a report on product shipments by month, broken down by type of distribution outlet. A report on one of the products leads you to conclude that the response of one of the market segments to a recent promotion campaign is far below projections. You have discovered a problem. Now you look for the cause. Testing a variety of hypotheses by running the "what-if" scenarios, you conclude that the promotion had targeted a wrong customer group.

You now wish to develop alternative solutions to the problem so that you can select the preferred course of action. To do this, you will construct a model. The graphics module of your DSS can produce, for example, a scatter plot of a product's sales from month to month correlated with various aspects of marketing tactics, such as discount percentage or amount spent on advertising. The user may then request that the system perform a regression analysis: The system will plot a curve and display a mathematical formula that best matches the points on the scatter plot. You will thus obtain a series of equations that show the response

Figure 10.4

Goal seeking with a marketing DSS (Drawn with modification from Efraim Turban, *Decision Support and Expert Systems,* 3rd ed., 1993, p. 143.)

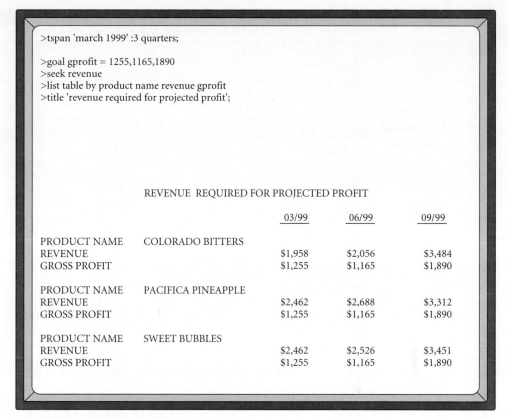

```
>tspan 'march 1999' :3 quarters;

>goal gprofit = 1255,1165,1890
>seek revenue
>list table by product name revenue gprofit
>title 'revenue required for projected profit';
```

REVENUE REQUIRED FOR PROJECTED PROFIT

		03/99	06/99	09/99
PRODUCT NAME	COLORADO BITTERS			
REVENUE		$1,958	$2,056	$3,484
GROSS PROFIT		$1,255	$1,165	$1,890
PRODUCT NAME	PACIFICA PINEAPPLE			
REVENUE		$2,462	$2,688	$3,312
GROSS PROFIT		$1,255	$1,165	$1,890
PRODUCT NAME	SWEET BUBBLES			
REVENUE		$2,462	$2,526	$3,451
GROSS PROFIT		$1,255	$1,165	$1,890

Figure 10.5

The decision-making process

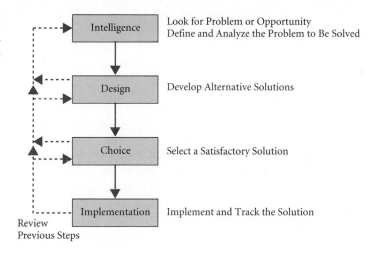

Intelligence — Look for Problem or Opportunity / Define and Analyze the Problem to Be Solved

Design — Develop Alternative Solutions

Choice — Select a Satisfactory Solution

Implementation — Implement and Track the Solution

Review Previous Steps

of various market segments (type of consumer, region, type of distribution outlet) to various promotional devices. This is the decision model you sought.

With the model, you can now compare alternative decisions and select one. Using the "what-if" mode, you can decide, for example, on the best way to spend a promotional budget of $500,000. (What if we spend $150,000 in print advertising in the northeast and

We Are Not Perfectly Rational Decision Makers

The classical model of a decision maker was formulated in economic theory and its origins are usually attributed to Adam Smith. The model makes the following very strong assumptions:

- The decision maker seeks to maximize the payoff from a decision, such as profit or market share to be attained by the firm.

- The decision maker knows all possible courses of action.

- The decision maker knows the outcome of each course of action.

In real-world situations, none of these assumptions is true. In fact, decision makers usually choose the first solution that moves them closer to their objective, without necessarily reaching the goal (such as maximization). As these incremental decisions succeed or fail, the objective itself may be adjusted.

Individual capability to make rational decisions is limited by a variety of biases. Individuals have *frames of reference* based on their experience, knowledge, and cultural backgrounds. These frames of reference filter out certain information or certain alternative courses of action, possibly taking away from the quality of decision making. Failing to gather the relevant and accessible information because you are sure of your assumptions is dangerous. Even when contradicting information is evident, people more readily accept information that confirms, rather than challenges, their assumptions.

Most people are highly averse to a possible loss and will take significant risks to prevent losses, even though they would not incur such risks when seeking gain. People frequently perceive a causal relationship between two factors, even when there are no grounds for doing so. Just because your sales are falling in a region where a significant part of the salesforce was recently changed does not mean that the change caused the fall (this suspicion needs to be investigated, of course).

Vivid events that are easily recalled or events in the more recent past are unjustifiably assigned higher probability and weigh more heavily in the decision. The form in which the information is presented influences people's understanding of it. For example, items listed first or last have greater impact than those in the middle.

All this means that people's decision making can be manipulated; frequently they themselves are the manipulators.

$350,000 in sales calls and discounting in the southwest? What if we spend the entire sum on sales calls?) You can also use the system in the goal-seeking mode: Given the goal of $50 million in sales in six months, how much should we spend on print advertising? You can introduce your own judgmental constraints. For example, you believe that the new sales manager in the northwest will need a boost and so the company has to spend at least $100,000 on discounting in that region over the next three months.

Having selected the course of action that appears most desirable, you proceed to implement the decision you have made with the assistance of the marketing DSS. You will continue to track the outcome closely by comparing the projections you have made with the incoming sales results.

Note how a decision support system supports the entire process of decision making rather than just one of the stages. Note also how the decision maker, rather than the system, renders the decision. Using a DSS, a decision maker can both develop a decision model and apply it to a particular situation. The decision maker needs to beware of biases, some of which are discussed in the preceding vignette.

The use of DSSs does not rid us of our biases, of course. However, by developing a pattern of challenging our own assumptions and investigating differing courses of actions with the use of a DSS, we can limit the effects of these biases. Designing several scenarios and investigating the possible outcomes under each of them helps us provide for contingencies, without knowing the future.

Features of DSS

DSSs have several features to offer in the general information system environment of an organization. Earlier we contrasted these systems with the other categories of management-oriented information systems, MRS and EIS, in Table 2.5. Specifically, DSS can:

1. Support decision making in ill-structured situations when, precisely owing to the lack of structure, problems do not lend themselves to full computerization. Yet the decision makers do require computer assistance for access to and processing of voluminous amounts of data.

2. Help to rapidly obtain quantitative results needed to reach a decision. A model for the structured part of the problem can be constructed rather quickly, and it can be flexibly deployed with data as needed during the decision-making process.

3. Operate in the ad hoc (as needed) mode to suit the current needs of the user, as opposed to operating on a pre-established schedule, as management reporting systems do.

4. Support easy modification of models, which increases the organization's responsiveness to the changing environment both within the firm and in the outside world.

5. Foster high-quality decision making by encouraging decisions based on the integration of available information and human judgment. DSSs give decision makers a degree of confidence in their decisions unavailable to a person who is wholly dependent on his or her judgment.

6. Facilitate the implementation of decisions, which frequently cut across departmental boundaries. By creating and exercising common models, decision makers in the involved organizational units develop common assumptions and, in general, learn to communicate at a deeper level. This helps to fight the "not-invented-here" syndrome, so common in organizations, that leads to the adoption of sub optimal solutions so long as they are one's own.

7. Support group decision making, particularly through group DSS (GDSS). These systems, which we will discuss further in the chapter, permit several people with a variety of experiences and areas of expertise to bring them to bear on a decision, leading to more effective, higher-quality decision making.

8. Be user friendly, a principal feature of a well-designed DSS. User-friendliness can make computer-supported problem solving attractive to individuals at all levels of an organization. The user can work with the system in the style that best serves him or her. This helps managers, professionals, and other knowledge workers to perform better. It also enriches their jobs, particularly at the operational level.

9. Give managers the opportunity to gain a better understanding of their business by developing and working with models.

Frequently, spreadsheets are used to construct relatively simple decision support models. However, spreadsheets do have limitations. They are limited in their data-handling capabilities and thus cannot work with large databases, and they do not allow for construction of more complex models. Also, as circumstances change, it is easier to modify a DSS model than a spreadsheet model. Keeping your spreadsheet consistent with everyone else's is virtually impossible.

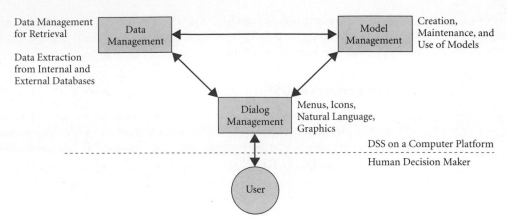

Figure 10.6

DSS subsystems and the capabilities they offer
(From Vladimir Zwass, *Management Information Systems,* Dubuque, IA: Wm. C. Brown, 1992, p. 533.)

10.3 | COMPONENTS OF DSS

Let us expand our discussion of DSS components, which were introduced to you in Section 2.4. The three principal DSS subsystems and their principal capabilities are shown in Figure 10.6. Various commercial systems support DSS development and package these DSS capabilities in a variety of ways by distributing them among a series of optional software modules.

Let us look more closely at the DSS subsystems.

The Data Management Subsystem

The **data management subsystem** of a DSS relies, in general, on a variety of internal and external databases. Indeed, we have said that the power of DSSs derives from their ability to provide easy access to data. This is not to say that a simple, usually spreadsheet-based DSS for the personal use of a manager cannot rely on the manager's limited personal database. It is just that maintaining the currency and integrity of a significant collection of personal databases is an impossible task.

On the other hand, it is usually undesirable to provide a DSS with direct access to corporate databases. The performance of the transaction processing systems that access these databases, as well as the responsiveness of the DSS, would both be degraded. Usually, therefore, the database component of DSS relies on extracts from the relevant internal and external databases. Some firms set up data warehouses that give end users access to the data extracted from the operational databases (see Section 6.11). The data management subsystem is shown in Figure 10.7.

The principles of database management discussed in Chapter 6 apply to the management of the database extract used by a DSS. The extraction procedure itself is generally specified by a specialist, such as the database administrator, rather than by an end user. The specialist needs to pay particular attention to data consistency across multiple decision support systems that extract data from the corporate databases. If extracts for the DSSs serving the same functional area or the same business process are made at different times, the extracted databases will differ and "battles of the printout" among the users may result. Data warehouses are used by many leading companies to support organizational DSS. Commercial data warehouses for decision support are emerging. For example, Source Informatics America makes its data warehouse that contains trillions of bytes of data on healthcare, along with a DSS, available to the industry over the Web as DSS Web (Gardner 1997).

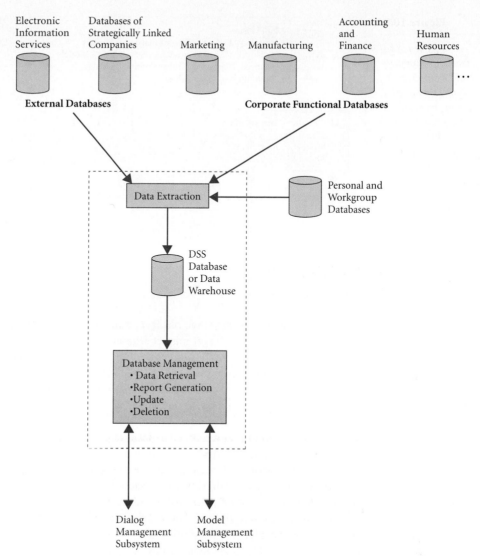

Figure 10.7

The data management subsystem of DSS (Modified from Vladimir Zwass, *Management Information Systems,* Dubuque, IA: Wm. C. Brown, 1992, p. 534.)

The Model Management Subsystem

The power of DSS rests on the user's ability to apply quantitative, mathematical models to data. Figure 10.1 illustrates a planning model that was used to obtain a pro forma income statement for a small company. Indeed, DSSs are primarily used for planning activities of varying scope and at various corporate levels. The analytical sophistication of DSS varies depending on the nature of the models employed.

Models have different areas of application and come from a variety of sources. Software packages for developing DSS (so-called DSS generators) contain libraries of statistical models. These models include tools for the exploratory analysis of data; that is, tools designed to obtain summarized measures such as mean and median values, to compute variances, to produce scatter plots, and so forth. Other statistical models help analyze series of data and forecast future outcomes by approximating a set of data with a mathematical equation, by extending the trend of a curve through extrapolation techniques, or by providing for seasonal adjustment. Other models help establish—or reject—causal

Figure 10.8

The model management subsystem of DSS (From Vladimir Zwass, *Management Information Systems*, Dubuque, IA: Wm. C. Brown, 1992, p. 535).

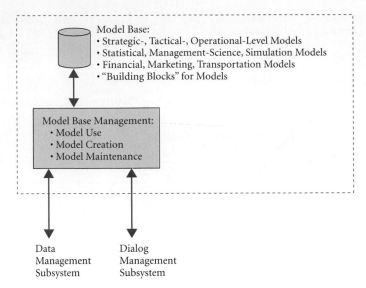

Model Base:
• Strategic-, Tactical-, Operational-Level Models
• Statistical, Management-Science, Simulation Models
• Financial, Marketing, Transportation Models
• "Building Blocks" for Models

Model Base Management:
• Model Use
• Model Creation
• Model Maintenance

Data Management Subsystem

Dialog Management Subsystem

relationships between various factors (for example, whether the drop in sales volume is caused by the aging of our target market segment).

We will discuss the types of models used in DSS in the next section. The capabilities of the **model management subsystem** of DSS are summarized in Figure 10.8.

A particular advantage of DSS is the decision maker's ability to use a model to explore the influence of various factors on outcomes (a process known as sensitivity analysis). Two forms of such analysis are the what-if analysis and goal seeking. We showed the results of both these analyses in Figures 10.3 and 10.4, respectively, when we introduced you to the decision support system in this chapter.

There is significant research interest in providing a degree of automated model management. With a system of this kind, the user is able to present the problem, and the system will automatically select an appropriate model or construct one from the existing models and software "building blocks." The capabilities of expert systems in selecting a proper model are being explored toward this end.

The Dialog Management Subsystem

Along with DSS's ability to apply models to large volumes of data from a variety of sources, another important advantage of DSS is the user-friendly and flexible interface between the human decision maker and such a system. This stands in contrast to management reporting systems, which provide little opportunity for user–system interaction.

The principal components of the **dialog management subsystem** are shown in Figure 10.9. The notable feature is support of multiple forms of input and output. By combining various input and output capabilities of a DSS, users can engage in the individually selected dialogs that best support their decision-making styles.

The field of artificial intelligence has made some notable contributions to dialog management, such as the ability to specify what is wanted in a subset of natural language or to activate the system by voice. The windowing capability enables the user to maintain several activities at the same time, with the results displayed in screen windows and the user employing a mouse to move between them. A variety of help and even training-by-example capabilities may be offered.

Figure 10.9

The dialog management subsystem of DSS (From Vladimir Zwass, *Management Information Systems,* Dubuque, IA: Wm. C. Brown, 1992, p. 537.)

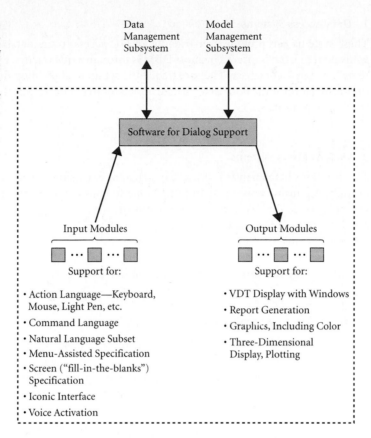

Significant attention has been devoted by researchers to the effectiveness of presentation graphics, as opposed to the tabular display of data. Graphs outperform tables when a large amount of information must be presented and a relatively simple impression is desired. This is very often the case and the main reason why executive information systems, discussed later in this chapter, rely heavily on graphics. Most business graphs are designed to answer just four questions:

1. Who is the biggest?
2. How do circumstances change over time (What is the trend)?
3. What is typical or exceptional?
4. How well does one factor predict another?

10.4 WHAT DSS CAN DO FOR YOU: CLASSIFICATION OF DSS

To see what a DSS can do, we will review these systems from the point of view of the degree to which the outputs of a given system can determine a decision (Alter 1980). This classification yields an entire spectrum of systems, ranging from the totally data-oriented to the more powerful model-oriented systems. Clearly, a given DSS often possesses a mix of these capabilities, in which case we would classify it with respect to its most powerful capability.

1. Data Access Systems

These systems can provide user-friendly ad hoc access to the database. This capability is equivalent to what is offered by most DBMSs through a query language. However, such systems "open up" a database. They are frequently set up to allow shop floor personnel to continuously monitor the floor or a particular piece of machinery; thus these DSSs help in controlling operations.

2. Data Analysis Systems

These systems help analyze historical and current data, either on demand (ad hoc) or periodically. An airline uses a system of this type to compare its performance with that of its competitors. The system's database contains the data on the quarterly performances of all airlines, submitted by them to the Civil Aeronautics Board of the federal government. Data analysis systems are frequently oriented toward the consolidation (aggregation) of data, such as summarizing the performances of a firm's sub-units and presenting the summaries in graphs. Only very simple models are employed in data analysis systems.

3. Forecast-Oriented Data Analysis Systems

These systems generally assist in developing product plans, including market segment forecasts, sales forecasts, and analyses of competitive actions. Their operation is based on access to a variety of internal and external marketing and product databases, including series of historical data. Ad hoc use for planning purposes by a staff analyst or a marketing manager is typical. The systems in this category include only the simpler of the variety of marketing models, which show how existing trends in the marketplace will extend in the future if similar conditions prevail.

4. Systems Based on Accounting Models

DSSs are used to consider alternative options for planning purposes, based on accounting definitions and relationships. Such systems typically produce estimated (pro forma) income statements, balance sheets, or other measures of financial performance. We saw an example of such a model in Figure 10.1. A system of this type accepts estimates of costs and revenues as inputs rather than forecasting them (for example, it would require a ready sales forecast submitted as an input). The "what-if" mode of operation is typically employed to compare alternatives.

5. Systems Based on Representational Models

These systems go beyond the use of ready standard formulas, such as those employed in systems that rely on accounting models. Rather, **representational models** show the dependence between a controllable variable, such as the price of a product, and an outcome, such as sales. These are frequently simulation models which yield probabilistic results. When we considered how you can use a marketing DSS to support the decision making earlier in this chapter, we mentioned a representational model of customer response to promotional devices. Another example is a risk analysis model, which considers such key factors as costs of resources (labor, raw materials, and so on) and product demand. We have seen how Houston Minerals used such a DSS to avoid an unacceptable degree of risk.

Figure 10.10

Types of DSS (Adapted in part from Alter, 1980, p. 76.)

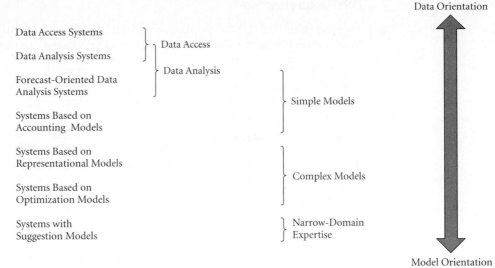

6. Systems Based on Optimization Models

Optimization models are developed by management scientists to determine optimal allocation of resources or best possible schedules. Using the techniques of linear programming, for example, one can establish the mix of products that must be produced to maximize an objective such as profit, subject to a variety of constraints. Using such a model, a company faced with temporary supply shortages was able to adjust the supply of raw materials it needed for its products to meet this temporary constraint.

7. Systems with Suggestion Models

These systems "push the envelope" of decision support systems by actually suggesting decisions, rather than merely responding to the user's request to evaluate an alternative. Systems with **suggestion models** suggest solutions within narrow domains of knowledge and sometimes combine a DSS with an expert system. Such a system may suggest product price, the rate of insurance renewal, or production volume.

This classification of DSS is summarized in Figure 10.10. Data-oriented DSS (or DSS components) primarily support earlier phases of the decision-making process, in particular the intelligence phase involving discovery of a problem or opportunity. The design and choice phases are supported by model-oriented DSS. The implementation of a decision is facilitated if the future implementers were involved in arriving at the decision with the use of DSS, or even in constructing the models employed in it.

10.5 | BUILDING A DECISION SUPPORT SYSTEM

Managers frequently build and use their own DSSs. Occasionally, a manager may have an intermediary, such as an assistant or a staff analyst, build and use the system. More complicated DSSs are built by information systems specialists, with the involvement of the intended end users and staff analysts. The DSS technology ranges from the specific DSS developed to solve a class of problems to the tools with which a DSS can be built.

DSS Technology

Three levels of DSS technology have been identified (Sprague 1980). We will consider them by progressing from the level closest to the actual DSS to the one most distant from it.

1. Specific DSS

A specific DSS is the actual system that a manager works with during the decision process. Our examples of DSS for marketing analysis, joint-venture evaluation, or police-beat allocation were systems of this type.

A specific DSS is constructed with the use of DSS generators or tools, which we will describe below. A variety of specific DSS are available in the software marketplace. However, they have to be customized to the actual environment in which they will be used. A DSS generally also undergoes extensive modification as it is used. Therefore, any specific DSS may be expected to evolve as time passes.

2. DSS Generators

A **DSS generator** is a software package that provides capabilities for building specific DSSs rapidly and easily. Capabilities of generators vary widely. Their common characteristic is that much of the processing and data accessing functionality needed in a specific DSS is already programmed into the generator and, therefore, building a specific DSS does not require much programming.

Elaborate DSS generators, such as EXPRESS and pcEXPRESS of Information Resources (of Chicago), incorporate a variety of tools for data analysis, financial modeling, and forecasting, combined with the capability of accessing multiple databases for querying and reporting. The generators also include comprehensive graphics packages. A widely used DSS generator, oriented toward financial planning, is IFPS of Comshare.

Spreadsheet packages, such as Excel (Microsoft), Lotus 1-2-3 (Lotus Development), or Quattro Pro (Corel), offer ever increasing capabilities for generating simpler DSSs. Specialized templates, that is, prewritten models for a specific area of application, and nonprocedural languages are available to simplify the use of spreadsheets for DSS generation. Nonprocedural, fourth-generation languages of various microcomputer-based DBMS, such as FOCUS, NOMAD2, or Ramis II, provide another avenue for generating a specific DSS. The main distinction between simply using a spreadsheet and producing a DSS is that in the latter there is a clear separation of the data from the models.

3. DSS Tools

A variety of tools may be employed as building blocks to construct a DSS generator or a specific DSS. These tools include programming languages with good capabilities for accessing arrays of data (for example, APL), simple spreadsheet packages, statistical packages, and DBMSs with a query facility.

Sometimes personal DSSs are indeed built with APL. We have observed many an actuary do so, and the builder would find the experience rewarding and stimulating. On the other end of the spectrum, a company may decide to use a tool such as a programming language to build its own DSS generator, specialized for its individual application area, from the ground up. The capability developed through the use of such a generator may contribute to a firm's competitive edge.

How a DSS Is Developed

By its very nature, a decision support system has a more customized orientation than a transaction processing or a management reporting system. A DSS is a collection of capabilities that support the decision-making process of a certain individual or a relatively small group of people. As the needs of these people change, the DSS should change with them—DSSs are truly built to be changed. We will distinguish three general approaches to building DSSs.

1. The Quick-Hit Approach

The **quick-hit** approach is the way most DSSs come into being. Indeed, most DSSs are built for the personal use of a decision maker. The initiative usually comes from an individual manager, so the DSS is built either by the manager or by the builders who belong to a more or less formal DSS group. Generally, a DSS generator is employed, frequently a spreadsheet with templates. The level of investment with the quick-hit approach is low and the payoff can be high.

2. Traditional Life-Cycle Development

As we will discuss in some detail in Part Five of the text, large software systems are generally built in a disciplined fashion with the use of a **life-cycle development** methodology. This process begins with detailed system planning and analysis, progresses through the design stages followed by coding and testing, and goes on to implementation—this is the development life cycle. The process is lengthy, and there is no partial system to work with before the system is completed.

This development methodology is suitable for complex systems, in particular those that affect many users and in which informational requirements can be established early through the analysis process. This is indeed the case when a DSS generator is to be built. Therefore, a DSS generator or a very large model-based organizational DSS that affects a number of functional units or business processes in an organization may be built using a life-cycle methodology. But in the development of a specific DSS, such usage is the exception rather than the rule.

3. Iterative Development

In DSS practice, the future user or group of users generally do not know what they want from the system. Moreover, an analysis process is not likely to surface a clear set of requirements. As in many other activities in life, we learn what we want from an activity by starting to perform it. To do so in the decision making with a DSS, we need a **prototype** of the system—a simple initial version that can be used to experiment with and learn about the desired features of the system.

Iterative (or evolutionary) **development** of DSS relies on the creation of such a prototype and its progressive refinement. The process begins when the future user and the DSS builder jointly define the problem to be solved and then discuss the system, perhaps only for a few hours. They identify the most useful screens. The builder then constructs a simple version of the system, ignoring many of its more advanced aspects. To construct the actual DSS, all three of its components (database, model, and dialog) will have to be built with the use of facilities offered by the DSS generator or with DSS tools. Particular attention is paid during the prototype development to the dialog component. Now the users have something to experiment with and react to.

The iterative, repetitive process of prototype refinement follows. End users offer suggestions for modifying the current version of the system. Builders analyze these suggestions and modify the emerging DSS. The prototype, refined over several such iterations, is tested and documented and eventually becomes the DSS. The process of iterative development is shown in Figure 10.11.

Figure 10.11

Development and adaptation of DSS

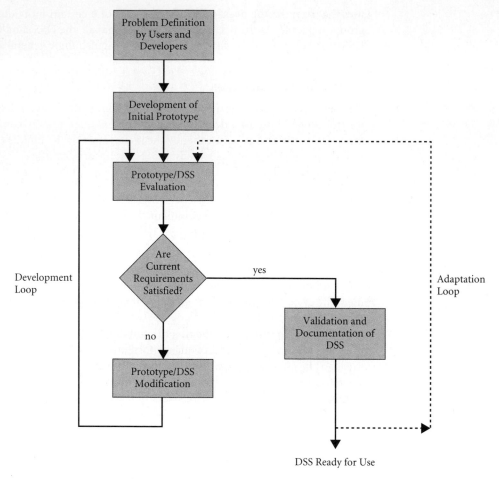

As the system is used it is adapted: Decision problems evolve and the users' needs change. The DSS is modified to satisfy these changing requirements. These renewed iterations are shown in Figure 10.11 as an adaptation loop. Each successive modification may thus be thought of as another iteration during the total evolutionary process of keeping DSS current with user needs.

10.6 | GROUP DECISION SUPPORT SYSTEMS

Group decision support systems (GDSS) are designed to support group communication and decision processes. In the developing information society, the volume of necessary decision making will continue to increase dramatically. Many decisions are complex and call for the participation of a number of experts working as a group. Contemporary organizational design relies on project-oriented teams as the fundamental structural units. More or less permanent groups, such as corporate boards, task forces, or teams of co-workers, increasingly form the basic work cells throughout an enterprise. All of these factors call for the support of group decision making. Competitiveness of organizations depends on creative decision making of the various groups that manage them and carry out their business processes.

Creativity in Group Decision Making

Recent analyses indicate that much creative decision making in organizations is performed or stimulated by groups, from a work team to the chief executive's "cabinet." Decision-making work in a group has to be carefully organized and there exists a large number (over 70 by one count) techniques for doing that (many of them described in Couger 1996). Information systems can stimulate creativity in decision making (MacCrimmon and Wagner 1994).

Probably the best known among group decision-making techniques is **brainstorming,** originated by Alex Osborn, a founder of one of the most successful U.S. advertising agencies. The goal of a brainstorming session is to generate ideas. Ideas need to be generated at several stages of the decision-making process: when the group is framing the problem or identifying the pertinent information, and particularly so when the group members are generating alternative solutions. A group of five to ten people participates (although much larger groups are present when electronic meeting systems are used), with one of the members acting as a recorder, listing ideas as they are presented. Brainstorming aims at fluency in the idea-generating process in order to produce a significant number of ideas. The ground rules of brainstorming are:

- No criticism—group members make no evaluation of ideas as they are freely generated.

- "Anything goes"—wild ideas are encouraged, and internal judgment by participants should be suspended.

- The more, the better—the more ideas the group generates, the greater the likelihood of coming up with several good alternatives.

- Build on the ideas of others—participants should feel free to combine or modify ideas generated by others and thus come up with superior ideas.

Another technique for creative problem solving, the **synectics** process, is more selective—only the best ideas are further considered as the process goes on. Synectics encourages thinking by analogy. For example, what can your experience playing baseball teach you about the way your project team should be organized? The **nominal group technique** addresses the needs of groups in which broad differences of goals and opinions are certain to lead to animosity and defensive argumentation. Therefore, large parts of these sessions are spent by participants working alone, and their ideas are then circulated and evaluated.

The **Delphi technique** is a method for soliciting the opinions of a group of experts and arriving at a consensus among them. The group members may be scattered around the globe. A questionnaire regarding the matter at hand, such as the forecast of the technologies that will have the greatest impact on your business within five years, for example, is distributed to them. The results are then tallied and sent out to the group members, perhaps with additional questions. The group members are invited to revise their opinions based on this feedback. This step is repeated until consensus is reached or until reasons for a lack of consensus emerge and additional information is sought. The entire Delphi process is anonymous.

Group decision making is not necessarily a fountainhead of creativity. Groups can also constrain individual creativity. The opposite of creative work in a group is known as *groupthink.* This drive for preservation of the group unity at the expense of grappling with the issues fosters over-optimism, the illusion of invulnerability, and collective rationalization of decisions and opinions that are not valid on rational ground.

Group decision support systems (GDSS) are designed to support some of the group decision-making processes.

Capabilities of GDSS

A GDSS should support a process that brings together a group of decision makers to share information, exchange ideas, explore alternative solutions with the use of models and data, vote, and negotiate in order to arrive at a consensus. Such a system consists of a number of software modules acting as tools that support an aspect of this process. A GDSS may support one or more of the creativity techniques we have discussed. Thus, the group moves along the path of the decision-making process shown in Figure 10.5 or works on one of its stages, such as choice. It is the objective of a GDSS to enable group members to bring their skills to bear on the decision process, while counteracting possible negative group dynamics.

Members of a GDSS-supported group work at their personal workstation, rather than directly interacting with one another. Since many group decision-making techniques require that the group members work simultaneously, the group as a whole is able to work faster than without the GDSS support. The anonymity of many GDSS interactions and the avoidance of direct interaction with others play a role in preventing dysfunctional group behaviors. For example, interactions in a GDSS setting frequently encourage group members who would have otherwise kept their counsel, or perhaps deferred to others, to participate actively in the decision-making process.

A group working with a GDSS is actually participating in a decision-related meeting. Electronic meeting systems (discussed in Section 8.5) provide the general infrastructure. Settings for a GDSS session range from a face-to-face meeting for an executive planning group to a "meeting" of widely dispersed sales agents of an insurance company. With the support of a GDSS, the agents can discuss the desirable level of new insurance rates through their VDTs and a telecommunications network.

Three levels of GDSS capabilities may be distinguished (DeSanctis 1987):

1. *Level-1 GDSS* facilitate communication among group members. They provide the technology necessary to communicate: decision rooms, facilities for remote conferencing, or both. These facilities were discussed in Section 8.5.

2. *Level-2 GDSS* contain the communication capabilities of the Level-1 GDSS and also provide support for the decision-making process. Thus, they furnish DSS modeling capabilities and software that support group decision processes. Level-2 GDSS thus facilitate activities involved in brainstorming, the Delphi technique, the nominal group technique, or other group processes.

Some of the software tools available to the participants in an electronic meeting using the GroupSystems (developed at the University of Arizona and available from Ventana Corporation of Tucson, Arizona) are:

- Session Manager that assists in meeting planning with an electronic questionnaire and with an agenda development tool.

- Electronic Brainstorming System that allows participants to enter comments simultaneously (and anonymously) into any of the topic files.

- Idea Organizers for combining ideas generated during brainstorming and moving to consensus.

- Prioritizing Tool for voting and ranking, with the ability to specify and assign weights to a set of criteria.

Figure 10.12 shows how the GDSS software tools may be used to come up with a set of prioritized and elaborated ideas for a problem solution (e.g., "How do we compete with Company X in California?").

Figure 10.12

A sequence of use of GDSS tools (From J. F. Nunamaker and others, "Electronic Meeting Systems to Support Group Work," *Communications of the ACM,* 34, no. 7, July 1991, pp. 40–61.)

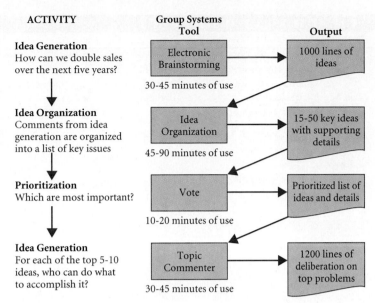

ACTIVITY	Group Systems Tool	Output
Idea Generation How can we double sales over the next five years?	Electronic Brainstorming 30-45 minutes of use	1000 lines of ideas
Idea Organization Comments from idea generation are organized into a list of key issues	Idea Organization 45-90 minutes of use	15-50 key ideas with supporting details
Prioritization Which are most important?	Vote 10-20 minutes of use	Prioritized list of ideas and details
Idea Generation For each of the top 5-10 ideas, who can do what to accomplish it?	Topic Commenter 30-45 minutes of use	1200 lines of deliberation on top problems

3. *Level-3 GDSS,* at this time still at the research stage, would formalize the desired patterns for group interaction, possibly by including expert systems that would suggest rules to be applied during a meeting. For example, Robert's Rules of Order may be automatically invoked by such a GDSS.

Characteristics of GDSS

Here are the distinguishing characteristics of GDSSs at their present stage of development:

1. Aside from the database, model, and dialog components of DSS, GDSSs also contain a communication component. This component, implemented with the organization's local or wide area communication facilities, or the Internet, may include electronic mail, teleconferencing, or various computer conferencing facilities. In this manner, GDSS may be integrated with groupware (discussed in Section 8.6).

2. GDSS should offer facilities for prompting and summarizing the votes and ideas of participants.

3. GDSS features, such as anonymity of interactions, the layout of the decision room, and the design of the dialog subsystem, should encourage both the formation of a cohesive group and the active participation of all its members.

4. GDSSs expand the model base to include models supporting group decision-making processes. Models for voting, rating, and ranking should accompany other statistical models. It should be possible to run a Delphi session with rounds of voting, anonymous opinion sharing, and arrival at a consensus; or a brainstorming session, by collecting the ideas from the participants, eliminating redundant ideas, and summarizing the results.

5. It should be possible to obtain the protocol of a group decision-making session for later analysis. A collection of such protocols from the more important decision-making sessions may be preserved as part of organizational memory.

6. GDSS should support a facilitator responsible for the orderly progress of a session. This individual should be able, for example, to route individual screen contents to the large common display. Some sessions also profit from the presence of a leader.

IN THE SPOTLIGHT

Using Group Support Technology to Develop the Economic Policy of New Zealand

The competitive position of New Zealand in global markets was of concern to the country's leaders. As the local market shrank due to a recession, it became more than ever obvious that the country's well-being depended on growth in export earnings. Cooperative efforts of companies in several industries, such as furniture, software, tourism, and agricultural technology, were required to upgrade their competitive position abroad.

Twelve meetings of the leaders of these and other industries were held. The meetings had four key objectives:

1. To involve a large number of the country's business leaders with a wide variety of backgrounds.

2. To assist business competitors to move beyond price competition in local markets and seek opportunities for joint action in order to upgrade the competitiveness of their industries in world markets.

3. To develop business opportunities for ethnic groups such as the Maori who were suffering from high rates of unemployment.

4. To develop an action plan containing five initiatives that the participants were committed to implement.

Because of the intended broad and diverse participation, a decision was made to provide GDSS assistance to the meetings. The meetings were held at the Decision Support Center at the University of Auckland, equipped with an electronic meeting facility. Every participant was working on a PC. GroupSystems software was used. The meetings were run by an independent facilitator.

All 12 meetings, involving from 14 to 33 participants, followed the same format. The purpose was brainstorming the ideas for gaining competitive edge for the country's industry and then building a consensus for common action. The work was based on the model of a nation's competitiveness devised by Michael Porter of the Harvard Business School. According to Porter, this depends on the production factors (such as skilled labor and infrastructure) for a given industry, home demand for the industry's products, the pres-

Continued

Figure 10.13

A screen of the Electronic Brainstorming System used to collect comments relating to the industry competitiveness in New Zealand during electronic meetings (From Sheffield and Gallupe, 1993–94, p. 103.)

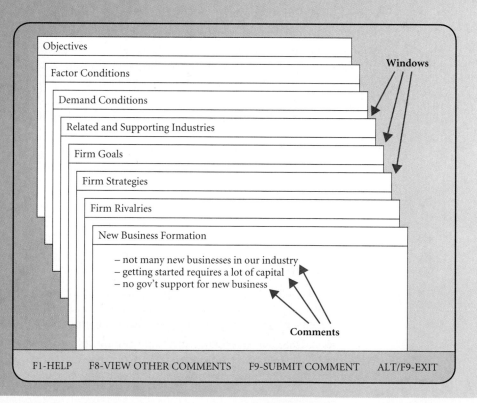

F1-HELP   F8-VIEW OTHER COMMENTS   F9-SUBMIT COMMENT   ALT/F9-EXIT

ence of strong supplier and other related industries, as well as the conditions for the creation, organization, and competition of companies. The Electronic Brainstorming System of GroupSystems was used to help generate ideas on the topics relating to these competitiveness factors (see Figure 10.13).

The participants, who could work anonymously, wrote comments into the appropriate windows, which could be viewed by all. They could elaborate on the comments of others. Some 25 minutes were spent on each topic, after which the topic was discussed. Voting was done with the prioritizing tool. The facilitator summarized the topic on a large whiteboard. Subsequently, the participants worked out an action plan and affirmed their commitment to its implementation, largely in personal discussions.

The electronic meetings were highly rated by the 240 participating business leaders. The meetings were found effective in generating action plans. They were also efficient, since the participants felt that during each meeting, three-days' work was accomplished in a single day. All action plans stimulated follow-on ac-

tivity and, two years after the meetings, action was continuing on 17 out of 36 plans.

Not all industries succeeded in furthering collective action. Yet, four industry groups—furniture, small business, software, and yachting—did. The project leaders in these industries ascribed much of the success to the ability to exchange information, fostering openness and trust, during the GDSS-assisted meetings. New joint business associations are implementing the action plans. Most participants felt that it was the intensity of the meetings, involving many participants and enabled by the electronic meeting tools, that resulted in long-term effects.

Based on Jim Sheffield and R. Brent Gallupe, "Using Electronic Meeting Technology to Support Economic Policy Development in New Zealand: Short-Term Results," *Journal of Management Information Systems,* 10, no. 3, Winter 1993–94, pp. 97–116; and "Using Group Support Systems to Improve the New Zealand's Economy, Part II: Follow-up Results," *Journal of Management Information Systems,* 11, no. 3, Winter 1994–95, pp. 135–154.

GDSSs are a very active area of research and development in the field of information systems (Jessup and Valacich 1993). They are also being actively used by such firms as Boeing and IBM. The preceding vignette illustrates how a series of electronic meetings with the use of GDSS technology contributed to the development of a country's economic policy.

10.7 | EXECUTIVE INFORMATION SYSTEMS

Characteristics of EIS

Executive information systems (EIS) provide a variety of internal and external information to top managers in a highly summarized and convenient form. EISs are becoming an important tool of top-level control in many organizations. They help an executive spot a problem, an opportunity, or a trend. We have encountered the use of an EIS in the extensive Case Study in Chapter 2 and you have seen how such a system helps executives to identify a problem, find its source, and establish a course of action leading to the solution. Some EISs also have forecasting capabilities that can be used in an "automatic-pilot" fashion: They access the database and adjust their forecasts to the changing data. With these capabilities, EIS becomes a strategic planning tool.

EISs serve people whose time is at a premium and who are responsible for the long-term vision of the company's future in the competitive marketplace. These executives develop long-term strategic plans for the company and exercise strategic control by monitoring the organization's performance. Executive information systems therefore have these characteristics:

1. EISs provide immediate and easy access to information reflecting the key success factors of the company and its units.

2. "User-seductive" interfaces, presenting information through color graphics or video, allow an EIS user to grasp trends at a glance. These systems generally are used directly (without intermediaries) by senior managers who cannot be expected to deal with complicated interfaces. Simple point-and-click devices and touch screens make keyboards unnecessary. Little or no training is needed to use the system.

3. EISs provide access to a variety of databases, both internal and external, through a uniform interface. Indeed, the fact that the system consults multiple databases is often transparent to the users. Along with tabular and graphical numerical information, textual informal information should be available as well. Such information may include notes, comments, opinions, and interpretations. External databases are available via the Internet and the electronic information services discussed in Section 8.4. Using them, EISs can provide news, data from securities markets, trade and industry data, and other up-to-date data and information. Through the use of intelligent agents (see Chapter 8) on the Internet's World Wide Web, it is possible to bring up-to-date information on the competitive environment into EIS in a systematic fashion (King and O'Leary 1996).

4. Both current status and projections should be available from EIS. Indeed, it is frequently desirable to investigate different projections for the future. In particular, planned projections may be compared with the projections derived from actual results (as we saw in the Case Study for Chapter 2).

5. An EIS should allow easy tailoring to the preferences of the particular user or group of users (such as the chief executive's cabinet or the corporate board).

6. EIS should offer the capability to "drill down" into the data. In other words, it should be possible to see increasingly detailed data behind the summaries.

EISs can be best understood by contrasting them with DSSs, which they complement. While DSSs are primarily used by middle- and lower-level managers to project the future, EISs primarily serve the control needs of higher-level management. The relationship between these two types of information systems, EIS and DSS, is shown in Figure 10.14.

Seen in the light of the structure of a decision-making process, EISs primarily assist top management in uncovering a problem or an opportunity. Analysts and middle managers can subsequently use a DSS to suggest a solution to the problem. More recently, EIS-type applications are coming into use by middle managers as well.

At the heart of an EIS lies access to data. EISs may work on the data extraction principle, as DSSs do (see Figure 10.7), or they may be given access to the actual corporate data-

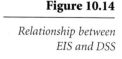

Figure 10.14

Relationship between EIS and DSS

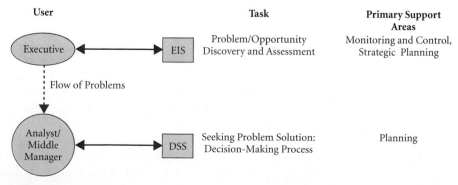

Selling an Executive Information System

Photo 10.1

"You can read these reports or you can get the information instantly with your executive information system," Douglas Stensvad of Nation-Bank's Dealer Financial Services told the executives (From Nick Wreden, "Sharpening the Corporate Vision," *Beyond Computing,* March–April 1994, pp. 29–32.)

Even though you may be persuaded about the advantages of EIS as you read this text, executives do not always flock to using such a system. Sometimes, a little selling is necessary. You can see in Photo 10.1 how Douglas Stensvad, vice-president of Nation-Bank's Dealer Financial Services (of Greensboro, North Carolina), did it.

"To illustrate the usefulness of our EIS," he tells us, "I took a box filled with 5,000 sheets of paper [reports] into a presentation and told the attendees they had two alternatives. They could wait for the box to arrive once a month and then look through all 5,000 sheets to find the necessary information, or they could use

our EIS and be able to analyze the most current information within 10 to 15 seconds."

Now, the executives of the company—a leading provider of auto loans—have all the data from the previous day available to them by 8:30 in the morning, summarized in the form they favor. The executives use the information to track interest rate yields, loan quality, expenses, and other performance indicators they select. Results that are below projections are displayed in red, while numbers that exceed forecasts are shown in green.

The bank's EIS has been developed using Focus/EIS for Windows generator from Information Builders. From their PCs, the executives can access the detailed loan data stored on a mainframe. Soon, the information will be distributed via a wide area network to regional offices as well. The implementation took more than two years, spent largely on getting the massive amounts of data into the system's database. At this time, the company wants to push the EIS down the ranks, making some of the data available to the marketing representatives who work out of their home or car.

Based on Nick Wreden, "Sharpening the Corporate Vision," *Beyond Computing,* March/April 1994, pp. 29–32.

bases or data warehouses. The first kind of EIS can fully reside on personal workstations. EISs, of the second kind need the power of servers to access corporate data. Any technical problems of EIS data access pale in comparison with the problem of potential resistance from managers below the top level, whose day-to-day performance becomes highly visible. Once an EIS has been set up, its executive users are able to obtain virtually instantly any information supported by the EIS data—unfiltered by and unbeknownst to their subordinates. Therefore, some organizations place a limit on the level of detail available via EIS. However, as the vignette above shows rather vividly, the concept of EIS also needs to be sold to their future executive users.

Developing EIS

What information should EIS provide? In the design of EIS, developers frequently rely on the **critical success factors (CSF)** methodology developed by John Rockart of MIT (Rockart 1979). He defined CSFs as "those few critical areas where things must go right for the business to flourish." With the use of this methodology, executives may define just the few indicators of corporate performance they need. Many executives have already fallen into the habit of reviewing these indicators on a regular, sometimes daily, basis. With the drill-down capability, they can obtain more detailed data behind the indicators. An executive who is experienced with such a system can perceive a trend (and a problem) in seconds.

As opposed to the CSF methodology, which relies on individual critical success factors, the **strategic business objectives methodology** of EIS development takes a company-wide perspective (Volonino and Watson 1991). Following the identification of the strategic business objectives of a firm, the critical business processes are identified and prioritized. Then, the information needed to support these processes is defined, to be obtained with the EIS

Figure 10.15

Competitive revenue analysis produced with an executive information system (EIS). Starting with the first screen, the decision maker "drills down" to obtain an increasingly detailed picture. We can see from the second screen that Competitor 1 has almost closed in on our company, and we can obtain the third screen to compare four financial ratios for our company and its two leading competitors in order to analyze the situation further. (The screens were obtained with Pilot EIS of Pilot Executive Software of Boston, Massachusetts.)

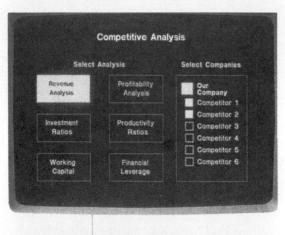

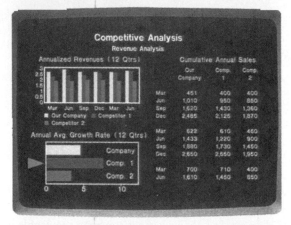

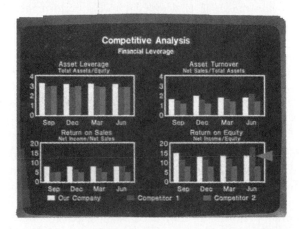

that is being planned. Finally, an EIS is developed to report on the CSFs. This methodology avoids the frequent pitfall of aligning an EIS too closely to a particular sponsor.

EISs are usually built with EIS generators, which help to configure a specific EIS. In the United States, Commander EIS (by Comshare of Ann Arbor, Michigan) and Pilot Command Center (by Pilot Executive Software of Boston) are the leading EIS generators. RESOLVE from Metapraxis (New York and of Kingston upon Thames, Great Britain) is a leader in Europe. After the information the EIS has to provide is established as discussed above, iterative development with prototyping is the methodology of choice for building these systems. Successful development usually requires an executive sponsor who supports the project.

Three screens from a Pilot EIS application, shown in Figure 10.15, bring home the principal features of EIS: use of graphics, crispness of presentation, strength in evaluating the competitive position of the company, and the ability to see the message at a glance (well, if you have some experience glancing).

Systems that combine the information-accessing capabilities of an EIS with the decision-support capabilities of a DSS are becoming available. They are known under the name of executive support systems.

S U M M A R Y

Decision support systems (DSS) are interactive information systems that assist a decision maker in solving ill-structured problems, when solutions require a combination of human insight and computerized support. DSSs permit the decision maker to apply an analytical model to a collection of data drawn from a database. A model is a simplified representation of a real-world entity which can help in understanding the entity. For example, a planning model can help us understand the financial operation of an enterprise.

By using a DSS in the "what-if" mode, the decision maker can develop several scenarios with different input values and compare the outcomes. By goal seeking, the decision maker can set a goal and determine which input values are necessary to achieve it.

Three principal components of a DSS are: data management that supplies data to which the models can be applied; model management that maintains the library of models; and dialog management that supports the user in applying models to data.

The principal classes of DSS are those that provide data access, support data analysis, enable the user to apply simple or more complex models, and those that include models that suggest decisions.

The three levels of DSS technology are: specific DSS, DSS generators, and DSS tools. DSS can be built by the quick-hit approach, through a life-cycle development, or via iterative development (with prototyping), the favored approach for personal DSS.

Group decision support systems (GDSS) support communication and decision making in a group. They help the decision-making group share information, exchange ideas, compare alternative solutions with the use of models and data, vote, and negotiate in order to arrive at an agreement. GDSS enable the group members to work simultaneously and anonymously.

Executive information systems (EIS) provide a variety of internal and external information to top managers in a highly summarized and convenient form. They help an executive spot a problem, an opportunity, or a trend. EIS should be easy to use and easy to tailor to the preferences of individual users. They should also permit the user to "drill down" into the detailed data. EIS should make it easy to track the critical success factors of the enterprise, that is, the few vital indicators of the firm's performance.

KEY TERMS

Decision support system (DSS)   *352*
Ill-structured problem   *352*
Model   *354*
"What-if" (scenario) analysis   *355*
Goal seeking   *355*
Decision-making process   *355*
Data management subsystem   *360*
Model management subsystem   *362*
Dialog management subsystem   *362*
Representational model   *364*
Optimization model   *365*
Suggestion model   *365*
DSS generator   *366*

Quick-hit development   *367*
Life-cycle development   *367*
Iterative development (prototyping)   *367*
Prototype   *367*
Group decision support system (GDSS)   *368*
Brainstorming   *369*
Synectics   *369*
Nominal group technique   *369*
Delphi technique   *369*
Executive information system (EIS)   *373*
Critical success factors   *375*
Strategic business objectives
   methodology   *376*

QUESTIONS

1. What are decision support systems (DSS)? What makes them different from other information systems?
2. How does the use of a DSS in a decision-making situation relate to the degree of the problem's structure? Give two examples of problems that would be ideally suited to the decision support approach. In each case, what part of the decision process would be handled by the DSS?
3. Which of the following should be implemented as decision support systems:
   a. A marketing lead subsystem that maintains information about the interest of prospective clients for various product lines.
   b. A manufacturing subsystem that helps allocate orders to several plants in the firm.
   c. An accounting subsystem that reports all the accounts receivable due for longer than 30 days.
   d. A human resources subsystem that assists in assigning overtime work to employees based on their earnings over the last quarter.
4. What is a model? Give a brief example of a model that can be used in a DSS.
5. How does "what-if" analysis with a DSS differ from goal seeking? Explain and give an example.
6. State three DSS features that you consider to be the most important. What is the organizational role of each of the features you have selected?
7. Show in a diagram the three principal DSS subsystems. Label the interconnections between them in terms of what data or information are being sent in each direction.
8. What are the best uses of presentation graphics in DSS?
9. Give three examples of DSS, each designed for solving a class of practical problems. One example should be a data analysis system; the second—a system based on a

representational model, and the last—a system based on an optimization model.
10. What is the relationship between a specific DSS and a DSS generator? Under what circumstances would you acquire a DSS generator for your company?
11. What is a prototype? Why is iterative development the most commonly recommended method for developing a DSS?
12. What are group decision support systems (GDSS)? How do they differ from DSS?
13. Name and describe two creativity techniques in group decision making. Under what circumstances would you use each of these techniques?
14. Name and describe three distinguishing characteristics of GDSS. What capability does each of them provide for the organization that deploys the GDSS?
15. What are executive information systems (EIS)?
16. Name three distinguishing features of EIS that you consider to be the most important. What capabilities does each of them offer the EIS users?
17. What is the relationship between DSS and EIS? Who is most likely to use each of the systems?
18. What are the two principal methodologies used in developing an EIS? What are their comparative advantages and drawbacks?

ISSUES FOR DISCUSSION

1. Discuss the possible effects of the use of DSS on the decision making in organizations. Consider both the individual DSS and the large organizational DSS.
2. Discuss what role the anonymity of the users plays in the effectiveness of GDSS use.
3. A vice-president of Kraft Inc., who is a user of EIS and whose division sells 500 products to 33,000 grocery stores, says that since he and his colleagues started to use

EIS, "we conduct our work lives differently." What, do you think, does he mean by that? Include a discussion of the possible effects of drill-down by top executives to investigate detailed activities of the organization's members. Do you believe ethical issues can be involved?

PROBLEM-SOLVING EXERCISES

1. Modeling with a Spreadsheet   Produce a worksheet of financial performance for your company, Technology Interests, Inc., for the next five years.

Assume that your sales will start at $100,000 annually and grow 20 percent a year. Your expenses include both production and nonproduction costs. Production costs consist of cost of materials (starting at $30,000 a year), cost of labor (starting at $15,000), and your overhead running at 40 percent of these two costs. Labor and material costs grow at 15 percent a year each. The nonproduction costs (R&D, engineering, marketing, and administration) make up 30 percent of sales. Your profit is your sales minus your expenses.

Your firm has to pay 40 percent tax on profits. You need to compute the profit after taxes for each of the five years and the profit-to-sales ratio based on this net profit.

a. Print a worksheet with the appropriate headings. The items in the worksheet should be: sales, production expenses (individual items and the subtotal), nonproduction expenses, total expenses, profit, taxes, profit after taxes, and profit/sales ratio for each of the five years.

b. Print out the worksheet with only its formulas showing.

c. Produce bar graphs of your profits and of the profit/sales ratio for the five years.

d. What if the taxes go up by 10 percent in the second year of operation? Produce the corresponding worksheet and the bar graphs.

e. Based on the analysis of the results of the previous situation, make a decision to lower some of your costs in order to compensate for the tax increase and to keep the profit after taxes growing steadily. Write a managerial summary of your decision.

2. Modeling with a DSS Generator   If you have access to a DSS generator, develop a simple planning model (similar to the one shown in Figure 10.1). Obtain printouts showing your use of the model to answer two "what-if" questions and a printout showing a solution to a goal-seeking problem. You may also perform this exercise with a spreadsheet.

Should you be able to perform the exercise with *both* a DSS generator and spreadsheet, compare the facilities offered by these two tools. Comment on the ease with which you were able to perform your task in each of the two environments.

3. Review the use of EIS in the Case Study for Chapter 2. Write a memo stating the conclusions of the problem-solving session at Diverse Industries and detailing the process through which the conclusions were arrived at.

TEAM PROJECT

Each two- or three-person team will study a selected group creativity technique. The book by J. Daniel Couger listed in the references is a good source; several relevant articles are also listed in the references for the chapter. Based on the review of a GDSS setting and GDSS features, the team will recommend how to best deploy a GDSS to stimulate group creativity using a given technique. The team should also analyze the potential limitations of GDSS use and suggest ways to overcome them. Desirable features for future GDSS may be suggested. Selected teams will make a report to the class, so that an integrated picture of GDSS use for group creativity can emerge.

SELECTED REFERENCES

Alter, Steven L. *Decisions Support Systems: Current Practice and Continuing Challenges,* Reading, MA: Addison-Wesley, 1980.

Belardo, Salvatore; Peter Duchessi; and John R. Coleman. "A Strategic Decision Support System at Orell Fussli." *Journal of Management Information Systems,* 10, no. 4, Spring 1994, pp. 135–158.

A case study describing the development and use of a DSS for strategic decision making by the 500-year-old Swiss printing company.

Benbasat, Izak, and Barrie R. Nault. "An Evaluation of Empirical Research in Managerial Support Systems." *Decision Support Systems,* 6, 1990, pp. 203–226.

Couger, J. Daniel. *Creativity and Innovation in Information Systems Organizations,* Danvers: Boyd and Fraser, 1996.

DeSanctis, Gerardine, and R. Brent Gallupe. "A Foundation for the Study of Group Decision Support Systems." *Management Science,* 33, no. 5, May 1987, pp. 43–59.

A foundational paper on GDSS.

DeSanctis, Gerardine; Marshall S. Poole; and George Desharnais. "Using Computing in Quality Team Meetings." *Journal of Management Information Systems,* 8, no. 3, Winter 1991–92, pp. 7–26.

Experience with using GDSS to support quality improvement programs.

Gardner, Dana M. "Cashing in with Data Warehouses and the Web." *Databased Advisor,* February 1997, pp. 60–63.

George, Joey F. "The Conceptualization and Development of Organizational Decision Support Systems." *Journal of Management Information Systems,* 8, no. 3, Winter 1991–92, pp. 109–125.

How to develop a DSS to support organizational decision making, rather than the individual decision makers.

Haley, Barbara J., and Hugh J. Watson. "Using Lotus Notes in EISs," *Information Systems Management,* Winter 1996, pp. 38–43.

How to combine the capabilities of the most popular groupware product with those of an EIS.

Jessup, Leonard M., and Joseph S. Valacich, eds. *Group Support Systems: New Perspectives,* New York: Macmillan 1993.

A collection of papers presenting the state of the art in GDSS.

King, David, and Daniel O'Leary. "Intelligent Executive Information Systems." *IEEE Expert,* 11, 6, December 1996, pp. 30–35.

How to regularly bring the relevant external information from the Internet into an EIS.

Lim, Lai-Huat, and Izak Benbasat. "A Framework for Addressing Group Judgment Biases with Decision Technology." *Journal of Management Information Systems,* 13, no. 3, Winter 1996–97, pp. 7–24.

How GDSS may be used to avoid biases in group decision making.

MacCrimmon, Kenneth R., and Christian Wagner. "Stimulating Ideas through Creativity Software." *Management Science,* 40, no. 11, November 1994, pp. 1514–32.

Nagasundaram, Murli, and Robert P. Bostrom. "The Structuring of Creative Processes Using GSS: A Framework for Research." *Journal of Management Information Systems,* 11, no. 3, Winter 1995–96, pp. 87–114.

Rainer, R. Kelly, Jr., and Hugh J. Watson. "The Keys to Executive Information System Success." *Journal of Management Information Systems,* 12, no. 1, Fall 1995, pp. 83–98.

What factors lead to successful development and operation of EIS, according to the practitioners who have achieved this success?

Rockart, John F. "Chief Executives Define Their Own Data Needs." *Harvard Business Review,* March–April 1979, pp. 81–93.

Silver, Mark S. *Systems That Support Decision Makers: Description and Analysis,* New York: John Wiley & Sons, 1991.

Analytical approach to DSS.

Simon, Herbert A. *The New Science of Management Decision,* New York: Harper & Row, 1960.

A classic work on managerial decision making.

Sprague, Ralph H., Jr. "A Framework for the Development of Decisions Support Systems." *MIS Quarterly,* 4, no. 4, June 1980, pp. 1–26.

A foundational paper.

Stohr, Edward A., and Benn R. Konsynski, eds. *Information Systems and Decision Processes,* Los Alamitos, CA: IEEE Computer Society Press, 1992.

A collection of papers surveying the field of DSS and offering future perspectives.

Turban, Efraim. *Decision Support and Expert Systems: Management Support Systems,* 4th ed., Englewood Cliffs, NJ: Prentice Hall, 1995.

A contemporary textbook.

Volonino, Linda, and Hugh J. Watson. "The Strategic Business Objectives Method for Guiding Executive Information Systems Development." *Journal of Management Information Systems,* 7, no. 3, Winter 1990–91, pp. 27–39.

Watson, Hugh J.; R. Kelly Rainer; and George Houdeshel. *Executive Information Systems: Emergence, Development, Impact,* New York: John Wiley and Sons, 1992.

A collection of essential papers on EIS.

CASE STUDY | How a Decision Support System Was Developed for Banking and the Lessons Learned

A large commercial bank engaged consultants, expert in DSS, to develop a system to support establishing prices the client bank would pay for money market deposits (we know these prices as interest rates). The system was expected to forecast future rate trends in the bank's local market for such short-term deposits and estimate the market share the bank would attain by setting the rates at various levels. Obviously, the higher the rate the bank would pay the depositors, the more deposits would flow to the bank rather than to its local competitors.

The interest-rate decisions were made weekly. Each decision had to be made quickly. The intended users of the system were the bank's product managers, who had no inclination to conduct long analysis sessions to set the rates. Therefore, the success of the system depended not only on accurate projections, but also on the ease and speed with which a product manager could use it. In other words, the complexity of statistical models that would result in satisfactory projections had to be hidden from its users.

Consequently, the developers divided the project into two parts. The first part was establishing a set of statistical models for generating projections. The models would be maintained through periodical review by a specialist in operations research. The second part of the project was to develop a user-friendly interface designed for the product managers who had to interact with the models.

The statistical models were built by an operations researcher from the historical data on interest rates and deposits (i.e., "so much money was deposited when the rates were at this level"), covering the client bank and its competitors. The data were obtained from the client bank and from the Federal Reserve Bank. The model equations were developed by using regression: arriving at the equation of the dependence between the deposits and interest rates, based on the available data points. The Minitab statistical package was employed to generate the equations.

The following general requirements were determined for the user interface:

1. Allowing the user to perform a wide range of activities, including projection of future rates, examination of impacts of interest rates decisions by the client bank or by competitors, sensitivity analysis (for example, how much can we vary a rate before the outcome would change significantly), reporting of findings, and updating the data.

2. Allowing both graphical and tabular presentation of historical and projected data.

3. Protecting the models and data from inadvertent modification by the user.

4. Ease of use and modification, with the following aspects:
   - Little training required before the product managers could use the system.
   - Quick response to the user, to encourage use of the system, and moreover, to encourage examination of alternative scenarios during such use.
   - Ease of system modification and documentation.

5. Developing the system with a software tool that the client bank already owned.

Based on the last requirement, it was decided to reject the development in a higher-level language, such as C, or in a DSS generator package, such as IFPS. Since the client owned and was familiar with the Lotus 1–2–3 spreadsheet, which has excellent graphics capabilities, the decision was made to develop the user interface in the spreadsheet's macro language. All the other requirements were judged to be satisfied by this choice. The system was to be used on managers' personal computers.

The user interface was developed by prototyping, since (as is most often the case) the users could not precisely define the system requirements. To save time to system delivery, the interface prototyping was to proceed in parallel with the model development. The initial prototype of the interface could be developed in a satisfactory fashion using a grossly simplistic model.

The user interface ultimately included 30 menus, 15 reports, and 20 graphs, generated by more than 1,000 lines of Lotus 1–2–3 macro code. More than one year of historical data

Figure 10.16

The graph, generated by the DSS in August, shows six months of historical deposits (March through August) and the projection for the next six months, based on a given scenario (in millions of dollars)

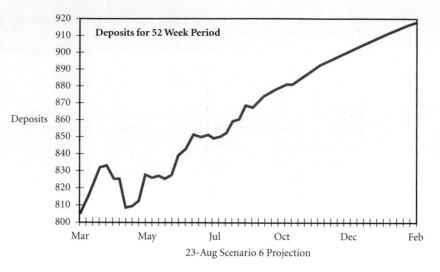

23-Aug Scenario 6 Projection

were included, with the ability to project and analyze up to two years of future data. A typical graph generated by the system is shown in Figure 10.16.

Sensitivity analysis is shown in a tabular form in Figure 10.17. You can see the projected average deposits for the future six-month period based on a small change in two variables: the interest rate paid by the bank and the bank industry average rate (reported by the Donoghue service). For example, if the bank does not change the interest rate it will pay during the period, while the average interest rate paid by all banks (as reported by Donoghue) also remains unchanged, the bank's deposits at the end of the period will be $895.2 million. However, should the bank lower the rate it pays by 0.1 percentage point, while the prevailing rate does not change, the amount of money market deposits in the bank will fall to an estimated $894.3 million. Thus, a drop of $900,000 is to be expected due to the decreased attractiveness of the interest rate.

As we can see, with this decision support system the bank's managers gained the ability to make informed decisions. However, many managers continued to reach their decisions based on their experience, without using the system. Actually, they used the system after the decision was reached, to see whether it supported their conclusions. When it did not, some managers questioned the system's usefulness. Yet, after several months of use by the bank, the DSS seemed to attract a growing number of users.

Aside from this important implementation lesson, here is what the consultants learned from the completed project:

1. As the prototype was being developed using simplistic models, it was difficult to keep the client focused on the properties of the user interface and the system capabilities, rather than discussing the output of the admittedly unfit model.

2. Because low-speed PCs were used by the product managers, sensitivity analyses (such as that of Figure 10.17) were taking 15 to 20 minutes to complete. This led the managers to avoid generating alternative "what-if" scenarios and use the system to "run the numbers" on the alternative already selected without using the system.

3. The graphical presentations were initially found impressive by the bank managers and bolstered their decision to continually fund the project. However, as we can see in Figure 10.16, the historical data shows the full actual drama with a jagged

		CHANGE IN RATE PAID BY THE BANK				
		0.20%	0.10%	0%	−0.10%	−0.20%
	0.20%	$895.6	$894.8	$893.9	$892.9	$891.9
CHANGE	0.10%	$896.3	$895.4	$894.5	$893.6	$892.7
IN	0.00%	$896.9	$896.0	$895.2	$894.3	$893.4
DONOGHUE	−0.10%	$897.4	$896.6	$895.8	$895.0	$894.1
	−0.20%	$898.0	$897.2	$896.4	$895.6	$894.7

Figure 10.17

The table, generated by the DSS, shows how sensitive are the projected average deposits (in millions of dollars) to changes in two variables: the interest rate paid by the bank and the average rate (reported by Donoghue service)

pattern (until August), while the projected data largely show a trend. This sharp contrast, a characteristic of forecasting techniques, decreased confidence in the forecasts. Tabular display or statistical smoothing of the historical data could have removed the contrast.

4. The decision to use a spreadsheet rather than a DSS generator was found questionable. Spreadsheet macros are not self-documenting; that is, they are difficult to understand. Even with the inclusion of generous comments, this relatively large-scale DSS resulted in code that is difficult to maintain (read, understand, and modify).

Based on Edward J. Cale, Jr., and Steven E. Eriksen, "Design and Implementation Issues for a Banking Decision Support System," *Journal of Systems Management,* April 1994, pp. 18–21.

CASE STUDY QUESTIONS

1. Describe the three fundamental DSS components as implemented by this system. Do you feel that (as described here) two of them were paid more attention than the third one? What are your suggestions for organizing this third component in a disciplined fashion?

2. Consider the problem-solving process, as shown in Figure 10.5.
   a. What was the intended use of the DSS in terms of this process? Map the intended rate-setting steps on the figure.
   b. How did some of the product managers use the system without taking full advantage of its capabilities? Map their steps on the figure.

3. How would you classify the types of problems for which this DSS was designed in terms of the degree to which they are structured? Explain.

4. Consider what was learned from the implementation of this DSS. What was each of the lessons and what would you do (with 20/20 hindsight) to correct each problem? What would be the foreseeable consequences of each such correction, however?

5. How can a system such as this DSS affect the future decision making in the user organization?

CHAPTER ELEVEN

Expert Systems and Applied Artificial Intelligence

OBJECTIVES

After you complete this chapter, you will be able to:

1. Define the field of artificial intelligence (AI).

2. Define an expert system (ES).

3. Specify and discuss the areas of ES application.

4. Specify the components of an expert system.

5. Define knowledge base and knowledge representation.

6. Explain what rule-based expert systems are.

7. Define fuzzy logic.

8. Specify the categories of expert system technology.

9. Define the roles in expert system development.

10. Specify the principal benefits and limitations of expert systems.

11. Name other applied fields of artificial intelligence and discuss their potential role in information systems.

12. Define neural networks and their capabilities.

OUTLINE

Delivering Marketing Expertise to the Front Lines

Customer service representatives (CSR) of a telephone company are the people you speak to when you order new products and services. AGT, a Canadian telecommunications company, headquartered in Edmonton, Alberta, realized that the golden opportunity to market its myriad products and services occurs when a customer calls with an order. However, reps are not trained marketers. Moreover, the turnover in CSR jobs is high and, with the increasing availability of new services, it is difficult to keep the reps up to date. To solve the problem, AGT has made marketing expertise available to the CSRs with an expert system called, naturally, CSR Advisor.

Use of the CSR Advisor at AGT is replacing the conventional customer-service process, during which the rep enters customer information, service and product selection as requested by the customer, and installation details, all as a series of numeric codes. Since the rep also has to perform a number of manual calculations to assess service charges, the process is error-prone and leaves little opportunity to market additional services.

In contrast, CSR Advisor makes the marketing expertise, provided by experienced marketers, easily available to the CSRs. This expertise, stored in the expert system's knowledge base, relates the characteristics of the customer to the service and product recommendations. In addition, marketing scripts that appear on the PC screen provide the justification for the recommendations the rep will make. For example, "Based on what you have told me about your business, I recommend that you add call forwarding to your service."

CSR Advisor introduces a consistent flow of marketing and order-taking for all CSRs. First, the reps collect information about the customer, then they recommend the services, and only afterwards explain the products that are needed to deliver these services.

Processing of recommendations is divided between the part of the expert system that is resident on the mainframe, where the customer database is also located, and the expert system part running on the PCs used by the reps. The marketing knowledge base, that is, the rules that relate services and products for recommendation to the characteristics of the customers, is also located on the PCs. Thanks to this set-up, marketing personnel can adjust the marketing rules to changing market conditions and to the feedback gained from the use of the knowledge base. A window-based graphical user interface makes the system simple to use even for novice reps. Seasoned CSRs can use a short-form interface instead of a full script.

An eight-week evaluation of CSR Advisor was conducted in one of AGT's business offices, to compare the sales performance achieved with the results from the use of the conventional method the year before. Also, a simultaneous comparison was made with another office. The results of the expert system-supported marketing surpassed expectations. The orders taken with the CSR Advisor generated $94 on average, as compared to $55 a year earlier, and compared to $24 for orders taken in an office where conventional order-taking was used. In addition, CSR Advisor reduced the training time for CSRs and the error rate in order taking. It will now serve as a test bed for new marketing tactics.

One problem was discovered during the trials: The marketing personnel were unable to modify the knowledge base without the assistance of a knowledge engineer.

Although order-taking with the extra marketing took slightly longer, the average revenue per minute rose by 35 percent.

Based on Clayton D. Stafford and Johannes de Haan, "Delivering Marketing Expertise to the Front Lines," *IEEE Expert*, April 1994, pp. 23–32.

The field of artificial intelligence (AI) extends a vibrant promise of a future machine with the human capabilities of perceiving and reasoning. The most important applied area of AI is expert systems— vehicles for gathering, organizing, and delivering knowledge in a specific limited domain. Other areas include natural language processing, robotics, vision systems, speech recognition, and machine learning. A different research approach produced neural networks. Fuzzy logic has been used to perform approximate reasoning in some expert systems. All of these systems are significantly limited when compared with the human capabilities they are expected to imitate—but developments proceed apace.

11.1 | WHAT IS ARTIFICIAL INTELLIGENCE?

The field of **artificial intelligence (AI)** is concerned with, as *Encyclopaedia Britannica* tells us, "methods for developing computer programs (or software-hardware systems) that display aspects of intelligent behavior" (Zwass 1988). Human intelligence itself remains poorly defined. In most general terms, intelligence is associated with goal-oriented, adaptive behavior. In other words, intelligence is the ability to understand a complex situation and respond to it successfully; the ability to learn; and the ability to bring knowledge and reasoning to bear in solving problems.

Characteristics of AI Systems

How do AI software systems compare with conventional software? How are they different from the technologies underlying management reporting or transaction processing systems?

1. Symbolic Processing

In AI applications (other than the artificial neural networks that we will discuss in the last section of this chapter), computers process symbols rather than numbers or letters. This is different from obtaining numeric values through a series of database accesses and arithmetic computations. It is also different from word processing, where words are manipulated without reference to their meaning. AI applications process strings of characters that represent real-world entities or concepts. The terms "customer" and "profit" are examples of such symbolic strings. Symbols can be arranged in structures such as lists, hierarchies, or networks. These structures show how symbols relate to each other. For example, an expert system relies on its knowledge base that shows the relationship among symbols in its domain of operation. Owing to their ability to process symbols, AI programs deal with the general domain of human thinking; we usually think in symbols, not numbers.

2. Nonalgorithmic Processing

Computer programs outside the AI domain are programmed algorithms; that is, fully specified step-by-step procedures that define a solution to the problem. The actions of a knowledge-based AI system depend to a far greater degree on the situation where it is used. For example, an action—such as an expert system's recommendation or the movement of a

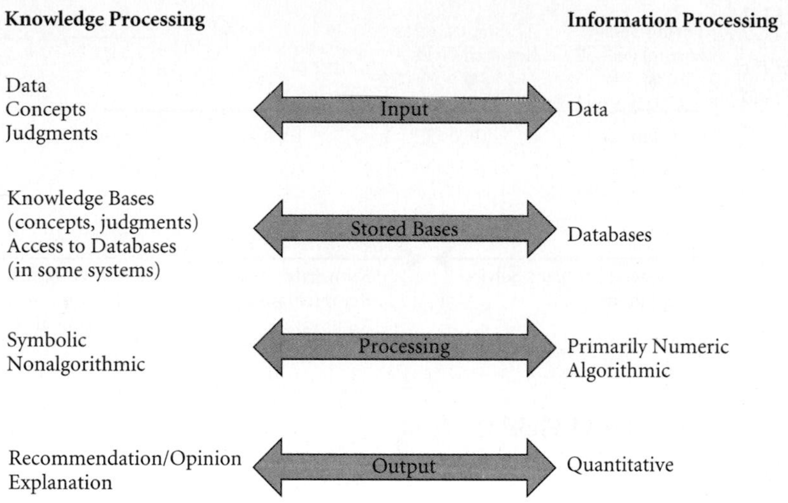

Figure 11.1

Knowledge processing contrasted with information processing

Knowledge Processing   **Information Processing**

| Data Concepts Judgments | Input | Data |

Knowledge Bases (concepts, judgments) Access to Databases (in some systems) — Stored Bases — Databases

Symbolic Nonalgorithmic — Processing — Primarily Numeric Algorithmic

Recommendation/Opinion Explanation — Output — Quantitative

robot's arm—is based on knowledge about the domain, procedures for knowledge processing, and facts about the situation at hand. A well-designed AI system works properly in situations not foreseen by its designer.

The distinctions between the information-processing approach of a system based on non-AI technologies and the knowledge-processing approach of an expert system are summarized in Figure 11.1.

The Field of AI

Artificial intelligence is a highly dynamic field of research, which can already point to a series of spectacular successes that have entered computing practice. A much longer path still lies ahead if AI is even to approach its ambitious goals. Paradoxically, the hardest, and as yet largely unsolved, problems of AI are those we think require no particular intelligence. For example, in understanding speech, comprehending a scene being viewed, or displaying common sense in an unexpected if simple situation, AI systems cannot match children.

A certain degree of controversy surrounding AI arose from hitching the field to the ill-defined concept of intelligence. We do know now that AI systems can reason about concepts—a signal feature of human intelligence. However, polemics persist over whether these systems "understand" concepts (do they really understand, or just manipulate character strings according to rules?). At this time, AI presents no clear and present danger to humans as the unique "thinking reeds." Humans can conceptualize, that is, create concepts—say, a concept of time, or the much simpler concept of a business meeting—and their thinking can be creative. Humans learn in many ways and can bring past experience to bear on a problem, while AI systems display only a very limited learning capacity. Most important, human cognitive and perceptive faculties are integrated into a whole that is greater than the sum of its parts: Each of us is a very general-purpose system. We operate in multiple domains, rely on several senses, and use our faculties for perception and communication, and our limbs for locomotion and a host of other activities.

An *artificial* intelligence system is narrowly focused on a specific domain, be it rendering a diagnosis of a specific eye disease or recognizing a scene in a theater of war. But such a system does have its practical advantages. It is permanently housed in a computer system, where it can be accessed relatively easily from many locations. It works consistently, and it thoroughly brings to bear all it "knows" on a situation.

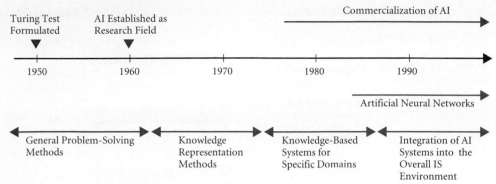

Figure 11.2

*The development of the
AI field*

How the AI Field Evolved

The idea of cognition as a form of computation—in other words, that computing machines can perform reasoning tasks—has its roots in the philosophical speculation of the seventeenth and eighteenth centuries. The ultimate potential of computers as intelligent machines was forecast by the brilliant British mathematician Alan Turing. In 1950 he formulated what is known as the Turing test: A machine performs intelligently if an interrogator using remote terminals cannot distinguish its responses from those of a human.

The early period of AI research culminated in the famous Dartmouth Conference of 1956, where the name "artificial intelligence" was coined. The principal characteristic of this founding period was the belief in a General Problem Solver (the actual name of a major program): a general problem-solving technique that would be usable across a variety of applications.

A major and extremely fruitful shift in thinking about AI occurred in the late 1960s. Researchers realized that the power of an AI system does not lie in its inferencing (reasoning) facility, but primarily in the knowledge methodically gathered, represented, and stored in its knowledge base. Knowledge-based expert systems were the result. For roughly the next decade, techniques of knowledge-based systems were developed and perfected in research laboratories.

Then, in the late 1970s, the era of AI commercialization began. It was led by the use of expert systems in a variety of business environments. An organizational environment where many and complex decisions have to be made calls for systems that can relieve humans of at least some of these tasks, and perhaps best humans in consistency and thoroughness. The declining costs of computer hardware have made some systems of this type cost-effective. At this time, AI systems are being integrated into such information systems as transaction processing and decision support systems.

In the mid-1980s, the so-called connectionist perspective on AI had become influential. It resulted in the practical development of artificial neural networks, resembling the interconnected neuronal structures in the human brain. While knowledge-based systems aim to imitate the *results* of human cognitive processes, the connectionist perspective relies on imitating the actual operation of the brain (in reality, of a small part of it).

Recently, AI approaches have been used to develop *intelligent agents,* software that performs assigned tasks on the user's behalf; this was previously introduced to you in Chapter 8. In particular, the agents find uses on the Internet's World Wide Web, where they can regularly seek out desired information, make purchases, or monitor specific events, according to the owner's preferences (Hendler 1996).

The development of the AI field is sketched out in Figure 11.2. We will survey the principal areas of applied AI after a thorough discussion of expert systems.

11.2 | CAPABILITIES OF EXPERT SYSTEMS: GENERAL VIEW

An **expert system** (ES) is a knowledge-based system that employs knowledge about its application domain and uses an inferencing (reasoning) procedure to solve problems that would otherwise require human competence or expertise. The power of expert systems stems primarily from the specific knowledge about a narrow domain stored in the expert system's **knowledge base**.

The name "expert system" evokes a feeling of exceptional, perhaps superhuman, expertise. Indeed, the best and the most expensive of these systems are truly expert in their performance. Over the course of a number of consultations (advice-seeking sessions) with such a system, we may obtain results surpassing the performance of experts in the field.

It would be a mistake, though, to believe that all expert systems have capacities equivalent to a human expert advisor. Some systems proffer decisions as a competent professional or paraprofessional would, within a narrow, highly focused task domain, such as diagnosing a product's quality defect or figuring out the best mailing service for a given package. A consultation with such a modest ES is shown in Figure 11.3. In general, expert systems are assistants to decision makers and not substitutes for them.

The use of expert system technology in an organization, as we will discuss further on, begins with finding reasonably (but not overly) ambitious projects that require an active knowledge delivery vehicle at the point "where the rubber meets the road." If you need a system to advise you how pertinent tax regulations could affect your company's investments,

Figure 11.3

Consultation with an expert system (Courtesy Computer Associates International, Islandia, New York.)

What type of package is it … Letter, Pak, Box, Tube?

= > Box

How much does the package weigh in pounds?

= > 4

Please tell me the state where you want to send this package.

= > CA

Which city? (If it's a suburb, enter the major city name.)

= > Los Angeles

What delivery services is required… Same day, Overnight, Two Day, Anytime?

= > Overnight

What is the combined length and girth of the package? I only need to know this if you think the sum of the length and girth exceed 84 inches. Otherwise, just press return.

= > <RETURN>

ATTN MR./MS. WARNER

After careful consideration, I have selected OTD as your best alternative, at a cost of $14.50. The selection was based on sending a 4 pound parcel with a delivery requirement of OVERNIGHT to LOS ANGELES, CA.

—Other Alternative Carriers—

EconoMail	*$26.56*
Fast Freight	*$21.00*
Overland Express	*$18.45*
Speed Shipping	*$23.00*

or how your existing personnel policies apply to a specific employment case, you would use an expert system. Such a system would draw on its voluminous knowledge about the domain (tax regulations or employment policies, respectively) and bring that knowledge to bear on the facts of the particular case, in a consistent fashion, with all the relevant factors.

The knowledge base of an expert system contains not only what one may call "book knowledge" about the domain. More important, it also contains **heuristic knowledge**— rules of thumb used by human experts who work in the domain. For example, a human credit manager might know that if an individual has had a poor credit history over the last five years, but has been employed for the last two with no adverse credit experiences during this period, then a credit transaction up to a certain limit should be approved. In the company's experience, known to its expert authorizers, this is a prudent policy. This rule can be incorporated into the expert system's knowledge base. Let us then look more closely at the application of expert systems.

11.3 | APPLICATIONS OF EXPERT SYSTEMS

Let us consider several examples of successfully fielded expert systems—systems that have actually been implemented in a business environment. This will give you a feeling for the capabilities of the technology. We will then classify the generic areas of ES application.

Minicases of Expert System Applications

1. Oracle Electronics Trading Company uses a Credit Advisor. The expert system identifies high-risk credit decisions based on the figures in a customer company's financial statement. It also makes about 90 percent of the credit-granting decisions in these cases, with the remaining 10 percent passed on to a top-level decision maker. The ES presents to the decision maker the reasons why the system had its doubts. Before the Credit Advisor was deployed, the decisions regarding credit were made by human decisions makers and passed on to the firm's chief executive for disposition. Now, the executives no longer have to spend time rendering credit decisions, the company's procedures manual no longer has to be consulted (and perhaps interpreted inconsistently by various people), and most credit-related decisions are made promptly.

Risk assessment is, in general, an area of ES strength. ESs that assess risks are used by banks and other credit companies to make loans and by stock traders to handle portfolios. Many firms do not publicly proclaim the capabilities of these systems, since the systems are believed to give their owner companies a competitive edge.

2. Expert systems are used to combine qualitative judgment with quantitative data in advertising decision making. A system developed for direct marketers analyzes each name on a mailing list. The system screens out unworthy names based on such data as the person's last direct-mail purchase, frequency of response to previous mailings, and demographic characteristics (such as age or zip code).

Potential marketing applications of expert systems can go beyond analyzing the contents of marketing databases. Expert systems can also help shape advertising strategies based on the system's judgment of the current strategies of the firm's competitors and of potential competitor responses to future changes in the industry environment. Expert systems can also assist in selection of the copy (that is, the text) and layout for advertisements based on voluminous qualitative research on the subject, or in allocating a budget for advertising a product brand among different media.

3. Expert systems shine in many aspects of manufacturing, where their use can contribute to higher productivity and quality. The fact that much factory work has shifted to knowledge work is stressed by the father of expert systems, Edward Feigenbaum, and his colleagues (1988), who tell us that factory "touch" work (all the machining, assembling, and handling) accounts only for approximately a third of total costs. A full two-thirds of the manufacturing costs can be chalked up to knowledge work: design, engineering, quality assurance, sales, and management. The productivity of the "touch" work can be increased by robotics; expert systems, along with other information systems, can have an even far more significant impact by reducing the other two-thirds of manufacturing costs.

An expert system implemented at Northrop Corporation, a major producer of jet fighter planes, is responsible for the planning of manufacture and assembly of up to 20,000 parts that go into an aircraft. A planner is able to enter a description of the engineering drawing of a part, and the ES will tell him or her which materials and processes are needed to manufacture it. The system speeds up the actual planning work by a factor of 12 to 18. The time needed to complete this task has been reduced from several days to about four-and-a-half hours, including a fifteen-minute session with the expert system. The payoff of the ES is easy enough to compute.

Generic Categories of Expert System Applications

We have discussed some illustrative cases. We can now classify the general areas where you should consider applying an ES. These categories of application are listed in Table 11.1 in the order of increasing difficulty. We will now illustrate these categories with examples of commercially fielded systems.

General Electric's Metal Analyst system identifies (that is, *classifies*) common metals and alloys, based on density, color, and simple tests that can be performed by a non-metallurgist. The knowledge base of the system contains 212 rules. To take a very different example, the U.S. Department of Energy uses an expert system to determine the security classification of documents.

Diagnosis systems, generally more complex than a simple classification (of faults, for example), are widely used in industrial settings. Indeed, the origins of ES are in medical diagnosis. Canadian Pacific Railroad uses an expert system to diagnose impending failure in its diesel locomotives (with 98 percent accuracy) based on the impurities found in a sample of engine oil. The American Stock Exchange uses its Market Surveillance expert system to

Table 11.1	**Application Area**	**Problem Addressed**
Generic areas of ES application (expanded and adapted from Hayes–Roth and others, 1983)	Classification	Identify an object based on stated characteristics
	Diagnosis	Infer malfunction or disease from observable data
	Monitoring	Compare data from a continually observed system to prescribed behavior
	Process Control	Control a physical process based on monitoring
	Design	Configure a system according to specifications
	Scheduling and Planning	Develop or modify a plan of action
	Generation of Options	Generate alternative solutions to a problem

IN THE SPOTLIGHT

Payback from Expert Systems

Insurance companies are among the most avid users of expert systems. The companies use the technology for fraud detection in both underwriting and in processing claims, in target marketing of insurance products, and in validating the applications for insurance made out in the field.

One insurer utilizing an expert system for evaluating risk exposure is The Hartford Steam Boiler Inspection and Insurance Company (HBS) of Hartford, Connecticut. The company's goal is loss prevention and so, in the words of its vice-president, "we proactively work with customers to take measurements of their equipment and, through data acquisition and data analysis, we report recommendations to customers." One of the expert systems developed by the company is DataAlert, which incorporates the rules used by HBS's most experienced prevention experts to evaluate the condition of rotating equipment—pumps, turbines, and generators. The measurements of vibration, temperature, and the condition of the lubricating oil are sent from the customer's site to headquarters via telecommunications networks and stored in an Oracle database. The expert system analyzes the data stored there and draws its conclusions, which are transmitted to the insured customers, who can then view on their PCs the developing trends in a graphical form.

Quick payback on DataAlert came during a single incident at a Texas oil refinery that HBS insures. The expert system found a turbine with high vibration levels. Thanks to the early detection, $20 million in losses in property damage and business interruption were avoided.

Based on Susana Schwartz, "Artificial Intelligence: Reviving the Love Affair," *Insurance & Technology*, August 1996, pp. 42–44.

---

diagnose whether a suspected trading irregularity (such as insider trading) warrants further investigation (Lucas 1993). In the Focus Minicase, we read how a Credit Advisor diagnoses high-risk credit decisions.

Monitoring can be thought of as continuous diagnosis. Westinghouse uses and sells expert systems for continuous on-line monitoring of steam turbines and generators. *Process control* expert systems monitor a production process and generate continuous messages to the operator aiming at optimizing operations; such real-time control is employed at one of the Nestlé food processing plants.

Allen-Bradley Company employs an expert system to *design* or *configure* sophisticated computer-integrated manufacturing (CIM) cells. A CIM cell, the hallmark of modern manufacturing, is automated machining equipment that can reconfigure itself under computer control to produce a wide range of parts in lots from one to thousands. The cell utilizes many types of sensors, controls, cutters, and other equipment, thus including over 300 possible types of components. A human expert configures a cell in about a day. A 1,500-rule expert system does the job in a few minutes, based on a salesperson's specifications. Fielded worldwide, the system is strategically important to maintain Allen-Bradley's competitive position.

Stone & Webster Engineering Corporation uses an expert system to *schedule* power production. This ES makes it possible to employ not only optimization routines but also heuristics, for example, those regarding the availability of start-up and maintenance crews. The particular strength of ES-based systems is the ability to reschedule promptly when a contingency or emergency arises (Sauer and Bruns 1997). Let us look at a very different example. During the Winter Olympics in Lillehammer, Norway, local police used an expert system to produce assignments that covered all venues adequately at all times, while complying with Norway's strict employment laws. After the Olympics, the system was rolled out to police and sheriff's offices throughout Norway.

The U.S. Space Command uses an expert system to *plan* satellite launches. The system also plans future launch capability to match the requirements for satellites. The five-year launch plan is maintained on a daily basis to assess the impact of such contingencies as failures during a launch or in orbit. We should note here that general organizational planning is too broad a task for expert systems at this time.

A group at IBM Los Angeles Scientific Center has developed an expert system designed to help business managers identify competitive applications of information technology. Using a framework for competitive market analysis similar to that presented in Section 3.5 and a knowledge base of cases of strategic information systems, the ES facilitates the *generation of options* in a search for potential strategic systems.

As the preceding vignette vividly illustrates, an expert system (diagnosis-oriented, in this case) can pay for itself in a single use.

11.4 | HOW EXPERT SYSTEMS WORK

The strength of an ES derives from its knowledge base—an organized collection of facts and heuristics about the system's domain. An ES is built in a process known as **knowledge engineering,** during which knowledge about the domain is acquired from human experts and other sources by knowledge engineers. The use of ES is often referred to as a consultation, which again stresses the role of the user in making the final decision. The two environments—knowledge acquisition and ES use—are shown in Figure 11.4, which also shows the interaction of the principal components of ES. The role of these components will be explained in this section. As we will see further on in the chapter, the facilities for expert system development and use are supplied by software packages (such as expert system shells). These facilities are combined with the knowledge base, which is specific to the given expert system.

The accumulation of knowledge in knowledge bases, from which conclusions are to be drawn by the inference engine, is the hallmark of an expert system. In this section, we will discuss how the ES consultation environment works; in other words, how knowledge is represented and how the reasoning is done. In the following sections, we will turn our attention to the development of ES, including knowledge engineering with the use of the knowledge acquisition facility.

Knowledge Representation and the Knowledge Base

As we already know, the knowledge base of an ES contains both factual and heuristic knowledge. **Knowledge representation** is the method used to organize the knowledge in the knowledge base. In contrast to knowledge bases, databases contain data of rather simple types—numbers, strings of text, or logical (true-false) values—organized into records that stand in quite simple relation to one another. Knowledge bases, on the other hand, must represent such notions as actions to be taken under different circumstances, causality, time dependencies, goals, and other higher-level concepts.

Several methods of knowledge representation can be drawn upon (see, for example, Zahedi 1993). Some of these approaches, such as frame-based systems, are employed for building very powerful ESs. A frame specifies the attributes of a complex object and frames for various object types have specified relationships. By far the most common method of knowledge representation used in business ES are production rules, which we will proceed

Figure 11.4

Structure of an expert system

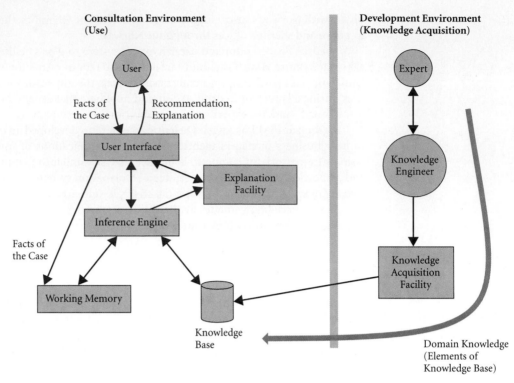

Consultation Environment
(Use)

Development Environment
(Knowledge Acquisition)

to describe. In the following discussion, therefore, we will concentrate on **rule-based expert systems:** expert systems in which the knowledge is represented by production rules.

A production rule, or simply a **rule,** consists of an IF part (a condition or premise) and a THEN part (an action or conclusion). We thus have this general form for rules:

IF condition THEN action (conclusion)

which is interpreted as:

IF the given condition occurs, THEN take this action (or draw this conclusion)

For example, a simple ES for selecting an advertising outlet for a product may contain, among others, these rules:

R5: IF product-category = toy
     or product-category = automobile
  THEN media = television.

R7: IF product-category = toy
     or product-category = baseball-cards
  THEN target-market = children.

R12: IF media = television
     and target-market = children
  THEN advertising-outlet = "Saturday Morning Cartoon".

R15: IF media = television
     and target-market = young-adult
  THEN advertising-outlet = "Late, Late Movie".

Rules are also used to identify the goal: what we are trying to establish with the use of the system. For example, in our case, we may have:

R1:   goal = advertising-outlet.

The rules are expressed in the language of the tool used to develop the particular ES. A simple ES contains 50 to 100 rules. During a consultation with the above system, the system will ask the user to supply the "product-category." Assuming that the user indicates "toy," the system will recommend that the "advertising-outlet" be "Saturday Morning Cartoon." Of course, the conclusions in useful systems are rarely so obvious.

The **explanation facility** explains how the system arrived at the recommendation. Depending on the tool used to implement the expert system, the explanation may be either in a natural language or simply a listing of rule numbers. For example, the recommendation of the advertising outlet may be explained as follows: "because of R5, R7, and R12." Explanations can help the users learn the domain covered by the expert system; they also increase the trust in the system (Dhaliwal and Benbasat 1996).

How are the rules of the knowledge base used to draw inferences? The rules are actually applied to the facts of the case by the inference engine of the expert system.

Inference Engine

The **inference engine** combines the facts of a specific case with the knowledge contained in the knowledge base to come up with a recommendation. In a rule-base expert system, the inference engine controls the order in which production rules are applied ("fired") and resolves conflicts if more than one rule is applicable at a given time. This is what "reasoning" amounts to in rule-based systems. The inference engine also directs the user interface to query the user for any information it needs for further inferencing.

The facts of the given case ("toy" in our example) are entered into the **working memory,** which acts as a blackboard, accumulating the knowledge about the case at hand. The inference engine repeatedly applies the rules to the working memory, adding new information (obtained from the rules' conclusions) to it, until a goal state is produced or confirmed. In our case, once the "advertising-outlet" is defined by R12, this goal state has been reached.

One of several strategies can be employed by an inferencing engine to reach a conclusion (or to reason, if you will). Inferencing engines for rule-based systems generally work by either forward or backward chaining of rules. The two strategies are contrasted schematically in Figure 11.5.

Forward chaining is a data-driven strategy: The inferencing process moves from the facts of the case to a goal (conclusion). The strategy is thus driven by the facts available in the working memory and by the premises that can be satisfied. The inference engine attempts to match the condition (IF) part of each rule in the knowledge base with the facts currently available in the working memory. If several rules match, a conflict resolution procedure is invoked; for example, the lowest-numbered rule that adds new information to the working memory is fired. The conclusion of the firing rule is added to the working memory.

In our example, if an input stating that the "product-category" is automobile then rule R5 will fire, and the value of "media = television" will be added to the working memory.

The inference engine repeatedly applies the rules of the knowledge base against the accumulating data in the working memory. In our example, if it had already been established through previous rule firings that the "target-market" is young-adult, rule R15 will fire to reach a goal state "Late, Late Movie" as the advertising outlet.

We may conclude that the forward-chaining inference method consists in repeatedly answering the question: What conclusions can be reached from the rules, given the data in the working memory?

A **backward-chaining** inferencing strategy works in the opposite direction: from a possible goal state to the premises that would satisfy it. Here, the engine attempts to match the assumed (hypothesized) conclusion—the goal or subgoal state—with the conclusion

Figure 11.5

Inferencing strategies

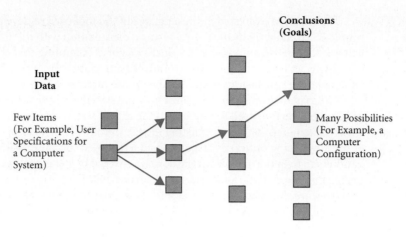

(a) Forward Chaining: IF–Part Matches Shown

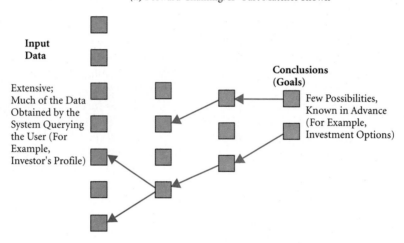

(b) Backward Chaining: THEN–Part Matches Shown

(THEN) part of a rule. If such a rule is found, its premise becomes the new subgoal. In an ES with few possible goal states, this is a good strategy to pursue.

For example, in our case the goal is to establish an "advertising-outlet." The first rule we have listed that matches the goal is R12; the goal state is "Saturday Morning Cartoon." The system will then back up and try to establish the validity of the two subgoals listed in the premises for this rule. If there is not enough information in the working memory to keep backing up, the system asks the user for information.

If a hypothesized goal state cannot be supported by the premises, the system will attempt to prove another goal state. Thus, possible conclusions are reviewed until a goal state that can be supported by the premises is encountered. Note that when the facts of the case are the same, both backward- and forward-chaining methods, of course, give the same results.

Backward chaining, more common in the expert systems currently developed, is best suited for applications in which the possible conclusions are limited in number and well defined. Classification- or diagnosis-type systems, in which each of several possible conclusions can be checked to see if it is supported by the data, are typical applications. These systems are, in general, simpler to write and use. They query the user as more data are needed to prove goals or subgoals.

Trying to Overcome the Brittleness of Expert Systems

Expert systems are notoriously brittle. When confronted with a situation unanticipated by its developers, an expert system is quite likely to reach a wrong conclusion. For example, a loan authorization system may approve a loan for an applicant whose "number of years at the current job" exceeds the applicant's age, or who applies for a loan from a penal institution. In these situations, a human would fall back on common sense.

A major attempt to build a knowledge base of human consensus knowledge (for example, what we mean by "buying"), intended to equip AI systems with common sense, is now under way. The project is led by Douglas Lenat. As part of the effort, Lenat and his colleagues scan newspapers and books, seeking what is *not* explained, since that is what readers are presumed to know and what needs to be stored in the huge knowledge base of this system.

Expert systems with access to this knowledge base (projected to include some 100 million rules) would be far less brittle. Business firms are beginning to use the results of this labor. Bellcore, for example, is working on an on-line expert assistant for customer advisers that would be far more flexible in "understanding" the problems faced by the telecommunication company's customers.

Started in 1984, Lenat's project Cyc (for en*cyc*lopedia) is expected to be completed in the early 2000s, with a chance of success estimated at 70 percent. The objectives of the project become broader as it continues: Researchers expect that the corpus of common knowledge they are compiling will help with the general tasks of information management. The system is considered a breakthrough technology, since it could provide the United States with a competitive advantage in the global marketplace.

Based on Douglas B. Lenat and others, "Cyc: Toward Programs with Common Sense," *Communications of the ACM,* 33, no. 8, August 1990, pp. 30–49; and R. V. Guha and Douglas B. Lenat, "Enabling Agents to Work Together," *Communications of the ACM,* 37, no. 7, July 1994, pp. 143–149.

Forward-chaining systems are commonly used to solve more open-ended problems of a design or planning nature, such as, for example, establishing the configuration of a complex product. The number of possible configurations is huge and, for practical reasons, not all configurations can be stated at the outset and then chained back from. Several powerful systems are of this nature.

The vignette above describes a most interesting project, whose results are supposed to overcome some of the limitations of expert systems.

Uncertainty and Fuzzy Logic

Many problem solutions with expert systems do not rely on exact knowledge. Rather, much of this knowledge is inexact and probabilistic. Since many knowledge rules supply such heuristic information, we can attach a *certainty* factor (CF) in the range from 0 (total uncertainty) to 100 (complete certainty) to them; for example:

R5: IF product-category = toy
         or product-category = automobile
       THEN media = television CF 90.

The certainty factor qualifies our confidence about the conclusion of the rule. The inference engine is able to perform a calculus of certainty factors and qualify the final recommendation by a cumulative certainty factor, which the user may then consider when acting upon the consultation.

An influential method of approximate reasoning is **fuzzy logic,** which is a method of reasoning with inexact propositions. It is the method of choice for handling uncertainty in

Fuzzy Logic Gives your Elevator that Fuzzy Feeling

We all complain about the irritating things elevators do. But some of us do something about it. Otis Elevator Company considered it a competitive necessity in the Japanese market to begin using fuzzy logic for finer elevator controls. The company installed its first elevators partially guided by fuzzy logic in a hotel in Osaka. This software controls the dispatching of elevator cars by aiming to minimize the wait time of passengers as well as to prevent crowding in the cars. It will not dispatch to a floor the car that is closest to it, if there is a less crowded car not much farther. Indeed, with fuzzy logic, more factors can be considered in controlling a device to increase the overall satisfaction of its users.

An interesting cultural observation was made when Otis's first elevator based on fuzzy logic, Elevonic 411, was installed in Osaka. The Japanese felt more strongly about reducing the longest waiting time than Americans do and it was necessary to adjust the logic

accordingly. The reason was that the persons who waited only a short time felt badly for a colleague who had to wait much longer. Reportedly, this problem was not encountered in New York.

Otis researchers are already developing the next generation of "smart" elevators. "Right now, elevators are reactive, not proactive," says Bruce Powell, a software engineer whose team is doing the development at the Farmington, Connecticut, headquarters of the world's largest elevator company. Neural networks, discussed further on in this chapter, will help the elevator to recognize patterns that may lead to congestion and prevent it.

Based on Jeanne B. Pinder, "Fuzzy Thinking Has Merits When It Comes to Elevators," *The New York Times,* September 22, 1993, pp. D1, D9; and Amal K. Naj, "Dumb Elevators Learn to 'Think' More Efficiently," *The Wall Street Journal,* April 15, 1996, pp. B1, B2.

some expert systems. It is also a hardware and software technology (used particularly broadly in Japan) aiming at more sensitive controls in camcorders, autofocus cameras, car brakes, heating and cooling systems in office buildings, and other applications. In all these systems, the input (which may be used as the "condition" for the IF part of a rule) is provided by sensors, and not by humans.

When we use fuzzy logic, we can express and use in reasoning such notions as "very high," "somewhat warm," or "reasonably good." In this logical system, we are not limited to the two, true or false, values of Aristotelian (or "crisp") logic. For example, if our system for rating suppliers considers companies with the total rating between 0.70 and 0.90 as "good" suppliers, how can we qualify a supplier with the rating of 0.68? It certainly would be wrong to classify the firm as not a good supplier. Fuzzy logic allows us to say (and use in further reasoning) that this supplier belongs to the set of good suppliers with a certainty factor of, say, 75.

Expert systems with fuzzy-logic capabilities thus allow for more flexible and creative handling of problems. These systems are used, for example, to control manufacturing processes (Gould 1995). Another, more common, use is illustrated by the vignette above. Among the development tools for such systems are TILSHELL of Togai InfraLogic (of Irvine, California), and Guru of MDBS (of Lafayette, Indiana).

11.5 | EXPERT SYSTEM TECHNOLOGY

As is the case with decision support systems, there are several levels of ES technologies, ranging from a specific expert system to programming languages. Simpler tools are quite accessible to end users, who indeed have developed a large number of smaller expert systems (containing on the order of 100 rules) in various enterprises. These tools generally run on personal computers. More elaborate tools require professional knowledge engineers in order to develop powerful systems.

The tool selected for the project has to match the capability and sophistication of the projected ES, in particular, the need to integrate it with other subsystems such as databases and other components of a larger information system. The tool also has to match the qualifications of the project team. Indeed, expert systems have been built to decide which expert system tools to use on a project! Various ES technologies are summarized in Figure 11.6 and are further discussed in this chapter.

Specific Expert Systems

Whenever you read about an expert system throughout this chapter, you were reading about a specific ES that actually provides recommendations in a specific task domain. A specific expert system can, of course, be more general in scope, or it can be specialized to a single model of an automobile engine so that it can diagnose malfunctions. Many companies believe that their expert systems provide them with a competitive edge, and their knowledge bases are thus kept confidential. Other specific ESs are marketed by their developers.

Historically, expert systems arose within artificial intelligence research as specific systems. Thus, MYCIN was developed at Stanford University as a rule-based expert system for the diagnosis of infectious blood diseases and for treatment recommendations. At some point, the researchers recognized the generic nature of the approach: Take away the knowledge base regarding blood diseases, and you are left with a shell that can inference from any appropriately represented knowledge base! They called the shell EMYCIN (for Empty MYCIN), and so expert system shells were born.

Figure 11.6

Expert-system technologies

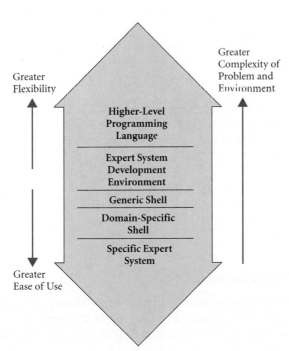

Expert System Shells

Expert system shells are the most common vehicle for the development of specific ESs. A shell is an expert system without a knowledge base. If we look again at Figure 11.4, we can conclude that such a shell furnishes the ES developer with the inference engine, user interface, and the explanation and knowledge acquisition facilities. Many of the end user-oriented shells also have an induction facility: You present a series of case examples with their conclusions and the system automatically builds the rules.

The capability to access databases is important in many applications. The fixed rules in the ES knowledge base are able to make recommendations based on the changing data in the database. Consider an ES for loan evaluation. Your expert system can process a database of loan applications, built up by a transaction processing system, once a week. Conversely, you can build an ES to decide whether an individual applicant qualifies for a loan based on a database of loan rates updated weekly.

Some shells offer a hypertext facility that allows for elaborate cross-referencing of information, a particular advantage in such applications as computerized policy manuals, on-line help facilities, or other reference systems.

As opposed to *generic shells* used to develop expert systems in any domain of application, **domain-specific shells** are actually incomplete specific expert systems, which require much less effort in order to field an actual system. For example, Picon, a domain-specific shell for oil-refinery applications, includes many knowledge rules about refinery operation and a user interface with icons useful in that environment. As another example, a Service Bay Diagnostic System built with a domain-specific shell for constructing diagnostic systems, required only 225 additional rules instead of the estimated 30,000 that would have been needed with a generic shell.

Some of the popular end user-oriented ES shells are listed in Table 11.2.

Expert System Development Environments

Expert system development environments, also listed in Table 11.2, expand the capabilities of shells in various directions. They run on engineering workstations, minicomputers, or mainframes; offer tight integration with large databases; and support the building of large expert systems. For instance, a system that runs in multiple hardware environments permits an ES to be developed on a personal computer and then ported to a mainframe for production use.

With development environments, knowledge bases can be modularized: Rules can be broken down into a set of modules, and these rule modules can be manipulated independently. Such systems also allow for sophisticated handling of uncertain information, support interaction of the ES with other programs, permit extensive customization of user interfaces, and offer many features that ensure the robustness of a professionally developed application for production use.

Development environments usually provide several alternative knowledge representations (for example, rules and frames) and several inferencing techniques beyond backward and forward chaining.

Higher-Level Programming Languages

Many original expert systems were developed with LISP, an AI language designed to process lists of symbols. Indeed, LISP was also used early in the commercial environment, particularly running on Symbolics workstations, which directly interpret and execute LISP code in

Table 11.2	Tool Name	Vendor
ES shells and development environments	*Rule-Based ES Shells for End-User PC Applications*	
	EXSYS EL	EXSYS, Albuquerque, New Mexico
	1st-Class	AICorp Waltham, Massachusetts
	Level5	Information Builders, New York, New York
	Personal Consultant Easy	Texas Instruments, Houston, Texas
	ES Development Environments	
	Aion Development System (ADS)	Aion Corporation, Palo Alto, California
	EXSYS Professional	EXSYS, Albuquerque, New Mexico
	Guru	MDBS, Lafayette, Indiana
	KBMS	AICorp, Waltham, Massachusetts
	KEE	IntelliCorp, Mountain View, California
	Personal Consultant Plus	Texas Instruments, Houston, Texas

hardware. Later, another influential AI language, Prolog, based on predicate calculus, began to be employed.

It is possible to develop an expert system with a general-purpose procedural language, and indeed, quite a few early systems were built in FORTRAN or PL/I. Several ES development environments have been rewritten from LISP into a procedural language more commonly found in the commercial environment, such as C or C++. This simplifies the integration of expert system technology with the more traditional information systems.

Considering the availability of shells and environments today, ESs are now rarely developed in a programming language. This is done only under special circumstances, in which particularly stringent performance or other special requirements that cannot be satisfied with higher-level tools are present. Even in some of these cases, custom programming may only augment the use of a development environment.

11.6   ROLES IN EXPERT SYSTEM DEVELOPMENT

Three fundamental roles in building expert systems are: expert, knowledge engineer, and user. When elaborate systems are built using flexible and complex tools such as development environments or using a higher-level programming language—and when integration with other systems is sought—the involvement of technical specialists proficient with these tools is essential.

1. Expert

The expert in the domain of a future ES is an indispensable person in its development. Much of the factual knowledge will be transferred into many a system from textbooks, manuals, policy statements, or bills of materials. However, it is the heuristic information, the problem-solving skills in the specialized domain, that will make the difference between success and failure of the system. Many an expert system is called "Mike-in-the-Box" or "Geoff's Book", since they reflect the distillation of an individual's many years of experience and application of knowledge. Large systems generally require multiple experts. It is crucial to identify individuals who not only perform in a superior fashion but who also have the desire and ability to transfer their knowledge to the system.

Culture Shocks

IBM Research Division was developing an expert system for financial marketing. Now successfully developed and fielded, the system assists marketing representatives of the company in financial marketing—generating a proposal for financing an expensive mainframe computer system to meet a customer's objectives. The expert system helps to design an acquisition plan attractive to a specific customer. The plan specifies the equipment and software that will be included, as well as details the financial impact of the acquisition on the customer's cash flow and budget.

A group of programmers was assigned to the project that until then was comprised only of knowledge engineers. The programmers were used to an orderly development of programs from the detailed specifications of what these programs were to accomplish. "When this group mixed with our AI developers, the cultural shock was evident to both sides," says one of the knowledge engineers. Due to the legitimate need to have a running system and to be able to respond to the demand for demonstration to various future users, the programmers wanted to see specifications, plans, and progress from one version of the system to another. The knowledge engineers, on the other hand, relied only on a very general statement of objectives for the system. They were busy learning the domain of the expert system and

trying out new ways to represent the knowledge. The orderly progress of system releases was not what they were interested in.

A culture clash arose also between the knowledge engineers and domain experts, whose knowledge needed to be tapped. The two groups simply did not speak the same language. The problem became manageable only when a reasonable prototype of the expert system was produced. The prototype served as a concrete reference for discussions. At the source of the problem were excessive expectations by domain experts, some of whom were also to be future users, as to the capabilities of expert systems. Some of the expertise was actually of too high a level to be implemented with the current state of the art in expert systems. As the development of the system progressed, it became impossible to implement computerized support for problem formulation and for special deals that would be applicable to certain customer situations. Support from the user organizations waxed and waned. Users' eagerness to use a prototype as if it were a finished system had to be resisted as well.

Based on James S. Griesmer, Se June Hong, and John K. Kastner, "How to Achieve FAME," in *Managing Expert Systems,* Efraim Turban and Jay Liebowitz, eds., Harrisburg, PA: Idea Group Publishing, 1992, pp. 389–421.

Acquiring knowledge from an expert is far from a trivial exercise. Much of the competence an expert displays is unconscious: it has become a habit honed over the years. Eliciting this tacit knowledge is difficult (Nonaka and Takeuchi 1995). Any systems analyst who has ever performed a user interview—which deals with far simpler and more objective questions than "What makes you think there is something wrong with the mixture in the vat?"—will appreciate the difficulties involved. Hence the need for a knowledge engineer.

2. Knowledge Engineer

The knowledge engineer has a dual task. This person should be able to elicit knowledge from the expert, gradually gaining an understanding of an area of expertise. Intelligence, tact, empathy, and proficiency in specific techniques of knowledge acquisition are all required of a knowledge engineer. Knowledge-acquisition techniques include conducting interviews with varying degrees of structure, protocol analysis (in which the expert performs the task and speaks about his or her thinking, which is recorded for subsequent analysis), observation of experts at work, and analysis of cases.

On the other hand, the knowledge engineer must also select a tool appropriate for the project and use it to represent the knowledge with the application of the **knowledge acquisition facility.** This facility is essentially a text editor, enhanced by the capability to check for inconsistencies. Thus, the knowledge engineer must be familiar with ES technology.

3. User

Expert systems are written for different categories of users. An advanced expert system is often used by another expert: The ES will provide an opinion which the human expert is able to set in context and evaluate. Physicians use diagnostic systems in this mode.

A non-expert may use an expert system as a domain consultant. A system that identifies alloys and metals for non-metallurgists acts in this fashion. A novice entering some field of endeavor can learn about the field from an expert system. The novice would do well to use the explanation facility and analyze its output.

A user may play all three roles (expert/knowledge engineer/user) at once. As we have already said, many simpler expert systems are actually developed by end users.

Larger systems are often developed with the assistance of programmers. The possible culture clashes among people playing different roles in ES development are described in the vignette on the preceding page.

11.7 | DEVELOPMENT AND MAINTENANCE OF EXPERT SYSTEMS

A system developed by an end user with a simple shell, with 50 to 100 rules in its knowledge base, is built rather quickly and inexpensively. Larger systems are built in an organized development effort. A prototype-oriented iterative development strategy is commonly used. ESs lend themselves particularly well to prototyping: A system with a few well-selected initial rules in its knowledge base can often do something sensible. This brings confidence and organizational capital to the developers. After the system is completed and placed in operation ("fielded"), it is maintained to remove imperfections and to keep up with changing requirements.

An iterative process for ES development and maintenance is shown in Figure 11.7.

Here are the steps of the methodology:

1. *Problem Identification and Feasibility Analysis.*   The problem has to be suitable for an expert system to solve. If you must smell the chocolate mixture in a vat in order to adjust the ingredients, it is unlikely that you can successfully implement an on-line ES control for the production process. James Martin, a well-known writer in the field of information systems, offers a telephone test: If you can fully describe how the problem is solved on the telephone, an expert system may be able to handle it.

Along with determining whether an ES is appropriate, system developers must find an expert (or experts who are in general agreement) for the project. At this stage, a subset of ES functionality that will go into the initial prototype should also be identified.

The cost-effectiveness of the system has to be estimated by establishing the approximate number of rules and determining the cost-per-rule in an environment similar to yours. The intangible benefits of garnering and saving the expertise of a retiring exceptional expert or the tangible benefits of rejecting fewer fundable loan applications are to be considered in determining cost-effectiveness.

2. *System Design and ES Technology Identification.*   At this stage, the system is actually being designed. In particular, the needed degree of integration with other subsystems and databases is established. Concepts that best represent the domain knowledge are worked out. The best way to represent the knowledge and to perform inferencing should be

Figure 11.7

*Development and
maintenance of expert
systems*

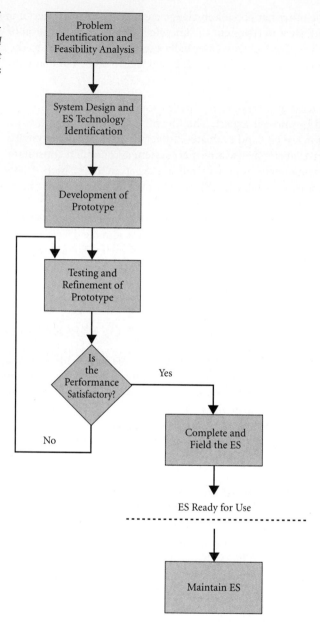

established with sample cases. The ES development tool is selected on the basis of these conclusions.

3. *Development of Prototype.*   Using the knowledge-acquisition facility, the knowledge engineer works with the expert to place the initial kernel of knowledge in the knowledge base. Knowledge acquisition techniques, discussed in the previous section, are used. The knowledge needs to be expressed in the language of the specific tool, such as the ES shell. The functionality of the prototype corresponds to that identified during Step 1.

4. *Testing and Refinement of Prototype.*   Using sample cases, the prototype is tested, and deficiencies in performance are noted. During the later stages of prototype refinement, end users make the best testers. The knowledge base continues to expand and be modified. To refine the knowledge base, knowledge engineers continue to work with experts. The end users ultimately test each new release of the ES. Throughout this stage, users need to understand that a prototype is not a completed system. The refinement cycles are repeated until the system achieves satisfactory performance on a variety of test cases.

5. *Complete and Field the ES.*   The interaction of the ES with all elements of its environment, including users and other information systems, is ensured and tested. A suite of test cases is run to validate the expert system and stored to validate future modifications. ES is documented and user training is conducted.

If the environment where the designed ES is running differs from the actual operational environment, the ES is installed in the latter. It is integrated with the organizational environment where it will operate, with the needed organizational changes carried out. Unless business processes are modified to take advantage of the system and unless user commitment is gained, the ES may fall into oblivion.

6. *Maintain the System.*   The system is kept current primarily by updating its knowledge base. However, with the exception of stand-alone systems, interfaces with other information systems have to be maintained as well, as those systems evolve. Large expert systems must be developed with maintainability in view—they will be maintained often and for a long time. Indeed, a number of successfully fielded expert systems proved to be unmaintainable and had to be abandoned (Gill 1995).

11.8 | EXPERT SYSTEMS IN ORGANIZATIONS: BENEFITS AND LIMITATIONS

Expert systems offer both tangible and important intangible benefits to owner companies. These benefits should be weighed against the development and exploitation costs of an ES, which are high for large, organizationally important ESs.

Benefits of Expert Systems

Expert systems assist individual knowledge workers much in the way colleagues, paraprofessionals, or instructors would. An ES is no substitute for a knowledge worker's overall performance of the problem-solving task. But these systems can dramatically reduce the amount of work the individual must do to solve a problem, and they do leave people with the creative and innovative aspects of problem solving.

Some of the possible organizational benefits of expert systems are:

- An ES can complete its part of the task much faster than a human expert. This may mean producing an immediate response for a customer asking for a credit decision or a lower downtime for an expensive piece of equipment being diagnosed.

- The error rate of successful systems is very low, sometimes much lower than the human error rate for the same tasks.

- An ES makes consistent recommendations. Given the same facts of the case, an ES will always proffer the same recommendation.

- ESs are a convenient vehicle for bringing to the point of application (via telecommunications networks, if needed) difficult-to-use sources of knowledge, such as voluminous procedure manuals or assembly instructions.

- An ES can capture the scarce expertise of a uniquely qualified (and possibly retiring) expert.

- An ES can become a vehicle for building up organizational knowledge, as opposed to the knowledge of individuals in the organization. This makes the company more independent of human vagaries, including personnel turnover. Knowledge bases become a part of organizational memory.

- When they are used as training vehicles, ESs result in a faster learning curve for novices.

- The company can operate an ES in environments hazardous for humans.

Both ES and decision support systems (DSS) address the crucial issue of organizations in the information society: coping with the rapidly increasing volume of complex decision making. They offer different, though complementary, capabilities. Table 11.3 summarizes and contrasts the capabilities of DSS and ES.

Limitations of Expert Systems

No technology offers an easy and total solution. While systems developed by an individual user for a limited task are surprisingly inexpensive, large systems are costly and require significant development time and computer resources. ESs also have their limitations. Among the limitations of expert systems and the concerns aroused by them are:

Table 11.3		**ES**	**DSS**
Comparison of ES and DSS (Modified from Turban 1995.)	Objective	Replicate a human expert	Assist human decision maker
	Organization Level	Mainly operational	Mainly managerial
	Who Recommends Decision?	The system	The human, assisted by the system
	Major Orientation	Automating use of expertise	Support of human decision-making process
	Problem Area	Narrow domain	Often a broad and complex domain
	Query Direction	System queries the human	Human queries the system
	Base of Support	Knowledge base of facts and heuristics (imprecise judgments)	Database of facts, largely numeric
	Manipulation	Symbolic reasoning	Numeric processing
	Explanation Capability	Major feature	Very limited
	Decision Problems Addressed	Repetitive	Ad hoc, often unique

1. Limitations of the Technology

The knowledge base of an expert system does not represent a causal model of the phenomena in its domain. The deep reasons for recommended actions are not investigated by an ES. This limits the class of applications of these systems (see Table 11.1) and precludes systems that require deeper analysis or approach creativity. The narrowness of the domain makes for brittle systems that cannot respond to situations an inexperienced user might expect them to be able to respond to. An expert system does not know what it does not know, and hence, care is required in its use.

Expert systems have no automatic learning capability. Improvement in performance has to come from system maintenance by knowledge engineers, which sometimes proves too costly. Good ESs perform impressively—but all of them make mistakes (just as human experts do).

2. Problems with Knowledge Acquisition

Tasks for an ES implementation have to be selected to ensure that:

- There is agreement on who the domain experts are.
- There is general agreement among experts in the domain on an effective approach to problem solving.
- A domain expert, recognized for his or her performance, is available and willing to work with knowledge engineers. The experts derive power from their knowledge and may be unwilling to cooperate, and they also have their primary jobs to do.

3. Operational Domains as the Principal Area of ES Application

Most expert systems support operational-level tasks and may be integrated with various transaction processing systems. Managerial roles (see Table 2.4) include few domains narrow enough to become the domains of expert systems.

4. Maintaining Human Expertise in Organizations

Paradoxically, reliance on an expert system may lead to a long-term weakening of innovation in the performance of the tasks the system is responsible for. Once they have acquired basic skills, people improve their performance by actually doing diagnosis, scheduling, or loan approving. If a large part of the task is handled automatically by an expert system, many workers do not acquire a "feel" for the actual task—and they may not be creative about it. Unquestioned assumptions, cast into expert systems, lead to a hardening of the organizational decision-making arteries. Organizational measures need to be taken to prevent this from happening. When you speak to the more thoughtful executives in companies where a strategically important system is 99 percent right, the executives express some of these rather surprising, but very real, concerns.

11.9 | OVERVIEW OF APPLIED ARTIFICIAL INTELLIGENCE

As we can see in Figure 11.8, expert systems are only one, albeit the most commercially prominent, of the areas of AI application.

Let us review other fields of AI research and as yet limited, but promising, practice.

Natural Language Processing

Computers have accustomed us to giving them instructions in a variety of "unnatural," computer-oriented programming languages, which we surveyed in Chapter 5. The time will

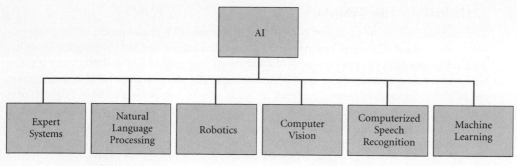

Figure 11.8

Applied fields of artificial intelligence

come, we hope, when we will design computers that can understand, to a large extent, our natural language, be it English or Japanese. Research on building natural language understanding into AI systems is flourishing, but the many levels of ambiguity and context dependence inherent in language make the general problem an extremely difficult one. What does "I saw a man on the hill with a telescope" mean, for example? Do I have the telescope or does the man have it? Who is actually on the hill?

However, limited-scope **natural language processing** systems are becoming rather common. The main application for a natural language system at this time is as a user interface for expert and database systems. For example, INTELLECT of Trinzic (Waltham, Massachusetts) enables business users to access information from corporate databases with requests in conversational English. Based on the vocabulary of an application and its own built-in dictionary, the system maintains a lexicon of terms it understands. The system paraphrases queries, "echoing" its interpretation of them to the user. It also recognizes ambiguous or unclear queries. Observe the user-system interaction shown in Figure 11.9. After the system establishes during the first query that the user means the city, rather than the state, of New York, it is able to correctly interpret the next reference to New York in that context.

Since the early days of computing, there has been hope for computerized translation of natural language. Present commercial translation programs can perform a rough translation in a specific technical field, producing an output that requires extensive human editing. The narrower the domain of the program, the better its performance.

Robotics

A **robot** with AI capability (simpler robots do not have it!) is an electromechanical manipulator able to respond to a change in its environment based on its perception of that environment. This implies that such a robot has a sensory subsystem (usually computer vision), and is programmed to interpret what it "sees" and to act upon the interpretation. For example, an industrial robot can manufacture one of many parts in its repertoire and manipulate it in order to inspect it for defects, recognizing very small departures from established standards.

Robots have been used extensively in the advanced industrial countries of the world, particularly in Japan (there are about 46,000 robots in the United States, but six to eight times as many in Japan). Robots are reliable, consistent, accurate, and insensitive to hazardous environments (see Photo 11.1). Also, let's face it, these "steel collars" do not do many things we wish their human counterparts would not do. However, the abilities of most robots are limited. For example, in a car assembly line, robots are employed only in such tasks as welding seams and installing windshields (Munakata 1994).

Figure 11.9

*The INTELLECT
natural-language query
system resolving an
ambiguity through
echo feedback*
(Intersolve, Inc.)

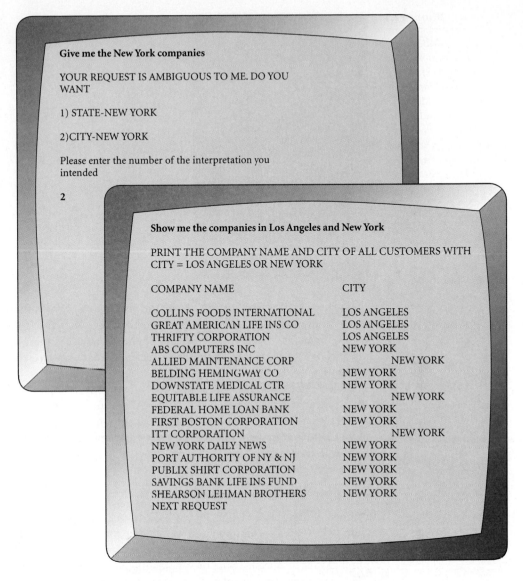

Give me the New York companies

YOUR REQUEST IS AMBIGUOUS TO ME. DO YOU
WANT

1) STATE-NEW YORK

2) CITY-NEW YORK

Please enter the number of the interpretation you
intended

2

Show me the companies in Los Angeles and New York

PRINT THE COMPANY NAME AND CITY OF ALL CUSTOMERS WITH
CITY = LOS ANGELES OR NEW YORK

COMPANY NAME	CITY
COLLINS FOODS INTERNATIONAL	LOS ANGELES
GREAT AMERICAN LIFE INS CO	LOS ANGELES
THRIFTY CORPORATION	LOS ANGELES
ABS COMPUTERS INC	NEW YORK
ALLIED MAINTENANCE CORP	NEW YORK
BELDING HEMINGWAY CO	NEW YORK
DOWNSTATE MEDICAL CTR	NEW YORK
EQUITABLE LIFE ASSURANCE	NEW YORK
FEDERAL HOME LOAN BANK	NEW YORK
FIRST BOSTON CORPORATION	NEW YORK
ITT CORPORATION	NEW YORK
NEW YORK DAILY NEWS	NEW YORK
PORT AUTHORITY OF NY & NJ	NEW YORK
PUBLIX SHIRT CORPORATION	NEW YORK
SAVINGS BANK LIFE INS FUND	NEW YORK
SHEARSON LEHMAN BROTHERS	NEW YORK
NEXT REQUEST	

At this time, a mass advent of robots with an appreciable degree of artificial intelligence is still a vision for the future. The two promising research directions pursue autonomous vehicles (such as the one in Photo 11.1) that can be guided by their own vision systems, and micro-electromechanical systems, micro-robots smaller than a cubed millimeter, that can, for example, cruise human blood vessels to perform surgery.

Computer Vision

The simulation of human senses is a principal objective of the AI field. The most advanced AI sensory system is **computer vision,** or visual scene recognition. The task of a vision system is to interpret the picture obtained, for instance, with a camera. These systems are employed in robots or in satellite systems, for example. Simpler vision systems are used for quality control in manufacturing. Such vision systems are applied particularly successfully to the inspection of silicon chips and circuit boards.

Photo 11.1

AMBLER, an autonomous robot designed to explore the surface of Mars (From Takeo Kanade, Michael L. Reed, and Lee E. Weiss, "New Technologies and Applications in Robotics," *Communication of the ACM,* 37, no. 3, March 1994, pp. 58–67, p. 60.)

After a camera obtains the image, the vision system scans it and breaks it down into pixels, that is, dots with fixed positions in the image. After that, the system determines the highlights of the object in the picture. Then, the object is matched with an image in an image database, and thus identified or rejected as unknown. Present systems work in a narrow domain of images.

Most digital image processing does not involve the complexity of computer-vision systems. Once the image has been digitized by the scanning process, many kinds of computerized image processing are possible (for example, undesirable faces can be edited out of the picture); but the AI component of computer vision is the actual recognition of the object—"scene understanding."

Computerized Speech Recognition

Understanding spoken language is a basic human faculty. The ultimate goal of the corresponding AI area is **computerized speech recognition,** or the understanding of connected speech by an unknown speaker, as opposed to systems that recognize words or short phrases spoken one at a time or systems that are trained by a specific speaker before use. The most successful general systems used today—for example, systems for automated telephone services—limit themselves to very small vocabularies of 10 to 20 words (digits, "yes", and "no" prevail). On the other hand, speaker-dependent dictation systems have vocabularies that range up to 60,000 words, as we saw in Chapter 4.

Speaker-independent recognition techniques for connected speech that rely on recognizing only individual words are inadequate. The best system of this sort today, SPHINX of Carnegie Mellon University, has an error rate of over 20 percent on a vocabulary of 1,000 words. Researchers are seeking further progress by incorporating higher-level knowledge sources, such as syntax, semantics, and pragmatics (knowledge of the context of the utterance) into the design of these systems. In other words, they are attempting to integrate speech recognition with natural language processing.

A future "intelligent typewriter" with built-in translation ability may become only one illustration of the general fact that, by combining the AI capabilities, we may be able to create any number of imaginative products. Some of them appear within our grasp, while others are still well beyond it.

Machine Learning

Probably the most fascinating area of AI research is the work on learning systems. What *is* learning? A system with learning capabilities—**machine learning**—can automatically change itself in order to perform the same tasks more efficiently and more effectively the next time.

The notion of learning is very broad. In the simplest interpretation of this capability, a system may "learn" by self-adjusting a few numerical parameters. A more advanced learning system is able to acquire new concepts and relate them to the knowledge already stored in its knowledge base. A learning capability can potentially be incorporated into any type of system falling into the AI domain. Because it would continually learn as it works, such a system would keep improving its performance. For example, a vision system could more accurately recognize scenes, and a rule-based expert system could develop new rules for its knowledge base and modify the existing rules.

A number of approaches to learning are being investigated (Liang 1993). One of these approaches is learning by problem solving. For example, as a rule-based expert system is applied to problems, it can accumulate "experience" about its rules in terms of their contributions to correct advice. The rules that do not contribute or those that are found to provide doubtful contributions could be automatically discarded or assigned low certainty factors.

Another approach is case-based learning: collecting cases (e.g., legal rulings and precedents) in a knowledge base and solving problems by seeking out a case similar to the one to be solved. Probably the most promising learning mode is inductive learning—learning from examples. In this case, a system is able to generate its knowledge, represented as rules, for example, from a collection of training cases. One such learning system was able to infer (that is, conclude from the available evidence) a usable set of rules for granting loans.

As we know, knowledge acquisition for larger expert systems is an expensive and time-consuming process which also presents difficulties, as we outlined earlier in this chapter. Benefits could be reaped if at least a part of knowledge acquisition could be automated by applying a learning system.

An AI perspective that is entirely distinct from symbolic processing is built on the principle of learning systems. These are neural networks, which we will discuss in the next section.

11.10 | NEURAL NETWORKS

The dominant symbolic approach to AI, based on logical reasoning and on the representation of knowledge with symbols, has more recently been challenged by another approach, known as the connectionist perspective, or neurocomputing. The AI researchers and practitioners who work in this field are trying to imitate the behavior of the network of neuron cells in the human brain by constructing artificial neural networks. They aim primarily to mimic the brain's ability to recognize patterns—voices, scenes, or handwriting.

A **neural network** is an array of interconnected processing elements, each of which can accept inputs, process them, and produce a single output with the objective of imitating the operation of the human brain. The output from a processing element may be passed on through a connection to another processing element or presented to the environment of the network (see Figure 11.10). The processing elements may be actual hardware components (for example, microprocessors), or their operation may be simulated by software. Over a hundred different neurocomputer designs have been built into hardware, but few are available as commercial products. Most of neurocomputing today is done with software

Figure 11.10

A neural network

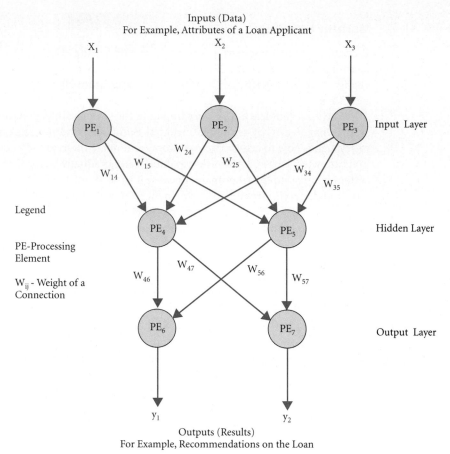

Inputs (Data)
For Example, Attributes of a Loan Applicant

Outputs (Results)
For Example, Recommendations on the Loan

running on conventional computers. Note that while the human brain contains billions of neuron cells, neural networks with more than a thousand processing elements are rare today. The action of processing elements differs significantly from what we know about the work of neurons as well.

Our interest in neural networks is motivated by their capability for learning. The operation of a processing element depends on the number of inputs to it that are currently activated and on their weights (see Figure 11.10). Other than in the input layer, the inputs to the processing elements are activated by other processing elements. Thus, knowledge is represented in a neural network by the pattern of connections among the processing elements and by the adjustable weights of these connections.

A network learns during a training process, during which it adjusts its weights in response to a collection of examples it is given. Each example contains the values of both the inputs and the outputs. In a classification task (say, the rating of loan applications), the encoded input describes the properties of sample cases (for example, income or home ownership) and the output is the specification of the category (for example, low-risk applicant). In other words, the network trains itself to recognize which attributes of applicants are most closely correlated with maintaining a good payment record and how strong that dependence is. The network strengthens, through greater weights, the appropriate connections, and weakens certain others. As soon as the network is able to perform sufficiently well on additional test cases, we can use it for new cases.

Neural Networks Learn about Fraud and Computer Viruses

Issuers of credit cards worldwide lose over $2 billion a year to the users of stolen and counterfeit cards. In detecting fraud, computer software looks for sudden changes in spending patterns. Expert systems have been used for several years in the task, but they tend to flag too many card users whose spending has changed only slightly. Customer irritation and waste of issuer resources may result.

Neural networks are able to narrow down the number of suspects sharply. They are far more discriminating than expert systems because they look at more factors in a more subtle way. Mellon Bank's Visa and MasterCard operation in Wilmington, Delaware, manages 1.2 million accounts. The neural network system introduced here fingers one-tenth of the number of potential defrauders as compared to the expert system that the net replaced and that made some 1,000 "accusations" a day. Now the bank can react quickly. In one case, it was able to notify a customer that her credit card was stolen before she herself noticed it. The neural network can spot a trend all on its own. Mellon's net noticed the so-called California scam. To test whether a card has been reported stolen, thieves would run a number of $1 transactions on it. The neural net promptly printed out a whole series of these transactions as suspect. The fraud-detection software paid for itself in six months.

Neural networks are also used in another security-oriented application: They are employed to detect computer viruses. These are hidden computer instructions that perform malicious acts and can replicate themselves through diskettes inserted into an infected PC (you will learn more about viruses in Section 14.3). Every day brings new viruses, which makes the detection difficult. Yet, the new viruses share subtle features with the known ones. Therefore, IBM has used fragments of known viruses to train a neural network to detect the unknown ones. The neural network for virus detection is marketed to clients, such as U.S. Trust.

Based on Gene Bylinsky, "Computers That Learn By Doing," *Fortune,* September 6, 1993, pp. 96–102; and Srikumar S. Rao, "The Hot Zone," *Forbes,* November 18, 1996, pp. 252–253.

Note that the network performs its own "knowledge engineering"—as a matter of fact, there is no such thing as a knowledge base or symbolic processing here. Neural nets are an alternative to expert systems in some applications. Once the network has "learned" from the data, its work will be based on the patterns it actually "observed," rather than on what an expert says is true through a knowledge engineer.

The strength of neural networks is in applications that require sophisticated pattern recognition. Ford Motor Company uses neural nets to spot faulty paint finish on a car and to recognize engine problems. The U.S. Navy deploys neural nets to identify submarines underwater based on the sound of their engine. Other neural networks have been trained to do quality control in a bottling plant, read handwritten zip codes (and they are working on learning signatures), and recognize a variety of patterns in financial data, such as credit-granting or stock-performance patterns. LBS Capital Management (of Safety Harbor, Florida) runs two investment funds with a hybrid neural network/expert system program, consistently beating market averages. The vignette above shows other interesting applications of neural networks.

Because of the way it works, a neural network does not furnish an explanation for its conclusions, a serious weakness in many potential applications.

Among the more powerful microcomputer-based neural network packages are Brainmaker from California Scientific Software (of Grass Valley, California) and Neuroshell from Ward Systems Group (of Frederick, Maryland).

SUMMARY

The field of artificial intelligence (AI) is concerned with methods of developing systems that display aspects of intelligent behavior. These systems are designed to imitate the human capabilities of thinking and sensing.

The most important applied area of AI is the field of expert systems. An expert system is a knowledge-based system that employs knowledge about its application domain in a reasoning (inferencing) procedure to solve problems that would require human competence or expertise. Expert systems are applied in such problems as classification, diagnosis, monitoring, process control, design, scheduling and planning, and generation of options.

An expert system consists of the knowledge base, the inference engine that performs the "reasoning," working memory, user interface, and explanation facility. To assist with knowledge acquisition during the process known as knowledge engineering, expert systems also contain a knowledge acquisition facility.

Expert systems work by applying a general inferencing (reasoning) procedure to a knowledge base specific to the task. The knowledge base of an expert system contains factual knowledge about its domain ("book knowledge") along with the rules of thumb used by the human experts who work in the domain. This knowledge base is organized with the use of a well-defined knowledge representation. By far the most common are rule-based expert systems, where the knowledge is represented as a collection of IF-THEN rules. Such a rule consists of a condition, specified in the IF part of the rule, and the conclusion, specified in the THEN part. Some systems implement fuzzy logic, which is a method of reasoning with approximate information.

Several levels of ES technology are available: specific expert systems, expert system shells, expert system development environments, and higher-level programming languages. Three principal roles in ES development are expert, knowledge engineer, and user. The process of development is generally iterative, based on continuing refinement of the initial prototype.

Among the principal benefits of expert systems are speed and error-free performance on tasks in limited domains, as well as ease of handling the acquired knowledge. The principal limitations include the narrowness of the application domain and problems with knowledge acquisition.

Other applied areas of AI are natural language processing, robotics, computer vision, computerized speech recognition, and machine learning.

Neurocomputing, an AI orientation that relies on artificial neural networks with learning capabilities, represents an important alternative approach to gaining for computers some of the pattern-recognition capabilities of the human brain. A neural network can be trained to recognize certain patterns and then apply what it learned to new cases where it can discern these patterns.

KEY TERMS

Artificial intelligence (AI)   *386*
Expert system (ES)   *389*
Knowledge base   *389*
Heuristic knowledge   *390*
Knowledge engineering   *393*
Knowledge representation   *393*
Rule-based expert system   *394*
IF-THEN rule   *394*

Explanation facility   *395*
Inference engine   *395*
Working memory   *395*
Forward chaining   *395*
Backward chaining   *395*
Fuzzy logic   *397*
Expert system shell   *400*
Domain-specific shell   *400*

QUESTIONS

1. What is artificial intelligence?
2. Why should businesses and other organizations be interested in the developments in artificial intelligence?
3. What is an expert system (ES)? Why are these systems called knowledge-based?
4. Consider the applications of expert systems at Oracle Electronics and Northrop, presented in Section 11.3. What business results does each of these systems bring to its owner corporation?
5. Give a realistic example of an expert system that can be used for such generic applications as classification, diagnosis, and design (i.e., three ESs should be described). What industries can your examples be used in?
6. What is knowledge engineering? Do you think it is a good name for the activity? Why or why not?
7. What is the function of each of the components of expert systems (as shown in Figure 11.4)?
8. What is the most common method of knowledge representation? Describe this way of representing knowledge.
9. Give an example of a rule for a diagnostic expert system and describe what will happen when this rule is applied during the operation of the system.
10. Which expert systems use forward chaining and which use backward chaining? Which way of thinking appears more natural to you?
11. What is fuzzy logic? What is its advantage over exact (true-false) logic? How does fuzzy logic relate to expert systems?
12. What tool is most commonly employed by end users to develop expert systems? What facilities does it offer?
13. What are the roles in ES development? What do people do in each of these roles?
14. What is the use of a prototype in ES development?
15. State in a table three principal benefits and three limitations of the business use of expert systems. Do you believe these limitations can be overcome with time?
16. List the five fields of applied AI, other than expert systems, that have significant potential in business. Give an example of a business application for each of these fields.
17. What is a neural network? How does it differ from an expert system with respect to knowledge representation?
18. How does a neural network learn?

ISSUES FOR DISCUSSION

1. Considering the present state of artificial intelligence, do you feel that AI systems pose threats to humans in a foreseeable future? If so, state what kind of threats and describe some possible countermeasures. If not, why not?
2. One may contend that expert systems will simply swallow decision support systems (DSS). In other words, one may claim that expert systems will be developed to include all of the DSS functionality, plus their own reasoning capability. What are the indications that this will happen—or not happen?
3. Discuss the notion of "learning" as evidenced by expert systems, neural networks, and the case-based reasoning systems we discussed when writing about machine learning in Section 11.9. How does this notion resemble or differ from what we generally mean by learning?
4. What ethical issues can arise when expert systems are used in providing healthcare?

REAL-WORLD MINICASE AND PROBLEM-SOLVING EXERCISES

1. **Expert Systems You Have Likely Corresponded With**
The Internal Revenue Service (IRS) has a big job. Each year, individuals and corporations file more than 200 million tax returns. Processing these returns, ensuring that they are consistent and complete, and communicating with tax payers, are monumental tasks. No wonder the IRS established an AI Lab in the mid-80s, which keeps fielding ever new applications. A number of expert systems have resulted and are helping the agency to cope. Here are some examples:

Employee/Contractor Determiner. The expert system determines whether the taxpayer is truly self-employed (and entitled to certain tax benefits) or is an employee of a company. The system then generates a letter that informs the worker and the firm of the worker's status. The Determiner is used nationwide, running in two centralized IRS processing centers. It is estimated that the expert system saves about $1 million a year and results in an increased revenue of about $22 million a year.

Reasonable Cause Assistant. Sometimes, a taxpayer who has not filed a tax return on time requests that no penalty be applied. The IRS must determine whether a reasonable cause existed for the late filing and a waiver is justified. The area is highly subjective and various IRS staffers produced inconsistent determinations. The expert system makes consistent and accurate recommendations (based on secret premises, of course).

Correspondence generators. Each year, the IRS sends out some 15 million letters to taxpayers through the Correspondence Expert System, which generates large chunks of letters automatically, drawing on a knowledge base to guide its users in selecting paragraphs and enclosures. The system now runs on about 8,000 PCs across the United States, eliminating approximately 60 percent of previous errors and saving an estimated $160 million over its 10-year life cycle. Another IRS system, the Letter Generation Module, automatically generates a letter—in English or Spanish—from a given set of facts. The letters are "computed text," rather than "canned": They answer the specific concerns of the taxpayer. As you may have expected, the AI Lab, now expanded and split into two parts, is also working on the detection of fraudulent returns claiming tax refunds.

a. Classify each expert system according to the classification of Table 11.1. Select the closest fit and provide an explanation, as necessary.

b. For each of the expert systems, find two other applications in a business context.

Based on Sara R. Hedberg, "AI & Taxes," *IEEE Expert: Intelligent Systems and Their Applications,* 11, no. 2, April 1996, pp. 4–6.

2. Assess the feasibility of implementing the following expert systems:

a. A system to select routes for delivery vehicles.

b. A system to plan the corporate budget.

c. A system to support the help desk assisting the users of corporate local area networks.

d. A system to assist the production of canned soup.

e. A system to assess the likely market response to your new product.

f. A system to rate the credit-worthiness of a potential customer.

 Explain your answers. If you feel that the given system can be developed with expert-system technology, think about the need to qualify your answer. What would be the principal elements of the knowledge base for each of the feasible expert systems? What facts would need to be presented for specific cases?

3. In Section 3.5 of this text, we described five competitive forces active in the marketplace. Expert systems may be wielded as a competitive weapon. Give an example of an expert system that could be used by a corporation to combat each of the five forces.

4. Select one of the fields of applied AI and perform literature research to determine the state of the art in this field as applied to business. Describe the state of "business maturity"

of the field. If you were the head of an Emerging Technologies group for your firm (specify the industry segment), would you recommend that a project bringing in this technology, new to your firm, be funded?

TEAM PROJECT

Each two- or three-person team will define a problem-solving task in a domain familiar to the team members. Each team will perform knowledge engineering by defining 20 to 30 rules about the domain. Outside experts may be consulted. If an ES shell is available, the team will state the rules as required by the shell; otherwise, the rules may be stated as shown in the chapter. Each team will describe its conclusions from this knowledge-engineering experience.

SELECTED REFERENCES

Back, Barbro, "Validating an Expert System for Financial Statement Planning." *Journal of Management Information Systems,* 10, no. 3 (Winter 1993–94), pp. 157–177.

 A case study that shows how to make sure that your expert system performs correctly.

Dhaliwal, Jasbir S., and Izak Benbasat. "The Use and Effects of Knowledge-Based System Explanations: Theoretical Foundations and a Framework for Empirical Evaluation." *Information Systems Research,* 7, no. 3 (September 1996), pp. 342–362.

El-Najdawi, M.K., and Anthony C. Stylianou. "Expert Support Systems: Integrating AI Technologies." *Communications of the ACM,* 36, no. 12, December 1993, pp. 55–65.

 How to integrate expert systems with decision support systems.

Feigenbaum, Edward; Pamela McCorduck; and Penny H. Nil. *The Rise of the Expert Company,* New York: Times Books, 1988.

 A number of case studies illustrating business uses of expert systems.

Gill, Grandon T. "Early Expert Systems: Where Are They Now?" *MIS Quarterly,* 19, no. 1, March 1995, pp. 51–81.

Gould, Lawrence. "If AI Ran the Zoo." *Byte,* December 1995, pp. 79–83.

 Using fuzzy logic and neural networks to control manufacturing processes.

Hayes-Roth, Frederick; Donald A. Waterman; and Douglas B. Lenat. *Building Expert Systems,* Reading, MA: Addison-Wesley, 1983.

Hendler, James A. (ed.) "Intelligent Agents: Where AI Meets Information Technology." Special Section, *IEEE Expert,* December 1996, pp. 20–59.

Kanade, Takeo; Michael L. Reed; and Lee E. Weiss. "New Technologies and Applications in Robotics." *Communications of the ACM,* 37, no. 3 (March 1994), pp. 58–67.

Liang, Ting-Peng. "Research in Integrating Learning Capabilities into Information Systems." *Journal of Management Information Systems,* 9, no. 4 (Spring 1993), pp. 5–15.

A brief and readable introduction to the present role of machine learning in information systems.

Lucas, Henry C., Jr. "Market Expert Surveillance System." *Communications of the ACM,* 36, no. 12, December 1993, pp. 26–35.

Munakata, Toshinori. Introduction to Special Issue on Commercial and Industrial AI, *Communications of the ACM,* 37, no. 3 (March 1994), pp. 23–25.

The issue contains several articles presenting the state of the art in applied AI.

Mykytyn, Kathleen; Peter P. Mykytyn Jr. ; and Craig W. Slinkman. "Expert Systems: A Question of Liability?" *MIS Quarterly,* 14, no. 1 (March 1990), pp. 27–42.

Measures to be taken to limit the legal liability arising from the use of expert systems.

Nonaka, Ikujiro, and Hirotaka Takeuchi. *The Knowledge-Creating Company,* New York: Oxford University Press, 1995.

How to convert tacit knowledge of the experts into organizational knowledge (the book does not deal with expert systems).

Sauer, Jurgen, and Ralf Bruns. "Knowledge-Based Scheduling Systems in Industry and Medicine," *IEEE Expert,* 12, no. 1, January–February 1997, pp. 24–31.

Tsai, Nancy; Charles R. Necco; and Grace Wei. "Implementing an Expert System: A Report on Benefits Realized." *Information Systems Management,* October 1994, pp. 26–30.

Users report that expert systems are most successfully deployed in well-defined applications, such as production, rather than those that require more reflective judgment, such as human resource management.

Turban, Efraim. *Decision Support and Expert Systems: Management Support Systems,* 4th ed., Englewood Cliffs, NJ: Prentice Hall, 1995.

An extensive textbook.

Turban, Efraim, and Jay Liebowitz, eds. *Managing Expert Systems,* Harrisburg, PA: Idea Group Publishing, 1992.

A collection of articles describing how organizations develop, utilize, and manage expert systems.

Zahedi, Fatemeh. *Intelligent Systems for Business: Expert Systems with Neural Networks,* Belmont, CA: Wadsworth, 1993.

A contemporary textbook.

Zwass, Vladimir. "Computer Science." *Encyclopaedia Britannica,* Macropaedia, Vol. XVI, 1988, pp. 629–637.

CASE STUDY | A Powerful Expert System Suite as a Strategic Resource

Customers demand products that suit their individual needs and businesses need to deliver these customized products cost-effectively—without being able to rely simply on the economies of mass production. To address this problem, the computer manufacturer Digital Equipment Corporation (DEC) developed its XCON expert system to electronically produce a properly working configuration of a VAX-11 computer system ordered by a client. Minicomputer models (of which there were many) of this series were notoriously difficult to configure and the expert system was a solution to a major business problem. Indeed, this expert system has become a legend in the industry. It also turned out to be the cornerstone of a suite of rule-based expert systems, known as XCON/XSEL, which became deeply embedded in the value chain of DEC over the years of VAX-11 manufacture.

As we shall further discuss in the conclusion of the case, XCON/XSEL was phased out of operation in the early 1990s when the VAX-11 computer series and related systems were discontinued. Its development and use have been, however, a learning laboratory for DEC, which now deploys similar expert systems for its new computer series, and for other companies that have emulated this success by developing their own configuration expert systems. We can also learn from this experience here.

DEC turned to expert systems in the early 1980s, when it confronted the difficulties of mass customization. Highly complex products were being developed and marketed with increasingly faster rates of change. Beyond that, most of the products had to be customized for the individual buyer. Yet the key elements of the business processes appeared weak.

Consider sales. A salesperson would take the customer's order, which could run to many pages. Multiple CPUs, a variety of peripheral equipment, software, interconnections, cabinets—all these had to work together and meet the customer's requirements. Technical editors (engineers) had to check whether the order was "clean"—that is, whether it would work. To tell the truth, if an order was complex, it was not at all likely to work. Drawing up this highly technical material required significant engineering expertise. The embarrassment of redrawing and renegotiating an order was a frequent experience. That was the sales problem.

There was also an order-delivery problem. After a "clean" order was manufactured, the company had to make certain the system would work when installed at the customer's site. To achieve this certainty, the order had to be assembled by field engineers at one of a number of final-assembly-and-testing plants. (Order components usually came from various DEC manufacturing plants.) Then the assembled order would be tested, corrected if necessary (and owing to human error in this complex environment, this was no rare occurrence), disassembled, and shipped to the customer, to be once again assembled at the customer's site. All of this was very costly and time-consuming.

With the growing product lines and complex customer requirements, there was no future in such processes. The development of organizational expert systems was the adopted solution.

The order-delivery problem was handled first by developing XCON (for eXpert CONfigurator), which became operational in 1981. It was rewritten in 1987 in a language of a new software-development environment that simplified the maintenance of the expert system, and then evolved a number of times. The sales problem was addressed a few years after XCON became operational by the interactive XSEL expert system, designed to work with XCON. XSEL reduced the time a salesperson would need to configure a system from between one and three hours to just 15 minutes. Configuration accuracy with the system reached 99 percent, and it had been 70 percent without. As one of the managers put it, "That 29 percent difference is what lets us stay in business."

The specifications of four principal expert systems in the suite were as follows:

1. XCON validates the technical correctness of the customer order, configures the order, and specifies its assembly. Among other things, XCON does the following:

- Configures hardware components, such as CPUs, memory components, power supplies, cabinets, and peripherals.
- Diagrams the complete system configuration.
- Determines full cabling.
- Generates warning messages if the order's technical validity is questionable.

2. XSEL is an interactive system that assists the salespeople in selecting the actual parts that will make up each customer's order. Thus, XSEL:

- Permits part selection by generic name.
- Performs a completeness check and suggests the addition of certain parts.

- Checks software compatibility.

- Provides the environmental requirements for the computer room.

- Is linked with the Automated Quotation System for pricing.

3. XFL diagrams the computer-room floor layout for the configuration. In doing so, it:

- Provides a "minimum footprint" floor layout.

- Allows the user to specify room dimension and equipment placement.

- Allows layout specifications for several systems on one site.

4. XCLUSTER helps to specify configurations of multiple nodes of a given equipment type. Indeed, many customers would require interconnected rather than stand-alone computer systems.

XCON consisted of over 10,000 rules. XSEL and the other two systems combined included approximately 6,000 rules. Rules themselves were complex, with many condition and action elements per rule (see Figure 11.11). The system also included five databases. For example, the Component & Template database contained data on over 30,000 parts, with an average of 40 attributes per part, as well as templates of their connectivity with other parts (for example, the number and size of slots). A software development methodology and an environment for expert system development (RIME) were created in-house to support the ongoing development and maintenance. The custom-made RIME simplified the expression of rules and produces significant execution-time efficiencies (an inferencing process with many very complex rules requires huge processing power).

The expert system suite handled the configuration of all the DEC products in the VAX-11 series. By the time a new product was due to be announced, the expert systems had to be updated. Thus, the company provided major releases of these systems once a quarter, with at least one update in the interim. About 40 percent of the rules in the knowledge base of the ES suite were changed every year. This was necessary owing to the continuous product innovation at DEC, which releases several hundred major new products each year and continually modifies the existing products. Maintenance of the expert system was very costly.

The use of the XCON/XSEL ES suite and its successors spans the firm's value chain:

- The expert systems are the fundamental tool for *Sales,* where they are used to generate quotations for customers and ensure that each order is technically valid.

- *Manufacturing* employs the systems to verify whether an incoming order can be built as specified, to determine which plants are to build the order components, to guide component assembly, and to determine which diagnostic routines should be run on an order. Plant technicians used elaborate diagrams produced by XCON to put assemblies together.

- Both *Engineering* and *Manufacturing* use the systems to identify potential problems in product design and manufacturability; they also learn how to design better products in the future.

- *Field Service* is supported in its need to assemble the order in the customer's environment, possibly integrating it with the systems already in place there. Service representatives also used the XCON-produced diagrams.

The expert systems are linked to many other information systems in DEC's worldwide operations, and many "indirect" users access them as well. The XSEL system, for example, was employed by DEC's OEM (original equipment manufacturer) customers. These firms

Figure 11.11	*Rule Name: Configure-Device:Propose:500b:Select-Container*

A sample XCON rule, expressed in the language of the RIME development environment (and simplified for presentation)

IF

C1	The current step of the process of configuring devices involves proposing alternatives;

C2	and there is at least one unconfigured device that needs to be placed inside a container;

C3	and no container has yet been chosen;

C4	and no device in which other devices can be placed has been chosen as a container;

C5	and the process of selecting a container has not yet been proposed;

C6	and there has been no problem identified concerning selecting a container;

THEN

A1	propose to go through the process of selecting a container.

Comments

The current activity of the system is to propose tasks that will ultimately result in the configuration of a device.

There are some large tape drives that have a compartment in the bottom suitable for disk placement.

If there is already an identified problem with selecting a container, the task should not be proposed again until the problem has been resolved.

add value to DEC's equipment by providing additional hardware and software for specialized markets and selling them as turnkey systems to their own clients.

A new system does not necessarily find immediate acceptance. Quite the contrary is true in many cases. For example, despite its obvious advantages, many salespeople did not immediately take to XSEL. They stayed with the tried-and-true method, taking orders and configuring systems by hand, until they had to change their ways. But it wasn't management that forced them to use the system—DEC's corporate culture is not stick-oriented. The fact was simply that within nine months in the 1980s, the company's product base was almost totally modified, and the best way for a salesperson to find out what had happened was to use the expert system, which was kept fully up-to-date. With the help of XSEL, salespeople could also give a customer a few configurations to choose from and create floor layouts with the other expert systems, in other words, they could sell more effectively. Complex (read "commission-generating") orders were won because the system could reliably configure and fully specify them in no time at all.

DEC was strategically dependent on its XCON configuration expert systems worldwide. The ability to provide a build-to-order system to customers, addressing their specialized needs rapidly, is considered a key competitive advantage. Customer satisfaction was also high because the configurations generated by XCON were optimal for the customer's needs. In addition, orders were configured in a consistent fashion.

With the expert systems, the technical accuracy of orders entering manufacturing became much higher than it had been before. When components configured by XCON reached the customer's site, the configuration was assured to work, without the need to assemble and disassemble them first at a DEC site.

The process of new product introduction was much simplified and shortened by the fact that the entire configuration information was available in one place—the expert system—in an active form (as opposed to manuals) by the time of the product introduction. This facilitated the training of field service people as well as the manufacturing of the product itself.

As the user constituency expanded, each new group would bring its own requirements. This, in turn, kept expanding the functionality of the systems. For example, when the plant technicians began to use the XCON-produced diagrams as basic blueprints for assembling computer components, specialized databases and procedural (non-ES) code had to be included for the purpose. Also, interaction with other non-knowledge-based systems was increasingly required. A production system of so wide a scope would draw on many experts (hundreds in the case of XCON). The development group of 60 people continually modified the system to keep it up to date. A steering committee, consisting of strategic-level managers from all of the system stakeholders, had been created to provide long-term direction.

The XCON system processed some 80,000 orders each year. The net annual return on these systems is estimated at $70 million. The expert systems suite both contributed to the strategic objectives of the owner company and provided large financial returns.

When the VAX-11 line was discontinued, two principal factors led to the phasing out of the XCON/XSEL suite. New computer systems were much easier to configure. In fact, the new system designs were produced with ease of configuration as a design objective. The second factor was the ever increasing cost of maintenance of the suite and the expected cost of its retargeting for the new computer systems.

Having gained experience with XCON/XSEL, DEC persists in developing and maintaining new expert systems for configuration purposes. Just as the computer systems are designed to be easier to configure, so the new expert systems are designed to be easier to maintain. Thus, the development and use of the expert system suite has been an important component of organizational learning at Digital Equipment Corporation.

Based on Dennis O'Connor and Virginia Barker, "Expert Systems for Configuration at Digital: XCON and Beyond." *Communications of the ACM*, 32, no. 3, March 1989, pp. 298–318; John J. Sviokla, "An Examination of the Impact of Expert Systems on the Firm: The Case of XCON." *MIS Quarterly*, 14, no. 2, June 1990, pp. 127–140; Frederick Hayes-Roth and Neil Jacobstein, "The State of Knowledge-Based Systems." *Communications of the ACM*, 37, no. 3, March 1994, pp. 27–39; and T. Grandon Gill, "Early Expert Systems: Where Are They Now?" *MIS Quarterly*, 19, no. 1, March 1995, pp. 51–81.

CASE STUDY QUESTIONS

1. Why is the XCON/XSEL suite considered an organizational system?

2. What competitive advantages did XCON/XSEL confer on its owner firm?

3. What stages of the company's value chain are directly affected by an ES suite such as XCON/XSEL? How?

4. How was the initial resistance to using the expert systems overcome?

5. Note that, as described, the system addressed operational rather than management concerns. What management information can be obtained from expert systems and how can this be done?

6. If you were the champion of this expert system suite, presenting its potential benefits, costs, and risks before the initial system was built, what specific points would you make? Remember, you need to manage expectations—don't overpromise!

CHAPTER TWELVE

Information Systems for Business Functions

OBJECTIVES

After you complete this chapter, you will be able to:

1. Specify the principal business functions to be supported by information systems and describe their interrelationship.

2. Specify the three classes of subsystems that make up a marketing information system.

3. Discuss the objectives of marketing-research and marketing-intelligence subsystems.

4. Discuss the objectives of each of the marketing-mix subsystems.

5. Specify and explain the characteristics of the new manufacturing environment to be supported by information systems.

6. Identify the subsystems of a manufacturing information system that support management and knowledge work.

7. Identify the subsystems of an accounting and financial information system.

8. Identify the transaction-processing subsystems of a human resource information system.

9. Identify the subsystems of a human resource information system that support management and knowledge work.

10. Discuss the motivation for the integration of functional information systems within a company and across its boundaries.

OUTLINE

Yes, You Can Make Money on the Web

Cisco Systems is a leading supplier of networking products that are a part of the backbone of the Internet and of corporate intranets. The firm has also learned how to make money by *using* the Internet. Its Web site, Cisco Connection Online (http://www.cisco.com), is considered by many the highest-impact Web site in business-to-business electronic commerce. Cisco uses the Web to deliver more than 70 percent of its customer support. Moreover, it is selling over $200 million worth of products a year on the Web and wants to increase this figure to $2 billion—about a third of its annual sales.

Peter Solvik, the company's chief information officer, tells us: "Most companies use the Web as a marketing tool. We're using it as a vehicle to move customer relationships to a new level. We want quantum-leap results: lower costs, higher customer satisfaction, leadership in service." Cisco is indeed getting the results. More than two-thirds of contacts with the existing customers—to report technical problems, check orders, download software—now take place electronically. Cost savings are easy to compute. Each of the 50,000 hits a month to the Web site instead of a phone call for technical assistance saves the average $200 cost of handling the call, for a total savings of $120 million a year. Selling on the Web is cheaper for Cisco and buying there is cheaper for its customers.

Every Cisco department that communicates with customers, including marketing, engineering, customer service, and technical support, is responsible for maintaining the Web site. This accounts for the speed; the day a new product is announced, all the manuals, marketing information, press releases, and service information go automatically to the Web.

Here are some of the information systems that support Cisco's Web site. The Marketplace enables customers to order products electronically by signing an "electronic commerce agreement." Web customers see up-to-date prices and available options; the system automatically generates applicable discounts and forwards the order for fulfillment. The Status Agent allows customers to track their order. The Software Library lets customers upgrade their software electronically, alerting them automatically when they select software that will not run on their hardware. The Troubleshooting Engine uses artificial-intelligence software to help customers diagnose and fix their problems.

Customer satisfaction levels are high. Internally, the corporate Web site and team intranets have become the focal points for integrating the firm's activities—always with superior service in mind.

Based on Eric Matson, "Two Billion Reasons Cisco's Sold on the Net," *Fast Company*, February-March 1997, pp. 34–36; http//:www.cisco.com.

You have read in the Focus Minicase how Cisco revolutionized its customer service with information systems supporting customer relationships over the World Wide Web. Today, all but very small organizations need information systems to support their principal business functions, such as marketing or production. Some of these systems process the transactions as organizational units perform the corresponding functions. Other information systems support the managers who run these functions and the professionals who contribute their knowledge work to them.

12.1 | SUPPORTING BUSINESS FUNCTIONS IN AN ENTERPRISE WITH INFORMATION

In supplying the marketplace with its products—goods or services—a business firm performs several distinct functions. The principal **business functions** are:

- Marketing and sales—ensuring that the firm's products meet the needs of the marketplace, developing a market for these products, providing them at the right place at the right time, and selling them.

- Production—creating or adding value by producing goods or offering services. In firms that produce goods, the production function is known as manufacturing.

- Accounting and finance—managing the funds of the enterprise.

- Human resources—developing the personnel of the firm.

As we know from Chapter 1, organizations have been traditionally structured along these functional lines. As you also read there, some of the leading companies organize themselves differently today. To compete effectively, many organizations are now subdivided into territorial (geographic), line-of-business, or other customer-oriented structures. The flatter organizations of the 90s rely less on middle management as the backbone of separate functions and more on information technology for integrating these functions. In some companies, functional specialists are distributed among the units performing the firm's business processes (Hammer 1996). Cross-functional teams, with the informational support we discussed in Section 8.6, have become the essential work units in a number of firms. Yet regardless of the organizational structure of the enterprise, information systems need to support the four principal business functions we listed above.

The investment in information technology for support of business functions has been increasing steadily. Indeed, with intensifying business competition, the information intensity of business processes, as well as of products and services, has been rapidly increasing in recent years (Konsynski 1993).

A general view of information systems supporting a company's operations and management is shown in Figure 12.1. As we can see, management support systems, that is, management reporting systems (MRS), decision support systems (DSS), and executive information systems (EIS), rest on the foundation of transaction processing systems (TPS) that support business operations. The latter are the major source of data used by the higher-level systems to derive information. Professional support systems (PSS) and office informa-

Figure 12.1

General view of information systems in a firm

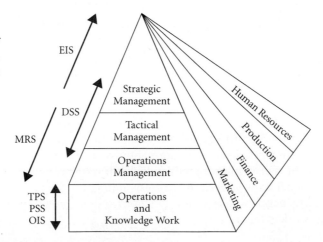

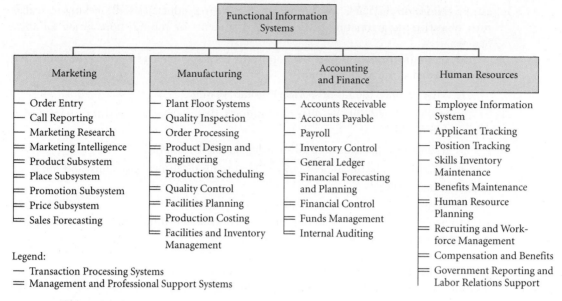

Figure 12.2

Functional information systems

tion systems (OIS), which support individual and group knowledge work, are also a part of this foundation.

As we will discuss in the last section of this chapter, the overall information system portfolio is more effective if the functional systems are properly integrated. Databases are the principal means of this integration. Creating information architectures in which various functional subsystems are able to access common databases supports informed managerial decision making. Higher-level systems, such as executive information systems, are often expressly designed to provide an integrated view of information across functional boundaries.

The principal functional information systems and their typical subsystems are shown in Figure 12.2. Various components of these systems support the appropriate level of management or operations and are implemented as TPS, OIS, PSS, MRS, DSS, or EIS. As we now proceed to discuss the functional systems in the present chapter, you will see that their general structure reflects the informational relationship between the transaction processing systems that supply data and management support systems that use the data, as illustrated previously in Figure 9.8.

Over several recent decades, business companies have moved from a production-and-sales orientation to a marketing orientation. This means that the driving force in these companies has been redirected from selling what the companies produce to producing with a high degree of both customization and efficiency what the companies could profitably sell. In keeping with this orientation, we begin our discussion with marketing information systems.

12.2 | MARKETING INFORMATION SYSTEMS

The Domain of Marketing Information Systems

Marketing activities are directed toward planning, promoting, and selling goods and services to satisfy the needs of customers and the objectives of the organizations. In a business firm, the most important objective is realizing a profit. Nonprofit organizations, such as universities or charitable institutions, market their products as well, seeking to realize such objectives as graduating better-qualified students or raising more funds for their beneficiaries.

Marketing information systems support the decision making regarding the **marketing mix,** expressed as the so-called four Ps:

1. What *products* (goods or services) should we offer?
2. At what *place* should we offer our products; that is, what should our distribution channels be?
3. What *promotion* (sales and advertising) should be conducted?
4. What should be the *price* of our products (with mark-ups, discounts, and other terms of sale)?

The outcome of this decision making is integrated into a sales forecast. This forecast used to be made for a year ahead but, in the environment of time-based competition, it is now often made for shorter periods.

The structure of the entire marketing information system is shown in Figure 12.3. As we can see, in order to support decision making on the marketing mix, a marketing information system draws on several sources of data and information. Let us proceed to discuss them.

Sources of Data and Information for Marketing: Boundary-Spanning and Transaction Processing Subsystems

By its very nature, a marketing information system relies on external information to a far greater degree than other organizational information systems. As we can see in Figure 12.3, it includes two subsystems expressly designed for boundary spanning: bringing into the firm data and information about the marketplace.

Figure 12.3

Marketing information system

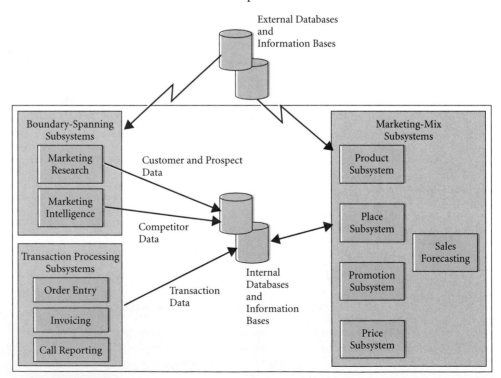

Marketing to an Internet's Community of Interest

Using the facilities of the Internet's World Wide Web and the technology of intelligent software agents, Boston-based Firefly Network Inc. has invented a new way to research and to finely segment a marketplace. Visitors to the company's Web site (http://www.firefly.com) adopt an alias to assure their privacy and begin to register their likes and dislikes in music and movies, which is what Firefly is promoting. The intelligent agents sift through these lists of preferences entered by the site visitors and locate "nearest neighbors" among them. In other words, the software agents identify clusters of people with similar tastes. Having identified these small affinity groups, Firefly recommends to them the appropriate new products, based on the expressed preferences of all of the "nearest neighbors."

The company sells CDs on-line. It has also attracted to its rapidly growing community of interest, now encompassing some 300,000 people, such major advertisers as AT&T and Columbia Records, which pay $100 for every 1,000 people who click on their ads. Based on the psychographic profile of its visitors, the site can place an advertiser's banner in front of those most interested in its products.

Firefly delivers much more value to its users than just a shopping list. The users can put their reviews up on the site; they can electronically chat with one another; and they can use the agents to find others with similar tastes. This sense of community makes people want to come back. The advertisers are able to build up an affinity group around their brands and to get their marketing information to the right people.

The services of Firefly are free—or, one can say that personal information is the currency here. Privacy of the visitors is stringently protected. Individuals do not have to share their real names or addresses, unless they choose to. Firefly has hired the accounting firm of Coopers & Lybrand to conduct twice-yearly audits of the confidentiality of the user profiles that are built by the intelligent agents.

Firefly considers the site to be a showcase for its intelligent agents, which are being licensed to others. For example, Reuters New Media will use the technology to help its subscribers locate news stories based on what "nearest neighbors" found relevant. The Firefly marketing site plans to go from movies and music to restaurants, books, and mutual funds.

Based on Paul C. Judge, "Why Firefly Has Mad Ave. Buzzing," *Business Week,* October 7, 1996, pp. 100–102.

The objective of **marketing research** is to collect data on the actual customers and the potential customers, known as prospects. The identification of the needs of the customer is a fundamental starting point for total quality management (TQM). These needs will be converted into quality targets for the products. Peter Drucker, a noted authority on management, has stressed the importance of gathering the data on non-customers, in order to understand why they do not patronize the firm's products. In doing marketing research, many firms gather their own data with surveys or interviews (for example, in focus groups, also conducted over the Internet), or by observing the actual buying behavior. The data garnered by observation are more reliable than the statements of intent or fact in surveys. Electronic commerce on the World Wide Web makes it easy to compile statistics on actual buyer behavior.

With the growth of the information economy, the availability of data from external sources has grown. Such data can be obtained from on-line databases, such as those listed in Table 8.3, or on magnetic or optical media (CD-ROM). Examples include the data gathered by the U.S. Census (available over the Internet) or collected by a market research company. Leading suppliers of data collected by point-of-sale (POS) scanners at supermarkets, pharmacies, and other mass merchandisers are Information Resources (via its InfoScan

Service) and Nielsen Marketing Research. These firms also supply software for analyzing the data.

Marketing research software supports statistical analysis of data. It enables the firm to correlate buyer behavior with very detailed geographic variables (such as a small community or several urban blocks), demographic variables (age, income, education, etc.), and even psychographic variables (such as the degree of conservatism or gregariousness). Geographic information systems, which we described in Section 6.11, are particularly helpful in visualizing the distribution of customers and non-customers. The vignette on page 427 shows how the capabilities of the Internet can be creatively used in marketing research.

Marketing (competitive) intelligence is responsible for the gathering and interpretation of data regarding the firm's competitors, and for the dissemination of the competitive information to the appropriate users. Most of the competitor information comes from corporate annual reports, media-tracking services (e.g., on-line databases or filtered news services that relay information based on client profiles), and reports purchased from external providers, including on-line database services. It is a vital function of sales call reporting to provide competitive information as well. And the Internet has become a major source of competitive intelligence (Cronin 1994).

As we have stressed, an important objective of transaction processing is to provide data for the higher-level information systems. Indeed, several transaction processing subsystems feed data into the marketing information system. These include primarily Order Entry, which provides data on customer orders; Invoicing, providing the billing and returns data; and Call Reporting, through which data on sales calls (including the competitive data collected by the salespeople) reaches the systems.

Marketing-Mix Subsystems

The marketing-mix subsystems support decision making regarding product introduction, pricing, promotion (advertising and personal selling), and distribution. These decisions are integrated into the sales forecast and marketing plan against which the ongoing sales results are compared.

1. Product Subsystem

Product subsystem helps to plan the introduction of new products. Continually bringing new products to market is vital in today's competitive environment of rapid change. As one example, Nike places on the market an average of more than one shoe style every single day (Lane 1996). New products differ in their degree of newness: They range from extensions to the current product lines and improvements to existing products to products that are new to the company or even new to the world. The higher the degree of newness, the higher the risk in introducing the product. The Product subsystem should support balancing the degree of risk in the overall new-product portfolio with more aggressive competitors assuming higher degrees of risk for a potentially higher payoff.

Although decisions regarding the introduction of new products are unstructured, information systems support this process in several ways. Professional support systems assist designers in their knowledge work. Decision support systems are used to evaluate proposed new products. With the use of a DSS, a marketing manager can score the desirability of a new product. To do this, he or she can consider the attributes of the proposed product, such as the appeal to non-customers for the existing product, its fit with the firm's strengths, like core competence in manufacturing or post-sale service, and its fit with the existing product line, such as utilizing off-season production capacity or exploiting the customer database.

Electronic meeting systems help bring the expertise of people dispersed in space and time to bear on a problem. Information derived from marketing intelligence and research is vital in evaluating new product ideas.

2. Place Subsystem

Place subsystem assists the decision makers in making the product available to the customer at the right place at the right time. In other words, the Place subsystem helps plan the distribution channels for the product and track their performance. Some products are sold through short channels: Machinery is usually sold directly to the industrial user; some manufacturers of consumer products such as Avon or Tupperware sell directly to the consumer. Longer distribution channels include brokers, wholesalers, and retailers, which provide such important marketing functions as product promotion, credit support, storage, and post-sale service. With longer channels, there is a need for more information processing in the Place subsystem.

The use of information technology has dramatically increased the availability of information on product movement in the distribution channel (Clemons and Row 1993). The bar-coded Universal Product Code (UPC) combined with point-of-sale (POS) scanning makes it possible to track every unit of merchandise. Electronic data interchange (EDI) is increasingly used to transmit price and promotion data, along with the electronic orders and invoices.

Customized delivery has become possible with the use of information systems. As customers increasingly demand just-in-time product delivery, the Place subsystem has to support precise deliveries against a pre-agreed schedule. However, it is also necessary to accommodate variations from that schedule, as requested by the customer. Specialized distribution companies relying on sophisticated information technology, such as FedEx and UPS, have become virtual partners of many manufacturing and merchandising firms. FedEx is also becoming an aggressive distributor of products acquired (often with the help of its software) over the Internet (Blackmon 1996). In some industries, such as retail, suppliers have to manage customers' inventories and the suppliers' information systems have to be integrated with those of their customers.

3. Promotion Subsystem

Promotion subsystem is often the most elaborate in the marketing information system, since it supports both personal selling and advertising. Media-selection packages assist in selecting a mix of avenues to persuade the potential purchaser, including direct mail, television, print media, and the electronic media such as the Internet and the World Wide Web in particular. The effectiveness of the selected media mix is monitored and its composition is continually adjusted. Point-of-sale (POS) systems bring timely and detailed data on sales, which are employed to direct advertising spending. For example, Kraft General Foods uses the POS data to analyze annual spending of a sample 12,000 households and to direct its $1.6 billion in advertising so as to reach the most promising prospects. Further up the supply chain, the POS data are used to pull in the appropriate products from Manufacturing and the appropriate input goods from the firm's suppliers.

Database marketing relies on the accumulation and use of extensive databases to segment potential customers and reach them with personalized promotional information (as we learned in Chapter 6). The frequent-flier database of British Airways, combined with the airline's data warehouse (whose combined capacity surpasses one trillion bytes), helps it ward off competition from discount air carriers by pampering the best customers. Airline representatives throughout the world, as well as flight attendants, have access to information about each of the customer's preferences in order to provide superior service (Foley

1997). A customer information system has furnished competitive advantage to Williams-Sonoma, a direct marketer and retailer of cooking and gardening equipment. Relying on its database of over 4.5 million customers that tracks up to 150 data items per customer, the company's two full-time statisticians can project the sales from each direct-mail catalog with 95 percent accuracy. The database also helps the company locate the most promising sites for new stores. Thanks to its customer information system, Fingerhut, the fourth largest mail-order company in the United States, succeeded where many others have failed. By capturing and analyzing as many as 1,400 data items about a household, the company is able to sell merchandise on credit to families with low annual income (Bessen 1993).

The role of **telemarketing,** marketing over the telephone, has increased. A telephone call costs about one-hundredth of the cost of an in-person sales call. Telemarketing calls are well supported by information technology. Better uses of telemarketing include careful selection of prospects based on marketing databases and automatic displays on the telemarketer's screen of the data regarding the prospect whose number has been successfully dialed. Telemarketing techniques offensive to many include automatic dialing followed by a computerized voice message.

Sales management is thoroughly supported with information technology. Customer profitability analyses help identify high-profit and high-growth customers and target marketing efforts in order to retain and develop these accounts. On the tactical level, plans are developed for the servicing of these key accounts and for general sales-call coverage and development of sales territory. Variances from these plans are monitored, analyzed, and become a stimulus for action. Operational planning involves, for example, weekly salesforce assignment. Operational control may be performed through weekly analysis of regional sales volume. By collecting the daily data on the sales of its products store by store, and combining these with the data on its competitors's sales, Frito-Lay is able to react rapidly to demand changes in the salty-snack market segment and has garnered competitive advantage (Rayport and Sviokla 1995).

Salesforce automation, equipping salespeople with portable computers tied into the corporate information systems, gives the salespeople instantaneous access to information and frees them from the reporting paperwork. This increases selling time and the level of performance. Access to corporate databases is sometimes accompanied by access to corporate expertise, either by being able to contact the experts or by using expert systems that help specify the product meeting customer requirements. Computerized ordering systems in healthcare and other industries, with the vendor's software for ordering installed on customer sites, reduce the need for salesforce.

4. Price Subsystem

Pricing decisions find a degree of support from decision support systems and access to databases that contain industry prices. These highly unstructured decisions are made in pursuit of the company's pricing objective. General strategies range from profit maximization (or charging what the market will bear) to forgoing a part of the profit in order to increase market share. Discounting and promotional devices, such as coupons, complicate the pricing task. Manufacturers often use promotions by lowering prices to retailers for a specific period or in a specific region. This sometimes results in investment buying by brokers, who stock up the goods for future sale or divert them to regions where no discount is available. Information technology is deployed by brokers in this arbitrage, which defeats the manufacturer's pricing purpose.

Information systems provide an opportunity to finely segment customer groups and charge different prices depending on the combination of product and service provided, as well as the circumstances of the sale transaction. Because of yield management systems (see Section 3.4), passengers in neighboring seats on the same airplane pay different prices, depending on such circumstances as advance purchase, length of stay, applicability of special rates, and qualification for such promotions as frequent flier. When you buy M&M candy, you may pay very different prices for the same weight. Indeed, its vendor, Mars, offers 76 different packaging formats and prices for its product (Goldman 1994).

5. Sales Forecasting

Based on the planned marketing mix and outstanding orders, sales are forecast and a full marketing plan is developed. **Sales forecasting** is an area where any quantitative methods employed must be tempered with human insight and experience. The actual sales will depend to a large degree on the dynamics of the environment.

Qualitative techniques are generally used for **environmental forecasting:** an attempt to predict the social, economic, legal, and technological environment in which the company will try to realize its plans. These forecasts play a broader role in the overall corporate planning than just supporting sales planning. Group decision-making techniques, such as the Delphi method discussed in Section 10.6, are used to elicit broad expert opinion. The use of these techniques may be supported by a GDSS. Another oft-employed qualitative forecasting technique is scenario analysis. Each scenario in this process is a plausible future environment. Royal Dutch/Shell, an oil company renowned for its preparedness when unfavorable market conditions occur, works out two to four scenarios, each reflecting a plausible combination of favorable and unfavorable future circumstances. A decision that would stand up under two or three future scenarios is favored. Decision support systems may be used to develop models for the scenarios.

The sales volume has to be forecast quantitatively, of course. Among quantitative forecasting techniques is the extrapolation (i.e., extension into the future) of trends and cycles through a time-series analysis. Many phenomena are cyclic, with the cycles repeating themselves over periods of a few years as well as seasonally. If the sales growth rate can be charted in this fashion, we can extend such a chart into the future. Figure 12.4 shows how a computerized projection for the coming year has been made by considering a time series for several years preceding. The projection is based on the fact that the time series for the earlier years shows both an upward trend and seasonal cycles.

Sales forecast is the foundation of a marketing plan. It must be stressed that any long-range planning in an environment fraught with uncertainties is not a blueprint. It is rather a continual process through which the company integrates its activities, devises targets to

Figure 12.4

A sales volume forecast

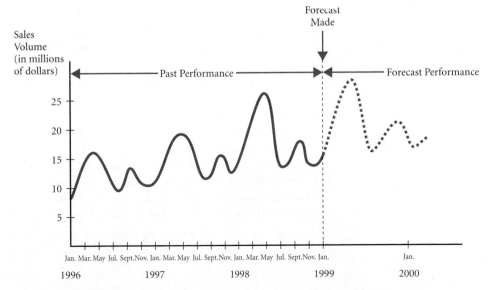

focus on, and learns to improve its performance. Once the marketing plan has been developed, managerial control can be performed by tracking variances from the key indicators. For example, managers might ask, "Which division was responsible for the large negative sales variance in the second quarter?" or "What should be done to narrow the gap between planned sales for the current year and possible projections considering the results we have so far?" We have seen the use of an executive information system to ask such questions in the Case Study for Chapter 2.

The marketing information system may be integrated with other organizational information systems. For example, corporate plans for various time horizons are an important input to the system, while the sales forecasts are a vital output from the marketing to the manufacturing information system.

12.3 | MANUFACTURING INFORMATION SYSTEMS

The New Manufacturing Environment

As the need for goods and for their customer-driven quality attributes is established by marketing, they have to be produced by manufacturing. Even though in this section we concentrate on manufacturing firms, all organizations deliver goods or services that must be produced in an organized fashion, using similar concepts, and with the operations supported by information systems.

Global competitive pressures of the information society have been highly pronounced in manufacturing and have radically changed it. The new marketplace calls for manufacturing that is:

- *Lean*—highly efficient, using fewer input resources (materials, human effort, energy, plant space) in production through better engineering and through production processes that rely on low inventories and result in less waste. In particular, "green" products are designed to be less environmentally invasive. Thus, for example, IBM microcomputers are designed for easy disassembly and recycling.

- *Agile*—fit for time-based competition. Both the new product design and order fulfillment are drastically shortened. Product design cycles (time-to-market) are cut by rapid prototyping with the use of computer-added design (CAD) systems and by concurrent engineering that supports parallel development of different aspects of the product. Moreover, products are expressly designed for easy manufacture and assembly. Customer-oriented manufacturing systems enable a firm to fill a manufacturing order almost immediately. For example, thanks to a computer-integrated manufacturing (CIM) system, Copperweld Corporation of Pittsburgh, a manufacturer of metal tubing, produces and ships a customer order within two hours.

- *Flexible*—able to adjust the product to a customer's preferences rapidly and cost-effectively. At the Allen Bradley plant in Milwaukee, Wisconsin, electrical contactors are efficiently produced in a lot size of one, with a six-second changeover time from one type of product to another. Similarly, Motorola's plant in Boynton Beach, Florida, produces pagers in lots of one. By varying the styles and colors of its pagers, the firm has been able to reach a very broad consumer market. This is known as **mass customization**—producing varied, often individually customized products at the cost of standardized, mass-produced goods (Pine 1993).

- *Managed for quality*—by measuring quality throughout the production process and following world standards (such as ISO 9000), manufacturers treat quality as a ne-

Figure 12.5

*Manufacturing
information system*

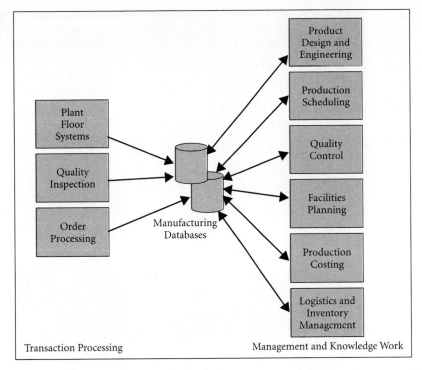

Plant Floor Systems

Quality Inspection

Order Processing

Manufacturing Databases

Product Design and Engineering

Production Scheduling

Quality Control

Facilities Planning

Production Costing

Logistics and Inventory Management

Transaction Processing

Management and Knowledge Work

cessity and not a high-price option. The so-called six-sigma technique, pioneered by Motorola, permits no more than 3.4 defects per million units of a product.

We will proceed to discuss manufacturing information systems that can contribute significantly to this manufacturing environment.

Structure of Manufacturing Information Systems

To achieve the results we have just described, information technology must play a vital role in the design and manufacturing processes. Virtually all the capabilities of information technology we discussed in Chapter 1 are called upon. Indeed, **manufacturing information systems** are among the most difficult both to develop and to implement. The general structure of manufacturing information systems is shown in Figure 12.5.

Transaction processing systems are embedded in the production process (such as plant floor systems and quality inspection systems) or in other company processes (such as order processing). The data provided by the transaction processing systems are used by management support subsystems, which are tightly integrated and interdependent. Let us consider these subsystems of the manufacturing information system.

1. Product Design and Engineering

Product design and engineering are widely supported today by **computer-aided design (CAD)** and **computer-aided engineering (CAE)** systems. A variety of products, from semiconductor chips to airplanes, are designed using similar principles of constructing geometric objects. CAD systems assist the designer with automatic calculations and display of surfaces while storing the design information in databases. The produced designs are subject to processing with CAE systems to ensure their quality, safety, manufacturability, and cost-effectiveness. If concurrent engineering is implemented, the designers develop the

Photo 12.1

*MicroStation software
(from Intergraph of
Huntsville, Alabama)
helps visualize on the
desktop the product
being designed*

functionality of the product at the same time as it is engineered for ease of manufacture, assembly, testing, and repair. CAD/CAE systems increasingly eliminate paperwork from the design process, while speeding up the process itself.

The product is designed in electronic form, visualized by the workstation graphics (see Photo 12.1). In many cases, design rules are prestored in a database to ensure that the designs are valid. Instead of producing costly and time-consuming physical prototypes, preliminary designs can be validated in electronic form. Simulation software allows the engineers to test the virtual product under the expected conditions of its operation. The technique known as stereolitography uses laser under computer control to produce a physical prototype of a product quickly by curing a liquid polymer layer by layer, until these cross sections stack up to the product shape. The combined techniques of CAD/CAE and rapid prototyping cut time-to-market.

With increasing frequency, product design is done in collaboration with the customer. Figure 12.6 shows how apparel makers are able to quickly respond to the demands of fashion by relying on such computer-based collaboration.

2. Production Scheduling

Production scheduling is the heart of the manufacturing information system. This complex subsystem has to ensure that an appropriate combination of human, machinery, and material resources will be provided at an appropriate time in order to manufacture the goods. The manufacture has to take place on an appropriate schedule in accordance with the sales forecasts, taking into account orders on hand and production for inventory.

1. Plain white, prepared-for-print fabric is shipped from the textile mill to the apparel manufacturer.

2. Apparel manufacturer designs garment on a computer workstation.

3. A digital file of the garment design is sent electronically to the retailer for approval.

4. Retailer approves design or transmits suggested changes.

5. After receiving approval, apparel manufacturer transmits digital garment file (including manufacturing instructions and design) to automated manufacturing equipment.

6. Garment is manufactured...

7. ...and shipped to the retailer.

Figure 12.6

Rapid response to the marketplace: electronic collaboration between manufacturer and retailer (From *Computerworld,* January 24, 1994, p. 68)

Production scheduling and the ancillary processes are today frequently controlled with a **manufacturing resource planning** system (also called **MRP II** or "big MRP," since it is an advanced version of material requirements planning, or MRP) as the main informational tool. This elaborate software converts the sales forecast for the plant's products into a detailed production plan (usually by quarter) and further into a master schedule of production, usually segmented into weekly periods.

Instead of relying on "push"-style manufacturing, driven by production schedules, some firms have converted to just-in-time (JIT) operation, driven ("pulled") by customer orders. In these cases, suppliers deliver materials just in time for production and, in turn, the production occurs just in time for delivery to customers. JIT operation helps reduce production costs by minimizing inventory of raw materials, in-process products, and finished products. The integration of value chains of several firms involved in supplier–customer relationship requires stringent coordination with information systems. Electronic data interchange (EDI) is necessary. In some cases, JIT features have been incorporated in the MRP II systems, which are able to accommodate both scheduled production and a sudden surge of orders. Other companies use specialized JIT manufacturing software.

Leading companies seek a total integration of their manufacturing value chain. **Computer-integrated manufacturing (CIM)** is a strategy through which a manufacturer takes control of the entire manufacturing process. The process starts with computer-aided design (CAD) and computer-aided engineering (CAE) and continues on the factory floor, where robots and numerically controlled machinery are installed—and thus **computer-aided manufacturing (CAM)** is implemented. A manufacturing system based on this concept can turn out very small batches of a particular product as cost-effectively as a

Figure 12.7

Integrated ordering and production system: fusion at Motorola
(Adapted from R. Strobel and A. Johnson, "Pocket Pagers in Lots of One."
IEEE Spectrum,
September 1993, p. 29.)

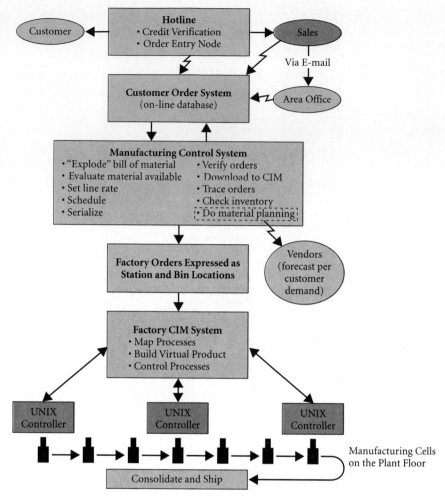

traditional production line can turn out millions of identical products. A full-fledged CIM is extremely difficult to implement; indeed, many firms have failed in their attempts to do so (Walton 1989).

The most advanced manufacturing systems are built today around the customer-oriented manufacturing system (COMMS) model, which may be used together with CIM. With such systems, when a customer's order is being taken, the customer can choose the desired product features and be given the price and the delivery date. The order is "translated" by the information system into a virtual product that exists only in the computer's memory and is sent to the plant floor while the customer is still on the phone. The Fusion manufacturing system used by Motorola to manufacture pagers in lots of one, shown in Figure 12.7, implements a COMMS model with CIM. A customer orders a pager over a telephone hotline. The order, given in plain English, is automatically translated into the data the factory needs, checked out by building the "virtual product" on a computer, and sent to the plant for fabrication, while the customer may still be on the line.

The following vignette shows how mass customization is entering the clothing industry.

**Mass
Customization
in Blue Jeans**

Levi Strauss has introduced mass customization of women's jeans in its Original Levi's Stores. A sales clerk measures the customer, using instructions from a PC screen as an aid. After the data are entered into the computer, the customer can see her future jeans on the screen and make the desired adjustments. All in all, 4,224 combinations of basic measurements are possible. Color and finish options, such as stone-washing, can be selected. The final measurements are relayed over the telecommunications network to a computerized fabric-cutting machine at the Levi's plant in Mountain City, Tennessee. As the fabric is cut, bar-code tags are attached to the components of the clothing, which is assembled, washed, and prepared for shipment.

The customized product costs about $10 more than a mass-produced pair, with an option of receiving the product directly from the plant via FedEx for an additional $5. The entire process takes two and a half weeks.

When this Levi's Personal Pair Jeans service was introduced at a Cincinnati store, sales of women's jeans jumped 300 percent. Although the store offers a money-back guarantee, the rate of returns for the customized jeans is far lower than for those off the rack. "Eventually, this could mean no inventory, no markdowns," says a marketing services manager for the company. "You are not mass-producing product and hoping it sells. You've already got a sale."

One year later, Levi Strauss has more than 60 so-called Personal Pair kiosks. The mass customization has been judged a success, largely because of the repeat business: Once the measurements have been stored, it is easy to order extra pairs (and one customer did order 43 of them). However, the program requires additional work from store clerks and slows down factory operations, which adds to the company's costs.

Based on Glenn Rifkin, "Digital Blue Jeans Pour Data and Legs Into Customized Fit," *The New York Times*, November 6, 1994, pp. A1, D8; and Bruce Caldwell, "Trading Size 12 for a Custom Fit," *InformationWeek*, October 28, 1996, p. 44.

3. Quality Control

Global competition has made product quality a necessary attribute of any product, not just of a high-priced one. The quality control subsystem of a manufacturing information systems relies on the data collected on the shop floor by the sensors embedded in the process control systems. Leading companies have instituted a total quality management program, based on the principles articulated by W. Edwards Deming, an American expert whose work was initially recognized in Japan.

Total quality management (TQM) is a management technique for continuously improving the performance of all members and units of a firm to ensure customer satisfaction. In particular, the principles of TQM state that quality comes from improving the design and manufacturing process, rather than "inspecting out" defective products. Robust products that will function properly over a wide range of uses and environmental conditions are designed. The foundation of quality is also understanding and reducing variation in the overall manufacturing process. Continued quality improvement, with broad training and participation of all—workers and managers—is a must. It is vital to give priority to those quality initiatives that will pay off by attracting customers.

Since one of the foundations of quality is avoiding variance from standards, statistical quality control is conducted, with continual measurement of the work-in-process as well as of finished products. Based on these measurements, graphs, histograms, and distributions of product sizes and their other attributes are obtained. Sources of variation from standards

Figure 12.8

Tracking quality improvement with on-the-screen information systems (From Richard J. Schonberger and Edward N. Knod, Jr., *Operations Management: Continuous Improvement*, 5th ed., Burr Ridge, Ill.: Irwin, 1994, p. 48.)

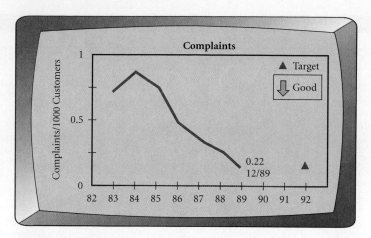

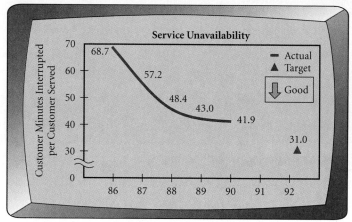

are sought and future variations are prevented by removing their root causes. At the same time, product designs are gradually adapted so that the products become more tolerant of minor variations. The improvements in quality are continually tracked with information systems, for example, with screen-based charts such as those in Figure 12.8. These graphs were obtained by Florida Power & Light, a utility company that was the first non-Japanese winner of Japan's Deming Prize for quality.

Innovative use of information technology in ensuring product quality may be illustrated by the warranty system implemented at Harley-Davidson. By linking the defect-surfacing database of this system with the motorcycle manufacturer's engineering and manufacturing systems, engineers are able to correct deviations from performance standards in the future designs.

4. Facilities Planning, Production Costing, Logistics, and Inventory Subsystems

Among the higher-level decision making supported by manufacturing information systems is facilities planning: locating the sites for manufacturing plants, deciding on their production capacities, and laying out the plant floors. Plant sites are selected primarily by considering the proximity to customers, suppliers, sources of labor, and access to transportation.

IN THE SPOTLIGHT

When Information Technology Brings Your Business to Its Knees

Retailers get very few shoes from Adidas America these days. Last month, the Portland, Oregon, company was able to fill only about one-fifth of roughly $50 million in orders, and even that was done with the help of direct shipments from overseas factories. The reason? Adidas's main U.S. warehouse is almost at a standstill because of the software problems in its new automated distribution system.

Adidas embarked on the automated warehouse project in 1993. The goals included increasing capacity, boosting productivity (in part, by halving the staff), and reducing the time for order fulfillment to 24 hours or less. Bar-coded items were to pass through a central tilt-tray sorter, which would drop the merchandise into a proper chute for either shipment or stocking. Workers would pick up items based on instructions from their armband-mounted wireless computers and from terminals placed on conveyor lines.

The problems stemmed from the software that was customized for the system. Having contracted software vendor Isle, which marketed a UNIX-based distribution system, Adidas decided that it was to be ported to the proprietary operating system platform of the fault-tolerant Stratus computers—because Adidas was familiar with that platform. The compatibility problems common to ported software emerged. The difficulties were compounded when Isle went out of business, leaving Adidas without adequate software documentation to fix the bugs. According to a former information systems manager of Adidas, "Adidas shot itself in the foot by insisting to go on-line when the project was only 90 percent done." (It is a well-known adage in computing that all that's left to do in projects that are 90% done is the other 90%.)

Eventually, Adidas decided to scrap the computer hardware and software of the distribution system, and to install an IBM RS/6000 server running warehouse management software from Exeter Systems in North Billerica, Massachusetts. That was the system that froze the warehouse. While both Adidas and Exeter claim transient delays of a "normal conversion process," it is expected that difficulties will continue for weeks or months. In the meantime, "they are killing us," says a manager of a West Coast retailer, whose sales of Adidas products are down 90 percent—because there are no products to sell.

Those who have followed the continuing saga (nightmare?) of the automated baggage-handling system at Denver International Airport, where software errors resulted in a 16-month delay in the airport opening at a cost overrun of $3 billion, have a sense of déja vu. Indeed the airport's system is still malfunctioning. It would appear that the complexity of coordinating the movement of objects (sneakers or suitcases) within the system of laser bar-code scanners, tilting trays, conveyor belts, and lifting equipment simply overwhelms the vendors of custom-produced distribution software.

Based in part on Marianne K. McGee and Doug Bartholomew, "Meltdown," *InformationWeek*, March 11, 1996, pp. 14–15.

The decisions are unstructured, but decision support systems can assist managers in arriving at them.

Manufacturing management requires a cost control program, relying on the information systems. Among the informational outputs of the Production Costing subsystem are labor and equipment productivity reports, performance of plants as cost centers, and schedules for equipment maintenance and replacement.

Managing the raw-materials, packaging, and the work-in-progress inventory is a responsibility of the manufacturing function. In some cases, inventory management is combined with the general logistics systems, which plan and control the arrival of purchased goods into the firm as well as shipments to the customers. We have noted that proper management calls for low levels of inventories: Inventory represents a temporarily frozen financial asset and is accompanied by carrying costs such as warehousing, insurance, and spoilage. On the other hand, inventory management seeks to avoid stockouts, the absence of materials needed to fulfill a customer's order. The implementation of these systems is not simple. The vignette on the preceding page tells a cautionary tale of the deployment of information systems in logistics. Reading it, you can see how dependent the firms have become on their functional information systems.

12.4 | ACCOUNTING AND FINANCIAL INFORMATION SYSTEMS

The financial function of the enterprise consists in taking stock of the flows of money and other assets into and out of an organization, ensuring that its available resources are properly used and that the organization is financially fit. The organizational use of computers originated with this function. However, their original role was limited to accounting, that is, taking stock of past performance in monetary terms. Since then, financial information systems have become more forward-looking and assist decision makers in planning and controlling the financial performance of the unit for which they are responsible. The general structure of **accounting and financial information systems** is shown in Figure 12.9.

Figure 12.9

Accounting and financial information system

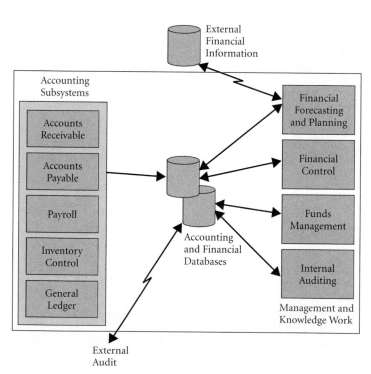

As we can see, the system incorporates the accounting subsystems, which are the transaction processing systems that we discussed in Chapter 9. The accounting subsystems serve to record, consolidate, and report financial events in a firm; that is, events that result in the flow of money and other assets into or out of the firm. The components of the accounting system were included in the general TPS shown in Figure 9.4. In particular:

- Accounts Receivable records amounts owed by customers.
- Accounts Payable records amounts owed to suppliers.
- Payroll records amounts owed to employees.
- Inventory Control records changes in inventory assets.
- General Ledger consolidates the data from all other accounting subsystems, which post the appropriate transactions to the ledger, and produce financial reports and statements. At the end of an accounting period (e.g., a year), General Ledger produces the balance sheet for the firm, listing its assets and liabilities and the firm's income statement, showing its revenues and expenses for the period.

In addition to the data produced by the accounting subsystems, financial information systems rely on external sources, such as on-line databases and custom-produced reports, particularly in the areas of financial forecasting and funds management.

Let us consider the essential functions that financial information systems perform.

1. Financial Forecasting and Planning

Financial forecasting is the process of predicting the inflows of funds into the company and the outflows of funds from it for a long term into the future (for example, for five years on a monthly basis). Outflows of funds must be balanced over the long term with the inflows. Since the sales of products are the principal source of funds, the inflow side of a financial forecast is based on the sales forecast generated by Marketing. Aside from the cost of sales, major investment projects—for example, building a new plant or developing a new market in Hungary—will be considered in the financial forecast as outflows. With the globalization of business, the function of financial forecasting has become more complex, since the activities in multiple national markets have to be consolidated, taking into consideration the vagaries of multiple national currencies. Scenario analysis, discussed above, is frequently employed in order to prepare the firm for various contingencies.

Financial forecasts are based on computerized models known as cash-flow models. They range from rather simple spreadsheet templates to sophisticated models developed for the given industry (known as vertical models) and customized for the firm or, in the case of large corporations, to specific modeling of their financial operations. Financial forecasting serves to identify the need for funds and their sources. Among possible fund sources are bank loans, debt financing (issuing bonds), equity financing (issuing stock), merger with another firm, or being acquired by a firm. Specialized expertise of investment bankers is generally employed when funds other than bank loans are sought.

Based on the long-term financial forecasts, financial plans are drawn up, generally for one year. Financial plans rely on planning models, which show the dependence of projected financial results on the values of input variables. Financial plans obtained with these models include a projected (pro forma) income statement and a pro forma balance sheet. You have seen a simple planning model, which may be specified with a DSS generator, in Figure 10.1, and the pro forma income statement obtained with the model in Figure 10.2. By considering various alternatives (what if's), we can vary the model's premises and compare the outcomes.

Figure 12.10

*A flexible budget
produced with a
spreadsheet program*

General Development Corporation				
Monthly Sales Volume for March 1997 (in thousands of dollars)				
	$100	$120	$140	$160
Expense Items				
Materials	$40	$48	$56	$62
Labor	$15	$18	$21	$24
Overhead	$8	$9	$10	$11
Production Costs	$63	$75	$87	$97
Research and Development	$5	$5	$5	$5
Engineering	$1	$1	$1	$1
Marketing and Sales	$15	$16	$18	$20
Administration	$10	$10	$10	$10
Nonproduction Costs	$31	$32	$34	$36
Total Costs	$94	$107	$121	$133
Profit	$6	$13	$19	$27
Profit/Sales Ratio	6.0%	10.8%	13.6%	16.9%

2. Financial Control

The primary tools of financial control are budgets. Budgets are a powerful means of expressing financial plans on tactical and operational levels. A **budget** specifies the resources committed to a plan for a given project or time period. For example, we may need to draw up a budget for converting a plant to a new manufacturing process or for the operations of the marketing department for the next six months. Fixed budgets are independent of the level of activity of the unit for which the budget is drawn up. Flexible budgets commit resources depending on the level of activity. Thus, the sales activity envisaged by a plan may be classified into three categories, depending on the success of the product, and three budget levels may be drawn up, depending on this activity.

Spreadsheet programs are the main budgeting tool—and budgeting is what made spreadsheets the leading personal productivity tool they are today. An example of a flexible budget for a small company, obtained with a spreadsheet program, is shown in Figure 12.10. Here, costs are budgeted for four possible levels of sales.

In the systems-theoretic view, budgets serve as the standard against which managers can compare the actual results by using information systems (as shown in Figure 2.5). Performance reports are used to monitor budgets of various managerial levels. A performance report states the actual financial results achieved by the unit and compares them with the planned results. This monitoring may be done with management reporting systems, as depicted in Figure 9.9. Senior managers increasingly use executive information systems to monitor budgets.

Along with budgets and performance reports, financial control employs a number of financial ratios indicating the performance of the business unit. A widely employed financial ratio is **return on investment (ROI)**. ROI shows how well a business unit uses its resources: Its value is obtained by dividing the earnings of the business unit by its total assets. Innovative companies are prepared to assume appropriate risk and suspend using the ROI indicator for a certain period with respect to a promising project. In particular, the use of ROI may be suspended when considering the development of a strategic information system.

3. Funds Management

Financial information systems help to manage the organization's liquid assets, such as cash or securities, for high yields with the lowest degree of loss risk. Some firms deploy computerized systems to manage their securities portfolios and automatically generate buy or sell orders. The globalization of business has resulted in the need to maintain positions in multiple currencies in order to conduct business in the corresponding countries. Companies do forward buying of a currency to be used in a payment to a foreign supplier in order to minimize the risk associated with the appreciation of that currency. The purchasing firm pays a fixed price for a certain amount of foreign currency to be delivered on a future date.

4. Internal Auditing

How do the firm's executives know whether the financial records of various units correspond to reality? How do investors or government organizations know whether the financial statements reported by the firm are true? The **audit** function provides an independent appraisal of an organization's accounting, financial, and operational procedures and information. All larger firms have **internal auditors,** answerable only to the audit committee of the board of directors. The staff of the chief financial officer of the company performs financial and operational audits. During a **financial audit,** an appraisal is made of the reliability and integrity of the company's financial information and of the means used to process it (including information systems). An **operational audit** is an appraisal of how well management utilizes company resources and how well corporate plans are being carried out. Today, of course, it would be impossible to render an opinion on the financial state of a firm or its unit without a thorough audit of information systems. The professional who evaluates the effectiveness of financial information systems is known as an information systems auditor. Audit software, such as Dyl-Audit (from Dylakor), EDP Audit (from Cullinane), or Pan Audit (from Pansophic Systems) is available to assist these auditors.

To certify that a firm's records and procedures are in "accordance with generally accepted accounting principles" (or find that they somehow diverge from them), external audits are performed by certified public accountants (CPAs). Audited financial statements are provided to the local, state, and federal governments in the United States, furnished by public companies to the financial community, and published in the annual reports. We will return to the audit function during our discussion of information systems controls in Section 14.6.

12.5 │ HUMAN RESOURCE INFORMATION SYSTEMS

Functions and Structure of Human Resource Information Systems

A **human resource information system (HRIS)** supports the human resources function of an organization with information. The name of this function reflects the recognition that people who work in a firm are frequently its most valuable resource (Clinchy and Cornetto 1996). The complexity of human resource management has grown immensely over recent

Figure 12.11

Human resource information system

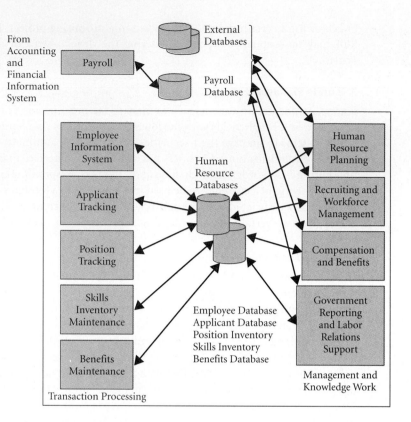

From Accounting and Financial Information System

Payroll

External Databases

Payroll Database

Employee Information System

Applicant Tracking

Position Tracking

Skills Inventory Maintenance

Benefits Maintenance

Human Resource Databases

Employee Database
Applicant Database
Position Inventory
Skills Inventory
Benefits Database

Human Resource Planning

Recruiting and Workforce Management

Compensation and Benefits

Government Reporting and Labor Relations Support

Transaction Processing

Management and Knowledge Work

years, primarily due to the need to conform with the laws and regulations of the U.S. federal government in providing equal employment opportunity, and a safe and healthy workplace. A firm's own efforts to ensure both equality and diversity of workforce call for enhanced information processing. The move of many companies to a multinational structure, with operations conducted in several countries, has further complicated their human resource management. Flexible organizational structures, such as project-oriented teams, require extensive computerized "inventories" of human skills and experience. To cite one outstanding example, thanks to its integrated PRISM system for human resource management, FedEx has been able to maintain tight control of its very rapidly growing workforce, realizing at the same time the economies of paperless operation (Palvia 1992).

The general structure of human resource information systems is shown in Figure 12.11.

An HRIS has to ensure the appropriate degree of access to a great variety of internal stakeholders, including:

- The employees of the Human Resources department in performance of their duties.

- All the employees of the firm wishing to inspect their own records.

- All the employees of the firm seeking information regarding open positions or available benefit plans.

- Employees availing themselves of the computer-assisted training and evaluation opportunities.

Figure 12.12

This applicant resume has been selected by Restrac Enterprise software (from MicroTrac Systems of Dedham, Massachusetts) based on a weighted list of selection criteria

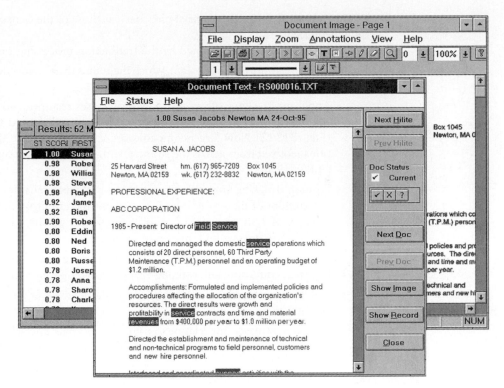

- Managers throughout the firm in the process of evaluating their subordinates and making personnel decisions.
- Corporate executives involved in tactical and strategic planning and control.

Transaction Processing Subsystems and Databases of Human Resource Information Systems

At the heart of HRIS are its databases, which are in some cases integrated into a single human resource database. The record of each employee in a sophisticated employee database may contain 150 to 200 data items, including the personal data, educational history and skills, occupational background, and the history of occupied positions, salary, and performance in the firm. Richer multimedia databases are now assembled by some firms in order to facilitate fast formation of compatible teams of people with complementary skills. Such databases include employee photographs and even brief interviews stored in a voice form.

Many HRISs maintain other databases as well. Applicant databases contain resumes and other data regarding applicants for positions. Position inventory describes all positions within the firm, both filled and unfilled. Skills inventories that describe job-related skills of the firm's personnel have become vital in proper staffing, including team assignments. Benefit databases describe the variety of available employee benefits, including health, insurance, vacation, stock-option, and retirement benefits. In addition to the internal databases,

HRISs rely on access to the external ones, such as those of the Census Bureau or local employment agencies.

The databases are maintained by the transaction processing systems, which include:

- Employee Information System, which maintains the employee database we described above.
- Applicant Tracking subsystem, which processes resumes and results of interviews. Many firms maintain the received resumes with specialized text-retrieval software (Figure 12.12). Now, larger companies are able to create central databases of applications received from across the country, with many of these coming over the Internet (Rifkin 1996).
- Position Tracking maintains the inventory of open positions along with the job descriptions of these positions. For example, the inventory may tell us that an open position of systems analyst has to be filled by a person with a master's degree in information systems and three years' experience.
- Skills Inventory Maintenance is necessary to keep track of the employees' skills as turnover, education, and training change the skill pool.
- Benefits Maintenance is needed to keep updating the ever growing variety of benefits available to employees.

In addition, transactions relating to payments of wages and salaries are handled by the Payroll subsystem, which is generally a part of the Accounting and Financial information system.

Information Subsystems for Human Resource Management

The information subsystems of HRIS reflect the flow of human resources through the firm, from planning and recruitment to termination. A sophisticated HRIS includes the following subsystems:

1. Human Resource Planning

To identify the human resources necessary to accomplish the long-term objectives of a firm, we need to project the skills, knowledge, and experience of the future employees. The geographical (in some cases, international) distribution of this future workforce has to be developed. Computerized workforce planning models are often employed. After considering the current workforce and the level of turnover, the number of positions that will need to be staffed in various job categories can be determined. This information can then be matched with the forecasts on the availability of human resources in the locales of projected company operations, which can be made based on external databases.

2. Recruiting and Workforce Management

Based on the long-term human resource plan, a recruitment plan is developed. The plan lists the currently unfilled positions and those expected to become vacant due to turnover. Internal sources, such as promotions and transfers, for filling these positions are considered. Resumes maintained by the Applicant Tracking subsystem are considered as well. Recruitment programs are drawn up in conformance with the applicable Equal Employment Opportunity/Affirmative Action (EEO/AA) laws and regulations. In order to enrich the external search, HRIS may maintain data on alternative sources of candidates with the ratings

Photo 12.2

At a Compaq plant in Houston, workers can check on their benefits and retirement plans at an electronic kiosk connected to the corporate intranet

of their effectiveness: schools and colleges, the Internet, advertisement media, employment offices, and so forth.

The life-cycle transitions of the firm's workforce—hiring, promotion and transfer, and termination—have to be supported with the appropriate information system components. The results of employee performance appraisal are maintained as part of their records. Partly based on the analysis of these transitions and appraisals, job analysis and design is performed. The objective is to develop job descriptions—requisite skills, experience, and knowledge—that would create a demanding yet satisfying workplace, thus leading to lower turnover and higher performance.

Employee training (skills development) and education (knowledge acquisition) are planned and supported. Many companies conduct their own internal training and education programs. Increasingly, computer-based training is employed, with a cycle of computer-assisted instruction and evaluation offered to the employees who wish to advance themselves in the firm. Multimedia just-in-time training is sometimes done right at the assembly line.

3. Compensation and Benefits

Information systems are used to develop and administer the firm's compensation plan. This plan specifies salaries, hourly wages, incentive pay, and profit sharing that go with a specific position in the firm's workforce. An increasing variety of benefits is available to employees. In firms that offer flexible (cafeteria-style) benefits, employees can design their own benefit package. Employees may be offered on-line access with electronic kiosks (see Photo 12.2) to review their options.

In designing a compensation package, decision support systems may be used by human resource specialists to compare various combinations of compensation and benefits in terms of the total cost per employee. With the use of external databases, these costs can be compared with the averages for the industry and for the geographical region.

4. Government Reporting and Labor Relations Support

Two principal external stakeholders have an abiding interest in the human resource policies of organizations. These are government and labor unions.

Provision of equitable and healthy workplaces is of concern to various levels of government. A variety of laws and regulations, administered by the Equal Employment

IN THE SPOTLIGHT

**The Seamless
Web of
Enterprise**

SAP AG, Europe's largest vendor of applications software, headquartered in Walldorf, Germany, has made a strong entry into the American market. Its forte is the software that helps an enterprise consolidate its business functions. For example, when a company using SAP software hires an employee, not only the human resource information subsystem but also payroll, accounting, and, say, production (if the employee goes to work there) are all automatically made aware of the change.

SAP R/3 software, which runs in a client/server environment, treats its various functional subsystems much like cells in a spreadsheet. When you change an item in one of the functional components, you automatically change the related items on other functions, much as a spreadsheet recalculates the related cells. Going from an order entry to inventory control, and then on to pricing schedules is almost as easy as moving a cursor through a spreadsheet.

The SAP software is also notable for its multinational capabilities, providing multicurrency and multilingual operation. "You can look at databases in Japanese, German, and French, all at the same time," says Charles Faust, vice-president of operations at Fujitsu Microelectronics, the semiconductor manufacturer. SAP software is built around the business processes, disdaining the functional subdivisions of the corporation. Thus, implementing SAP has to be preceded by business reengineering, with a major redesign of business processes, the SAP way.

Going beyond the corporate boundaries and toward interorganizational information systems, SAP has released enhanced R/3 software that works over the Internet. The R/3 systems of two cooperating companies can be linked to process orders in real-time. When the first company's system sends an order, it automatically triggers transactions (such as an inventory check) in the second company's R/3 system.

The software is expensive, with customers paying well over $1 million for a typical installation. It is famously difficult to implement, which causes $5 consulting fees for each $1 in software licensing fees. Some very large multinationals are known to have spent over $200 million to roll out an R/3-based system. And yet SAP's North American subsidiary, located in suburban Philadelphia, keeps showing dramatic growth in sales. This indicates that customers' need to integrate their functions is great enough to make the expenditures worthwhile.

Based on David S. Fondiller, "Client Serving," *Forbes,* July 4, 1994, p. 130; John J. Xenakis, "Taming SAP," *CFO,* March 1996, pp. 23–30; and Julia King, "SAP AG Boards 'Net Bandwagon," *Computerworld,* March 11, 1996, p. 4.

Opportunity Commission (EEOC), require reporting to establish that equal opportunity is provided to minorities, women, handicapped, and older employees. Occupational Safety and Health Administration (OSHA) requires that information be available regarding employee health and safety, and that each work accident and work-related illness be reported. In addition to these two federal agencies, a variety of state and local government agencies require reporting as well.

Where appropriate, HRIS should support management negotiations with labor unions. Information necessary for this is based on the data provided by the Compensation and Benefits subsystem, as well as the Accounting and Financial information system. To put the firm's compensation in perspective, the data from external databases on industry averages, competitor pay, and similar comparative figures have to be accessed. During the actual negotiations, a variety of ad hoc reports may be needed by the negotiating team on short

IN THE SPOTLIGHT

Failure to Connect

Sometimes the failure to integrate information systems has very tangible and unfortunate effects. Take hospital information systems. A few years ago, several hospital patients died from a bad batch of the drug protamine. Yet the problem could not be traced to its source. The reason? In about 70 percent of hospitals, the pharmacy information subsystem is not integrated with the treatment information system. There is no way to establish which vendor supplied the drug administered to a particular patient, let alone establish the batch number that went into the treatment.

Various departments in most hospitals have implemented their own systems on a piecemeal basis. Under pressure to lower the costs of the healthcare they deliver, many of these hospitals give low priority to the integration of various existing subsystems. As the result, pharmacy information cannot be linked to information about treatment outcomes. Yet patients with adverse drug reactions have to stay in the hospital an average of two extra days (assuming no outcome worse than that), at a cost of some $2,000. Sometimes these costs have to be absorbed by the hospital. Prevention—by system integration—appears well worth the investment.

Based on Mitch Betts, "Drug Data Fails to Connect," *Computerworld*, January 17, 1994, p. 68.

notice. Negotiation support systems are currently being developed as a form of electronic meeting systems (Lim and Benbasat 1992–93) and have been used experimentally to facilitate the process.

12.6 | INTEGRATING FUNCTIONAL SYSTEMS FOR SUPERIOR ORGANIZATIONAL PERFORMANCE

Functional information systems rarely stand alone. This reflects the fact that the functions they support should, as much as possible, connect with each other seamlessly in order to serve the firm's customers. Today's companies compete on the package of product–service–information they provide to their customers, rather than on the product "thrown over the wall." Customers expect timely order delivery, often on a just-in-time schedule; quality inspection to their own standards; flexible credit terms; post-delivery service; and often, participation in the product design process. As we noted at the beginning of this chapter, this demands that the specialized functions interact closely, driven by customer requirements. Powerful software supporting integration of business functions is now available from SAP AG, Oracle, and PeopleSoft (Frye 1997). Its use is illustrated by the vignette on page 448, which will make the meaning of integration more tangible to you. As that vignette shows, the IS-enabled integration of business functions is expensive but, as the vignette above illustrates in a very different domain, it may indeed be necessary.

Integration of business functions is more and more frequently going beyond the boundaries of an individual firm. Let us consider two telling examples. SmithKline Beecham Consumer Brands of Pittsburgh manufactures over-the-counter healthcare products. The firm used information technology to respond to the intense competitive cost-cutting pressures in its industry. SmithKline's IS specialists implemented an information system that integrates planning for the entire supply chain, including what is supplied to the firm and what the firm supplies to its customers. Corporate plans are integrated with those of the principal suppliers and customers of the firm. Sales forecasting has been integrated with manufacturing and distribution planning. Planning is now based on what the customers say they will need in the future, rather than on what the company produced in the past. The redesigned planning process resulted in significant savings by reducing inventory and cutting transportation costs. Even more important, it resulted in better customer service. There are fewer instances of products not being available for filling orders, and any problem can be detected several days prior to the intended shipment date and corrected. The time between order receipt and product shipment has been cut. Production schedules are more stable. It is the timely flow of information throughout the entire supply chain that has made possible this improvement of customer service combined with cost cutting (Santosus 1993).

Information technology can also help a firm integrate its operations with those of its suppliers and customers. As our next example, Campbell Soup (of Camden, New Jersey) runs a continuous product replenishment program for its wholesale and retail customers. Thus, Campbell Soup in effect manages their inventories for the customers. Receiving through EDI the daily sales data from the customers, the Campbell's order-management program automatically analyzes their remaining inventory and orders shipments. In this way, the supplier's marketing and sales system is integrated with the customers's ordering and inventory systems. The tight relationship with customers helps sales: the sales growth to customers participating in the program is much steeper than to others.

Going even further than the two companies just described, Wal-Mart has integrated its own functional systems and the systems of its major suppliers to such a degree that it is able to provide each of these suppliers with a profit-and-loss statement for the goods received from that supplier (Darling and Semich 1996).

Based on the several business examples in this section, we may conclude that information technology provides vital support for integrating internal business processes, cutting across functional lines, and for integrating operations with the firm's business partners, its customers and suppliers.

SUMMARY

The principal business functions to be supported with information systems are marketing and sales, production (known as manufacturing in goods-producing firms), accounting and finance, and human resources.

Marketing information systems encompass three classes of subsystems: transaction processing subsystems that include order entry, invoicing, and sales-call reporting; boundary-spanning subsystems; and marketing-mix subsystems.

Boundary-spanning subsystems bring into the firm data and information about the marketplace. Marketing research collects data on the actual and prospective customers. Marketing intelligence gathers and helps interpret data on the firm's competitors and disseminates the data to the appropriate users.

Marketing-mix subsystems include product, place, promotion, and price subsystems, as well as sales forecasting. Product subsystem helps to plan introduction of new products. Place subsystem helps to plan distribution channels for products and assists in tracking their performance. Promotion subsystem supports personal selling of products and advertising. Price subsystem helps in establishing product prices. Sales forecasting helps to forecast the expected sales based on the future marketing mix established by the other four subsystems and on the existing orders.

The new manufacturing environment that needs to be supported with information systems is lean in that it uses fewer input resources; agile in that it relies on short product design cycles and rapid order fulfillment; flexible in that it is easy to adjust a product to a customer's preferences; and managed for quality to satisfy the needs of the customers with respect to the attributes of the products they are expected to purchase. The subsystems of a manufacturing information system which support management and knowledge work are product design and engineering, production scheduling, quality control, facilities planning, production costing, and logistics and inventory management.

An accounting and financial system includes the following accounting subsystems: accounts receivable, accounts payable, payroll, inventory control, and general ledger. It also includes the following financial subsystems: financial forecasting and planning, financial control, funds management, and internal auditing.

A human resource information system includes the following transaction processing subsystems: employee information system, applicant tracking, position tracking, skills inventory maintenance, and benefit maintenance. It also includes systems supporting management and knowledge work: human resource planning, recruiting and workforce management, compensation and benefits, government reporting, and labor relations support.

Companies increasingly integrate their internal functional information systems as well as integrate their systems with those of their suppliers, customers, and business partners. This is done to assure fast and cost-effective response to the specific customer demands for products with the quality attributes desired by the customer.

KEY TERMS

QUESTIONS

1. What are the four principal business functions that need to be supported with information systems?
2. What are the boundary-spanning subsystems of marketing information systems and what is the objective of each of them? What capabilities of information systems (see Section 1.5) make them important in these subsystems?
3. What are the marketing-mix subsystems of marketing information systems and what are their objectives?
4. What is database marketing? Describe its competitive potential. What are the threats it poses from the ethical point of view?
5. What role does information technology play in sales-force automation?
6. What are the four characteristics of the new manufacturing environment? Describe each of them in one sentence.
7. List the manufacturing information systems that support management and knowledge work. State the objective of each of them in one sentence.
8. What is manufacturing resource planning (MRP II)?
9. What is just-in-time operation in manufacturing? What are its advantages and drawbacks? Would it be possible without information systems and, if so, to what extent?
10. What is computer-integrated manufacturing (CIM)? Why is it difficult to implement?
11. What is mass customization? How does it relate to the use of information systems in manufacturing?
12. What are the objectives of total quality management (TQM)? What is the role of information systems in it?
13. List the information systems supporting management and knowledge work in the area of accounting and finance. State the objective of each of these systems.
14. What are the principal budgeting tools? How do budgets relate to the concept of responsibility reporting (which was discussed in Section 9.6)?
15. What are the transaction processing subsystems of a human resource information system (HRIS)?
16. What subsystems of HRIS assist management and knowledge work? What databases do they rely on?
17. What is the effect of government regulation on the informational needs in the area of human resource management? Give specific examples.
18. Specify the functional information systems and, if possible, their subsystems that would be involved in the processing of these transactions:
    a. Hiring a new employee.
    b. Entering a new customer company into the information system.
    c. Processing an order for an existing customer company.

Specify what information is used and/or modified in each of these systems or subsystems by the transaction.
19. Specify point by point the objectives of intra- and interorganizational integration of functional information systems.

ISSUES FOR DISCUSSION

1. Discuss the most promising uses of expert system technology in the systems supporting business functions. Use specific examples in each of the business areas to make your points. What business results can be expected from the use of each of the systems?
2. What are the principal influences of the use of information systems on the competitive environment in manufacturing?
3. Why does integration of functional information systems in a firm usually present great difficulties? Discuss the behavioral and organizational factors, as well as the technological ones.
4. Discuss the ethical issues that can arise during the use of a human resource information system. Is there a way to design the system to prevent the issue from arising or to make the issue capable of being handled properly?

REAL-WORLD MINICASE AND PROBLEM-SOLVING EXERCISES

1. Moving to Electronic Commerce at Campbell Soup   As you read in Section 6 of the chapter, Campbell Soup has become an inventory manager for many of its customers through an automatic replenishment system. "Many" in this case means 30 percent. The remaining 70 percent of the company's customers are not comfortable with the supplier making their purchasing decisions for them. Yet, orders that are not processed by the replenishment system have been until now paper-based and prone to end up in the wrong plants and offices of Campbell Soup.

To handle these orders, Campbell Soup is phasing in a new electronic commerce system. It will be based on an IBM RS/6000 parallel processor, running a relational DBMS from Oracle Corporation. The software will consist of two essential components. An order-processing application from Industri-Mathematick in Sweden will let Campbell centralize all orders, now scattered throughout 13 regional offices. A second application, from Manugistics (of Rockville, Maryland) will help in sales-order forecasting and thus assist inventory planning for Campbell soup and for its customers.

The electronic commerce system will work as follows. The customers will send their orders via E-mail. The order-processing subsystem will process them, enter them into the database, and direct them to an appropriate plant. At the same time, the orders will be routed to the inventory planning subsystem, which will help sales managers decide how much of which products to make and where. The subsystem will also track the inventory of individual customers and advise them by E-mail when to replenish. The decision to do so belongs, however, to the customer. When the goods are to be dispatched, the customer will be electronically informed about the shipment and its arrival time.

a. What business functions are being integrated by the system described here?

b. What business results can Campbell expect from the implementation of the electronic commerce system?

c. What more advanced electronic commerce facilities can Campbell Soup use in the future?

d. Do you believe the use of this system by Campbell's customers is a stepping-stone to the use of automatic replenishment in the future? Why or why not?

Based on Mark Halper, "Campbell Soups Up Inventory," *Computerworld Electronic Commerce Journal,* April 29, 1996, pp. 11–12.

2. You are responsible for computerizing the marketing function of a newly formed health maintenance organization. Produce a memo describing how a geographic information system (GIS) can be used to assist the firm's marketing efforts. The memo is directed to the vice-president of marketing, who is not an information systems specialist. Make sure to include (as the front matter) a brief executive summary of your findings.

3. Using a spreadsheet, develop a template for the budget report shown in Figure 12.10. Print out the template. Create a bar graph for the profit/sales ratio and print it out.

4. Show graphically how the life-cycle transitions of a company's employees can be supported with HRIS.

5. Using the strategic cube, presented in Section 3.5, describe a manufacturing and a marketing information system that can both be used as strategic systems in the Differentiation–Present Competitors–Internal Innovation subcube.

TEAM PROJECT

The information systems supporting the management of corporate human resources have been undergoing profound change. Each two- or three-person team will investigate an aspect of this change. Possible topics will include the integrated management of life-cycle transitions of company's employees, the use of multimedia in HRIS, skill development-oriented HRIS, use of the Internet and intranets in HRIS, and outsourcing of HRIS. Selected teams will make a presentation to the class so that a general picture of trends can emerge.

SELECTED REFERENCES

Bessen, Jim. "Riding the Marketing Information Wave." *Harvard Business Review,* September–October 1993, pp. 150–161.

Blackmon, Douglas A. "FedEx Plans to Establish a Marketplace in Cyberspace." *The Wall Street Journal,* October 9, 1996, p. B3.

Bylinsky, Gene. "The Digital Factory." *Fortune,* November 14, 1994, pp. 92–110.

Cassidy, Peter. "The Point of Most Return." *CIO,* April 1, 1994, pp. 46–56.

How point-of-sale technologies are changing the way companies sell.

Clemons, Eric K., and Michael C. Row. "Limits to Interfirm Coordination through Information Technology: Results from a Field Study in Consumer Packaged Goods Distribution." *Journal of Management Information Systems,* 10, no. 1, (Summer 1993), pp. 73–96.

Clinchy, Kenneth, and Michael Cornetto. "Help for Those Doing the Hiring." *InformationWeek,* March 11, 1996, pp. 47–56.

Cronin, B., and others. "The Internet and Competitive Intelligence: A Survey of Current Practice." *International Journal of Information Management,* 14, no. 3, (June 1994), pp. 204–222.

Darling, Charles B., and J. William Semich. "Extreme Integration." *Datamation,* November 1996, pp. 48–58.

Foley, John. "Market of One: Ready, Aim, Sell!" *InformationWeek,* February 17, 1997, pp. 34–44.

Fredenberger, William B.; Art DeThomas; and Howard N. Ray. "Information Needs of Firms in Financial Distress." *International Journal of Information Management,* 13, October 1993, pp. 326–340.

Discusses corporate needs for financial information, which applies not only to the turnaround companies.

Frye, Colleen. "PeopleSoft Goes Global." *Software Magazine,* March 1997, pp. 62–66.

How global companies integrate their business functions using specialized software.

Goldman, Steven L.; Roger N. Nagel; and Kenneth Preiss. *Agile Competitors and Virtual Organizations,* New York: Van Nostrand Reinhold, 1994.

Hammer, Michael. *Beyond Reengineering: How the Process-Centered Organization is Changing Our Work and Our Lives.* New York: HarperBusiness, 1996.

Konsynski, Benn. "Strategic Control in the Business Enterprise." *IBM Business Journal,* 32, no. 1, (1993), pp. 111–42.

Lane, Randall. "You Are What You Wear." *Forbes,* October 14, 1996, pp. 42–46.

Lim, Lai-Huat, and Izak Benbasat. "A Theoretical Perspective of Negotiation Support Systems." *Journal of Management Information Systems,* 3, no. 9, Winter 1992–93, pp. 27–44.

"Manufacturing A La Carte: Agile Assembly Lines, Faster Development Cycles." Special Issue, *IEEE Spectrum,* September 1993.

The articles in this special issue are an excellent introduction to the new manufacturing environment.

Palvia, Prashant C.; James A. Perkins; and Steven M. Zeltmann. "The PRISM System: A Key to Organizational Effectiveness at Federal Express Corporation." *MIS Quarterly,* 16, no. 3, (September 1992), pp. 277–292.

A detailed description of a leading-edge human resource information system.

Pine, B. Joseph II; Bart Victor; and Andrew C. Boynton. "Making Mass Customization Work." *Harvard Business Review,* September–October 1993, pp. 108–121.

Rayport, Jeffrey F., and John J. Sviokla. "Exploiting the Virtual Value Chain." *Harvard Business Review,* November–December 1995, pp. 75–85.

How to move your company's operations from the marketplace into a "marketspace" created with information systems.

Rifkin, Glenn. "Virtual Recruiter: Software That Reads Resumes." *The New York Times,* March 24, 1996, p. B12.

Santosus, Megan. "Rethinking the Distributive Principle." *CIO,* December 1, 1993, pp. 32–41.

Schonberger, Richard J., and Edward M. Knod, Jr. *Operations Management: Continuous Improvement.* 5th ed. Burr Ridge, Illinois: Irwin, 1994.

A comprehensive contemporary textbook that stresses total quality management (TQM).

Walton, Richard I. *Up and Running: Integrating Information Technology and the Organizations,* Boston: Harvard Business School Press, 1989.

Shows how the same information technology can have positive and negative organizational effects. Also shows how to manage the implementation of information systems for positive effect.

Winkler, Connie. "The New Line on Managing People." *InformationWeek,* May 23, 1994, pp. 60–69.

Discusses human resource information systems and their integration with other functional information systems.

Wozny, Michael J., and William C. Regli eds. "Computing in Manufacturing." Special Issue, *Communications of the ACM,* 39, no. 2, (February 1996), pp. 32–85.

Several articles describing the implementation of shared manufacturing services via World Wide Web, rapid design of wearable computers, virtual prototyping and virtual enterprises, and other uses of IS in manufacturing.

CASE STUDY | # Making Mass Customization Possible at Andersen

Andersen windows are a symbol of quality. Many a real estate agent will begin telling you about a new house by mentioning the view you will get through its Andersen windows. These windows are made by Andersen Corporation of Bayport, Minnesota, a private manufacturer of wooden-frame windows and patio doors with a 100-year tradition. With over $1 billion in sales and 4,000 employees, Andersen works with more than 100 distributors, including some in Europe and on the Pacific Rim, as well as with thousands of retailers.

Hans Jacob Andersen, founder of the company, set up an assembly line in his factory in 1904, creating mass production nine years before Henry Ford. But mass production, even of high-quality products, is now no longer satisfactory. Consumers and commercial end customers demand products that satisfy their special requirements. Therefore, along with the mass-produced, standard items, in the 1980s Andersen started to deliver customized and made-to-order windows. Sales of these profitable items began to climb rapidly. From 1985 to 1991, the number of different products offered by Andersen grew from 28,000 to 86,000. Here is where the problem began. Surely, products did have the usual Andersen quality. But if the right product could not be delivered to the right place at the right time, all the custom casements, colors, and low-energy glass in the world could not satisfy the customer. In 1991, when the problem reached its critical level, 20 percent of all deliveries contained at least one shipping or invoicing mistake. As we know, a product today combines the physical good with the service—and the service was unsatisfactory.

The problem was diagnosed at Andersen as a failure of the business processes, aimed at economies of scale of standardized mass production. Andersen managers realized that they would have to move to a new business model, that of mass customization, achieving economies across a wide range of related products. It was necessary to revamp the company's business processes. It was also apparent from the very beginning that the new business processes have to be enabled by new information systems. After all, Andersen had lost control of much of its product and, as we know, information systems are a potent control tool.

Take the critical order-fulfillment process that includes all the lower-level processes between the time an order is received and the moment the finished product is shipped to the customer. The process is highly information-intensive. In 1992, custom products (that is, variations of standard windows) and unique products (built-to-order from the ground up) generated 25 percent of sales but accounted for over half of the more than two million line items—product components that had to be recorded, tracked, and verified as the orders were being filled. Yet Andersen did not have a standard process for labeling, tracking, and distributing such components and products.

At the same time, the company was doing well. During the 1980s, Andersen tripled its business volume, serving both residential and commercial markets. But to gain control of its present operations and to create a base for future development, Andersen needed to become proactive.

In 1990, a business reengineering effort was started, focusing on order fulfillment and, in particular, on the internal distribution within the firm. The goal, according to Mike Tremblay, who heads the firm's 150-member IS group, was "to improve service so that our customers like doing business with us better than anyone else." An unusually active role was assigned to Tremblay's IS people. The IS group developed a standard methodology for reengineering projects at Andersen. The methodology identified the individual processes—such as internal distribution of materials, semi-finished, and finished products within the firm—rather than concentrating on functions, such as picking and loading. Each process was evaluated for improvement potential with a clearly stated business objective. Based on this evaluation, it was decided whether the process had to be completely reengineered or simply improved with a technique such as total quality management. The firm's managers believe that the methodology was critical to the ultimate success.

Each process within the standard, custom, and built-to-order lines of business was assessed with a report card. It became readily apparent that the internal distribution process had to be completely reengineered. A multidisciplinary team was assembled, including the members of internal staff and consultants from Ernst & Young. The team created a bar code-based product identification system. Each physical item, such as a casement or a glass pane, handled in the firm's plant was linked through an affixed bar code to a line item on a customer order.

The team proceeded to develop a PC-based application to provide on-line shipment verification for customer orders. The old manual process of reporting shortages went like this: Oops, a picker discovered that a product is missing and the order can't be shipped—unless we disrupt the manufacturing line to produce the missing item in time for loading. With the on-line system, manufacturing knows in real-time what needs to be produced to complete orders due for shipment. The complexity is daunting: Each day 60,000 transactions take place among receivers, pickers, and loaders of the ordered merchandise. Loaders were involved in prototyping and designing the information system. Indeed, the loaders demonstrated and explained the system to the company's board of directors. This reinforced the loaders's sense of ownership in the system and led to their involvement in its future improvement.

The customer-order database runs on a hardware system consisting of multiple Sequent minicomputers, where it was moved from a Unisys mainframe. A local area network, with a fault-tolerant Stratus minicomputer serving as a communications processor, links the Sequent minis with the PCs distributed throughout the company. The fast network uses optical-fiber interconnections. Handheld and forklift-mounted terminals in the distribution area communicate with the network via radio-frequency signals.

The results of coordinated order fulfillment are readily apparent. As the number of unique items is multiplying, the shipping mistakes that once plagued the company have been almost eliminated. In 1992, Andersen shipped 6.5 million cartons containing 23.7 million parts and 108,000 unique items with a shipping discrepancy rate of less than 1 percent.

Now, a new IS application is being developed in order to ensure continuous flow of material and to eliminate the remaining discrepancies. The picking function will be eliminated and the picked stacks of products will no longer be left in front of the shipping docks for a shift or two waiting to be loaded. The software will allow the loaders to do both picking and loading.

The greater variety of products calls for greater efficiency in using warehouse space. As the shipment verification system was being developed, inventory was consolidated from 22 sites to 5. Thanks to the efficiencies reached with the new processes, supported by information systems, Andersen will be able to avoid building an additional warehousing facility and will save at least $12 million in construction and $5 million in annual operating expenses. Elimination of discrepancies saved Andersen's customers the expense of verifying Andersen's shipments and correcting problems.

"We've succeeded in eliminating many of the economies of scale that we relied on," says Kim Korn, manager of production planning. Andersen's managers feel that the company is well on its way to achieving a new core competency in mass customization: achieving efficiency in handling many custom products.

The internal distribution process is not the only one to be redesigned. As the company learns how to handle the expanding product lines, it also wants to sell more of the custom and made-to-order products. So the firm has developed an information system that could

Photo 12.3

With a multimedia point-of-sale kiosk connected to a product database, what you see is what you get (From Santosus, "No Pane, No Gain," *CIO*, November 1, 1993, pp. 47–52.)

Figure 12.13

Generating an order with Andersen's Window of Knowledge System (From Charles D. Winslow and William L. Bramer, *Future Work: Putting Knowledge to Work in the Knowledge Economy,* New York: Free Press, 1994, p. 171.)

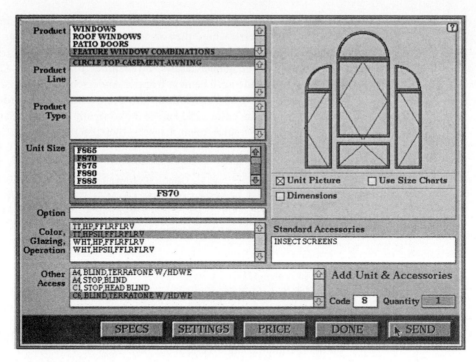

help distributors and retailers configure and price these products. In order to do this, 10 of these customers were invited to work with the firm's IS developers to design interfaces to a desktop PC-based system. "We asked them, 'How would you sell your products if you did not have any limitations,' " says Tremblay. As the result, a point-of sale kiosk (Photo 12.3) was developed.

The kiosk is actually the delivery vehicle for Andersen's Window of Knowledge (WOK), a multimedia system based on an Apple Macintosh equipped with an optical disk and connected to an Oracle database (running on another Sequent mini) with more than 500,000 product records. Full-motion video is provided. The entire kiosk costs about $4,000. In addition, a UNIX-based publishing network is available, over which product and pricing information are sent. Using an in-store WOK terminal, a salesperson can sit down with a consumer and create a representation of what the desired custom product would look like (see Figure 12.13).

Using WOK, a price quote is available within seconds. It is no simple matter. A quote for an arch window used to take an hour and a half to prepare. Many customers could not take that much time, particularly if several different windows were involved. The system has been sold to 100 distributors and 350 retailers. Actually, the cost of hardware is subsidized by Andersen, which also provides software and telecommunications, and offers ongoing training and support. Virtually all the distributors and retailers report increased accuracy; 46 percent say that WOK has increased their sales by an average of 20 percent. Retailers report that WOK draws a crowd. Customers "enjoy playing with the system," according to one retailer. "Often customers bring their kids back to the store to use it—future customers in the making."

Recently, it has become possible to transmit the orders directly from retailers' PCs into the corporate computers, where they are entered into the customer-order database. Each window is assigned a unique "license-plate number," which can be tracked using bar-code technology. With the reengineered sales and manufacturing system, Andersen has moved to on-demand manufacturing. The next frontier Andersen wants to conquer is batch-of-one manufacturing: making all the windows components exactly to order. This will dramatically reduce the parts inventory and enable the company to compete aggressively in the $15-billion-a-year window-replacement market—by replacing the windows originally made by Andersen's competitors.

Based on Megan Santosus, "No Pane, No Gain," *CIO,* November 1, 1993, pp. 47–52; Linda Wilson, "The Online Economy," *InformationWeek,* July 4, 1994, pp. 35–54; Charles D. Winslow and William L. Bramer, *FutureWork: Putting Knowledge to Work in the Knowledge Economy,* New York: Free Press, 1994; and Justin Martin, "Are You As Good As You Think You Are?" *Fortune,* September 30, 1996, pp. 142–154.

CASE STUDY QUESTIONS

1. What prompted business reengineering at Andersen?

2. Which business processes have been singled out for redesign at Andersen and why?

3. What do you think the effects are of the redesign of the described business processes on the manufacturing function?

4. What does Kim Korn mean by eliminating economies of scale? Explain how Andersen has moved from economies of scale to economies of scope.

5. Discuss the possible effects of on-demand manufacturing on the firm, its suppliers, its immediate customers (distributors and retailers), and its end customers.

PART FOUR

Acquiring and Managing Information Systems

Organizational information systems are acquired in support of business initiatives in order to obtain specific business results. Many firms implement a planned information systems architecture as a platform for the delivery of information services. This part of the text will discuss how information systems are planned and acquired, and how the firm's information services are managed and controlled.

Chapter Thirteen will show how information systems can enable business reengineering and describe how to plan an overall information systems architecture. As there are many information system projects calling for funding, it is necessary to assess the relative worth of these possible future systems—and we will see how this can be done. Once the priority information systems (IS) are identified, they have to be acquired. There are four principal avenues of information system acquisition; we will describe and compare them here. Thus, we will discuss how systems can be developed internally in a firm by IS professionals or, in some cases, by end users. We will also discuss the acquisition of information systems and services from outside vendors by outsourcing or through the purchase of a software package. System acquisition does not necessarily result in its successful use. We will conclude the chapter by analyzing the process of system implementation that should lead to success.

Chapter Fourteen will show how the Information Services function in a firm can be organized, managed, and controlled. Most organizations today depend heavily upon the proper operation and security of their information systems. To ensure the viability of organizational functioning, it has become critical to pay significant attention to a variety of measures, called collectively, information system controls. For this reason, these controls and the audits that, in turn, ensure that the controls remain effective will be described in the chapter in some detail.

CHAPTER THIRTEEN

Business Reengineering, Information Systems Planning and Acquisition

OBJECTIVES

After you read this chapter, you will be able to:

1. Demonstrate understanding of the role information systems play in business reengineering.

2. Specify the contents of a master plan for information systems.

3. Identify the methods for planning the information system architecture in a firm and explain their principles.

4. Outline the Business Systems Planning (BSP) methodology.

5. Identify the methods that can be used to assess the business value of information systems and explain their principles.

6. Identify and contrast the four avenues of information systems acquisition.

7. Outline the systems development life cycle and explain the objective of each of its stages.

8. Explain the idea of prototyping and its role of rapid application development.

9. Explain the principal benefits and risks of end-user development.

10. Explain the benefits and drawbacks of the outsourcing of information systems.

11. Use the scores-and-weights method to select an application package.

12. Explain the success factors in the implementation of information systems.

OUTLINE

Focus Minicase. Information Services as a Business Partner

13.1 Business Innovation with Information Systems

13.2 Planning the Information System Architecture for a Firm

13.3 Assessing the Business Value of Information Systems

13.4 Avenues of Information Systems Acquisition

13.5 Information Systems Development: Life Cycle versus Prototyping

13.6 End-User Development of Information Systems

13.7 Acquisition of Information Systems and Services from Vendors

13.8 Implementation of Information Systems

Case Study. Shape Up or Ship Out for Information Systems

Information Services as a Business Partner

U.S. Bancorp of Portland, Oregon, is the largest banking company in the Pacific Northwest, with $21.4 billion in assets and over 400 branch offices in five states. But staying Number 1 is getting increasingly difficult, as the profit margins of the corporation are declining in the competitive marketplace. Constant innovation is a necessity. U.S. Bancorp is turning to the "noninterest" forms of revenues, offering ever new services for which it can charge fees as a steadier source of revenue.

To decide which services can be profitably offered, business units of the banking firm call on the Information Services department. The IS specialists advise the banking experts on what kind of support the existing information systems can provide and what additional investment in information technology would be necessary to offer a particular new service.

For example, when the bank decided to convert some of the trust assets to investments in mutual funds, the trust officers together with the IS specialists determined what information the bank's employees would need to offer these investments. The IS specialists determined what additional information technology would be needed to support the much higher transaction processing requirements, provide the reporting necessary to satisfy the regulations by various levels of government, and maintain customer information. The IS professionals then devised several options for expanding the IS capabilities. They developed the technological and staffing requirements for each option, performed a cost-benefit analysis, evaluated the options, and put together requests for proposals that went to the selected hardware and software vendors.

The IS professionals also weigh whether a new service should be provided by an outside IS vendor under an outsourcing arrangement in order to lower costs or to seek out a special competence. If so, the IS group helps find an outsourcing partner, negotiate the contract, and monitor the service once it is in place. The IS department is paid by the business units for its consulting services. A chargeback system has been implemented to identify and recover the costs of information services from the revenues of the company's operating units. The final decision as to the selected option for information systems support of a service belongs to the business unit. The role of IS is to furnish the correct and detailed information in its area of expertise. This is the foundation of the partnership between business units and information services at U.S. Bancorp.

Based on Leslie Goff, "I Walk Aligned," *Computerworld,* August 8, 1994, pp. 68–69.

You have just read how Information Services are regarded as partners with other corporate units in producing business results. As with any other major organizational resource, a firm's information systems should be planned to support its objectives. Today, in the environment of vigorous competition, these objectives frequently depart far from "business as usual." Rather, they often include reengineering the firm's business processes to reach for such values as significantly lower costs of doing business, very high product quality, nimbleness in bringing to market new products and services, and serving customers with speed and precision. In order to pursue these objectives and other business results specified earlier in Table 1.1, firms have to take advantage of the capabilities offered by information systems.

Table 13.1

Typical business processes in a manufacturing firm
(From Thomas H. Davenport, *Process Innovation: Reengineering Work through Information Technology,* Boston: Harvard Business School Press, 1993, p. 8.)

Operational Processes

Product development
Customer acquisition
Customer requirements identification
Manufacturing
Integrated logistics
Order management
Post-sales service

Management Processes

Performance monitoring
Information management
Asset management
Human resource management
Planning and resource allocation

In this chapter, we will see how information systems can enable business reengineering, which leads to new ways of doing business. The information systems architecture is planned in many cases to support the new business processes rather than, in a trenchant metaphor, "pave the cowpaths" of the old corporate ways. After discussing how information systems architecture is planned, we will review the methods of assessing the business value of proposed information systems. This assessment identifies the systems most worthy of acquisition. We will then see what the various ways are for an organization to acquire a new information system and discuss how new systems are implemented for successful use in the organization.

13.1   BUSINESS INNOVATION WITH INFORMATION SYSTEMS

The Role of Information Systems in Business Reengineering

Information systems have changed the realm of the possible in business and organizations. These systems offer capabilities that enable companies to redesign their business processes. As we learned in Section 1.6, such redesign is performed by a number of leading firms during a radical business reengineering that aims at major gains by lowering costs, raising quality of products, and cutting the time-to-market for new goods and services.

As you may remember from Section 1.6, a **business process** is a set of related tasks performed to provide a defined work output, such as a newly designed product, a customized order delivered to the buyer, or a business plan. This outcome of a business process should deliver a well-defined value to a customer. The customers of many processes are external to the firm; this is, of course, our traditional understanding of the word. However, the customers of other processes are internal. For example, the planning process delivers plans that are used internally in the firm; the product development process delivers product specifications to the firm's manufacturing unit. Table 13.1 will refine your understanding of what a business process is.

Information technology has come to play a crucial role in the performance of business processes. Consider order management. Many manufacturers receive orders via electronic data interchange (EDI) from the customer's computer. The receipt may automatically trigger another order, sent via EDI to the firm's supplier for the materials necessary to produce the ordered goods. At the same time, the firm's manufacturing information system is automatically notified to schedule the production and the logistics subsystem is notified to schedule the delivery. To take another example, many insurance companies have delegated their claim approval process for each type of insurance policy to a team. The members of the team deal with an electronic version of the claim, produced by digital image processing. This claim is routed to an appropriate team member at an appropriate time by workflow software. As we can see, information systems can enable new levels of process performance.

However, in most firms the current business processes are a holdover from the days when information systems were not yet capable of such process support. Today, the processes can be radically changed to take advantage of the capabilities offered by information systems. Process innovation can be applied to processes both large and small. The greater the scope of process redesign, the larger are the benefits that may be expected— and the greater the risk of the project. Indeed, many reengineering efforts fail, but those that succeed dramatically improve the performance of the company (Hammer 1996). Leveraging the capabilities of information technology to achieve new levels of organizational performance under the conditions of global competition has become the hallmark of the 1990s.

To identify the processes through which your firm delivers value to customers, you may use the value-chain analysis, which we discussed in Chapter 3. It is vital in such an analysis not to be hamstrung by the existing departmental divisions within a firm, but to concentrate instead on the content of the process. You may note how close the operational processes listed in Table 13.1 are to the stages of the value chain shown in Figure 3.14. Even large companies have been able to break down their activities to no more than 20 major processes (for example, IBM identified 18 and Xerox 14 such processes).

We showed the typical directions of business process redesign in Table 1.3 in Chapter 1. We also described how each of these directions exploits a capability offered by information systems. When redesigning a business process, the firms should pursue specific business results, rather than focusing on information systems. For example, cutting the time necessary to process a routine insurance claim from seven business days to 20 minutes is a business objective. This objective is realistic, since the process can be supported with the use of an expert system precisely in order to achieve this business result. Today, information systems are the enabler of virtually all business processes. Beyond that, information systems enable coordination of multiple processes in the enterprise. Further, they make it possible to coordinate the firm's processes with those of its business partners, such as customers and suppliers.

Before we discuss these broader targets, it is best to follow through a reengineering project.

Example of a Business Reengineering Project

Bell Atlantic of Philadelphia provides telephone service to the mid-Atlantic states in the highly competitive environment of today's telecommunications (Hammer and Champy 1993). A principal business of the firm, accounting for almost half of its profits, is providing carrier-access services. Such service amounts to providing, on a customer's request, a link between customers and their selected long-distance carrier, such as AT&T, MCI, or Sprint. Processing a request from a residential customer used to take about 15 days. Corporate customers requiring high-speed data communications, perhaps involving multimedia transmission, would, in some cases, wait for 30 days to be hooked up to a service. The delay was due to a long chain of handoffs: The business process of servicing customer requests was distributed among different functional work groups, as shown in Figure 13.1a.

In the competitive environment created by the new entrants to the telecommunications business who could process service orders in a quarter of the time Bell Atlantic did, the firm lost most of its core business to these competitors. The company recognized that an incremental change would not do and that business reengineering was necessary.

A reengineering team was formed and quickly recognized that customers expected the company to provide service hookup with close to "zero cycle time"—which means on demand. Analyzing the assembly-line chain with its multiple handoffs through which a customer request was processed (Figure 13.1a), the team established that out of the 15 days that the process took, the actual work time was only 10 hours. This indicated a significant opportunity for redesign. The radical target of zero cycle time was set.

A new process was designed (Figure 13.1b) and set in action to service customers in a part of central Pennsylvania. All the tasks of the process were integrated in one location and turned over to a multifunctional team—the case team. The team was given access to the necessary information systems, which were integrated to support the team. Thus, the team had immediate access to the customer records and the information system that specified the connections to carriers. Within several months, the team reduced the request handling cycle to a few days, and in some cases, a few hours. The handling costs were lowered dramatically. The quality of the service improved dramatically as well: The self-managed team "owned" the process and its members had a greater commitment to service excellence than the participants on the "assembly line."

Bell Atlantic is moving further toward zero-cycle processing. By equipping the request-approval cell with information technology and by providing extensive training, the firm aims to replace the case team with a single case worker. The information technology will

Figure 13.1

Redesign of the business process "Provide Carrier-Access Service" at Bell Atlantic

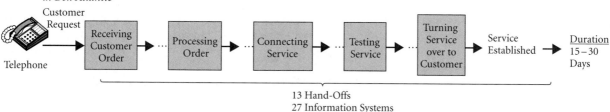

(a) Before Redesign: Assembly-Line Approach

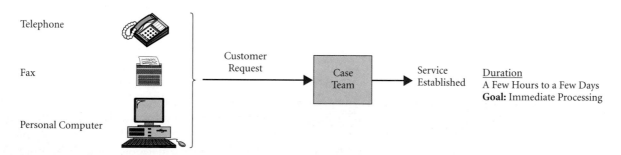

(b) After Redesign: Multifunctional Team Approach

allow the case worker to use his or her workstation to electronically make all the connections necessary to establish the service immediately, while the customer is still on the phone.

The Scope of IS-Enabled Business Reengineering

We have seen how Bell Atlantic drastically cut the order processing time. Business reengineering also cuts time-to-market for new products. Extensive business reengineering programs have cut fielding a new car model by Ford Motor Company from four years to two or three years, with deployment of computer-aided design (CAD) and computer-aided engineering (CAE) systems. Beyond that, the functioning of entire business networks consisting of multiple supplier and customer firms can be reengineered by cooperating firms. Thus, Ford's suppliers participate in the total production cycle of the automaker, from design through distribution. They share several information systems with Ford, such as those supporting design and engineering, and those supporting just-in-time delivery of supplies.

The suppliers for Wal-Mart and Kmart now replenish the retailers' shelves every three to five days, instead of three to five weeks as before. The coordination of these processes is enabled by information systems. As the items are being sold, the data from the point-of-sale terminals pull in the goods from the immediate suppliers, the suppliers' suppliers, and so forth, backwards through the supply chain. The grocery industry alone expects annual savings on the order of $30 billion when such "Efficient Customer Response" grounded in information technology is implemented throughout the industry ("H. E. Butt," 1995).

Radical process innovation through business reengineering differs from the continual quality improvement of business processes under a program such as total quality management (TQM), in which information systems also play a major role, as we learned in Chapter 12. Through business reengineering, firms seek to raise productivity by factors of two or more in their key business processes. Considering its magnitude, a major process innovation in a large firm usually takes no less than two years (Davenport 1993) and is a high-risk project, as is any innovation. Quality improvement programs, on the other hand, generally aim for a steady improvement of 5 or 10 percent annually in the performance of business processes. Quality improvement of processes—such as elimination of unnecessary steps and reduction in product variance—is conducted continually, with the broad participation and initiative of all the involved members of the firm. There is no conflict between process innovation and quality improvement. As soon as a process has been redesigned and the organizational change has been implemented, a quality improvement program can be started.

Business reengineering is an extensive process of planned organizational change, generally led by top corporate executives. Since information technology enables most such efforts, information systems specialists must be partners with business experts on the reengineering team. Only some firms, of course, perform a radical reengineering of their operations. However, to compete in the 21st century, all organizations find it necessary to plan and develop a flexible information technology platform from which new information services can be offered to support operations and management. We will now discuss how to plan such an information system architecture.

13.2 | PLANNING THE INFORMATION SYSTEM ARCHITECTURE FOR A FIRM

To be effective competitors in the information society, many companies increasingly find it vital to have models for the future of their information systems. Such a high-level model of the firm's information systems is known as the **information system architecture** of the firm. We have discussed the IS architecture in Section 7.9 of this text. The principal vehicle for bringing this vision into life is a long-term master IS plan, the product of strategic IS planning. The master IS plan has to be linked to the firm's long-term (strategic) business plan.

We will first discuss the principal contents of an IS master plan and how to link it with the corporate long-term business plan. We will then present the principal methodologies for establishing the long-term IS requirements of an organization. Many firms, and small companies in particular, do not perform orderly long-term planning. The development of information systems in such companies is project-driven, with priorities sometimes established by political interplay. It is far more difficult in these circumstances to use information technology for competitive initiatives and for business process redesign.

Contents of a Master Plan for Information Systems

Information systems are a major corporate asset, both with respect to the benefits they provide and their costs. A number of businesses have become strategically dependent on these systems: Their role in the marketplace depends on information systems. Therefore, the future of information systems in an organization has to be planned for the long term.

Information systems planning helps to ensure that the firm's business initiatives and business processes will receive the requisite informational support. This planning also helps to allocate IS resources in a way that benefits the corporation as a whole, with the information systems most critical to the organizational objectives receiving priority (Lederer and Sethi 1996).

The **IS master plan**, a formal document, should be drawn up for three to five years. It should assess the current state of organizational information systems and make a projection for the future. The master plan should include:

1. A statement of objectives.
2. Projection of the future information technology environment.
3. Projection of the future user environment.
4. Projection of the future industry environment.
5. Definition and evaluation of strategic IS alternatives in relationship to the organization's strategic plan and selection of the preferred alternative.
6. If appropriate, a plan for outsourcing (contracting out) a well-defined part of the IS function.
7. A general plan for the portfolio of the company's IS applications.
8. Infrastructure plan, outlining the general design of the firm's computer systems, telecommunications, and databases.
9. A human-resources plan for IS specialists.
10. A plan for the organizational structure of the IS function.
11. A financial plan.
12. An action plan for the implementation of the strategic plan, possibly including the budget for the next year.

Figure 13.2 shows these contents in conceptual terms.

To be effective, a long-term IS plan has to be aligned or coordinated with the corporate long-term business plan. What does this mean? The coordination of IS plans with business plans should take place along three dimensions: content, timing, and the people involved in

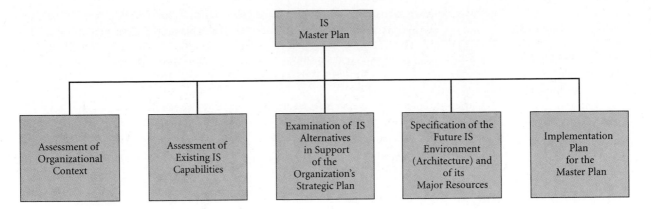

Figure 13.2

Contents of a master plan for organizational information systems

the planning process (Lederer and Mendelow 1989). More specifically, we have achieved the linkage if:

- The corporate business plan states information needs.
- The IS plan refers to the requirements of the business plan and is checked against the business plan.
- Non-IS managers participate in the process of IS planning, while IS managers are involved in corporate business planning.
- Corporate and IS planning calendars conform with each other.

As with any long-term plan, the IS master plan is reviewed both periodically (every six months or every year) and as warranted by developments. If it is not reviewed, the plan rapidly becomes invalidated by environmental changes.

How do we establish long-term IS requirements for an organization and thus set the course for the master plan? This question may be rephrased as follows: What information do we need in order to support the business objectives, strategies, and processes of our organization? We will now describe three methodologies that may be employed to answer this question.

Deriving Information Systems Requirements from Long-Term Organizational Objectives and Plans

If an organization has a strategic business plan, a long-term IS plan may be derived directly from this larger plan (Davis and Olson 1985). Thus, each general goal, strategy to achieve the goal, and specific objective stated in the business plan is analyzed to derive the required IS support. An example of such a derivation is shown in Table 13.2. Note that a goal often generates several strategies and a large number of specific objectives.

After all the components of the long-term business plan are analyzed in this way, the derived IS plan components are consolidated into the IS master plan.

Enterprise Analysis with Business Systems Planning (BSP)

An elaborate and comprehensive methodology for planning enterprise-wide IS requirements is **Business Systems Planning (BSP)**. The objective of BSP is to ensure that the data necessary to support a firm's business processes are available and that a relatively stable information systems architecture has been developed to serve the firm for years to come. The components of the BSP process are shown in Figure 13.3.

Table 13.2

Deriving IS plan components from a business plan

		Business plan component	Derived IS plan component
	Goal	Supply exceptional quality space heaters to a narrow market segment.	Provide information systems for marketing and sales to the narrow market segment. Provide a quality-control information system.
	Strategy	Identify the market segment; ensure top-quality product and after-market service.	Establish customer database. Establish quality-control database. Establish a service information system.
	Objective	Run a direct-mail promotion campaign from 9/1 to 11/1/XX.	Customer database system to be operational by 4/1/XX. Pilot mailing to be performed by 5/15/XX.

The key components of BSP are:

1. Defining Business Processes

The BSP study team identifies principal business processes of the firm. As we saw earlier in the chapter, a business process is a set of related activities required to produce a specified output. Such a business process is the principal entity to be supported with appropriate information. A business process is identified independently of the organizational unit or units that perform its work. This ensures that the planners are guided by business requirements and not by the current organizational structures. An example of a business process in a manufacturing firm is "Control Raw Materials Inventory," which includes the receipt, inspection, storage, and accounting of this inventory. As we have discussed earlier in the chapter, redesigning business processes prior to equipping them with informational support may be vital to the competitive health of an organization.

2. Defining Business Data

Figure 13.3

Key components of information systems planning with BSP

Classes of data that will need to be maintained about each business entity are identified. Business entities include persons (for example, customers or employees), places, things (such as plants or equipment), concepts, and events. Data classes describe business entities. For example, the data class "Inventory Record" describes inventory and may include the

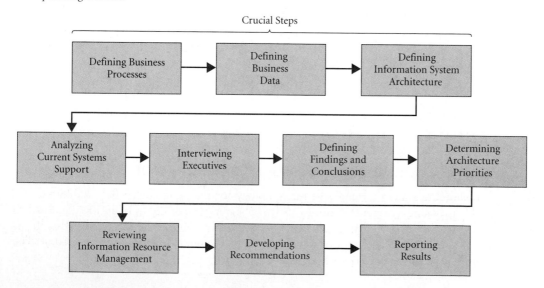

stock-keeping number, name, location, quantity in stock, lead time for restocking, and average price of each item in the inventory.

3. Defining Information System Architecture

The relationship between business processes and data classes is established. The planners identify the data classes each process will create and which data classes it will use. All processes are listed in a column and all data classes in a top row. This results in a process/data class matrix, shown in Figure 13.4. Each data class ought to have a single creating process (denoted by a "C") that is responsible for keeping it up to date. A data class can be used by a number of business processes; these processes are identified by "U" in the matrix. After that, data classes are ordered in the matrix from left to right in the sequence in which the processes create these data (note the sequence of "C"s in the figure).

Process groups with similar patterns of data usage are identified as boxes in the matrix (this step requires experience). These process groupings, based on common data use, will be supported with specific databases, to which the appropriate users will have access. The need

Figure 13.4

Process/data-class matrix (Reprinted by permission from *Business Systems Planning: Information Systems Planning Guide, IBM,* GE20-0527-4. Copyright © 1984 by International Business Machines Corporation.)

Processes \ Data Classes	Objectives	Policies & Procedures	Organization Unit Desc	Product Forecasts	Bldg & Real Estate Reqt	Equipment Requirements	Organization Unit Budget	G/L Accounts Desc & Budget	Long-Term Debt	Employee Requirements	Legal Requirements	Competitor	Marketplace	Product Description	Raw Material Description	Vendor Description	Buy Order	Product Warehouse Inventory	Shipment	Promotion	Customer Description	Customer Order	Seasonal Promotion Plan	Supplier Description	Purchase Order	Raw Material Inventory	Production Order	Equipment Description	Bldg & Real Estate Desc	Equipment Status	Accounts Receivable	Product Profitability	G/L Accounts Status	Accounts Payable	Employee Description	Employee Status
Establish Business Direction	C	C	C								U	U	U																			U	U			
Forecast Product Requirements	U			C																	U		U													
Determine Facility & Eqt Reqts	U		U		C	C		U																				U	U	U						
Determine & Control Fin Reqts	U		U				C	C	C																							U				
Determine Personal Reqts		U	U		U	U	U	U		C	U																									U
Comply with Legal Reqts		U					U				C			U																					U	U
Analyze Marketplace	U											C	C					U																		
Design Product	U									U	U			C	C						U															
Buy Finished Goods			U											U		C	C																		U	
Control Product Inventory														U			U	C	U							U										
Ship Product																		U	C			U					U									
Advertise & Promote Product													U	U				U		C																
Market Product (Wholesale)													U	U						U	C	U														
Enter and Cntrl Customer Order														U				U	U		U	C									U					
Plan Seasonal Production			U											U									C				U								U	U
Purchase Raw Materials															U								U	C	C	U									U	
Control Raw Materials Inventory															U										U	C	U									
Schedule & Control Production														U	U									U		U	C	U		U					U	U
Acquire & Dispose Fac & Eqt					U	U																						C	C							
Maintain Equipment																											U	U		C						
Manage Facilities																													U							
Manage Cash Receipts																					U	U									C					
Determine Product Profitability							U						U	U				U							U	U						C	U		U	U
Manage Accounts								U								U									U							U	C	U		U
Manage Cash Disbursements								U								U	U		U					U	U									C	U	U
Hire & Terminate Personnel	U	U			U					U	U																								C	U
Manage Personnel	U																																		U	C

to provide the databases and access to them gives rise to the information systems necessary to support business processes.

The subsequent stages of the BSP process involve analysis of what is currently available as compared to what has been identified as needed, setting priorities on the development or modification of individual systems, reviewing current information management policies in consideration of the new requirements, and developing an action plan for implementing the long-term master plan.

Used to develop a comprehensive, long-term organizational IS plan, BSP requires a major commitment of resources. It aids in developing an enterprise-level IS architecture and helps to identify high-priority areas.

Critical Success Factors (CSF) Methodology

As opposed to the massive enterprise-wide effort involved in BSP, the **critical success factors (CSF)** methodology derives organizational information requirements from the key information needs of the individual executives or managers. The CSF approach was developed by John Rockart of MIT, who defined CSFs as "those few critical areas where things must go right for the business to flourish" (Rockart 1979). There are usually fewer than 10 such factors that each executive should continually monitor. Frequently, they are monitored with executive information systems, which we discussed in Chapter 10.

CSFs of individual managers are identified through a series of interviews. By combining the CSFs of these managers, we can obtain factors critical to the success of the entire enterprise. These aggregated success factors are used to modify the organizational processes and structure, and to develop an organization's informational requirements. The CSF

Figure 13.5

CSF methodology for establishing organizational IS requirements

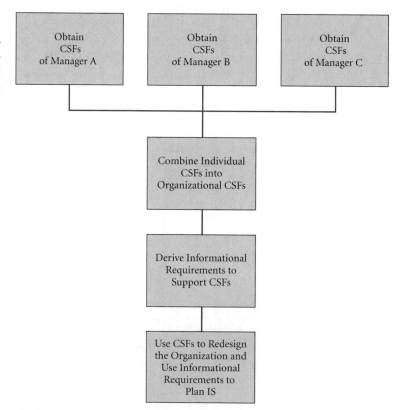

Table 13.3	**CSF**	**Key Information to Support CSF (Examples)**
Critical success factors and derived informational requirements in a healthcare organization	Access to services	Type and number of patients referred to other institutions because of lack of resources in place
	Continuous care	Quality of the follow-up on patients as they go from one treatment to another
	Adequate response to clients' needs	Use rate of services offered, identification of unsatisfied needs
	High-quality care	Compatibility between the results achieved and recognized standards
	Detailed knowledge of population's health status	Epidemiological data on mortality and morbidity in the target population

methodology for establishing organizational (rather than individual) informational requirements is shown in Figure 13.5.

There are four sources of CSFs: (1) the industry that the firm is a part of, (2) the enterprise itself, (3) the business environment, and (4) the firm's current situation (such as, for example, an excess of inventory at the present moment). Some of the eight CSFs identified for a healthcare organization (Bergeron and Bégin 1989), along with the derived informational requirements, are shown in Table 13.3 as examples. Here we see how the information identified with CSF methodology can be used to control the quality of healthcare service.

The CSF methodology is oriented toward supporting a company's strategic direction. Generally, only the CSFs of the top executives are considered during the process, which limits the amount of information produced as compared to BSP methodology. The needs for operational information are much more broadly covered by the BSP methodology. Critical success factors are time-dependent and must therefore be reviewed periodically, with informational support adjusted accordingly.

Both the CSF and the BSP methodologies are supported by software planning tools, such as PC Prism from Intersolv Corporation. An example of a professional support system, this software helps IS planners specify organizational units, business processes, critical success factors, projects, and data objects specific to the organization.

Organizational information system plans produce broad outlines of the firm's information resources. These outlines are filled in with specific information systems. The business value of every system has to be assessed before starting the system acquisition. We will proceed to discuss how such an assessment can be made.

13.3   ASSESSING THE BUSINESS VALUE OF INFORMATION SYSTEMS

How Can the Relative Worth of Applications Be Determined?

Based on the long-term IS plan and on requests for information systems by their prospective users, by corporate management, or by IS specialists, applications that appear worthy of development or acquisition from outside the firm are identified. Project priorities then have to be set. Certain projects require immediate implementation, for example, in order to

Table 13.4	Method	Criteria for Evaluation
Methods for evaluating the relative worth of applications	Cost-benefit analysis	Projects with highest payoff are given priority.
	Portfolio approach	The overall portfolio of projects should be *balanced* in terms of risk, support for the firm's strategic directions, and other identified criteria. Projects that are necessary for maintaining competitive parity also receive priority.
	Contribution to the firm's competitive position	Projects expected to enhance the competitive position of the firm are favored.
	Chargeback	Are users willing to "buy" the application?
	Ranking by steering committee	Projects are selected based on negotiations of executives who represent various organizational interests.

satisfy a new government reporting regulation or to interface with a new customer's system. Others may have high priority owing to the competitive edge the system may give the company or the high payoff the system promises. Resources, such as people, funds, and equipment, are allocated to projects, and project schedules are drawn up.

Not all systems that appear needed will produce sufficient business results to justify their acquisition. How can we evaluate the worth of prospective applications? The approaches most often employed to identify applications worthy of implementation and to rank them in order of importance are summarized in Table 13.4.

Cost-benefit analysis is used to estimate the expected payoff from a proposed system by comparing the costs of its acquisition with the expected benefits from its use. We will further discuss the application of this highly popular technique to IS projects in this section. However, the approach has its limitations. It is far more difficult to apply such analysis to systems supporting knowledge work than to those performing transaction processing. The benefits of individual systems that support managerial decision making (decision support systems, for example) or communication and coordination (such as office information systems) are frequently difficult to quantify. Rational resource allocation for such projects may be done using the portfolio approach.

The **portfolio approach** was adapted for information systems evaluation from the field of securities analysis by F. Warren McFarlan of the Harvard Business School (McFarlan 1981). When using this approach, the analysts attempt to devise a portfolio of application development projects whose overall degree of risk and expected payoff is appropriate for the firm. Indeed, development projects carry different degrees of risk. Projects more likely to fail are those involving large systems, technology unfamiliar to the organization, or a great deal of organizational change. System failure has many faces. The principal risks include the following:

- System implementation may fail due to technological or organizational reasons, such as user resistance.

- Cost overruns and implementation delays may significantly decrease the payoff from the system.

- The expected benefits from the system may not materialize, for example, due to the moves by competing firms.

IN THE SPOTLIGHT

How Much Does a Networked PC Cost the Owner Company?

The Gartner Group, a leading information technology consultancy, computes the total cost of owning a personal computer connected to a local area network (LAN) at close to $13,000 a year. Here are the costs that make up this figure:

- About 21 percent, or $2,730, is the amortized (prorated over the time of ownership) cost of the PC and LAN hardware and software.

- About 27 percent, or $3,510, is the cost of providing technical support to the user.

- About 9 percent, or $1,170, is the cost of administering the system.

- About 43 percent, or $5,590, is the surprisingly high cost of the so-called end-user operations—the time spent trying to figure out how to use the system and various software, installing software, organizing disk files, and in general "messing" with the machine. Several authorities find the inclusion of this last figure debatable.

Although the cost structure in your organizational environment may be different, it is good to be aware of how much higher the costs of ownership can be than the simple costs of the acquired system resources.

Based on Nina Munk, "Technology for Technology's Sake," *Forbes*, October 21, 1996, pp. 280–288.

However, if high-risk projects promising valuable benefits are not implemented, the effectiveness of organizational IS may suffer. Risk management is a necessity with organizational information systems ("IT Risk" 1996). The portfolio approach assesses the riskiness of each proposed project, after which it assesses the riskiness of the overall portfolio of proposed projects. A balance of risk and potential benefits should be maintained. Organizations that use information systems to compete should take on a riskier applications portfolio than those that use information systems merely to support their operations.

Indeed, even though the firm might not conduct a full portfolio analysis, the projects that credibly promise to *enhance the firm's competitive position* may be favored among the projects proposed for development. The areas where competitive advantage can be sought may be identified with the value-chain analysis, discussed in Chapter 3.

The accounting **chargeback** mechanism, whereby the cost of the system is charged back to the users, can be employed to enable the prospective users to express their need for a proposed application. The firm's IS unit pursues the IS project only if the future users are willing to pay for the acquisition. The "payment" may in actuality be made by allocating an appropriate amount from the budget of the user unit.

In some companies, priorities for systems acquisition are established by the IS steering committee. An **IS steering committee** is a high-level policy-making unit whose members are executives representing the major functions or business processes of the organization, including the information services function. The steering committee acts as a board of directors for the organizational information systems. This committee combines the business expertise of the line-of-business managers with the information systems know-how of IS managers. A steering committee sets the overall direction for a firm's IS function; allocates major informational resources (for example, by reviewing requests for projects estimated to cost more than a given amount); monitors the progress of major projects; and, last and perhaps most crucial, resolves conflicts among various claims on resources.

Since cost-benefit analysis is used most frequently to assess the worth of information systems, we will proceed to discuss the technique at length.

Table 13.5	Systems Costs	Tangible Benefits of Systems
Costs and tangible benefits in cost-benefit analysis of information systems	*Fixed Costs* (one-time resource acquisition) Hardware acquisition Software purchase and development Establishment of databases Establishment of telecommunications Training and hiring of personnel Establishment of new procedures	
	Operating Costs (for example, annual) Labor (operation and maintenance) Facilities Supplies Leases	*Savings* (for example, annual) Reduced labor costs Reduced hardware costs Reduced purchasing costs Inventory reduction *Revenue Increases* Increased sales in existing markets Market expansion

Cost-Benefit Analysis of Information Systems

Cost-benefit analysis is a technique that is often applied to estimate the expected payoff from an information system. Acquisition of such a system is a capital investment and needs to be economically justifiable. Cost-benefit analysis helps to establish whether the benefits to be received from a proposed information system will outweigh its expected cost. It should be remembered that the figures employed in this analysis are estimates. In particular, the figures meant to reflect the expected benefits should be carefully seen in this light.

The basic stages of cost-benefit analysis as applied to information systems acquisition are as follows:

1. Identification of the Costs of the Acquisition and Operation of the Proposed System

Some of the expenses incurred will be **fixed costs,** one-time costs of acquiring systems resources, including the costs of systems development or customization. Generally, these expenditures need to be made before the system becomes operational—and thus before any benefits can be derived from it. **Operating costs,** on the other hand, will be steadily borne after system implementation. In the case of personal computers, for example, the fixed cost of system acquisition, generally ranging between $3,000 and $5,000, is widely recognized. However, the operating costs of a networked PC are often forgotten. The vignette on page 473 offers a surprisingly high figure for these costs.

Table 13.5 shows the typical information systems cost categories, along with the tangible benefits such systems provide. Note that both operating costs and benefits start only after system implementation.

2. Identification of Benefits that Will Be Derived from the Use of the System

Benefits fall into two categories: (1) **tangible benefits** that are easy to express in dollars and (2) **intangible benefits** that are difficult to quantify. Tangible benefits include savings and revenue increases, as shown in Table 13.5. Intangible benefits, which are often of overriding

Table 13.6	
Important intangible benefits of information systems	Improved customer service
	Achieving specific strategic advantage in the marketplace
	Higher quality of products
	Availability of higher-quality information
	Higher utilization of assets
	Improved work coordination
	Improved planning
	Improved resource control
	Assimilation of promising new information technology
	Improved working environment
	Increased organizational flexibility
	Higher-quality decision making
	Streamlined operations
	Increased reliability and security of IS operations
	Satisfying legal requirements
	Higher employee morale

importance in the case of information systems, by definition cannot be readily expressed in dollars. Even though analysts may express some of them in quantitative terms, at least in part (ingenuity abounds), they may have to settle for stating many others verbally, in as precise terms as possible, in the final cost-benefit statement. Some of the categories of intangible benefits are listed in Table 13.6.

The various aspects of information quality that may be enhanced by an information system, such as timeliness or relevance, were discussed in Chapter 2 (see Table 2.1). The oft-claimed benefit of higher asset utilization may be illustrated by an airline or hotel's ability to adopt a yield-management approach and to enter reservations and cancellations more rapidly to increase the utilization of the available capacity. A project may be part of the assimilation process that brings a new technology (such as object-oriented development) into the firm and its relatively high cost may be justified by new opportunities. This is similar to a research and development expenditure.

In general, valuation of benefits is difficult, and it so happens that while costs are generally more certain, benefits are usually more risk-prone. It is far easier to evaluate the benefits of transaction processing systems or clerically oriented office information systems than it is to place a value on the benefits of a decision support or executive information system. That is why other evaluation techniques shown in Table 13.4 are frequently employed for these types of systems.

3. Comparison of Costs with Benefits

After the costs, tangible benefits, and those aspects of intangible benefits that can be "dollarized" are quantified, a cost-benefit evaluation technique is applied. The time frame in which a cost is incurred or a benefit is obtained needs to be kept in mind. Information systems are frequently considered to offer benefits for five years after their implementation, under the assumption that they will be replaced or significantly modified after this period (even though in actuality many systems serve significantly longer).

The present value of all of the future money flows must be established. For example, if the organization can invest its capital at a 10 percent return, then $100 it would receive in benefits a year from now is worth only about $91 today. In other words, the value of future cash flows is discounted, that is, multiplied by a present value factor based on the discount rate used by the given organization and the number of years until the future amount will be received. Should the same $100 be coming in two years from now, it would be worth at present only about $83, at a discount rate of 10 percent, since the present value factor is 0.826. Spreadsheet packages contain a function that computes the present value of a series of cash flows over a period of time.

The most commonly used cost-benefit analysis technique is the **net present value approach.** Using this method, the net present value of a system is computed by subtracting the present value of the costs from the present value of the benefits over the lifetime of the system. If a positive value is obtained, the project has merit. The net present value technique is illustrated in Figure 13.6.

Figure 13.6

Cost-benefit analysis for an information system: net present value technique

It is estimated that:

* The development time of the information system will be 18 months
* The system will remain in operation for 4.5 years

After the costs and tangible benefits have been listed and quantified, the following schedule of costs and benefits is obtained:

	Costs	
	Fixed	**Operating**
Year 1:	$50,000	
Year 2:	$30,000	$10,000
Year 3–6:		$20,000

	Benefits
Year 1:	0
Year 2:	$30,000
Years 3–6:	$80,000

The discount rate, as used by the finance department at the firm, is 12 percent.

The spreadsheet of the net present value computation is:

	Year Effective					
	1	**2**	**3**	**4**	**5**	**6**
Costs	50,000	40,000	20,000	20,000	20,000	20,000
Benefits	–	30,000	60,000	60,000	60,000	60,000
Net Values	−50,000	−10,000	40,000	40,000	40,000	40,000
Present Value Factor	1	.893	.797	.712	.636	.567
Net Present Values	−50,000	−8,930	31,880	28,480	25,440	22,680

Net present value of the system: $49,550.

IN THE SPOTLIGHT

Assessing the Business Value of IT: How They Really Do It

Today, business managers are highly sensitive to the payoff from information systems. Most of them do believe that the use of information technology has enhanced the productivity of their firms. However, it is difficult to quantify results brought by the use of information systems such as quality of customer service, variety of services provided, or responsiveness to customer needs. Analytical techniques are combined with an understanding of business problems to arrive at a decision as to whether or not an information systems project is justified. Let's see how some companies do that.

Inifi, Inc. has equipped 20 salespeople with $3,000 worth of laptops each, with a total investment in hardware, software, support, and training of $75,000. The salespeople now have all the information they might need during a sales call available to them and they can upload sales orders directly to headquarters. Jerry Moore, vice-president of IS at the Greensboro, South Carolina-based company, says that "our management has bought off on the project because the information's more timely. But I don't know that we can break down [the benefits] into dollars and cents. If we can't justify an investment in hard dollars, we get the management together and present the facts. If management buys it, we do the project."

The chief information officer of a major industrial company, on the other hand, tells us that "we do a strict return on investment analysis on every project over $75,000."

At Ace Hardware Corporation, headquartered in Oak Brook, Illinois, "we allocate [information technology] resources based on the business plan," says the firm's Vice-President of IS Don Schuman. "Once the officer responsible for the functional area decides this is a priority, he gets the resources to do it."

"Our top management is not in love with [information technology], but we are adamant about quality, customer service, and being low cost," says John Mitchell, director of information services at Cooper Tire & Rubber Company in Findlay, Ohio. "We pursue every investment with this in mind."

With fewer and fewer IS projects providing simple cost savings by replacing people, some savvy IS people shift the responsibility to end users through a chargeback. "We charge [end users] for everything we do," says W. Ben Kuenemann, senior managing director of information services at the Bear Stearns brokerage house in Whippany, New Jersey. "Why should I be held responsible for the productivity of the user community?" Indeed, in the brokerage business, the information services are tightly woven into the business fabric. "In this business, until we can automate a product, we don't *have* a product," says Kuenemann.

And then consider what Frank Barbee, manager of information technology for Phillips Petroleum in Bartlesville, Oklahoma, can tell us: "We ask 'Is it feasible?' We define costs, risks, manpower requirements . . . But we know we're going to do the project, because the CEO said so."

Based on Paul Gillin, "Pressure to Produce," *Computerworld Premier 100*, September 19, 1994, pp. 10–12; and E. B. Baatz, "Digesting the ROI Paradox," *CIO*, October 1, 1996, pp. 32–34.

As an alternative cost-benefit analysis technique, some firms use the **break-even method** (also known as the payback method) to establish when the use of the system will pay for its acquisition. When this is done, the graphs for annual benefits and costs (their present values, of course) are charted for the lifetime of the project. The point where they intersect shows when the system becomes profitable. The organization would establish a threshold known as a hurdle of, say, two years. If the system can pay back the original investment within this period, the project has merit.

The valuation of the impact of information technology on organizational performance remains a "hot" research topic. Recent studies by MIT researchers show that, on the average, computers improve productivity significantly more than other types of investment (Brynjolfsson and Hitt 1993). At the same time, there is high variance in obtained results, with some firms losing money on their information technology investments. Frequently, this results from failing to introduce a new information system as a component of a larger organizational change, such as business process redesign, or from improper implementation (see Section 8 of this chapter). The vignette on page 477 shows how various companies cope with assessing the value of information systems.

Once we know the information system is worthy of acquisition, we need to decide on the way it will be acquired. As we will read in the next section, today there are four principal options for doing so.

13.4 | AVENUES OF INFORMATION SYSTEMS ACQUISITION

The fundamental decision to be made when a system has to be acquired is: Make or buy? Actually, this decision is never as simple as that. It is almost never possible to buy exactly the information system you want. Of course, the hardware and systems software are purchased or leased from vendors. There exist, however, several avenues for acquiring "apps"—the applications software that makes up the specialized components of an organization's information systems. These applications, in effect, model the way your firm operates and, therefore, are to a degree specific to your needs.

The alternative avenues to IS acquisition are shown in Figure 13.7. Two of the methods shown in the figure rely on the internal development of the system within the organization. Traditionally, information systems have been developed by systems professionals. This has remained the way large organizational systems are developed internally. As familiarity with computers and information systems has grown into information systems literacy and as powerful tools for end-user development have become available, end-user computing has become an important part of organizational computing.

Another major trend is resolving the "make-or-buy" dilemma by outsourcing the running of organizational information systems, sometimes also including information systems

Figure 13.7

Avenues of information system acquisition

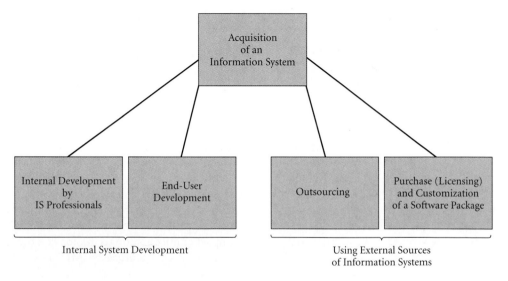

development, to a specialized vendor. A more traditional version of such outsourcing is the use of outside contractors to develop specific information systems for the firm.

A common form of availing yourself of outside expertise is the purchase of a software package. Other than the simple personal productivity systems, such packages usually have to be customized to satisfy the firm's specific requirements. The customization may be done internally or by an outside contractor.

We will now proceed to review these four methods of IS acquisition. After we learn about them in more detail, we will be able to compare their characteristics. The methods are not mutually exclusive; more than one of them may be used to acquire a specific information system.

13.5 | INFORMATION SYSTEMS DEVELOPMENT: LIFE CYCLE VERSUS PROTOTYPING

The traditional methodology of developing large information systems relies on a life-cycle organization of the development process: a sequence of development stages that ultimately produce an operational system. More and more frequently, life-cycle development is replaced by rapid system development that relies on prototyping. By developing and refining the system prototype as a preliminary working version of the system, it is possible to better establish the user requirements. We need to appreciate that in some development projects the two methodologies are combined: a prototype is produced during the systems analysis to determine user requirements, after which the life-cycle development takes place.

Developing Large Organizational Systems with Life-Cycle Methodologies

Large organizational systems come into being through a systematic process. As we know, the acquisition of such a system should be preceded by a broader process of strategic IS planning or, in other words, determining the organization's long-term informational requirements and its IS architecture. The responsibility for the process rests with the IS planners and, ultimately, with the top IS management of the firm. In many firms, the IS steering committee plays a significant role in channeling organizational resources toward the strategically vital or highest payoff information systems.

Consistent with the long-term objectives of the IS strategic plan, and in response to requests for systems, the applications to be acquired are identified and their relative priorities are established. Many firms set these priorities for shorter terms with tactical (e.g., for a year) and operational (e.g., for several months) planning. Based on this lower-level planning, projects may be initiated in order to develop individual organizational systems. This is shown in Figure 13.8.

Large organizational systems, such as transaction processing systems or management reporting systems, may then be developed internally in a process consisting of well-defined stages and are known as **systems development life cycle.** This process, which will be discussed in more detail in Part Five of the text, consists of four conceptually different stages: system analysis, system design, programming (coding and testing), and installation. As we will see in Chapter 15, these stages have to be further broken down in practice. The work is done by project teams, whose composition will depend on the nature of the project and will generally vary from stage to stage. The idea of a development life cycle is to match the complexity of a large information system to be developed with a development process containing well-defined stages, deliverables, and quality controls.

Figure 13.8

Planning, development, and operation of information systems (From Vladimir Zwass, *Management Information Systems,* Dubuque, IA: Wm. C. Brown, 1992, p. 702.)

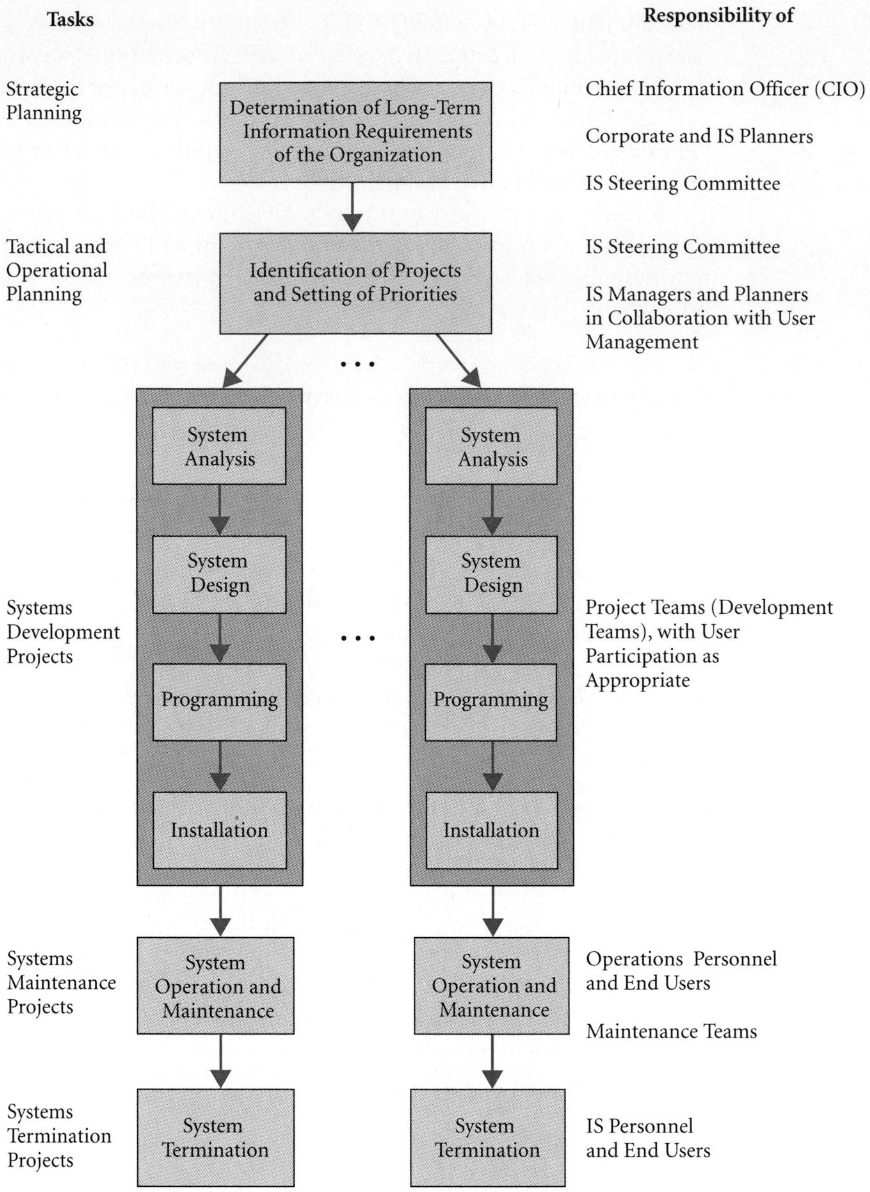

Tasks		Responsibility of
Strategic Planning	**Determination of Long-Term Information Requirements of the Organization**	Chief Information Officer (CIO) Corporate and IS Planners IS Steering Committee
Tactical and Operational Planning	**Identification of Projects and Setting of Priorities**	IS Steering Committee IS Managers and Planners in Collaboration with User Management
	● ● ●	
Systems Development Projects	System Analysis → System Design → Programming → Installation ● ● ● System Analysis → System Design → Programming → Installation	Project Teams (Development Teams), with User Participation as Appropriate
Systems Maintenance Projects	System Operation and Maintenance System Operation and Maintenance	Operations Personnel and End Users Maintenance Teams
Systems Termination Projects	System Termination System Termination	IS Personnel and End Users

We can see the four principal stages of the development life cycle in Figure 13.8. The principal objective of **system analysis** is to provide a detailed answer to the question "*What* will the new system do?" The next stage, **system design,** answers the question "*How* will the new system be organized?" During the **programming** stage, the individual software modules of the system are coded and tested, and then integrated into an operational system as further levels of testing proceed to ensure continuing quality control. System documentation is produced as the project progresses. **Installation** includes final testing of the system in the actual environment where it will be deployed and conversion of operations to fit the new systems.

The implementation process for a major information system goes beyond system development. It is a broader process of achieving organizational objectives with the use of the system, which we will discuss in Section 8 of this chapter.

An implemented system is handed over to the end users and the operations personnel. It will be extensively modified over its useful life in a process known as **system maintenance,** discussed in Chapter 16. If the development process of a large system has taken 2 years and involved perhaps 30 professionals, the system will likely be used and maintained for some 5 to 10 years. The primary objective of maintenance is to adjust the system to the organization's changing informational requirements, and to the new hardware and software platforms on which the system will run. Another objective is, unfortunately, the removal of development errors.

After the useful life of the system comes to an end, the system should be terminated and replaced. The IS portfolios of many organizations, however, contain large numbers of so-called legacy systems, some of which have been in operation for 10 to 15 years and which no longer satisfy the organizational requirements. This leads, in many cases, to figurative and literal (for IS managers) maintenance nightmares.

Prototyping and Rapid Applications Development

Systems development life cycle has been frequently faulted for its long development times, its voluminous documentation requirements, and for failing to meet the actual user requirements at the end of the long development road. Companies seek faster development techniques for systems that lend themselves to less cumbersome approaches than a life cycle-based development. These techniques rely on prototyping the system to be developed.

A **prototype** is a preliminary working version of an application (or one of its parts) that is built quickly and inexpensively, with the intention of modifying it. The capabilities of the initial prototype are limited as compared to those intended for the final system. Development of a prototype is particularly helpful in the development of the user interface of an information system. The prototype is turned over to the users, who work with it and make suggestions for modifications. During this learning process, both users and developers discover the actual user requirements. The objective of **prototyping** is to successfully develop more complete prototypes and thus obtain a functional specification of what the intended system is supposed to do and, possibly, evolve the prototype into the system to be delivered to the users. A methodology of evolving a prototype into an operational system is known as **rapid applications development.** This methodology relies on Joint Application Development (JAD) to bring together users and developers in a series of workshops (see Section 15.1).

Just as a car manufacturer produces a prototype automobile, so system developers can rapidly place a system prototype before the users. An early prototype generally includes the user interface, such as screens and reports, and some of the principal system functions. The costs of producing a prototype are kept low by ignoring in the first version such aspects of the final application as nonessential functions, validation of input data, system controls, exception handling, and efficiency considerations. Fourth-generation programming languages (4GL), discussed in Section 5.5, and computer-aided software engineering (CASE) tools that will be discussed in Chapter 16 make prototyping fast and economically attractive. Indeed, such software tools are imperative for effective prototyping.

A general view of the prototyping process is shown in Figure 13.9. As you can see, a prototype may be used as a tool in establishing user requirements in a life-cycle

Figure 13.9

Prototyping

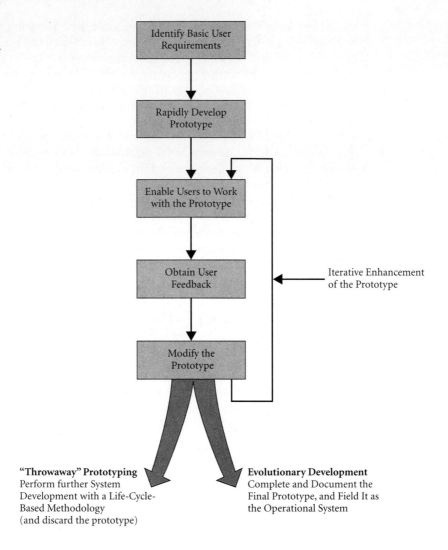

Identify Basic User
Requirements

Rapidly Develop
Prototype

Enable Users to Work
with the Prototype

Obtain User
Feedback

Iterative Enhancement
of the Prototype

Modify the
Prototype

"Throwaway" Prototyping
Perform further System
Development with a Life-Cycle-
Based Methodology
(and discard the prototype)

Evolutionary Development
Complete and Document the
Final Prototype, and Field It as
the Operational System

development methodology. After requirements have been established, the prototype is discarded; this is known as "throwaway" prototyping. A different way to use prototypes is to evolve a series of them into the final system. Known as evolutionary prototyping or rapid applications development, it results in faster system delivery. This is the preferred methodology for developing decision support and expert systems, as we discussed in Chapters 10 and 11, as well as other systems of limited scope.

Let us consider two typical prototyping scenarios.

Scenario 1

Our bank's IS department needs to develop a new on-line system for checking account inquiries. This elaborate transaction processing system (TPS) will have to be developed to meet very high standards of efficiency, reliability, maintainability, security, and auditability.

It will also have to interact with the existing information systems and accommodate a large number of users. The TPS will therefore be built through a complete life-cycle process.

However, to establish user requirements, we build a prototype. The prototype produces data entry screens and report screens as well as hard copy reports. The bank officers should be able to enter the data identifying the account by various means. They need screens and reports that present basic account information, show credit history for the account, give instant statements for any past period, and show activity for the current period.

Mock-up screens, which do not draw data from a database, are created by system developers with a prototyping tool such as a fourth-generation language (see Section 5.5). The prototype is installed on user workstations. The users work (or "play") with the prototype for several days, trying to imitate practical situations. They see how easy—or difficult—it is to enter data, how well the screens are designed, and how many screens they have to navigate to complete a typical transaction. The users then provide feedback to the developers, who modify the prototype, perhaps repeatedly.

At this stage, a "dummy" database of customer accounts may be established and principal processing routines may be written in a simplified form, without error checking or exception handling. The users attempt to run their typical transactions on the enhanced prototype, and another series of enhancements follows until the users are satisfied with the operation. Throughout the process, the developers make it abundantly clear to the users that the prototype is *not* a working system and that it serves only to establish their needs.

After the prototype has served this purpose, the actual system is designed and programmed in the language of choice, such as C or C++. All the necessary features of so-called production systems, such as data validation, efficient database accessing, and controls are included. Complete documentation is produced. The prototype is a "throwaway." Since it was only used to establish user requirements, it is now discarded.

Scenario 2

The IS group of our company's Human Resources department is asked to develop a decision support system (DSS) to help in the comparison of the alternative packages of wages and benefits. Having spent several hours with the middle-level managers who are the intended users, the developers produce an initial version of the application. The prototype is developed in the nonprocedural language (4GL) of the database management system used to manage the human resources database. It is then turned over to the users, who try it to support typical decisions. They write their comments into a text file set up for the purpose. Several iterations of the cycle follow—enhancement (by developers), exercising (by users)—until a satisfactory DSS is produced and subsequently documented. When the next round of labor negotiations comes around, it turns out that some other features are desirable. The DSS is rapidly modified to satisfy the need. This prototype has become the working system, and the prototyping process was actually the system development process.

The benefits of prototyping include faster development, flexibility in making changes to the system under development, and the ability to establish the *real* user requirements owing to an extensive user involvement throughout the development process. A prototype makes the future system more real to all involved. It is easier to determine the organizational changes that will be necessary for successful system implementation, and an early start in these directions can be made. Users are trained and learn as they work with the prototype; thus, training is begun early as well.

Problems emerge when prototyping is used for unsuitable purposes or when it is used inappropriately. The following are typical problem areas:

1. Inappropriate Evolutionary Development via Prototyping in the Case of Large Organizational Systems

Large systems that are to serve major organizational units and perhaps cross a number of organizational boundaries are not good candidates for evolutionary development. However, the requirements for these systems may be clarified by using "throwaway" prototypes.

2. Prototyping as a "Quick-and-Dirty" Development

Before systems development life cycle was introduced, systems had been developed largely by programming and testing, with not enough attention paid to analysis and design. It is important that prototyping does not degenerate into this "development" mode.

3. Behavioral Problems

When the scope and purposes of prototyping are not made clear to the users, behavioral problems may emerge. In instances when "throwaway" prototyping is intended, for example, the users may want to use the prototype instead of waiting for the final system, and the quality of their work will suffer. Users may also be dissatisfied with the system because the developers are unable to accommodate the users' growing appetite for improvements. Too many iterations of prototype enhancement are costly and may sorely try the patience of all involved. The developers should be careful to limit the number of prototype versions.

When life-cycle development is combined with prototyping, hybrid methodologies emerge. Some developers attempt to loosen the excessively rigid development life cycle by incorporating a process for accepting requirements changes as the system is being developed. Others provide more structure for the prototyping process. The spiral development process is an important variant: Prototypes are constructed at the conclusion of individual life-cycle stages in order to limit the risk of the development project.

While life-cycle development is the domain of information systems specialists, prototyping is frequently employed by end users when they are developing their own systems. We will now turn to end-user development as a general component of organizational computing.

13.6   END-USER DEVELOPMENT OF INFORMATION SYSTEMS

The Role of End-User Development

With appropriate software tools at their disposal and with training, some end users are able to develop their own systems. Applications development by end users has become an increasingly important part of end-user computing.

End-user computing has three dimensions: sophisticated use of information technology by end users; end-user control of systems (that is, the authority to acquire and operate information systems resources); and end-user development of certain applications. End-user systems development has been enabled by fourth-generation languages (4GL) such as query languages, report generators, and application generators, which we discussed in Chapter 5. With the help of generators, end users often develop decision support and expert systems for their own or their team's use, as we discussed in Chapters 10 and 11. Visual programming languages, such as Visual Basic from Microsoft, and generators, such as Delphi from Borland International, which we discussed in Chapter 5, play a large role in end-user computing.

End-user development is often highly productive and can place systems into the users' hands more quickly than an IS department can. By developing their own systems, end users

**One Company
and Two Views
on End-User
Computing**

Commercial Office Supply Division of 3M Co. of St. Paul, Minnesota, has a long history of spectacular innovations—from scotch tape to post-it notes. Two years ago, Bob Wolf, a product development engineer, joined the new 20-member team created in the division to develop the next generation of innovative products. Wolf is the end-user computing specialist in the group. Let's compare his view of his role with the view of an IS specialist.

1. End-User View

Wolf develops and maintains the applications that track the group's research and survey results using the group's own database (maintained with Microsoft's Access database management system), determines configurations of the desktop workstations for his group, takes care of the local area network and Windows for Workgroups software that runs on it, and orders all the hardware and software for the group. Wolf also acts as liaison between his group of engineers and the IS department. Last but not least, he also performs his "real" job of product development. And that job always comes first.

Wolf acquired some experience in information technology as he worked his way through college at a computer store. His end-user responsibility has developed gradually. He simply filled the gap that developed between what his fledgling team needed and what the busy Information Services department could provide. Also, "we are the ones who really understand the business," says Wolf.

Wolf discusses all the acquisitions of information technology he makes for his team with his IS counterpart, John Winterhalter, to avoid any conflict with corporate standards.

2. Information Services View

John Winterhalter, manager of information services for the division, says that the company has divided the information services into two categories: (1) core and common activities and (2) end-user computing. Core and common activities include organizational systems that are key to business and that usually process operational data. These systems are developed by the IS professionals and the IS department is overwhelmed with this organizational responsibility.

"We've selected users such as Bob to help bring technology to bear on business problems at the end-user level," says Winterhalter. According to him, the mix of the organizational and end-user computing is paying off in productivity gains.

Based on Alice LaPlante, "The End-User Invasion," *Computerworld*, July 18, 1994, pp. 93–98.

avoid the multi-year backlogs of systems development projects awaiting the attention of IS units in many firms. A combination of the functional expertise possessed by end users and the technological competence of IS specialists, who often assist end users during systems development, may result in superior systems. As another important benefit, the communication gap between the user and the developer disappears.

End-user development coexists with, rather than replaces, systems development by IS professionals. Applications that lend themselves best to end-user development have characteristics listed in Table 13.7. You can see the role end-user computing plays in one business department in the vignette above.

Managing Risks of End-User Development

More and more systems are successfully developed by increasingly information-system literate users. However, end-user development has limitations and carries certain risks. The following organizational risks should be counteracted by appropriate management controls:

Table 13.7	
Characteristics of applications that are most suitable for end-user development	1. The application is of limited size and complexity with respect to information technologies (as opposed to the demands it may make on the functional expertise of end users).
	2. Expertise of end users is important to understand the application.
	3. The application may be developed by evolutionary prototyping.
	4. A fourth-generation language may be used to develop the application.
	5. The application will be for personal use, or for the use of a limited group, as opposed to organization-wide use. There are no extensive documentation demands.
	6. No high security, privacy, or data integrity demands are present.
	7. The application has a management-support, rather than transaction-processing, orientation.

1. Ineffective Use of Financial Resources

Limited-size user-developed systems tend to "creep up" on the organization. Some foresight is needed to organize some of these development projects into larger ones, producing systems of wider scope. An assessment of the business value of larger end-user development projects is necessary.

2. Inappropriate Selection of Hardware and Software

Organizational benefit is achieved through information systems that can work together, through quantity purchases of resources from vendors, and through the lowering of maintenance costs by using as uniform hardware and software as possible. It is usually counterproductive, for example, if three different microcomputer DBMSs are used in various units of a firm. Networking places further demands on the interoperability of hardware and software. Enterprise-wide standards should be established for hardware and software acquisition. Departures from such standards can be made only for valid reasons.

3. Threats to Data Integrity, Security, and Privacy

Policies for providing end-user access to corporate databases, downloading snapshots (extracts) from these databases to end-user workstations, and uploading data from end-user workstations (which is generally undesirable) must be established. End users who use extracts of corporate data for their management-oriented systems should be assisted with regular procedures for updating the extracts. Rigid backup procedures should be instituted. Security and privacy precautions should be followed in extracting the data.

4. Errors in Systems Analysis

End users, unaided by systems analysts, can make errors of several kinds, including:

- Solving the wrong problem.
- Applying an inappropriate analytical method to the right problem.
- Over-analysis in a time-consuming search for perfection.
- Applying the wrong software tool.

Training and consulting by IS specialists are the primary methods of managing these risks.

5. Lack of Quality Assurance in Systems Development and Operation

Many user-developed systems are poorly constructed, insufficiently tested, do not provide for data validation and audit trails, and are accompanied by virtually no documentation. Many of the methods and controls applicable to professionally developed systems (which we will discuss in Chapter 14) have to be adapted for end-user developed systems.

6. Proliferation of Private Systems

Private systems, which can conceal information from others instead of contributing to the overall information environment of an organization, may be outright harmful. They may also contain suspect data and lead to contentious discussions about whose information is right.

7. Undesirable Information-Related Behavior

There are a variety of behaviors in the end-user development environment which may be counterproductive to an organization's goals. Users may develop systems to keep information "just in case," or for its symbolic value, related to prestige or in order to gain a reputation as a rational manager. Some may even collect information to put their own spin on issues (sometimes to the extent of verging on misrepresentation). This work may also detract users from their primary tasks. As one member of senior management said in regard to the money managers in an investment firm: "We pay these people a great deal of money to make good investment decisions, not to write programs in Lotus."

Many of these risk exposures are caused by the absence of checks and balances associated with traditional, professional systems development. The management of end-user computing should combine the approaches fostering its expansion with those ensuring management control. Support is often provided to the end users with information centers and help desks.

Information Centers and Help Desks

A frequent source of support for end-user computing is the **information center,** an organizational unit that provides training, consulting, and other assistance to end users. Information centers assist end users with selecting, installing, and maintaining PC hardware and software. They also help users with accessing the corporate databases, in some cases by defining the appropriate extracts for decision support systems. Information centers are also often responsible for local area networking. These centers provide assistance with the use of the resources of the Internet. Some information centers develop complete applications with end-user facilities; others lend consulting assistance to the end-user developers. As end-user computing matures in a firm, the task of the information center evolves from training novices and assisting them with acquiring microcomputers and personal productivity software to assisting sophisticated users with developing, maintaining, controlling, and integrating their information systems.

Help-desk software is increasingly employed to provide basic support to the users, most frequently by answering questions relating to the use of software packages. This software often includes expert systems for troubleshooting. It also logs and tracks user requests for help. A number of firms have placed their help desks on the intranets for easy access (King and Jacobs 1996).

Internal systems development, whether done by information systems specialists or by end users, has an alternative—acquisition from an outside vendor. We will now discuss two avenues available for such an acquisition.

Table 13.8	
Principal guidelines for outsourcing	1. Don't outsource your strategic systems.
	2. Maintain the capability for business innovation with information systems.
	3. Negotiate the outsourcing contract with great care.
	4. Provide for a way back from outsourcing.
	5. Oversee closely the delivery of outsourced services.

13.7 | ACQUISITION OF INFORMATION SYSTEMS AND SERVICES FROM VENDORS

The "make-or-buy" decision increasingly results in organizations buying some of their information systems and services. The more radical form of this trend is outsourcing: contracting a significant part of a firm's IS operations and development to external vendors. Only some firms outsource their IS. But owing to the development of the software industry, virtually all firms purchase software packages for at least some of their information processing requirements.

Information Systems Outsourcing

The use of contract programmers to develop systems, rather than a firm's employees, is a long-established practice. So is contracting with specialized firms to develop systems or to provide information services. More recently, the scope of this practice has been significantly expanded by a number of organizations. Known as **outsourcing,** this is the practice of contracting out the operation of a firm's data centers, telecommunications networks, or applications development to external vendors. Some firms elect to outsource only some of these assets and services; others outsource all of them. In many outsourcing arrangements, the information systems resources, including personnel, are transferred to the vendor under a contract that typically runs for 10 years.

From the point of view of systems development, an outsourcing arrangement may give the firm access to experienced IS specialists working for the vendor. Owing to specialization and economies of scale, the vendor may be able to deliver services of higher quality and at a lower cost than can be done internally by the client firm. By buying services from an outsourcing vendor, a firm may invest its resources more productively elsewhere. If the outsourcing contract is skillfully written, the client firm is able to pay only for the IS services it actually uses, resulting in further economies and flexibility, as compared to running an underutilized data center.

Studies (such as Lacity and Hirschheim 1993) show that satisfaction with their outsourcing arrangements is not shared universally by all the firms that have gone that route. Sources of dissatisfaction stem from loss of control due to a dependency on the outsourcing vendor, lack of expected access to the technological talent, and unrealized savings. In some cases, the managers of client firms concluded that they would have been better off restructuring their own IS function. In opting for IS outsourcing, the firm should heed the guidelines summarized in Table 13.8.

Here are the key elements of successful outsourcing:

- The information systems that are a source of competitive strength for the firm should not be outsourced. Strategic systems should be considered proprietary information by a firm and, when transferred to an outsourcer, it may become vulnerable to a disclosure. As we stressed throughout the text, strategic systems remain a source of competitive strength for the firm by being constantly modified to challenge competitors in the marketplace. If the firm sheds its ability to do this internally, it gives up a vital competitive capability. Companies that deploy information systems as a strategic weapon encounter difficulties in finding a good fit with an outsourcing vendor (McFarlan and Nolan 1995).

- In general, the long-term interest of many firms requires maintaining the capability to innovate with information systems. Qualified personnel are necessary to accomplish this. If this capability is lost, it is very expensive to restore.

- As a long-term arrangement affecting an important aspect of a company's operations, the outsourcing contract should be negotiated with utmost care. Such a contract is usually written for the delivery of so-called baseline services, with extra payments, known as excess fees, for any services that exceed them. The baseline services are usually the ones that a firm delivers internally at the time the contract is signed. It is crucial to carefully evaluate the nature, volume, and quality of the baseline services (e.g., over a six-month period), in order to avoid excess fees in the future.

- It is important to consider how the outsourcing decision can be reversed if, in the future, the arrangement does not work out. Appropriate contractual provisions are necessary, but not sufficient, for this contingency. Indeed, termination services to be delivered at the conclusion of the contract should be considered a part of an outsourcing contract (Appleton 1996).

- It is vital that the firm closely oversee the delivery of the outsourced services. In no way can it abdicate the responsibility for the delivery of quality computing!

The IS outsourcing trend is part of a general movement of companies in the postindustrial economy to specialize around their core capabilities and to contract with other firms for other services. In successful cases, long-term corporate partnerships emerge, with both sides avoiding opportunistic behavior and aiming at trust and mutual satisfaction. Major companies that provide outsourcing services (they are also known as systems integrators) include Electronic Data Systems, IBM, Andersen Consulting, Computer Sciences Corporation, and TRW.

Purchase of a Package

Information systems outsourcing is a major change in a firm's governance. Relatively few undertake it. On the other hand, just about all organizations choose, in many instances, to purchase a software package that satisfies most of their relevant requirements, instead of developing their own application. Of course, personal productivity software and many types of office information systems are generally purchased as packages. These packages are designed for the so-called horizontal markets; that is, relatively independent of any specific line of business. A number of packages for the so-called vertical markets, that is, for various lines of business, are also available commercially from software vendors.

The purchase of a business package is actually the purchase of a license to use the package. The customer-licensee pays a one-time charge for the right to use the product to a specified extent, and then continues to pay an annual sum for the updates and service provided by the vendor.

This proprietary software generally has to be modified to fit the needs of a user company. Thus, the "buy" option is usually the "buy-and-modify" case. Modifications may be performed by the licensee, that is, the firm that acquires the software; however, in most cases the vendor does not support modified packages. To get around this problem, the firm that acquires a package may develop additional programs that work with the package and become part of the resulting customized information system. Less frequently, a vendor may modify the package for the licensee. It should be noted that modifications are expensive. Every effort should be made to avoid them; for example, by adjusting the noncritical company procedures to fit the applications package.

When the purchase of a proprietary software package is being considered, **requests for proposal (RFPs)** are sent to the potential package vendors, following an initial study of user requirements. An RFP outlines the requirements of the organization and asks questions about how the vendor's systems may satisfy them. A thorough investigation of needs, expectations, performance benchmarks, and other aspects of the intended package use has to precede sending out an RFP (Conger 1994). A study of independent package evaluations and interviews and visits with the vendor's clients who are currently using the package are the primary means of information gathering. The package selection process is best performed by the **scores-and-weights method** that allows us to score the attributes of a package and assign our own weights to these attributes, in order to arrive at a comparative figure of merit. This is also a learning process, important in discovering the specific requirements of the firm. The method is shown as the general procedure in Figure 13.10.

First, all the attributes of the package to be selected are analyzed and broken down into more detailed subaspects. We thus obtain a tree of object attributes (usually shown horizontally). Based on an analysis of our own needs, we establish the percentage weights by answering the question: Just how important is the given aspect *to us?* These weights add up to 100 percent on each tree branching point. In the process, we learn both about the package and our envisaged uses for it.

For each candidate package, we score the tips of the tree—the aspects which are not further broken down—and 0 to 10 scoring is convenient. The scores should be totally independent of the weights and should also be based on our investigation of the particular product. While the weights are subjective (they reflect our own needs), the scores are objective (they reflect the quality of the candidate package). In the process, we may totally eliminate from further consideration any candidate packages that obviously do not satisfy our major objectives; for example, those that are not compatible with our existing environment.

The total figure of merit for a candidate package is obtained by going up the tree and multiplying scores by weights, as shown in the example of DBMS selection in Figure 13.11. In most situations, figures of merit are meaningful only in a comparative sense, and only significant differences between these figures point to a decision.

In the process of selecting applications packages, the sources of information may be demonstrations (particularly in a similar environment), reports from companies specializing in software evaluation (such as Gartner Group of Stamford, Connecticut), online databases, user groups (including those active on the Internet), or consultants. The package cost is an important factor as well. It is vital not to limit oneself to considering only the technical characteristics of various packages. The way the use of the software will affect the work environment has to be analyzed to make sure that a desirable change will result. Ultimate user acceptance is a principal selection criterion. For example, certain types of groupware were rejected by the users who saw them as imposing undesirable commitments on them or forcing them to share information with others in the firm without compensation. We will see in the next section that both internally developed systems and acquired

Figure 13.10

Scores-and-weights method

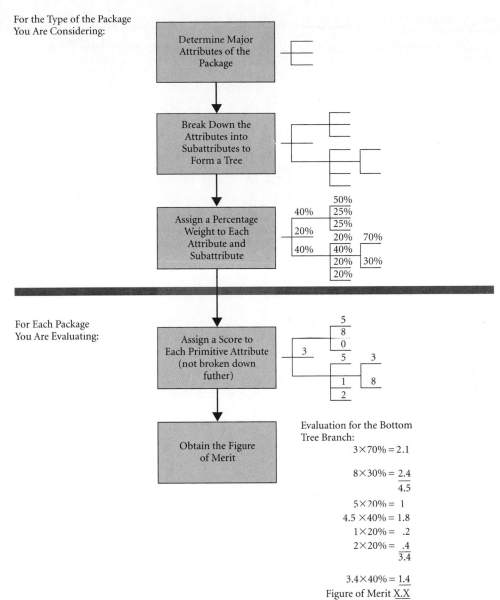

For the Type of the Package You Are Considering:

Determine Major Attributes of the Package

Break Down the Attributes into Subattributes to Form a Tree

Assign a Percentage Weight to Each Attribute and Subattribute

For Each Package You Are Evaluating:

Assign a Score to Each Primitive Attribute (not broken down futher)

Obtain the Figure of Merit

Evaluation for the Bottom Tree Branch:

$3 \times 70\% = 2.1$

$8 \times 30\% = \underline{2.4}$
4.5

$5 \times 20\% = 1$
$4.5 \times 40\% = 1.8$
$1 \times 20\% = .2$
$2 \times 20\% = \underline{.4}$
3.4

$3.4 \times 40\% = \underline{1.4}$
Figure of Merit <u>X.X</u>

packages are subject to the process of organizational implementation that goes well beyond simple installation.

A principal advantage of package purchase over internal development is that the purchase is generally far less expensive. Among its disadvantages is loss of flexibility in adapting the software to the evolving needs of the enterprise. A measure of control is exercised by the user firms that associate into user groups, partly to influence the evolution of the packages they acquire (Williamson 1997). Proprietary software purchase is now increasingly preferred to in-house development. Training is often available from the vendor or a third party. Across industry segments, the use of vertical software prevents duplication of effort

Figure 13.11

Applying scores-and-weights method to select a database management system (DBMS)

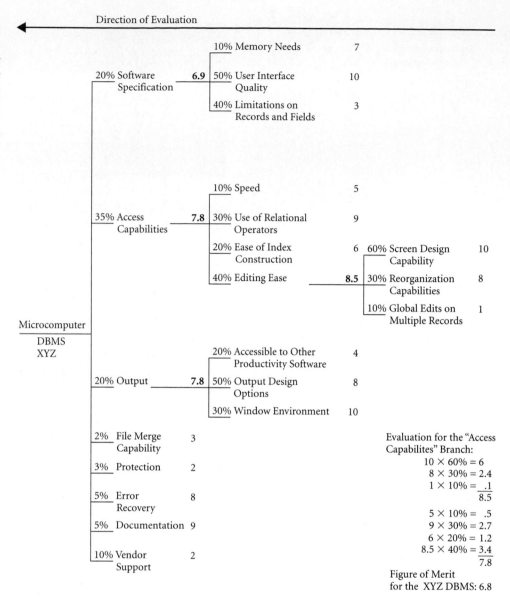

Direction of Evaluation

20% Software Specification	**6.9**
	10% Memory Needs — 7
	50% User Interface Quality — 10
	40% Limitations on Records and Fields — 3

35% Access Capabilities	**7.8**
	10% Speed — 5
	30% Use of Relational Operators — 9
	20% Ease of Index Construction — 6
	40% Editing Ease — **8.5**

60% Screen Design Capability — 10
30% Reorganization Capabilities — 8
10% Global Edits on Multiple Records — 1

Microcomputer DBMS XYZ

20% Output	**7.8**
	20% Accessible to Other Productivity Software — 4
	50% Output Design Options — 8
	30% Window Environment — 10

2% File Merge Capability   3
3% Protection   2
5% Error Recovery   8
5% Documentation   9
10% Vendor Support   2

Evaluation for the "Access Capabilites" Branch:

$$10 \times 60\% = 6$$
$$8 \times 30\% = 2.4$$
$$1 \times 10\% = \underline{.1}$$
$$8.5$$

$$5 \times 10\% = .5$$
$$9 \times 30\% = 2.7$$
$$6 \times 20\% = 1.2$$
$$8.5 \times 40\% = \underline{3.4}$$
$$7.8$$

Figure of Merit for the XYZ DBMS: 6.8

and sometimes results in very significant savings and avoidance of the risks that accompany in-house systems development.

Comparison of Systems Acquisition Methods

Let us compare and contrast the principal methods of information systems acquisition that we have discussed. This comparison is offered in Table 13.9.

Note that these approaches are not mutually exclusive. Thus, end-user developers generally rely on prototyping; the contribution of a systems integrator may be combined with the internal development of a proprietary system part; and the prototyping approach may be used just to establish user requirements during the initial phases of a life cycle-oriented development process.

Table 13.9	**Method**	**Description and Principal Characteristics**
Principal characteristics of IS acquisition methods	Internal development with a life-cycle methodology	System developed in stages, reflecting the analysis–design–programming cycle.
		Advantageous for large organizational systems, such as TPS. Supports project planning and control, organization of team development effort, and production of maintainable systems. Relatively inflexible with respect to user requirements that change during the development cycle; results in voluminous documentation; time-consuming.
	Internal development through evolutionary prototyping (rapid applications development)	System developed by gradually modifying an initial prototype based on feedback from users.
		Relatively fast development, with early availability of a first version of the system. Advantageous when user requirements are uncertain. Principal technique for limited-size systems that need to evolve continually, such as DSS and expert systems. Unless precautions are taken, may evolve into a "quick-and-dirty" system, hampering maintenance.
	Internal development via end-user computing	Relatively simple systems developed by end users, generally for their own (rather than organizational) use.
		May result in faster development and does not tax IS resources. End user-oriented development tools needed. Users committed to system because they get what they believe they need. Care required in selecting appropriate systems and controlling their impact on the firm.
	Outsourcing	External vendor develops systems and, possibly, operates the firm's IS infrastructure.
		Relieves the company from the resource commitment to IS. May result in access to expertise and savings. May lead to loss of control, hamper organizational learning, and prevent gain of competitive strength.
	Purchase of a package	Package that satisfies most user requirements acquired from external vendor.
		Rapid placement into operation at a relatively low cost; cost largely known at outset. The work within the organization often has to be adjusted to use the package. More reliable and better documentation than internally produced systems provide. Package may need extensive modification. May cause company to forgo competitive edge that could be realized with information technology.

Figure 13.12

Key agents in systems development and implementation, with their agendas

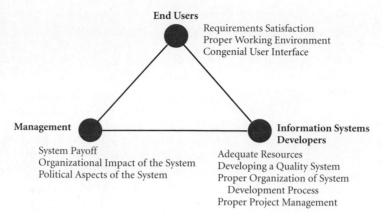

End Users

Requirements Satisfaction
Proper Working Environment
Congenial User Interface

Management

System Payoff
Organizational Impact of the System
Political Aspects of the System

Information Systems Developers

Adequate Resources
Developing a Quality System
Proper Organization of System
    Development Process
Proper Project Management

13.8 | IMPLEMENTATION OF INFORMATION SYSTEMS

What Is System Implementation and Who Is Involved in It?

The **implementation** of an information system is the process of preparing people in an organization for a new system and introducing the system into the organization. In other words, it is an ongoing process that should start early during system development (or even precede the actual development) and result in the intended use of the new system and its continuing modification to meet new requirements. Similar activities should be undertaken to introduce systems acquired from outside the firm.

The success of an information system is not at all assured by its technical qualities alone. We know from Chapter 1 of the text that the sociotechnical perspective requires that we go well beyond the technology to reach for implementation success. This success will depend on a variety of organizational measures and processes that are collectively called system implementation.

Introduction of a major system is a process of organizational change that involves three key agents. These agents are the intended users of the systems, its developers, and the corporate management. These three groups have well-defined interests, which have to be reconciled to the benefit of the organization. Their agendas are shown in Figure 13.12. Of course, each of these groups is not uniform itself.

As we can see, the principal interests of the users lie in the satisfaction of their job-oriented requirements and the provision of a proper working environment. Corporate managers are interested primarily in the organizational impact of the system. IS developers need the resources, such as the adequate budget and time, to develop a quality system. Mutual understanding of the interests of all three parties assists in successful system implementation.

A fully developed system may become a technical success but be an organizational failure (Keen 1981). To its developers, the system "works," but it remains unused. Here is an example. Bank tellers are provided with a new system for entering account transactions. Management wants it used as soon as possible. The system is complex, but the tellers are given a cursory two-hour orientation, and they make multiple errors as they navigate the several densely filled screens that are needed to open a new account or renew a certificate of deposit. As a result, the tellers make mistakes. Adjustments to the accounts have to be made at a later time, which further increases the load on the system. Response time goes up, and the frustration level is high. The system is judged to be a failure.

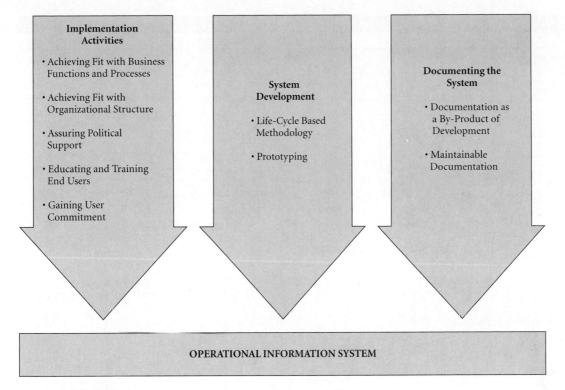

Implementation Activities

- Achieving Fit with Business Functions and Processes
- Achieving Fit with Organizational Structure
- Assuring Political Support
- Educating and Training End Users
- Gaining User Commitment

System Development

- Life-Cycle Based Methodology
- Prototyping

Documenting the System

- Documentation as a By-Product of Development
- Maintainable Documentation

OPERATIONAL INFORMATION SYSTEM

Figure 13.13

Implementation activities should accompany system development and documentation

The need to begin implementation activities before systems development begins and to continue these activities as the development progresses (and as the system is documented) is illustrated in Figure 13.13.

Throughout the development of a large organizational system, the developers and the two other principal agents involved in the process should interact on a regular basis. The developers must be assured of continuing management support and must gain user commitment to the system the users will be expected to work with. This interaction with future users occurs naturally during prototyping, when users and developers collaborate in development; users of management-oriented systems developed in this fashion are most often the managers themselves. In end-user development, it is frequently important to involve IS professionals to counteract the discussed risks of these systems.

Implementation Success and Failure

The implementation of an information system is considered successful if most of the following results are obtained:

1. High level of system use—most of the expected users do indeed use the system.

2. The system is used to its full potential rather than superficially.

3. Users are highly satisfied (the satisfaction level can be measured by administering validated questionnaires).

4. The original objectives of the system are achieved. The success of the system should be gauged in terms of achieving the results stated during the analysis of its expected business value.

Why Did this Information System Project Fail?

Swissair's Personnel Information and Salary (PISA) on-line system was approved for development to replace a 15-year-old batch payroll system with limited functionality. The Swiss airline wanted PISA to be built around an extensive database.

The airline employees who were supposed to develop the system were required to work with two user departments. Payroll was the responsibility of the Finance Department and personnel information was needed by Human Resources. The two departments had different objectives with respect to the envisaged information system. The Finance Department wanted a simple and economic upgrade of its old system while Human Resources wanted a technologically advanced system. The differences in the future owners' perspectives led to contradictory system requirements. The need to elicit and reconcile such requirements from two conflicting sources made systems analysis a very expensive exercise.

In addition, the database management system that was to be used for the PISA database was also needed to support a mission-critical information system for the airline engineering application. Since no hardware upgrade was provided for in the project, it became obvious that both systems would suffer from degraded performance. As PISA was less critical to the core activities of Swissair, it was more likely to be sacrificed.

The development of major systems at Swissair was overseen by a project policy board, normally chaired by the vice-president of the user department for which the system was being developed. However, the vice-president of finance delegated this responsibility to his deputy. The deputy did not believe the system could be developed economically. Moreover, he was chairing at the same time a task force aiming to combat the effects of an impending recession on the firm—a cost-cutting program, in other words. This was hardly consistent with his chairing a steering committee for a spending project.

Two years after its inception, the requirements for three-quarters of the system had been specified in detail, with half of the system programmed. In technological terms, the progress was satisfactory. However, when the recession unfolded, a financial review of all IS projects was undertaken. The review of PISA revealed that in addition to the initial budget of 5.3 million Swiss francs, a further 3.6 million was required. This would reduce the return on investment from 3 percent to zero. The Payroll Department proposed scrapping the payroll part of the system. The Human Resources Department was unable to provide financial justification for continuing alone, and the project was terminated.

Based on Chris Sauer, *Why Information Systems Fail: A Case Study Approach*, Henley-on-Thames, England: Alfred Waller, 1993.

5. The system is institutionalized. This means all of the following: The system is continually modified to meet new needs. New generations of users emerge, supported by ongoing training. The business processes and organizational structures around the system evolve continually as well.

The failure of information system projects has many faces. Some examples of failures that many organizations could (but are not eager to) recount include the following situations:

• Owing to political opposition, resources are diverted from a system development project, which is never completed.

• Development costs and time wildly exceed original estimates.

• Intended users ignore the operational system and do their job the old way.

- The system produces disappointing business results.
- The system falls into disuse as soon as its original users are transferred elsewhere—and the list could go on.

The vignette on the preceding page tells you that a failure may have several causes.

How to Achieve Successful IS Implementation

A number of factors determine the success or failure of an information system. It is vital that we know what leads to success. Figure 13.14 shows the principal factors, which we will now consider.

1. Organizational Fit

The planning processes we outlined earlier in the chapter need to ensure that the information system's objectives are in line with organizational objectives. The specific tasks and even the entire job of all the people who will work with the system may have to be redefined, and the system has to be built to match the desired job design. For instance, if teamwork is to be encouraged, a groupware system must be selected and customized to match the pattern of the work in the group. This could provide an opportunity to define meaningful tasks for each individual, with a high degree of autonomy and perceived significance of performed tasks (Davenport 1994). In broader terms, the redesign of business functions has to precede system development. Change processes, discussed below, must be initiated to gain commitment from the individuals whose workplace will be affected by the system.

2. Management Support

Absence of support at higher management levels has doomed many a worthy project. Corporate management has to make appropriate resources available to the project, including qualified personnel, funds, computer resources, and sufficient time for system development.

Figure 13.14

Factors in successful system implementation (From Vladimir Zwass, *Management Information Systems*, Dubuque, IA: Wm. C. Brown, 1992, p. 748.)

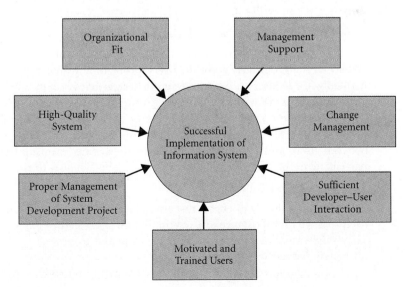

Figure 13.15

Process of organizational change

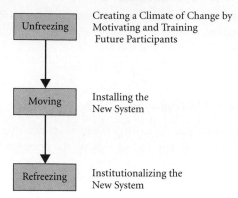

Objectives

Unfreezing — Creating a Climate of Change by Motivating and Training Future Participants

Moving — Installing the New System

Refreezing — Institutionalizing the New System

3. The Process of Change Management

The introduction of a new system is an organizational change. Systems analysts act as change agents. Most people resist change, which brings uncertainty, and perhaps threatens their positions and roles. The process of **organizational change** is needed for change management during the introduction of a new information system. The process is shown in Figure 13.15.

This process first creates a climate for change by motivating and training the affected parties (and, if necessary, neutralizing those who cannot be motivated). Evidence of commitment to the process by senior managers is crucial. Only after this "unfreezing" phase can the new system be installed during the "moving" phase. After a change is introduced, the system must be institutionalized in the "refreezing" phase. Thus, the change has to be buttressed by new procedures, additional training, and, if necessary, system modification to gain full acceptance and its proper level of broad use.

Throughout the implementation process, it is very important to manage the expectations of the prospective users and of corporate management. No unrealistic promises should be made and all involved should be informed of the progress of the development project.

4. Sufficient Interaction between Users and Developers

The involvement of intended users in system development is important to ensure that the system will appropriately solve the users' problem and that it will be successfully implemented with the users' full commitment. User participation in system development generally leads to higher user satisfaction with the delivered system (McKeen and Guimaraes 1997). Developers are increasingly helping users define their problems rather than trying to offer solutions. Prototyping approaches to systems development are a form of collaboration between users and developers that can remove many a misunderstanding. Users often participate in the life cycle system development, particularly during the analysis phases.

5. Motivated and Trained Users

It would be foolhardy to expect that user participation in the development process will in itself remove user resistance to a system that the users perceive as a threat to their interests. They might instead embark on a variety of tactics to protect these interests and so may ultimately subvert the implementation.

Users should see a clear picture of how the new system will help them do (and, perhaps, keep) their jobs. User training is an important factor in allaying user fears of the unknown caused by the new system. New skills may be acquired through formal instruction, through self-study with a system prototype or a training system, or through a combination of both. Training has to be an ongoing process as new employees are hired, systems are modified, and skills need to be refreshed.

6. Proper Management of a System Development Project

Information system projects are notorious for such problems as drastic cost overruns and dramatic schedule slippages (Keil 1995). Project management tools should be used to control a project. The more ambitious the scope of a project and the newer the technologies to the organization, the more likely the project will fail. To lower the project risk, a complex undertaking should be broken down into stages to be implemented step by step. "Grand designs" fail more often than a series of incremental projects.

7. System Quality

A "working" system often falls into disuse because of its low quality. Some quality problems are:

- *Poor usability.* Users face long response times in on-line systems, poor screen designs, or long and confusing menu sequences.
- *Poor data quality.* Reliable information cannot be generated from inaccurately entered data, from data that are not entered on a timely basis, or data that are simply unavailable.
- *Poor quality of information provided.* Inaccurate data introduced into databases give rise to inaccurate information. Similarly, irrelevant information hardly helps users in their decision making. Information overload may result from frequent and voluminous reports. Information provided too late for decision making is useless.
- *Operating cost overruns.* High costs of system use may make it cost-beneficial to abandon the system.
- *Operational problems.* The system "goes down" frequently and takes a long time to repair.

We will discuss the general attributes of quality software in Section 15.1.

As one may conclude from a review of these success factors, many of them are interrelated, making the implementation of an information system a complex process indeed.

SUMMARY

The capabilities of information systems enable redesign of business processes, which is sometimes conducted through radical business reengineering. Relying on information systems, organizations can dramatically improve the quality of their products, cut the time-to-market, or shorten the order processing time. Whether to support a business reengineering effort or to provide a platform for delivery of their information services in the future, many organizations find it necessary to develop a long-term plan for their information systems architecture.

A master plan for organizational information systems includes the statement of objectives, projections of the future environment, evaluation of alternative ways of delivering information services in the future, along with selection of a preferred alternative, and a plan for the portfolio of the firm's IS applications. The specification of the IS infrastructure, of the IS human resources, a financial plan, and an action plan are also included.

The information systems architecture and the long-term IS requirements of a firm can be established with one of four methods. They can be derived from the long-term organizational objectives or plans by analyzing all goals, strategies, and objectives. Enterprise analysis with the Business Systems Planning (BSP) methodology can be conducted to establish business processes, the data needed to support them, and the information system architecture necessary to create the data and to process the data in order to obtain information. The Critical Success Factors (CSF) methodology can be used to derive organizational information requirements from the key information needs of individual executives.

The following techniques may be used to assess the business value of information systems: Cost-benefit analysis compares the costs of the system acquisition and operation against the tangible and intangible benefits of its use over the information system's lifetime. The portfolio approach assembles a portfolio of application development projects that balances the total risks of developing new systems with the desired benefits. Through a charge-back mechanism, end users can pay for systems development. The priorities for systems acquisition can be established by the IS steering committee comprised of the key managers of the firm.

Once established as worthy of acquisition, information systems may be acquired through internal development by IS professionals or, if appropriate, end users. Alternatively a firm may outsource this development effort to outside vendors or acquire a package that may be customized as desired.

Systems development life cycle serves to develop large organizational information systems through a process of systems analysis, systems design, programming, and installation activities. The operational system then goes into maintenance. In order to speed up the development process and to elicit user requirements for the new system more reliably, an initial prototype of the system may be built. In a process known as rapid applications development, the prototype may be evolved into an operational information system.

End-user computing has three dimensions: (1) sophisticated use of information technology by end-users, (2) end-user control of systems, and (3) development of certain applications by end-users. The benefits of end-user development include high productivity, when the functional expertise of the developers is combined with appropriate software tools, as well as the more likely acceptance of the finished systems by the users who developed it themselves. The principal risks of end-user development are ineffective use of financial resources; inappropriate selection of hardware and software; threats to data integrity, security, and privacy; errors in systems analysis; lack of quality assurance; proliferation of private systems; and undesirable information-related behavior, such as being distracted from their own primary tasks. Information centers are a source of support for end-user computing.

Information systems may be acquired from outside the firm by outsourcing or by the purchase and customization of an application package. Outsourcing is the practice of contracting out the operation of a firm's data centers, telecommunications networks, or applications development to external vendors. To select a package that best meets the firm's needs, the scores-and-weights method may be used. Using this method, we score the attributes of a package and assign our own weights to them in order to arrive at a comparative figure of merit.

In order to introduce an information system into the organization and prepare people for using it, an implementation process is necessary. To be successfully implemented, the information system has to fit the way the organization intends to operate, it must receive management support, and it should be introduced through a process of change management. End users need to interact with the system developers and be motivated and trained. System development projects have to be properly managed. There is no substitute for the quality of a new system.

KEY TERMS

Business process   *462*

Information system architecture   *466*

Master IS plan   *466*

Business Systems Planning (BSP)   *467*

Critical Success Factors (CSF) methodology   *470*

Cost-benefit analysis   *472*

Portfolio approach   *472*

Chargeback   *473*

IS steering committee   *473*

Fixed and operating costs   *474*

Tangible and intangible benefits   *474*

Net present value approach   *476*

Break-even method   *477*

Systems development life cycle   *479*

System analysis   *480*

System design   *480*

Programming   *480*

Installation   *480*

System maintenance   *481*

Prototype   *481*

Prototyping   *481*

Rapid applications development   *481*

End-user computing   *484*

End-user development   *484*

Information center   *487*

Help desk   *487*

Outsourcing   *488*

Request for proposal (RFP)   *490*

Scores-and-weights method   *490*

System implementation   *494*

Organizational change   *498*

QUESTIONS

1. State the objective and the typical most important output of two operational and two management business processes listed in Table 13.1. How is providing this output related to information or information systems (if at all)?

2. What is the role of information systems in business reengineering?

3. Consider the business reengineering project at Bell Atlantic, described in Section 13.1. Using Table 1.3, specify the generic directions that were taken to redesign the "Provide Carrier Access Service" process. What capabilities of information systems were exploited?

4. What is the difference between business reengineering and total quality management? Are the two compatible? What is the relationship between them? Can you show this relationship graphically with "time" on the horizontal axis? How does the role of information systems in these two initiatives differ?

5. What are the contents of a master plan for organizational information systems?

6. What are the principal differences between the Business Systems Planning and the critical success factors methodologies?

7. What do you believe are the critical success factors of a corporate vice-president for marketing (you may select a specific industry you are familiar with)? What information is needed to support each of the factors?

8. What are the methods for evaluating the relative worth of applications? State the principal approach in each of these methods.

9. Name five important intangible benefits of information systems. What capabilities of information systems (see Table 1.2) can be exploited to produce these benefits? Why are the major benefits of strategically important information systems often intangible?

10. What is the difference between the net present value (NPV) and break-even methods of cost-benefit analysis?

11. What are the four principal ways in which information systems can be acquired by a firm? What are the general advantages and drawbacks of using an external source as opposed to the internal development of an information system?

12. What are the principal tasks involved in planning, developing, and operating information systems? What is the objective of each of these tasks?

13. How does life-cycle development of information systems differ from rapid applications development with prototyping? What types of systems lend themselves best to development with each of these methodologies?

14. What possible pitfalls of prototyping should be avoided?

15. What is end-user computing? Name five characteristics of applications that are suitable for end-user development.

16. What risks of end-user development have to be managed?

17. Which of the following projects are *not* likely candidates for end-user development? Why?

    a. An expert system that will help its developer, the geologist at an oil exploration company, classify the deposits brought up from a well.

    b. An organizational decision support system that will rely on a data warehouse, which also has to be developed as part of the project.

    c. A management reporting system for the marketing group of the company.

d. A front-end system that will present information from the database in a form convenient for the quality assurance group in a manufacturing firm.

18. What is an information center? What is a help desk? How are the two related?

19. What is information systems outsourcing? Is it part of a general business trend you can describe?

20. What are the principal motivations for outsourcing?

21. What are the outsourcing pitfalls to be avoided?

22. What is request for proposals? What factors would you consider in selecting a vendor (rather than selecting a specific product)?

23. In a table, list the principal advantages and disadvantages of each of the four methods through which information systems can be acquired.

24. Who are the key agents in the implementation of information systems? What are their principal agendas? Is it possible that two, or even three, agents become one? Under what circumstances? What would be the agenda of the "collapsed" agent?

25. List the principal activities that should be undertaken during the implementation of an information system. What is the objective of each activity? Can its achievement be measured and how?

26. What major factors does a successful implementation of an information system depend upon?

27. What are the stages of the process of organizational change? What is the objective of each stage? What would you do specifically at each stage to implement a new system supporting the platform officers who are responsible for dealing with consumers in a bank's branch office?

ISSUES FOR DISCUSSION

1. A central database of student records has been proposed for your college or university. The database will include not only the records of the present students but also the records of all the known past students and those of potential future students whom the university intends to recruit aggressively. What will be the sources of the costs of establishing and maintaining the database? What will be the tangible benefits of having such a database and how can they be evaluated? What will be the intangible benefits? Are there any ethical issues that can arise and how should they be handled?

2. Suppose you have been promoted to the position of IS director by your employer, a midsize distributor of specialty foods. You are expected to reduce the backlog of applications awaiting development. What methods of system acquisition will you recommend? What drawbacks of these methods will you need to control?

3. Discuss the relationships between the culture of an organization on the one hand and its methods of information systems planning and preferred avenues for systems acquisition on the other.

REAL-WORLD MINICASE AND PROBLEM-SOLVING EXERCISES

1. A Tale of Woe   When Unocal converted its internally developed mainframe accounting system in 11 months to a client/server package, Oracle Financials from Oracle Applications, the oil company was truly proud of what it called fast implementation. The success story even appeared in a full-page ad Oracle placed in *The Wall Street Journal.*

The new accounting system however, proceeded to wreak havoc on Unocal's nearly 1,000 retail gasoline dealers, causing billing errors and long invoicing delays. The dealers, doing business under the Union 76 brand, say they are being charged erroneously for oil, tires, and other nongasoline goods they never purchased. Hundreds, and sometimes thousands, of dollars, were falsely transferred from the dealers' accounts to Unocal.

Unocal tried to remedy the situation by installing a new release of Oracle Financials, but the software was still "buggy," that is, it contained errors, according to a technical support manager at Unocal. Officially, Unocal blames the problems on the gaps in Oracle's software functionality. "We found that some of the EDI [electronic data interchange] and EFT [electronic funds transfer] capabilities of Oracle were not there," says Rod Starr, manager of accounting systems development at Unocal's Houston office that directed the Oracle project. Several Oracle employees have been assigned to Unocal to help with delivering these services.

a. What is the difference between conversion and implementation? Was the difference perceived here?

b. What could have the Unocal IS managers done to prevent the situation from arising?

Based on Doug Bartholomew, "Stalled at the Pumps," *Information-Week*, April 29, 1996, p. 16.

2. Cost-Benefit Analysis   Using a spreadsheet, perform cost-benefit analysis for an information system development project with these characteristics:

- Development time—one year.
- Time the system will be in operation—five years.
- Fixed costs—$50,000.
- Operating costs—$10,000/year.
- Annual benefits when operational—$25,000.
- Discount rate—10 percent.

Use the net present value method and make a recommendation, assuming that there are no significant intangible benefits.

3. Request for Proposal (RFP)   Write a request for proposal (RFP) for an applications package to be acquired by your firm. The package should support your human resources function. You should first determine the likely vendors by using the resources of the Internet and by reading articles and ads in the relevant periodicals (See Table 1.4). Section 12.5 will help you identify the capabilities you will seek in the application. You will need to define the user population, the hardware and systems software environments, and the operational characteristics of the packages you wish to acquire. For the details of the RFP contents, you may consult (Conger 1994) or another text on systems development.

TEAM   PROJECT

Each two- or three-person team will select a specific type of a software package, equipment (such as notebook computers), or information service. Study the evaluation of this type of resource in the periodical literature. Determine the environment in which your resource will be deployed. Using the scores-and-weights method, specify the attributes of the resource and weigh them from the point of view of the selected environment. Develop scores for two or three specific resources in your category. If possible, contact the current users to obtain the scores. Compute figures of merit and make a selection decision. Present the results to the class and discuss whether meaningful distinctions among products have been found.

SELECTED   REFERENCES

Alavi, Maryam; R. Ryan Nelson; and Ira Weiss, "Strategies for End-User Computing: An Integrative Framework." *Journal of Management Information Systems,* 4, no. 3, (Winter 1987–88), pp. 28–49.

What are the effective organizational strategies with respect to end-user computing?

Appleton, Elaine L. "Divorce Your Outsourcer?" *Datamation,* August 1996, pp. 60–62.

What happens if the outsourcing contract is not working out?

Barr, Stephen. "Grinding It Out: Why Reengineering Takes So Long." *CFO,* January 1995, pp. 26–31.

Describes several practical cases of business reengineering and the difficulties that need to be overcome.

Bergeron, François, and Clermont Bégin. "The Use of Critical Success Factors in Evaluation of Information Systems: A Case Study." *Journal of Management Information Systems,* 5, no. 4, (Spring 1989), pp. 111–24.

Boar, Bernard H. *The Art of Strategic Planning for Information Technology: Crafting Strategy for the 90s,* New York: Wiley, 1993.

Discusses several methodologies for the strategic planning of IS and the execution of the strategic plans.

Brynjolfsson, Erik, and Lorin Hitt. "Is Information Systems Spending Productive? New Evidence and New Results." in Janice I. DeGross, Robert P. Bostrom, and Daniel Robey, eds. *Proceedings of the Fourteenth International Conference on Information Systems,* Orlando, FL, 1993.

The evidence of the business value of information systems.

Conger, Sue. *The New Software Engineering.* Belmont, CA: Wadsworth, 1994.

Contains a thorough and contemporary discussion of systems planning and development. Includes a good description of requests for proposals (RFP).

Davenport, Thomas H. *Process Innovation: Reengineering Work through Information Technology.* Boston: Harvard Business School Press, 1993.

An essential and detailed book on business process redesign.

Davenport, Thomas H. "Saving IT's Soul." *Harvard Business Review,* March–April 1994, pp. 119–131.

Davenport, Thomas H., and Michael C. Beers. "Managing Information about Processes." *Journal of Management Information Systems,* 12, no. 1, (Summer 1995), pp. 57–80.

The authors find that managing the information about business processes is crucial to their redesign and describe how the leading firms manage this information.

Davis, Gordon B., and Margrethe H. Olson. *Management Information Systems: Conceptual Foundations, Structure, and Development.* New York: McGraw-Hill, 1985.

Fink, Dieter. "Information Systems Planning in a Volatile Environment." *Long Range Planning,* December 1994, pp. 108–113.

Compares the use of various long-term IS planning methodologies and includes three case studies.

Hammer, Michael. *Beyond Reengineering: How the Process-Centered Organization Is Changing Our Work and Our Lives.* New York: HarperBusiness, 1996.

Hammer, Michael, and James Champy. *Reengineering the Corporation.* New York: Harper Business, 1993.

Along with Davenport's book, a principal source on business process redesign.

"H.E. Butt Grocery Company: A Leader in ECR Implementation." Harvard Business School Case 196-061, 1995.

"IT Risk Management," Special Section. *CIO,* April 15, 1996, pp. 36–60.

Keen, Peter W. "Information Systems and Organizational Change." *Communications of the ACM,* 24, no. 1, (January 1981), pp. 24–33.

An essential paper on IS implementation.

Keil, Mark. "Pulling the Plug: Software Project Management and the Problem of Project Escalation." *MIS Quarterly,* December 1995, pp. 421–448.

King, Julia, and April Jacobs. "Help Desk to Workers: Don't Call Us, Use the Net." *Computerworld,* June 3, 1996, pp. 1, 28.

Lacity, Mary C., and Rudy Hirschheim. *Information Systems Outsourcing: Myths, Metaphors, and Realities.* Chichester, United Kingdom: Wiley, 1993.

A thorough evaluation of the pros and cons of information systems outsourcing.

Lederer, Albert L., and Aubrey L. Mendelow. "Coordination of Information Systems Plans with Business Plans." *Journal of Management Information Systems,* 6, no. 2, (Fall 1989), pp. 5–19.

Lederer, Albert L., and Vijay Sethi. "Key Prescriptions for Strategic Information Systems Planning." *Journal of Management Information Systems,* 13, no. 1, (Fall 1996).

McFarlan, F. Warren. "Portfolio Approach to Information Systems." *Harvard Business Review.* September–October 1981, pp. 142–50.

McFarlan, F. Warren, and Richard L. Nolan. "How to Manage an IT Outsourcing Alliance." *Sloan Management Review,* Winter 1995, pp. 9–23.

McKeen, James D. and Tor Guimaraes. "Successful Strategies for User Participation in Systems Development." *Journal of Management Information Systems,* 14, no. 2 (Fall 1997).

Regan, Elizabeth A., and Bridget N. O'Connor, *End-User Information Systems: Perspectives for Managers and Information Systems Professionals.* New York: Macmillan, 1994.

Discusses many practical aspects of end-user computing.

Rockart, John F. "Chief Executives Define Their Own Data Needs." *Harvard Business Review,* March–April 1979, pp. 81–93.

A description of the Critical Success Factors (CSF) methodology.

Swanson, E. Burton. *Information System Implementation: Bridging the Gap Between Design and Utilization.* Burr Ridge, Illinois: Irwin, 1988.

Williamson, Miryam. "Powers of Persuasion." *CIO,* January 15, 1997, pp. 46–53.

CASE STUDY | # Shape Up or Ship Out for Information Systems

Information Systems group at Novus Financial in Riverwoods, Illinois, was in deep trouble. This consumer finance unit of Dean Witter, Discover & Co., makes consumer loans for mortgages and automobile purchases. It was facing increasingly stiff competition from banks, credit unions, and other sources of financing. The pressure to cut costs, create new products, and offer customers flexible services was intense. But the firm's information systems were shackled by mainframe-based legacy applications written in COBOL and even in IBM assembly language. The systems were costly to operate and difficult to modify in order to respond to new business demands. There was an additional cause of inflexibility: All applications were run on the mainframes managed by Dean Witter's parent company at the time—Sears and Roebuck.

Aroon Maben, vice-president of technology at Novus, faced a stark choice: Replace all the legacy systems with a new information system architecture, based on downsized, client/server systems with open systems software—or face outsourcing. Indeed, Novus has already evaluated the outsourcing option and received quotes from several companies in the business, including EDS and Perot Systems. All outsources claimed they could match the current IS functionality for 25 to 30 percent less than the cost of the internal IS services at Novus.

But Maben had a different plan: to reinvent the internal IS department as a much smaller group and to use the $4 million savings to fund the transition to a downsized and flexible new system. The decision to go ahead with the proposal was not easy. When Maben's plan was adopted in 1991, permanent IS personnel was cut from 48 to 20 people (see Figure 13.16). As the chief information officer, he chose to work in the future with people who he felt could face the drastic change, could anticipate user needs, and were not simply order-takers. Maben had to create an organization that could move fast and take chances, risking an occasional mistake. He hoped that the IS developers who stayed on would be the people who could face the disruption caused by the necessary layoffs, quickly learn the new technologies, and work 12-hour days necessary to accomplish the rapid transition. The gamble paid off: All 20 developers did stay through the migration.

The former hierarchical structure of the IS department was replaced by several self-managed project teams. All members of the teams were encouraged to explore and bring in new technologies. The veteran IS professionals on the new teams were offered intensive training in UNIX, C, and relational database technologies, and they gained marketable skills. For the first time, the organization started to use outside consultants, both to help with the actual systems development and to act as on-the-job instructors in the technologies new to the company.

A sequence for migrating the IS applications to the new environment was developed, with the most critical systems moved first. Thus, the first to be modified was the loan-origination system used by 150 employees to process loan applications. It was also an application that would get the process off to a quick start. In the anticipation of redesigning the origination system, the developers at Novus had already defined the user requirements. Also, a package that met most (though not all) requirements was identified. That was Creditrevue, a UNIX-based origination application from Credit Management Solutions of Columbia, Maryland. The package was relatively easy to modify, because it was written in a non-procedural 4GL. The origination system went into full production in eight months.

The origination system was followed by a new office information system that offered E-mail and standard spreadsheet and graphics applications, integrated with the origination system.

In January 1994, some two and a half years into the downsizing project, the teams delivered the extensive document-preparation, loan-servicing, and collection system. In this case, Novus decided against adapting a packaged solution. Here, the company wanted to build maximum flexibility into the system, which was seen as a potential source of competitive advantage. At the heart of the system is the database maintained with the Oracle relational database management system. The CASE tools supplied with the Oracle DBMS were used in the development process. The system is deployed to monitor, maintain, and report on 400,000 customer accounts in Novus's $1.3 billion loan portfolio.

The new architecture relies on four servers (MIServers from Pyramid), interconnected with client PCs via an Ethernet local area network. The most significant problems encountered during the system implementation stemmed from the developers' inexperience with UNIX. The problems related to configuring the system and tuning the applications for performance.

Figure 13.16

Downsizing of the IS unit of Novus Financial (Modified from Jeff Moad, "Shock Therapy Cures Fossilitis," *Datamation,* June 1, 1994, p. 57.)

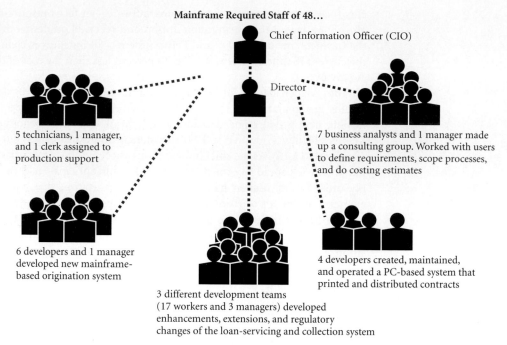

Mainframe Required Staff of 48...

Chief Information Officer (CIO)

Director

5 technicians, 1 manager, and 1 clerk assigned to production support

7 business analysts and 1 manager made up a consulting group. Worked with users to define requirements, scope processes, and do costing estimates

6 developers and 1 manager developed new mainframe-based origination system

3 different development teams (17 workers and 3 managers) developed enhancements, extensions, and regulatory changes of the loan-servicing and collection system

4 developers created, maintained, and operated a PC-based system that printed and distributed contracts

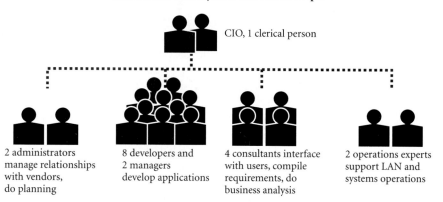

...But Client/Server System Runs with 20 People

CIO, 1 clerical person

2 administrators manage relationships with vendors, do planning

8 developers and 2 managers develop applications

4 consultants interface with users, compile requirements, do business analysis

2 operations experts support LAN and systems operations

Throughout the transition, Maben both motivated the members of the new IS organization and ensured that they got the necessary resources from the company. The IS specialists showed total commitment to the project. "To get to where we are today would have taken us ages if we hadn't done what we did," says Joe Nevins, a 28-year IS veteran. "It was hell for two years, but it's paying off now."

There is more to learn. Novus's developers have yet to introduce system prototyping and rapid applications development and gain experience in developing graphical user interfaces. However, the confidence is there. Costs have dropped by 21 percent—comparable to what the outsourcers offered the company. At the same time, the firm has control of its IS destiny. "It's not just a choice between maintaining a large [IS] organization or outsourcing," says Maben. "There's a middle ground, provided you're willing to change and take risks."

Based on Jeff Moad, "Shock Therapy Cures Fossilitis," *Datamation,* June 1, 1994, pp. 57–59.

C A S E   S T U D Y   Q U E S T I O N S

1. What were the options in providing IS services at Novus Financial and what would be the consequences of each of these options for the firm's IS unit and for the firm at large?

2. What were the reasons for the IS downsizing at Novus Financial?

3. What did downsizing mean for the IS organization and what did it mean for the information technology in the firm?

4. How were the multiple sources of IS acquisition combined at Novus?

5. Do you believe that the crash project was necessary during the downsizing? What were the advantages and the costs of the "shock therapy"?

CHAPTER FOURTEEN

Managing and Controlling Information Systems

OBJECTIVES

After you complete this chapter, you will be able to:

1. Compare and contrast the centralized and decentralized organizations of the Information Services department.

2. Provide basic job descriptions of such information systems specialists as systems analyst, designer, programmer, and chief information officer (CIO).

3. State the basic objectives of IS operations.

4. State the relationship between the identification of threats to information systems, information system controls, and audits of information systems.

5. Define information system security, privacy, and confidentiality.

6. State the nature of the threats to information system security.

7. Give examples of threats related to computer crime and abuse.

8. Explain the nature of computer viruses.

9. Define information systems controls and distinguish between general and application controls.

10. Specify the types of general controls.

11. Define encryption and describe public-key encryption.

12. State the areas that are covered by application controls.

13. Explain what an information systems audit is.

OUTLINE

Focus Minicase. With Benchmarking, You Know How You Rate

14.1 Managing Information Services in a Firm

14.2 Managing Information Systems Operations

14.3 Threats to Security, Privacy, and Confidentiality in IS Operations

14.4 General Information Systems Controls

14.5 Application Controls

14.6 Auditing Information Systems

Case Study. Diary of a Disaster Recovery: Walking the Walk

FOCUS MINICASE

With Benchmarking, You Know How You Rate

Benchmarking is the process of continuously measuring and assessing your firm's products and practices against those of world-class corporations or your top competitors. Benchmarking helps the firm adapt best practices to its own needs. Today, many firms are benchmarking the way they market their products and the way they deliver them to the customers, the way they process orders, and the way they handle accounts receivable.

As information technology becomes more deeply embedded in business processes, companies are also benchmarking information services. By using the data from industry reports and databases, from user groups, from associations devoted to IS productivity, and from specialized consulting firms, the companies compare the quality and cost of the information services they provide with those of the best-of-breed. In some cases, after identifying the four or five leading companies, often in noncompeting industries, the firm's teams spend a day on their site, sharing data on applications, time and cost of systems development, methodologies used to develop and maintain the applications, and the methods of quality assessment.

Thomas Walsh, a director in the management information systems department of Champion International, a Hamilton, Ohio-based maker of paper goods, tells us: "My mission is to make information technology a low-cost, high-quality service provider and to make sure that service is a nonissue to all our internal customers." The IS department Walsh runs constantly compares its services to the selected quality providers in various industries. By instituting a program of self-measurement and benchmarking and acting on its results, Champion's IS department has decreased the costs of processing a computerized transaction from $1 to 39 cents, achieved a 99.9 percent on-time information delivery rate, and obtained customer ratings of "excellent" in 99.5 percent of service agreements. All this was done while the work volume increased by 200 percent and the data center budget decreased by 33 percent, yielding savings of $4 million. And, you may note, the people at Champion know all of this precisely—thanks, again, to their measurement and assessment program.

Based on Lois Slavin, "Benchmarking Information Technology: How Do You Rate?" *Beyond Computing*, July/August 1994, pp. 45–47.

As with any other corporate function, the delivery of information has to be managed and controlled. As information systems have become critical to the functioning of organizations, so has the proper management and operation of these systems become vital to the firms.

14.1   MANAGING INFORMATION SERVICES IN A FIRM

Organization of Information Services Units

The corporate **Information Services (IS) department** is the unit responsible for providing or coordinating the delivery of computer-based information services in an organization. These services include developing, operating, and maintaining organizational information systems, as well as facilitating the acquisition and adaptation of software and hardware. Increasingly, this corporate unit coordinates the delivery of many of these services, rather than providing all of them itself. As we have seen in Section 13.4, some services are outsourced to outside vendors; others may be provided by end users themselves.

Firms organize their Information Services function in very different ways, reflecting the nature of their business, their general structure and business strategy, their history, and the way they wish to provide information services to the business units. Most of the IS departments remain centralized. The traditional organization chart of such a unit is shown in

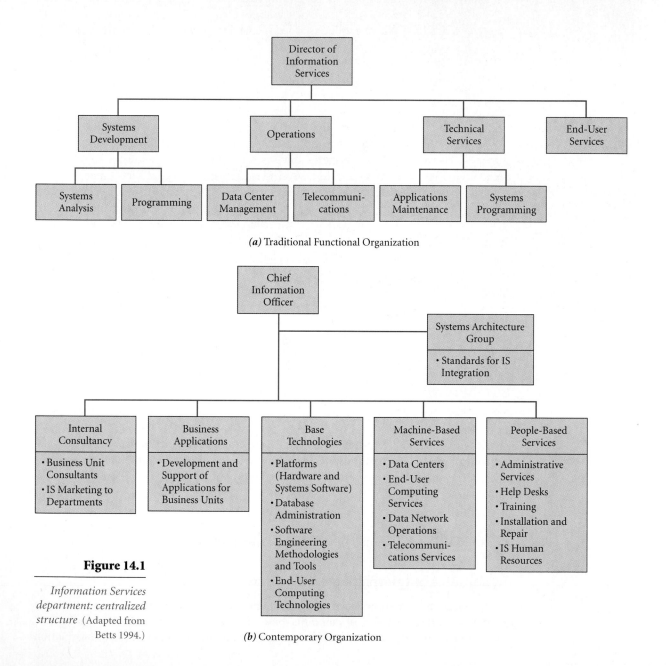

(a) Traditional Functional Organization

Figure 14.1

Information Services department: centralized structure (Adapted from Betts 1994.)

(b) Contemporary Organization

The Mission of an Information Services Unit

At ITT Hartford insurance company, the Information Services function is centralized as a 1,500-person Information Management Division with a $160 million-a-year budget. Yet teams of IS staffers are assigned to the company's lines of business, whose systems they develop and maintain. Within these business units, they work side by side with the users. The Information Management Division is proud of its mission, vision, and statement of goals that have withstood a six-year test of time. We can learn from this statement, reproduced below.

Our Mission

Our Mission is to support the business goals and objectives of The Hartford by doing the following:

- Maintaining production performance at a level that reflects a "service excellence" philosophy.
- Seeking out and implementing solutions that effectively satisfy business requirements and creatively exploit business opportunities.

Our Goals

- To establish customer service as the distinguishing characteristic of information management.

- To establish information management as a leading contributor to ongoing corporate expense control and reduction efforts.
- To enable The Hartford to improve its competitive position through automation that is tailored to the specific needs of each market segment and business group, and adaptable to changing business requirements and technological opportunities.

Our Vision

Our highest priority is to satisfy our customers' needs and expectations through responsive, courteous, high-quality service delivered at the lowest possible cost.

Our aim is to promote a dynamic, energetic, and productive working environment in which achievement is recognized, creativity is encouraged, and teamwork is fostered through relationships based upon trust and respect.

Based on Julia King, "Interview with the Coach," *Computerworld,* October 10, 1994, pp. 95–97.

Figure 14.1a. The more contemporary structure of a centralized IS unit is shown in Figure 14.1b. The new structure is far better suited to servicing a firm's business units with specialized consulting and end-user oriented services. The vignette above shows how some companies combine their centralized IS unit with specialized support of the corporate lines of business, and as well, presents the mission of an IS unit.

Centralized IS departments are giving way in many firms to the IS function decentralized to the business units of the firm, such as shown in Figure 14.2. This decentralization is often a by-product of moving from the mainframe-based legacy systems to the "rightsized" distributed systems, such as the enterprise-wide client/server configuration.

In a decentralized structure, the corporate IS department is principally responsible for the corporate information system infrastructure; that is, for the telecommunication networks and management of corporate databases. Other responsibilities include developing and maintaining corporate information systems standards, supervising systems integrators who perform information services for the firm under outsourcing arrangements, and interacting with vendors to ensure quantity discounts and other benefits of corporate scale.

Figure 14.2

Decentralized structure of Information Services

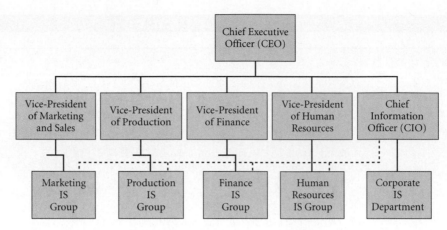

The "dotted-line" authority of the top corporate information officer (sometimes bearing the formal title of chief information officer, or CIO) with respect to the departmental IS groups ensures the coordination of the overall corporate information technology effort. However, since these groups are answerable directly to the heads of their business units, their members are familiar with the unit's specific needs and responsive to its concerns. This is the primary advantage of decentralization. As we know from the previous chapter, many firms rely on a steering committee of senior functional managers for coordinating their information services. Frequently, IS departments create multi-skilled teams for particular projects, involving the line-of-business specialists such as marketers or manufacturing engineers, as well as information technology experts.

Members of the Information Services units, whom we broadly call information systems specialists, actually possess a wide variety of skills, from the highly technical to those of generalist–managers. Owing to the vital role information technology plays in doing business, most of these people need to combine their technology expertise with an understanding of the corporate business lines they serve. With the increasing role of outsourcing and acquisition of software packages, the IS units of most firms are expected to become smaller over time, yet its specialists will have to offer enhanced expertise in both technology and business processes (Rockart 1996). We will now proceed to discuss different categories of these specialists.

Information Systems Specialists

Who are the information systems professionals? Let us discuss the occupational categories of IS specialists. Although the two principal occupations are analyst and programmer, a variety of other specialists is also often needed. The IS specialist functions are summarized in Table 14.1.

A **systems analyst** analyzes the users' information requirements, develops system prototypes, and often also designs information systems based on the requirements specifications. Analysts play the key role in translating business problems and opportunities into information systems. Analysts provide a liaison between the users and other IS specialists. An analyst is a problem solver who can perform a variety of tasks relating to defining, developing, and exploiting information systems. He or she must combine business knowledge with a keen understanding of the potential of technology in order to communicate effectively with end users on the one hand and technical specialists, such as system designers or

Table 14.1	Job Categories and Titles	Job Descriptions
Job descriptions of information systems personnel	*IS Managers*	
	Chief information officer (CIO) or IS director	Responsible for the organization's Information Services function.
	Data administrator	Manages the organization's data as a corporate resource.
	IS project manager	Responsible for a project, such as the development of an information system.
	Team leader	Manages development or maintenance team.
	System Developers	
	Systems analyst	In collaboration with users, determines their information requirements and designs a system that would satisfy them (though system designers may be employed for design tasks instead).
	Systems designer	Designs systems based on requirements specifications provided by systems analysts.
	Programmer/analyst	Performs both the analyst's and the programmer's functions.
	Applications programmer	Codes and tests programs based on systems analyst's (or designer's) specifications.
	Maintenance programmer	Modifies existing programs to meet changing needs or to improve system's performance.
	Technical Specialists	
	Systems programmer	Maintains or develops systems software.
	Telecommunications specialist	Designs and maintains telecommunications networks; develops telecommunications software.
	Database administrator (DBA)	Creates the physical design of databases and ensures their efficient operation and control.
	Operations Personnel	
	Computer operator	Operates computers in a data center.
	Control clerk	Responsible for input (such as magnetic tapes to be mounted) and output (such as reports) in a data center.
	Data entry clerk	Enters data through a terminal.
	Librarian	Maintains tapes and disk volumes and delivers them to the operator.
	Information Center Personnel	
	Director of office and group information systems	Plans and coordinates the use of OIS.
	Microcomputer coordinator	Develops standards and policies for the use of PCs and personal productivity software.
	Education specialist	Trains end users.
	IS Auditors	Assess whether information systems safeguard assets, maintain data integrity, and perform in an effective and efficient fashion.
	Webmasters	Maintain corporate electronic sites on the World Wide Web.

programmers, on the other. Senior systems analysts frequently act as project managers during system development.

Systems designers and programmers implement the analysts' specifications. A **systems designer** translates these specifications of what the system is expected to do into high-level specifications for the needed system components. A **programmer** develops, that is, codes and tests the programs that satisfy the requirements established by the analysts, using the design specifications worked up by the designer. Programmers will also maintain the programs. These **applications programmers** are supported by **systems programmers** who maintain systems software and have considerable technical expertise. In many cases, the functional distinction between programmer and analyst is blurred. This is formalized in some firms in **programmer/analyst** positions, often held by senior programmers who perform both tasks.

Since IS units in large firms are often also large, a hierarchy of managers has evolved. The levels range from the first-level managers of programming teams and project managers, who may be responsible for several teams, to the top corporate officer responsible for information services. This top officer often has a vice-presidential rank and, in some companies, is given the formal title of **chief information officer (CIO)**, analogous to a chief financial or operating officer. The CIO coordinates the entire corporate IS effort and has the primary responsibility for linking the IS plans and implementation to the company's business plans. The role of the top IS executive is to focus the attention of top corporate management on the contribution that information technology can make to the firm's business. The vignette on the next page will tell you more about this role.

In addition to analysts, programmers, and managers, IS personnel include a variety of specialists in various aspects of computer and telecommunication technologies (such as client/server, for example), operations personnel responsible for running data centers where larger computers are housed, and other support personnel. A more recent addition are Webmasters who establish and maintain corporate electronic sites on the World Wide Web; their qualifications usually include experience in graphics design.

The basic workforce unit that develops and maintains information systems is a project team. The composition of a team, which usually includes no more than 10 professional members, varies depending on the task. Large projects involve several teams. A team includes information systems professionals, such as analysts and programmers, and may at various stages of its work on the system include end users (who assist in systems analysis) and technical specialists, such as telecommunications or database experts. We will come back to software development teams in Section 16.9.

Now that we know how information services are managed as a whole, we need to learn about managing their basic aspect, namely, the day-to-day operations of information systems.

14.2 | MANAGING INFORMATION SYSTEMS OPERATIONS

Objectives of IS Operations and a Typical Case

The objective of the **IS operations** staff is to keep information systems running smoothly: to process transactions with an acceptable response time, deliver reports on time, and ensure reliable and efficient operation of data centers (the physical location of larger, non-personal computers) and telecommunication networks. In the face of the general trend toward distribution of the information processing function and the growth of end-user

Let Us Hear from a Quintessential CIO

Colin Crook (see Photo 14.1) is the Senior Technology Officer and CIO of Citicorp in New York. He is now in the process of consolidating 25 data centers and 100 disparate wide area telecommunications systems of the global bank into the new platform, known as the Global Information Network. With 8,000 information system specialists spread over 90 countries, his job is not made easier by the bank's strategy of taking a leadership position in the move to electronic commerce. Indeed, Colin Crook himself is very actively involved in that initiative.

Here is Crook's brief job description: "Establishes technology policy and standards, introduces new technology, evaluates the quality and direction of IS efforts, and directs change throughout the corporation."

Now, Colin Crook will share with you his understanding of the CIO's role:

How far ahead do you plan IT strategies at Citicorp? We look ahead three years, but we are taking a much more operational view of planning by rolling it forward [making changes as necessary]. We're trying to change the notion of a series of static plans by using three-year plans to rationalize, converge, and standardize our existing infrastructure. But we'd like to become much more real-time in our planning horizons.

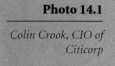

Photo 14.1

Colin Crook, CIO of Citicorp

You have spoken of the value of an adaptive, enabling infrastructure. What is its chief characteristic? An infrastructure is not a utility; it is the core of a business. . . We run big, global networks. We put a premium on global architecture, which is the framework for adaptation and change. [We] drive ruthlessly toward a core infrastructure that is standardized and aligned to the external world. When the external world changes, our internal infrastructure changes too.

What does a new-style CIO do differently? I am in the business of driving change. I am judged on my ability to introduce new thinking and, from a technology standpoint, to get this company organized for the 21st century as a global corporation. I've got to partner with the business units—to persuade, cajole, and preach to them. And I've got to form a partnership with the chairman and his senior people.

Indeed, Colin Crook works closely with Citicorp's chairman, John Reed, who himself is known as a leader in using information technology in banking. Colin Crook deeply believes that any outsourcing of IS should be considered only after the corporation itself transforms its own IS infrastructure.

Based on the interview with Colin Crook by John Whitmarsh, *CIO*, September 15, 1996, p. 88; and author's meeting with Colin Crook, December 1993.

computing, corporate data centers retain their vital role as repositories of corporate databases. Like any other major corporate asset, information systems must be controllable. As we know, some companies have outsourced their IS operations to specialized vendors. For others, these operations are a major concern of IS departments. This is very clearly reflected in corporate IS budgets. A typical budget structure is that of Nissan Motor Corporation, U.S.A., shown in Figure 14.3 (McNurlin and Sprague 1989).

As we can see, of the total annual IS budget of $30 million, $10.3 million is spent on systems and programming. Out of this sum, 30 percent goes to the development of new systems while 70 percent is spent on the maintenance of existing systems. The remaining $17.3 million is spent on operations. Thus, over half of the annual IS budget of the firm is devoted to operations, which is comparable to the budgets of IS departments elsewhere.

What is it that the IS department at Nissan (or elsewhere) actually operates? The firm's operations include computer systems at 64 locations, such as ports, parts warehouses, and sales offices—a typical situation in today's distributed computing environment. They also include the networking infrastructure that connects these locations and provides access to

Figure 14.3

Annual budget of the IS department of Nissan Motor, U.S.A.

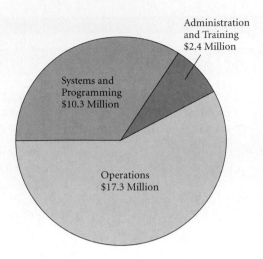

the external networks, such as the Internet. A large part of the budget is used up by the personnel at the data centers where computer and telecommunications equipment must be kept operational.

Functions of IS Operations

The principal concern of IS operations is to ensure that information services are delivered in an uninterrupted, reliable, and secure fashion. This poses a special challenge in the distributed hardware environment of today. Another set of challenges is provided by the variety of possible organizational designs for the IS function itself, with the many options for centralization and decentralization, and on to partial or total outsourcing. The design must be selected to match corporate objectives and then this design must be modified as the objectives change.

Here are the major functions of IS operations:

- Data entry—introducing validated data into the system using a variety of data entry equipment, preferably with automatic data capture at the source to avoid keyboarding (as discussed in Chapter 9).

- Operation of computer systems in data centers, for example, via control consoles.

- Operational support for the equipment in the hands (or on the desks) of end users and support of end users with information centers and help desks.

- Maintenance of wide area telecommunication links and local area networks.

- Maintenance of databases, including periodic reorganizations for efficiency's sake.

- Production control in data centers—scheduling, running, and monitoring jobs, including mounting the necessary tape and disk volumes; ensuring backup; and initiating restart and recovery in the case of operating problems.

- Production support—maintenance of data libraries in archival storage volumes (tapes and disks) and providing a flow of necessary supplies.

- Ensuring the physical security of operations, including the operation of firewalls against unauthorized access over the Internet.

- Controlled distribution of information output, such as reports, perhaps in an electronic form.
- Dealing with vendors and consultants, in particular, supervising the vendors to whom services have been outsourced.
- Planning the necessary processing and telecommunication capacities.

As organizations have become highly dependent on the secure functioning of their information systems, a principal function of the IS operations is protecting the systems from a variety of threats to this security.

14.3 | THREATS TO SECURITY, PRIVACY, AND CONFIDENTIALITY IN IS OPERATIONS

The operation of information systems is constantly vulnerable to a number of threats, from earthquakes to human error (Neumann 1995). Computer crime, one of the threats to IS security, has called forth a veritable fountainhead of ingenuity. Controls need to be instituted to counteract these threats, and periodic auditing of these controls is necessary to see that they remain effective. Privacy and confidentiality of information rely on security measures as technical safeguards.

Vulnerabilities, Controls, and Auditing of Information Systems

Most of today's organizations are dependent on the reliable operation of their information systems. It has been estimated that financial institutions could not survive a total failure of their information processing capacity for longer than a day or two. Electronic funds transfer systems (EFTS) these institutions rely on handle immense amounts of money that exist only as a bit stream or as a minute spot on a magnetic disk. Intensive care units and air traffic control systems are dependent on computers to function reliably. Yet information systems would be highly vulnerable without the measures that are taken to protect them from threats. When you read a software package from a diskette into a personal computer that handles sensitive correspondence, how do you know the package does not contain a surreptitious code that will send copies of your correspondence over the network to your competitor? Vital systems may malfunction for a variety of reasons, and functioning information systems are the target of ingenious and high-stakes crime.

It is necessary for an organization to identify the nature of possible threats to its information systems and establish a set of measures, called *controls,* to ensure their security (and, beyond that, to also ensure the privacy and confidentiality of information stored in the systems). It is then necessary to continually control the controls with the auditing process. Figure 14.4 illustrates the conceptual relationship between threats to information systems, necessary controls, and auditing.

Information system security is the integrity and safety of its resources and activities. **Privacy** is an individual's right to retain certain information about himself or herself without disclosure. Comprehensive security safeguards are a prerequisite for the privacy of individuals with respect to the information stored about them in information systems. However, while such security is necessary, it is not sufficient. We will further discuss the issue of privacy in Chapter 17. **Confidentiality** is the status accorded to data (be it the data about an

Figure 14.4

Threat identification, controls, and auditing in Information Systems

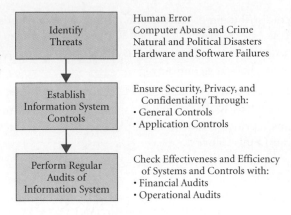

Identify Threats

Human Error
Computer Abuse and Crime
Natural and Political Disasters
Hardware and Software Failures

Establish Information System Controls

Ensure Security, Privacy, and
   Confidentiality Through:
• General Controls
• Application Controls

Perform Regular Audits of Information System

Check Effectiveness and Efficiency
   of Systems and Controls with:
• Financial Audits
• Operational Audits

individual or about a new product development project), limiting its use and dissemination. Thus, we may keep certain data confidential to enforce our privacy policies. In enforcing our policies, we must rely in part on information systems controls.

In this section, we will concentrate on threats to information systems, after which we will analyze the nature of possible controls, concluding the chapter with a discussion of information systems auditing.

Information Systems Security and Threats to It

The security of information systems is maintained by measures taken to prevent threats to these systems or to detect and correct the effects of any damage. We will discuss these controls in the next section. Information system security aims to protect corporate assets or, at least, to limit their loss. Security measures limit access to information to authorized individuals; there can be no privacy or confidentiality of data records without adequate security.

Security measures are often costly and, moreover, often at odds with other objectives of information systems. Obviously, the more secure the system, the less accessible it is. This is why we often hear of intruders invading university computers, where accessibility is a primary objective. Likewise, the integration of databases, which may be desirable for a particular business opportunity or for the efficient functioning of government agencies, raises valid concerns about privacy. Telecommunications networks, and the widely used Internet in particular, have opened most organizational information systems to a threat of invasion from outside the firm (Baker 1995).

Security threats have four principal sources, summarized and exemplified in Table 14.2.

Although instances of computer crime receive the greatest attention, human error is estimated to cause far greater losses in information systems operation. This security threat should be considered particularly carefully, therefore, in setting up a system of controls. Disasters such as earthquakes, floods, or fires are the particular concern of disaster recovery planning, which we will discuss in the next section. A contingency scheme is also necessary in case of a major equipment failure, such as the failure of a corporate server or of a network (or its segment) that is part of a corporate information system.

The ingenuity involved in computer crime warrants a closer look.

Table 14.2	Nature of Threat	Examples
Threats to information systems	Human error	Wrong input data keyed in. Errors in program development or maintenance. Operator error (for example, mislabeling of tapes).
	Computer abuse or crime	Using a system to steal. Sabotaging the system. Unauthorized access to or modification of data.
	Natural and political disasters	Earthquake, flood, hurricane. Fire. War.
	Failures of hardware or software	Failure of equipment in a data center. Network failure. Power failure. Systems software malfunction.

Computer Crime and Abuse

Computer crime is estimated to cost the U.S. economy billions of dollars annually. However, this well-publicized phenomenon still resists definition, and the legal system finds it difficult to deal with its high-technology nature and the novel issues it presents (Westland 1996–97). We may define **computer crime** as any illegal act in which a computer is used as the primary tool. **Computer abuse** is unethical use of a computer; we will learn more about the ethical issues in information systems in Chapter 17.

Here are the more widespread security threats related to computer crime or abuse.

1. *Impersonation:* Gaining access to a system by identifying oneself as another person. Having defeated the identification and authentication controls employed by the system, the impersonator enjoys the privileges of a legitimate user.

2. *Trojan horse method:* Concealing within an authorized program a set of instructions that will cause unauthorized actions.

3. *Logic bomb:* Unauthorized instructions, often introduced with the Trojan horse technique, which stay dormant until a specific event occurs (or until a specific time comes, as the instructions may keep checking the computer's internal clock), at which time they effect an unauthorized act. The act is often malicious, for example, erasing files. A well-known case involved a programmer who placed a logic bomb in his company's personnel system; should his name ever be absent from the human resources file (indicating his dismissal), the entire file would be erased.

4. *Computer viruses:* Segments of code that are able to perform malicious acts and insert copies of themselves into other programs in the system and onto the diskettes placed in the "infected" PC. Because of this replication, a virus will progressively infect "healthy" programs and systems. Close relatives of viruses are *worms:* independent programs that make and transmit copies of themselves through telecommunications networks. Computer viruses have become a pervasive threat in personal computing, which is why we describe them in more detail in the following section.

5. *Denial of service:* Rendering the system unusable by legitimate users. For example, an Internet server can be overloaded by writing a program that continually sends the request for a Web page located there.

6. *Data diddling:* Changing data before or during input, often to change the contents of a database. An example of this simplest and most common threat is the operation of a payroll clerk of a railroad company who succeeded over several years to bypass system controls and enter an excessive amount of overtime for himself.

7. *Salami technique:* Diverting small amounts of money from a large number of accounts maintained by the system. These small amounts, like thin slices disappearing from a salami sausage, will not be noticed. A well-known example was provided by programmers who rounded down the interest on account balances to the nearest cent—and transferred the accumulated fractions into their own accounts.

8. *Spoofing:* Configuring a computer system to masquerade as another system over the network in order to gain unauthorized access to the resources the system being mimicked is entitled to.

9. *Superzapping:* Using a systems program that can bypass regular system controls to perform unauthorized acts. The name comes from the IBM Superzap utility, available to systems managers. Superzap utilities are provided to handle emergency situations, such as restoring system operation after a malfunction that cannot be handled with a regular recovery method.

10. *Scavenging:* Unauthorized access to information by searching through the residue after a job has been run on a computer. Techniques range from searching wastebaskets or dumpsters for printouts to scanning the contents of a computer's memory.

11. *Data leakage:* A variety of methods for obtaining the data stored in a system. The data may be encoded into an innocuous report in sophisticated ways, for example, as the number of characters per line.

12. *Wiretapping:* Tapping computer telecommunications lines to obtain information.

Note that some of the techniques may be used for a direct gain of financial resources, others for industrial espionage, while yet others simply for destructive purposes. The above list is not exhaustive. Probably the most important unrecognized threat today is the theft of portable computers with access codes and information in their memories. Direct losses suffered by major U.S. corporations due to computer crime are estimated at $800 million a year (Fialka 1996). Even this high figure in dwarfed by the losses due to the theft of intellectual property, such as software, product development information, customer information, or internal corporate documents, estimated to cost U.S. corporations $24 billion annually (Radcliff 1997). We will come back to the protection of intellectual property in section 17.6.

Computer Viruses

Computer viruses are the most frequently encountered threats to end-user computing and the best-known form of computer threat. A **computer virus** is a piece of program code that attaches copies of itself to other programs and thus replicates itself, much like its organic counterpart. The attacked program may work properly, but, at some point, will perform a malicious or destructive act intended by the attacker who wrote the virus. Although a computer virus may attack a multi-user system with shared disk facilities, viruses are best known for their rapid spread in a personal computer environment. In this environment, they proliferate through infected diskettes or programs downloaded from the Internet or other networks.

Most viruses are insidious, and their presence is not obvious after the infection. In the meantime, they infect other programs. After a period of dormancy, the virus activates itself (on the logic-bomb principle) and may display a message on the display monitor ("It's Friday the 13th!") or erase all the data files.

Two principal types of viruses are boot infectors and program infectors. Boot infectors replace the contents of the first sector of the diskette or hard disk. (Since the sector contains the so-called bootstrap loader that loads the operating system, it is known as the boot sector, thus giving the name to the virus). These are the viruses that most commonly occur in personal computing. The sequence of events through which such a virus gets into the system is shown in Figure 14.5.

Program infectors, instead of copying themselves into a disk's boot sector, copy themselves into the executable (binary) files stored on the hard disk.

Protection against viruses requires the following measures:

- Only original manufacturer's diskettes or reliable Internet sites should be used for any program introduced into the system. Pirated software, which should be avoided on ethical grounds, can also lead to the spread of viruses.

- Commercial "antiviral" software (such as Norton AntiVirus of Symantec) should be used regularly (see Figure 14.6) to scan the system. Moreover, recent versions of such software should be used, since ever new virus strains are being spread by attackers.

Figure 14.5

How a boot infector virus spreads (Modified from Corey Sandler, "Virus, They Wrote," *PC Computing,* September 1994, p. 213.)

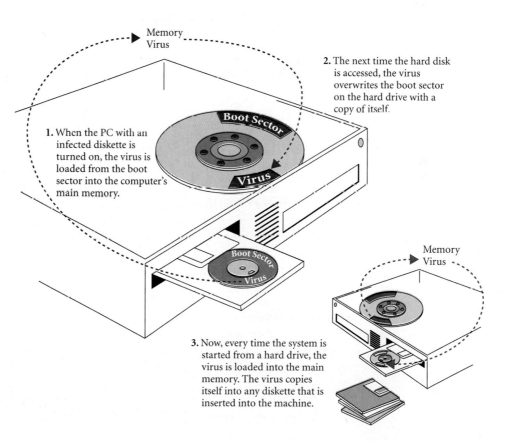

Memory Virus

1. When the PC with an infected diskette is turned on, the virus is loaded from the boot sector into the computer's main memory.

2. The next time the hard disk is accessed, the virus overwrites the boot sector on the hard drive with a copy of itself.

Boot Sector

Virus

Boot Sector Virus

Memory Virus

3. Now, every time the system is started from a hard drive, the virus is loaded into the main memory. The virus copies itself into any diskette that is inserted into the machine.

Some of the Rich Virus Lore

There are an estimated 4,100 different strains of computer viruses around. IBM estimates that up to five new viruses are written every day. Viruses certainly existed before Fred Cohen, a graduate student at the University of Southern California, coined their name in his doctoral dissertation in 1983. But the spread of personal computing and of computer networking gave these viruses the playing field they enjoy today. With names like Stoned, (c)Brain, Lehigh, Jerusalem, and Michelangelo, computer viruses have created two communities, those of attackers and those of security experts. Or, as some would have it, a single community of crackers and their pursuers, who all share common interests.

Let us listen to the 18-year old Metal Militia, one of the virus generators (or virogens),

who blames the users: "If they don't back up, it's their own fault. They're the ones using pirated software. They're the ones not using antivirus software." Here is what perhaps the best-known attacker of all times, Dark Avenger, who started as a computer science student at the University of Sofia in Bulgaria, has to say: "The idea of making a program that would travel on its own and go to places its creator could never go was the most interesting thing for me." We do not know the identities of these attackers. We do know they could find a better outlet for their creative energies.

Based on (Kane 1994), Corey Sander, "Virus, They Wrote," *PC Computing*, September 1994, pp. 207–214, and (Nance 1996).

- To guard against viruses in files downloaded from the Internet, one should use utilities such as McAfee Associates WebScan, which can work with browsers.
- Regular backup of files will help restore them if a virus is detected.
- A contingency plan for a virus attack is necessary.

The mentality of the attackers who write computer viruses comes through in the vignette above.

Risk Assessment in Safeguarding Information Systems

In a distributed systems environment, with virtually every employee of an organization having some form of access to systems, security threats are an extremely serious concern. Multiple connections to the Internet open the field to interlopers all over the world. Possible sources of threats are summarized in Figure 14.7.

Once the extent of security exposures in information systems is appreciated, it is easy to see that no system is perfectly secure and that no IS manager can devote to this vital aspect of IS operations the amount of resources necessary to even approach the goal. What to do?

A system of controls can be based on a **risk assessment** procedure: a methodical evaluation of the probability of losses due to security exposures and the extent of these losses. Risk is defined as the product of the amount that may be lost due to a security exposure and the probability that such a loss will occur. This probability can be estimated by the frequency of such occurrences in the past. A threat that could occur once a month, with a maximum loss of $100,000, is well worth counteracting with a control that costs $10,000 to develop and $5,000 a year to maintain. Another method of assessing vulnerabilities is a scenario analysis, sometimes involving simulated attacks on the system.

Figure 14.6

A possible result of a scan performed with Norton AntiVirus (From Norton AntiVirus documentation)

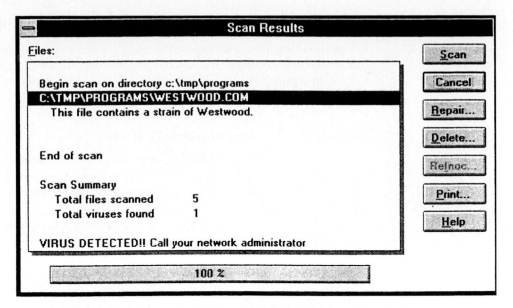

Figure 14.7

Threats in distributed information systems

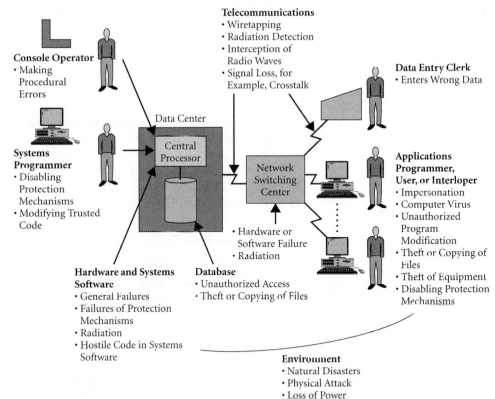

Controls which safeguard against the greatest exposures are instituted, including last-resort methods of insurance and disaster recovery planning. The variety of controls available is described in the next section.

14.4 | GENERAL INFORMATION SYSTEMS CONTROLS

Information systems are safeguarded through a combination of general and application controls. In this section, we will describe general controls, which apply to the entire IS activity of an organization. We will follow this in the next section with a discussion of controls specific to given applications.

The Role of Information Systems Controls

To ensure secure operation of information systems and thus safeguard assets and the data stored in these systems, and to ensure that applications achieve their objectives in an efficient manner, an organization needs to institute a set of policies, procedures, and technological measures collectively called **controls.**

Some of the IS controls *prevent* an error or an attack from taking effect; for example, when data are entered into the system, they may be validated to prevent erroneous entry. Other controls help *detect* a violation: a log of all amounts payable above a certain amount will help detect embezzlement. Yet a third category of controls will both *detect* and *correct* an exceptional situation: when a power failure is detected, an uninterruptible power supply (UPS) may automatically take over to maintain operations for a period of time.

A comprehensive set of internal controls in a public company must conform with the Foreign Corrupt Practices Act (of 1977), which requires that:

- All transactions be authorized.
- All transactions be recorded.
- Access to systems, including access to data stored in them, be controlled.
- Data produced by information systems be correct and verifiable.

Information systems controls are classified as **general controls,** that is, controls applying to the whole of an organization's IS activity, or as **application controls,** which are specific to a given application, such as order processing or accounts payable. The boundary line between these control types is rather flexible, particularly in client/server systems where a single application may be run on several computers. An effective combination of general and application controls should ensure an adequately secure processing environment.

Types of General Controls

General controls cover all the systems of an organization or one of its subunits. The roles played by general controls are summarized in Table 14.3. In the remainder of this section, we will discuss general controls in more detail.

Administrative Controls

Administrative controls aim to ensure that the entire control framework is instituted, continually supported by management, and enforced with proper procedures, including audits.
Administrative controls include:

- A *published controls policy* which makes it obvious that IS controls are taken with utmost seriousness by an organization's top management.
- *Formal procedures,* such as a systems development life cycle process, with standards for operator manuals, backup and recovery procedures, and regulations for managing archival data.

Table 14.3	**Type of Control**	**Principal Roles**
General controls	Administrative controls	Published formal control policies Published procedures and standards Screening and supervision of personnel Separation of duties in job design Disaster recovery planning
	Systems development and maintenance controls	Auditing of systems development process to ensure systems controls and auditability Postimplementation review Ensuring that only authorized maintenance is performed Documentation audits
	Operations controls	Control of access to data centers Control over operations personnel Control over equipment maintenance Control over archival storage
	Physical protection of data centers	Environmental controls Protection against fire and flooding Emergency power supply (for example, UPS—uninterruptible power supply) Radiation shielding
	Hardware controls	Error detection circuitry Protection measures implemented as hardware mechanisms Fault-tolerant computer systems
	Controlling access to computer systems	Identification and authentication of users Firewalls
	Controlling access to information	Encryption
	Controls of last resort	Disaster recovery plan Insurance

- Careful *screening* of personnel during the hiring process, followed by orientation and necessary training.

- Continuing *supervision* of personnel, including paying particular attention to deviations from expected behavior. Cases have been known of maintenance programmers parking their Ferraris in the corporate lot without anyone questioning their sources of income.

- *Separation of duties* as a fundamental principle of job definition, so that no single individual would have access to a complete process that could lead to abuse. User duties must be separated from those of the IS personnel (this places obvious limitations on end-user computing), and duties must be separated within the IS function itself. Duties may also be periodically rotated to prevent personnel members from becoming bored and succumbing to the temptation to tamper with the system as a challenge. Beyond that, many financial institutions require that employees take annual vacations, during which they may not enter the institution's premises.

526 Part Four Acquiring and Managing Information Systems

Instilling norms of *ethical behavior* with respect to information and information systems is an important management responsibility. We will discuss the ethical issues involved in Chapter 17.

Systems Development and Maintenance Controls

Internal IS auditors should be a party to the entire systems development process. They should participate in major milestones and sign off on the appropriate deliverables. Their participation is crucial at the sign-off on the system requirements specifications, when they need to ensure that the system will be not only secure, but also auditable. IS auditors should also be principal participants in the postimplementation review that follows the system being placed in operation. As part of their concern for the system as a corporate asset, the auditors must check that the appropriate system documentation is developed and maintained.

During system maintenance, auditors need to ensure that only authorized changes are made to the system and that the appropriate version of the system goes into operation.

Operations Controls

Operations controls are the policies, procedures, and technology established to ensure that data centers are operated in a reliable fashion. Included among these controls are:

- *Controls over access to the data center.* Access should be strictly limited to authorized personnel. Both the personnel who work in the data center and escorted visitors should be appropriately identified. Protective measures include guarded entry, identification using badges or coded cards, sign-in/sign-out registers, and closed-circuit monitors connected to a panel monitored by security personnel.

- *Control over operations personnel.* Procedures manuals should be available, and their instructions regarding running processing jobs strictly followed. Operating logs (console logs), which record all of the system's messages and operator instructions, should be maintained, on magnetic disk or tape for example. An equipment log showing how processing time is utilized should also be kept.

- *Control over maintenance of computer equipment.* System downtime due to equipment maintenance should be minimal; only authorized personnel should perform maintenance.

- *Control over archival storage.* All movement of tape and disk volumes should be logged; the volumes should be securely stored.

Physical Protection of Data Centers

Operations controls in data centers must be supplemented by a set of controls that will protect these centers from the elements and from environmental attacks.

Normal operating conditions should be ensured with environmental controls (such as air conditioning, air filtering, humidification, and dehumidification), as required by the equipment. Drains and pumps should be installed in case of fire or flood. Fire detection and extinguishing systems are necessary.

It is vital that emergency power sources be available. A battery-based **uninterruptible power supply (UPS)** should be installed to provide continuous operation in case of total or partial power failure. Depending on its capacity and cost, a UPS will be able to maintain uninterrupted operation for a few minutes to about an hour, which should be enough time to shut down the system without loss of data integrity. Systems that must be operated continuously for economic or functional reasons (such as life support systems in hospitals) require an independent power generator.

When operating, computers emanate radio frequency waves that can be picked up by detection equipment located at a significant distance from the data center. If this level of security is warranted, the equipment, the wiring, and the computer rooms themselves must be shielded to contain this radiation.

Hardware Controls

A computer's central processor contains circuitry for detection and, in some cases, correction of certain processing errors. A rudimentary example of such a measure is a *parity check.* Each byte in storage contains an additional bit, called a parity bit, which helps detect an erroneous change in the value of a single bit during processing. Processor hardware usually has at least two states: a *privileged state,* in which any operation can be performed (for example, setting the internal clock), and a user state, in which only some operations can be done. A user cannot enter privileged state, which is reserved for system software.

Fault-tolerant computer systems are important in environments where interruption of processing has highly undesirable effects, such as in hospital information systems or in securities trading. These systems will continue to operate after some of their processing components fail. Fault-tolerant computer systems are built with redundant components; they generally include several processors in a multiprocessing configuration. If one of the processors fails, the other (or others) can provide degraded, yet effective, service. Among the most frequently used fault-tolerant computers are systems produced by Tandem Computers and Stratus Computer.

Identification, Authentication, and Firewalls: Controlling Access to Corporate Computer Systems

In today's computing environment, with the organizational information systems widely networked and connected to the Internet, users as well as interlopers may attempt to access the system from virtually anywhere. Yet we need to ensure that only authorized accesses take place.

A user first identifies himself or herself to the system, typically with a name or an account number. The system then looks up the authentication information stored for the identified user and does a double-check. It requests the user to provide a password or another means by which he or she can be authenticated. The principal means of **identification** (user's knowledge) and **authentication** (user's possession or a personal characteristic) are summarized in Table 14.4.

The most traditional scheme, using passwords, puts excessive reliance on the user's willingness to select a nonobvious password, remember it, and keep it secret. A simple defense against a person who is masquerading as a legitimate user is to limit the number of repeat access trials and trigger an alarm. Many systems, such as automatic teller machines and other electronic fund transfer systems, rely on a combination of a personal identification

Table 14.4	**Means**	**Implementation**
Means of user identification and authentication	User's knowledge	Name, account number, password
	User's possession	Card with a magnetic strip, smart card (with a microprocessor), key
	Personal characteristic (biometrics)	Fingerprint, voiceprint, hand geometry, iris or retinal scanning, signature

number (PIN) with the means of authentication, for example, a magnetic-strip card or a smart card.

A variety of security features are implemented to increase the effectiveness of passwords. The features include regular and frequent password changes, use of a combination of letters and digits in a password, and prevention of the use of a common word, easily associated with the user. Users' possessions (e.g., smart cards) may, of course, be improperly handled in a variety of ways. This is one reason why the use of so-called biometric access de-

Photo 14.2

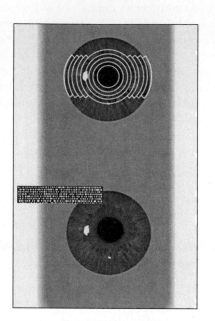

Every iris has a unique texture. In a prototype iris recognition system from IriScan (of Mount Laurel, New Jersey), a videocamera captures the image of the iris, from which the salient features are extracted in several zones outlined in white. These features are digitized and converted into a 256-byte code, corresponding to the bar code shown. Once stored, the legitimate user's iris features can be used for authentication (Based on John E. Siedlarz, "IRIS: More Detailed Than a Fingerprint," *IEEE Spectrum,* February 1994, p. 27.)

Figure 14.8

Firewall: all accesses to and from the Internet must pass through the firewall computer

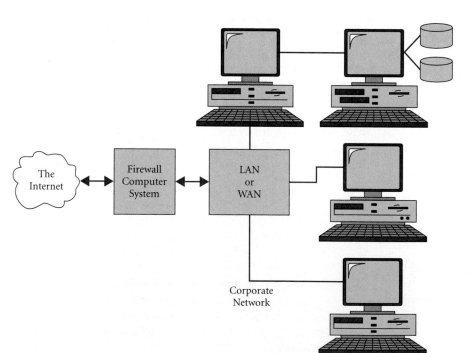

**Guardians of
the Internet**

Did you ever think about who guards the largest network in the world, the Internet, shared by millions of users? The Computer Emergency Response Team (CERT), run by the Software Engineering Institute of Carnegie Mellon University, does. CERT helps the Internet users identify and fix the damage done by crackers who break into the systems connected to the Net by going around the authorization and authentication measures. The 14-member team is managed by Dain Gary, former director of corporate data security at Mellon Bank of Pittsburgh.

The most famous incident on the Internet occurred in 1988, when a Cornell University student, Robert T. Morris, Jr., released a software worm that sneaked its way through some 3,000 of the Internet computers. Because of the bug in his program, Morris forced major portions of the network to shut down, causing by some estimates over $100 million damage in computing time lost and work not done. Morris was convicted in a court of law and sentenced to a probation term and a fine. In response to his misdeed, the Department of Defense created CERT.

CERT responds to the calls (at 412-268-7090) and messages (at cert@cert.org) from Internet users who sense that their system has been compromised. The 24-hour hotline rings more than three times a day. Since its founding in 1988, CERT has responded to several thousands of security incidents, leaving the tracking and prosecution of the crackers to the agencies of the Department of Justice. For $20,000 a year, the CERT Affiliates Program offers technical advice on how to prevent computer break-ins and how to deal with them if they do occur.

The nature of break-ins is changing. In the 1980s, most intruders were joyriders, breaking into remote computers for the thrill and the challenge. Now many of them attempt destructive attacks. A computer crime detective from the British Scotland Yard has reported the first deaths attributable to such break-ins. An attack on a computer running weather forecasting programs stopped weather forecasts in the English Channel, which led to the loss of a ship at sea.

With many millions of computers connected to the Internet all over the world, and the number growing explosively, plans are in place to expand the staff and the activities of CERT. The only certainty we have is that there will be more break-ins to respond to in the future.

Based on Joseph C. Panettieri, "Guardians of the Net," *InformationWeek,* May 23, 1994, pp. 30–40; Clinton Wilder, "How Safe Is the Internet?" *InformationWeek,* December 12, 1994, pp. 12–14; and Jeffrey Rothfeder, "Hacked! Are Your Company's Files Safe?" *PC World,* November 1996, pp. 170–182.

vices that rely on each user's personal characteristics, such as the fingerprint or the iris scan, is growing rapidly. In Photo 14.2, you can see how authentication can be based on iris scanning.

The ubiquitous use of the Internet has forced organizations to employ firewalls in order to protect access to their information resources. A **firewall** is the hardware and software placed by a firm between its own network and an outside network, such as the Internet, to insure that only authorized traffic passes through the firewall (Cheswick and Bellovin 1994). The typical implementation is a computer system, sometimes a router, set up as the gateway between the Internet and the corporate network. All the traffic from outside to inside, and vice versa, has to pass through the firewall (see Figure 14.8). The firewall software employs identification and authentication to screen the incoming network traffic (such as packets), allowing only the authorized accesses to the corporate information resources. Firewalls generally allow the traffic to pass freely from the corporate sites to the outside of the firm, unless specific limiting policies are in effect.

Since today's networking environment is a fundamental infrastructure that also creates many security exposures, it is good to take a look at the vignette above to see what is done to guard the Internet.

Encryption: Controlling Access to Information

A different way to prohibit access to information is to keep it in a form that is not intelligible to an unauthorized user. The technique long used in the three traditional forms of international intercourse—diplomacy, war, and espionage—is encryption. **Encryption** is the transformation of data (or any text in general) into a form that is unreadable to anyone without an appropriate decryption key. In computing, the key is a bit pattern. Encryption has been pressed into the service of computer security and is gaining particular importance as electronic commerce over telecommunications networks is gaining momentum. All the schemes for a future electronic cash—or electronic tokens that could be used to pay for goods, services, and information over the Internet—rely on encryption.

Encryption renders access to encoded data useless to an interloper who has managed to gain access to the system by masquerading as a legitimate user (and so has passed through the identification and authentication schemes), or to an industrial spy who can employ a rather simple receiver to pick up data sent over a satellite telecommunications link. Thus, the technique is important not only in the protection of the system boundary but also in the communications and database controls, discussed in the next section. The two most common encryption techniques are the private-key Data Encryption Standard (DES) and public-key encryption. Both methods use an encryption key in executing an algorithm that performs a complex transformation of the message into a cipher. In both cases, the decryption key is private and secret.

DES is the encryption algorithm most often used in business and government applications that warrant this protection. The system relies on software or hardware implementation of the DES algorithm and on a user-supplied 64-bit-long key. Using the key, the DES algorithm encodes 64-bit-long blocks of data into scrambled cipher through a series of complex computational steps. The receiver applies the same secret key and the DES algorithm "in reverse" to restore the original data. The DES approach based on the 64-bit key has been challenged on the grounds that owners of powerful supercomputers can try all the key combinations in order to break the code, and more elaborate DES-based schemes are used today.

A major disadvantage of cryptosystems such as DES, which rely on private (secret) keys both for encryption and for decryption, is that the keys must be distributed in a secure manner. Since the keys must be changed rather frequently, this represents significant exposure. Also, a prior relationship between the sender and the receiver is necessary in order for them to share the same private key. An alternative is a public-key encryption. In a **public-key system,** *two* keys are needed to ensure secure transmission: one is the encoding key and the other is the decoding key. Because the secret decoding key cannot be derived from the encoding key, the encoding key can be made public. Therefore, a user can generate both keys and publicize only the encoding key and thus be able to receive encoded messages from anyone. This is convenient for conducting business transactions on open networks, such as the Internet. However, public-key encryption and decryption are more time-consuming than the private key systems, and can significantly degrade performance of transaction processing systems (Balderston 1997).

If the recipient wants to be able to authenticate the sender or, in other words, to obtain a "digital signature" for the message, the sender keeps the encoding key secret and makes the decoding key public. To send both secure and authenticated messages, the two techniques are combined, with two keys per user, as shown in Figure 14.9. Note that the private keys need not be distributed, and the knowledge of a public key is insufficient to break the code.

Encryption is the essential technique for ensuring privacy of communications. A program known as Pretty Good Privacy, accessible over the Internet, has become a de facto standard in E-mail encryption (Garfinkel 1995). We will return to encryption in Section 17.4, when discussing privacy issues in information systems.

Figure 14.9

A public key encryption for secure transmission and for a "digital signature"

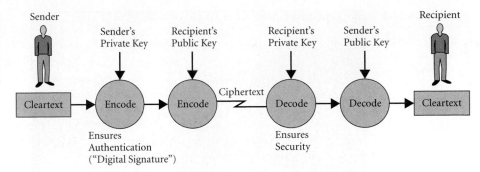

Controls of Last Resort: Disaster Recovery Planning

Notwithstanding safeguards, a disaster may strike or an attack on the system may succeed either because management has not foreseen it or because it has decided to accept the risk of this attack. Two controls of last resort should be available. One of them is adequate insurance for the residual risk (unless the firm chooses to self-insure the risk, that is, absorb any possible losses). The other control is a necessary component of a general control system: a disaster recovery plan.

A **disaster recovery plan** specifies how a company will maintain the information services necessary for its business operations in the face of disaster. A fire or an explosion in a data center would bring the business of most financial corporations (and many other types of firms) to a standstill. Information services are, in other words, vital to their operations. In addition, a disaster plan may be required by regulatory agencies or to obtain insurance.

In disaster recovery planning, the first task is to identify the necessary business functions to be supported by the plan, since covering less vital functions is, in general, too costly. A disaster recovery plan for these functions should contain four components: an emergency plan, a backup plan, a recovery plan, and a test plan. Here are their roles:

1. An *emergency plan* specifies the situations when a disaster is to be declared and the actions to be taken by various employees.

2. A *backup plan*, the principal component of a disaster recovery plan, specifies how information processing will be carried out during the emergency. It details how backup computer tapes or disks are to be maintained and specifies the facility, called the recovery site, where they can be run on very short time notice. Also, backup telecommunications facilities need to be specified. Some companies maintain a telecommunications link between their data centers and the recovery site in order to have access to the latest data if disaster strikes (Dash 1997).

The alternatives for a *recovery site* include:

- A company-owned backup facility, distant geographically from the data center. In a distributed processing environment, operations may be structured so that each data center is backed up by another.

- A reciprocal agreement with a company that runs a compatible computer system.

- A hot site or a shell (cold site) offered by a disaster recovery firm under contract. A **hot site** is a facility that operates computers compatible with the client's, who may use the site within 24 hours of disaster. **Shells** (or **cold sites**) are computer-ready buildings, available to accept equipment on very short notice. Two leading firms offering such services are Comdisco Disaster Recovery Services of Rosemont, Illinois, and Sungard Recovery Services of Wayne, Pennsylvania; IBM offers these services as well. These vendors also operate mobile recovery sites (see Photo 14.3).

Photo 14.3

*Major disaster recovery
vendors operate mobile
recovery sites*

3. A *recovery plan* specifies how processing will be restored on the original site, including detailed personnel responsibilities.

4. A *test plan* specifies how the other components of the disaster-recovery plan will be tested. A plan that is not periodically tested through simulated emergencies generally turns out to be useless in a real emergency. Chase Manhattan Bank (of New York), for example, follows the generally recommended procedure of testing its plan twice a year without warning.

For many companies, disaster recovery planning is part of a broader process of business resumption planning, which aims to ensure that all the activities of an enterprise (and not only its information processing) can be resumed after a disaster.

14.5 APPLICATION CONTROLS

Application controls are controls implemented specifically for a particular information system, for example, accounts payable or an order processing system. Both the automated and the manual aspects of processing need to be controlled. The principal areas of concern of application controls are summarized in Figure 14.10. We will now describe the principal measures undertaken in application controls.

Figure 14.10

*Areas covered by
applications controls*

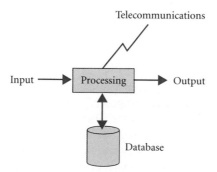

Input Controls

Data input is the area where most controls are applied, since significant exposures exist for both abuse and error. The purpose of input controls is to prevent the entry of incomplete, erroneous, or otherwise inappropriate data into the information system. These controls must ensure the following results:

1. Accuracy of Data

In order to ensure accuracy of data, system developers should:

- Provide for direct data entry (as discussed in Chapter 9) whenever possible.
- If data are keyboarded from documents, design both the documents and the screens so as to minimize the number of errors which could be made by the data entry personnel.
- Include in the codes that identify transactions and other entities the so-called check digits, which enable a computer to check whether a code has been entered correctly.

2. Completeness of Input

The main tools for checking whether all transactions have been entered are batch controls. In a batch processing system (see Chapter 9), we actually have a *physical* batch of transactions. Therefore, a manual count of transactions to be entered may be compared against the count for the batch produced by the computer. Alternatively, financial totals for the batch might be compared for the transaction fields that contain dollar amounts.

In the much more frequent on-line systems, *logical* batches may be created. For example, each data entry clerk may keep the count of transactions she or he enters, while the system groups the transactions entered by each clerk into a logical batch. The two totals may then be compared.

3. Validation of Input

Input routines, known as edit routines, perform a variety of checks, such as:

- Format checks (for example, if a customer's name contains digits, the format is improper).
- Reasonableness of the value (if an invoice amount is over $10,000, it may be considered suspect in the particular system).
- Code checks, using check digits, as we just discussed. The system may compare the code in the transaction with a table of valid codes.

Extensive validation which cross-references input data with the database contents may be performed, if it is feasible in terms of speed and cost. The result of validation, as shown in Figure 14.11, is an error file and an error report for human inspection.

Figure 14.11

Validation of input

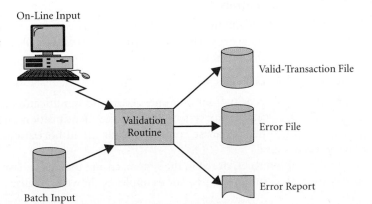

Processing Controls

An application system should be developed in such a way that processing errors are prevented from occurring in the first place. But, as we know full well, problems will occur and controls are necessary. Processing controls include:

- Crossfooting—two independent computations of a total figure can be made and compared. For example, in a payroll program, control totals may be calculated for net pay, deductions, and gross pay of all employees. At the end of the payroll run, gross pay should equal net pay plus deductions.

- Reasonableness check—after an employee's deductions have been computed, they may be compared against a table of reasonable values.

- Rounding off—correct rounding off of financial data can avoid a possible salami-technique attack, which we discussed before.

- Functional checks—this check can make sure you are not sending off an invoice for $0.00 (as many have done)!

Database Controls

Information systems files and databases hold the very data we seek to protect from destruction and from improper access or modification. The following are the principal measures for safeguarding data stored in systems.

1. Backup and Recovery

The primary concern is to be able to recover a file or database in case of a system failure. This concern is addressed by a **backup and recovery** policy: We maintain a version of the database from some prior time and a log of transactions (changes to the database) from that time on. The importance of maintaining backup files in personal computing cannot be overemphasized.

In a batch system, the master file, prior to the transaction file being run off against it, serves as an excellent backup file. In an on-line system, it is necessary to dump (copy to tape, for example) the database periodically to create such a backup file. To recover from the failure of the database (for example, as the result of a disk crash), logged transactions are run off against the previous version or against the dump.

It is common for organizations to maintain multiple backup versions (dumps) of their database with the corresponding transaction files, some of them in vaults on highly secure remote sites (including former salt mines in Utah). This file retention policy should be clearly stated and adhered to.

2. File Handling Controls

File handling controls aim to ensure that an appropriate storage medium (tape or disk volume) is mounted in the drive. Header and trailer records, as well as the control total stored with the file, serve this purpose.

3. Access Authorization

A certain level of security from improper access and modification is reached by enforcing general access control to the system. Beyond the identification and authentication safeguards thus furnished, database controls include an authorization system. Encryption is also sometimes used.

Authorization rules, stored in the system, ensure that users have access to information strictly on a need-to-know basis. For example, as shown in Figure 14.12, access privileges

Figure 14.12

Access control in databases (Based on Ron Weber, *EDP Auditing: Conceptual Foundations and Practice,* 2nd ed. NY: McGraw-Hill, 1988, p. 516.)

Human Resources Database

Name	Location	Salary	Home Address	Performance Rating
Smith	Production	28000	16 Park St., Anytown	2
Jones	Accounting	22000	2 Odd St., Anytown	4
Brown	Marketing	32000	26 Small Lane, Somewhere	1
Thomas	Research	34000	84 March St., Anytown	1

Payroll Clerk   Human Resources Clerk

stored in the system for payroll clerks would permit the clerk to read the name, department location, and salary of each employee, but no more, while a Human Resources clerk could access the home address field as well and modify the values stored in any of these four fields.

More sophisticated authorization rules prevent access to a data item depending on its value (for example, the payroll clerk could be prevented from accessing the salary field if the value stored there exceeds $50,000). In so-called statistical databases, the purpose of which is to furnish only aggregate statistics (for example, average values), it is necessary to ensure that a snooper would not be able to get at individual values by designing a series of queries and then deducing confidential information from the multiple responses.

Telecommunications Controls

Telecommunications are the most vulnerable component of information systems. An infiltrator can gain access to transmitted information by intercepting radio frequency waves in wireless systems. By tapping into a physical line with a terminal, the interloper can perform active attacks—inserting, deleting, or modifying messages by masquerading as a genuine user who is currently connected to the system. The technique for securing telecommunications is to render any intercepted information useless to the attacker by encrypting it. Authenticity is guarded by assigning to the messages sequence numbers and authentication codes such as "digital signatures," which are, of course, also encrypted.

Output Controls

Output controls are largely manual procedures aimed at ensuring that the information presented in reports and screens is of high quality (see Chapter 2), complete, and available only to authorized individuals. The techniques employed include:

- Review of documents and reports by qualified individuals to confirm that output values balance back to the inputs from which they are derived, to check reasonableness of figures, and to perform a variety of spot checks on the printed information.
- Making sure that all documents and reports have been produced as scheduled.

- Proper report design, including a distribution list, production date, and retention time, and an indication whether special security procedures are to be followed in report accessing.

- Making sure that any printed output is distributed and that electronic output is accessible in conformance with the rules of security (for example, negotiable instruments, such as checks), privacy (for example, payroll or employee health information), and confidentiality (for example, data on pricing).

14.6   AUDITING INFORMATION SYSTEMS

Information systems auditing has evolved into both a profession and an organizational function. An audit process consists of two fundamental steps—compliance testing and substantive testing—and is supported by extensive specialized software.

What Is an Information Systems Audit?

The effectiveness of information systems controls is evaluated through a process known as **IS auditing.** The process of verifying an organization's accounting records and financial statements, known as auditing, has, of course, been around for years (see Section 12.4). Today, it would be unconscionable to render an opinion on the financial state of a firm without a thorough audit of information systems, which are the primary tool for managing these records. Because the expertise required to analyze all the controls is very extensive, IS auditing has evolved into a profession in its own right.

Information systems are audited by external auditors, who render their opinion on the veracity of corporate financial statements, and by internal auditors, who work for the organization itself. As we discussed in Section 12.4, in addition to performing *financial audits* and thus rendering an opinion on the financial health of various corporate units, internal auditors perform *operational audits* to evaluate the effectiveness and efficiency of IS operations.

The requirements of the Accounting Standards Provision of the Foreign Corrupt Practices Act of 1977 have led to a significant strengthening of internal controls in organizations. At the same time, a trend has developed toward strengthening internal auditing as a means of *management* control. An independent audit department exists in most of the country's large businesses. Such a department now often includes a group that performs information systems audits as well.

Information systems have to be auditable by design. This means that every transaction can be traced to the total figures it affects, and each total figure can be traced back to the transactions which gave rise to it. In other words, an **audit trail** must exist, making it possible to establish where each transaction originated and how it was processed. Transaction logs provide a basic audit trail.

As end-user computing proliferates, audits of systems developed and controlled by end users are conducted increasingly often. Lack of auditability is one of the faults generally associated with many of these systems, unless appropriate policies and controls are enacted and audited on a regular basis.

How Is an Information Systems Audit Conducted?

IS auditors primarily concentrate on evaluating information system controls, on the assumption that if a system has adequate controls that are consistently applied, then the information produced by it is also reliable. They perform both scheduled and unscheduled audits.

At the beginning of the audit, auditors study the information system and its documentation, inputs and outputs, and interview the key users and IS personnel. They study both the general and application controls in detail. Then, the auditors select a sample of the transactions processed by the system and trace their processing from the original documents (or transaction sets in EDI) on to the totals they affect. Auditors replicate the processing done by the system, and if the results they obtain are in compliance with those produced by the system, they gain some confidence in the controls the system is supposed to have. In other words, reasonable assurance exists that assets are being protected and that the information furnished by the system is reliable.

This so-called compliance testing is followed by substantive tests to independently validate the totals contained in the financial records. The extent of substantive testing depends on the results of compliance testing: If controls were found operative, then a limited substantive testing will be sufficient. On the other hand, in the areas where controls were inadequate, extensive validation of financial totals is necessary. One example of an action that may be taken during substantive testing is requesting that the company's suppliers verify that their accounts payable are represented properly by the audited company. An audit is concluded by reporting the findings to corporate management, with a detailed statement of all the control deficiencies discovered.

One would expect IS auditors to use audit software to help them. Indeed they do. Generalized audit software is available to specify a variety of accessing, analysis, and reporting operations on databases in a higher-level language. Among these packages are Dyl-Audit from Dylakor, EDP Auditor from Cullinane, and Pan Audit from Pansophic Systems. In operational audits, software and hardware monitors are employed to gauge how efficiently the IS equipment is utilized.

S U M M A R Y

The Information Services (IS) department is responsible for providing or coordinating the delivery of computer-based information services in a firm. A centralized IS department provides most of these services. In a decentralized organization, most of the services are provided by the IS groups of the individual business units and coordinated by the central IS department.

There are numerous job categories of information systems specialists who manage, develop, and operate information systems. Systems analysts analyze users' requirements, develop system prototypes, and often design information systems. The latter function is sometimes performed by specialized systems designers. Programmers code and test the programs that satisfy the requirements established by the analysts. The top manager of Information Services in a firm, who may bear the title of chief information officer (CIO), coordinates the corporate IS efforts.

The basic objectives of information systems operations is to keep information systems running smoothly to process business transactions and deliver the information necessary to operate and manage the enterprise.

The operation of information systems is vulnerable to a variety of threats. It is necessary for an organization to identify the nature of these threats, establish a set of controls to ensure the security of the systems, and continually check the effectiveness and efficiency of systems and controls with information systems audits.

Information system security is the integrity and safety of its resources and activities. Privacy is an individual's right to retain certain information about himself or herself without disclosure. Security safeguards are necessary to protect the privacy of the individuals with respect to the information stored about them in information systems. Confidentiality is the status accorded to data and information, limiting their use and dissemination.

The sources of threats to information system security are human error, computer abuse or crime, natural and political disasters, and failure of hardware or software. Examples of threats related to crime and abuse are impersonating a legitimate user, causing the denial of service to legitimate users, concealing illegitimate instruction within an authorized code by using the Trojan horse technique or a logic bomb—introducing into the system unauthorized instructions that stay dormant until a specified event occurs. A pervasive threat is computer viruses: hidden segments of computer code that are able to perform malicious actions and replicate themselves onto other programs and computer systems, thus "infecting" multiple systems.

Information systems controls are policies, procedures, and technological measures instituted to ensure secure operation of information systems. General controls cover the entire IS activity of the firm, while application controls are specific to a given application.

General controls are of the following types: administrative (for example, separation of duties), covering systems development and maintenance, covering IS operations, physical protection of data centers, built into hardware and systems software, controlling access to the system and to information (such as user identification and authentication, firewalls, and encryption), and controls of last resort (such as a disaster recovery plan). Encryption is scrambling data, or any text in general, into a cipher that can be decoded only if one has the appropriate key (i.e., bit pattern). It renders the encoded data useless to an interloper. Public-key systems do not require secure distribution of keys between parties prior to their communication.

Application controls are implemented specifically for a particular information system. They include input, processing, database, telecommunications, and output controls. In particular, a backup and recovery policy is a vital database control.

The effectiveness of information systems controls has to be regularly evaluated during IS audits. In particular, these audits establish where every transaction recorded by the information system originated and how it was processed.

KEY TERMS

QUESTIONS

1. What are the two principal ways of organizing the Information Services unit? What are their comparative advantages and disadvantages?
2. What is the division of responsibilities between the corporate group and the functional units in a decentralized Information Services function?
3. List the principal functions of a systems analyst.
4. What is the relationship among a systems analyst, a systems designer, and an applications programmer?
5. List five principal functions of IS operations.
6. What is information systems security? What is privacy and how is it related to the security of information systems? What is confidentiality?
7. How are information systems controls related to threats to the systems and to IS audits? Give an example of a threat and of a control aiming to contain it.
8. What are the four categories of threats to computer systems? Give an example of each.
9. Give three examples of computer crime or abuse possible in the Internet setting.
10. What is computer virus? What are the two types of viruses?
11. Why do we need risk assessment in safeguarding information systems?
12. Define general and application controls. What is the relationship between the two?
13. What types of general controls are there? Give a specific example of each type.
14. Why do we need both identification and authentication to control access to an information system? Describe how these controls work in a system you are familiar with.
15. What is a firewall?
16. What is encryption? Why, do you think, is this usually a favored method of protection?
17. What are the advantages and drawbacks of public-key encryption?
18. What is a "digital signature"? What benefits can be obtained from having a "digital signature" on a message in electronic commerce?
19. What are the principal components of a disaster recovery plan?
20. What are the four areas covered by applications controls? Give an example of controls from each of these areas.
21. Why do we need access authorization as a database control even though we have implemented identification and authentication as general controls?
22. What is the objective of information systems audits? What is the difference between financial and operational audits?
23. What are the steps in an information systems audit and what is the objective of each step?

ISSUES FOR DISCUSSION

1. Based on articles in the current periodicals, compare the way information systems are managed by two companies. Select one firm with centralized IS and a firm with decentralized IS. If the information is available, identify the role end-user computing plays in each of these firms.
2. Discuss how the use of the Internet, and the World Wide Web in particular, has influenced the information system operations in several companies, based on a survey of literature and Web sites. Include a discussion of new threats to corporate IS operations.
3. One way to learn about the security mechanisms in information systems is to "hack" a system, that is, to experiment with it in order to break in through any loopholes in its protection schemes. Do you believe such hacking should be encouraged as a part of instruction in information systems? Is it ethical for an instructor to award a grade in a course, for example, based on how clever a student was in invading a system?

REAL-WORLD MINICASES AND PROBLEM-SOLVING EXERCISES

1. When It Comes to Computer Crime, Frank Clark Has Seen It All   Frank Clark, now a criminal investigator for the Pierce County prosecutor's office in Tacoma, Washington, has gained a reputation as one of the country's leading enforcement agents in the area of computer law. Here are some lessons from his experience:

Question. How worried should IS managers be about employees committing cybercrimes?

Answer. About 80 to 85 percent of computer crime losses are caused by insiders. Very often they're committed by the lowest-paid people who have the lowest investment in the business. Sometimes they're committed by data processing folks who have the greatest computer access.

Question. What should IS managers look for if they suspect an employee of being a cybercriminal?

Answer. There is nothing about these people that makes them easy to identify. What we have seen are employees who seem to be very motivated and spend a great deal of time, even unpaid time, working on a computer. Usually they are people who have a grudge because they have been overlooked in the business or passed over for promotions. Often they exceed their authority: They help others to use the computer, and in doing so, gain access to parts of the [information systems] they would not have access to in their jobs.

Question. If an IS worker is hacking from the employer's system [that is, acting without the employer's authorization to gain access to information systems owned by others], what kind of liability does the employer face?

Answer. That's a gray area. We don't have much case law dealing with computer thefts, piracy, and hacking yet. . . We have a major pornography bulletin board being run out of a Fresno hospital computer system unbeknownst to the system's managers. . .

Question. What problems do cybercrime investigators face when dealing with business?

Answer. Most computer crimes go unreported. Businesses are reluctant to report them because they lack confidence that law enforcement will investigate and prosecute the crimes successfully. Their second concern is damage to their business reputations if they report the crimes. Those are both valid reasons, but I think things are changing for the better when it comes to reporting computer crime because losses are becoming really widespread. And law enforcement is getting better at investigating.

Based on what you learned from Clark's experience and applying the knowledge you gained from this chapter, describe the measures you would undertake in your organization to guard your information systems against insider crime and abuse. You should produce a systematic report.

Based on Steve Alexander, "The Long Arm of the Law," *Computerworld,* May 6, 1996, pp. 99–100.

2. From the source available to you, including the daily press, collect information about an instance of computer crime or abuse. One notable example is the case of Stew Leonard, owner of the famed Stew Leonard's grocery store in Norwalk, Connecticut. The store, which sells $88 million in merchandise a year by carrying a limited range of items with low prices and also provides amusement park-like attractions for customers, had been hailed as an example of a successful company. It is still successfully run by the children of the owner, who is serving a 52-month jail term. Stew Leonard had hired computer specialists to design a software system that would automatically eliminate evidence of the receipts from a certain number of the store's cash registers. For some 10 years, he would collect the cash and carry it out of the country when going to his Caribbean vacation home on St. Martin, bypassing the Internal Revenue Service in the process (Berman 1996).

Describe the controls and other measures that could have prevented this occurrence or any other occurrence you find yourself.

3. Describe all the controls that may be applicable to an Accounts Receivable subsystem. State how these controls should be applied.

TEAM PROJECT

In two- or three-person teams, interview IS professionals at a local business, or at your college or university, about the general and application controls used in their installations. (Naturally, some controls remain effective thanks to their not being publicized.) Write a report.

SELECTED REFERENCES

Baker, Richard H. *Network Security: How to Plan for It and Achieve It.* New York: McGraw-Hill, 1995.

Balderston, Jim. "SET 2.0 on the Way." *Infoworld,* April 21, 1997, pp. 1 and 28.

Berman, Phyllis. "Like Father, Like Son." *Forbes,* May 20, 1996, pp. 44–45.

The case of a major computer crime.

Bernstein, David. "Secure the Virtual Office." *Datamation,* January 15, 1995, pp. 49–51.

Security for mobile computing.

Betts, Mitch. "Dotted Lines and Crooked Arrows." *Computerworld,* January 3, 1994, pp. 16–17.

New ways of organizing the IS function.

Cheswick, William R., and Steven M. Bellovin. *Firewalls and Internet Security.* Reading, MA: Addison-Wesley, 1994.

The best source on firewalls.

Dash, Julekha, "Crash!" *Software Magazine,* February 1997, pp. 48–51.

Earl, Michael J., ed. *Information Management: The Organizational Dimension.* Oxford: Oxford University Press, 1996.

An important collection of articles describing the organizational role and functioning of the IS unit.

Fialka, John J. "Intrusions by Computer Hackers Cost Big Business $800 Million in 1995." *The Wall Street Journal,* June 6, 1996, p. B7.

Ganesan, Ravi, and Ravi Sandhu, eds. "Securing Cyberspace." Special Section. *Communications of the ACM,* 37, no. 11, (November 1994), pp. 28–65.

Several articles about security measures in telecommunications networks.

Garfinkel, Simson. *PGP: Pretty Good Privacy.* Sebastopol, CA: O'Reilly & Associates, 1995.

Kane, Pamela. *PC Security and Virus Protection Handbook.* New York: M&T Books, 1994.

McNurlin, Barbara, and Ralph H. Sprague, Jr. *Information Systems Management in Practice,* 2nd ed. Englewood Cliffs, NJ: Prentice Hall, 1989.

Nance, Barry. "Keep the Networks Safe from Viruses." *Byte,* November 1996, pp. 167–175.

What policies should be enacted to keep organizational networks virus-free.

Neumann, Peter G. *Computer-Related Risks.* Reading, MA: Addison-Wesley, 1995.

The most comprehensive discussion of threats to information systems, with many examples.

"PC Security Threats." Special Issue of *PC Today,* May 1996.

Radcliff, Deborah. "Network Security: Mission Impossible." *Software Magazine,* January 1997, pp. 60–66.

Rockart, John F., Michael J. Earl; and Jeanne W. Ross. "Eight Imperatives for the New IT Organization." *Sloan Management Review,* Fall 1996, pp. 43–55.

Weber, Ron. *EDP Auditing: Conceptual Foundations and Practice,* 2nd ed. New York: McGraw-Hill, 1988.

An exceptionally thorough discussion of IS controls and auditing.

Westland, Chris. "A Rational Choice Model of Computer and Network Crime." *International Journal of Electronic Commerce,* 1, no. 2 (Winter 1996–97), pp. 109–126.

CASE STUDY | # Diary of a Disaster Recovery: Walking the Walk

Having a disaster recovery plan is one thing. Actually recovering from a disaster is another. Luckily, few IS managers have to walk this walk. Charles Peruchini, director of information systems at aluminum wheel manufacturer Superior Industries International of Van Nuys, California, did.

At 4:30 a.m. on Monday, January 17, 1994, when an earthquake registering 6.6 on the Richter scale hit the northern suburbs of Los Angeles, Superior's data center found itself less than five miles from the epicenter and stopped working. Six U.S. sites of the $325-million (in sales) company depend on that data center for computing services. Peruchini got into gear to start his day early; the day was to end 39 hours later.

10 a.m. Peruchini is the only IS employee to reach the data center that morning. The systems manager has slashed his leg on broken glass and the programming supervisor cannot drive her car out of the smashed garage. Others cannot be reached by phone. Power is out throughout the area.

Peruchini finds extensive damage to the data center. Debris is scattered throughout. The AS/400 F60 minicomputer "walked a little bit, but it didn't turn over." All of this does not matter anyway—there is no power to run any systems.

Peruchini begins doing something he has only practiced before: setting up operations at a hot site of a company specializing in disaster recovery, XL/Datacomp. He contracted for the site in October of the preceding year. The hot site is in Anaheim, more than 60 miles away from Van Nuys.

1 p.m. After conferring with Superior's plant managers in the midwest, whose information services depend on the Van Nuys site, Peruchini notifies XL/Datacomp that he is declaring a disaster emergency. He locates a backup tape of the operating system, stored in an off-site storage facility, and an applications backup tape, stored with Superior's security guards in a nearby company building.

3:30 p.m. While awaiting delivery of the operating system tape, Peruchini dives under his desk in response to a powerful aftershock.

6:30 p.m. The hot site is ready to start loading the operating system and applications onto its AS/400 Model D70. But by 8 p.m. Peruchini discovers that the 8mm backup tapes containing applications and data cannot be read without an EMC Corporation's tape drive compatible with the one at his own data center. The Los Angeles office of EMC locates such a drive at Del Taco, in neighboring Orange, California. Del Taco's IS director goes to work at 9:30 p.m. to deliver the drive to Peruchini. The drive will be returned the next day.

10:30 p.m. Peruchini starts loading his data center's manufacturing, financial, and distribution applications. He loads all 99 of them, since he is not sure which are the most critical. He is assisted by two staffers of XL/Datacomp, flown in from Dallas.

Noon, Tuesday, January 18. All systems are operational, except for the 19.2 Kbit per second modems that XL/Datacomp sent to Superior's remote sites in Arkansas, Tennessee, and Kansas. The network interfaces between the local area networks of PCs at the remote sites and the long-distance telecommunications lines have to be reconfigured, because they were set to support higher-speed telecommunications.

3:30 p.m. The hot site is ready to run. But it is past the time when Superior's plants in the east close for the day. Also, by this time—two days after the quake hit—Superior's own data center in Van Nuys is back up and running. Despite all the work on the hot site, nothing was really processed there. But, "it's a comfortable feeling to know that we were able to recover from this catastrophe," says Peruchini, in hindsight.

6 a.m., Wednesday, January 19. The AS/400 located at the Van Nuys data center, surrounded by fallen ceiling tiles and other debris, is processing information for Van Nuys and for one of the remote plants.

10:30 a.m. Four other remote plants regain their links to the data center after a long-distance line outage is repaired. Now all information services at Superior Industries International are restored.

Based on Jean S. Bozman, "Diary of a Disaster Recovery," *Computerworld*, February 14, 1994, pp. 61 and 66.

CASE STUDY QUESTIONS

1. What elements of disaster recovery did you find unexpected?

2. What went right in the disaster recovery at Superior?

3. If you were Charles Peruchini, what would you do differently in your future disaster recovery planning, based on the described experience?

4. Following the disaster, Superior's operations managers in the midwest have suggested installing a second AS/400 in a plant outside California to avoid a repeat of the outage. What would be the advantages and the drawbacks of such a step?

PART FIVE

Developing Quality Information Systems

This part of the book will describe how to develop and maintain quality information systems. You will see what is meant by software quality and learn about the quality assurance techniques applicable to software development. You will also learn how to structure and manage the development process.

Chapter Fifteen will explain what we mean by quality software and show the relationships between total quality management and information systems. Systems development life cycle, a complete methodology of systems development, will be presented. The chapter will go on to discuss in detail the objectives and techniques of systems analysis, the vital initial task of the development life cycle, during which user requirements are specified with the use of structured analysis tools.

Chapter Sixteen will continue the discussion of information systems development, taking it from design to conversion and postimplementation review. The chapter will also discuss systems maintenance through which the system is kept current with changing user requirements and information technology platforms. Computer-aided software engineering (CASE) and object-oriented development will be explained as the two important approaches to constructing quality information systems.

CHAPTER FIFTEEN

Development Life Cycle and Systems Analysis

OBJECTIVES

After you complete this chapter, you will be able to:

1. Explain the role information systems play in total quality management.

2. State and explain the attributes of software quality.

3. State the principal components of quality assurance for information systems.

4. Identify the principal tasks of systems development life cycle and their main deliverables.

5. State the objectives of systems analysis.

6. Distinguish the goal of feasibility study from the goal of requirements analysis.

7. Identify the principal techniques of information gathering during systems analysis.

8. Draw up a context diagram and a data flow diagram for an information system.

9. Explain the leveling process for data flow diagrams.

10. Design a decision table and a decision tree.

11. Understand the role of the data dictionary during systems development.

OUTLINE

Focus Minicase. Quality at the Ritz

15.1 Quality Information Systems: Vital to Total Quality Management

15.2 Stages of the Systems Development Life Cycle

15.3 Systems Analysis

15.4 Techniques and Tools of Structured Systems Analysis: Data Flow Diagrams

15.5 Techniques and Tools of Structured Systems Analysis: Description of Entities

Case Study. Developing a System for a Client and Its Discontents

Quality at the Ritz

Ritz-Carlton hotels are renowned for the quality of their service. In fact, the Atlanta-based chain of luxury hotels was the second service company to win the prestigious Malcolm Baldrige National Quality Award (FedEx was the first). This level of service was made possible in part by a unique guest recognition system that collects data on guest preferences from all employees and makes the information available when the guest comes back.

Vice-president of information systems at the Ritz-Carlton, Bruce Speckhals, recalls how, several years ago, all managers had to pitch in to check out the guests who were hurrying to catch a morning plane. Yes, the hotel did provide good service then, but it was all done as crisis management. That problem was solved first. Now, the company uses Reserve, a custom-developed reservation system, thanks to which each hotel knows when a guest will arrive and check out. Front desk staffing and other services can be planned accordingly.

But, that is not all the hotel did. The guest recognition system was implemented next. If a guest has stayed at any of the 28 Ritz-Carlton hotels at least once, she or he is now known to Ritz-Carlton. The data about each customer's preferences are collected by desk clerks, waiters, and other staff members, and entered by data clerks into the guest recognition system. The hotels also conduct surveys of their guests. Hotel-based PCs are linked over a wide area network so that a guest's preferences can be made known to all the Ritz Carlton hotels. Now the staff knows whether the guest prefers chardonnay or champagne and which newspapers to provide in the guest's room. The quality of service the hotel chain is trying to create is best described as follows: "A Ritz-Carlton guest never has to ask for anything."

The Information Services department of the hotel chain does not operate information systems. They are outsourced to Covia, a consortium run by United Airlines, which developed both the reservation and the guest recognition systems. But the IS department plays a vital business role as a manager in the quality-of-service process, coordinating the work of third-party providers of information services. "My major responsibility is developing and overseeing guidelines and making sure all of our hotels follow certain standards in providing quality information," says Bruce Speckhals.

Based on Julia King, "Quality Conscious," *Computerworld,* July 19, 1993, pp. 89–91.

As the business functions of enterprises become increasingly dependent on sophisticated information processing, quality information systems play an ever more important role in organizational performance and in total quality management. You have just read how this linkage presents itself at the Ritz-Carlton hotels. Large organizational systems are usually built in the process known as systems development life cycle. This chapter will describe the initial major phase of this process—systems analysis—which aims to establish in detail the user requirements for the new system.

15.1 | QUALITY INFORMATION SYSTEMS: VITAL TO QUALITY MANAGEMENT

Information Systems in Total Quality Management

Heightened global competition has made it imperative for organizations to deliver products—goods and services—of consistently high quality. The principles of **total quality management (TQM)**, introduced in Section 12.3, recognize that consistent product quality results from designing and executing business processes so as to remove error and waste. One does not ensure quality just by testing the end product. Rather, product quality is the result of customer focus, introduction and continuous improvement of business processes and product-development processes that reduce variations, creation of a company-wide quality culture through motivation and training of all its members, and continuous measurement and analysis of the accomplished results.

Information systems today are deeply embedded into both operations and management. Quality information systems are therefore vital to total quality management, because:

- Business processes of the firm depend on information systems (as we described in Chapter 12) and, therefore, their quality depends to a large degree on IS quality.

- Information systems enable most projects of business process redesign. This IS-enabled streamlining of processes gives fewer opportunities for error, thus leading to higher quality of the processes' outputs.

- Information systems are a necessary component of the feedback loop in managing an enterprise (see Figure 2.5). IS are necessary to continually gauge any deviations from the expected norms (such as plans or budgets) in the firm's performance and thus help reduce variance in performance. Some firms use the methodology known as Quality Function Deployment to identify their products' features that most critically meet their customers' needs. They devote special attention to these features by tracking them with information systems.

Many companies, particularly in the manufacturing sectors, comply with the **International Standards Organization's (ISO) 9000** group of quality standards (Tingey 1997). Such compliance is mandatory for those selling any of a broad range of products to the countries of the European Union. Some other countries also require this certification. The standards aim to ensure quality of products by certifying quality assurance during business processes, such as product design, manufacturing, delivery, and service support. Extensive quality-oriented information processing is a prerequisite for a certification of compliance. Indeed, as the following vignette illustrates, the process of obtaining the certification requires assistance from the Information Services department.

Software is not the strongest link in the TQM process, however. The relative youth of the software industry and the complexity of large software systems have made software quality assurance a particular concern. Here are only some in the litany of problems:

- Systems development time and cost are frequently woefully underestimated, which may lead to "runaways"—development projects that are abandoned after significant expenditures.

- The delivered systems do not satisfy the actual user requirements ("a wrong system has been delivered").

- Because of errors, ranging from the analysis and design errors to code defects known as "bugs," systems can work unreliably.

Yet Another Way Information Systems May Help in a Quality Drive

To obtain a certificate of compliance with the ISO 9000 quality standards, an organization needs to maintain prodigious amounts of documentation. The standards do not specify what kind of quality assurance system a company must have. They simply say that the company must have effective and well-documented quality assurance procedures. It fell to Steve DiMartino, manager of quality assurance for the Process Systems Group of Air Products and Chemicals of Allentown, Pennsylvania, to be in charge of the corporate drive to obtain the certification. As required by the International Standards Organization, the firm's internal quality program has to be audited by an independent inspector.

Just a few weeks before the inspection, DiMartino realized that because the company's programs were documented on paper and managed by hand, there was no easy way to display, disseminate, or change the information. It was necessary to convert the documentation to an electronic form—straightaway. At DiMartino's request, in less than a month, the IS unit of the company developed an application that allowed 550 employees of the division to view on-line all 450 documents required by ISO 9000. The application was developed in the PowerBuilder fourth-generation language from Powersoft of Burlington, Massachusetts, and it made the documentation accessible on PCs via a local area network using an SQL Server database.

Thanks in part to the promptly developed system, the operations and engineering units of the Process Systems Group received ISO 9000 certification. And the Information Services department at Air Products and Chemicals are now applying the lessons learned from the certification program to raise its own quality assurance standards.

Based on Jeff Moad, "How ISO 9000 Quality Programs Affect IS," *Datamation,* August 1, 1993, pp. 65–66.

- System performance (e.g., response time) is unsatisfactory, particularly during peak-use periods.
- The system is difficult to use.

The objective of a system development process is to produce quality software to satisfy organizational needs and user requirements (Zahedi 1995). Software quality assurance is the crucial concern of the development process. And just as you cannot ensure quality in a car by testing the product after it leaves the assembly line, you cannot assure that a software system is of high quality by simply testing the code. Quality applications emerge from a planned process, carried out with proper techniques and tools, with results checked continually as the development proceeds.

We will now discuss what we mean by software quality. We will then see how the principles of total quality management can be applied to information systems. We will come back in Section 16.4 of the next chapter to the specific measures of software quality assurance.

Software Quality

There are many attributes of software quality (Zwass 1984). These attributes are summarized in Figure 15.1.

The primary software characteristic, *effectiveness,* refers to the satisfaction of the user and organizational requirements as established during an analysis of these requirements,

Figure 15.1

What we mean by software quality

possibly including prototyping. The ease with which the intended users can use the system, dependent on the proper user-system interface, is known as **usability.** *Efficient* operation is reflected mainly in how economically hardware resources are used to satisfy the given effectiveness requirements. Software *reliability* refers to the probability that the information system will operate correctly; that is, according to specifications over a period of time. It may also be defined as the mean time between failures. Software reliability is rooted in its freedom from defects. If a system must run on different hardware or systems software platforms, **portability** should be included as a desired attribute.

Rapidly changing organizational environments require, today more than ever, that software be *maintainable:* easy to understand, modify, and test. *Understandability* is achieved by readable and well-commented system code and by documentation, which includes the requirements specifications, system documentation, user manuals, and, sometimes, special maintenance documentation. This documentation is more and more frequently delivered in an electronic form. *Modifiability* means that it is relatively easy to identify and change any part of the system that requires maintenance without affecting its other parts. *Testability* is the ease with which we can demonstrate that a modification resulted in a quality system.

Applying Total Quality Management to Information Systems

Applying the principles of total quality management to the information systems software broadens and institutionalizes the established approaches to software quality assurance (Kan and Basili 1994). The following are the principal aspects of the TQM-oriented quality assurance for information systems:

1. Customer focus is achieved by involving end users in the IS development process, particularly during its early stages when the requirements for the system are being defined. System prototyping and joint application development (JAD) are the principal techniques applied to this end.

Joint Application Development (JAD) is an organizational technique for conducting meetings between the prospective users of an information system and its developers. A JAD workshop usually lasts from three to five days and consists of several sessions. It is generally conducted during the initial stages of system analysis, with the objective of establishing user requirements for the system. Sessions are facilitated by a leader and the results are transcribed by a scribe. When successful, JAD creates a partnership between users and developers that lasts throughout the system development and subsequent maintenance. JAD has particularly good results when combined with the development of a system prototype that helps to identify users' requirements.

2. The life-cycle oriented systems development, with the inclusion of prototyping, is a process that lends itself to control, measurement, and continuous improvement. Support with computer-aided software engineering (CASE) tools, which we will discuss in the next

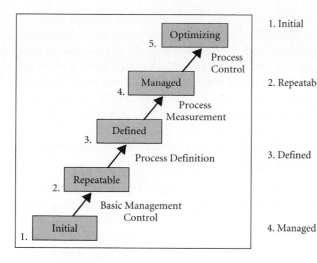

1. Initial — The development is performed ad hoc, and the process is often chaotic. There is no development methodology, no formal procedures, cost estimates, or plans. Development tools are not used systematically.

2. Repeatable — Project management controls with respect to costs, schedule, and making changes to the system under development have been introduced. A consistent systems development methodology has been introduced.

3. Defined — Software development process has been formally defined, with all the specific tasks and deliverables. A database has been established to track the process, and all the developers have been trained in its use for process improvement.

4. Managed — A comprehensive program of measurements is introduced, beyond that of measuring costs and schedules. The measurements of the attributes of software quality (e.g., defect rate) and of the development process (e.g., its productivity) have been introduced.

5. Optimizing — The development process is optimized proactively, by using the experience from other projects, collected in the process database, to prevent delays and problems in the current projects. A continual quality improvement process is in place.

Figure 15.2

Process maturity levels for assessing the software development process. Arrows show the measures necessary to move to a higher level (Based on Watts S. Humphrey, *Managing the Software Process*, Reading, MA: Addison-Wesley, 1990.)

chapter, helps to ensure product quality. Continuing quality control throughout this development process needs to:

- Validate that *we are building the right system;* that is, a system satisfying user requirements.

- Verify that *we are building the system right;* that is, what we do in the current stage of development agrees with what was done during the previous stage. For example, the program code produced during the programming stage needs to correspond to the design specifications.

We will discuss the techniques of software quality assurance used during the development life cycle in the next chapter.

3. Software development and maintenance teams are the primary human element in ensuring software quality. We will discuss team organization in the next chapter.

4. The quality measurement program can assist in consistent striving for higher quality levels. Such a program rests on the foundation of software metrics. **Software metrics** include techniques for measuring the attributes of software (e.g., the number of defects identified per thousand lines of code) and techniques for measuring the attributes of software development process (e.g., productivity expressed in terms of the development effort expended for a software product). We shall also encounter these metrics in the next chapter.

To help organizations assess their own or their contractors' ability to produce quality software, the Software Engineering Institute of Carnegie Mellon University has developed a framework of **process maturity levels** used for assessing software development (see Figure 15.2).

A firm whose IS development is at the initial level employs no well-defined development methodology. By progressive introduction of project management and quality control, technical reviews, result measurement, and error prevention, the organization moves to the higher levels of quality assurance. It should be noted that very few firms have as yet reached even Level 3 of the framework. The use of the framework (described in detail in Humphrey 1990) can help a firm remove, step by step, the deficiencies in the development of its information systems. This has led to significant business results in a number of firms (Fox and Frakes 1997).

We will overview the systems development life cycle in the next section and devote the remainder of the chapter to its initial stages, those of systems analysis.

15.2 | STAGES OF THE SYSTEMS DEVELOPMENT LIFE CYCLE

Large systems development projects involve a number of people over an extensive period of time. Thus, to develop a transaction processing system, such as an on-line order processing system that supports hundreds of terminals, two project teams, consisting of 10 people each, may need to work for about two years. Such a significant commitment of organizational resources has to be managed in a formal fashion. The systems development life cycle (SDLC) was introduced to you in Section 13.5 as an alternative to rapid applications devel-

Figure 15.3

Systems development life cycle

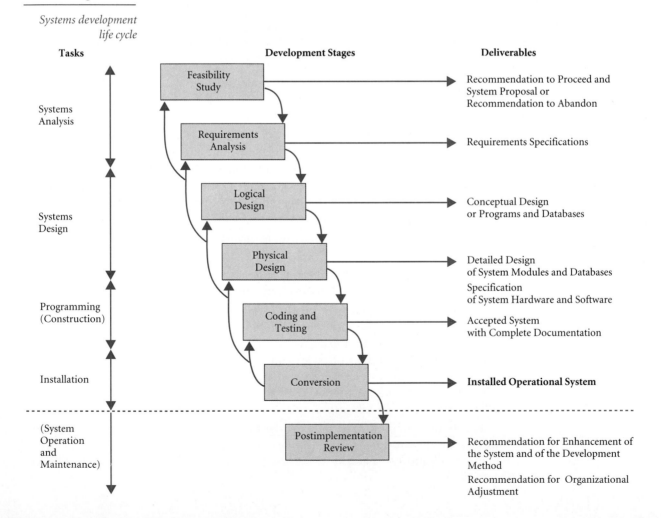

opment via prototyping. SDLC gives organizations a means of controlling a large development project by dividing it into manageable stages with well-defined outputs. SDLC consumes a significant amount of resources itself: It takes time and money to manage projects in such an elaborate fashion.

In a life-cycle oriented development, every stage is defined in terms of the activities and responsibilities of the development team members. Each stage terminates in a milestone defined in terms of the subproducts to be delivered, such as system requirements specifications or coded and tested software modules. The development life cycle can be shown as the so-called waterfall model of Figure 15.3. Note that the arrows in the figure point in both directions, down but also up the "waterfall." This reflects the fact that developers often need to rework the deliverables produced at earlier stages in the light of the experience they gain as the development effort progresses and to accommodate legitimate user requests for change. The later phases of the life cycle should be accompanied by the system implementation activities discussed in Section 13.8.

In this part of the text, along with the discussion of the stages of the development life cycle and of the deliverables shown in the figure, we will also discuss the tools and techniques most frequently used during these stages. Both systems analysis and systems design move from the more abstract level to more detailed levels through a process known as stepwise refinement (gradual fleshing out with detail, in other words). Specific graphic tools are employed for the analysis and design stages. Narrative descriptions are avoided, as they generally prove both ambiguous and difficult to maintain as the system is modified in the future. Effort is concentrated on these early stages, rather than on coding, in order to avoid errors in establishing user requirements (chiefly during analysis) and to produce a system that could be relatively easily modified during maintenance. A typical distribution of development effort is shown in Figure 15.4. You may conclude that the actual program code does not appear until well into the project— a feature that business-oriented managers need to understand.

The effort expended on developing an information system is generally surpassed by the efforts needed for the system's maintenance, which may cost over time twice as much as the development. Indeed, many organizations spend 60 to 70 percent of their IS budgets on systems maintenance. It pays, then, to develop systems that will be easier to maintain. Producing extensive system documentation during the development is necessary to support maintenance. Moreover, it is desirable that the documentation necessary for system operation and maintenance be produced as the by-product of the development process. For example,

Figure 15.4

Distribution of systems development effort
(From Marvin V. Zelkowitz, et al., *Principles of Software Engineering and Design,* © 1979, p. 3. Reprinted by permission of Prentice Hall, Inc., Englewood Cliffs, NJ.)

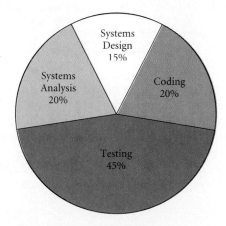

IN THE SPOTLIGHT

Offshore Development

Unable to spare its U.S.-based IS staff for a two-year application development project, The Chase Manhattan Bank of New York struck a deal with Tata Unisys in Bombay, India. The Indian software development company will coordinate the entire project: The application and the database design will be done in the United States and in Hong Kong, while most of the programming will be done in India.

Access Computers in Detroit had trouble finding experienced programmers at home for developing future versions of Wintegrity, its multimedia point-of-sale software, written in Visual C++. The firm found them in Bombay and will depend almost fully on offshore development for future versions of its product. The company expects to slash development costs by one-fifth.

As we can see, savings are not the only reason for offshore development of information systems anymore. Indeed, foreign labor is significantly less expensive. However, in the past, the savings were often difficult to realize because of the complexity of managing projects involving systems developers in countries such as Hungary, India, or Ireland. Recently, some of these countries have overhauled their telecommunications infrastructures and trained their workers in skills that make them attractive partners.

High-speed telecommunications and videoconferencing facilities are a key reason Chase's project is proceeding well, according to the bank's executives. Software technology parks constructed across India in Bombay, Bangalore, Calcutta, and Delhi house many software firms and feature 64 Kbit per second satellite-based telecommunications, and Internet access. Thanks to this, work can be instantly distributed and supervised. Training in state-of-the-art client/server and object-oriented technologies and conformance with the ISO 9000 quality standards make some foreign developers desirable partners. However, drawing up detailed system requirements specifications, usually before going offshore, is absolutely critical to the success of an offshore project.

The prerequisites for a country's success as a major offshore development site include the following:

- Capability to market its software development services in high-cost locations, such as the United States and Japan.
- Good telecommunications between the development sites and clients.
- Strong protection for intellectual property, such as copyrights.
- Fluency in English and other international business languages.
- Good support from the national government.
- Adequate capitalization to get started.

Offshore development of information systems raises concern and creates controversy in the United States. While some feel that the ever growing needs of the software industry and the natural limitations of spreading the work geographically will not result in a massive flight of work from the United States, others are less sanguine.

Based on Martin LaMonica and Elizabeth Heicher, "Operation Offshore," *Computerworld,* August 8, 1994, pp. 73–80; G. Pascal Zachary, "U.S. Software: Now It May be Made in Bulgaria," *The Wall Street Journal,* February 21, 1995, pp. B1, B12; and Capers Jones, "In Software, the Fight Will Be Fierce," *IEEE Spectrum,* July 1996, p. 43.

data flow diagrams that are used to analyze the system become an essential part of its documentation. Computer-aided software engineering (CASE) tools, which we discuss in Section 16.8, assist in producing the documentation. To reduce the very significant costs and save time, today some U.S. firms rely on offshore developers for some of their systems development and maintenance needs, as the vignette above illustrates.

We will proceed to discuss in the remainder of the chapter the details of systems analysis, a fundamental task to ensure that the right system will be built.

15.3 | SYSTEMS ANALYSIS

Objectives of Systems Analysis

The task of **systems analysis** is to establish in detail *what* the proposed system will do (as opposed to *how* this will be accomplished technologically). This includes establishing the objectives of the new system, conducting an analysis of its costs and the benefits to be derived from it, and outlining the process of system implementation. Detailed systems analysis must also establish who the system users are, what information they should get and in what form, and how this information will be obtained from the incoming data and from the databases. In other words, the flow of data into the system, data transformation and storage by the system, and the delivery of information to users are subject to a detailed analysis.

The first of the systems analysis stages is the feasibility study (also known as the preliminary investigation), which may actually result in abandoning the project, should it be found undesirable. The main analysis stage is the extensive requirements analysis, which results in the requirements specifications for the system—a detailed statement of what users expect and what developers will deliver (Siddiqi and Shekaran 1996).

These two analysis stages (shown in Figure 15.3) are performed by systems analysts, in close collaboration with the intended system users. Users are routinely consulted as information is gathered for this phase. Several users may be members of a liaison team that facilitates communication between users and developers, or they may be active participants in the analysis process. In some firms, users and developers work together in developing systems requirements during the joint applications development (JAD) sessions, as discussed above. User involvement is often critical to the success of a system development project.

The principal quality assurance activity during systems analysis is validation—making sure that the system to be produced will satisfy user requirements. As requirements analysis progresses, it is also necessary to verify that the more detailed specifications of the system correspond to the earlier ones.

Feasibility Study

The main objective of the **feasibility study,** the introductory phase of development, is to establish whether the proposed system is feasible or, to be more accurate, desirable, before resources are committed to the full-scale project. If all systems proposals could be the result of careful longer-term planning, the scope of feasibility studies would be limited. The realities are different, however. Most proposals for new systems stem from business problems and opportunities—as they are encountered—and require a preliminary evaluation to make sure that we are solving the right problem and that the solution we are proposing is feasible.

In a feasibility study, systems analysts perform a preliminary investigation of the business problem or opportunity represented by the proposed system development project. Specifically, they undertake the following tasks:

- Define the problem or the opportunity which the system will address.
- Establish the overall objectives of the new system.
- Identify the users of the system.
- Establish the scope of the system. A structured analysis tool such as a context diagram, discussed in the next section, may serve this purpose.

Here is an example of an executive summary which briefly establishes a system development project in these terms:

> The project will address the need for a system that presents the total relationship of our company with each customer firm. The objective of the system is to assist the marketing department in devising the appropriate promotion for the customers, as well as to enable the sales department to price orders appropriately. The users of the system will be marketing planners, and sales managers and representatives in the field. The system will interface with the present order processing system and the customer database.

In addition, the systems analysts perform the following tasks during the feasibility study:

- Propose general hardware/systems software options for the new system (for example, a client/server configuration), which is necessary to size the project.
- Perform a make-or-buy analysis for the application.
- Perform a value assessment, such as the cost-benefit analysis, based in part on the estimate of the development project size.
- Assess the project risk.
- Recommend whether to proceed with the project (perhaps assigning a priority rating as well), or whether to abandon the project.

It is vital at this early stage to address the business problem the new system is expected to solve, rather than to simply automate an existing way of doing business. As we said in Section 13.1, business process redesign or business reengineering is in some cases performed prior to detailed systems analysis.

The assessment of system feasibility may be based on a narrative system description, perhaps supported by a context diagram, or it may be supported by an initial system prototype. The five essential aspects of feasibility study are shown in Table 15.1.

In the cases when the *legal feasibility* of the proposed system is in question, the developers need to consult with legal experts to establish that the system will conform with applicable laws. In some cases of systems that pass this feasibility test, steps need to be taken to limit a potential legal liability during the system's use (Bordoloi 1996). The system's development may raise no legal issues; however, it may involve questionable ethics. The *ethical feasibility* study will answer this principal question: Will the system violate the rights of others? For example, a system that will violate the privacy of people about whom and unbe-

Table 15.1	**Feasibility Aspect**	**Issues That Need Evaluation**
Aspects of a feasibility study	Legal	Will the proposed systems conform to laws and regulations?
	Ethical	Will the proposed system conform to the norms of ethics?
	Technological	Do we have the technology and skills needed to develop and operate the system?
	Economic	Will the system result in competitive advantage or another payoff to the enterprise?
	Organizational	Will the organizational change result in an acceptable quality of working life for those affected by the system? Will the political changes caused by the system be accepted? Will the organization benefit as a whole?

knownst to whom it will maintain data in its database will not pass that test. We shall discuss ethical issues arising in the development and use of information systems in Chapter 17.

The *technological feasibility* study aims to answer the question: Do we have the capability to develop this system? This involves an assessment of IS personnel capabilities and the hardware and software environment available for development. Lack of appropriate technological capabilities and experience qualifies the project as a high-risk undertaking and may call for outsourcing of the project. In addition, certain technological solutions may lead to undesirable risk exposures. For example, a centralized database may be undesirable for some firms in this respect.

The *economic feasibility* of the project is evaluated by comparing its costs with the envisaged benefits, as discussed in Section 13.3. Strategic business considerations may, however, override pure comparison of costs with quantifiable benefits.

Organizational feasibility has two aspects: The system has to be accepted both by the users and by the managers of the affected units. The sociotechnical approach, for example, mandates an investigation of the impact of the system on the quality of the users' working life. It is necessary to establish whether the organizational change that will accompany system implementation is desirable and, if so, whether it can be managed, and then to plan and set in motion the implementation process we discussed in Section 13.8.

Based on the estimated size of the system, the novelty of the technology for the given organization, and the extent of required organizational change, a system risk assessment may be made, to become a part of portfolio analysis (as discussed in Section 13.3). A project plan is also produced during this stage: This plan lays out the schedule and the budgets for the remaining stages of the project. The succeeding stages of the project are subject to management approval of a recommendation to proceed and to commit resources to the project.

Typically, a feasibility study consumes 5 to 10 percent of a project's resources; that is, of the time that will be spent on the development and the development cost. Among the tools that may be used at this stage, along with the cost-benefit analysis, are interviews, questionnaires, observation, and participation. We now proceed to discuss these general tools of systems analysis as part of the systems requirements analysis, when they are used extensively.

Requirements Analysis

The principal objective of requirements analysis, the main systems analysis stage, is to produce the **requirements specifications** for the system, which set out in detail what the system will do. Requirements (also known as functional) specifications establish an understanding between the system developers, its future users, the management and other stakeholders (for example, internal auditors). This understanding may be treated as a formal contract between the parties.

Requirements analysis needs to establish:

- What outputs the system will produce, what inputs will be needed, what processing steps will be necessary to transform inputs into outputs, and what data stores (files or databases) will have to be maintained by the system.

- What volumes of data will be handled, what numbers of users in various categories will be supported and with what levels of service, what file and database capacities the system will need to maintain, and other quantitative estimates of this type.

- What interface will be provided for the users to interact with the system, based on the skills and computer proficiency of the intended users.

- What control measures will be undertaken in the system (these measures were discussed in Chapter 14).

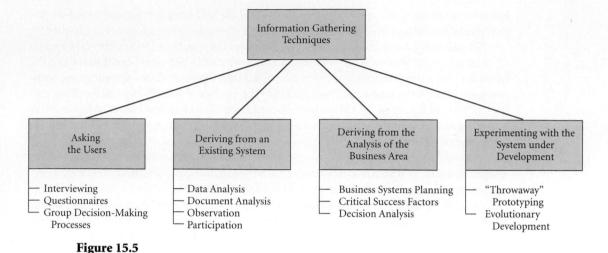

Figure 15.5

Techniques for information gathering in systems analysis

The next section will present the systems analysis tools, such as data flow diagrams and entity descriptions for data dictionaries. Here, we will concentrate on the techniques that can be used in the massive information gathering effort that the stage entails. To describe these techniques, we will employ the framework proposed by Gordon Davis of the University of Minnesota (Davis 1982). The techniques for gathering information during systems analysis can be grouped into four categories, shown in Figure 15.5. A combination of these approaches is usually employed.

Let us discuss these techniques in order of increased uncertainty on the part of the users as to what they want from the proposed system, an important criterion for the selection of techniques for the project.

1. Asking the Users

Interviewing the users requires considerable skill and preparation. Interviews are a very rich but costly and time-consuming communication channel. Both open-ended ("How could order processing be done better?") and closed-ended ("Do you maintain an audit trail for this type of transaction?") questions may be employed where appropriate. While open-ended questions aim to draw the user out into a longer explanation or opinion, closed-ended questions can be answered with yes, no, or a specific brief response.

The interviewing process must be planned, since managers at several levels may have to be questioned. The analyst has to prepare for each interview by establishing the position, activities, and background of the interviewee. In a structured interview, the analyst relies on a prepared list of questions. In an unstructured interview, the direction unfolds as the person being interviewed answers the largely open-ended questions; follow-up questions are then asked.

During an interview, the analyst must convey a clear understanding of the purpose of the interview, ask specific questions in terms understandable to the interviewee, listen rather than anticipate answers, control the interview but be open to a suddenly discovered rich source of information, and create a record (notes or a tape recording) of what is learned. An interviewer learns how the interviewee makes decisions (frequently, the interviewee actually learns this during the interview as well). The analyst should analyze the results immediately following an interview session.

While the analyst may learn from managers what information they need to make decisions, an experienced claims clerk will be the best source of information on how insurance claims are actually handled and on ideas for how they may be handled more expeditiously.

Operational supervisors generally know best the volume of various transactions that the system will be expected to handle.

Questionnaires are an efficient way of asking many users at once, particularly users who are dispersed in the field, such as insurance agents, for example. Increasingly, questionnaires are distributed on diskettes or intranets. An easy-to-fill-out questionnaire with concise and closed-ended questions is most likely to meet with success. Simple yes/no questions and checklists are preferable. Questionnaires have limitations as compared with interviews, in part because of their requisite simplicity. For instance, any clarification of questions or follow-up is generally difficult. And, to begin with, it is necessary to motivate an addressee to actually fill out a questionnaire. Generally, questionnaires are employed together with other, more powerful, means of eliciting user requirements.

Group decision-making processes such as the Delphi method, brainstorming, and nominal group technique, which we discussed in Section 10.6, may also be used in search of creative new solutions. These techniques are sometimes used during a joint application development (JAD) session.

2. Deriving the Requirements from an Existing Information System

The requirements for a proposed system may be derived from an existing information system. The possibilities are:

- The system (manual or computerized) that will be replaced by the proposed system.
- A system similar to the proposed one that has been installed elsewhere and is accessible to the analyst.
- A proprietary package, whose functionality may be analyzed.

In the approach known as *data analysis,* the requirements for the proposed system are derived from the data contained in the outputs of the existing system (reports, worksheets, documents, and so forth) and inputs to it (orders, invoices, time cards, and so on). The data can also be obtained from the existing programs and system documentation, such as procedures manuals, organization charts, file descriptions, operations manuals, and so forth.

Document analysis concentrates on the analysis of business documents, such as orders or invoices. Document analysis usually accompanies the "asking" methods, since documents are difficult to interpret independently; for example, documents are frequently consulted during an interview. By sampling the incoming documents (orders, for example) over a period of a day, an analyst may establish the necessary processing capacity for the proposed system. It is important that the documents be used merely as a point of departure rather than "frozen" into the new system. For example, the format of an order will change radically when conversion is made to electronic data interchange.

By *observing* the work of an intended user or by actually *participating* in the work, the analyst learns first-hand about the inadequacies of the existing system. For example, by observing a securities processing area in a bank, the analyst may note the job fragmentation imposed by the existing system and, in consequence, the lack of responsibility the users take for the results. At the same time, the analyst is also able to establish the volumes of the incoming securities and peak processing times. The need to redesign the business function and to integrate its fractured parts into a system that supports a workgroup become apparent to the analyst.

3. Deriving the Requirements from the Analysis of the Business Area

The information system we are developing will assist a manager in making decisions or make a business unit more effective in its operations. If we take this point of view, we may then use the methodologies applicable to the organization's IS planning (as discussed in

Section 13.2) to derive the requirements for a particular information system as well. Specifically, informational analysis of the business unit to be served by a system may be carried out with *Business Systems Planning (BSP)*. On the other hand, using the *critical success factors (CSF)* methodology, analysts can establish the CSFs of the individual managers and support them with information.

A method that will also help establish the informational needs of an individual manager is *decision analysis*. It consists of the following steps:

- Identify the key decisions that a manager makes.
- Define the steps of the process whereby the manager makes these decisions.
- Define the information needed for the decision process.
- Establish what components of this information will be delivered by the information system and what data will be needed to do so.

4. Experimenting with the System as It Is Being Developed

Experimenting with the system under development is the prototyping approach, discussed in Section 13.5. An initial system version that embodies some of the requirements is built. The users are then able to define their requirements in an "as-compared-to-something" manner—which is much easier than defining them without such a comparison. The prototype may be discarded after it has been put to such use, or it may evolve into the system to be delivered.

As the systems analysts gather information, they can perform structured analysis by a stepwise refinement of the context diagram obtained during the feasibility study stage. We now proceed to discuss the tools and techniques of this process, known as structured systems analysis.

15.4 | TECHNIQUES AND TOOLS OF STRUCTURED SYSTEMS ANALYSIS: DATA FLOW DIAGRAMS

The purpose of systems analysis is to devise a logical model of the proposed system. In other words, we wish to specify the new system in business terms, independent of its physical implementation. Using the methodology known as **structured systems analysis,** we graphically describe the system as interacting processes that transform input data into output data. These processes may then become code modules as the system is further designed and programmed.

Data Flow Diagrams

The principal tool used in structured analysis is the **data flow diagram** (DFD), which graphically shows the flow and transformation of data in the system. A DFD representation of a system is the graphical depiction of what the system will do. Yet this is not simply graphics—this is what will ultimately become the system itself! There are only four symbols employed by a DFD (as shown in Figure 15.6).

1. A **process** is shown as a circle, also called a bubble (although some analysts prefer rectangles with rounded corners). A process, as the term is used in structured analysis, transforms its inputs into outputs. For example, a *Compute discount* process will transform the data about the customer and the order into a discount percentage. The name of the

Figure 15.6

Symbols of data flow diagrams

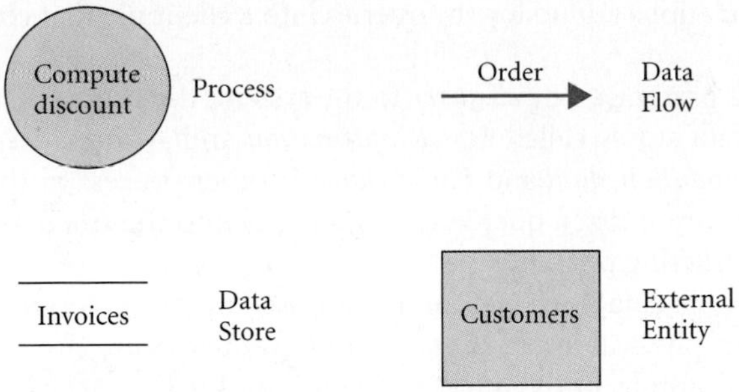

Compute discount — Process

Order → Data Flow

Invoices — Data Store

Customers — External Entity

process very briefly explains what the process does. Since the processes are the "active" components of the system (they are likely to ultimately become program modules), their names reflect this. Therefore, the name of a process generally consists of a verb ("Compute") and an object ("discount"). All processes in a DFD are numbered.

2. A **data flow,** shown as a line ending in an arrow, represents a flow of data into or out of a process. In general, data flows show the movement of data between all the components of a DFD. Although during the initial analysis we may consider physical data flows in the existing system (for example, a report or an invoice), ultimate analysis will deal with their logical data content (such as customer data or order data).

3. A **data store,** shown as parallel lines (although some analysts use a rectangle open on the right), shows a repository of data maintained by the system. Such a repository may become a data file or a database component—such decisions are made during system design. Both data stores and data flows are data structures; note the similarity in the way they are named and further analyzed. Data store names are frequently in the plural (for example, *Invoices*), to distinguish them from data flows.

4. An **external entity,** represented as a square (or a rectangle) is a source from which the system draws data or a receiver of information from the system. These entities are external to the system; they are beyond the system boundary. Thus, *Customers* may present an *Order* to the system and receive an *Invoice* from it. External entities may also be other systems with which the given system interacts.

Let us first familiarize ourselves with DFDs by reviewing (walking through) the simple diagram shown in Figure 15.7. The objective of our Travel Information System (other than introducing DFDs to you in their simplest form) is to respond to queries regarding flights

Figure 15.7

Data flow diagram of a Travel Information System

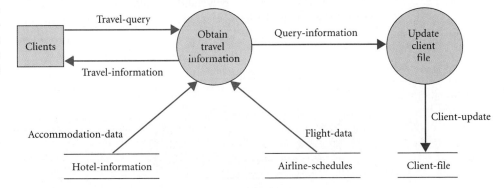

and accommodations and to log the queries into a client file that could be used for marketing purposes.

As *Clients* present a *Travel-query* to the system, the process *Obtain travel information* accesses the data stores called *Hotel-information* and *Airline-schedules* to obtain, respectively, *Accommodation-data* and *Flight-data*. Another process of the system, called *Update client file*, logs summarized queries and responses into the *Client-file*, a data store that will be used for marketing purposes.

Note that this data flow diagram is expressed in logical terms. We are not committing ourselves to any physical implementation of how queries are entered or how data stores are designed. For example, both *Hotel-information* and *Airline-schedules* may be part of a single database. All we know is that our system does not maintain these data (note that there are no inputs to the stores from the system's processes); they may be provided by a third-party vendor. The process of analysis must produce such a DFD for the new system—this is a logical model of the system. Indeed, since a DFD is a logical model of the system, a comparison of the DFD of the old system (if available) with the DFD of the new system can be used to assess the extent of change involved in a business process redesign (Lucas 1996). The implementation of this DFD will be decided on later, during the design stages.

We will now consider how DFDs are used to analyze larger systems.

Using Data Flow Diagrams: From Context Diagram to Level-0

Our fundamental requirement concerning tools for systems development is that they lend themselves to a process of progressive refinement, bringing in the details gradually. This helps manage the complexity of the analysis process. DFD leveling is such a process of progressive refinement.

We start structured systems analysis with a special kind of DFD called the **context diagram** of the system, which is generally the product of a feasibility study. This diagram shows only the system interfaces (inputs and outputs) flowing to or from external entities. A context diagram shows the system as a single process bearing the system's name, with its principal incoming and outgoing data flows, as they are known at this early stage of analysis. If there are too many to show, a table may be employed to show inputs and outputs in two columns. A context diagram of a simple *Order Processing System* is shown in Figure 15.8.

As we can see from the context diagram, our *Order Processing System* accepts customer orders and produces the invoices sent to customers; it also prints picking labels, which are sent to the warehouse. A picking label directs warehouse pickers to the bins where the product is located so that an order can be assembled for shipment. Instead of an invoice, a customer may receive an order-rejection notice (rejection may be for a variety of reasons, including absence of good credit standing), or an out-of-stock notice. All or most of the data flows will probably be implemented in an electronic form. Our simple system does not han-

Figure 15.8

The context diagram of the Order Processing System

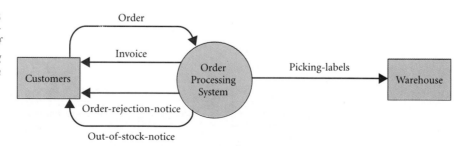

dle backorders: Our warehouse is restocked periodically and all the goods that we are able to deliver to customers are there.

Using this context diagram, let us now produce a level-0 DFD, which shows the major functions of the system. We will first walk you briefly through this DFD, shown in Figure 15.9, and then discuss the rather simple principles of leveling (decomposition) of DFDs.

The main line of the DFD, which shows the processing of a valid order for available products, is laid out from left to right for easy understanding. The appropriate processes (1 to 5) check order validity and product availability, update the inventory file for the quantities that will be removed for the order, determine the price, and produce the invoice.

Note that we need to ensure sufficiency of data for a proper process operation. It would be an error, for example, if the only information passed on by the *Check order validity* process to the subsequent processes were an indication whether the order is valid or not. The process should, rather, pass on the appropriate data about the order itself. Observe that we show only a net flow from a data store. For example, we do not show that the *Check product availability* process must send the product identifier to the *Inventory-file*; the objective of access is to get the *Product-quantity-on-hand*, and that is what is shown in the DFD.

Note that the external entity *Customers* is repeated for readability. Indeed, we can replicate like this any external entity or data store (but not a process or a data flow). With the exception of these repetitions, each entity must have a distinct name. Careful and proper naming of entities to reflect their meaning in the system is important. A DFD should be correct, complete, and consistent and it ought to show what the system is supposed to do in the best possible way. Do not forget that DFDs are communication tools; you should be able to show them to future system users, and they should be able to comment on them. Computer-aided software engineering (CASE) tools, which will be discussed in the next chapter, provide assistance in drawing up consistent DFDs.

Figure 15.9

Level-0 DFD of the Order Processing System

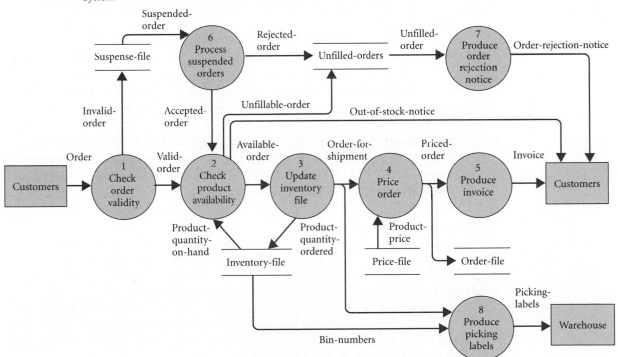

Orders that are found invalid by the *Check order validity* process (we do not at this time have to determine exactly what criteria will be used, but we know that a credit check will be included) are placed in the *Suspense-file*. They will be further reviewed (perhaps manually?), and an *Order-rejection-notice* may have to be produced. Placing any *Suspended-order* in a data store makes it possible for the two processes that access the store to operate at different times. Likewise, an *Out-of-stock-notice* will be sent if the product is not currently available. For an order to be shipped, a set of *Picking-labels* for the *Warehouse* will be generated. To do so, the *Inventory-file* will be accessed to determine the *Bin-numbers* indicating where the products are located.

Leveling Data Flow Diagrams

Going from the context diagram to the level-0 DFD, we have encountered the first instance of DFD leveling. **Leveling** is the gradual refinement of DFDs, which brings more and more detail into the picture. In doing so, it is necessary to ensure quality by following these basic principles of DFD leveling:

1. The top-level DFD is the context diagram of the system. Subsequent levels are obtained by progressively breaking down individual processes into separate DFDs.

2. Decomposition is governed by the balancing rule, which ensures consistency. The **balancing** rule states that data flows coming into and leaving a process must correspond to those coming into and leaving the lower-level DFD that shows this process in more detail. Observe the balancing rule in action in Figures 15.8 and 15.9 with respect to the *Order Processing System* process which is being decomposed: all five data flows in Figure 15.8 match the appropriate flows in Figure 15.9 (actually, we did not have to show the external entities in the level-0 DFD but, at that top level, this is frequently done for readability's sake). Sometimes, minor data flows are added on lower levels but do not appear at the higher level.

3. No more than 10 processes should be shown on a given DFD to prevent cluttering the diagram—use leveling!

4. Not all processes have to be broken down—only those whose complexity warrants it. Typically, you stop decomposing a process if you feel that you can describe what it does in detail in procedural terms (as you will see in the next section) in about a page.

5. The leveling process is not over until it's over, to use Yogi Berra's immortal phrase. That is, as you introduce more detail into the analysis by leveling, you will note omissions in higher-level DFDs—and you will correct them.

6. The numbering rule for processes is as follows. Use 1, 2, 3, and so on in the level-0 DFD. If you decompose, say, process 3, the processes shown on process 3's level-1 DFD will be numbered 3.1, 3.2, 3.3, and so on. Therefore, if you see a process numbered 5.1.4, you know that it belongs to a level-2 DFD of process 5.

Let us now look at leveling on a more detailed example of the *Check order validity* process, as shown in Figure 15.10.

Since our system handles only known customers, an order will be rejected if the *Customer-file* contains no customer record or if the *Evaluate customer credit* process comes up with a deficient credit rating, based on access to the *Credit-information*. This data store contains a variety of "soft" data on customers' and potential customers' credit standings, as well as an overall rating of customers' creditworthiness. A separate data store for credit information is maintained due to the sometimes sensitive nature of the data contained there. Note that while our system obtains the data from both data stores, it does not store the data; the data stores are maintained by another system.

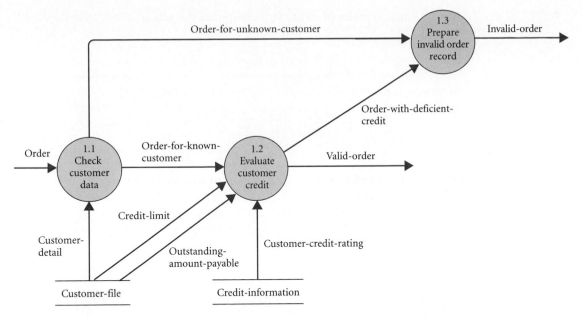

Figure 15.10

Level-1 DFD for the process Check order validity

We did not have to show the stores used by the *Check order validity* process on a higher-level DFD, since they are used internally rather than being used to interface this process with others (as the *Suspense-file* does, for example). Sometimes we may choose to show a data store used by a single process in order to make a DFD more readable (as we chose to show *Credit-information*, for example).

A DFD description of the system is the higher-level model in structured analysis. We still must describe the primitive processes, as well as the data structures contained in the data flows and data stores. Now let us see how this is done.

15.5   TECHNIQUES AND TOOLS OF STRUCTURED SYSTEMS ANALYSIS: DESCRIPTION OF ENTITIES

The entities that appear in the data flow diagrams are described in further detail in a data dictionary. Originally used to store only descriptions of data, **data dictionaries** have evolved into powerful tools as repositories of descriptions of all project entities. Such dictionaries are available as specialized software packages; a dictionary facility also lies at the heart of CASE tools.

Description of Processes: Basic Logic Constructs

To show how the primitive DFD processes transform their inputs into outputs, we must describe their logic. The principal tool for this specification is **structured English,** which is a form of **pseudocode;** that is, a code describing the processing logic to a human rather than to a computer. Structured English is more readable and less detailed than a code expressed in a programming language for computer execution. As any structured code, structured English relies on imperative sentences (orders for a computational action) and three fundamental programming structures expressing how these computational orders are to be applied.

Here are some examples of orders for a computational action as they might appear in structured English:

```
Compute Tax = 6.25 • Sale-total
Read Customer-record from Customer-file
Add Sale-amount to Sale-total
Delete Supplier-record from Approved-supplier-file
```

Just three fundamental constructs are sufficient to express any processing logic: sequence, loop, and decision. An additional construct represents multiple choice. Each of these constructs is itself an action. This fact enables us to express any procedural logic, since the constructs may be expanded by detailing these actions, again using the same constructs (we say that the constructs are nested). These constructs, along with their explanatory flowcharts, are shown in Figures 15.11 through 15.14.

Let us explain and illustrate these constructs:

1. **Sequence** specifies that one action be carried out after another (Figure 15.11).

For example, here is a sequence of two actions:

```
Read Supplier-record from Approved-supplier-file
Print Supplier-address
```

Figure 15.11

Sequence

Action 1
Action 2

Action 1

Action 2

Figure 15.12

Loop

DO WHILE condition is true
    Action(s)
END DO

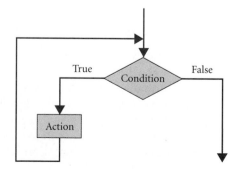

Figure 15.13

Decision

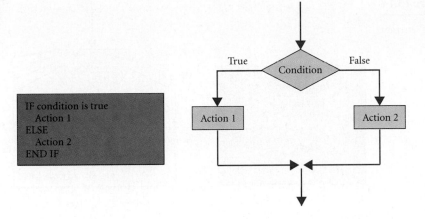

```
IF condition is true
    Action 1
ELSE
    Action 2
END IF
```

2. **Loop** specifies that certain actions be carried out repeatedly while the given condition holds (Figure 15.12).

   For example:

   ```
   DO WHILE there are more records in Customer-file
       Read next Customer-record from Customer-file
       Write Customer-address onto Mailing-list
   END DO
   ```

3. **Decision** specifies alternative courses of action, depending on whether a certain condition holds or not (Figure 15.13). It expresses this thought: "If a given condition exists, one action (or actions) should be taken, or else the alternative action(s) should be carried out."

   For example:

   ```
   IF Customer-credit-rating is satisfactory
          Write Customer-order into Valid-order-file
   ELSE
          Write Customer-order into Suspense-file
   END IF
   ```

4. Frequently, a need arises to choose one of a set of several actions, based on a condition that may have more than two outcomes. Though this situation may be expressed with nested IF constructs, it is far easier to express it with the multiple selection (CASE) construct shown in Figure 15.14 on the next page (do not confuse this construct with CASE tools!).

Figure 15.14

Multiple selection

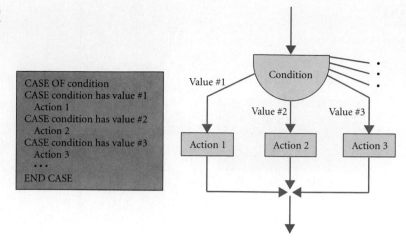

```
CASE OF condition
CASE condition has value #1
    Action 1
CASE condition has value #2
    Action 2
CASE condition has value #3
    Action 3
    • • •
END CASE
```

For example:

```
CASE OF Customer-state
CASE Customer-state = "New Jersey"
   Set Sales-tax to 0.0725
CASE Customer-state = "New York"
   Set Sales-tax to .0825
CASE Customer-state = "New Hampshire"
   Set Sales-tax to 0
END CASE
```

Note the following:

- The data entities referred to in the constructs must be defined in the data dictionary. They will be data flows, or their components, or records of data stores. Data items which are local to a process, as is *Order-total* in the process *Evaluate customer credit* described next, do not have to be entered in the dictionary.

- The scope of a construct is shown by indentation (ENDs are sometimes omitted).

As we said, an "action" in any of these structures may be any other structure. Thus, by nesting these structures within one another, we can express the needed process logic. On the next page you can see the specification of a process from the DFD shown in Figure 15.10, which employs all of the above structures (and where some ENDs are skipped for readability). It may be noted that while the structured English could be considered rather clumsy, it is eminently readable to end users.

Quite frequently, a process specification requires that a complex decision, based on several factors, be specified. In those cases, a decision table or decision tree may be employed, as we will show in the next section.

```
1.2 Evaluate customer credit
Obtain Customer-credit-rating
CASE OF Customer-credit-rating
CASE Customer-credit-rating = 1
    Mark Order-for-known-customer as Valid-order
    Indicate "Credit granted" on Valid-order
CASE Customer-credit-rating = 2
    Read Outstanding-amount-payable from Customer-file
    Read Credit-limit from Customer-file
    Set Order-total to 0
    DO WHILE there are more Order-items
        Add Item-amount to Order-total
    Mark Order-for-known-customer as Valid-order
    IF Outstanding-amount-payable + Order-total < Credit-limit
        Mark "Credit granted" on Valid-order
    ELSE
        Mark "COD payment" on Valid-order
CASE Customer-credit-rating = 3
    Mark Order-for-known-customer as Order-with-deficient-credit
END CASE
```

Description of Complex Decisions in Processes: Decision Tables and Trees

Decision tables and decision trees help us consider all the possible actions that need be taken under a given set of circumstances in a complete and unambiguous fashion.

A **decision table** specifies in tabular form the actions to be carried out when given conditions exist. A decision table has the general format specified in Figure 15.15.

To design a decision table:

1. Specify the name of the table as its heading, and insert a reference to it at the place in the process description where the table applies.

2. List all possible conditions in the condition stub.

3. List all possible actions in the action stub.

4. Fill in the condition entries by marking the presence (Y) or absence (N) of the conditions. The number of rules, that is, entries in the right-hand side of the table, equals the number of possible combinations of conditions. Thus, two conditions may have up to four rules, three conditions up to eight, etc. Impossible or unneeded conditions may be eliminated. Indeed, the use of decision tables frequently helps simplify complex logic by identifying irrelevant conditions.

Figure 15.15

*General format of
decision tables*

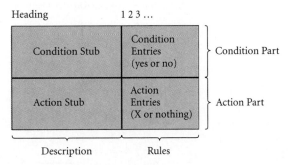

5. For every condition entry, mark with an X an action entry opposite the action(s) to be taken under these circumstances.

Let us apply these rules to the following example:

To compute an employee's weekly pay, apply the standard hourly rate for 40 or fewer hours worked on weekdays. Apply overtime rates to the weekend work and work beyond 40 hours on weekdays. Print out the names of employees who only worked at overtime rates (i.e., on weekends).

The table in Figure 15.16 results from applying the above rules. You can trace how they have been applied. If the first rule is considered impossible under our circumstances, it could be eliminated.

Decision trees present conditions as branches of a tree, going from left to right. The decision tree for the same sample problem is shown in Figure 15.17. As you can see, no action needs to be taken if an employee did no work during a particular week.

Decision trees are easier to read than are decision tables, but the greater the number of conditions, the more tedious they are to draw up. Also, decision tables are better for checking the completeness of the policy represented.

Figure 15.16

Decision table for Weekly Pay

Weekly Pay

	1	2	3	4
1. Worked Weekdays up to 40 Hrs	N	N	Y	Y
2. Worked During Overtime Periods	N	Y	N	Y
1. Compute Pay at Standard Rate			X	X
2. Compute Pay at Overtime Rate		X		X
3. Compute Total Pay				X
4. Print Out Employee's Name		X		

Figure 15.17

Decision tree for Weekly Pay

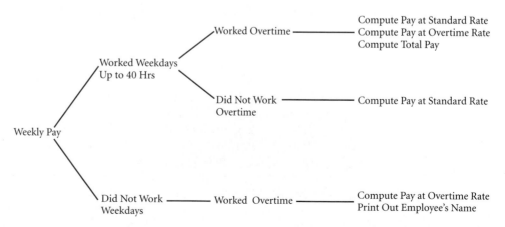

Data Dictionaries and the Description of Data

All the descriptions of the DFD entities are entered into the data dictionary of the project. In particular, data are the crucial ingredient of information systems. We need to plan what data and what relationships among data are stored in an organization's databases. To be able to do this, we need to store and manage a description of the data in addition to the data values. The principal vehicle for managing data is the data dictionary. We know from Chapter 6 that a data dictionary plays a crucial role in data administration and in database administration.

It is the data dictionary of our project that will explain to the user reading a data flow diagram what the analyst means by *Picking-label* or by *Unfilled-orders.* The composition of each data store and data flow appearing in the DFDs must be described in the dictionary. Generally, both data flows and the records in data stores are data structures; that is, they are composed of more elementary data entities.

Let us take the *Valid-order* data flow that appears in the DFD shown in Figure 15.9. This data flow would be described in the data dictionary as follows:

```
Valid-order = Order-number
            + Customer-data
            + {Product-data}
            + (Comment)
```

The symbols used in the data dictionary permit the analyst to describe the composition of the data entities in rather simple terms. Thus, our data dictionary uses the following symbols:

= means "is composed of"

+ means "and" (this is not an arithmetical symbol here!)

{} means "several"

() means "optional"

We may, then, interpret our data dictionary description as follows. The data flow *Valid-order* consists of the *Order-number* and the *Customer-data,* several *Product-data* entries, and sometimes a *Comment.*

Some of the entities are elementary data items that are further described in the data dictionary as to their physical makeup. Thus, *Order-number* may be described as a numeric item of a particular length (say, seven digits).

Data dictionary software is available as part of DBMS packages, CASE tools, or as a stand-alone facility. As we said, data dictionaries are employed not only to store "data about data," but more broadly to store all the information about system entities that emerge during analysis (such as process descriptions) and during later development stages (such as descriptions of the system modules). This makes data dictionaries powerful tools for a systems developer. An example of a data dictionary description of an elementary data item (*Order-number*) is shown in Figure 15.18.

As we know, systems analysis concludes with the acceptance of the requirements specifications by the future system users and management. We will discuss the subsequent phases of systems development life cycle in the next chapter of the text.

Figure 15.18

A data element description in a data dictionary

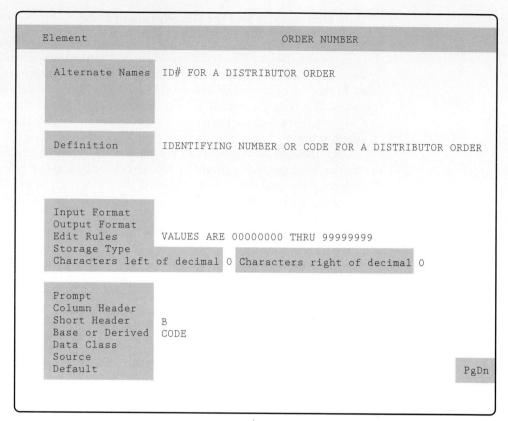

Element	ORDER NUMBER
Alternate Names	ID# FOR A DISTRIBUTOR ORDER
Definition	IDENTIFYING NUMBER OR CODE FOR A DISTRIBUTOR ORDER

```
Input Format
Output Format
Edit Rules              VALUES ARE 00000000 THRU 99999999
Storage Type
Characters left of decimal 0  Characters right of decimal 0

Prompt
Column Header
Short Header            B
Base or Derived         CODE
Data Class
Source
Default                                                      PgDn
```

SUMMARY

Information systems play a vital role in total quality management, since these systems enable most of the business processes of a contemporary organization and are the technological foundation of business process redesign. The principal software quality attributes include: effectiveness, usability, efficiency, reliability, and maintainability. To develop quality software, we need to involve end users in the development of the system that will serve their needs. We also need to organize software development with a well-defined methodology, such as systems development life cycle; we need to structure development teams, and to monitor software quality with a measurement program.

Systems development life cycle comprises the following tasks. Systems analysis delivers requirements specifications for the new system. Systems design delivers the design of programs and their modules, the design of the database, and the specifications of the hardware and systems software platform for the application to be developed. Programming delivers the fully tested, documented, and accepted application. During conversion, the new system is installed. During the postimplementation review, recommendations are made for future improvements of the system and the development methods.

The task of systems analysis is to establish in detail what the proposed application will do. As the first of the two analysis stages, the feasibility study establishes whether the proposed system is desirable from the legal, ethical, technological, economic, and organizational standpoints. The second analysis stage, requirements analysis, produces a detailed specification for the system.

The principal techniques of information gathering during systems analysis include obtaining information from the end users, deriving requirements from the existing systems and from the analysis of the business area to be affected by the new system, and experimenting with the system under development by prototyping.

Data flow diagrams (DFD) show the flow and transformation of data in the system. They rely on only four symbols: process, data flow, data store, and external entity. The initial DFD, called context diagram, shows only the flows of data into the system from external entities and the flows from the system to these entities. The more detailed DFDs are obtained by gradual refinement of the context diagram with the technique known as leveling.

The elementary processes shown in DFDs are further described in structured English, a form of pseudocode. Complex decisions in processes may be graphically described with decision tables or decision trees that illustrate what actions are taken under all possible conditions. All the descriptions of data and processes are entered into the data dictionary of the project.

KEY TERMS

Total quality management (TQM)   *546*
ISO (International Standards Organization)
   9000 standards   *546*
Usability   *548*
Portability   *548*
Joint Application Development (JAD)   *548*
Process maturity levels in software
   development   *549*
Software metrics   *549*
Systems analysis   *553*
Feasibility study   *553*
Requirements specifications   *555*
Interviewing   *556*
Questionnaires   *557*
Document analysis   *557*
Structured systems analysis   *558*

Data flow diagram (DFD)   *558*
Process (in a DFD)   *558*
Data flow   *559*
Data store   *559*
External entity   *559*
Context diagram   *560*
Leveling a DFD   *562*
Balancing rule   *562*
Data dictionary   *563*
Structured English   *563*
Pseudocode   *563*
Sequence, loop, and decision
   in programming   *564-5*
Decision table   *567*
Decision tree   *568*

QUESTIONS

1. Why are quality information systems vital to total quality management (TQM)?

2. What are the attributes of software quality? What quality attributes make software maintainable?

3. What is Joint Application Development (JAD)? How does it relate to achieving software quality?

4. What are software metrics? How do they relate to software quality?

5. What are the organizational advantages of developing information systems using the systems development life cycle (SDLC)? What are the drawbacks of SDLC?

6. What are the stages of SDLC and what are the principal deliverables of each stage?

7. What are the objectives of systems analysis? What are the principal differences between the two stages of systems analysis?

8. What are the five aspects of a feasibility study? What issues does each of them address?

9. What are the requirements specifications for an information system?

10. What are the four principal techniques of gathering information during systems analysis?

11. Compare and contrast interviewing and the use of a questionnaire as a source of information during systems analysis. How would you go about gathering information from sales representatives working in the field? What role can the Internet and intranets play in the application of each technique?

12. What is the principal tool of structured systems analysis? What are the symbols used in structured analysis and what do they stand for?

13. Classify these as DFD components in a business firm's analysis:
    a. *Salary*
    b. *Determine payback period*
    c. *Prospect-records*
    d. *Social Security Administration*

14. What is a context diagram? What does it show? How does it relate to the systems approach we discussed in Chapter 2?

15. What is accomplished by leveling a data flow diagram? Will all DFDs have the same number of levels? Why or why not?

16. What are the basic logic constructs? Give an example of each construct and provide comments.

17. What is the relationship between structured English and decision tables (or trees)?

18. What is the data dictionary of the project? What information is stored there?

ISSUES FOR DISCUSSION

1. Consider the attributes of software quality. Discuss the results of an applications software *not* having each of these attributes, one by one.

2. Discuss how an organization can improve its software development process stage by stage, based on the software maturity levels.

3. Discuss the differences between data flow diagrams (DFDs) and system charts, introduced in Chapter 9. What are the advantages of DFDs as an analysis tool?

4. Do you believe that software quality can be an ethical issue? If so, why? Who bears the responsibility?

PROBLEM-SOLVING EXERCISES

1. Incorporate a backorder function into the Order Processing System discussed in this chapter. In order to do so, you will need to modify the data flow diagrams shown in Figures 15.8 and 15.9.

   Assume that the system ought to order a preestablished quantity of a product as soon as the current inventory level falls below a certain (also preestablished) threshold quantity. Products are ordered from one of several distributors that your firm deals with. State any assumptions you need to make.

   (*Hint:* Make all the necessary modifications to the context diagram and then modify the level-0 diagram accordingly. Check whether the two diagrams balance and modify the context diagram again, if necessary.)

2. Develop a context diagram and a level-0 DFD for an on-line Accounts Receivable (A/R) System. If you have access to a CASE tool, you may use it to solve this problem.

   The A/R System maintains the records of all invoices you have sent to customers, both those that have been paid and those that remain to be paid. The system receives two principal inputs: invoices from the Order Processing System (such as the one discussed in this chapter) and receipt records from a Payment Acceptance System. The A/R System sends monthly statements to customers. A statement lists all the invoices that were outstanding at the beginning of the month, all the payments that were received against these invoices during the month, and all invoices sent out during the month at the close of which the statement is rendered.

   The system maintains an Accounts-receivable master file, which contains records of all the transactions for each customer (identified by account number); that is, records of invoices sent and payments received. The system also has access to the Customer-file maintained by the Order Processing System, where all the particulars about the customer are specified. When an invoice is paid, its record is transferred to the Paid-invoices file (but make sure it shows on the proper monthly statement!).

3. Customers often query us on the total amount they owe. Present a structured English specification for the process that determines the total amount the customer owes the company in the following fashion:

   Produce the total amount of all outstanding invoices for a specified customer, considering the following adjustments. Customers who have done business with our company for five or more years receive a 5 percent discount on the total amount of the purchase; those of two to five years standing receive a 2 percent discount. No discount is offered if there is an invoice more than 30 days old. All customers pay 15 percent interest on any amount outstanding over 30 days.

4. Represent the following Sales Personnel Pay policy in a decision table and a decision tree:

   The salespeople are paid monthly. The pay consists of the individual's salary and a commission. If a salesperson sells more than $50,000 worth of goods, he or she receives a commission of 5 percent of the sales amount. A salesperson who has been with the firm for more than two years and sells less than $50,000 worth of goods a month receives a commission of 3 percent. On the other hand, a salesperson who has been with the firm for two years or less receives an additional bonus of 2 percent on any amount sold over $50,000. The total monthly pay needs to be determined.

   Compare how easy it is to produce and to understand the two documents and state your conclusions.

TEAM PROJECT

Using a CASE tool, if available, each two- or three-person team will produce a feasibility study, the context diagram, and a level-0 DFD for a selected information system of a limited scope. The team will select and use the tools of requirements analysis most appropriate for the project. The project report will include the description of the techniques employed for information gathering, along with sample documents together with the context and data flow diagrams.

SELECTED REFERENCES

"Achieving Software Quality." Special Issue, *CIO,* February 15, 1995.

Bordoloi, Bijoy; Kathleen Mykytyn; and Peter Mykytyn, Jr. "A Framework to Limit Systems Developers' Legal Liabilities." *Journal of Management Information Systems,* 12, no. 4, (Spring 1996), pp. 161–186.

Davis, Gordon B. "Strategies for Information Requirements Determination." *IBM Systems Journal,* 21, no. 1, (January 1982), pp. 4–30.

Fox, Christopher, and William Frakes, eds. "The Quality Approach: Is It Delivering?" *Communications of the ACM,* 40, no. 6, (June 1997), pp. 24–61.

Several papers illustrate how the practice of quality oriented software development leads to business results.

Grady, Robert B. *Practical Software Metrics for Project Management and Process Improvement.* Englewood Cliffs, NJ: Prentice-Hall, 1992.

Humphrey, Watts S. *Managing The Software Process.* Reading, MA: Addison-Wesley, 1990.

Humphrey, Watts S. *A Discipline for Software Engineering.* Reading, MA: Addison-Wesley, 1995.

Hutchings, Anthony, ed. "Software Process and Quality." Special Issue, *Digital Technical Journal,* 5, no. 4, (Fall 1993), pp. 6–80.

Several articles describing how to build quality into the software development process.

Kan, S.H., V.R. Basili; and L.N. Shapiro. "Software Quality: An Overview from the Perspective of Total Quality Management." *IBM Systems Journal,* 33, no. 1, 1994, pp. 4–19.

Kendall, Kenneth E., and Julie E. Kendall. *Systems Analysis and Design,* 3rd ed. Englewood Cliffs, NJ: Prentice-Hall, 1995.

A thorough textbook.

Kettelhut, Michael C. "JAD Methodology and Group Dynamics: Improving Group Decision Making." *Information Systems Management,* (Winter 1993), pp. 46–53.

Kitchenham, Barbara, and Shari L. Pfleeger, eds. "Software Quality: The Elusive Target." *IEEE Software,* 13, no. 1, (January 1996), pp. 12–71.

Several articles describing the avenues to quality software and the business value derived from achieving this quality.

Lucas, Henry C., Jr.; Donald J. Berndt; and Greg Truman. "A Reengineering Framework for Evaluating a Financial Imaging System." *Communications of the ACM,* 39, no. 5, (May 1996), pp. 86–96.

How to use DFDs to assess the extent and benefits of a business process redesign.

Siddiqi, Jawed, and M. Chandra Shekaran, eds. "Requirements Engineering: The Emerging Wisdom." *IEEE Software,* 13, no. 2, (March 1996), pp. 15–64.

A collection of several articles describing the state of the art in systems analysis.

Tingey, Michael O. *Comparing ISO 9000, Malcolm Baldrige, and the SEI CMM for Software.* Upper Saddle River, NJ: Prentice-Hall, 1997.

Compares the three leading methodologies for assessing the quality of software development process.

Zahedi, Fatemeh. *Quality Information Systems.* Danvers: Boyd & Fraser, 1995.

An extensive textbook treatment of the subject.

Zwass, Vladimir. "Software Engineering," in *The Handbook of Computers and Computing.* Arthur R. Seidmann and Ivan Flores, eds. New York: Van Nostrand Reinhold, 1984, pp. 552–67.

CASE STUDY | # Developing a System for a Client and Its Discontents

American Student Assistance Corporation (ASA) of Boston is in the business of guaranteeing student loans. ASA belongs to a highly regulated industry, and also an industry where the spirit of public service is far stronger than business-oriented thinking. Indeed, as the firm's internal auditor, Missy Hagemeier, tells us, "this [is] the most cumbersome, complex, poorly structured industry that I have ever been involved in." ASA had always relied on others for information services, delivered until now by another firm from an IBM ES/9000 mainframe, with applications written in COBOL. As ASA's customers became increasingly unhappy with its (or, actually, its outsourcer's) information-processing capabilities and revenues began to decline, action was taken. While other firms were outsourcing their information systems services, ASA decided to insource by developing its own IS capabilities.

ASA hired the Tradewinds Information Strategies consultancy of Cambridge, Massachusetts, to redesign its business processes, based on state-of-the-art information technology. The promise was a faster, leaner enterprise, ready to pursue new business opportunities. Tradewinds, in turn, hired Marble Associates, an information systems developer, to develop a client/server system relying on the newest object-oriented development methodologies.

The project was started in the winter—and it got off to a slow start. The deadlines became completely meaningless when most members of Marble Associates' senior management team were killed in a plane crash in March. In June, ASA hired its first director of information technology, David Seisel. Now that some of the actors had disappeared from the scene and others had joined it, and as the project had no hope of meeting the June 30 deadline for implementing the first part of the system, a serious soul-searching and finger-pointing began. We can learn much from it.

First, there was a problem of mutual expectations, rooted in the culture clash between ASA and Tradewinds, whose responsibility it was to manage Marble as its subcontractor. Philip Pyburn, managing director of Tradewinds, simply found ASA too slow. He reels off a list of tasks ASA was responsible for which were not completed by the agreed-on deadlines. They include leasing a site for the development project, buying the hardware for development (done on NextStep PCs with the Sun Sparc 10 as the server), and hiring an information technology chief early in the project.

Pyburn expected that the tragic accident affecting Marble would spur ASA into fast action. But, according to Pyburn, the operational staff at ASA lacked project management skills. The habit of ASA's president, Daniel Cheever, to manage by consensus does not foster swift action. "What they think of as acting quickly seems to be measured in months rather than days or weeks," says Pyburn. "They've got a bunch of Gandhis over there when what they need is a Patton," whose generalship, Pyburn appears to believe, was required in the crisis due to the sudden deaths at Marble. There was no true owner of the project at ASA, someone who would be rewarded for success or fired for failure. Tradewinds, a hungry new consultancy, driven by business results measured in money and time, was used to customers of the same ilk.

Missy Hagemeier says that Pyburn did not evaluate the ASA environment properly, going on the assumption that the firm's executives were familiar with information processing. "He came in and [. . .] said, 'Well, all you guys do is process information.' So Phil structured his time line and his project management plan on that thinking, and that was not realistic at all." Cheever concedes that ASA has been slow at times, but Tradewinds, as the contractor, was responsible for delivering an acceptable system on time. Since Marble was the subcontractor to Tradewinds, the problems at Marble did not concern ASA.

Throughout the project, a management steering committee met regularly with Pyburn and a dedicated user group worked with Pyburn's associate Peer Neilsen. A missing element was a more frequent and direct interaction between developers and users. The development methodology adopted was evolutionary prototyping, whereby the system would be implemented through several releases. But it was not made clear to the users just what consecutive system releases would contain. Also, users were involved largely when a release was to be delivered. An unpleasant surprise emerged several months into the project, when the developers delivered a system component that was nothing like what the users had requested. The developers fixed the problem, "yet, because we hadn't seen anything and then it was so clearly wrong, it caused a feeling of consternation [among the users]," says a manager of a user area, "If you don't have it [well documented] and you don't have it to touch and feel, then you don't have a handle on it."

Pyburn blames the communication gap on the unsophistication of the future users regarding the development of large-scale applications. But he also concedes that selecting prototyping as the principal development method was probably a mistake. Since then, the project has been reorganized along the lines of systems development life cycle methodology, with some prototyping added in, and has enjoyed success with the users. Also, since Seisel came on board as the IS chief at ASA, project management has much improved. "We're more able to get the information that we need from the [developers] because he can help ask the questions the right way," one of the users tells us. Seisel has also mapped out an elaborate quality assurance procedure that, while postponing the system's use, will help prevent problems down the line.

In early August, a major project review was initiated, the code was audited, the discovered errors were removed, the documentation was worked up, and the plan for finishing the project was agreed on. This took additional time, but led to increased confidence in the project. Tradewinds, whose speciality is consulting rather than systems development, was dropped under an option written into the original contract. Indeed, the consultants did not intend to stay once ASA acquired capabilities to work directly with the developer. Marble Associates were again selected by ASA to finish the project, but the company is now responsible directly to ASA. Although the project is now four to six months late, it is largely on budget.

The future system seems to be indeed attracting business opportunities: Three New England-based loan guarantors expressed interest in handing over their loan processing to ASA. Yet, to listen to Pyburn: "If you look at it with a little bit of a gimlet eye, you'll say, 'Yeah, you've changed. But a lot of other organizations have changed a lot faster.'"

Based on Leigh Buchanan, "In for a Penny," *CIO*, November 15, 1994, pp. 44–51.

CASE STUDY QUESTIONS

1. Characterize ASA as a company prior to its embarking on the insourcing, particularly with respect to its use of information technology and the managers' familiarity with its capabilities.

2. What were the principal roots of the problems encountered during the system development project?

3. How did different cultures of ASA and its contractor Tradewinds lead to different expectations with respect to the development project?

4. Why did Pyburn conclude that systems development life cycle should have used for the project?

5. What quality assurance measures should have been implemented?

6. What lessons do you think ASA management has learned from the development project?

7. What lessons did the Tradewinds consultants learn?

CHAPTER SIXTEEN

From Design to Maintenance of Information Systems

OBJECTIVES

After you complete this chapter, you will be able to:

1. Explain the objectives of the logical and physical systems design.

2. Understand the structure chart as the principal tool of structured design.

3. Specify the objectives of programming.

4. Explain the techniques of software quality assurance.

5. State the methods of converting operations to a new system.

6. State the objectives of postimplementation review.

7. Identify the three components of software maintenance.

8. Explain the relationship between the "front-end" and the "back-end" computer-aided software engineering (CASE) tools.

9. State the main principle of object-oriented development and relate this development methodology to software reuse.

10. Explain the relationship between estimating system development effort and project scheduling.

11. State the principles of two organizational structures for software project teams.

OUTLINE

Focus Minicase. Here is a Runaway—Project That Wasn't Managed

16.1 Systems Design

16.2 Techniques and Tools of Structured Systems Design

16.3 Programming

16.4 Software Quality Assurance

16.5 Conversion

16.6 Postimplementation Review

16.7 Maintaining Information Systems

16.8 Technologies Assisting the Development of Information Systems

16.9 Management of Information Systems Projects

Case Study. Managing a Mission-Critical Information System Project Very Carefully

Here Is a Runaway—a Project that Wasn't Managed

A long time ago, in 1982 in fact, Allstate Insurance contracted Electronic Data Systems, a systems integrator, to develop a strategically important information system. Allstate hoped that by using this system it would be able to cut the development time for new types of insurance from several months to as little as a day. This would give the insurer a competitive edge in its industry. The system was estimated to cost $8 million and to take five years to develop.

Both the cost and time estimates were exceeded by more than a wide margin: The system was completed in 1993–11 years after the development started—and at a cost of some $130 million. The worst of it was that during the 11 years, the business environment changed. Having run the system for a short time in 1993, Allstate had to withdraw it from service as useless. The company is now trying to decide which parts of the system can be adapted to its current ways of doing business. Here is what an industry expert says about the way the development effort was estimated and tracked: "That Allstate project started at $8 million, but didn't get any attention until the budget hit $64 million. It was a $130 million job all along. They just didn't know when they started."

If you think these are large amounts to be lost to a runaway information system project, consider the Tax System Modernization Project of the Internal Revenue Service. Having spent $4 billion on the project so far, IRS has "basically nothing to show for it," in the harsh words of the chairman of the House of Representatives committee that approves IRS funding. According to some estimates, this failure results in the inability to collect some $50 billion annually in taxes.

Based on Robert X. Cringely, "When Disaster Strikes IS," *Forbes ASAP*, August 29, 1994, pp. 60–64; and Gary H. Anthes, "IRS Project Failures Cost Taxpayers $50 Billion Annually," *Computerworld*, October 14, 1996, pp. 1, 28.

We will proceed here to discuss the stages of the systems development life cycle that follow systems analysis. We will then describe systems maintenance that follows the development. We will also discuss the important new approaches to building information systems: computer-aided software engineering (CASE) and object-oriented development. We will conclude the chapter by describing how information system projects are managed. In the Focus Minicase for this chapter, you have read about a typical result of a project mismanagement—a runaway information system project.

16.1 | SYSTEMS DESIGN

Objectives of Systems Design

The objective of **systems design** is to produce the design specifications for the system that will satisfy the requirements defined during the systems analysis. These specifications should be detailed enough to become inputs to the programming stage that follows the design. The design process is usually broken down into two parts. Logical design produces the general specification of the resources that will make up the system. Physical design produces a complete, detailed specification of the named program components, called modules, which are to be programmed, and of the databases to be maintained by the system.

The following system aspects have to be determined and described in the appropriate documentation during the system design:

- Hardware and systems software platforms for the application.
- Programs that will constitute the application and the modules that will make up the programs.
- Specification of individual software modules.
- Design of the database.
- Design of user interfaces.
- Procedures for system use.

We will now proceed to discuss logical and physical systems design. In the next section, we will present the techniques and tools of structured design to support this design process.

Logical Design

During the **logical design,** the developers create the general specification for the information system's resources, often taking the existing system as a point of departure. Thus, the developers will devise alternative major solutions to the problem identified during the analysis phase and recommend one of these solutions for implementation.

These activities are included in logical design:

- The components of the hardware and systems software environment for the system are specified.
- System outputs and the inputs needed to produce these outputs are identified.
- The **user interface,** that is, the means whereby the user interacts with the system, is specified. Attractive interfaces have become increasingly important with the pervasive use of the graphical user interfaces (GUIs) on personal computers (Preece and others 1994). Carefully designed windows and menu trees, that is, hierarchies of menus that help select the desired activity, are furnished in the user interface (GUI).
- The logical design of the database is developed. This design was described in Chapter 6.
- The programs that will compose the system and the modules that will make up the programs are designed. A structured methodology for this major task of logical design is described in the next section.
- The procedures to be employed in operating the system are specified.
- The controls that will be incorporated in the system are specified, with information systems auditors participating in the process. Information systems controls were described in Chapter 14.

Let us consider an example. We need to design a payroll processing system for a large manufacturing enterprise with three plants. We can consider two alternatives: fully centralized payroll processing at headquarters and, on the other hand, a system that would disperse all payroll processing to the individual plants. We settle on a distributed payroll processing system that is shown in Figure 16.1. System charts, which we introduced in Section 9.1, are commonly used to show the principal physical components of a system, and their use is illustrated by the figure.

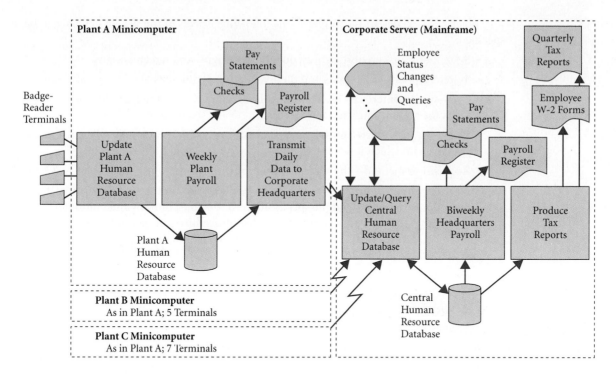

Figure 16.1

System chart of a payroll processing system—a product of logical design

The system chart shown in the figure will be accompanied by the following explanatory narrative:

1. Employee payroll data are collected as each employee inserts her or his badge into a terminal upon entry to each of the three plants. The data are entered into the human resource database at each of the plants.

2. Weekly payroll processing is done on the plant minicomputers.

3. At the end of each day, each plant minicomputer transfers the work data for all three shifts to the headquarters server (a mainframe).

4. The headquarters payroll is produced biweekly by the headquarters mainframe.

5. The headquarters server produces all the tax reporting.

6. The central human resource database, maintained at headquarters, is also used for management support systems, which are separate from the payroll system.

Individual subsystems of the payroll system may be acquired by combining several methods. Some existing systems will be modified and incorporated into the design, certain proprietary software will be purchased (for example, payroll programs are rather common), and the remaining application subsystems will be developed in-house.

Physical Design

The objective of **physical design** is to produce a complete specification of all system modules and of interfaces between them, and to perform physical design of the database (as discussed in Chapter 6). Structured design methodologies help specify module logic during this stage, as discussed in the next section.

When physical design is completed, the following aspects of the system will have to be specified:

- System outputs—report layouts, document designs, and screen designs.
- System inputs—data inputs and their validation procedures.
- User–system interface—exact protocols of user–system interaction (menu trees, icons for graphic interfaces, and so forth).
- Platforms—hardware and software platform(s) on which the system will run and the systems with which it will interface.
- Acquisition method—the way each component of the application will be acquired.
- Modular design of the programs that will be developed for the application, interfaces between the modules, and the specifications of the logic of individual modules. This means that the algorithms (strictly specified procedures for computer execution) to be implemented in the modules are selected. We will discuss this crucial aspect of systems design in the following section.
- Detailed test plan—the plan for various levels of testing to be conducted during the later stages of development and a test suite containing the sets of tests for these levels.
- Database—logical and physical designs. Needed capacities of files and databases have been estimated.
- Controls—application-specific controls, as well as the necessary general controls.
- Documentation—a full set of documentation to be delivered with the system is specified. The documentation will include the user manual, systems and operation documentation, and maintenance documentation, as needed. The documentation items produced up to this point, notably the system requirements specification and the system design documentation, will be included in the documentation package.
- Conversion plan—the plan for converting the present way of doing things to the new system, including the design of any programs that may be needed for conversion (of databases, for example).

It is crucial to sustain the processes of organizational change connected with system implementation. This includes reorganizing the affected units of the firm, redesigning the jobs of people who will be affected by the system, enhancing user motivation, and conducting user training.

We will now turn to the discussion of the techniques and tools that can be used during the structured design of the programs for the new information system.

16.2 | TECHNIQUES AND TOOLS OF STRUCTURED SYSTEMS DESIGN

Disciplined, structured design is a widely used methodology of logical systems design. The principal objective of **structured design** is to specify the structure of the programs in the system in such a way that the system will be relatively easy to program and modify.

The principal product of the logical design stage of structured design is the structure charts of the programs that need to be coded and tested. A **structure chart** specifies the modules that the program will consist of and the interfaces between them. An interface is a call by a higher-level module: It calls a lower-level module to do part of the task. An example is shown in Figure 16.2.

In the figure, you can see the structure of the principal program of the *Order Processing System* which we analyzed in Section 15.4 (suspended orders are handled by another

Figure 16.2

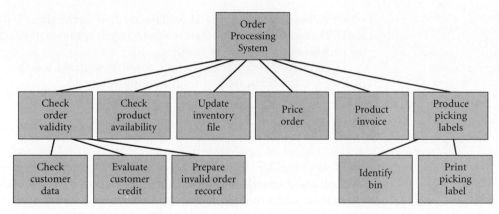

program that is run at the close of the day). Each box corresponds to a **module,** a named program routine that is handled as a unit. The main module of the program will call six others, as shown in the figure. These six modules handle different aspects of processing an order. For two of these lower-level modules, we have also shown the next-level modules which they will in turn call to perform subtasks. Thus, the *Check order validity* module calls three other modules. We can see a close relationship between the structure chart and the DFD on which the design is based.

This design method, grounded in systems theory (discussed in Section 2.2), rests on two basic principles:

1. Modular Structure

Programs must be constructed of modules—relatively short segments of code that are invoked (called) by their names during program execution. In such a call, certain data are usually passed between the two modules. For example, the module *Check order validity* needs to have the *Order* passed to it. A module ought to perform completely a well-defined function in the overall system. Many processes shown in a data flow diagram become modules in the system. A module should be short enough so that its logic is relatively easy to understand. This logic may be presented as a page of pseudocode (such as structured English). Structured design entails selecting solutions leading to modules that are relatively independent from one another and, thus, a modification of some of them during maintenance will scarcely affect other modules.

2. Hierarchical Design

Program modules are identified top-down; thus, a hierarchical program structure emerges. We start with the single top module that provides the overall control. We then break down its function into lower-level functions and so identify the modules it must call. This step-wise refinement, based on the DFDs produced during the analysis, results in a structure chart for the system. The designer thus starts with an abstract view of the program and introduces more and more detail as the lower-level modules are specified. During system maintenance, the maintainer will be able to understand the program structure by studying the structure chart and relating it to the program code.

You may think of a module hierarchy as analogous to an organizational chart, where the subunits of a larger unit handle specific tasks that add up to the task of that larger unit.

After the logical design stage, the processing steps to be carried out by individual modules are specified during the physical design stage. Specification is done in pseudocode, which we discussed in Section 15.5. Many modules derive directly from their corresponding DFD processes, and their logic is already largely specified in structured English, including perhaps decision tables or trees.

The resultant structure charts for a system's programs, together with the pseudocoded module specifications, are now ready for programming.

16.3   PROGRAMMING

At this stage of its development, the system is coded, tested, and debugged in a process called programming. **Programming** is writing instructions for computer execution and testing the written code to ensure that it performs according to specifications. The objective of programming is thus to produce reliable software based on appropriate design specifications. At this point, programmers take over from system analysts or designers, unless programmer/analysts have been developing the project and hence will continue it.

To be more specific, programming tasks include:

- Coding the software module specifications produced during system design into statements in a programming language. The programmers will be working from the pseudocode and other documentation produced before.

- Testing at several levels, beginning with testing individual modules as they are programmed and culminating in acceptance or installation testing before the system is placed into operation. Problems discovered during testing are tracked down to their source in the code and removed through a process known as **debugging.** Program testing is a principal component of software quality assurance which we discuss in the next section.

As we discussed in Chapter 5, most applications programming is performed today in a higher-level language, or a nonprocedural, fourth-generation language (4GL). The 4GL approach exploits the fact that hardware resources are inexpensive relative to programmers' time. However, more complex systems do not lend themselves to the 4GL approach.

To ensure quality of the product, the discipline of **structured programming** is essential. Structured programming relies on a small number of programming structures, introduced in Figures 15.11 through 15.14, for organizing the logic of the program. This makes the program code relatively easy to understand, test, and modify. In addition to using these structures, good programming practices demand that the code be laid out in a readable fashion and thoroughly commented on.

16.4   SOFTWARE QUALITY ASSURANCE

We have introduced you in the first section of this part of the text to the issues of software quality. **Software quality assurance** includes a variety of techniques aimed at producing a software product that satisfies user requirements and organizational objectives. Let us discuss how quality assurance is performed during the development process.

Importance of Early Error Detection

The use of a disciplined system development methodology, such as structured development—preferably supported by CASE tools—is in itself a crucial measure for producing quality software. When using such a methodology, early detection of errors is the basis of cost-effective software quality assurance. The severity of errors varies. The following vignette provides one classification.

The Consequences of Software Errors

Software errors (which some prefer to call, rather softly, bugs) may result in a mild displeasure or in a catastrophe. Table 16.1 gives you one classification of the consequences of software errors.

While we may quibble about the adjectives used in the classification, we can clearly see the range of the outcomes of software errors. To prevent some of the more dire consequences, the team that produces shuttle-control software at NASA carefully documents and records in a database every error made while developing the software. The objective is to not only get rid of the errors, but to study them and to remove their source. Thanks to the development methodology adopted at NASA, in each of the last three versions of this software, some 420,000 lines long, just one error was discovered.

Based on Boris Beizer, *Software Testing Techniques*, New York: Van Nostrand Reinhold, 1983, pp. 15–16, and Charles Fishman, "They Write the Right Stuff," *Fast Company*, December–January 1997, pp. 95–106.

Table 16.1

Possible consequences of software errors

1.	Mild	An esthetic offense, such as a misspelled output or misaligned report.
2.	Moderate	Misleading or redundant output; somewhat degraded system performance.
3.	Annoying	The system's behavior is dehumanizing: truncated names; bills for $0.00 sent; users must trick the system into proper response.
4.	Disturbing	The system refuses to handle legitimate transactions (your credit card is not accepted at the bookstore).
5.	Serious	System loses transactions and there is no record that they ever occurred.
6.	Very serious	The system executes a wrong transaction (your deposit becomes a withdrawal).
7.	Extreme	Problems 4 to 6 occur frequently and arbitrarily.
8.	Intolerable	An unrecoverable corruption of the database occurs and is not apparent.
9.	Catastrophic	The system fails and cannot be operated.
10.	Infectious	The software system corrupts other systems, such as the physical environment or radiation treatment equipment; a system that kills.

Early detection of errors is necessary. Let us study Figure 16.3, based on actual experience with a large number of software systems (Boehm 1981). Note the rapidly increasing numbers on the vertical axis. Early errors that are not detected right after they are made are expensive to correct later. The figure shows that an error made during the early system development stage—requirements analysis—will cost perhaps 100 times more to fix if it is discovered during system operation rather than during the analysis stage itself! Indeed, if there are major errors committed during systems analysis, the software may be entirely useless. It "works," but it does not do what is required.

The principal means of software quality assurance in the early development stages are walkthroughs and inspections. These quality assurance techniques retain their importance

Figure 16.3

Dramatic increase in the cost to fix an error as a system development progresses

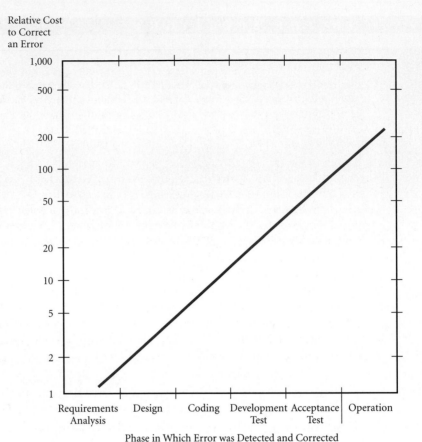

Relative Cost
to Correct
an Error

Phase in Which Error was Detected and Corrected

in the programming stage, but the essential means of quality assurance when the program code is available is software testing.

Walkthroughs and Inspections

A **walkthrough** is a review by a small group of people of a system development product presented by its author. Walkthroughs should be scheduled frequently during systems development so that a manageable piece of work—such as a data flow diagram, a structure chart, or code listing—can be thoroughly reviewed in one to two hours. Walkthroughs thus include:

- Specification walkthroughs, where the group looks for errors, omissions, and ambiguities in the data flow diagrams at various levels, in the data dictionary entries, and in other components of requirements specifications.

- Design walkthroughs, where structure charts and the pseudocode of individual modules are inspected.

- Code walkthroughs, where program listings are studied.

- Test walkthroughs, to ensure that the test cases are prepared thoroughly for all the testing levels we will discuss further on.

Who participates in the walkthrough? That depends on what is being "walked." Thus, for example, during a specification walkthrough, users, analysts, a systems designer, and perhaps an invited expert (such as an auditor) may participate, since all of them will be able to make a contribution.

A walkthrough is scheduled in advance, so that all participants can come prepared, after studying the work the author will "walk" them through. The walkthrough is generally conducted by a coordinator, who mediates any conflicts that might arise and who maintains a collegial spirit. The purpose is not to put the author on the spot; rather, everyone should understand that finding inadequacies in the "walked" product is in the common interest. To further this attitude, no error correction is performed during the walkthrough.

It is crucial for the effectiveness of walkthroughs that they be established as a quality assurance tool as opposed to a management tool for evaluating the performance of IS professionals. When regular walkthroughs are conducted, the intellectual integrity and uniformity of style of the ultimate product can be maintained. Since all the participants become familiar with the work of other developers, fewer problems will emerge if one of them leaves the project in midstream.

An **inspection** is similar to a walkthrough in its objectives, but it is a more formal review technique. In an inspection, a review team checks a data flow diagram or a program against a prepared list of concerns. At the heart of code inspection is the paraphrasing technique: An inspector verbally expresses the meaning of one or more lines of code at a time, with other participants striving to detect errors in this code. Inspections also include formal rework and follow-up stages to see that the discovered errors were corrected.

Testing

In **testing,** system components, and later the entire system, are run for the purpose of finding errors, which are then removed by debugging—locating the source of the errors and correcting them. As soon as programming begins, the resulting code should be tested. As we have pointed out, testing plans are drawn up in the earlier development stages. To achieve a desired level of confidence in a software system, a variety of tests are performed. Testing levels are summarized in Figure 16.4.

Figure 16.4

Software quality assurance: testing levels

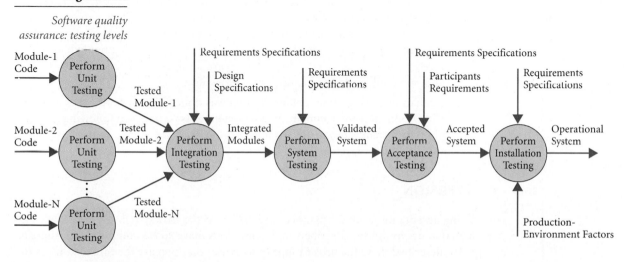

Before we discuss these tests in detail, let us specify the general principles of testing:

- A test plan must be prepared to specify the sequence in which the modules will be coded, individually tested, and then integrated into the program.

- Test cases must be prepared as part of the plan. Each test case should include a specification of the data to be submitted as inputs, as well as—and this is crucial!—a specification of the expected results of the test.

- All test results should be studied and recorded.

- Test cases should be prepared for both valid and invalid input conditions. We expect the program not to fail when improper input is submitted.

- Software tools are available to support testing and debugging; their use significantly increases the effectiveness of the process.

The following are the principal levels of software testing:

1. **Module (Unit) Testing.** After a module has been coded, the code is thoroughly reviewed and then tested with predesigned test cases.

2. **Integration Testing.** After individual modules are coded and unit-tested, they are integrated into the overall program. Generally, one module at a time is added to the structure (such as that shown with the structure chart in Figure 16.2) and the resulting partial product is tested.

3. **System Testing.** Now that all the system's programs have been tested, the functioning of the system and its performance are tested next. The system is validated against its functional specifications, in an environment and under loads that resemble the actual operation as closely as possible. The system is subjected to stress loads to see whether it degrades gracefully. We establish the system's compatibility with other systems it will have to interact with. Controls and recovery procedures are also tested. It is very important to test the documentation that will accompany the system along with the system itself.

    Sometimes, a **beta test** of software is performed (particularly by software vendors). Early copies of software are offered to end users in order to uncover problems in actual use. The name of beta testing indicates that it follows a thorough testing by the developers, considered an alpha test.

4. **Acceptance Testing.** Before the system is "placed into production," all parties—users, developers, future maintainers, management, and auditors—must perform a set of system tests to ensure that their requirements have been satisfied. A suite of tests validating the overall system operation is identified, documented, and preserved for maintenance purposes. These **regression tests** will be used to revalidate the system following each maintenance procedure.

5. **Installation Testing.** If acceptance testing was done before a system was installed in its production environment, a set of system tests is run again following installation. The system is now ready for operation; indeed, we need to convert our operations to the new system.

16.5 | CONVERSION

Following acceptance testing, a planned **conversion** to the new system is performed. The implementation measures, described in Section 13.8, have to be completed during this stage. We described there the broad range of activities that prepare the intended users for

Figure 16.5

Conversion methods

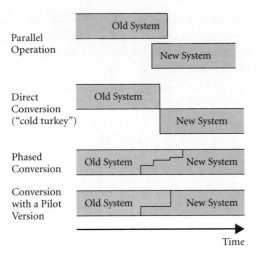

work with the new system and for "owning" it. Conversion is done close to the completion of these activities. The four common conversion methods are illustrated in Figure 16.5.

The **parallel operation** method is the safest: The old and the new systems run simultaneously until sufficient confidence is gained in the new system. Of course, the method can be used only if there is an "old" system in place; it is also expensive to run both systems. In the event that the new business processes and thus the new system significantly depart from the old, it is impossible to do the conversion this way. As opposed to parallel operation, **direct conversion** is the most risky (and thus potentially the most expensive). At a certain point, the old system is completely replaced by the new one.

The two other methods involve gradual conversion and are a compromise between the first two extremes. During a **phased conversion,** the new system is introduced in incremental stages, which are divided by function, organizational units served, the hardware on which the new system will reside, or some other factor. The **pilot version** method relies on introducing a part of the system into one carefully designated organizational area, learning from this experience, and then introducing the complete system.

After full conversion to the new system has been completed, the system becomes operational. However, we still need to make sure that it has been successfully implemented.

16.6   POSTIMPLEMENTATION REVIEW

The final phase of the development life cycle is actually conducted during systems operations. Its objective is to assess both the system and the development methodology, and it is a vital aspect of organizational learning. This stage is called the **postimplementation review.** This review should take place after the system has been used for several months to allow for the "burn-in" period.

A properly conducted review pursues several objectives:

- The organizational impact of the system is studied and further effort is made to ensure successful implementation (unless the system is recognized to be an outright failure which, unfortunately does happen). The review may trigger adjustments in organizational structure, business processes, and job designs.

- A major system development project should be a source of organizational learning: We want to improve future system implementations based on the experience (Stein and Vandenbosch 1996). Systems development methodology may be modified in the future in light of these results.

- The system's performance and controls are evaluated, with the IS auditors participating. Requests for maintenance frequently follow this evaluation.

If properly conducted, with the results analyzed and disseminated throughout the organization and stored in an accessible repository, postimplementation reviews can be an important component of organizational learning, leading to improved performance on future projects (Collier 1996).

During the system's operational life, it will certainly need maintenance. Let us now turn to this lengthy stage of the overall system life cycle.

16.7   MAINTAINING INFORMATION SYSTEMS

What Is Involved in the Maintenance of Information Systems?

Operational information systems must be maintained. **Maintenance** is the process of modifying an information system to continually satisfy organizational and user requirements. There is a vast difference between hardware and software maintenance in costs as well as in objectives. The purpose of maintaining computer system hardware is to keep the equipment in working order without changing its functionality. Traditionally, this aspect of system maintenance has been covered by maintenance contracts with equipment manufacturers.

Figure 16.6

Software maintenance dominates life-cycle costs of software (From James Martin and Carma McClure, *Software Maintenance: The Problem and its Solutions*, © 1983, p. 7. Reprinted by permission of Prentice Hall, Inc., Englewood Cliffs, NJ.)

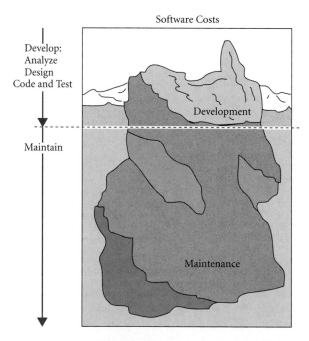

What Has to Be Maintained—a Few Figures

The worldwide investment in existing software is estimated at over $2 trillion. There are 80 to 100 billion lines of (just!) COBOL code being maintained today across the world. It is estimated that $30 billion is spent worldwide on maintenance, one-third of that amount in the United States alone. According to other estimates, the worldwide software spending in the year 2000 will be close to $600 billion, much of it stemming from maintenance.

The average age of a business system in the United States is 6 1/2 years, with some 25 percent more than 10 years old. The average Fortune 100 company maintains 35 million lines of code and adds 3.5 million more lines a year just as maintenance, without including newly developed systems.

Based on Kathleen Melymuka, "Managing Maintenance: The 4,000-Pound Gorilla," *CIO,* March 1991, pp. 74–82; and Hossein Saledian, "An Invitation to Formal Methods," *Computer* 29, no. 4, April 1996, pp. 7–14.

The principal effort in system maintenance is directed at maintaining the applications software. Software maintenance includes all modifications of a software product after it has been turned over to operations. The cost of this maintenance over the useful life of an application is typically twice the development cost. The preeminent costs of maintenance are graphically illustrated in Figure 16.6, while the vignette above will give you a more precise idea about the extent of software maintenance.

The perception of maintenance as the repair or replacement of defective parts applies only in part to software maintenance. The principal objective of software maintenance follows from the very objective of having software: to provide flexible systems in the face of changing needs. But there are other, less cheerful, reasons for the high costs of maintenance.

Software maintenance actually consists of three types of activities:

1. *Perfective* Maintenance. Enhancing and modifying the system to respond to changing user requirements and organizational needs, improving system efficiency, and enhancing documentation.

2. *Adaptive* Maintenance. Changing the application to adapt it to a new hardware or software environment. Adaptive maintenance may involve, for example, moving an application from a mainframe to a client/server environment, or converting it from a file to a database environment.

3. *Corrective* Maintenance. Correcting an error discovered during operations.

Figure 16.7 illustrates the distribution of effort that goes into these three maintenance components (Lientz and Swanson 1978). It must be stressed that classification of a maintenance activity is not always easy. In particular, if the maintainers and developers are the same people, there is a strong tendency to disguise correcting an error made during systems analysis by classifying its fixing as perfective maintenance.

Even if, as Figure 16.7 shows, most of the maintenance resources are expended on improving the system rather than correcting its imperfections or adapting it to new environments, the total maintenance expenditures are nevertheless very high. For example, recent efforts to fix the "year 2000 problem"; that is, to modify the existing software written for two-digit years (e.g., 78 or 79) to work correctly once year 2000 comes, are estimated to cost over $70 billion (Jones 1997).

Figure 16.7

Distribution of effort in software maintenance

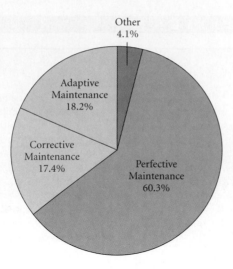

The Dynamics of Software Maintenance

A **software maintenance** procedure consists of three steps:

1. We need to *understand* the software to be modified and identify the parts targeted for maintenance. This often proves the most difficult task.

2. We must then *modify* the appropriate components of the application system without adversely affecting the rest of the system.

3. Finally, we must *test* and thus validate the modified components, as well as the entire system. During the system testing following the modification, we use the regression tests we described in Section 16.4.

If we look back at Figure 15.1, we will see that software maintainability is one of the principal qualities we seek when we develop a software system. We can also see there that maintainability has three aspects (understandability, modifiability, and testability) that correlate directly with the three maintenance steps. As we stressed earlier, a primary objective of the development process should be to develop software that is easy to maintain.

The high costs of software maintenance today are in large part due to the need to maintain the so-called legacy systems that underpin information processing in many organizations. Some of these, although certainly not all, were developed without the use of proper development methodologies and are poorly documented. Such systems are difficult to understand. Because such a system lacks proper modular structure and contains unstructured code, it is difficult to modify one part of it without affecting others. As a consequence, it is difficult to devise an appropriate sequence of tests to validate the modified system. As we will see in the next section, the use of computer-aided software engineering (CASE) tools can contribute to better maintenance.

Maintenance costs are frequently increased by low morale on the part of the maintainers, with resultant low productivity. This is a consequence of the lower status accorded by many organizations to maintenance work as compared to development. Most systems analysts are trained to develop new systems rather than to maintain existing ones. Yet system maintenance can be a rewarding experience, thanks to the close working relationship that can develop between the users and the people who maintain their information systems. The

IN THE SPOTLIGHT

Establishing a Software Reuse Program

Motorola has recognized that reusing previously developed software can lead to increased productivity and higher quality since the already deployed software has been extensively tested. As a part of the company-wide software reuse program, a pilot reuse initiative has been introduced at Motorola Israel. An important component of the initiative is an incentive program bearing cash rewards.

To encourage the developers to share their software components, the program awards $100 for each approved item added to the library of reusable software. Each time a software component is retrieved from the library for reuse, an additional award, proportional to the resulting savings, is given. The developer receives 40 percent of the award and the reuser receives 60 percent. A schedule of rewards has been established, tying them to the resulting savings. For example, savings in the range of $250 to $500 result in the award to the in-

volved developers of up to $60. When the savings go up into the $2,501 to $50,000 range, the maximum bonus is $2,500. In just one example, the reuse of a software set saved the company an estimated $15,000 and resulted in an $847 bonus to the three software engineers involved in the project. The savings are calculated by a software project manager, based on the staff–months saved.

The support of top management, combined with the incentives, has been responsible for the success of the reuse program, which has already more than paid for itself. The Motorola Israel facility has been designated as the premier example of software reuse in Motorola. It shares both its reuse experience and reusable components with other company's facilities throughout the world.

Based on Rebecca Joos, "Software Reuse at Motorola," *IEEE Software*, September 1994, pp. 42–47.

jobs of software maintainers must be designed properly: Their responsibility for a meaningful unit of work and the factors that will signify their success should be clearly defined. To enhance their professionalism, Frito-Lay of Dallas holds annual symposia for its software maintainers, where workshops covering the developments in the field are conducted. The symposia have resulted in establishment of a task force that facilitates sharing ideas, techniques, and tools among maintenance groups in various functional areas of the company. And the work of the task force has, in turn, resulted in changes in the corporate software maintenance procedures, and in increased efficiency of maintenance.

16.8 | TECHNOLOGIES ASSISTING THE DEVELOPMENT OF INFORMATION SYSTEMS

Two relatively new technologies offer particular promise to raise the productivity of information systems development and enhance the quality of the resulting product. Computer-aided software engineering (CASE) technology offers development tools that automate important aspects of the software development process. The other technology, object-oriented development (OOD), is a software development methodology that offers the all-important possibility of large-scale software reuse: an ability to build up a collection of basic software components from which larger and larger systems may be constructed, just as it is done in hardware manufacturing (Williamson 1997). Several leading companies have recognized that software reuse can lead to significant savings and they are doing something about it, as the vignette above illustrates.

The two technologies—CASE and OOD—are in many respects complementary. For example, many CASE tools have been built using the OOD methodology, just as CASE tools are available to support the building of applications with the use of OOD methodology. A warning is in order—both technologies are complex and require a significant investment of training and experience.

Computer-Aided Software Engineering (CASE)

For a long time software developers had been in the proverbial role of the shoemaker's barefoot children. While they supported the knowledge work of others with their software, their own work had to rely on methodologies supported by only rudimentary tools. Finally, in the mid-1980s, computer-aided software engineering (CASE) began to come into its own. An analogy can be drawn between this technology and the computer-aided design (CAD) systems used in hardware engineering.

Computer-aided software engineering (CASE) tools assist software developers in planning, analyzing, designing, programming, and maintaining information systems. The principal advantage of a CASE tool is that it offers an integrated package of capabilities for several of these tasks. Ideally, we might imagine a developer producing a set of data flow diagrams with a supporting data dictionary using a CASE system; the system would then generate the program code automatically. Though integrated CASE tools of limited capabilities have begun to appear (such as MicroSTEP of Syscorp International of Austin, Texas), general cradle-to-grave CASE support is not yet available. In other words, executable specifications (or, if you will, fully automatic programming) are still a rather remote possibility.

The best-known CASE tools assist the developer in creating a complete set of the requirements specifications for a system, with all the data flow diagrams and with the entities defined in the data dictionary. The tool subsequently supports the development of structure charts. Alternative development methodologies (such as object-oriented development) and the design of databases are also supported. Many of these tools run on personal computers.

CASE tools combine several technologies:

- Software development methodologies, such as structured systems development.

- Fourth-generation languages (4GLs) for nonprocedural coding ("state what the computer is to do rather than how to do it" for a certain range of tasks).

- Graphical user interfaces.

The capabilities of CASE tools are illustrated in Figure 16.8. When we refer to CASE, we most often mean the **"front-end"** tools that support the earlier phases of systems development, such as analysis and design. However, CASE tools also include the **"back-end"** tools, such as the code generators—software that produces program code from a terse specification. As we said, automatic code generation from a specification produced with a "front-end CASE" is not, in general, possible at this time. As is shown in the figure, the specifications produced by a front-end CASE tool must be translated into a form acceptable to "back-end CASE" tools. The dotted line in the figure indicates that some of these specifications can be "picked up" by a back-end tool, but much of the work needs to be done by the developer.

Comprehensive CASE packages include both front-end and back-end tools. Today, front-end CASE systems are able to assist the developer in producing complete and consistent system specifications, which are then entered into the information repository offered

Figure 16.8

"Front-end" and "back-end" CASE tools

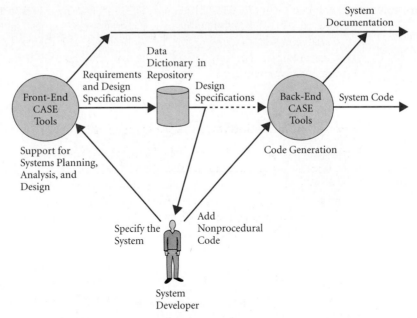

by the tool. Documentation, the preparation of which is a significant drain on resources when structured techniques are used, is generated automatically by the CASE tools.

Back-end tools may be used independently of front-end tools. The general objective of these code generators (also known as application generators and introduced to you in Section 5.5) is to generate code from the specifications of the database structure and from screen and report layouts. The programmer can often use a simple fill-in-the-blanks interface to input this information, which the generator uses to produce executable code. This code may then be refined by the programmer.

CASE tools are an excellent vehicle for rapid applications development through prototyping. They help to develop the hierarchy of menus for the user interface and specify screens and reports, all of which can be done in consultation with the users. The code generator then produces the necessary code.

Figure 16.9 summarizes the key facilities offered by CASE tools. As you can see, the focal facility of a CASE tool is the **information repository,** a central database for storing and managing project data dictionaries, which can contain all the information about the systems being developed. This information begins with the plans and goes on to the entities that appear in data flow diagrams, on to the code, and even to the project management information. We have shown how an entry is made in the data dictionary in Figure 15.18. Thanks to the complete development information available in electronic form, CASE tools facilitate traceability—the ability to relate program code to the analysis and design entities it implements.

CASE tools provide automatic assistance for checking the consistency and completeness of the products as the development goes on. The availability of this information makes it easier to introduce modifications in a consistent fashion at any time during system development or maintenance.

Indeed, the use of CASE tools can also contribute significantly to improved maintenance of information systems. In the first place, the use of CASE during the development means better documented systems, with essential documentation kept in the repository and

Figure 16.9

The key components of a CASE tool (Modified from Elliot J. Chikofsky and Burt L. Rubenstein. "CASE: Reliability Engineering for Information Systems" in *IEEE Software* 5, no. 2. March 1988. Copyright ©1988 IEEE. Reprinted by permission.)

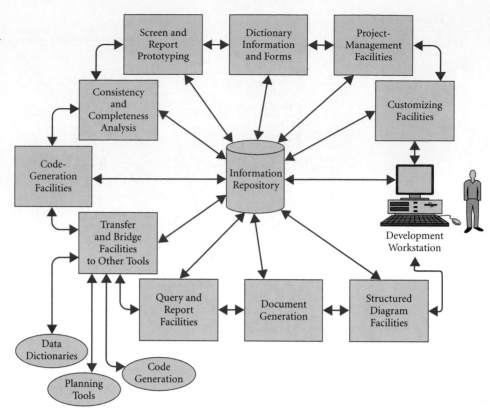

thus relatively easy to maintain. It is possible to trace a user's request for an enhancement from a data flow diagram to the code modules to be modified and thus to determine the impact of the change. Further, CASE tools make it possible to maintain system specifications as they are changed during maintenance.

Certain CASE tools are expressly designed for maintenance activities. Some of these tools have evolved from the far simpler utilities that have helped programmers to *restructure* programs. Such packages automatically recast a program from unstructured code, which is difficult to understand, into a structured format that relies on the disciplined programming constructs we presented in Section 15.5.

More elaborate CASE packages for maintenance support **reverse engineering:** developing analysis and design specifications from the program code. This approach derives from the well-known method of analyzing a competitor's product, such as a new car model. Once a design specification—for instance, a structure chart—has been produced from the program with the aid of a CASE tool, the program is far easier to maintain than if the maintainers were faced only with page upon page of the code printout.

The capability to develop software faster thanks to the use of CASE technology has been touted as one element in the formula for significantly reducing time-to-market for products and services. However, CASE is a complex technology, requiring organizational and individual learning. Quality improvements are likely to come before increases in productivity of systems development or maintenance. Indeed, some studies have found that even though the users are more satisfied with systems produced using CASE, the develop-

Table 16.2	Tool	Vendor
Selected CASE tools	Excelerator	Intersolv Cambridge, Massachusetts
	Foundation	Andersen Consulting Chicago, Illinois
	Information Engineering Facility	Texas Instruments Plano, Texas
	Information Engineering Workbench	KnowledgeWare Atlanta, Georgia
	Teamwork	Cadre Technologies Providence, Rhode Island

ment process may actually take longer (Guinan 1997). The complexity of CASE tools and the lack of integrated support for systems development have limited their adoption.

Several powerful CASE tools are listed in Table 16.2.

Today, CASE tools are often used to support system development with object-oriented methodology, which we will now discuss.

Object-Oriented Development

Object-oriented development methodology is rooted in the concepts of object-oriented programming, discussed in Section 5.6. Instead of focusing on the flow of data through the system to be developed, as is done in the structured development methodology, OOD aims to build a software model of the real-world system. This explicit modeling is done by defining and implementing classes of objects using the vocabulary of the business that will be supported by the information system.

The central principle in **object-oriented development (OOD)** is building the system as a collection of interacting objects. If program objects represent real-world objects, we obtain a rather close correspondence between the program components and their real-world equivalents. Much of the development proceeds by defining the classes of objects for the information system. Classes are templates of objects and, conversely, objects are instances of classes. The classes and objects that information systems deal with are relatively permanent in their behavior (e.g., respectively, *Customers* and *Customer for Shipment*). Therefore, code libraries can be built up, to be used as needed.

The ability to build up libraries of reusable code has long had an understandable appeal. Instead of rediscovering the wheel with each new software project, developers are able to reach for software components developed for other systems—and tested through prior use.

The following will briefly sketch out the idea of object orientation, introduced to you in Chapter 5 together with object-oriented languages. As we develop a human resource information system, we may define a class of objects called "Employee." Each object would have the general attributes that describe our employees, such as education and previous experience. We would also define operations that can be meaningfully applied to this object, say Hire, Promote, Move, Fire. We will program that object by *encapsulating* the employee attributes and operations together, as opposed to separating the data and instructions as in traditional methodologies. Computation is done by objects sending messages to other objects: A message tells an object which operation to apply to data.

The power of OOD consists in large degree in our ability to define a hierarchy of object classes of interest in the given application. Thus, in our system we can define subclasses of "Applicant," "Active Employee," and "Retired Employee." Thanks to the crucial *inheritance* feature, these subclasses inherit the properties of the more general object class "Employee" and add their own special properties. We can thus derive new classes from the existing ones. Ideally, we would assemble programs from prewritten classes and objects.

Producing reusable software components is only one of the potential benefits of the object-oriented approach. The process of systems analysis and design based on object orientation is a powerful technique for gaining understanding of a business system and casting this understanding into modifiable software components. With OOD, there is a smooth transition from analysis to design: Both of these development tasks deal with objects and classes of objects. Likewise, when a library of objects has been built up, the development of new systems is much like the maintenance of the existing systems, since both rely on reusing existing classes and objects.

OOD is especially promising for:

- Graphical user interfaces, where objects such as icons are common.

- Complex applications running on several computers, such as client/server systems, where different objects can be allocated to different processors.

- Multimedia applications, which need to support a variety of objects, such as text, voice, image, and video. This leads to the interest in object-oriented databases, introduced in Section 6.11.

As you may conclude, OOD requires a totally different thinking about information systems; this is both its promise and the difficulty of introducing it into the information systems environment. Indeed, learning difficulties are a serious barrier to the adoption of OOD (Sheetz 1997).

16.9 | MANAGEMENT OF INFORMATION SYSTEMS PROJECTS

Proper management of a large software development or maintenance project has three main aspects: estimation of the effort needed to develop the system, project planning (or scheduling), and the organization of development teams.

Estimation of System Development Effort

The effort needed to develop a system (or to perform major maintenance), from the initial planning phase through delivery, is best expressed by a snail-shaped curve showing the number of people needed to work on a project relative to its development schedule (see Figure 16.10). The area under the curve represents the total number of person–months needed to develop the system. As we can see, in general, projects start with a small number of people in the initial stages of systems analysis and design. The number then peaks during the coding and testing stage. The actual shape of the curve—that is, the staffing pattern over the

Figure 16.10

Project staffing throughout the development life cycle

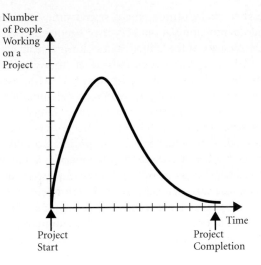

project's duration—depends on a variety of factors. Thus, incremental development, achieved by releasing initial partial versions of the system to users flattens the curve.

There are several ways to go about estimating the development time and cost for a software system. Often, estimating is done by analogy with a previously developed system. If the previous system was developed in the same environment, this rather simple technique often gives reasonable results. Yet, this is not a general method of estimating.

The time and cost necessary to develop an information system may be estimated by establishing a measure for the software product and by determining the relationship of this measure to the cost and time of software development. A frequent measure is the estimated count of lines of the code to be delivered. When combined with the knowledge that our developers deliver on the average, say, 20 instructions of fully tested code per day (when the entire development life cycle is taken into account), this measure allows us to estimate the cost and the time. The general problem with such a metric based on code is that a reliable estimate of this sort is obtainable only late in the life cycle. Yet, some companies do rely on software models based on these metrics, such as COCOMO (Boehm 1981).

An important newer method of cost estimation is the **function points** technique. This method makes it possible to estimate the required effort early in development by considering the number and complexity of the system inputs, outputs, inquiries, and files. A significant experience, databases, and software support for the technique have been accumulated. Using these, analysts determine the estimated number of function points in the system under development. This figure can be then translated into the number of lines of code, if desired. Experience indicates that one function point equals approximately 100 noncomment statements in a system to be developed (Jones 1996). As the sophistication of estimation techniques grows, efforts are made to develop methods that would establish the impact of proposed information systems on the business outcomes of a firm, such as profitability or time-to-market for the firm's products.

The measures of software product, such as lines of code or function points, are also used in software quality improvement. By driving down with each successive project the number of defects per function point or per thousands of lines of source code, we are increasing the reliability of information systems.

It is rather easy to underestimate the cost and time necessary for software development. The internal study by the National Security Agency (NSA), whose mission is to provide support for the security of the United States, shows that an average person–day of software development at the agency yields only seven to eight lines of code, at a cost of approximately $70 per line (Drake 1996). Although NSA is more exacting in its software development than an average organization, these figures are not far removed from the general experience, when the work necessary for systems analysis and design is taken into account.

Once the total development effort on the project has been estimated, a project schedule may be established. A schedule breaks the project up into stages (such as those of SDLC), which may be further broken down into lower-level activities. Major activities terminate in a milestone, which is defined in terms of completed deliverables. In the earlier development stages, a deliverable may be a development document or an operational prototype. For example, the systems analysis stage is terminated by the delivery of requirements specifications. During the later stages of systems development, the deliverables are operational subsystems or, ultimately, the complete information system.

Project Scheduling and Tracking: Use of Software Tools

There are hundreds of activities to be carried out as a project progresses. In scheduling these activities and controlling the project, software developers employ methods long established in project management, notably **PERT/CPM**.[1] To use this method, we first list the specific activities that make up the project and their estimated durations. Along with each activity, we list its immediate predecessors; that is, the activities that must be completed before any given one can be started. Using PERT/CPM, we may then answer questions such as these:

- How much total time will be needed to complete the project?
- What are the scheduled start and finish times for each activity?
- Which activities are critical and must be completed exactly as scheduled?
- How long may noncritical activities be delayed?

Let's take a simple example. For a small part of a project, we might come up with the activity list shown in Table 16.3.

Note that if activities A and B are both started at the same time, activity B is *critical:* any delay in this activity will cause the entire project to be delayed. Activity C is also critical. On the other hand, a noncritical activity, such as A, may be delayed. In our case, the maximum delay possible without adversely affecting project completion is two days for activity A: It will be then finished at the same time as activity B. This permissible delay is called *slack*.

Based on such activity lists presented as input, the software tools for project management that implement PERT/CPM may be used to answer the questions we listed. These

Table 16.3	Activity	Description	Duration(Days)	Predecessors
An activity list for a part of a software project	A	Code and test module XYZ	3	—
	B	Code and test module MNP	5	—
	C	Integrate modules XYZ and MNP	2	A, B

Figure 16.11

A PERT chart.

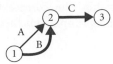

packages may also be used to display a PERT chart, such as that in Figure 16.11, which shows the precedence relationships among the activities listed and the numbered completion events (milestones). The *critical path,* which consists only of critical activities, has been highlighted. Any delay in an activity on this path will cause project delay.

Another, simpler, tool made available by project management packages is the **Gantt chart** (also known as a time chart): This is a graphical bar representation of project tasks over time. An activity's duration is shown as a black bar and its slack may be shown as a white bar; critical activities are, of course, solid black (see Figure 16.12). As we know from Section 8.6, project management is often supported by groupware.

As the project progresses, PERT and Gantt charts need to be constantly updated to identify new project bottlenecks. Recovering late projects by "throwing people at them" is limited by what is known as "Brooks's law": Adding people to a late software project will

Figure 16.12

Gantt chart produced with Timeline project management package (Courtesy of Applitech Software, Cambridge, Massachusetts.)

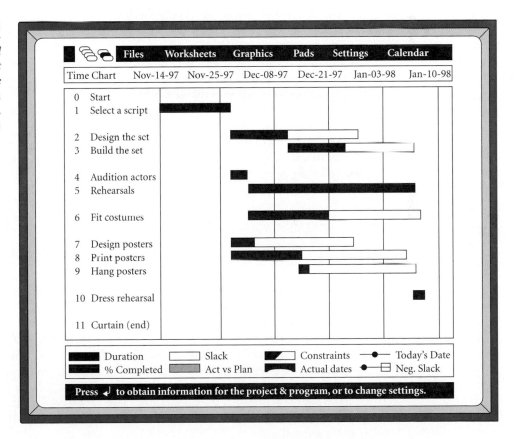

delay it further (Brooks 1995). The reason for this is the complexity of software development: The effort required to bring additional people up to date becomes greater than their potential contribution.

Software Project Teams

Most software projects, in both development and maintenance, are carried out by teams. This reflects what we already know about teams being highly effective contributors in a modern firm. Team composition varies depending on the development phase: Initially, it may include largely systems analysts, but in the end it will consist chiefly of programmers. It is generally recognized that teams should be small (no more than 10 people), since the development of a complex product such as an information system calls for intense communication among team members. Two organizational structures for a team, representing opposite extremes, are the chief programmer team and the democratic team.

The **chief programmer team** is built around an outstanding software developer, the chief programmer, who personally defines the requirements specifications and design for the system and programs the key modules. This professional is assisted by others, such as a back-up programmer of almost equal qualifications, an administrator responsible for the managerial aspects of the project, the project's software librarian responsible for the documentation and keeping current with new program versions, and by several other professionals. The team is built hierarchically, with all the members answering to the chief programmer.

On the opposite end of the spectrum is the **democratic team.** In such a structure, all the team members bear equal responsibility for the project, and the relationships between them are informal. There is much more communication among team members in a democratic team than in a chief programming team. Team members are assigned fixed roles, which may be rotated as the situation requires. Frequently, decisions are made by consensus. Because the team's operation is highly dynamic, it is vital to preserve group memory as the work on the project progresses. This role is assigned to the project librarian, who maintains all the project information in an accessible computerized form.

The chief programmer team is more applicable to a large project involving a known set of technologies. The democratic team lends itself better when new technologies are applied in smaller, exploratory projects. In practice, software project teams generally combine the features of both of these structures.

S U M M A R Y

Systems design follows systems analysis during the development life cycle of applications. The objective of the logical design is to produce the general specifications of the hardware and systems software platforms on which the application will run and the modular structure of the programs that will make up the application. During the physical design, a complete specification of all the program modules and databases is completed. As the principal tool of structured design, structure charts show graphically the program modules and interfaces between them.

During programming, the application's instructions are written in the selected programming language and the code is tested incrementally to ensure that it performs according to specifications.

The techniques of software quality assurance include walkthroughs, that is, reviews of a system development product (such as a data flow diagram or a structure chart) by a small group of people with a purpose of error detection. A more formal review technique is inspection, which is followed up by scheduled reviews of corrected products. Several levels of testing, from unit testing of individual program modules to acceptance and installation testing, are performed to discover and remove errors.

Operations can be converted to the new system by parallel operation, direct conversion ("cold turkey"), phased conversion, or by initially running a pilot version and only then converting to the complete new system. After the system is operational, its performance and use, as well as the development methodology, are assessed during the postimplementation review.

Software maintenance includes all the modifications of an operational application. The three types of activities during maintenance are perfective maintenance, to enhance the system and keep it in line with changing user requirements; adaptive maintenance, aiming to adapt the system to new hardware or systems software; and corrective maintenance, to remove errors as they are discovered during operations.

Computer-aided software engineering (CASE) tools assist software developers in planning, analyzing, designing, programming, and maintaining information systems. The "front-end CASE" tools support analysis and design by assisting the developers in producing requirements specifications and structure charts for the application. The "back-end CASE" tools produce the code for the application from terse higher-level specifications.

Object-oriented development aims to build an application as a collection of interacting objects that correspond to the real-world objects in its domain. This development methodology enables developers to build up libraries of reusable code, potentially resulting in savings and higher software quality.

Estimation of the effort needed to develop an application or to perform maintenance, such as time and cost, is based on the measure of the software product to be delivered, for example, on function points. Based on this effort estimate, a schedule of the project can be devised with a method such as PERT/CPM. Software projects are carried out by teams. A chief programmer team is organized to support an outstanding software developer who performs most of the key work on the project. Members of a democratic team bear equal responsibility for the project's outcomes. Most teams combine the features of these two organizing principles.

KEY TERMS

QUESTIONS

1. What is the objective of system design? What are its two principal stages? What is the essential distinction between them?
2. What are the principal activities performed during the logical design?
3. What aspects of the information system have to be specified at the conclusion of physical design?
4. What tool is used in structured design to specify the structure of a program? Describe what the boxes and lines stand for in this representation of a program.
5. What are the two principles of structured design? Explain them briefly. How do these principles relate to systems theory discussed in Chapter 2?
6. What is programming? What is the scope of this activity as compared to the scope of the overall system development?
7. How does programming relate to debugging?
8. What are the principal measures of software quality assurance? Which of them rely on people and which rely on computers?
9. What is the difference between a walkthrough and an inspection? Which is more costly?
10. What are the levels of software testing? Who should participate in accepting the system?
11. Can testing guarantee the absence of errors in the program?
12. What are the methods of conversion to a new system? What do you think are the advantages and the drawbacks of each?
13. What is the objective of postimplementation review?
14. What is the maintenance of an information system? Why are the costs of maintaining a system usually much higher than the costs of developing it?
15. What are the objectives of each of the three types of activities during software maintenance? Which activity directly supports adjusting the system to the demands of the changing marketplace on the owner firm?
16. What are CASE tools?
17. What are the differences between the front-end and the back-end CASE tools?
18. What is the basic principle of object-oriented development?
19. What benefits can be expected from moving to object-oriented development?
20. How can you estimate the development effort for a software project? What is the advantage of the function-point technique as compared to the counts of the lines of code?
21. What is a PERT chart?
22. Compare and contrast a chief programmer team and a democratic team.

ISSUES FOR DISCUSSION

1. Based on this chapter and the preceding one, state and discuss the measures that can be taken to assure quality of information systems throughout the process of their development and maintenance.
2. Discuss the variety of measures that can be taken to cope with the ever increasing number of information systems that have to be maintained in a typical organization. Consider all the possible ways of "coping," using "out-of-the-box" creative ideas as well.
3. Discuss the relationships between computer-aided software engineering and object-oriented development. Which technology, do you think, is more easily introduced in a firm and why? If possible, illustrate your points with examples found in current periodicals.
4. The manager of the functional unit insists on converting the operations of the unit to a new information system that the IS professionals who developed it find insufficiently tested. Are the IS professionals absolved of ethical responsibility for the likely negative outcome? Discuss.

REAL-WORLD MINICASE AND PROBLEM-SOLVING EXERCISES

1. Does Load-Tested Equal Road-Tested?   As applications grow in complexity, they are also becoming more mission-critical, an ever riskier combination. Network-based client/server information systems run stock exchanges, banks, and airports. When these systems go down, the havoc is immense. Liability suits follow. Both the outsourcers and the in-house developers want to see to it that when the system is moved from the five-user pilot environment to regular deployment by 5,000 users, it will not collapse under the load. The Internet is a factor that aggravates the situation: As companies enable outsiders, such as customers, to access corporate data, controlled access to corporate systems by a limited number of well-trained users is becoming a thing of the past.

Load testing of information systems is supposed to simulate their real-world operational environment. It can be employed to determine what happens if many more users than expected log on, or if the system's memory requirement is exceeded. It is, essentially, a stress test. Many and complex DBMS queries are generated, creating heavy traffic on the network and resulting in a large number of transactions arriving at the server.

Load-testing software is available from several companies. It includes tools such as Automated Test Facility from Softbridge of Cambridge, Massachusetts, KEY:TestPro from Sterling Software of Atlanta, Georgia, and V-Test from Performance Software of Newburyport, Massachusetts. The tools cost $2,000 to $3,000 per seat license, and many projects require that multiple human testers be supported. The software generates the load according to a script developed by the testers. As the load is being increased, the software measures responsiveness of the system and its throughput, that is, the number of transactions handled per unit of time.

Developers frequently tack on load testing just prior to releasing the system for deployment. The following questions can then be answered: Is the proposed server powerful enough to handle all the client PCs? Can the server manage simultaneous log-ons by all the users on the network? Will minimum performance requirements be met under heavy load? However, more experienced IS development teams use load testing at far earlier stages, in order to obtain a proof of concept. They may even use load testing with an early system prototype to see whether the particular DBMS can support the number of transactions estimated for the application.

"IS managers are desperate for any kind of certainty they can get," says Curtis Franklin, the director of Client/Server Laboratories, an independent testing company in Atlanta, which performs load testing for a number of clients.

a. Answer the question posed in the title. In other words, do you believe that load testing is a fair simulation of the real operating conditions of complex systems, such as described in the Real-World Minicase? Argue for your answer.

b. Discuss the role load testing can play during the development of the information system architecture for an organization.

Based on Mary Hanna, "Load Tested Equals Road Tested," *Software Magazine*, May 1996, pp. 88–94.

2. Modify the structure chart shown in Figure 16.2 to include the backorder function described in Exercise 1 in the preceding chapter.

3. Produce a structure chart for the Accounts Receivable System described in Exercise 2 in the preceding chapter.

T E A M   P R O J E C T

Each two- or three-person team should research a system development methodology and its support with CASE tools. If possible, the use of the methodology in a local organization should be investigated. If there is no such access, trade magazines and vendor's literature should be researched. The team should study the following:

• During what stages of the software development and maintenance process can the development methodology and the CASE tool be applied?

• What deliverables are produced?

• What is the cost per license?

• What is the breadth of market penetration?

• Who are the lead users?

The lead users, whom the vendors frequently use as a reference, may be contacted for their opinion. Selected analyses should be presented to the class so that the state of the art in CASE and development methodologies—and the state of their assimilation by specific firms—can emerge.

E N D N O T E

1. The method combines the Program Evaluation and Review Technique (PERT), developed in the 1950s for the Polaris missile project, with the Critical Path Method (CPM) developed for running industrial projects.

S E L E C T E D   R E F E R E N C E S

Baecker, Ronald M., and others. *Readings in Human-Computer Interaction: Toward the Year 2000.* 2nd ed. San Francisco: Morgan Kaufman, 1995.

A collection of excellent papers on developing user interfaces for information systems.

Boehm, Barry. *Software Engineering Economics.* Englewood Cliffs, New Jersey: Prentice-Hall, 1981.

A classic.

Booch, Grady. *Object-Oriented Analysis and Design with Applications,* 2nd ed. Redwood City, California: Benjamin/Cummings, 1994.

An excellent textbook.

Brooks, Frederick P., Jr. *The Mythical Man–Month: Essays on Software Engineering,* 2nd ed. Reading, Massachusetts: Addison-Wesley, 1995.

Classic essays by an experienced software manager and scholar.

Collier, Bonnie; Tom DeMarco; and Peter Fearney. "A Defined Process for Project Postmortem Review." *IEEE Software,* 13, no. 4, (July 1996), pp. 65–71.

How to conduct postimplementation reviews.

Constantine, Larry L., and Lucy A.D. Lockwood. (Eds.) "Project Organization and Management." Special Section, *Communications of the ACM,* 36, no.10, (October1993), pp. 30–113.

A series of thorough articles describing the organization of software development teams, customer-centered development, and software project planning.

Drake, Thomas. "Measuring Software Quality: A Case Study." *Computer,* November 1996, pp. 78–87.

Guinan, Patricia J.; Jay G. Cooprider; and Steve Sawyer. "The Effective Use of Automated Application Development Tools." *IBM Systems Journal,* 36, no. 1 (1997), pp. 124–139.

Jones, Capers. "Software Estimating Rules of Thumb," *Computer* 29, no. 3, (March 1996), pp. 116–118.

Very helpful for quick, initial estimating.

Jones, Capers. "Year 2000: What's the Real Cost?" *Datamation,* March 1997, pp. 88–93.

Lientz, B.P.; E.B. Swanson; and G.E. Tompkins. "Characteristics of Application Software Maintenance." *Communications of the ACM,* 21, no. 6, (June 1978), pp. 466–71.

Preece, Jenny and others. *Human-Computer Interaction.* Wokingham, England: Addison-Wesley, 1994.

An excellent and comprehensive sourcebook on the design of user interfaces to information systems.

Sheetz, Steven, and others. "Exploring the Difficulties of Learning Object-Oriented Techniques." *Journal of Management Information Systems,* 14, no. 2, (Fall 1997).

Stein, Eric W., and Betty Vandenbosch. "Opportunities for and Obstacles to Organizational Learning During Advanced System Development." *Journal of Management Information Systems,* 13, no. 2, (Fall 1996), pp. 115–136.

Vaughan, Jack. "CASE Kids Grow into Object Veterans" *Software Magazine,* February 1995, pp. 88–91.

Introducing object-oriented development into CASE environments.

Williamson, Miryam, "Software Reuse." Special Section, *CIO,* March 1, 1997, pp. 34–64.

CASE STUDY | # Managing a Mission-Critical Information System Project Very Carefully

Standard & Poor's (S&P) is in the business of analyzing risk: The New York-based company has been rating bonds and credit since 1916. It is no wonder then that we can learn a lot from the way the company managed its own risks when it decided to move to a new information system platform.

The stock-market crash of 1987 was a wake-up call for the company. Assessing the firm's vulnerabilities in the aftermath of the crash, its executives realized that S&P needed to expand its basic business beyond that of rating debt in the United States marketplace—or be threatened in the globalized economy by competitors with a broader business profile. In 1991, an offsite meeting of the company's senior executives produced a new vision and a new mission statement. The vision was to apply the company's core competencies—risk analysis and information services—to financial instruments other than bonds, and to international markets as well as the domestic one.

Unfortunately, the company's information system architecture was not adequate to support this business diversification. The company operated a mainframe-based system with outdated hardware and software technology. The only people who directly used the system were those working for the Information Services department. To access information from S&P's databases, its risk analysts (that is, the people who produced the risk ratings) had to describe their needs to a programmer and wait 48 hours or more for a report. Or, increasingly, the analysts would work on their own PCs, using the data they hoarded locally. "Analysts were spending more time getting information than they were analyzing it, and critical information wasn't shared across the company," says Ken Moskowitz, who was hired as CIO in 1992. In the words of Executive Vice-President Robert Maitner, "Two-thirds of our costs are associated with people, but we were paying our analysts to do data management rather than analysis."

The executives realized that a mission-critical information system project had to be initiated. Indeed, the success of the company's new mission of serving global markets and assessing varied financial instruments would depend on the success of this project. The project's success would affect every knowledge worker in the firm. Information Services (IS) of the firm had to be reengineered from a mainframe custodian into a service-oriented shop. A flexible computing platform had to be developed which could be modified as the company's evolving business needs demanded. The company needed to invest in all of the IS resources: networks, PCs, servers, systems and applications software, designing and populating new relational databases, hiring of new IS specialists, and massive training and broader organizational learning.

Maitner, Moskowitz, and Chief Ratings Officer Leo O'Neill committed to a project that would take years and cost millions of dollars. The company also decided to invest in expertise: It hired the Chicago-based management and technology consultancy, Booz, Allen & Hamilton, which was to be paid $1.5 million for a continuing involvement in the project. The role of the consultants was clearly defined at the outset. They were to help S&P with the strategic planning for the new information system platform, with developing the database architecture, and with staffing and recruitment for the project. Indeed, strategic planning teams included S&P managers, Booz, Allen specialists, and the S&P IS staff members. The S&P departments used the Booz, Allen people as a liaison between the user and the technology communities. The consultants were able to talk with the S&P risk analysts on a peer-to-peer level to determine their data needs. This was the foundation for rebuilding the legacy databases into flexible business-oriented relational systems.

A central committee, consisting of S&P's financial officer, CIO, and operations directors as well as Booz, Allen representatives, devised a plan for the new client/server information system. S&P's Information Services specialists, assisted by Booz, Allen-supplied project managers and developers where necessary, would build and populate relational databases (using Oracle DBMS) to contain current and historical risk ratings as well as the data on various organizations and financial instruments. These would be placed on the powerful servers. After that, a series of client applications would be developed. These applications would use the database and would be customized for different types of users. For example, risk analysts would use an application with a familiar spreadsheet-like interface. The data management staff would use, on the other hand, applications that would mimic a DBMS interface.

The project was apportioned among three major coordinated team groups. The Corporate Repository (CORE) group was responsible for the conversion from the legacy data repositories to new databases. The application and class library development group was to develop a library of business object classes, since object-oriented development methodology was to be deployed. The information dissemination group was to develop the programs related to S&P's 60 publications that are produced for a company's clients, as well as for the programs needed to support the on-line client services.

By using Powersoft's PowerBuilder to develop a company-wide library of reusable software objects for the applications, programmers would be able to leverage their work for one business unit to develop or modify applications quickly for another business unit. For example, a software object that extracts data from spreadsheets could be added to the library after it was built and used where necessary in other applications. "When someone takes an object out of the library, it's been tested and debugged, so you know it works," says Moskowitz.

Chris Rousseau, who began work on the project as a Booz, Allen employee and is now S&P's vice-president of applications development, headed four development teams: applications development, data conversion, publications, and reporting and inquiry. One early challenge, he says, was to resist the temptation to simply reprogram old work patterns into a client/server architecture. The legacy system produced over 300 different reports. Yet, it turned out that a majority of these reports were produced because the legacy system had no ad hoc inquiry capability. Most of the reports became unnecessary once the client-side inquiry tools became available. "Now we have 20 standard reports that are used with great frequency, plus a handful of more complex reports," says Rousseau.

To maintain the quality of development and to contain the project risk, careful planning of the overall project was done. The project combined iterative prototyping during the early stages of development with parallel conversion in the finishing phase. Thus, successively enhanced versions of the prototype were produced, with much of the resulting code used in the final system. The working prototype of the database and of the related applications was produced. The database was loaded with both real and specially developed test data. The working prototype helped define the scope of the project and real business requirements. It also helped build consensus. At first, "people would think there was agreement when there wasn't," says Moskowitz. "But when people got to see something and physically use it, they'd say: 'Oh, that's what I said, but it isn't what I meant.' And we could fix it, rather than have to wait three months and then redo it." The prototype also made it easier to pinpoint trouble spots. "[Testers] could say, 'See? Watch how long it takes me to perform this function.'" And the function could be redesigned.

To test the prototype as it evolved, nine terminals were set up in a large conference room and one in a separate building to mimic the future actual LAN connections. Risk analysts, data managers, directors of operations, and other "friends of the project" were asked to work with and comment on the evolving prototype. "We tested actual working sessions with groups of people," recalls Moskowitz. "We ran the most demanding transactions while we were running reports in the background [with lower priority]. We learned which transactions were the most time-consuming and where the system was being stressed."

While Rousseau's teams were programming, another group was outfitting some 1,300 desktops with PCs, installing servers, and providing connections among these computers. Then, systems software was installed. This included Windows NT on the PCs, Banyan Systems' network operating systems for LANs, wide area networking with Sun Microsystems' UNIX client/server operating system, and the TCP/IP protocol for the Internet access. Personal productivity software, such as word processing programs, spreadsheets, calendaring, and real-time news feeds were also installed. The task proved monumental. "The logistics involved in a a large rollout are always underestimated," says Moskowitz. To manage the huge number of hardware and software elements required by such a large project, the team responsible for the installation, training, and user support, led by Doug Taggart, S&P's vice-president of business technologies and support, built an inventory database, listing each desktop PC's complete configuration. This will also enable consistent future updates.

The system was rolled out and tested in several releases. By upgrading the system over time, the teams gained the experience they would need to ultimately switch from the legacy mainframe system to the new platform.

End-user training was viewed as an ongoing enterprise throughout the project. "We had to make sure people were trained in the applications we were rolling out, but we needed to make sure they knew how use a PC and Windows first," says Moskowitz. The support team coordinated training with upgrades of the system. Upon returning to their desks from a training session for a new application or service, the users would find that same software installed, along with end-user help and documentation. This not only helped build up competence and increase user buy-in, but also reduced the workload at the help desk. "Without training, we learned, people using a new application would be calling within five minutes. There were a lot of misspent hours at the help desk," says Taggart. "Now, we won't permit a [software] install to take place if someone hasn't shown up to class." During the peak period of the rollout, four staff instructors (three in New York and one in Europe) were teaching five classes a day, organized by business unit.

As the project was nearing completion in February 1995, three months of parallel operation started, to avoid any surprises after the conversion. For users in some departments, parallel operation during the conversion testing meant doing the same job twice. As part of parallel operation and final testing of the new system, S&P actually produced two sets of some of its client publications—one using the legacy system and the other using the new platform. Proofreaders were hired to compare them. "We did find we had some deeply buried inconsistencies that were not obvious to anyone during our normal acceptance testing," says Moskowitz. As the result of the parallel operation, some of the data definitions and relationships had to be refined and, in some cases, workflow had to be adjusted.

Almost three years after the inception of the project (see Figure 16.13), S&P now has a client/server information system architecture, anchored by the relational database with 12 Gbytes of data on approximately 55,000 organizations and 4 million financial ratings. There are two large suites of applications, one for analytical operations and the other to support publication and on-line information dissemination to clients. Risk analysts can now perform a wide range of on-line queries and create customized reports almost instantly. They can respond more quickly to the events that affect financial markets, run what-if scenarios, and spend their time analyzing data, rather than trying to collect the data.

The company is able to produce its ratings more rapidly and is more efficient in its operations. S&P can respond more quickly to the needs of the marketplace by leveraging its

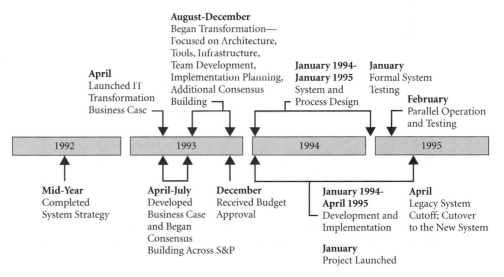

Figure 16.13

The time line of Standard & Poor's information system project (Based on Tracy Mayor, "Proceeding with Caution," *CIO*, October 19, 1996, pp. 68–75.)

past work. The company has built up a library of software objects that will help it to do that and to develop future applications. Standard & Poor's has built a flexible platform from which it can launch future products and services.

Based on Tracy Mayor, "Proceeding with Caution," *CIO*, October 15, 1996, pp. 68–75.

CASE STUDY QUESTIONS

1. Why was the new information system considered mission-critical by Standard & Poor's?

2. What measures did Standard & Poor's information system developers use to manage the risks of the project?

3. What quality-assurance measures were built into the development project?

4. What measures were undertaken to facilitate the implementation of the system? Classify these measures in terms of the framework in Figure 13.14.

5. What were the advantages of object-oriented development to the project?

6. What measures undertaken during the development project will facilitate the maintenance of the system?

PART SIX

Ethical, Societal, and Global Issues in Information Systems

We will begin this concluding part of the text by discussing the ethical issues that arise when information systems are developed and used. We will see that proper or improper uses of information technology may have weighty effects both on individuals and on society. This part of the book will also describe the role information systems play in the globalization of business—in reaching for international marketplaces and in seeking needed resources internationally.

Chapter Seventeen will discuss the domain of ethics and the fundamental ethical issues in information systems. It will show how ethical approaches and specific codes of ethics should guide problem solving with information systems. The chapter will also present the impacts of information technologies on the workplace, showing both the opportunities these technologies bring and the threats they create.

Chapter Eighteen will discuss the role information systems play in business globalization and show how specific companies are expanding their international horizons using these systems. Global strategies, worldwide corporate structures, and global business drivers will be shown to determine the way specific firms are exploiting information technologies for global reach.

CHAPTER SEVENTEEN

Ethical and Societal Issues in Information Systems

OBJECTIVES

After you complete this chapter, you will be able to:

1. Understand why ethical considerations should guide you in making decisions regarding the use of information technologies.

2. Know what the codes of ethics relevant to the development and use of information systems are.

3. Apply ethical theories to the decision-making situations.

4. Define privacy and understand how individual privacy may be threatened by the use of information systems.

5. Explain how information accuracy can become an ethical issue.

6. Specify property issues involved in the use of information systems and the means of property protection.

7. Identify the access issues in the use of information systems.

8. Specify the potential positive and negative impacts of information technology on the workplace.

9. Describe how computer-based work monitoring can be employed productively.

OUTLINE

You May Be Well, but Will It Be Good for You?

Next to the Adolph Coors brewery in Golden, Colorado, stands the company's 23,000-square foot Wellness Center, devoted to keeping workers healthy. The center has a state-of-the-art gym, medical clinic, and counseling center. It is good for the workers' health and it saves the company some $2 million a year in sick leave and medical costs.

A lot of information related to the workers' health is being collected in the databases maintained at the center. Here is how one of the firm's subsidiaries, Coors Ceramics, kept track of one employee, Richard Fletcher. The company registered in its database that the worker had mumps at the age of eight, a vasectomy in 1962, smelly feet, and that he smoked 30 cigarettes a day. When Fletcher died in 1992 at the age of 54, his widow filed for survivor's benefits, available in many states if a worker's death is job-related. Since Richard Fletcher died two weeks after having been demoted from a desk job to manual labor and his wife had found him sobbing on the floor shortly after the demotion, she thought she had a strong case.

But Coors argued that Fletcher died from smoking. To argue the case, the company used the records from Wellness Center, which indicated that the deceased employee had smoked a pack-and-a-half a day since the age of 14. An administrative judge denied the widow's benefits and she is appealing the case. Should the information collected for the needs of an internal wellness program have been used for another purpose? Is an ethical issue involved? If so, what individual right has not been protected?

Based on Ellen E. Schultz, "Medical Data Gathered by Firms Can Prove Less Than Confidential," *The Wall Street Journal*, May 18, 1994, pp. A1, A5.

Each of us would like to lead a life we can be proud of, making choices that agree with our notions of right and good. We do not want shortcuts of momentary expediency to detract us from the long-term goals of enjoying a reputation as a good person, feeling good about ourselves, or upholding principles that are dear to us. Our notions of morality help in realizing these goals. However, we need more direct guidelines to assist us in making the choices for right in our professional lives. This is the objective of the present chapter.

Ethics is a branch of philosophy that deals with the issues of right and wrong, just and unjust, proper and improper. The treatment of workers in a wellness program, described in the Minicase above, is an example of a situation that raises such a question. Computers and telecommunications play a vital role in our information society, and work with information systems raises a well-defined set of ethical issues that will be discussed in this chapter. Both the developers and the users of these systems need to be aware of the nature of these issues in the context of general ethics as well as ways of coping with ethical dilemmas that invariably arise and the recommendations of the appropriate codes of ethics.

Information technology is a source of material progress and can contribute to the well-being of all of us: It generates opportunities for a society. It can also harm us. It threatens employment in some job categories. It may be used to invade our private life and to make our workplace less congenial. Ethical issues are tightly interwoven with societal issues aimed at furthering the well-being of all members of society. The fundamental question is: How do we employ our sense of right and wrong to gain the benefits of this technology while protecting the rights of those who are affected by it? Here, we will attempt to help you to answer this question for yourself.

17.1 | THE DOMAIN OF ETHICS

Information technology is a potent tool that can be used to further organizational goals, pursue national interest, or support environmentally sustainable development. The same technology can also be used to hold employees or citizens in fear of the omnipresent surveillance supported by information systems with databases on all aspects of their lives. The way the technology is deployed in organizations depends on our decisions as managers, computing professionals, and users of information systems. All of us, therefore, should make these decisions guided not only by the organizational and technological aspects of information systems, but also in consideration of their effects on individuals. Our knowledge of ethics helps us in making such decisions.

Ethics and Codes of Ethics

Ethics is a study of the principles of right and wrong that ought to guide human conduct. Ethics is about which values are worth pursuing in life and which acts are right (or wrong)—thus, ethics is a study of morality. How do ethical issues relate to legal ones? Is an ethical breach punishable by law? If there is no law that penalizes a certain conduct, does it mean that you are always right behaving in that way?

Human behavior and decision making fall into three domains, shown in Figure 17.1. As we develop and use information systems to solve organizational problems or to respond to opportunities, we need to make sure that our solution is proper with respect to each of these domains. The legal domain governs a variety of relatively well-described behaviors, specified by law and enforceable in the courts of a given country or within a local jurisdiction. As we discussed in Section 15.3, during the preliminary feasibility study of the system to be developed, we need to make sure that the proposed system is *legally* feasible. Com-

Figure 17.1

Investigating an information system solution to a problem or opportunity

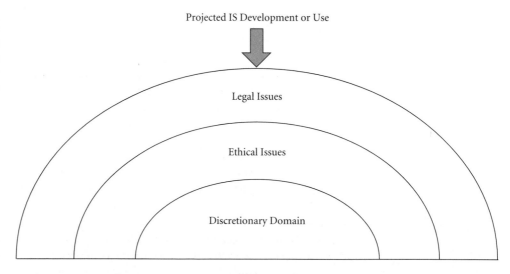

Projected IS Development or Use

Legal Issues

Ethical Issues

Discretionary Domain

puter crime and abuse, discussed in Section 14.3, are breaches of law and fall into this domain.

However, just because an action is legal, it does not follow that the action is ethical. The domain of ethics is governed by the general norms of behavior and by specific codes of ethics. To see whether your decision making in a given case involves an ethical issue, apply the "sunshine principle": What if I read about my decisions and subsequent actions in tomorrow's paper? Ethical considerations go beyond legal liability.[1] This chapter will help you make decisions in those cases when you do perceive that an ethical issue is involved. Only if the action is both legal and ethical does it fall into the discretionary domain, where we act properly entirely according to our preferences. In this domain, we can apply such criteria as organizational desirability or cost-benefit analysis.

Knowledge of ethics as it applies to the issues arising from the development and use of information systems helps us make decisions in our professional life. Professional knowledge is generally assumed to confer a special responsibility within its domain. This is why the professions have evolved **codes of ethics,** that is, sets of principles intended to guide the conduct of the members of the profession. The principal codes of ethics for information systems professionals are the ACM Code of Ethics and Professional Conduct, binding on the members of the Association for Computing Machinery (ACM), and The Code of Ethics and Standards of Conduct adopted by the Data Processing Management Association (DPMA). These codes should also be familiar to the managers and end users whose professional life is affected by information systems. We have reproduced the fundamental statements of the ACM Code of Ethics and Professional Conduct in Figure 17.2. We will come back to these statements throughout the chapter.

Although the ethical codes are not enforceable in the courts, a human society would be intolerable in their absence. Therefore, societies (and, on a smaller scale, professional societies) have evolved mechanisms that in various ways penalize a breach of ethical norms. But what is to guide us in selecting a course of action? How do we act in an ethical dilemma, a situation where each course of action appears ethically less than desirable? To answer these questions, we will turn to ethical theories.

Ethical Theories

Ethical theories give us the foundation from which we can determine what course of action to take when an ethical issue is involved. At the source of ethics lies the idea of reciprocity. There are two fundamental approaches to ethical reasoning:

1. Consequentialist theories tell us to choose the action with the best possible consequences. Thus, the utilitarian theory that represents this approach holds that our chosen action should produce the greatest overall good for the greatest number of people affected by our decision. The approach is often difficult to apply, since it is not easy to decide what the "good" is and how to measure and compare the resulting "goods." In our pursuit of the greatest resulting good, we may also sacrifice the interests of a minority to those of the majority. Indeed, there are certain acts that are wrong in themselves and should be always avoided. Misstating the truth, or lying, is such an act. The ACM Code of Ethics and Professional Conduct states the general moral imperative to "be honest and trustworthy." Unethical acts interfere with the rights of others, rights which may be derived from the other principal group of ethical theories.

2. Obligational (deontological) theories argue that it is our duty to do what is right. Your actions should be such that they could serve as a model of behavior for others—and,

Figure 17.2

Fundamental statements of the ACM Code of Ethics and Professional Conduct (Courtesy Association for Computing Machinery.)

Association for Computing Machinery
Code of Ethics and Professional Conduct

General Moral Imperatives

- Contribute to society and human well-being
- Avoid harm to others
- Be honest and trustworthy
- Be fair and take action not to discriminate
- Honor property rights including copyrights and patents
- Give proper credit for intellectual property
- Respect the privacy of others
- Honor confidentiality

More Specific Professional Responsibilities

- Strive to achieve the highest quality, effectiveness, and dignity in both the process and products of professional work
- Acquire and maintain professional competence
- Know and respect existing laws pertaining to professional work
- Accept and provide appropriate professional review
- Give comprehensive and thorough evaluations of computer systems and their impacts, including analysis of possible risks
- Honor contracts, agreements, and assigned responsibilities
- Improve public understanding of computing and its consequences
- Access computing and communication resources only when authorized to do so

Organizational Leadership Imperatives

- Articulate social responsibilities of members of an organizational unit and encourage full acceptance of those responsibilities
- Manage personnel and resources to design and build information systems that enhance the quality of working life
- Acknowledge and support proper and authorized uses of an organization's computing and communications resources
- Ensure that users and those who will be affected by a system have their needs clearly articulated during the assessment and design of requirements. Later the system must be validated to meet requirements
- Articulate and support policies that protect the dignity of users and others affected by a computing system
- Create opportunities for members of the organization to learn the principles and limitations of computer systems

in particular, you should act as you would want others to act toward you. Our fundamental duty is to treat others with respect, and thus not to treat them *solely* as a means to our own purposes.

Treating others with respect means not violating their rights. It is, therefore, vital that we recognize the rights of each human individual. The principal **individual rights** are:

a. The right to life and safety.

b. The right of free consent: Individuals should be treated as they freely consent to be treated.

   c. The right to privacy: Individuals can act freely away from work and can retain private information about themselves without disclosure, while having other information about them properly safeguarded by those to whom it was disclosed.

   d. The right to private property.

   e. The right of free speech, extending to the right to criticize truthfully the ethics or legality of the actions of others.

   f. The right to fair treatment: Individuals who are similar in the aspects relevant to a given decision should be treated similarly.

   g. The right to due process: Individuals have a right to an impartial hearing when they believe their rights are being violated.

The application of ethical theories is best illustrated by considering practical cases, which we will now proceed to do.

17.2   SCENARIOS IN THE ETHICAL DOMAIN

Consider the following three scenarios (adapted from Parker 1990). As you read each of these Minicases, you will probably have a sense of unease: Your moral antennae will pick up a signal. Jot down on the margin any ethical issues you perceive. We will come back to these scenarios throughout the chapter and discuss them in Section 8 of this chapter.

1. Transactional Information on Smart Cards

A manager of the smart-card division of a financial institution has developed a new debit card containing a microprocessor chip. Unbeknownst to its holder, detailed information about the purchase transactions in which the card was used was stored on the card. As a result, any merchant presented with the card could evaluate the credit history of the cardholder. The financial institution was further considering seeking competitive advantage with this application by allowing the merchants to upload the information from the smart cards to their own computers. This would enable the merchants to use personal information about their customers for mail-order and other promotions.

Consider these questions: Do you believe that there are any ethical issues involved? Was there anything wrong with developing and fielding such a system? If so, what ethical principles were breached?

2. Who Owns Electronic Mail?

A firm had a policy allowing employees, upon approval, to use their networked PCs for personal purposes. When a possible acquisition of the company by another one was announced, rising employee unrest was suspected. The president of the company ordered the security department to monitor all the PC activities of the employees, including the contents of their memos, E-mail messages, budgets in preparation, and so forth. Reports prepared by the security department detailed what the employees produced both during their work and during private use of their PCs. The monitoring and reporting was done without employees' knowledge.

Was the action of the company management ethical or unethical in allowing personal use of information systems by employees? How about the president's monitoring decision?

3. Let's Just Release This System

A project leader was assigned by her manager, the vice-president of sales for the retail company where they both worked, a task to develop a billing system. When the work was being assigned, the project leader thought that the time and human resources provided were adequate to complete the project. However, due to an unexpected turnover of computing specialists, it became clear that the system could not be completed as designed within the available budget and time frame. The project leader warned her superior about the impending problem. She was forced to deliver a "bare bones" system, without error detection, exception handling, security safeguards, and audit trail. When the system was fielded, it became a source of problems in customer service. Many customers received incorrect statements and, following heated exchanges, switched suppliers. Cases of fraud were discovered, but proved impossible to trace. Business losses resulted and the project leader was blamed.

Was the action of the project leader ethical in knowingly implementing an inadequate system? How would you evaluate the actions of her superior in ordering an inadequate system into production?

Keep in mind these scenarios as you read the subsequent sections. We will come back to discuss the issues involved in Section 8.

17.3 │ ETHICAL ISSUES IN THE DEVELOPMENT AND USE OF INFORMATION SYSTEMS

The welfare of individuals and their specific rights, postulated by the ethical theories we discussed, need to be safeguarded in the environment of an information society. The principal ethical issues of concern with regard to information systems have been identified by Richard Mason (1986) as the issues of privacy, accuracy, property, and access (PAPA, for short). These are the issues that will be discussed throughout the chapter.

We have shown these principal ethical issues as the four circles in Figure 17.3. As you may see in the figure, we can trace these issues to their sources: (a) the pervasive role and immense capabilities of systems for collecting, storing, and accessing information in our information society, (b) the complexity of information technology, and (c) the intangible nature of information and software. The figure also shows the specific individual rights whose potential violation brings the issues to a head.

Figure 17.3

Ethical issues, their sources, and the underlying individual rights

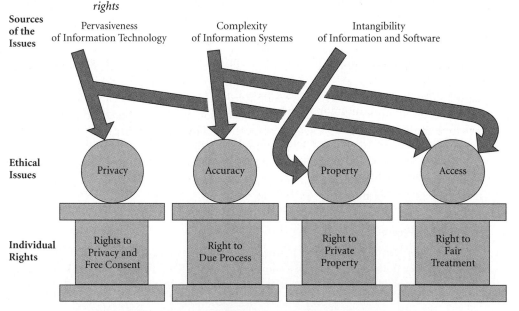

Tracing an ethical issue to its source and the understanding of which individual rights could be violated helps us understand the issue. For example, the intellectual property rights embodied in software are relatively easily violated because software is intangible and can be easily copied. Since information technology pervades so many aspects of our lives, our privacy can be more easily violated than in the absence of this technology. Indeed, without computerized databases, fed by information systems that process our purchases, loan applications, insurance policies, and other transactions, it would hardly be possible to assemble the detailed record of our lives within seconds. At the same time, those dispossessed of access to the technology are impaired in many of life's pursuits and their right to fair treatment is violated. We will now proceed to consider the four ethical issues in the following sections.

17.4   PRIVACY

You obtained a major credit card and have faithfully paid your bills for two months. Then you receive a telephone call from the card's issuer. Your credit privileges have been suspended because the balance in your bank checking account is too low to pay your next bill. Indeed, you gave the credit card company your bank reference in order to establish the credit—but not to continually monitor your checking account without your consent. "I felt violated," says a cardholder to whom this actually happened.

When the controller at a New Jersey company sided with his employer in a dispute with a bank, he did not think about the fact that he had recently applied for a personal loan there. The bank got even: It divulged to the controller's employer that he owned two luxury cars (which he listed on his loan application) and suggested that the employee was moonlighting. The controller was fired.

Both cases represent an invasion of privacy. Privacy is the most important ethical issue raised by information systems. **Privacy** is the right of individuals to retain certain information about themselves without disclosure and to have any information collected about them with their consent protected against unauthorized access. When our privacy is invaded, we are embarrassed, diminished, and perceive a loss of autonomy—a loss of control over our lives. Invasion of privacy is a potent threat in an information society. Individuals can be deprived of opportunities to form desired professional and personal relationships, or can even be politically neutralized through surveillance and gathering of data from the myriad databases that provide information about them.

Concern about privacy had existed for many years before the computer-based information technology entered human affairs. But computers and related technologies create possibilities to endanger privacy that had not existed before. Massive databases containing minute details of our lives *can* be assembled at a reasonable cost and *can* be made accessible anywhere and at any time over telecommunications networks. It is necessary to uphold the right to privacy as a basic individual right. Justice Louis Brandeis, a century ago, called this right "the most valued by the civilized man." Even though this right is not guaranteed by The Bill of Rights in the United States, that constitutional document stresses that other rights, beyond those enumerated there, are retained by the people. The right to privacy is such a right. To uphold the right to privacy, we need to learn what kind of safeguards individuals have with respect to their privacy.

Collection, storage, and dissemination of records concerning individuals from computer databases are necessary to our business, government—indeed, to the very fabric of our lives. Yet the quality of our lives has to be protected by legislation and by an ethical approach to the acquisition and use of these records. Several laws regulating record keeping are in force in the United States. The most prominent of these are the Fair Credit Reporting Act of 1970, which limits access to the credit information collected by credit agencies and gives individuals the right to review them, and the Privacy Act of 1974, which bars federal agencies from allowing the data they collect to be used for purposes other than those for which they were collected. However, both legislative acts contain loopholes that defy their already feeble enforcement. Gaps in legislation and enforcement make it difficult to protect privacy through the legal system and leave much of the privacy issue in the domain of ethics.

The Privacy Act serves as a guideline for a number of ethics codes adopted by various organizations. It is also being looked upon as a model for protecting the privacy of electronic medical records ("Electronic Threats" 1997). The act specifies the limitations on the data records that can be kept about individuals. The following are the principal privacy safeguards specified:

- No secret records should be maintained about individuals.
- No use can be made of the records for other than the original purposes without the individual's consent.
- The individual has the right of inspection and correction of records pertaining to him or her.
- The collecting agency is responsible for the integrity of the record-keeping system.

The volume of personal records stored in various databases is staggering. The agencies of the U.S. federal government have collected more than 4 billion records. In the private sector, the most prodigious collectors of personal data are credit bureaus, which play a vital role in the facilitation of credit decisions. The three largest credit bureaus, TRW, Trans Union Credit Information, and Equifax, have assembled over 400 million records on 160 million individuals. The proliferation of new technologies, such as point-of-sale systems, while a boon to marketers, generates volumes of individually identifiable records. Any transaction that is identifiable to you—even by name only—may end up in a permanent database. You do not own the record of the transaction. And it has proven virtually impossible to control the uses of these databases.

Ensuring privacy in the face of rapidly expanding technological possibilities for its invasion is not easy. Controversies arise; two of these are described in the following vignette. We can see from the examples in the vignette that privacy issues have significant economic implications. Scrapping a product that defies the common expectations of privacy protection was costly for Lotus Development. The competitiveness of several U.S. industries that would rely on a government-supported encryption standard, such as the Clipper chip, is called into question.

Two database phenomena create specific dangers. The first, **database matching** makes it possible to merge separate facts collected about an individual in several databases. If minute facts about a person are put together in this fashion in a context unrelated to the purpose of the data collection and without the individual's consent or ability to rectify inaccuracies, serious damage to the rights of the individual may result. The dispersion of personal data among several independent databases is one safeguard against invasion of privacy. The other concern relates to **statistical databases** that contain large numbers of personal records, but are intended to supply only statistical information (the U.S. Census database is the best example). A snooper, however, may deduce personal information by constructing and asking a series of statistical queries that would gradually narrow the field down to a specific individual. To prevent such disclosure, limitations on the allowed queries need to be placed (for example, a query would not be answered if the answer would refer to fewer than 10 persons).

IN THE SPOTLIGHT

Controversies in Privacy

A *Marketplace that Did Not Happen* In 1990, Lotus Development Corporation (now a part of IBM) announced its intent to release, on CD-ROM disks, a database containing names, addresses, consumption patterns, and estimated incomes of some 80 million households and 120 million individuals in the United States. Called *Lotus Marketplace,* the database was compiled from the records of the Equifax credit bureau. The database would be sold to any "legitimate business" in pursuit of new customers, whose marketing profiles would be available at low cost. The consumers whose personal data were the contents of the database had never granted their permission for this use of the data. An uproar resulted. Faced with negative publicity and requests from over 30,000 people to have their names excluded, the company canceled the intended product release.

The Clipper Chip
The controversy over the *Clipper chip* has attracted the attention of the computing community during recent years. The issue is access of law enforcement agencies to encrypted information. As we discussed in Section 14.4, encryption is the primary means of protecting communications sent over the telecommunications networks from interlopers. The use of encryption for electronic commerce over the networks and for messaging in general has grown rapidly. Under United States law, law enforcement agencies authorized with a court warrant have the right to conduct electronic surveillance in investigating serious criminal activities. That is, the agencies have the right to read electronic messages surreptitiously. Yet, encoded messages are practically impossible to understand without the key that has to be used to unscramble them.

The Clinton administration proposed an encryption system that would address the needs of law enforcement. The system would rely on a hardware chip, called Clipper chip, that would perform encryption and decryp-tion using a classified algorithm. A Clipper chip would be embedded in computers and telephones so that both digital information and voice communications could be encoded. Each chip would have a unique serial number and a secret encoding key that would be split into two parts. Each part of the key would be stored with a separate escrow agency, designated by the Attorney General. Given a court warrant, a law enforcement agency could obtain the two parts of the key and decrypt the message. The administration would facilitate the use of the Clipper system, although use would be voluntary.

A number of concerns are involved in the Clipper chip controversy. Fear of the government playing Big Brother in intercepting private communications alarms civil libertarians. Would the ability to gain access to people's electronic communications always be used lawfully? Would alternative encryption schemes ultimately be outlawed? Even though the standard is meant to be voluntary, if it is used in most or all government transactions, then the enormous buying power of the U.S. government would, in effect, force the country's businesses to use the standard. Would the ability of U.S. businesses to compete in world markets be endangered? A diverse and bipartisan committee of the National Research Council concluded in May 1996 that escrowed encryption entails significant risks of its own and should not be implemented. The debate continues and the proposal is certain to be significantly modified, if not scrapped altogether.

Based on Peter G. Neumann, *Computer-Related Risks,* Reading, Mass: Addison-Wesley, 1995; Chuck Appleby, "Making Security a Reality for All," *InformationWeek,* January 2, 1995, pp. 38–40; Gary H. Anthes, "Elite Panel Slams U.S. Crypto Policy," *Computerworld,* June 3, 1996, p. 15; and John Markoff, "Compromise Is Offered on Computer Security Codes," *The New York Times,* October 2, 1996, pp. D1, D8.

Databases are not the only locus of exposure and controversy when privacy is concerned. E-mail messages and myriad other forms of individual expression or information become accessible to others in the cyberspace created by computers and telecommunications. We will further discuss the workplace use of E-mail in the last section of this chapter.

Information systems have made it possible to conduct systematic surveillance of persons and groups. This surveillance by law-enforcement agencies and other authorized bodies may be justifiable in protecting people and property (and those, we remember, are very legitimate individual rights), and in prevention of fraud and abuse, both in the public and the private sectors. However, because of its intrusive nature, surveillance involving information systems requires far greater justification in the specific cases when it is applicable, and far greater safeguards, than those currently present in the legal domain.

The ACM Code of Ethics obligates information systems professionals to "respect the privacy of others," and goes further to offer specific guidelines on how to do that. This obligation directly addresses the problem that emerged in the first scenario in Section 2 above: Computing professionals who are expected to become involved in a project that will breach individual privacy have an obligation to speak out. They may indeed serve their employer well if they do so. We will discuss a specific privacy issue arising in the workplace—computer-based employee monitoring—in the last section of this chapter.

Legislation and enforcement in the area of privacy in the United States are behind those in a number of other countries. The countries of the European Union offer particularly extensive legal safeguards of privacy. In the environment of business globalization, this creates difficulties in the area of transborder data flow, or transfer of data across national borders. Countries with more stringent measures for privacy protection object to a transfer of personal data into the states where this protection is more lax. The United Nations has stated the minimum privacy guarantees recommended for incorporation into national legislations. There is a concern about a possible emergence of "data haven" countries, where information could be collected, stored, and accessed in an unethical manner.

Privacy protection relies on the technical security measures and other controls (discussed in Chapter 14) that limit access to databases and other information stored in computer memories or transmitted over the telecommunication networks.

17.5 | ACCURACY

Pervasive use of information in our societal affairs means that we have become more vulnerable to misinformation. **Accurate information** is error-free, complete, and relevant to the decisions that are to be based on it. With respect to the last issue, the concern about the accuracy of information about individuals is frequently related to a concern for privacy.

When Robert Corbey applied for a home improvement loan, his prospective lender refused, citing unpaid mortgage bills and an Internal Revenue Service lien against him and his wife, Ann. Since Corbey's mortgage had been paid off and he had never been married to a person named Ann, Corbey protested. The information turned out to be erroneous: It came from a credit report provided by Equifax, whose information systems simply confused him with another Robert Corbey. But it took the present Robert Corbey more than eight months to clear his credit record (Schwartz 1992). Perhaps he had fallen prey to a "credit doctor" (as individuals who "cure" credit problems are called), who sold his credit history to an individual with a poor credit record, who then proceeded to continue that record. Although stories about inaccurate information surface most frequently with regard to the credit-reporting industry, they reflect a generally low level of data quality control throughout the public and private sectors of the economy.

An inaccurate credit report can prevent you from getting a credit card or a job. When people rely on inaccurate information, other people may be deprived of their right to due process. An incorrect medical record can threaten your life. A weather report that incorrectly forecast the trajectory of a storm because the data from a failed buoy were unavailable to the computerized model did send a sailor to his death (Mason 1986). French police officers, in hot pursuit of a car recorded as stolen in their database, opened fire and wounded a law-abiding driver. The records of the car recovery by the legitimate owner and of the subsequent sale of the car were missing from the database.

Is the development of information systems that provide accurate information just a question of professional competence? In the third scenario presented in Section 2, a "bare-bones" system was knowingly forced through by a firm's executive and knowingly implemented by a project leader. Similar events could have been behind any of the systems that led to the loss of individual welfare in the cases we just described. There exist various sources of possible bias in information systems, and the information system professional should be aware of that (Friedman and Nissenbaum 1996). Professional integrity is one of the guarantors of information accuracy.

An ethical approach to information accuracy calls for the following:

- A professional should not misrepresent his or her qualifications to perform a task.

- A professional should indicate to his or her employer the consequences to be expected if his or her judgment is overruled. The ACM Code of Ethics and Professional Conduct speaks of the professional's obligation to "avoid harm to others" by carefully assessing potential impacts of any information system to be implemented.

- System safeguards, such as the controls and audits we discussed in Chapter 14, are necessary to maintain information accuracy. Regular audits of data quality should be performed and acted upon.

- Individuals should be given an opportunity to correct inaccurate information held about them in databases.

- Contents of databases containing data about individuals should be reviewed at frequent intervals, with obsolete data discarded.

The quality of data in federal databases raises many concerns. One study (Laudon 1986) examined the quality of data in the criminal record systems of the United States. Street detention by police and employment opportunities in many occupations depend on the contents of these systems' databases. One of the Federal Bureau of Investigation databases examined contained at the time of the survey 74.3 percent of records with significant quality problems. Thus, only 25.7 percent of records were complete, error-free, and unambiguous. Absence of adequate organizational and technological controls, such as periodic sampling for quality, was a principal reason for this.

Accuracy problems have wider societal implications. A claim has been made that the absence of proper controls in some computerized election systems may threaten basic constitutional rights. Indeed, several examples of irregularities have been reported (Neumann 1995). For example, in Ventura County, California, yes and no votes were reversed by an information system on all the state propositions in the 1992 elections. After a series of errors, computer-based elections had to be abandoned in Toronto, Canada.

17.6 | PROPERTY

The right to property is largely secured in the legal domain. However, intangibility of information is at the source of dilemmas which take clarity away from the laws, moving many problems into the ethical domain. At issue primarily are the rights to **intellectual property:** the intangible property that results from an individual's or a corporation's creative activity. As plummeting costs of computer hardware render much of it a relatively inexpensive commodity, the value of many information systems resides largely in their software, databases, and knowledge bases. Yet while all of us would label taking someone's laptop without permission theft, few of us would even consider the contents of its storage.

Intellectual property is protected in the United States by three mechanisms: copyright, patent, and trade secret. These means serve to protect the investment of an innovator and to ensure public good by encouraging disclosure so that further innovations can be made by others. Indeed, the copyright and patent laws are designed to assist in public disclosure and thus further technological progress.

Copyright registration, which is easy to obtain, protects the form of expression (for example, a given program) rather than the idea itself (for example, an algorithm). Because the underlying problem solution is more valuable than its coded expression, this is a limited protection. **Patents,** which are more difficult to secure, protect novel and nonobvious discoveries that fall within the subject matter of the Patent Act. Many patent applications for software failed to prove that they qualify under this "subject matter" criterion. However, in August 1994, a U.S. Federal Appeals court affirmed the patentability of sufficiently innovative software. Because of the limitations of copyrights and patents with respect to their intangible product, software developers most often rely on trade secret protection. **Trade secret** law protects the confidentiality of intellectual property through licenses (such as those you generally neglect to read on software packages) or nondisclosure agreements.

An elaborate software system, be it an expert system or a personal productivity package, is expensive to create. The same system can be copied at a negligible cost. Moreover, it may be falsely claimed that the overall welfare has been increased by such replication: The original owner is still in possession of the original system. Such is the nature of intellectual property. Books, a more traditional form of intellectual property, have better natural safeguards, stemming from a well-defined authorship and the barrier of publication. Yet, as book publication begins moving in part from the paper medium to that of CD-ROM, and as it is now a simple matter to post the text of a book (written by someone else) on the Web, this pursuit also moves within our area of concern.

In the ecology of personal computing, unauthorized copying of software is a widespread phenomenon. The high cost of software is the frequent excuse (Cheng 1997). Illegal copying of computer software, known as **software piracy,** is theft. A number of companies have introduced stringent policies against such illegal copying. Software piracy in the form of selling illegally reproduced applications has become a serious problem in international trade. In a number of countries, more than 75 percent of sales of U.S. software packages are illegal copies. Worldwide software piracy is estimated to cost the U.S. software industry $10 to $12 billion annually (Anthes 1993).

Because the legal system trails the pace of technology and because ethical guidance is sought in framing the legal issues, many controversies spill over into the ethical domain. To "honor property rights" is one of the eight general moral imperatives of the ACM Code of Ethics. The legal system and the ethicists are grappling with the following unresolved issues:

- To what extent can information be considered property?
- What makes one software product distinct from another?
- Can the look-and-feel of software be protected as property? The emerging interpretation of the copyright law protects the way the program looks to its user on the screen and the way it works, rather than the specific code of the program, but controversy on the subject persists.
- Would computer-generated works have a human author? If not, how would the property rights be protected?

The issues arising with regard to expert systems go beyond those of the rights of the software or knowledge engineer. How do we account for the intellectual property of the experts, whose knowledge is the fundamental resource that becomes "disemminded" (as in disembodied) in those systems? Yet another issue is that of property rights to electronic collections of data, such as directories. At this time, the courts have ruled that the copyright law protects only the collections that display some creativity in the selection or arrangements of the data and does not protect such labor-intensive but nonoriginal collections as telephone white pages.

The property issues of concern to us here are not limited to intellectual property. What about the electromagnetic spectrum that belongs to everyone and that gets crowded with the varieties of telecommunications? To invest, businesses require property rights to transmission channels. Yet how are these rights to be allocated? A public auction by the government is one means of doing so.

As we may conclude, many legal issues regarding intellectual property remain unresolved (Ross 1996). This is why it is particularly important to approach this property from an ethical standpoint to ensure that our decisions do not violate property rights of others.

17.7   ACCESS

It is a hallmark of an information society such as ours that most of its workforce is employed in the handling of information, and most of the goods and services available for consumption are information related (as we discussed in Chapter 3). To gain access to the benefits of such a society, an individual must possess at least three things: (1) the intellective skills to deal with information, (2) access to information technology (e.g., a PC with a modem and a telecommunications link), and (3) access to information. If we consider these issues on the national and global scales, we will see that inequalities persist. Because each of us in a society draws an economic benefit from the equality of opportunity, and because each of us is ethically concerned about fairness, the issue of capable access to information and information technology redefines our concern for literacy.

Information technology does not have to be a barrier to opportunities. Quite to the contrary, when deployed purposefully it can *provide* opportunities that were not accessible before. For example, electronic mail is being successfully used to teach functionally illiterate adults to read and write (Chira 1992). Internet access can bring some of the contents of the world's libraries to a remote location. Thus, computer literacy can become the road to traditional literacy and to education.

With the phenomenal growth of personal computers, the Internet, and on-line information services, the accessibility of information technology has grown vastly. But it has not grown equally. Economic inequality is, of course, a major reason. But it is not the only one. A broad issue of access arises in relation to people with disabilities. Information technologies can be potent tools in bringing the handicapped into the social and economic mainstream. They can also be a barrier to employment or enjoyment of equal access to societal benefits. Several major legislative acts fostering access to information technology in the workplace have been enacted in the United States, the most important being the Americans with Disabilities Act (ADA) of 1990. The act indicates that some 43 million Americans have one or more physical or mental disabilities—which shows the weight of the issue.

Intensive work is being done on developing **assistive technologies** that enhance access for the handicapped to information technology and, in many cases, to the world at large through that technology. Assistive technologies for the blind include screen displays that work in an auditory mode through screen-reading software and speech synthesizers and screens that work in a tactile mode with the use of a Braille display. Assistive technologies for people with impaired mobility rely on programs that modify the operation of the keyboard. There are specialized word processing programs that automatically monitor the text for errors typically made by people who are hearing impaired. A broad series of products

IN THE SPOTLIGHT

Information Technologies Can Broaden Access to the Workplace

Personal computing has significantly increased the opportunities for access to the workplace by handicapped people. Several companies have assumed leadership in providing this access. Apple Computer has espoused the view that people with disabilities do not need a *personal* computer, but rather a *personalized* computer, enhanced to suit their particular disability. To make such enhancements widely available, Apple Computer has opened "Aisle 17," a mail-order "one-stop shop" for Macintosh computers enhanced with assistive technology. Specific packages are recommended for people with various disabilities and furnished at highly competitive prices.

Microsoft's Active Accessibility program makes Internet browsing easy for people with impaired vision. Its flagship program, Internet Explorer, contains program code that enables the screen-reader software used by the blind community. The Explorer works with synthesizers, Braille displays, and other assistive tech-

nology. Another software vendor, The Productivity Works, wrote a special Web browser for the blind. Called pwWebSpeak, the browser has a built-in speech processor and can verbalize the contents of Web pages through a speech synthesizer (see Figure 17.4).

As a large employer, United Parcel Service (UPS) has a systematic program of integrating people with disabilities into the workplace. To accomplish that, the company created its ADA Committee in 1992. One of the committee's first tasks was to review 28 of the most common jobs at 2,000 UPS work sites, carefully distinguishing the essential job functions from those that could be modified or assigned to someone else. Now, interviewers consider only the core job tasks when discussing a position with an applicant with a disability. The use of computerized assistive technologies is considered when matching a person with a job. An organization called Job Accommodation Network of Morgantown, West Virginia, helps employers such as UPS identify effective assis-

Figure 17.4

A Web browser for the vision-impaired (Courtesy of The Productivity Works.)

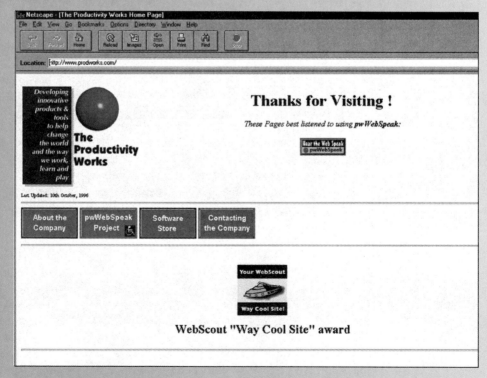

tive technologies for specific circumstances, drawing on the experience of hundreds of other employers.

According to the statement of principle enunciated by Oz Nelson, the chief executive of UPS, we must "provide opportunity to people on the basis of what they can do, rather than denying it based on what they cannot do." Computer-based assistive technologies expand the domain of the possible.

Based on "The New Competitive Advantage," Special Advertising Section, *Business Week,* May 30, 1994; and Joe Lazzaro, "Browse the Web with Your Eyes Closed," *Byte,* December 1996, p. 36.

for people with disabilities, called Independence Series, has been made available by IBM. The preceding vignette illustrates the efforts some corporations make to integrate people with disabilities, assisted by information technologies, into the workforce.

The issue of access has focused on the proposed "information superhighway"—a National Information Infrastructure that is expected to achieve speeds in computer communications surpassing 1 gigabit per second. Hundreds of times faster than today's public networks, it would be able to transmit the text of the entire *Encyclopaedia Britannica* across the United States in seconds. The future network calls for massive investment. Intended originally to support universities and schools, the initiative has been reoriented to also support U.S. companies in their continuing quest for global competitiveness. Concerns arise for the protection of the interests of educational institutions, and indeed, individuals, seeking knowledge who would share such a network with powerful commercial interests. Many believe that the Internet will gradually evolve to serve the goals of the information superhighway. The cost of linking all the U.S. schools and libraries to the Internet is estimated at $2.5 billion annually for five years (Lohr 1996). The magnitude of the sum indicates that equality of access will come, at best, sometime in the future.

17.8   MAKING ETHICAL DECISIONS

Let us consider how we can make decisions applying ethical principles—and then let's do so under the scenarios we presented in Section 2 above. The following decision-making sequence can be adopted:

1. Examine the issues to see whether they fall in the ethical domain. Seek appropriate professional guidance if the issues seem to be in the legal domain. Apply the "sunshine test" to see whether the issue is ethical or discretionary: Would your decision withstand a public disclosure?

2. If you believe that ethical issues are involved, would a course of action you are considering violate individual rights? Would the action violate a professional code of ethics?

3. Choose the course of action that would not result in an ethical breach.

Let us now view our three scenarios from Section 17.2 in light of this decision making.

Transactional Information on Smart Cards

The ethical issue of privacy is involved. It is not apparent that the action is illegal. However, the developers and the users of the system invaded the privacy of the debit-card holders with the system that gathered and released information about them without their knowledge. People may consent to specific information being stored about them for a specific purpose; however, no such consent was sought. The individuals were also deprived of their right to inspect and, if appropriate, correct the information stored about them. Furthermore, the financial institution's prospective plans imply an even broader breach of privacy by indiscriminate, uncontrolled release of transactional information to further parties and should not be pursued.

A breach of ethics may have financial consequences. A possible consumer outcry may render the system useless. Such an argument may indeed carry the day, if you need to defend your recommendation to not go ahead with developing such a system.

Who Owns Electronic Mail?

Certainly, the management decision to allow employees the use of their workstations for personal purposes violates no ethical principles. We could judge this to be a discretionary action, and not an ethics issue. But the monitoring of information, some of it personal by agreement, was undertaken without employees' knowledge and we can clearly see that it is a violation of their right to privacy and thus highly unethical. However, employers have a right to set policy—and employees should be aware of their terms of employment. Indeed, some employers enable their employees to label certain communications as personal, with the employer undertaking an obligation to respect their rights.

Let's Just Release This System

The vice-president not only made a poor business decision (that would place the issue in the discretional domain) but by knowingly forcing the development of a defective system, he violated his duty to do what is right. The good of the company's employees and other stakeholders is threatened by the vice-president's decision. What about the action of the project leader? The DPMA Code of Ethics states that a professional is obligated to guard his or her employer's interests, and the ACM code obligates a professional to "give comprehensive and thorough evaluations of computer systems and their impacts, including analysis of possible risks." The project leader failed to do so in this case by agreeing to implement a defective system and by failing to call her superior's action to the attention of higher authorities.

These three scenarios show not only that ethical decision making protects your sense of your own integrity but also that the expediency of "cutting ethical corners" often produces adverse business results.

17.9 IMPACTS OF INFORMATION TECHNOLOGY ON THE WORKPLACE

All of the issues we have discussed have their impact on the workplace, where they emerge in the light of the right of employers to set policies and practices for the organization. Due to the pervasive use of information technology and its dual potential to be used for good or bad, we need to consider the specific issues that arise when people work with information systems.

Positive and Negative Potential of Information Technology

So profound are the changes that advanced technologies bring to the working life that many effects of information technologies cannot be anticipated. There is, however, a body of experience that permits managers and computing professionals to implement systems promising positive impacts. The ACM Code of Ethics and Professional Conduct commits computer professionals to "design and build information systems that enhance the quality of working life."

It has been established that people experience job satisfaction when (*a*) they have a sense that their work is meaningful, (*b*) they feel a sense of responsibility for the results of their work and have a sense of autonomy and control, and (*c*) they receive feedback about their accomplishments. Sociotechnical design of information systems is performed in recognition of these crucial factors of employee motivation. Information systems with very similar functionalities can have positive or negative consequences in a workplace. Table 17.1 contrasts some of these impacts and provides examples of systems which may have the listed consequences.

As we can see from Table 17.1, the same information technology can have different impacts, depending on the way it is used in an organization. Based on her study of several organizations, Shoshana Zuboff of the Harvard Business School (1988) stresses that an "informating" (rather than automating) organization deploys information technology to create a learning environment, where information is made broadly available to its members to enable them to do their work better and to have a sense of autonomy. Today's organizations compete by best developing and deploying their intellectual capital, whose principal components are the people working there, and the information and knowledge these people are able to apply in their work (Stewart 1997).

Certain widely forecasted effects of technology on the workplace have taken place as the technology has matured. These effects have significant societal implications. The use of computers has displaced workers in middle management (whose primary purpose was to

Table 17.1	Potential Positive Impacts	Potential Negative Impacts	Examples of System Types
Potential positive and negative impacts of information systems	Increase ability to exercise individual skills; provide opportunity to develop individual skills	Deskilling: decreased value of individual's skills	Expert systems
	Provide an intelligent assistant to an individual	"Disemmind" individual's knowledge	Expert systems
	Disperse information to promote autonomy	Monitor to control rigidly	Management reporting and executive information systems
	Provide feedback information for self-supervision to individuals and teams	Routinize work and pace it	Performance monitoring systems
	Provide for social interaction	Isolate individuals	Groupware
	Integrate work into meaningful tasks	Fracture work	Positive impacts promoted by sociotechnically designed information systems
	Empower people with disabilities	Create health hazard	All PC-based systems

IN THE SPOTLIGHT

Portable Work and Nomadic Workers

When IBM consulting networking specialist Walter Barlow arrived for work recently at the company's office in Cranford, New Jersey, he first walked up to the PC in the front lobby and entered his telephone extension. The computer told him he would be assigned desk number 135 that day. At the desk, Barlow plugged his IBM ThinkPad portable computer into the wall jack and logged onto the local area network. The jack into which he plugged had been assigned his extension number when he signed in in the lobby. Barlow's E-mail messages appeared on the screen. He opened his briefcase and was in business.

Actually, by far most of Barlow's business and the business of many of his IBM colleagues is done outside of the office, helping customers solve their problems. All seven of IBM's regional U.S. markets are converting their offices into "productivity centers." Gone are the private offices. The nomadic specialists and managers are out in the field, working with customers. Equipped with laptops, cellular phones, and text pagers, they have been untethered from the office. Actually, they carry their office with them. Studies show that almost three-quarters of IBM's employees have become more productive as nomads, with the biggest gains achieved in customer-related ac-

tivities. Savings in office space are, of course, part of the achieved business results.

And then there are the "lone eagles," the professionals who move to desirable locales to become freelance consultants, relying on the computing and telecommunications technologies to produce and deliver their work. Lee Taylor moved to Telluride, Colorado, an old mining town turned ski resort, where he does technical writing for several clients. Buffalo, Wyoming, is another out-of-the-way place that has attracted lone eagles. Several desirable small towns are upgrading their telecommunications facilities to do so.

Work can move almost as easily as the workers. Offshore outsourcing, the move of software development for information systems to countries with high skill levels and low labor costs, keeps programmers in Bangalore, India, working for Texas Instruments and software developers in Ireland working for Boeing Computer Services.

Based in part on Sandra D. Atcheson, "The Care and Feeding of 'Lone Eagles,'" *Business Week,* November 15, 1993, p. 58; Paul Gillin, "Look Who's on the Cutting Edge," *Computerworld,* May 30, 1994, p. 67; and Jenny C. McCune, "PC Power," *Beyond Computing,* October 1996, pp. 22–24.

gather and transfer information) and in clerical jobs. Some categories of work, such as nonelectronic typesetting, have virtually disappeared. Business reengineering has resulted, in most cases, in IS-supported efficiencies that a reduced workforce needs. Some analysts (for example, Reich 1991) fear that the information society world over may create a permanent underclass that will not be able to compete in the job market.

Information technology has changed the workplace. Many workforce changes result from the ability to work from remote locations, as we discussed in Chapter 1. The vignette above shows important directions of change.

As yet, **telecommuting,** that is, work at home and other locations distant from the office, enabled by the computer and telecommunication technologies, has not substantively replaced work at the office. Social needs and the ability to be visible in the organization have taken precedence over convenience. Yet, as we can see from the preceding vignette, work has been consistently moving to locations remote from traditional corporate offices. In these offices, an issue of particular importance is the increasing use of information technology to monitor employee performance, and we will now turn to it.

Computer-Based Work Monitoring

An employee stands in a different relationship to a workplace than a consumer does to a marketplace. Monitoring the performance of employees is a necessary tasks of management. Indeed, 4 to 6 million workers in the United States have their work evaluation based at least in part on the reports produced by computer-based performance monitoring systems. Many companies consider E-mail messages sent or received by their employees via company's computers to be company property. "E-mail is monitored by our people to make sure it is being used for Intel purposes," says the spokesperson for the Intel Corporation of Santa Clara, California. "It is a widely known policy within the company." (Samuels 1996). When a Compaq computer employee logs onto the corporate telecommunications network, a message is flashed which notes that the company reserves the right to read all messages sent over the network, including E-mail (Rigdon 1996).

Computer-based work monitoring and, related to it, telephone call accounting and service monitoring (for example, by listening to telephone conversations) is practiced to ensure the quality of customer service and to provide objective evaluation of employee performance. The aggregate information gained from these information systems is necessary for management as a means of planning and control. However, when used improperly, these systems can not only raise ethical concerns but actually be counterproductive. Invasive use may result in increased employee stress ("technostress") and a sense of lack of autonomy. When the gathered information is inappropriately applied to individual employees, such usage raises questions about privacy and quality of working life. As shown in Figure 17.5, a great variety of employees' behaviors, and even their personal characteristics, may be subjected to monitoring.

Figure 17.5

Categories of employee performance, behavior, and characteristics subject to monitoring or testing (Based on U.S. Congress, Office of Technology Assessment. *The Electronic Supervisor: New Technology, New Tensions,* OTA-CIT-333, Washington, DC: Government Printing Office, September 1987, p. 13.)

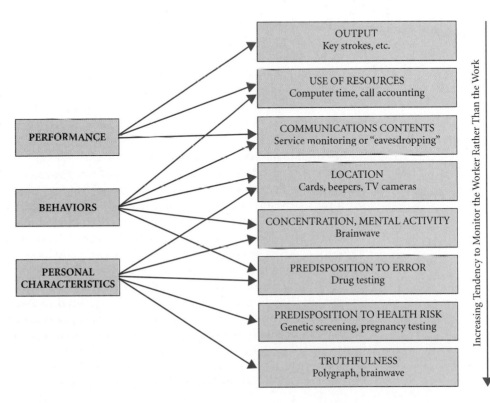

As Figure 17.5 clearly indicates, certain types of monitoring, particularly those that measure behaviors and personal characteristics of employees rather than their performance, are highly invasive. Content-based monitoring (for example, of telephone calls or E-mail) is more invasive than monitoring of output or of use of resources. It should be a primary goal of managers and computing professionals to lower the invasiveness of monitoring. Certain firms, such as Aetna Life & Casualty of Hartford, Connecticut, have formulated corporate guidelines for electronic work monitoring, based on ethical principles. These guidelines include the following highlights:

- Measure only the factors essential for meeting business objectives.
- Make sure employees understand the objectives of the monitoring program and how the measurement is done.
- Give employees access to their records.
- When analyzing electronic work-monitoring data, be careful to distinguish between short-term and long-term trends.
- Do not use electronic monitoring to have a machine pacing people's work.
- Be careful about using work-monitoring statistics to inspire competition.
- Give employees supportive feedback based on the results of the monitoring.

You should carefully consider these guidelines when deploying a performance-monitoring system.

Emerging Technologies: Opportunities and Threats in the Workplace

The emerging new technologies keep offering opportunities to improve the effectiveness and efficiency of people's work—and present new threats to their rights. Here are some examples.

The active badge is a clip-on computer roughly the size of an employee I.D. card that can keep track of the person wearing it. These badges send infrared signals to sensors placed throughout a building. Researchers at Xerox Palo Alto Research Center see great potential for the technology as part of a broad program of ubiquitous computing. Thanks to a badge, you will never miss a call: It will be forwarded to you wherever you are. Proper doors will open for you (and the room may even greet you by name); and any computer workstation you intend to use will automatically retrieve your preferred settings. Your organization knows where you are at all times. But what about your privacy?

Network management programs allow managers of local area networks to access the directories of individual microcomputers connected to the net, and read, modify, or delete files from their hard disks. Programs from XTree of San Luis Obispo, California, and from other software vendors will let managers seize control of any personal computer connected to the network and run it remotely. Software such as WinWhatWhere (from the corporation of the same name) enables managers to monitor what is currently being typed on any keyboard and what every mouse is being clicked on, as well as logs every Web site visited from a corporate computer (Wildstrom 1996). The software does have a privacy protection feature: It signals users that they are being monitored and gives each of them an option to prevent the monitoring. With the personal information management software such as Lotus Agenda or with groupware such as Lotus Notes, virtually all the knowledge worker's activity can be visible through the computer. What privacy protection measures should be used?

Of course, the use of any technology is a conscious decision. At Cypress Semiconductor Corporation of San Jose, California, a groupware program known as "killer software" constantly monitors the performance of each business unit in the corporation. The software does this by accessing the information stored in a uniform format on the personal computers of the units' managers. When the killer software finds a unit whose performance is slipping behind its projected targets, it simply turns off their computers!

Continuing uninterrupted use of computer workstations may have negative effects on employee health. Prolonged keyboarding in clerical occupations, such as data entry, may result in repetitive strain injuries. The most frequent disorder of this kind is carpal tunnel syndrome, which affects tendons in the wrist causing compression of the nerves serving the hand and producing persistent pain and numbness in fingers. Eyestrain, backaches, and suspected effects of radiation by video display terminals are among other health hazards.

A workplace has to be designed in accordance with the principles of **ergonomics,** the study of physical relationships between people and the things they use. One of these principles, for example, demands that we type on the keyboard with our wrist held flat. Alternative designs of keyboards have been produced, yet their beneficial effects remain unproven. Companies address the problem by providing ergonomically designed work stations that offer lower back support, adjustable seats, and armrests. U.S. West has been conducting a training program for its personnel, teaching the workers proper keyboarding skills. In Japan, regulations limit the time a worker can spend at a keyboard and mandatory rest periods are set.

As discussed above, recent legal acts and new assistive technologies have resulted in renewed possibilities for integrating people with disabilities into the workplace.

According to the full text of the ACM Code of Ethics and Professional Conduct, a computing professional has an obligation "to report any signs of system dangers that might result in serious personal or social damages." If one's superiors do not act on the warning, the professional may find it his or her ethical obligation to report the violations outside of the organization—an act known as **whistle-blowing.** However, an extremely careful assessment of all the relevant aspects of risk and responsibility must precede such an act. Otherwise, the reporting itself may be harmful (and not only to the reporter).

Ethical behavior of employees is highly dependent on the corporate values and norms—on the corporate culture as a whole. Open debate of ethical issues in the workplace and continuing self-analysis help keep ethical issues in focus. Many corporations have codes of ethics and enforce them as part of a general posture of social responsibility. Do those who do good do well? Evaluations of relationships between the financial and social performance of firms have been contradictory. Encouraging results, indicating somewhat better performance by socially responsible firms have been reported (McGuire and others 1988). This is an indication that social responsibility does not have to be a competitive burden.

SUMMARY

As information technologies have the power to significantly affect the quality of our private and working lives, all knowledge workers, and particularly computing professionals, face problems related to information systems whose solution requires an ethical consideration. Ethics is the study of what we ought to do, the study of what is right and what is wrong in human conduct.

Ethical principles may be derived from one of the two principal perspectives. The consequentialist theories tell us that we should act in such a way that the end result would have the best possible consequences for the largest number of people involved. The deontological (obligational) theories argue that it is our duty to treat others with respect and uphold their rights as individuals. The principal individual rights that should be protected include the right to life and safety, rights of free consent and free speech, rights to privacy and private property, and rights to fair treatment and due process. To safeguard these rights, most professional societies and many corporations have codes of ethics which their members are expected to follow. Two important codes operative in the area of information systems are the ACM Code of Ethics and Professional Conduct and the DPMA Code of Ethics and Standards of Conduct.

Four principal ethical issues are paramount with regard to information systems: privacy, accuracy, property, and access. Privacy is the right of individuals to retain certain information about themselves without disclosure. Information systems offer unprecedented opportunities for invading personal privacy, due to the availability and the relatively low cost of the use of databases and telecommunications. Ethical principles obligate us to use individual data only for the purposes to which the individuals consented, and to give individuals the right of inspection and correction of their records, along with maintaining other safeguards.

Information systems should be built to assure accuracy of information. Economies achieved at the expense of proper validation of data and information derived from the data are wrong. Intellectual property, represented by software, databases, and knowledge bases, should be respected. The principal means of protection of intellectual property are copyrights, patents, and trade secrets. Unauthorized copying of software, known as software piracy, is wrong.

One should strive to broaden the access of individuals to the benefits of information society. This implies broadening access to skills needed to deal with information by further enabling literacy, access to information technology, and the appropriate access to information itself.

In the workplace, the use of information technology may have positive or negative impacts on the worker, depending on the way the technology is deployed. Potential positive impacts include the increased ability to develop and exercise individual skills, and integration of work into meaningful tasks that can be performed with a large degree of autonomy. Potential negative impacts include deskilling, routinization of work, and excessive monitoring of workers. Sociotechnical system design strives to avoid negative impacts. Ergonomic design of workplaces and access by people with disabilities to the electronic workplace are specific concerns. Widespread computer-based performance monitoring of workers should be made as noninvasive as possible and should be organized in accordance with ethical principles. Ethical principles should be inculcated in the workplace as a component of the corporate culture.

KEY TERMS

QUESTIONS

1. Why should you learn about ethical issues in information systems?
2. What is ethics? What is a code of ethics?
3. What is the difference between the ethical and the legal domains? Why do many issues arising from the development and use of information systems fall into the ethical domain?
4. What type of ethical theory argues that we should act to produce the greatest good for the greatest number of people? What type of theory argues that we should act out of our duty to respect the rights of others? Discuss the differences and the similarities between the two approaches.
5. State five individual rights that we should respect. Use the Internet to provide examples of the issues that arise in connection with these rights.
6. Which statements in the ACM Code of Ethics and Professional Conduct (Figure 17.2) can serve as guidelines in each of the three situations described in Section 17.2?
7. What are the principal ethical issues pertaining to information systems? What individual rights need to be protected when addressing each of these issues?
8. What is privacy? Why has privacy emerged as a principal ethical issue involving information systems? What are the dangers of an invasion of privacy?
9. What are the privacy safeguards specified in the Privacy Act?
10. How does database matching threaten an individual's privacy?
11. What is the role of the privacy concerns in the globalization of information systems?
12. Why is accuracy of information considered an ethical issue, rather than strictly an issue of technological competence?
13. What are the specific measures of an ethical approach to information accuracy?
14. What is intellectual property? How does the wide use of the World Wide Web bring this issue into focus?
15. What are the three mechanisms of protecting intellectual property? How does each of them protect the property?
16. How *well* does each of the three protection mechanisms protect the intellectual property such as software and information bases, in your opinion? How do ethical considerations relate to this protection?
17. Describe two specific instances of software piracy you are familiar with from your own observation or from readings.
18. What are the three necessities for access to the benefits of an information society?
19. How do assistive technologies broaden access? Give two specific scenarios.
20. Consider expert systems and groupware. How can the use of each of these types of information systems improve or worsen the conditions in a workplace?
21. Describe three scenarios of telecommuting. What information technology supports the worker in each of them? What are the potential positive and negative impacts of this technology on each of these workplaces?
22. What are the specific differences between the proper and improper use of computer-based work monitoring?
23. What is whistle-blowing? Give a scenario in which an information systems specialist may rightly consider whistle-blowing. What assessment would the specialist need to make in the situation you describe?

ISSUES FOR DISCUSSION

1. Discuss, in general terms, the *beneficial* aspects of information technology in a society.
2. Discuss how privacy can be safeguarded in a society in the face of growing numbers of databases containing records about individuals and of the proliferating means of access to these databases.
3. Consider the Internet. What beneficial and deleterious impacts may we expect from its expanding use in the workplace?
4. A network computer (described in Section 4.2) is a device without local secondary storage (i.e., without a hard disk), whose main objective is to access the Internet and its resources. In particular, personal productivity and other software may be obtained from the Internet as needed. Some proponents of the concept claim that the organizational use of the device will help control how workers spend their time with computers. Discuss the foreseeable effects of the use of the network computer on the workplace.

REAL-WORLD MINICASES AND PROBLEM-SOLVING EXERCISES

1. Privacy and the Internet   Several companies are devising efficient ways to track the Internet newsgroups and the World Wide Web sites you frequent. If you give your E-mail address to a Web site, the site's software can deposit a special file (called a "cookie") in your computer system. This file can connect your name to any future visits—so you can build up a track record. A California company, Email America, collects and sells E-mail addresses. According to the company's ad, you can buy "5 MILLION of these same addresses in an easy-to-use plain ASCII text format for only $99!" Other companies copy E-mail addresses from newsgroups to develop targeted mailing lists. Some solicitations are targeted more precisely; others are plain "spamming" of everyone in sight (or on the list) by sending unsolicited messages to them. Receiving unwanted E-mail may be an inconvenience to a consumer, or this mail may clog a corporate E-mail system.

a. Do you think the privacy of the Internet users is being violated by the practice described?

b. What are the actual components of the described practice and which of them is, or are, more invasive than other(s)?

c. How can Internet marketing be made less invasive? Suggest several means.

Based on Lawrence Magid, "Caring About Online Privacy," *InformationWeek,* April 29, 1996, p. 94; and Stephen H. Wildstrom, "They're Watching You Online," *Business Week,* November 11, 1996, p. 19.

2. Consider the Following Situation (Based on Parker 1990): The director of information systems of a university decided to test the security of a shared computer system to which all students had access. The director adopted the following procedure: All authorized students were encouraged to compromise the system by gaining from it improper privileges (for example, enabling themselves to use computer time and other resources beyond their proper allocation). The students were asked to report any weaknesses they found, which would gain them public recognition. A free-for-all in attacking the system resulted. One of the students discovered a means of compromising the system and reported it. However, the vulnerability was not corrected. The student continued to exploit the vulnerability to obtain more computer time and disk space than allowed.

Use the ACM Code of Ethics and Professional Conduct to help you provide answers to these questions:

a. Was the director acting ethically in encouraging students to break into the system?

b. Was he acting ethically in not correcting the discovered vulnerability?

c. Was the student acting ethically in taking advantage of the vulnerability she discovered?

3. Discuss the Ethical Issues Involved in the Following Scenario (Based on Parker 1990): While working on a project for a client, a consultant was asked to copy a copyrighted utility program that would help in performing the assignment. The consultant explained to the client that her employer's policy, as well as her own ethical standards, forbade doing that. The client copied the program right then and there and gave it to the consultant. The consultant used the pirated software to perform her assignment.

What would you do if you were the consultant?

TEAM PROJECT

Each two- or three-person team should interview representatives of a local business about the policies of the firm with respect to software piracy. Are there such policies in place? If so, how formal are they and how are they publicized? How are they enforced? Assess the policies and comment on the results.

ENDNOTES

1. Illegal acts may be committed on ethical grounds. Examples of such acts include conscientious objection during a war.

SELECTED REFERENCES

Anthes, Gary H. "Study Cites Software Industry Growth, Piracy Problems." *Computerworld,* March 29, 1993, p. 119.

Branscomb, Anne W. *Who Owns Information? From Privacy to Public Access.* New York: BasicBooks, 1994.

How to reconcile the public's right to access with the rights to intellectual property and to privacy,

Cheng, Hsing K.; Ronald R. Sims; and Hildy Teegen. "To Purchase or Pirate Software: An Empirical Study." *Journal of Management Information Systems,* 13, no. 4, (Spring 1997).

What are the principal motivations for software piracy?

Chira, Susan. "Linked (at Last) by the Word," *New York Times,* March 25, 1992, p. A16.

Collins, W. Robert, and others. "How Good Is Good Enough? An Ethical Analysis of Software Construction and Use." *Communications of the ACM,* 37, no. 1, (January 1994) pp. 81–91.

"Electronic Threats to Medical Privacy," *New York Times,* March 11, 1997, p. A22.

Friedman, Batya, and Helen Nissenbaum. "Bias in Computer Systems," *ACM Transactions on Information Systems,* 14, no. 3, (July 1996), pp. 330–347.

Specifies the potential sources of bias. (persistent discrimination against certain categories of individuals and groups) in information systems, which negatively affects the accuracy of information they provide.

Johnson, Deborah G. *Computer Ethics,* 2nd ed. Englewood Cliffs, New Jersey: Prentice-Hall, 1994.

A slim volume, but a fundamental work on computer ethics.

Kling, Rob, ed. *Computerization and Controversy: Value Conflicts and Social Choices,* 2nd. ed. San Diego: Academic Press, 1996.

An extensive collection of shorter articles concerning information systems ethics and policy making.

Laudon, Kenneth C. "Data Quality and Due Process in Large Interorganizational Record Systems." *Communications of the ACM,* 29, no. 1, (January 1986), pp. 4–11.

Lohr, Steve. "A Nation Ponders Its Growing Digital Divide," *The New York Times,* October 21, 1996, p. D5.

McGuire, Jean B., Alison Sundgren; and Thomas Schneeweis. "Corporate Social Responsibility and Firm Financial Performance," *Academy of Management Journal,* 31, no. 4, (December 1988), pp. 854–72.

Does ethical behavior pay off for a firm?

Mason Richard O. "Four Ethical Issues of the Information Age." *MIS Quarterly,* 10, no. 1, (March 1986), pp. 5–12.

Mason Richard O., Florence M. Mason, and Mary J. Culnan. *Ethics of Information Management.* Thousand Oaks, California: Sage, 1995.

A fundamental guide to ethical decision making in cases related to information systems and management.

Neumann, Peter G. *Computer-Related Risks.* New York: ACM Press, 1995.

The most inclusive discussion of risks stemming from the use of information systems.

Parker, Donn B.; Susan Swope; and Bruce N. Baker. *Ethical Conflicts in Information and Computer Science, Technology and Business.* Wellesley, Massachusetts: QED Information Sciences, 1990.

Reich, Robert B. *The Work of Nations: Preparing Ourselves for 21st Century Capitalism.* New York: Knopf, 1991.

Will the information society consist of the empowered "symbolic analysts" and a large permanent underclass?

Rigdon, Joan I. "Curbing Digital Dillydallying on the Job." *The Wall Street Journal,* November 25, 1996, pp. B1, B9.

Ross, Philip E. "Cops Versus Robbers in Cyberspace." *Forbes,* September 9, 1996, pp. 134-139.

Protecting intellectual property in the age of the Internet.

Samuels, Patrice D. "Who's Reading Your E-Mail? Maybe the Boss," *New York Times,* May 12, 1996, Business Page 11.

Schwartz, Evan I. "It's Time to Clean up Credit Reporting," *Business Week,* May 18, 1992, p. 52.

Stewart, Thomas A. *Intellectual Capital: The New Wealth of Organizations.* New York: Doubleday/Currency, 1997.

Wildstrom, Stephen H. "They're Watching You Online." *Business Week,* November 11, 1996, p. 19.

About the privacy concerns in the age of the Web.

Wood-Harper, A.T., and others, "How We Profess: The Ethical Systems Analyst." *Communications of the ACM,* 39, no. 3, (March 1996), pp. 69–77.

Outlines an ethical approach to systems analysis and presents a healthcare case study to illustrate the use of the approach.

Zuboff, Shoshana. *In the Age of the Smart Machine: The Future of Work and Power.* New York: Basic Books, 1988.

An important work, showing the potential of information technology for fruitful use in the workplace, as well as illustrating misuse of this potential.

Zwass, Vladimir. "Ethical Issues in Information Systems," *Encyclopedia of Computer Science and Technology,* Vol. 29, Suppl. 14, New York: Marcel Dekker, 1993, pp. 119-137.

CASE STUDY | ## Unethical Behavior Compounds a System Development Failure

Reservation systems are strategically important to firms in the travel industry. In 1988, a consortium of three firms, Hilton Hotels, Marriott, and Budget Rent-A-Car contracted the development of a comprehensive reservation system to AMR Information Services (AMRIS), a subsidiary of American Airlines. The system was to rely on leading-edge technology to enable the traveler to make one-call reservations for air travel, hotel stay, and a rental car. American Airlines, the developer of its famed SABRE computerized reservation system, was a natural choice as the contractor. Three-

and-a-half years after the project had begun and after a total of $125 million had been spent, the project was canceled. A malfunctioning partial system was the only—unusable—result.

In his letter to employees, Max Hopper, the head of AMRIS and, as the father of SABRE, one of the best-known IS executives wrote this: "Some people who have been part of CONFIRM's management did not disclose the true status of the project in a timely manner. This has created more difficult problems—of both business ethics and finance—than would have existed if those people had come forward with accurate information. Honesty is an imperative in our business—it is an ethical and technical imperative." Since this system failure was thus placed squarely in the ethical domain, let us follow through the developments.

AMRIS had intended to leverage the success of SABRE, one of a handful of the most successful strategic information systems, by developing reservation systems for others. In March 1987, AMRIS representatives made a presentation to Marriott executives about a new reservation system AMRIS intended to develop. Called CONFIRM, the system would be used by hotels and car rental companies which would become AMRIS's business partners. Thanks to the interfaces with airline reservation systems, simultaneous airline, hotel, and car rental reservations would be possible through a single system. AMRIS assured Marriott executives that CONFIRM would be superior to any existing reservation system in the industry and would be completed in time to outpace competition.

In October 1987, Marriott, Hilton, and Budget formed a consortium with AMRIS, called Intrico. The consortium was to implement the CONFIRM system. In May 1988, the development of the system began and the partners started to commit money to the project. In September 1988, the three firms signed a partnership agreement with AMRIS, designated "Managing Partner, Development." The partners agreed to pay AMRIS $55.7 million for the development of the reservation system. Each partner was to appoint a professional team to be stationed in Dallas, at the AMRIS headquarters. The teams would test and evaluate the system as it was being developed. The agreement allowed seven months for system analysis and design, with the entire development to be completed within 45 months of the signing of the agreement. The system was thus to be delivered at the end of June 1992.

When, at the end of December 1988, AMRIS presented the functional specifications of the system, Marriott found them inadequate. Similarly, the partners found the specifications and design documents presented in March 1989 unacceptable. After further work, AMRIS completed the preliminary system design in September 1989. At that time, the company increased the price of the project from $55.7 to $72.6 million. It also stated that the cost per reservation would be $1.30 (instead of the original $1.05) during the first year of operation, to decline to $0.72 and $0.40 in the fourth and the fifth years.

According to the contract, at that point the partners could have withdrawn from the project after paying a relatively minor penalty. The estimated cost per reservation was the information crucial to their decision making. A later analysis of the pro forma financial statements that AMRIS presented to its partners showed the statements to be false, since they understated the projected costs of system operation. The projected cost per reservation should have been stated as $2.00. Based on the falsified statements, the partners made a decision to stay with the project.

In February 1990, AMRIS missed the milestone for completing the first of the project stages, that of complete system analysis. However, the developers redefined the unfinished work of that development stage as part of the next stage, system design. In May 1990, despite the internally obvious delays, AMRIS made a presentation to its partners, claiming the project was on time and would be completed by the deadline. When the firm's employees responsible for developing and tracking the project schedule estimated that the deadline would be missed, they were instructed by their managers to change their estimates to conform with the original project calendar. According to the claims made by Marriott in a subsequent law suit, those AMRIS employees who refused to change the real schedule were reassigned to other projects, resigned, or fired.

In August 1990, AMRIS declared the system analysis complete but declined to show its deliverables to the Marriott representatives. Finally, in October of that year AMRIS admitted that the project was a year behind schedule, yet continued to claim that the original deadline would be met.

In February 1991, AMRIS presented a "Re-Plan" to replace the original development plan. According to it, only Hilton would be able to use the system by the original date of June 1992, with Marriott receiving a complete system in March 1993. The new price tag for the system was $92 million. AMRIS employees were aware that the new schedule could not be met and that their managers had lied to the firm's partners. By the summer of 1991, about half of the people assigned to CONFIRM were looking for new positions. A consultant was hired by AMRIS to evaluate the project. Dissatisfied with his report, the firm's vice-president "buried" it and dismissed the consultant.

When the initial version of the system was made available to Hilton in April 1992 for beta testing, major problems surfaced. The integration of the newly developed system with the existing airline reservation system turned out to be impossible. The project was recognized as being two years behind schedule. AMRIS fired eight top executives and replaced another fifteen employees.

In July 1992, the project was abandoned and Intrico disbanded. Several legal suits and countersuits were filed. By January 1994, AMRIS reached out-of-court settlements with its former partners. According to some sources, the amounts paid to them approached $160 million. Beyond that, company's rivals believe that the CONFIRM debacle will hurt the firm's information-technologies service business. "Our business is really reputation. You don't get in the business of suing your customers," says an executive of one of AMRIS's competitors.

Technological issues aside, it appears, and is alleged in Hopper's letter, that unethical behavior contributed to the extent of the failure. As we saw, a number of employees realized that the project was in trouble and that the partners–clients were being misinformed about the state of affairs. The dishonesty ultimately hurt not only AMRIS's clients, but also the company itself.

Based on Effy Oz, "When Professional Standards Are Lax: The CONFIRM Failure and Its Lessons," *Communications of the ACM*, 37, no. 10, (October 1994), pp. 29–36; and Wendy Zellner, "Portrait of a Project as a Total Disaster," *Business Week*, January 17, 1994, p. 36.

CASE STUDY QUESTIONS

1. Do you agree with Max Hopper that ethical issues contributed to the extent of the system development failure? If so, in what way?

2. What breaches of ethics did the managers of the provider of information services—AMRIS—commit? What signals did these breaches send to the company's employees who were aware of the situation?

3. What options did AMRIS's employees face? What would you have done in their situation?

4. Do you believe that the partners–clients of AMRIS were blameless in the described situation?

5. State the measures you would undertake to prevent a similar "runaway project."

CHAPTER EIGHTEEN

Innovating with Information Systems for Global Reach

OBJECTIVES

After you complete this chapter, you will be able to:

1. Define business globalization and describe its relationship to information systems.

2. State and discuss the three forces that shape the competitive posture of multinational corporations.

3. Describe the three strategies of global competition and the principal role information systems play in each of them.

4. Identify principal global business drivers.

5. Identify principal challenges to globalization and discuss their relationship to the organizational information systems.

6. Identify principal factors in building a global information systems architecture.

OUTLINE

Global Business Calls for Global Suppliers

An oil company with worldwide operations sought an information services vendor that would help it establish a corporate-wide office information system. The system would be based on a network that would interconnect 60 countries where the oil company does business. The hardware would include mainframes and minicomputers as servers as well as personal computers for the desktops of some 20,000 users worldwide. The hardware and software would be installed and maintained by the vendor's various country offices. But the customer intended to plan and develop the system out of its own U.S. offices. The vendor would then be responsible for the system's operation. The ongoing billing for this operation was to be subdivided and made to the customer's several regional offices. The system was to use identical user workstations throughout the world, but with the capability to handle the local language for screens and printed reports. All user documentation was required to be in the local language.

This is an example of a requirement that today's global customers make on vendors. Any vendor whose worldwide operations are organized as autonomous national units, with their own operating procedures, billing and commission structures, and installation plans, would be unable to meet the requirements of this customer. As business becomes global, companies need to change their strategies, structures, and operations. Information technology is a powerful tool in this change.

Based on Blake Ives and others, "Global Business Drivers: Aligning Information Technology to Global Business Strategy," *IBM Systems Journal,* 32, no. 1, 1993, pp.143–161.

Throughout this text, we have seen that today's business is carried out in a global context. Many Minicases and examples have demonstrated that corporations need to address any local market in the context of a worldwide competition—for customers, for suppliers, for qualified people, for capital. In particular, the Minicase you have just read showed that in order to compete for business in this environment, many companies *must* be global. Virtually all larger companies, and many surprisingly small firms, are multinational, running operations in more than one country. Information systems enable these businesses to coordinate their operations across borders and oceans. Forces of globalization drive business processes and the information system architecture necessary to support them.

It is the worldwide information technology infrastructure that enabled the globalization of business. This technology may also become an enabler for a firm to become a superior competitor in the global marketplace—or an obstacle to the firm's success.

In this chapter, we will discuss business globalization and the fundamental ways in which a multinational corporation can be supported by information systems. We will discuss the drivers through which this globalization affects a firm's business processes. We will see how these processes can be supported with an information system architecture. We will discuss a major business example that gathers the themes of this book: innovation, business reengineering, total quality management—all in the context of reaching for the global marketplace.

18.1 | GLOBALIZATION OF BUSINESS: THE NEW CORPORATE ENVIRONMENT

As we enter the 21st century, a paramount characteristic of the economic environment is increasing **business globalization:** the emergence of the worldwide market as the arena of corporate activities. Virtually all large firms, and many smaller ones, acquire labor (and locate plants) where it is cost-effective, find intellectual and financial capital anywhere it is available, and pursue markets across the globe. The costs of developing and marketing many products, such as cars, computer hardware and software, or drugs, have to be recouped by going far beyond the local market to sell them. Business partnerships among corporations headquartered in different countries are common. World trade grows much faster than the total of products and services produced around the world (measured by the world gross domestic product): A 6-fold increase in production over the past four decades has been accompanied by a 15-fold increase in trade volume (Ruggiero 1997).

Since the last World War, and particularly in the last decade, business has become increasingly international (Waters 1995). Political and economic developments have resulted in relatively free flows of goods, capital, equipment, and knowledge (in the form of technological, managerial, and entrepreneurial skills and in the form of intellectual property rights) across borders. These changes have had a mutually reinforcing relationship with the development of a global infrastructure of transportation and of computer-enabled telecommunications. Thus, information technology is an enabler of globalization and this globalization, in turn, stimulates the use of emerging information technologies.

A global economy has developed, with several regions defining the competitive environment. The United States provides the anchor for North America. Several major countries of Latin America are vigorously developing their free market economies. The economic development in the Pacific Rim is no longer largely the story of Japan. The newly industrialized countries of Hong Kong, Singapore, South Korea, and Taiwan (known as the four dragons) are being joined by Malaysia, Thailand, and Vietnam. China has entered its own path of rapid development. The most economically powerful countries of Western Europe are ever more closely allied in the European Union; several others are members of the European Free Trade Association, closely collaborating with the European Union. As the countries of Central and Eastern Europe, emerging from decades of Soviet domination or from being a part of the Soviet Union, build their own market economies, several of them may be expected to become part of the European Union. The new global world order still leaves behind all too many countries in several regions. However, it is clear that the competition and cooperation among corporations take place on an international scale.

In the environment of business globalization, many products lose their nationality. The value chain for a product, that is, the chain of activities through which a firm adds value to the input materials (see Chapter 3), can be distributed to several countries, according to the comparative advantage the country enjoys. Skills and resources—such as product design and engineering, supplies, capital, manufacturing facilities, transportation—come from a country where they can be obtained at the best terms. For example, semiconductor chips are moved from country to country between such production stages as fabrication, packaging, assembly, testing, and delivery. Thus, a device that costs less than a dollar may travel 20,000 miles in various stages of production before it reaches the customer (Ives 1993).

Service companies have followed the manufacturers in globalizing their operations. Consider the movement of goods. The worldwide net of freight mega-carriers, such as express operators, airlines, and freight forwarders, makes the necessary transportation cost-effective (Browne 1992). Such carriers as FedEx or UPS have become business partners of many major corporations which even share their business plans with them. In many cases, corporate logistics has been outsourced to these carriers. The operations of these worldwide carriers are enabled by information systems, including electronic data interchange (EDI), cargo reservation systems, tracking and tracing systems (relying on bar codes), and vehicle routing and scheduling. Another service industry going global is the temporary help business. For example, responding to the need of its global client, Northern Telecom, for "one bill, and contracting company, and one point of contact," the Milwaukee-based global leader in "flexible staffing," Manpower, supplies the company with temporaries for all of North America through a single toll-free telephone number. Now, Manpower will also be providing temporary workers for Northern Telecom overseas (Rose 1996).

Another, less obvious, phenomenon makes work much more mobile in our information society. It is not only that there are facilities for moving the work around. The very content of work has changed. As we have stressed throughout the text, it is knowledge work that accounts for most of the production costs today. Indeed, only 3 percent of the cost of a semiconductor chip is the cost of raw materials. Most of a chip's value derives from the design, engineering, financing, marketing, and similar activities. We can say that the knowledge, or information, intensity of the products has increased vastly. Knowledge work can be easily moved around the world with the use of telecommunications networks.

We may conclude that the business opportunities, threats, and everyday problems today are to a great extent defined by the global business environment. As we show in Figure 18.1, business globalization calls for global strategies and fitting corporate structures. In pursuing such a strategy, a firm needs to identify the specific drivers, that is, the essential aspects of its business that can benefit from globalization. Here is an example of such a driver: managing the firm's human resources so as to benefit from the skills and wage differentials available throughout the firm's field of operations. The firm needs to design its business processes and information systems to support the drivers that are vital to its business.

We will now proceed to discuss the strategies that corporations pursue in the global marketplace and the general roles information systems play in these strategies. We will then turn to the specific drivers that shape business processes and global information systems, and to the challenges to the systems' globalization that need to be overcome. In an extensive case, we will see how a global firm uses information systems to innovate on a global scale. We will then discuss the elements of global information system architecture.

Figure 18.1

How business globalization drives business processes and information system architecture

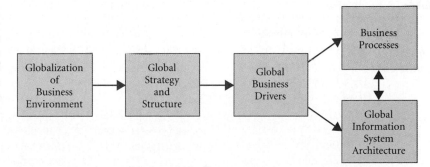

18.2   THE ROLE OF INFORMATION SYSTEMS IN GLOBAL CORPORATE STRATEGIES

Multinational Corporations in the Global Marketplace

Business firms become involved in international business to a different degree. Some firms engage only in exporting and importing, selling and buying goods and services, or trading technical and managerial skills through licensing agreements and management contracts. In a more advanced stage of international involvement, a domestically based firm begins to produce some goods or services abroad. When a corporation owns and operates companies located in more than one country, it becomes a **multinational corporation.**

Multinational corporations have become a principal driving force of business globalization as they have grown rapidly in size and number since World War II, although some firms were already involved in similar activities during the Industrial Revolution. These firms generally locate their headquarters in a parent country and their subsidiaries or other subunits in various host countries. As they grow, some of the multinationals lose ties to a domestic market (because most of their activity is abroad), and many host countries develop their own industrial base with companies that have the capability to compete with a foreign multinational. It is then that the relationships between multinational organizations and the nations where they are headquartered and where they do business become rather complicated.

Information systems have a vital role to play in a multinational corporation. To perform and innovate successfully in a global marketplace, organizations need to develop superior coordination skills. "Coordination involves sharing information, allocating responsibility, and aligning efforts," says Michael Porter of the Harvard Business School (Porter 1990). As we know, a principal capability of information systems is that they can serve as a means of coordination. Worldwide corporations also need to diffuse innovations internationally. If a corporate site in Ireland, for example, has developed a superior capability in object-oriented systems development, the entire corporation should use the experts from this site to develop systems and, which is even more important, to spread their knowledge to other sites. Thus, a technological or managerial innovation in one location should be leveraged across the organization. We may conclude that organizational designs and the use of information systems should facilitate the processes of coordinating and innovating.

Table 18.1	Goal	Business Opportunity	Information Systems Response
Goals of multinational corporations	Global integration	Efficiency: economies of scale and scope	Developing global core information systems
	Local differentiation	Flexible response to local requirements	Identifying and maintaining systems to support regional and local business processes
	Worldwide innovation	Leveraging impact of local knowledge across the corporation	Supporting knowledge work with globally accessible databases, message handling, teleconferencing, and groupware

Indeed, three forces shape the competitive posture of multinational corporations (Bartlett and Ghoshal 1989). The first is the need for *global integration* in order to achieve efficiencies, such as economies of scale from a large-scale production of a given product, and economies of scope, from a large-scale production of several related products. The second force is the need for *local differentiation* among the units located in different countries in order to respond to the requirements of local markets. The third, and increasingly important, force is the need for *worldwide innovation*—to develop and diffuse technological and organizational innovations on a global scale. If we review the capabilities of information systems which we discussed in Chapter 1, we will see that these systems can contribute to harnessing all three of these forces. The corporate goals and the information systems strategies needed to meet them are summarized in Table 18.1.

Multinational corporations differ with respect to the goals they actually pursue. We will now proceed to discuss the principal strategies of these corporations.

Strategies of Worldwide Corporations

There are three principal strategies and corresponding structures of worldwide organizations. Each of the strategies balances the three goals we discussed differently (see Table 18.2). Companies pursuing the traditional **multinational strategy** are primarily oriented toward building a strong presence in the host countries by responding to local needs. The units operating in different countries are almost independent, so long as they operate in a satisfactory manner. The central unit performs financial control of the entire enterprise. On the other hand, with a **global strategy,** the corporation treats the world as a single market and aims to realize efficiencies of scale and scope over its territory of operations.

The **transnational strategy** offers the greatest promise and many corporations are moving to implement it. A transnational corporation integrates its overseas components into the overall structure across several dimensions: Each of them can become a source of specialized innovation, integrated into the overall corporate web of the firm. Under this strategy, joint innovation by headquarters and by some of the overseas units leads to the development of relatively standardized and yet flexible products that can capture a number of local markets. For example, Japan's NEC Corporation combined the hardware expertise of its central development group in Japan with the knowledge of telecommunications software at its U.S. subsidiary to develop a superior and adaptable line of digital switching equipment. Transnational strategy often leads the company to a flexible network organizational structure, in which each unit becomes a node contributing its own core competence, something it does best.

Transnational companies often enter into strategic alliances with their customers, suppliers, and other business partners. As long-term partnerships, these alliances may bring to the firm specialized competencies, relatively stable and sophisticated market outlets that help in honing its products and services, or stable and flexible supply sources. Forming an alliance saves time and capital. A virtual organization, consisting of several independent firms that collaborate to bring products or services to the market, may emerge as a result.

Rosenbluth International Alliance is an example of such a virtual corporation (Miller 1993). Created by Rosenbluth Travel, one of the largest U.S. travel agencies with sales over $1.3 billion and headquartered in Philadelphia, the alliance responds to the growing needs of a global corporate traveler. The alliance includes 34 locally owned partner agencies with a strong presence in 37 countries. Each agency has access to the extensive information systems of Rosenbluth Travel that provide the general airline and hotel reservation information as well as the records of all of the firm's clients. Thanks to this access, each of the

Table 18.2

Corporate strategies and roles of information systems in the global business environment

Business Strategy (and Structure)	Principal Characteristic	Decision-Making Characteristics	IS Role	IS Architecture
Multinational (decentralized federation)	Foreign operations regarded as a portfolio of relatively independent businesses	Decision making decentralized to subsidiaries; informal relationships between headquarters and subsidiaries	Financial reporting by subsidiaries to headquarters for control purposes	Decentralized: primarily stand-alone systems and dispersed databases
Global (centralized federation)	Foreign operations regarded as pipelines for delivery of goods and services to a unified global market, in search of economies of scale and scope	Decisions made at the center; knowledge developed and retained at the center	Tight central control of subsidiaries through centralized planning, control, and general decision making	Centralized systems and databases
Transnational (integrated network)	Differentiated contributions by all units to integrated worldwide operations	Decision making and knowledge generation distributed among units	Vital coordination role at many levels: knowledge work group decision making, planning and control	Integrated architecture with distributed systems and databases, supporting management and knowledge work across the organization

independently operating agencies can treat the traveler in any of the countries where the members of the alliance operate as though the agency were a branch of Rosenbluth Travel. At the same time, each agency brings to the table its extensive local contacts that facilitate local arrangements. Rosenbluth Travel would not be able to acquire the foreign agencies— and thanks to the coordinating role of information technology, it did not need to.

Using Information Systems to Pursue a Worldwide Strategy

As shown in Table 18.2 and illustrated in Figure 18.2, information systems play different roles and have a different structure in companies pursing various strategies in global markets (Karimi and Konsynski 1991).

Figure 18.2

The roles of IS in worldwide corporations pursuing different business strategies (Adaped from Jahangir Karimi and Benn R. Konsynski. "Globalization and Information Management Strategies," *Journal of Management Information Systems*, 7, no. 4 (Spring 1991), pp. 7–26.

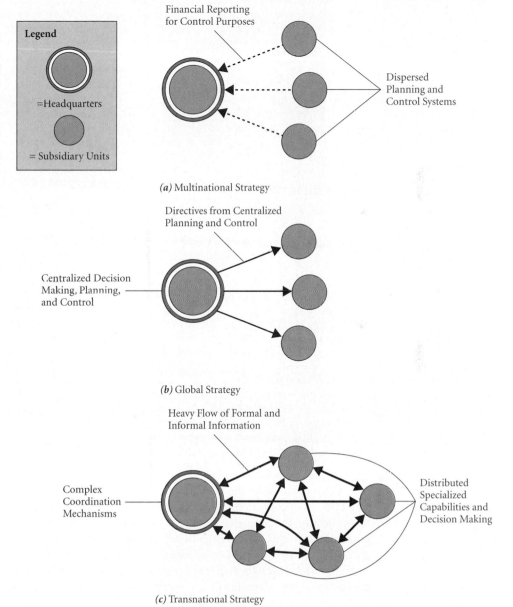

Legend

= Headquarters

= Subsidiary Units

Financial Reporting for Control Purposes

Dispersed Planning and Control Systems

(a) Multinational Strategy

Directives from Centralized Planning and Control

Centralized Decision Making, Planning, and Control

(b) Global Strategy

Heavy Flow of Formal and Informal Information

Complex Coordination Mechanisms

Distributed Specialized Capabilities and Decision Making

(c) Transnational Strategy

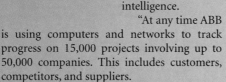

IN THE SPOTLIGHT

"Every Company is an Information Technology Company"— Percy Barnevik

Percy Barnevik (see Photo 18.1), who until 1997 ran ABB Asea Brown Boveri, is one of the world's most respected executives. He created the present corporate structure of the corporation that in a recent poll of European managers tied with England's Marks & Spencer as the most admired company in Europe. Here are some of his opinions on the role of information technology (IT).

"IT changes everything in your life, whether it's manufacturing, distribution, or retailing. Soon, there will be no non-IT companies. The writing is on the wall. Globalization of business demands global organization. You can't begin to do that without IT. Nor can you think about efficiency improvements, product development, service. The most traditional products contain more and more intelligence.

Photo 18.1

Percy Barnevik as the chief executive of ABB Asea Brown Boveri

"At any time ABB is using computers and networks to track progress on 15,000 projects involving up to 50,000 companies. This includes customers, competitors, and suppliers.

"We spend about $700 million on information system resources and have 5,000 employed in this area. The budget breaks down like this: development/application, 35%; operation/communication, 55%; training, 10%. We have 50,000 PCs and terminals and 45,000 E-mail users. Eighteen months ago, to facilitate doing more interactive work globally, we became users of Lotus Notes. We're up to 8,000 users.

"ABB *must* reduce all of its cycle times. We have set big goals: engineering, 30%; manufacturing, 60%; field work, 90%.

Engineering reductions come from computer simulation, which is far more reliable than prototype building. Manufacturing reductions are even greater. Computer simulation up front reduces the potential for mistakes on the back end. Robots directly reduce time and costs. . . Finally, supply management—the integration of fewer suppliers and faster inventory turnover—adds to speed. Fieldwork reductions are most dramatic: 90%, because of zero defects in engineering and manufacturing.

"In my business, if you don't have an understanding of speed in the world and the impact of IT on business, now and in the future, you are going to be a loser.

"There's another aspect of IT: not how to make products, but how to sell them. . . Forty percent of everything we sell is based on IT. Today, you can show a customer a plant configuration on a computer screen. You can walk [the customer] through the plant. You can customize technical specs and immediately show the effect on price. You can connect [the customer] to specialists with video links."

". . . every company is an IT company."

In May 1997, Barnevik became the chairman of Investor, one of the largest European holding companies, which controls some of the world's most famous brands, such as the Saab automobile.

Based on Rich Karlgaard, "Interview with Percy Barnevik," *Forbes ASAP*, December 5, 1994, pp. 65–68; and Charles Wallace, "Percy Barnevik Gets a Shot," *Fortune,* June 9, 1997, p. 166.

As we move down the table and the figure, we can see the increasing role of information systems in coordinating the operations of the enterprise (note the thickening lines interconnecting the business units). The architecture of the company's information systems corresponds to this role. Multinational strategy, which treats the subsidiary units almost as a portfolio of independent companies, requires only periodic financial reporting to headquarters. Global strategy requires a centralized planning and control to support centralized decision making. The units of a transnational company create a network relying on everyday communication among many members of the organization. This communication has to be supported with an extensive distributed systems architecture relying on a global telecommunications network. Indeed, in some transnational corporations, the word "headquarters" is banned, and the size of the headquarters has been shrunk. For example, ABB Asea Brown Boveri, a global giant in electrical power industry with annual revenues of more than $28 billion earned in 140 countries and with over 213,000 employees around the world, has fewer than 200 staff members working at its Zurich headquarters in Switzerland. In the vignette on the preceding page, the company's chief executive tells us about the role of information technology in a global company.

As corporations pursue their worldwide strategies, the marketplace presents ever new demands that shape, in turn, the firm's information systems. These demands create global business drivers, which we will now discuss.

18.3 | BUSINESS DRIVERS IN THE GLOBAL ENVIRONMENT AND HOW TO ENABLE THEM WITH INFORMATION SYSTEMS

It is very important for you as a future manager to understand the general forces of globalization. However, specific investment and operational decisions are made in response to a specific problem or opportunity, not a generality. How do the forces of globalization translate into the specific business problems and opportunities? This happens through specific business drivers. **Global business drivers** are the aspects of the firm's business that can benefit from the global economies of scale or scope. By analyzing whether a specific driver is important to your business, you can identify the data and information that need to be shared globally. This leads, in turn, to the definition of the shared databases, shared information systems, and the telecommunications infrastructure necessary to provide access to them.

Table 18.3, based on the work of Blake Ives and his colleagues (Ives 1993), presents the major drivers, the questions that lead you to identify a driver as vital to your business, and the major examples of databases and systems that need to be shared to enable the driver.

Let us discuss the individual drivers:

1. People (call them *human resources*) are the most important asset of an enterprise. This is particularly so as many products acquire high information intensity, that is, these products are the result of specialized and varied knowledge work. This means, in turn, that much of the work on a product can be electronically moved to the knowledge workers as opposed to the traditional way of moving people to the work. Employee skills can be drawn upon on the global corporate scale and international teams can be organized. For example, IBM develops software faster with multinational teams by moving the work with the clock. When the team in the company's facility in Hursley, England, is finished for the day, the design database is transferred via telecommunications to San Jose, California, and from there to Tokyo, Japan, only to be moved again to Hursley when the Japanese team completes the day's work (Deans and Kane 1992).

Important categories of information systems that enable this driver are teleconferencing, electronic meeting systems, intranets, and electronic mail. As more and more knowledge work takes place in teams, groupware that makes collaboration possible becomes particularly important. Human resource information systems need to include detailed skills and experience inventories for the members of the organization so that task-oriented teams can be formed.

Table 18.3	**Global Business Driver**	**Why Is This Driver Important to Your Business?**	**Databases and Systems to Be Globally Shared**
Frequent global business drivers (Adapted from B. Ives, S.L. Jarvenpaa, and R.O. Mason, "Global Business Drivers: Aligning Information Technology to Global Business Strategy," *IBM Systems Journal*, 32, no. 1, 1993, pp. 143–161.)	Shared human resources	Can you manage skills globally? Can you move knowledge work electronically to countries with the requisite skills and favorable wage levels? Can you build and support globally dispersed teams?	Skills inventory Experience inventory Project histories
	Distributed operations	Can you coordinate production around the world? Can you move production from one country to another? Can you share production resources around the world to best use their capacity?	Manufacturing resource planning on a global scale
	Global products	Can you identify opportunities for global products? Can you launch a product in several countries? Can you derive maximum efficiencies from global products?	International product standards Marketing plans
	Quality	Can you trace the source of a defective component? Can you perform global quality benchmarking?	Product database Performance standards
	Risk management	Can you analyze country risk? Can you manage your foreign exchange exposure?	Environmental scanning Asset management
	Suppliers	Can you determine your global position with a supplier? Can you negotiate volume discounts based on the global relationship?	Purchasing database Supplier database
	Customers	Can you ensure consistent product, service, and information to your customers worldwide? Can you provide seamless worldwide ordering, order tracking, and billing around the world? Can you identify global opportunities to serve your customers better?	Customer information Order database Marketing database

   2. In a manufacturing firm, it should be possible to *distribute the operations* in a product's value chain internationally to the greatest possible advantage, based on the availability of capital equipment, skills, or supplies. To accomplish that, it is necessary to coordinate production and to provide the necessary logistics to move semi-finished products. It should be possible to move production from one country to another based on the consideration of capacity utilization, or if unfavorable business or political conditions emerge in a given location. Global manufacturing resource planning and global logistics systems are necessary to support such very complex operations.

3. *Global products* that are the same (or nearly the same) anywhere in the world where they are sold become more common. Why? Consumers around the world that emerged from the geographical isolation and the cold war, stimulated by travel and info-tainment, demand many similar products. Business customers demand similar products anywhere they do business. Your firm, of course, prefers to supply a global product, or a product that requires only minor modifications for a local market, since this leads to in-creased economies of scale.

Your information systems should help you identify opportunities for global products and help launch such products in several countries. Your marketing research should be sup-ported by access to several external information sources and your own databases that support information systems for scanning the business environment. You should have the capability to coordinate marketing plans across multiple countries or even regions.

4. *Quality* has become a required, not an optional, attribute of products sold in the world markets. Total quality management (which we discussed in Chapter 12) is practiced by an increasing number of firms. Information systems are necessary to establish the at-tributes of quality that international customers demand. To achieve the highest levels of these attributes of quality, you have to be able to benchmark all aspects of your operations against those of the top performers in the world and within your own firm. Databases of benchmarks, of your own standards, and of the actual product quality achieved have to maintained. To follow up on a problem, you need the ability to track a defective product to its source—a supplier, a worker, or a machine. Product databases and bar coding of indi-vidual products are vital in the task.

5. International operations bear additional *risks.* Extensive environmental scanning is necessary in order to be apprised of country risks—the exposure to a political or eco-nomic downturn in a given country where you do business. Since you will need to do busi-ness in several currencies, you also need to manage your foreign exchange exposure. What if the value of the currency in which you have to pay your supplier a year from now goes up significantly in the meantime? Many firms maintain sophisticated asset management sys-tems for the purpose, protecting themselves against possible unfavorable changes in the value of foreign currencies.

6. Increasingly, large companies find that they are able to deal in several countries with the worldwide entities of the same *supplier.* It is of great advantage to you if you can determine the overall global volume of your purchases from a given supplier. As a large cus-tomer, you can negotiate volume discounts and influence the attributes of the future prod-ucts supplied to you. Global purchasing and supplier databases are necessary to do so.

7. The most important subsystem in your global information system architecture should be your customer information system that will enable you to integrate all the infor-mation about your dealings with each customer. As your *customers* do more business around the world, they will expect you to provide a consistent level of service anywhere. If you are to be able to do that, you need information systems that support worldwide trans-action processing for transactions originating anywhere you wish to do business. Globally accessible customer and order databases are necessary. Global access to "soft" information about present or potential customers, which may be secured with groupware, such as Lotus Notes, is also necessary. Soft information is different from the "hard" numbers of reports. It includes opinions, speculations, assessments, and rumors. Such soft information will tell you about the problems a prospective customer is experiencing with its current suppliers, or about the likely personnel changes in the regional purchasing division of your existing customer. You need to be proactive—to analyze both the "hard" and the "soft" information

IN THE SPOTLIGHT

In Europe, 3M Thinks Globally and Acts Regionally

"We need information systems that will tell us the status of all the orders a customer has with us and systems that will tell us what the customer has been buying across Europe," says David Drew, the information technology chief at 3M of St. Paul, Minnesota. This company believes in regionalization as a means to strike a balance between local autonomy and central control. And that is no whimsical creed. The company's customers themselves have become regionalized. When a French business expands production and markets to other European countries, it wants to deal with its supplier as a single firm. Therefore, country-focused processes and the information systems that support them had become a roadblock. For example, an order placed in Austria used to take seven days to reach the 3M plant in the United Kingdom because it had to be entered and transmitted several times as part of a batch file.

With its EUROMS pan-European information system, whose first version was fielded in 1991, 3M has integrated order processing and production planning in 17 countries.

Now, an Austrian order is routed directly to the British factory—in seconds.

But regionalization is not the final answer. Now, the firm's European customers are globalizing: They do more and more business all over the world. And they may wish to deal with 3M in their own country to do so. This means that a Swedish customer may wish to place orders through 3M's marketing office in Sweden for the customers' factories in Europe, but also in Japan and in the United States. The regional system becomes insufficient. Thus, 3M is driven by its customers to develop truly global information systems.

In order to support its international initiatives, 3M has one-third of its IS staff deployed overseas and consisting of local nationals. Senior IS managers also live and work outside of the United States, to develop insight and sensitivity to local conditions and cultural imperatives.

Based on Allan E. Alter, "Continental Divides," *CIO*, October 1, 1993, 62–68; and Anne Stuart, "As the World Shrinks," *CIO*, August 1996, pp. 100–108.

about the customers and the noncustomers globally in order to identify new opportunities.

The vignette above shows how one company is meeting the expectations of its international customers with information systems.

18.4   CHALLENGES TO GLOBALIZATION

It would be naive to believe that the world has permanently moved to a new order in which nation–states and national cultures and economies blend into a global society espousing market economy and liberal democracy as the way of life. Significant and deeply rooted differences of culture and value systems exist among the world's regions and nations. Moreover, many of these nations are committed to maintaining these differences rather than to see them disappear. It is rather premature to speak about the "twilight of sovereignty," the decline of national governments, precipitated by the information revolution (Wriston 1992). The uneven economic development throughout the world has produced deep differentials between the economic endowments and technological capabilities of its nations. These differences in some cases offer business opportunities that can be reached for with information technology. However, to exploit these opportunities one must overcome various challenges to the implementation of global information systems.

We summarize the barriers to a globalization of information systems in Table 18.4. We will concentrate here on the cultural, political, and socioeconomic differences that present

Table 18.4	Challenge	Manifestations	Response
Challenges to globalization of information systems	Nationalism	Importation of foreign IS managers into a host country. Limitations imposed by the host country on the use of foreign information technology.	Sensitivity to the local concerns, training and promotion of local personnel. Long-term incentives to the host country.
	Language barriers	Inability to communicate in information systems planning and systems development. Problems with system use by knowledge and information workers.	Personnel selection and language training. Localized system interfaces.
	Cultural traditions	Different approaches to time, uncertainty, hierarchy, community.	Personnel exchanges, videoconferences, multinational teams, process benchmarking on best-in-the-world.
	Political (country) risks	Exposure to adverse legislation and political unrest.	Monitoring country risk and maintaining flexible operations.
	Uneven economic development and skills shortages	Absence of skills needed to implement, maintain, and work with an advanced information system.	Gradualism, education, and continual benchmarking.
	Differences in tax laws and accounting procedures	Inability to implement uniform global information systems.	Using localized systems along with specialized applications for consolidation of financial results.
	Legal differences	Differences in laws regarding transborder data flows.	Structure information systems to obey the local laws.
	Different technology standards	Different EDI, telecommunications, and hardware standards.	Employing hardware and software that translate protocols. Furthering international standardization.
	Differences in telecommunications capabilities	Difficulties in implementing global networks.	Matching the local nets with the local capabilities.

challenges to the global information systems. We will come back to the technological issues in the last section of the chapter.

Cultural differences go to the very root of the national identity. Even managers in the most developed countries that have long espoused market economies display striking differences in their values and priorities (Hampton-Turner and Trompenaars 1993). At their worst, these differences express themselves as nationalism, the belief that one's own nation would benefit from acting autonomously, rather than by harmonizing its initiatives with other members of a global community. A multinational corporation that consistently imports information systems managers into a host country displays nationalism, and so does a host country that imposes unreasonable limitations on the use of foreign equipment or software. Only by understanding the long-term incentives of the global division of labor can the nations and their decision makers overcome the tendency toward self-sufficiency and opportunism.

Language barriers are often absent at the management level, but they manifest themselves acutely when information workers are expected to use systems with foreign language interfaces (Roche 1992). Internationalization of software, with interfaces in local languages, is beginning to catch up with the needs (Taylor 1992). More difficult to overcome are the culture-based differences, such as perceptions of how absolute are time commitments, or the loyalty one owes the community versus loyalty to the employer. Personnel exchanges and multicultural teamwork create better understanding and the ability to work around the differences. This understanding can be maintained by collaboration using various forms of teleconferencing and electronic meeting systems.

Multinational operations create by their very nature additional risks. Firms trying to take advantage of the opportunities that emerged from the fall of the Soviet empire find shifting legislation, punitive tax codes, and instability of authority in many of the new countries (Zwass 1992). Labor unrest or a threat to data centers can emerge in a given host country and it should be possible to move operations elsewhere rapidly.

One of the many adverse effects of uneven economic development of the countries in which multinational companies operate is inability to implement a strategic information system in a country unprepared for such development. For example, although it may be possible to implement an operational information system for order processing, it may be difficult to deploy an executive information system based on critical success factors. The interest in "leapfrogging," bypassing the intermediate development stages, often arises. This is in many cases difficult to do, because of the lack of acculturation to the advanced information technology, absence of the proper educational and technological infrastructure, and lack of requisite skills on a broad base.

Local capabilities of the less economically advanced countries can be raised by offshore outsourcing of information systems development to some of them. This need not sound paradoxical. Since these countries have far lower wages than the advanced ones, but have at the same time pockets of highly skilled experts (Hungary, India, and Russia may serve as examples), they offer comparative advantages. Such offshore outsourcing of information systems development furthers the international diffusion of information technology. However, projects that require extensive ongoing interactions between users and developers should be developed at the user location.

Differences in tax reporting and accounting procedures among countries of the world may be expected to become narrower, but not disappear. In order to produce uniform consolidated results necessary for global coordination, it is necessary to deploy specialized information systems that perform such translation. For example, the U.S. multinational firm Tambrands uses in its operations in Kiev, Ukraine, the accounting program SCALA from a Swedish company Beslutsmodeller, which translates the local results into the language of U.S. accounting.

National laws and regulations differ widely, of course. Particularly pertinent are the distinctions with respect to the labor laws and the protectionist laws trying to shield local information industry from the international competition. We will come back later in the chapter to the issue of laws limiting transborder data flow—the ability to bring data and information into and out of a country. We will also investigate more fully the primary technological obstacle to global networking—the widely differing national telecommunications capabilities and regulations. We should note that in some countries of operation it may be necessary to deviate from the corporate hardware and software standards and acquire products of local vendors in order to accommodate expectations of good corporate citizenship.

It is possible to identify several regional clusters consisting of countries with a similar approach to information systems management (Watson 1997). As you can read in the following vignette, there are meaningful differences in the information systems culture of the United States, Europe, and Japan.

Cultural Differences in the Use of Information Technology

The United States and Europe are the leading regions in the deployment of organizational computing. Forces of globalization are moving European and U.S. information systems ever closer together. Increasingly, companies in both parts of the world compete in the same markets, face similar business problems, and adopt similar information systems architectures to solve them. The firms use the same information technologies and the same products, from client/server systems to Windows and Lotus Notes.

Yet, some differences remain. If you ask the European managers, they will tell you that their U.S. colleagues are much quicker to deploy a hot new information technology product. The Europeans tend to be more planning-oriented, focusing on the projected business benefits of a technology or, if you will, simply more cautious. In Europe, "they'll implement the technology if they can control it. It's a risk-free approach. People in the U.S. might just say, 'Go for it,'" Cedric Thomas, head of a Paris-based consultancy, tells us.

Other differences stem from the geopolitics. "Europe is more fragmented, so European companies support extensive decentralized processing strategies. That puts much more focus on the overall IT architecture," says the director of information systems at the large Belgian retailer Delhaize. The structure of European telecommunications, with national telecommunications authorities maintaining high costs of telecommunications, also leads to decentralized solutions. But then several European countries, most notably Germany, are privatizing their telecommunications.

"In the U.S., upper management is more comfortable with [information] technology," says another European IT chief. User expectations in the United States are also seen to be higher than in Europe. And since the key IT suppliers are largely U.S.-based, users in the United States benefit from working more closely with the suppliers' product development teams.

Japan, so justly acclaimed for its use of information technology in production processes, has not been a leader in using information systems in management and office operations. In the consensus-driven corporate cultures, few Japanese companies have a chief information officer who would be responsible for the corporate deployment of information technology. Long-standing practices of keeping tight reins on the flow of information hamper the development of organizational telecommunications networks. Face-to-face communication almost excludes electronic mail. In general, the technology is seen as taking away from the warmth of human contact. As Toshiyuki Mori, a senior executive involved with information technology at the cosmetics manufacturer Shiseido, tells us, most senior managers there have a "serious allergy" to computers which prevents them from touching a finger to a keyboard. "We are very far behind the U.S. in managing information systems," says Kiyoshi Asakawa, a general manager at Nikko Securities.

At times, there is high price to pay for the lack of adequate computerization. When a trader in copper futures, Yasuo Hamanaka, racked up losses of $1.8 billion in unauthorized trades in 1996, his activities did not trigger any computerized watchdog programs at the firm that employed him. This was because the employer, the giant Japanese trading company Sumitomo, did not have appropriate information systems for auditing purposes, as a similar U.S. firm would. While such auditing systems offer no guarantee that a transgression would be promptly discovered, they provide an important layer of compliance checking.

Now, leaders in the use of IT, such as Shiseido, Japan's largest and oldest cosmetics company, and Nikko Securities, a top brokerage house, are emerging. Driven by the new generation of managers, these firms are attempting to carefully blend information technology with the corporate culture.

Based on Paul Tate, "Hands Across the Borders," *Information Week,* October 10, 1994, pp. 188–192; Kathryn Graven, "The Eastern Front," *CIO,* October 1, 1994, pp. 46–52; David P. Hamilton, "Unplugged: Sumitomo Scandal Suggests Japanese Don't Use Computers Enough," *The Wall Street Journal,* June 26, 1996, pp. B1, B15; Shuji Honjo, "Catching On?," *Computerworld/NetworkWorld,* September 9, 1996, p. 11; and David Kirkpatrick, "Europe's Technology Gap Is Getting Scary," *Fortune,* March 17, 1997, pp. 26–27.

18.5 | GLOBAL BUSINESS PROCESS INNOVATION WITH INFORMATION TECHNOLOGY

As multinational corporations attempt to extend their global reach in pursuit of new markets or a deeper penetration of the existing ones, they turn to information systems as a principal tool in this pursuit. As we discussed earlier in the chapter, information systems can support all three aspects of the transnational strategy evolving in many leading corporations.

When an established multinational firm starts this pursuit, it does not begin it in a "green field" of no information systems, to which the appropriate new technology can be moved. Rather, the firm's operations are supported by a cacophony of existing legacy systems spread around the world, which served the units of the company adequately when the traditional multinational model was being pursued. These legacy systems are often difficult to modify in order to adapt them to new needs. It is, indeed, neither feasible nor necessary to replace the entirety of the existing corporate information systems with a new globalized one.

As Figure 18.3 shows, only some of the corporate information systems, those dealing with the core global business processes, have to be designed on the global scale. The nature of these processes corresponds to the global business drivers. For example, driven by global customers, many companies have developed global order processing systems. Other systems serve a limited geographical region rather than spanning the globe. In particular, as we have seen in the 3M vignette on page 650, pan-European systems are often developed. At the same time, either due to the specific local conditions, or due to external limitations (such as those on data export), some systems do not need to go beyond the confines of a specific country and remain local.

Let us follow through a path of innovation taken by a well-known firm, Tambrands. Let us remember that in order to innovate, we have to break away from established patterns. Such breaking away is never easy—the paths are uncharted and the established patterns are comfortable grooves for many, often powerful, occupants. The risk of innovation is particularly high when an international scale is involved. Local operating units and their managers are used to enjoying a high degree of autonomy; solutions that come from abroad can

Figure 18.3

Structure of a corporate global information system (Adapted from Edward Roche, *Managing Information Technology in Multinational Corporations*, New York: Macmillan, 1992, p. 50)

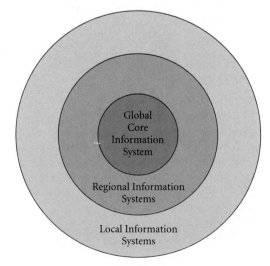

Global Core Information System

Regional Information Systems

Local Information Systems

be immediately branded as not meeting local needs; and maintaining a working relationship throughout a long-term transformational project requires the goodwill of many parties.

When we discuss the initiatives at Tambrands, we are considering a case of an organizational innovation in developing a global information system core that throws in focus several major themes of the contemporary IS environment.

1. The Company and the Primary Global Business Driver

Tambrands, based in White Plains, New York, is a single-product company: It manufactures and markets Tampax tampons (Buchanan 1994). The company has manufacturing plants in 7 countries and sells in 135 countries. In 1997, the company has been acquired by Procter & Gamble. The operational units of the firm had been traditionally independent and their processes differed widely. The organization was perceived as difficult to manage and its costs were relatively high. As a manufacturer of a global product and, moreover, a single one, the overriding objective of Tambrands in the emerging global marketplace is to secure maximum efficiency in the value chain of its product. For example, the firm moved early into the emerging European labor markets by opening a plant in Kiev, Ukraine. This move was, of course, not a solution to the general problem of unmanageability and high costs. By pursuing a transnational strategy, the company expects to combine the advantages of global integration with significant local contributions to the corporate business processes.

2. Global Business Process Reengineering Combined with Total Quality Management

To pursue its strategy, Tambrands undertook to reengineer its core business processes globally. A transnational solution, resting on the principles of total quality management, was adopted: The firm set out to identify the best practices throughout its global units for each process, in order to use them as a foundation for global reengineering. Internal benchmarking, introducing the best practices of various units throughout the firm, was to be the basis for reengineering. This was expected to lead to a uniform performance of major common tasks, such as manufacturing and logistics, in the best way. From the outset, it was decided to rely on global teams for identifying the best practices. As we know, teamwork is another principle of total quality management. Training in total quality management was initiated throughout the corporation.

It was recognized at the outset that information technology would play a major role in the implementation of the reengineered processes. The reengineering was sponsored by the top executives of the firm—indeed, the firm diagnosed the former lack of such sponsorship as the reason for its relative backwardness in the deployment of information technology. Needed investment in the technology had been postponed for a long time.

3. Role of Information Systems

Under the leadership of the chief financial officer and the chief information officer of the company, a strategic four-year plan for drawing up an information technology platform under the new strategy was devised. In terms of Table 18.1, the principal objectives were global integration and worldwide innovation based on the best local practices. The reengineering process was to be driven by the business needs rather than information technology.

The task was simplified by the single-product (with minor local variations) nature of the company and by the fact that largely the same hardware had been used throughout the corporation. When the reengineering started, the midrange IBM AS/400 systems were the hardware of choice. The systems were consolidated into two data centers, in Europe and in the United States, each with two processors. However, software and operating procedures differed widely among the geographic divisions.

4. Experience with Implementing Global Reengineering

To respond to the most critical need, the first process to be reengineered was that of financial management reporting. Because of widely differing local reporting, the company had been unable to compare its financial performance for various countries and regions, or to compare its cost structures throughout the world. Indeed, the situation had been so bad that internal benchmarking proved unsatisfactory in this area and it was necessary to rely on external expertise. As the result of reengineering, the streamlined cost- and profit-center reporting enabled the firm to cut the book-closing time (that is, the time needed to obtain consolidated financial results) by more than half. Financial systems changed the role of the financial group from number crunchers dealing with past results to analysts who could offer solutions for the future.

Internal benchmarking proved successful in reengineering the manufacturing processes. With the help of the information available through the previously reengineered financial processes, the teams were able to benchmark internally throughout the world the inventory systems, productivity per employee, purchasing costs, and production costs. External benchmarks were also employed, with the help of a consulting firm. In addition, informal sharing of plant information helped identify the plants where best results were obtained.

Local business needs were used to determine which site would begin the reengineering of what process. For example, a site where reengineering of order processing was the highest priority became responsible for that process. A lead team would be created on such a site, with the responsibility to reengineer the process locally and to transfer the process and its enabling information technology to other sites. In this way, a center of excellence for a process became responsible for how well the process would work throughout the firm. In this way, the European division reengineered the manufacturing processes, and the U.S. division redesigned order processing.

As reengineering progressed on a site, teams from overseas locales were continually involved: thus, they could both contribute and learn, in order to cut the implementation time on their own site. Moreover, this involvement, along with the management review committees, ensured that the lead location considered the requirements of other sites in the definition of global business processes and data structures. The timetable for transferring a project was determined by the priorities of the receiving site.

The identified core business processes were implemented by modifying software packages acquired from specialized vendors. For example, PRISM (from Marcam of Newton, Massachusetts) was used for manufacturing resource management and order fulfillment.

5. Allowing for Local Differences

To avoid a "cookie-cutter" approach, room for local software differences was allowed, as long as the local systems had common general functionality. Limitations in human resources and technology were also considered. For example, the sites in China and in Ukraine relied on local area networks of microcomputers, instead of mid-sized AS/400s. In the Ukrainian plant, where accounting practices differed widely from the U.S. and European ones, it proved best to use a software package that translated their results into those conforming to Western practices. It was also necessary to temporarily bring in some Western expertise. As a process was being reengineered locally, it was assigned a local owner, the manager responsible for the success of implementation—a crucial factor in such success.

6. Evaluation

The firm found that the cultural differences were initially compounding the usual regional and functional prejudices. Indeed, in some cases, such differences were claimed as a convenient excuse. However, as the teams worked together, their common business objectives and responsibility for results took precedence.

Operating in the market where it is difficult to achieve meaningful product differentiation, Tambrands has positioned itself to become a low-cost manufacturer. We need to recognize that many of the global business drivers (summarized in Table 18.3) remain to be satisfied. As an example, flexible production or risk management were not part of the original design. But the firm is now in a position to pursue these goals. The transformation of information system architecture is in progress. In particular, the company is considering a further consolidation of its two data centers in support of its redefined business processes.

18.6 | BUILDING GLOBAL INFORMATION SYSTEM ARCHITECTURE

Business processes that have to respond to the demands of the global business environment have to be supported with a **global information system architecture.** Such an architecture is largely defined in terms of the backbone telecommunications network—this is why we discussed it in Chapter 7. However, as shown in Figure 18.4, aside from the telecommunications, architectural plans need to include the processing hardware and software, as well as the design and siting of databases. In addition, global information systems development projects are more difficult because of greater variability of circumstances as the projects are carried out, the need to work in environments unfamiliar to some of the developers, and the complexity arising from these different environments (Tractinsky and Jarvenpaa 1995). Let us first discuss the specific problems that make developing a global information system architecture a major challenge. We will then describe the global communications network of a firm that has successfully responded to this challenge over two decades.

Special Considerations of a Global Information System Architecture

Moving to a global information system architecture presents a series of challenges that we will now discuss.

1. Hardware and Software in Global Architecture

The barriers to a global information technology platform that are presented by the variety of computer equipment, and by the variety of systems and applications software, are not that different from the barriers encountered in a distributed system that is local to a single nation. There are the existing legacy systems to contend with and there are parochial interests of local management. However, in addition, a hardware or software selection for a given

Figure 18.4

Components of global information system architecture

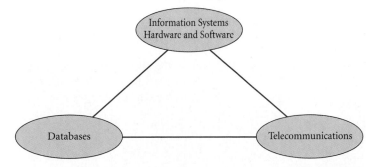

country may be limited by the following considerations:

- The resource of choice may not be locally supported by its vendor or a service company.

- The host country government actively encourages, or even legislates, the use of locally produced information systems resources, of resources with a partial local content (that is, partly produced locally), or of resources available from a local distributor.

- In the case of software, many governments mandate that products sold locally have local language capability.

- The local price of a desired resource, after the import duties and other costs, makes its deployment not cost-effective.

- Unavailability of qualified staff may restrict the available options.

- The climate, the quality of the electric power, and other limitations call for equipment that can withstand these inclemencies.

As business globalization progresses, **localized software** packages that have user interfaces in the local language and conform to the local cultural tradition are increasingly produced by vendors (Greenwood 1993). Thus, going beyond the user interfaces in the national language (you can see an example in Figure 18.5), such a package displays dates, time,

Figure 18.5

The Japanese version of the Microsoft Windows 95 interactive demo (From John Golding, "Windows 95 Versus Macintosh 88," *Multilingual Computing,* November 1995, pp. 18–20.)

Photo 18.2

The programmers of Digital Equipment Corporation in India are adapting the company's software to the needs of the Japanese market. This is part of a broad process of software localization. (From *Forbes,* May 23, 1994, p. 132.)

and numbers according to local custom, and its design may consider the significance of color in the culture (red signifies danger in the United States, but happiness in China), and the local style of group work, among other things. Some packages also conform to local business practices while delivering a common functionality. Unicode, the standard universal character code that we introduced in Chapter 4, assists in producing software that can be localized for any language (Fowles 1997).

Since, in general, managerial and other professional knowledge workers know English, the lingua franca of software, while other workers do not, user interfaces in the local language are particularly vital for the clerical and plant workers. In Photo 18.2 you can see Digital Equipment Corporation's programmers adapting the company's software to the Japanese market.

2. Databases

Added challenges and limitations present themselves with respect to the corporate databases. Thus, the challenge of defining a uniform structure of data for all business units across multiple national boundaries is more daunting than in a national case because of a greater variance among local business practices. The considerations of country risk, such as a potential threat to data centers, may necessitate other than the technologically optimal choice for the database sites, more stringent backup and disaster recovery policies, and a replication of databases.

A specific additional challenge is that of restrictions some countries impose on the **transborder data flow:** the transmission of data across (primarily out over) their boundaries. In general, such nations consider the data created in their country to be a resource that should be protected or exploited (or both) by the country. The restrictions take different form and have different sources in various countries (Carper 1992).

By limiting the data flow out of their territory, some countries pursue the issues of political and economic sovereignty. For example, Canada requires approval from its government for processing abroad data originating from transactions within the country; France requires every database maintained in the country to be registered with the government and imposes duties on data transfers. Other countries, such as Brazil, impose duties and restrictions on data transfers in order to protect their own information technology industries. Privacy protection is the main concern in the Scandinavian and certain other European countries, which limit the transfer of data regarding specific individuals to countries that do not have privacy legislation matching their own. This may severely restrict options in the design of a human resource management system, for example. All these restrictions present challenges that go well beyond the technical problems of specifying an organizational database design.

Storing multilingual nonnumeric data in databases presents challenges as well. To address the issue of software internationalization, the SQL standard for relational databases was revised in 1992 to support multiple character sets.

3. Telecommunication Networks

A global telecommunications network is the principal platform of the corporate information system architecture of a multinational corporation. It is also the component that presents the toughest challenges. Here are the most frequently encountered obstacles:

1. Countries and regions differ widely in the quality (for example, capacity and reliability) of their telecommunications infrastructure.

Consider some examples. Western Europe has emerged as the leading region in implementing Integrated Services Digital Network (ISDN) and in evolving the necessary standards for mobile telecommunications. In Eastern Europe and in Russia, wireless networks are proving the only solution to many telecommunications problems. While in the United States 40 percent of the offices are wired for networks, in Japan only 5 percent are network-ready (McMullen 1994).

2. Telecommunications services in many countries are dominated by a PTT (postal, telegraph, and telephone) monopoly run by the country's government. This leads to very high telecommunications costs (in some European countries, 10 times higher than in the United States), limited availability of telecommunications services, and limited flexibility, since acquisition of leased lines may take months or even years. The 1997 international agreement, negotiated under the auspices of the World Trade Organization, is expected to lead to lower telecommunications prices and enhanced services over several years.

3. Conflicting standards on various protocol levels—from the electric connections to the electronic data interchange (EDI)—make it necessary to deploy hardware and software for protocol conversions.

4. The great variety of cost tariffs (i.e., prices associated with various telecommunications services) and supplier offerings call for a thorough evaluation of options.

It is not surprising that many firms choose to outsource running their global networks to outside vendors. However, there are signs of improvement. Several European countries have privatized or are in the process of privatizing their telecommunications supplier. Virtual private networks have emerged as an important option for the firms that spend over $25,000 a month on telecommunications. In such an arrangement, against a minimum guaranteed level of usage by the user firm, the carrier guarantees the firm access on demand to a given level of service (transmission speed, performance, and access points). Virtual private networks combine the flexible cost of pay-per-use of a public network with the availability and control of a private network. With the Internet's emergence as a global information utility, even if far more widely used in the United States than in most other countries, it is being adopted for the needs of global electronic commerce (Lavin 1996).

A Global Telecommunications Network as a Backbone of Information System Architecture

Let us look at the global telecommunications network of a leader in using globally distributed information systems for competitive advantage—Texas Instruments (see Figure 18.6).

The principal objective of Texas Instruments's information system architecture is to support managing the company as a single entity and a "global factory" (Keen and Cummins 1994). Thus, the network has to enable the company to set up and operate factories, warehouses, and design facilities anywhere in the world, with linkages to the data center in Dallas and to any of the over 60,000 user workstations throughout the world. Indeed, giv-

Figure 18.6

Global telecommunications network of Texas Instruments— crucial component of the company's information systems architecture
(From Peter G.W. Keen and J. Michael Cummins, *Networks in Action: Business Choices and Telecommunications Decisions,* Wadsworth: Belmont, CA, 1994, p. 342.)

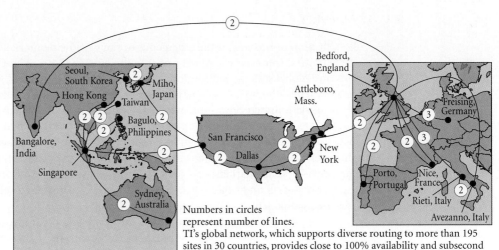

Numbers in circles represent number of lines.
TI's global network, which supports diverse routing to more than 195 sites in 30 countries, provides close to 100% availability and subsecond response times between Dallas and the company's locations worldwide.

ing each user access to information worldwide and to other knowledge workers in the firm (rather than just supporting core business processes) is a top priority. Thanks to this, local innovation can have impact anywhere. Permanent links with the leading global customers and suppliers are also very important to the firm.

The company's telecommunications capability evolved over more than 20 years and relies today on the backbone network of 85 T1 digital circuits, each with a capacity of 1.544 Mbytes, which connect to local area networks. The U.S. network hubs are in Dallas, New York, and San Francisco. Three regional hubs are located in Bedford, England; Miho, Japan; and Singapore. For the purposes of reliability, all hubs are interlinked with two T1 circuits (operating via satellite and fiber optics); each hub has two data centers; and there is more than one way to route from one node to another (a technique known as diverse routing).

The Texas Instruments architecture was drawn up in response to the uncontrolled growth of local area networks and relies on a number of corporate standards. The standards emerged since all local area nets connecting to the backbone need to be able to transmit to a remote LAN. The company's managers meet monthly with its common carriers and international value-added network (IVAN) providers. Together they run quality management programs, based on detailed performance measurements. Texas Instruments also shares the appropriate plans with these carriers, to support future developments. We can say that the carriers are truly the firm's business partners.

Approximately one million E-mail messages are transmitted each day on the network, with the end-to-end delivery time under three seconds. The company is a recognized leader in electronic data interchange (EDI), linking to over 2,000 trading partners in 20 countries. Many of the over 11,000 EDI transactions a month are routed directly to an appropriate transaction processing system supporting a core business process.

Business results are scrupulously measured. Relying on its global telecommunications, the semiconductor group of Texas Instruments reduced the cycle time from receiving an order to delivery by 39 percent in 1993 alone (Sager 1994). Flexible transnational operations are the main reason: Chips may be ordered in Sweden, developed in Texas, and manufactured in the Philippines. Using the network, designs and equipment setup instructions can be transmitted anywhere in the world the company maintains its plants.

We may conclude that, owing to its global information system architecture, Texas Instruments is a formidable global competitor and an able collaborator with its business partners.

SUMMARY

Globalization of business is the emergence of the worldwide market as the arena of corporate activities. Information systems enable the coordination of internal corporate operations on a global scale, as well as global cooperation with customers, suppliers, and business partners. Thus, the use of information technology reinforces globalization of business.

Multinational corporations, which own and operate companies in more than one country, are a principal driver of globalization. The three forces that shape the competitive posture of multinational corporations are the pursuit of global integration of the firm—to achieve efficiencies of scale and scope; the pursuit of local differentiation—to meet the requirements of local markets; and the need for worldwide innovation—to develop and diffuse technological and organizational innovations accomplished within the corporation's units on a global scale.

Three principal strategies are pursued by worldwide organizations. The multinational strategy treats foreign operations as independent businesses that can be supported with decentralized, stand-alone information systems. With the global strategy, foreign subsidiaries are centrally controlled from headquarters, with support of centralized information systems and databases. The transnational strategy aims to leverage competencies and innovations developed in any part of the firm over the entire corporation. The transnational strategy is supported by an integrated information system architecture and systems supporting corporate knowledge work.

Principal global business drivers are the need to share corporate human resources, to flexibly distribute operations among the worldwide units, to develop global products, to maintain quality on a global scale, to manage risks, and to develop worldwide relationships with suppliers and customers.

Challenges to globalization include cultural, political, and socioeconomic differences among the nations of the world, as well as differences in technology standards and telecommunications capabilities. Most of these distinctions should not be expected to disappear.

To operate on a global scale, realizing its strategy and responding to the specific business drivers, a corporation needs to develop a global information system architecture. The principal factors are the selection of appropriate hardware and software, the design of a corporate database (responding to the limitations on transborder data flow), and, most important, the development of a global telecommunications network.

KEY TERMS

Business globalization   *640*
Multinational corporation   *642*
Multinational strategy   *642*
Global strategy   *642*
Transnational strategy   *642*

Global business drivers   *647*
Global information system architecture   *657*
Localized software   *658*
Transborder data flow   *659*

QUESTIONS

1. What do we mean by business globalization? How does it relate to information technology?
2. What effects does business globalization often have on the value chain of a product? How does information technology enable these changes?
3. How does information technology enable the pursuit of each of the three goals of multinational corporations?

4. What are the three principal corporate strategies in the global business environment? What is the role of information systems under each of these strategies?
5. Which information systems types and components do you believe to be mission-critical for each of the three strategies of multinational corporations?
6. What could be the specific reasons for creating virtual organizations in globalizing a firm's business?
7. What are the advantages of the transnational strategy?

How does the structure of information systems in an organization pursuing this strategy differ from the IS structure in organizations pursuing the other two strategies (taken together)?

8. What are global business drivers? Specify and briefly describe these drivers.

9. What role can information systems play in the global sharing of a firm's human resources?

10. What role can information systems play in satisfying global customers of a company?

11. Specify three challenges to globalization you consider the strongest. How do they manifest themselves? How can they be addressed? What role can information technology play in this effort?

12. What are the global core information systems in a firm? Why do only some systems belong to this core?

13. What were the principal objectives pursued by Tambrands in its global reengineering of business processes? How was the site where the reengineering would start selected? How was the experience transferred to other sites?

14. What special considerations need to be taken into account when developing a *global* information systems architecture?

15. What is localized software?

16. What is transborder data flow? What challenges does this issue present to the globalization of information systems?

17. What are the challenges to global telecommunications networks?

ISSUES FOR DISCUSSION

1. Discuss the advantages of the transnational approach to worldwide business. How do the challenges listed in Table 18.4 limit the possibilities of this approach? What, do you think, will be the influence of the global penetration of the Internet? What obstacles to the effective global use of the Internet will need to be overcome?

2. Based on articles in the current periodicals, evaluate the status of off-shore outsourcing of software development to professionals in other countries. How, do you think, will it develop in the future and what will be the outcomes? (*Hint:* You may seek out the two books Edward Yourdon, a well-known programming consultant, wrote on the subject, with the second one, published in 1996, reversing the conclusions of the first.)

3. Discuss the possible influences of information systems on future trends in business globalization.

4. What are the possible ethical issues that IS professionals who are temporarily assigned to their company's unit in a less developed country face? How would you handle each of these issues?

REAL-WORLD MINICASE AND PROBLEM-SOLVING EXERCISES

1. Global Sourcing: Far Easier Said than Done Global sourcing is the contractual purchase of products and services from a selected supplier on a worldwide basis. Information Services units of large multinational companies are themselves major purchasers of hardware, software, and various services. Global sourcing from a major international supplier can save these multinational customers time, money, and headaches caused by incompatible acquisitions. But it is far from easy. "It's a lot of work. . . but we are saving between 30 and 40 percent on the initial purchase cost of our PCs, servers, and software," says Mark Dickens of FedEx (see Photo 18.3).

Charged with conducting a definitive global sourcing survey for all future purchases of these resources at FedEx, Dickens did not realize how difficult the task would prove to be. His group was seeking a strategic supplier relationship with a vendor that would deliver annually at least 30,000 PCs and tens of millions of dollars worth of other goods and services worldwide. Dickens's group sent out 46 detailed requests for proposal (RFPs) to domestic and international companies. He was shocked to see these RFPs largely ignored, and the proposals actually received proved unacceptable because of inflated prices.

Photo 18.3

Mark Dickens of FedEx was charged with global sourcing for the firm's Information Services— and found the task daunting (From Marsha W. Johnston, "Buy Global, Skip Local," *CIO,* April 1, 1996, pp. 30–38.)

So Dickens and his people went around the world themselves to visit vendors in Japan, Korea, Taiwan—and in North America, where they met with the representatives of every major PC vendor. When they were finished, they knew more about the PC business than the individual vendors, and that put them in a powerful negotiating position.

After the appropriate global vendor partners were found, the internal purchasing authority at FedEx was recentralized. Now, instead of calling a favorite dealer or distributor, every FedEx employee must place an order for one of several approved product groups through a Memphis-based FedEx purchasing unit. "It was a major cultural change," says Dickens. "But it's important as companies become more networked. The systems need to work together."

a. What kind of information systems could facilitate global sourcing and how? Would their use entirely replace Dickens's travels?

b. What uses can the World Wide Web be put to in seeking global sourcing?

c. Would you allow for exceptions to the need to buy information products and services from a contracted global source? Under what circumstances?

Based on Marsha W. Johnston, "Buy Global, Skip Local," *CIO,* April 1, 1996, pp. 30–38.

2. Select a global business driver in a specific industry. Discuss in detail how information systems may be used to enable it.

3. Research the special considerations of setting up telecommunications in a selected foreign country.

TEAM PROJECT

Each two- or three-person team will select a case of an international business initiative by an organization, supported by information technology. The case may be selected in a local firm or through readings. Describe the strategy the company appears to pursue, the global business drivers that are most prominent, the IS support for these drivers, and the apparent elements of the firm's global information systems architecture.

SELECTED REFERENCES

Bartlett, Christopher, and Sumantra Ghoshal. *Managing Across Borders: The Transnational Solution.* Boston: Harvard Business School Press, 1989.

This book introduced the concept of transnational corporation.

Bradley, Stephen P.; Jerry A. Hausman; and Richard L. Nolan. *Globalization, Technology, and Competition: The Fusion of Computers and Telecommunications in the 1990s.* Boston: Harvard Business School Press, 1993.

A collection of papers on the mutual influences between business globalization and information technology.

Browne, Michael. "Freight Mega-Carriers in the 1990s: The Strategic Importance of Information Technology in the Race for Global Scale." *International Information Systems,* 1, no. 2, (April 1992), pp. 59–76.

Buchanan, Leigh. "A Process-Change All-Star Team." *CIO,* March 15, 1994, 46–52.

Carper, William. "Societal Impacts and Consequences of Transborder Data Flows." in Shailendra Palvia; Prashant Palvia; and Ronald M. Zigli (eds.). *The Global Issues of Information Technology Management.* Harrisburg, PA: Idea Group Publishing, 1992, pp. 427–449.

Deans, P. Candace, and Michael J. Kane. *International Dimensions of Information Systems.* Boston: PWS-Kent, 1992.

Deans, P. Candace, and Dirk Karwan, eds. *Global Information Systems and Technology: Focus on the Organization and Its Functional Areas.* Harrisburg, PA: Idea Group Publishing, 1994.

A collection of articles describing how companies use information systems to change their operations in the global marketplace.

Fowles, Ken. "Unicode Evolves." *Byte,* March 1997, pp. 105–110.

Greenwood. Timothy G. "International Cultural Differences in Software." *Digital Technical Journal,* 5, no. 3, (Summer 1993), pp. 8–20.

Hampton-Turner, Charles, and Alfons Trompenaars. *The Seven Cultures of Capitalism.* New York: Doubleday, 1993.

You will be surprised by the depth of cultural differences among the seven leading capitalist societies described in this book.

Ives, Blake; Sirkka L. Jarvenpaa; and Richard O. Mason. "Global Business Drivers: Aligning Information Technology to Global Business Strategy." *IBM Systems Journal,* 32, no. 1, 1993, pp. 143–161.

Karimi, Jahangir, and Benn R. Konsynski. "Globalization and Information Management Strategies." *Journal of Management Information Systems,* 7, no. 4 (Spring 1991), pp. 7–26.

Keen, Peter G.W., and J. Michael Cummins. *Networks in Action: Business Choices and Telecommunications Decisions.* Belmont, California: Wadsworth, 1994.

Lavin, Douglas. "Internet is Assuming Global Proportions." *The Wall Street Journal,* March 15, 1996, p. A6.

McMullen, Melanie. "Wireless Lands." *LAN,* June 1994, pp. 40–44.

Miller, David B.; Eric K. Clemons; and Michael C. Row. "Information Technology and Global Virtual Corporation." in Bradley and others (above). 1993, pp. 283–37.

Porter, Michael E. *The Competitive Advantage of Nations.* New York: Free Press, 1990.

Roche, Edward. *Managing Information Technology in Multinational Corporations.* New York: Macmillan, 1992.

Rose, Robert L., and Martin du Bois. "Temporary-Help Firms Start New Game: Going Global." *The Wall Street Journal,* May 16, 1996, p. B4.

Ruggiero, Renato. "The High Stakes of World Trade." *The Wall Street Journal,* April 28, 1997, p. A18.

Sager, Ira. "The Great Equalizer." The Information Revolution 1994, Special Issue, *Business Week,* pp. 100–107.

Samuelson, Pamela. "Intellectual Property Rights and the Global Information Economy." *Communications of the ACM,* 39, no. 1, (January 1996), pp. 23–28.

Problems of harmonizing intellectual property rights across many countries of the world.

Taylor, David. *Global Software: Developing Applications for the International Market.* New York: Springer, 1992.

Tractinsky, Noam, and Sirkka L. Jarvenpaa. "Information Systems Design Decisions in Global versus Domestic Context." *MIS Quarterly,* 19, no. 4, (December 1995), pp. 507–529.

Waters, Malcolm. *Globalization.* London: Routledge, 1995.

Describes social, economic, and political aspects of globalization.

Watson, Richard T., and others. "Key Issues in Information Systems Management: An International Perspective." *Journal of Management Information Systems,* 13, no. 4 (Spring 1997).

Wriston, Walter. *The Twilight of Sovereignty: How Information Revolution Is Transforming Our World.* New York: Scribners, 1992.

Contends that in the information society power ebbs from the national governments and flows to large multinationals.

Zwass, Vladimir. "Between the Plan and the Market: Soviet Computing at an Impasse." *International Information Systems* 1, no. 2, (April 1992), pp. 111–24.

CASE STUDY | # Global Solutions for Nestlé

Nestlé SA is known for the variety of its food and drug products—be it Perrier water, Nescafe coffee, Carnation ice cream, Stouffer frozen foods, or Alcon eye care pharmaceuticals. In fact, Nestlé is the largest food company in the world. In the business world, the multinational company with close to $50 billion in sales is also known for the variety of its operations: It is made up of close to 300 operating companies spread in over 100 countries. Ninety-eight percent of these sales are made outside of the home country, Switzerland. In November 1995, the United Nations ranked Nestlé as the company with the highest global exposure in the world out of 100 of the largest global firms, compared in terms of their overseas sales, assets, and employment. We may say, therefore, that Nestlé is the ultimate in globalization.

Since its founding in 1866, Nestlé has had to go beyond the borders of small Switzerland to look for growth. The company has developed a tradition of patiently building up markets in the developing countries, expecting that the improvement in living standards will make new customers. The virtues of ethical business are strongly enforced from the top. "Run your company so that everything you do is fit to be published in tomorrow's newspaper," is the rule of Helmut Maucher, the chief executive officer. A lean staff of only 1,600 runs the 220,000-employee firm from the headquarters in Vevey, on the shores of Lake Geneva. Below a panorama of Alpine peaks, Vevey is probably the most picturesque company town in the world.

The small headquarters staff is a good indication of the independence traditionally given to the operating companies. This independence was found to be less than a good thing for the firm's information systems. Indeed, it is said that Nestlé prefers its brands to be local, its people regional, but its technology global. Here was the problem to be solved, according to Jeri Bender, the firm's IS methodology coordinator: "We have almost 2,000 developers worldwide. Besides having natural language problems in the different countries, we had a problem with redundant work and a lack of common methods. You name a language, database [management system], 4GL, platform, and methodology, and we had it. There was no way for developers to communicate with one another, and analysis means something different to every developer."

There are about 3,000 IS staffers throughout the firm, with an annual information systems budget of $350 million. In January 1991, a directive was sent down from headquarters: Find a common way to develop applications and build synergy among all of the companies in the Nestlé family.

With the old approach, each country or region (known at Nestlé as a "market") was responsible for defining its IS needs and developing the applications to respond to them. As a result, a worldwide "one of everything" mix of hardware and software includes equipment from IBM (many AS/400 mid-range systems in particular), Digital Equipment, and Hewlett-Packard, running both proprietary systems of the individual vendors and open systems.

Now, a few years since this directive to coordinate information systems on the corporate scale, the change is obvious. Nestlé has created an information system architecture and a standard systems development environment. The first worldwide application development projects are well under way. Software development costs are cut by eliminating redundancies.

The adopted enterprise-wide information system architecture will be based on distributed client/server systems, run under the UNIX operating system. A relational database management system from Oracle will be used to create databases. A key element is the use of the integrated software suite R/3 from the German vendor SAP AG to run the business functions of the firms, from logistics to accounting.

To develop new applications, Nestlé is using the Navigator process management software for systems development from Ernst & Young. After all, software development is also a process. Such process management software supports the management of software projects in which a systems development methodology is used. Navigator can support various development methodologies. The software provides assistance in the most time-consuming initial phases of systems development, when the business problem to be solved with the projected system is defined, the system is planned and analyzed, and the system development project is planned as well.

A key advantage of Navigator and similar process management software is the independence of the development it supports from the future physical implementation of the system. Using it, you analyze what the future system will do, and then you can generate the code for the system to work on any hardware and software platform. Therefore, the developers can concentrate on the logical business side of the problem, before any programming begins. To design and implement the systems that have been analyzed, Nestlé uses the computer-aided software engineering (CASE) tool PowerBuilder from Powersoft.

This platform-neutral nature of Navigator was important for the years of transition from the legacy systems needing to be supported before the changeover to client/server. The approach allows Nestlé to supply the users of the legacy AS/400 systems with new applications, while also being able to move these applications to the new client/server environment. However, Bender and her international team of developers did not select Navigator only for its independence of the development methodology and of actual implementation. Nestlé also needed development software that was available and supported worldwide. Ernst & Young, the accounting and consulting firm with a global presence, is a vendor that can ensure this. Now, in hindsight, Bender is satisfied with the firm's technology and consulting work. But there did emerge a problem that drove the initial costs up. The vendor failed to train its people worldwide in the Navigator methodology fast enough and Nestlé had to import the vendor's consultants from outside Europe to help implement Navigator.

Although the headquarters executives can force any Nestlé's business unit to move to the standards (for example, by blocking a budget expenditure for software or hardware that does not conform to it), this seldom happens in reality. Instead, standards are recommended and the decision as to when to begin following them is left to the local managers. People in Vevey realize that they do not know all the circumstances in the local unit in the Philippines. Manfred Kruger, Nestlé's assistant vice-president of management services, tells us about the company: "There is a culture of working together. We pull in experts from all over the world. Nothing works if you don't get key players to agree on an idea."

In the new environment, the core global information systems are developed by teams in Vevey and other locations, often assisted by experts in specific technologies from inside Nestlé or employed by the vendors. After the principal functionality of the application has been analyzed and developed, the application may be sent to a field IS organization for further adaptation to the local conditions. Once modified to meet the local requirements, the applications are deployed internationally. Being able to develop solutions that are adaptable to several markets is the key to Nestlé's economies of scale and scope in all their operations, not only IS.

Here is an example of a successful worldwide development project. Nestlé will soon begin deploying a set of applications, code-named Harmonization, throughout its Latin American region that will run the business units's commercial, financial, budgeting, and procurement operations. First, the business rules in Chile, one of Nestlé's principal markets in the region were determined with the use of Navigator. Then an international team was assembled in Switzerland, made up of Belgian, Italian, and Swiss designers to design and generate the code for the system. The software was piloted in Italy, and only then a rollout in Latin America was begun. "The individual markets can add something to that core, but the core has to conform to the Nestlé standard," says Jeri Bender.

Maintaining a close relationship with suppliers is another general Nestlé philosophy that has been adapted to the needs of information systems. For example, the firm has set up "centers of expertise" together with SAP AG of Walldorf, Germany, the immensely successful developers of R/3 integrated business applications software. The centers assist in the worldwide rollout of the software at Nestlé. "As you get further from the headquarters, things get worse," Ronald Kronemann, SAP's global account manager for Nestlé, tells us without going into detail. But for Ernst & Young, this means that as new Nestlé "markets" have to be supported, members of its consulting staff have to be pulled from other countries and sent to train Nestlé's IS personnel. Because of the wide scope of its operations, Nestlé finds that only large software vendors with well-developed international operations can become its strategic partners.

The standards-based approach did not take root painlessly, says Manfred Kruger. In the beginning, the regional managers claimed that the standardization plan went against the specific culture of their markets. Yet, they came around—but not in all specifics. Indeed, at one point the central IS staff recommended a specific PC vendor. This created an outcry and Nestlé's units can now choose from a list of recommended PCs. It appears that you cannot simply send the standards down—particularly in a company that prides itself on decentralized operations.

Based on Joshua Greenbaum, "Nestlé Makes the Very Best. . .Standard?" *InformationWeek,* August 23, 1993, pp. 22–26; Joshua Greenbaum, "Nestlé's Global Mix," *InformationWeek,* April 25, 1994, pp. 44–46; Richard J. Barnet and John Cavanagh, *Global Dreams: Imperial Corporations and the New World Order,* Simon & Schuster, New York, 1994; Janet Barnet, "Automating Process Trims Software Development Fat," *Software Magazine,* August 1994, pp. 37–46; author's meeting with Nasser Farschchian at Nestlé, Vevey, August 30, 1994; Francoise Hecht, "Nestlé Takes on the World," *EuroBusiness,* February 15, 1996, pp. 18–23; and Greg Steinmetz and Tara Parker-Pope, "All Over the Map: At a Time When Companies Are Scrambling to Go Global, Nestlé Has Long Been There," *The Wall Street Journal,* World Business Supplement, September 26, 1996, pp. R4–R6.

CASE STUDY QUESTIONS

1. Which corporate strategy is Nestlé pursuing in its global business? Do you find that it is also adapting to its needs the elements of other strategies? What are these strategies and their elements?

2. What principal areas are covered by the information systems standards adopted by Nestlé? Why is process management software for systems development important?

3. What were the obstacles toward the implementation of the standards? What were the factors mentioned in the case that motivated local managers to adopt the standards? What other factors could have played a role in the adoption? Is there some flexibility in the standards?

4. Why are the selected software vendors called strategic partners of Nestlé?

5. How is a global core of information systems emerging at Nestlé?

6. What are the principal distinctions between the IS problems that Nestlé has to solve as a multinational corporation as compared to a firm located at multiple sites within a single country?

Glossary

Accuracy of information The degree to which information corresponds to the reality it describes.

Action document Document directing that an action take place (e.g., airline ticket).

Adhocracy Organizational structure in which the principal work units are the temporary and permanent teams of people who contribute their distinct knowledge and experience.

Administrative controls Information systems controls that aim to ensure that the entire framework of *controls* is instituted, continually supported by management, and enforced with proper procedures, including audits.

Algorithm An unambiguous and terminating procedure for solving a class of problems.

Analog signal Signal transmitted as a continuous wave.

Application controls Information systems controls specific to a given application.

Application generator Software that makes it possible to specify an entire application, consisting of several programs, without detailed coding.

Applications software Programs that directly assist end users in doing their work.

Artificial intelligence (AI) Methods for developing computer programs (or software–hardware systems) that display aspects of intelligent behavior.

Assembler A translator for converting an assembly language program into machine language.

Assistive technologies Specialized technologies that enhance access of the handicapped to the information technology and, in many cases, to the world at large.

ATM (asynchronous transfer mode) Fast *packet switching* that transfers very short fixed-length packets, called cells, over high-capacity networks.

Audioconferencing An extension of the conference call, without the need for an operator to establish the connection between remote conference sites.

Audit function An organizational unit that provides an independent appraisal of an organization's accounting, financial, and operational procedures and information.

Auditing information systems. Evaluation of the effectiveness of information systems *controls* in an organization.

Audit trail Data that make it possible to establish where each business transaction originated and how it was processed.

Automating Replacing human labor, for example, with information systems.

Backward-chaining Expert-system strategy for "reasoning" by assuming a possible conclusion and proving or disproving it based on the facts of the specific case.

Bandwidth A measure of a transmission channel capacity expressed as the range of signal frequencies that can be transmitted over the channel.

Bar-code scanner Input device that reads bar codes.

Batch processing Processing programs or transactions in batches, without a user's interaction.

Beta testing Testing of the early copies of software by the intended end users in order to uncover problems in actual use.

Bit The elementary unit of digital representation (short for *b*inary dig*it*), whose value can be 0 or 1.

Boundary-spanning information systems Systems through which an organization receives intelligence about its environment and provides computerized information for its customers, suppliers, and the public at large.

Brainstorming A group decision-making technique aiming at unfettered generation of ideas.

Break-even method A cost-benefit analysis technique that establishes the point in time when the system will become profitable.

Bridge Hardware and software that interconnects two telecommunications networks of the same type.

Browser A program that enables its users to access electronic documents included in the World Wide Web on the Internet.

Budget Resources committed to a plan for a given project or time period.

Business process A set of related tasks performed to achieve a defined work product.

Business process redesign (BPR) Rethinking and streamlining business processes of a firm in order to produce business results. BPR is an important avenue to achieving payoff from the use of information technology.

Business reengineering Radical redesign of major business processes of an organization, aiming at major gains in costs, quality, or time-to-market for the firm's products.

Business Systems Planning (BSP) A methodology for establishing the enterprise-wide information systems requirements.

Byte Sequence of eight *bits* used to represent a character in computer systems.

Cache memory Fast semiconductor memory, into which blocks of data and instructions may be transferred from the main memory prior to their use by the central processing unit.

CD-ROM (Compact Disk-Read Only Memory) Optical disk used to distribute prerecorded information: once written ("mastered"), the contents of the disk cannot be changed.

Cellular radio Radio transmission that switches the mobile user from cell to cell, each cell with its own broadcasting antenna.

Central processing unit (CPU) The component of the computer which executes (that is, interprets and causes to be carried out) machine instructions.

Channel capacity The potential transmission speed of telecommunications media, expressed in bits per second (bps).

Chargeback Charging the cost of an information system to the users at whose behest the system is developed.

Chief information officer (CIO) Top executive responsible for information services in a corporation.

Chief programmer team A team structure for information system projects built around an outstanding software developer, the chief programmer,

who defines the requirements specifications and design for the system and programs the key modules.

Class In software, a template from which *objects* are created.

Client/server computing A model of computing in which the processing of a given application is split up among a number of client computers (usually PCs), serving individual users, and one or more servers, providing access to databases and doing most of the computing.

Cluster controller A device that manages several terminals in a telecommunications network, connecting them to a single telecommunications link, and performs communication tasks for them, such as screen formatting, code conversion, and error checking.

Cluster organization See *adhocracy*.

Coaxial cable A communications medium that consists of a relatively thick central conductor shielded by several layers of insulation and the second conductor just under the cable's shell.

Code of ethics A set of ethical principles intended to guide the conduct of the members of the profession or the employees of an organization.

Common carrier A company licensed by a country's government to provide telecommunications services to the public.

Communications software Software that enables the user to connect to a telecommunications network in order to send or receive messages.

Competitive intelligence Collecting and analyzing the information on the company's markets, technologies, customers, competitors, suppliers, and other external *stakeholders*.

Compiler Systems software that translates the program written in a higher level language, known as the source program, in its entirety into the binary machine language of the computer.

Computer An electronic general-purpose information processor.

Computer abuse An unethical use of a computer.

Computer-aided design (CAD) Design process relying on information systems that support creation, testing, and revision of designs, particularly with sophisticated graphics.

Computer-aided software engineering (CASE) Partial automation of software engineering with tools that assist software developers in planning, analyzing, designing, programming, and maintaining information systems.

Computer-based work monitoring Monitoring employee performance with the use of information technologies.

Computer crime An illegal act in which a computer is used as the primary tool.

Computer-integrated manufacturing (CIM) Manufacturing strategy relying on the computerized control of the entire manufacturing process.

Computer system A set of devices that can accept and store programs and data, execute programs by applying their instructions to the data, and report the results.

Computer telecommunications network (or computer network) A system of computers and telecommunications.

Computer teleconferencing Systems that support meetings distributed in time as well as in space.

Computer virus A segment of software code that is able to perform malicious acts and insert copies of itself into other programs in the system and onto the diskettes placed in the "infected" personal computer.

Confidentiality The status accorded to data, limiting its use and dissemination.

Consequentialist theories Ethical theories that tell us to choose the action with the best possible consequences (compare with *obligational* theories).

Context diagram The initial *data flow diagram* that shows only a system's interfaces (inputs and outputs) connecting it to the external entities.

Controlling Measuring performance against the planned objectives and initiating corrective action if needed.

Controls Policies, procedures, and technological measures taken to ensure the security of information systems and thus of the organization's assets and information.

Coordination Harmonizing the work of teams or other organizational units, entire organizations, or several collaborating organizations, in a common effort. Involves sharing information, communicating, and allocating responsibility.

Copyright A method of protecting *intellectual property* that protects the form of expression (for example, a given program) rather than the idea itself (for example, an *algorithm*).

Core competence A specific capability that distinguishes the firm and that is valued by the marketplace.

Cost-benefit analysis A method of estimating the expected payoff from a proposed information system by comparing the costs of its acquisition with the expected benefits from its use.

Cost focus Competitive strategy of serving a narrow market segment with a product or service that the firm offers at a significantly lower cost than its competitors.

Cost leadership Competitive strategy of offering the firm's product or service at a cost significantly lower than the offerings of its competitors.

Critical success factors (CSFs) Several crucial objectives and indicators of corporate performance.

Cylinder Set of all tracks on a magnetic disk that can be accessed when the read/write heads move to a certain position.

Data Raw facts that can be processed to obtain *information*.

Data administrator (DA) Person who has the central responsibility for an organization's data.

Database An integrated collection of interrelated data that serves a number of applications in an enterprise and is managed by a database management system (DBMS).

Database administrator (DBA) A database professional who creates the database and carries out the policies laid down by the *data administrator*.

Database management systems (DBMS) Systems software that provides assistance in managing large databases that are shared by many users.

Database marketing Accumulation and use of databases to segment potential customers and reach them with personalized promotional information.

Database matching Merging separate facts collected about an individual in several databases; may be a threat to *privacy*.

Data definition language A language for defining database objects.

Data dictionary (1) Description of the data stored in a database; (2) tool that stores the descriptions of all the entities defined during a system's development.

Data flow diagram (DFD) A graphical tool of *structured analysis,* which shows the flow and transformation of data in the system.

Data manipulation language A language for manipulating the data stored in a database.

Data mart A scaled-down *data warehouse* that provides the data required by a workgroup on its own server.

Data model A method for organizing databases on the logical level, i.e. on the level of the *schema* and the *subschemas.*

Data warehouse A subject-oriented, integrated collection of data, both internal and external, accumulated over time and maintained in support of managerial decision making.

Debugging Tracking down to their source and removing software errors discovered during testing.

Decision room Electronic meeting system facility for same-time-same-place meetings.

Decision support systems Information systems expressly designed to support individual and collective decision making by making it possible to apply decision models to large collections of data.

Decision table In describing a decision, a tabular specification of the actions to be carried out when given conditions exist.

Decision tree In describing a decision, presents conditions as branches of a tree and specifies the actions to be taken when these conditions exist.

Delphi technique A method for soliciting the opinions of a group of experts and arriving at a consensus among them.

Democratic team A team structure for information-systems projects, in which all the team members bear equal responsibility for the project, and the relationships between them are informal.

Denial of service An attack on a computer system that renders it unusable by legitimate users.

Desktop presentation software Personal productivity software that assists its user in designing professional presentations, such as a series of slides with graphics and a variety of text styles.

Desktop publishing software Personal productivity software that assists a designer of publications requiring layout, graphics, images, and control of multiple fonts and typefaces.

Detail report Extract from the database that lists the records satisfying particular criteria.

Dialog management A subsystem of *decision support systems* that provides a variety of user interfaces.

Differentiation Competitive strategy of distinguishing the firm's product or service from that offered by the competition.

Digital image processing Information technology that converts a document to a digital form and stores it electronically for retrieval.

Digital signal Signal sent as a stream of on-off pulses.

Direct access Accessing a record by its identifying value (key) rather than in the order that the records are stored.

Direct conversion The most risky conversion approach, whereby at a certain point the old information system is completely replaced by the new one.

Direct file organization Storing records for *direct access* by hashing their primary key.

Disaster recovery plan A plan specifying how a company will maintain the information services necessary for its business operations in the face of disaster, such as fire or flooding.

Distributed database A database stored in several physical locations.

Divisional organizational structure A structure where the company divisions are formed based on the groups of products or services they deliver, geographic region they cover, or the customer segment they serve.

Downsizing In information systems, transferring some or all of the organization's computing from centralized processing on mainframes or minicomputers to systems built around networked microcomputers (often in a *client/server* configuration).

Drill down The ability to move from summary data to ever lower levels of detail (usually provided in *executive information systems*).

Effectiveness The extent to which a system achieves its objectives.

Efficiency A measure of the consumption of resources in producing given system outputs.

Electronic bulletin board Means of many-to-many communication, through which users can post messages via E-mail to an open electronic mailbox or scan messages posted there by others.

Electronic commerce Sharing of business information, maintaining business relationships, and conducting business transactions by means of computer telecommunications networks.

Electronic data interchange (EDI) Computer-to-computer interchange of electronic transaction documents, involving at least two trading partners.

Electronic information services Commercial information services available over computer telecommunications networks.

Electronic mail (E-mail) Sending and receiving messages from personal workstations over computer telecommunications networks.

Electronic meeting systems Information technology that supports meetings that may be distributed in space and time.

Encryption The transformation of data (or any text in general) into a form that is unreadable to anyone without the decryption key.

End-user computing A component of organizational computing with three dimensions: sophisticated use of information technology by end users, end-user control of systems, and end-user development of certain applications.

End users The people who use information systems or their information outputs; that is, the majority of people in organizations.

Entity-relationship (E-R) diagram Tool for logical design of databases.

Environmental forecasting Attempt to predict the social, economic, legal, and technological environment in which the company will work to realize its plans.

Ergonomics Study of physical relationships between people and the things they use (such as information systems).

Error (or edit) report List of transactions found to be in error during the processing.

Ethics Study of the principles of right and wrong that ought to guide human conduct.

Exception report Report produced only when preestablished "out-of-bounds" conditions occur and containing only the information regarding these conditions.

Executive information systems Information systems that support the long-term, strategic view that senior executives and company boards need to take of the business they are in charge of. Provide easy access to summarized company data, often against a background of external information.

Expert system System that employs knowledge about its application domain and uses an inferencing (reasoning) procedure to solve problems that would otherwise require human competence or expertise.

Explanation facility A facility of an *expert system* that explains how the system arrived at its recommendation.

Facsimile (fax) Long-distance copying technology.

Fault-tolerant computer system System that continues to operate after some of its processing components fail.

Feasibility study The introductory phase of system development, whose objective is to establish whether the proposed system is feasible or desirable, before resources are committed to the full-scale project.

Feedback Outputs of a system that are transformed back into inputs in order to control the system's operation.

Fiber optic cable High-capacity communications medium that consists of many strands of pure glass with a data-carrying core in the middle, surrounded by a reflective coating and a protective sheath.

Field The smallest named unit of data in a database.

File (1) A collection of records of the same type; (2) a named unit of information maintained in secondary storage.

Financial audit An appraisal of the reliability and integrity of the company's financial information and of the means used to process it (including information systems).

Financial forecasting Process of predicting the inflows of funds into the company and the outflows of funds from it for a long term into the future (for example, for five years on a monthly basis).

Firewall A hardware and software facility that prevents access to a firm's intranet from the public Internet, but allows access to the Internet.

Focused differentiation Competitive strategy of identifying a segment of the market (a niche) whose special needs the firm can serve better than its competitors.

Formal information systems Systems relying on procedures, established and accepted by the organizational practice, for collecting, storing, manipulating, and accessing of data in order to obtain information. Usually computerized.

Forward chaining Expert-system strategy for "reasoning" by starting with the facts of the case and arriving at a conclusion.

Fourth-generation languages (4GLs) Programming languages that specify what needs to be done rather than detailing steps for doing it.

Frame relay Fast *packet switching* that checks a packet for errors only at the entry and exit *nodes* of the telecommunications network, thus reducing transmission delay.

Functional organizational structure Structure in which people who perform similar activities are placed together in formal units and thus the organization is subdivided in accordance with the functions of the enterprise.

Function points Technique of estimating software development effort early in development by considering the number and complexity of the system inputs, outputs, inquiries, and files.

Fuzzy logic Method of reasoning with inexact propositions that is implemented for handling uncertainty in some *expert systems* and device controls.

Gantt chart Graphical tool for project management that represents project tasks over time as a bar chart.

Gateway Hardware and software that interconnects two widely differing telecommunications networks.

General controls Information systems *controls* that apply to the whole of an organization's information services.

Geographic information system (GIS) Software that supports the presentation of geographically distributed data on maps.

Global business drivers Aspects of the firm's business that can benefit from the global economies of scale or scope.

Globalization of business Emergence of global markets as the arena of competition and cooperation among firms.

Global strategy Strategy of *multinational corporations* under which the corporation treats the world as a single market and aims to realize efficiencies of scale and scope over its territory of operations.

Goal seeking Establishing the input factors necessary to achieve specified goals (usually with a *decision support system*).

Graphical user interface (GUI) A user interface where commands to the computer system are issued with a pointing device against icons or menu selections on the screen.

"Green" products Products (e.g., personal computers) designed to be less environmentally invasive.

Group decision support systems (GDSS) *Decision support systems* that are designed to support group communication and decision processes.

Groupware Software that supports a business group whose members work on interconnected personal workstations. Groupware offers support for communication and collaboration among group members, and supports the *coordination* of group work.

Hardware Physical devices employed in computer systems (contrasted with *software*).

Help-desk software Software that provides basic support to end users by answering questions relating to the use of software packages and other components of personal computing.

Hierarchical data model Representing the data in a database as a number of trees.

High-level language Programming language in which each statement is translated into several machine-language instructions.

Horizontal packages Applications software that performs a certain general function, such as accounting or office automation, for a range of businesses.

Hot site A disaster recovery site that operates computers compatible with those of the client company, which may use the site within 24 hours of disaster.

Human resource information system (HRIS) The information system supporting the human resources function of an organization with information.

Hypermedia Multimedia database that includes links between related information items.

Hypertext Form of an electronic document (or information base) in which nodes with textual information are interconnected by meaningful links to allow nonsequential access to the text.

Ill-structured problem Problem whose solution does not lend itself to full computerization, and therefore a person–machine system is required for solution.

Image scanner Input device that digitizes and enters into computer memory images of figures, photographs, or signed documents.

Impact printer Output device in which the printing element strikes the paper to produce the impression.

Impersonation Gaining access to a system by identifying oneself as another person.

Implementation of an information system Process of preparing people in an organization for a new system and introducing the system into the organization.

Index In file and database organization, a table that shows where records are located in secondary storage.

Indexed-sequential file organization Storing records in their primary key sequence and, in addition, providing indexes for direct access to records.

Inference engine Facility of an *expert system* that combines the facts of a specific case with the knowledge contained in the knowledge base to come up with a recommendation.

Information An increment in knowledge. May be obtained by processing *data* into meaningful and useful content and form.

Information center An organizational unit that provides training, consulting, and other assistance to end users of information systems.

Information document Document confirming that a transaction has taken place or informing about one or several transactions (e.g., voucher sent with a payment to explain it).

Information repository Central database for storing and managing project data dictionaries.

Information Services (IS) department Unit responsible for providing or for coordinating the delivery of computer-based information services in an organization.

Information society Society where most of the people active in the economy are employed in the handling of information and most of the produced goods and services can be classified as information- (or knowledge-) related.

Information system An organized set of components for collecting, transmitting, storing, and processing data in order to deliver information.

Information system architecture High-level model of the organization's information system.

Information systems literacy The knowledge needed to apply information technology in a business setting to support the individual's own work, the work of his or her team, and the operations of the organization at large in pursuit of its competitive goals.

Information systems master plan A formal document that assesses the current state of organizational information systems and makes a long-term projection for their future.

Inheritance In *object-oriented programming,* classes lower in the hierarchy inherit properties of the classes higher in it.

Inspection Formal review by a small group of people of a system development product (such as a data flow diagram or module code) against a prepared list of concerns.

Installation of an information system Final testing of the system in the actual environment where it will be deployed, and conversion of operations to fit the new systems.

Intangible benefits Benefits that are difficult to quantify and express in financial terms (for example, higher-quality customer service).

Integrated Services Digital Network (ISDN) A digital telecommunications network standardized by an international committee (CCITT).

Intellectual property Intangible property that results from an individual's or a corporation's creative activity.

Intelligent agent Software that acts as a user's personal agent in a telecommunications network, assisting the user with an assigned task.

Internet Global network of networks that has become the worldwide information utility.

Interorganizational systems Information systems that help several firms share information in order to coordinate their work, collaborate on common projects, or sell and buy products and services.

Interpreter Systems software that translates and sends for execution a higher-level language program, statement by statement.

Intranet Internal corporate network that deploys the Internet facilities, primarily those of the World Wide Web.

Joint Application Development (JAD) An organizational technique for conducting meetings comprising the prospective users of an information system and its developers in order to define the requirements specifications for the system.

Knowledge base The specific knowledge about a narrow domain of an *expert system.*

Knowledge engineering Process during which knowledge about the *expert system's* domain is acquired from human experts and other sources in order to construct the knowledge base for the system.

Knowledge management Organizational methods, procedures, and information systems used to collect the knowledge and experience of the members of the organization and bring them to bear on problems and opportunities.

Knowledge representation Method used to organize the knowledge in the knowledge base of an *expert system.*

Knowledge work Work with abstract information rather than with tangible materials.

Leading Inducing the people in the organization to contribute to its goals.

Learning system System that can automatically change itself after performing a task, so as to perform the same task more efficiently and more effectively the next time.

Legacy system An older information system built around a minicomputer or a mainframe, often a candidate for *downsizing.*

Leveling Gradual refinement of *data flow diagrams* during structured system analysis.

Local area network (LAN) Privately owned network that interconnects processors, usually microcomputers, within a building or on a campus site that includes several buildings.

Localized software packages Packages that have user interfaces in the local language and conform to the local cultural tradition.

Logical design (1) In database design, designing the schema and the subschemas; (2) in systems design, the general specification for the information system's resources (compare with *physical design*).

Logical view of data The way the data appear to a user or an application (opposite of *physical view of data*).

Logic bomb Unauthorized instructions introduced into software, which stay dormant until a specific event occurs.

Magnetic disk Secondary storage device that affords the capability of both direct (random) and sequential access to data records.

Mainframe The largest computers in general use.

Main memory Electronic component of the computer system that serves to store the programs to be executed and the data these programs require.

Maintenance Process of modifying an information system to continually satisfy the organizational and user requirements.

Management reporting systems Information systems that support the management of organizations by producing reports for specific time periods, designed for managers responsible for specific functions or processes in a firm.

Manufacturing resource planning (MRP II) Software that converts a sales forecast into a detailed production plan and into a master schedule of production.

Marketing Activities directed toward planning, promoting, and selling goods and services to satisfy the needs of customers and the objectives of the organizations.

Marketing research Collecting data on actual and potential customers.

Mass customization Producing varied, often individually customized, products at a cost close to that of standardized, mass-produced goods.

Massively parallel computers Computer systems that deploy hundreds, or even thousands, of microprocessors working in parallel.

Metropolitan area network (MAN) Telecommunications network that interconnects various local area networks within a metropolitan area, that is, within approximately a 50-mile range.

Microcomputer A computer for personal use, built around a microprocessor.

Microprocessor A *central processing unit* on a single semiconductor chip.

Minicomputer A midrange computer with power, memory, and peripherals falling between the microcomputer and the mainframe.

Model A simplified representation of a real object or phenomenon that helps to understand or develop the modeled object.

Model management A subsystem of *decision support systems* that assists the user with selecting an appropriate model.

Modem Device that converts a digital signal into an analog one for transmission and then back to digital on the receiving end (stands for *mo*dulator-*dem*odulator).

Module A named program routine that is handled as a unit.

Mouse Input device used to control the cursor that appears on a video display and to send commands to the computer system by clicking a button while the cursor points to the corresponding icon.

Multimedia authoring software Personal productivity software that enables its user to design multimedia presentations.

Multimedia computing Technology that integrates various media, such as text, graphics, sound, and video, in the same application.

Multinational corporation A corporation that owns and operates companies located in more than one country.

Multinational strategy Traditional strategy of *multinational corporations* under which the units operating in different countries are almost independent, subject only to the financial control of the central unit.

Multiplexing Combining several lower-capacity transmissions into a single transmission, which is split at the receiving end.

Multiplexor Device combining the data sent to it over local low-speed links into a single stream for transmission over a high-speed telecommunications channel.

Multiprocessor A computer system with two or more *central processing units* sharing the main memory.

Multiprogramming Executing several programs concurrently on the same processor by having one of the programs using the processor while others are performing input or output.

Multitasking Computer system's ability to run several tasks at once on behalf of a user.

Net present value approach A cost-benefit analysis technique whereby the net present value of a proposed information system is computed by subtracting the present value of the costs from the present value of the benefits over the lifetime of the system. If a positive value is obtained, the project has merit.

Network computer A diskless microcomputer designed for accessing the Internet.

Network data model Representing the data in a database as a network of interlinked records, with the links identifying relationships among the records.

Network organization An organizational structure in which a firm becomes the core of an extended virtual organization that includes long-term corporate partners, supplying goods and services to the core firm.

Network protocol A set of rules that all nodes in a telecommunications network follow.

Network switching Establishing the connection between two nodes in a telecommunications network.

Network topology The arrangement of nodes and links in a telecommunications network.

Neural network An array of interconnected processing elements (usually simulated by software) in which knowledge is represented by the pattern of interconnections among them and by the adjustable weights of these connections.

Nodes Computers, switches, and terminals interconnected by links in a telecommunications network.

Nonimpact printer Output device that does not rely on striking the paper for printing an image. Widely used are laser printers and ink-jet printers.

Normalization Simplification of the logical view of data in relational databases.

Notebook (laptop) computer Battery-powered microcomputer that combines all components, including peripherals other than the printer, in a single package weighing between four and seven pounds.

Object In software, a program component that models a real-world object by encapsulating data and instructions that work with these data.

Object-oriented databases Databases that help manage *objects* that belong to various *classes*.

Object-oriented development (OOD) Designing and building the information system as a collection of interacting *objects*.

Object-oriented programming (OOP) Programming software that consists of *objects*, with these objects communicating—and accomplishing their task—by sending messages to each other.

Obligational theories Ethical theories arguing that it is our duty to do what is right (compare with *consequentialist theories*).

Office An environment where the management and administration of an organization take place and an arena of social action where people play out work roles, make decisions, and exchange information.

Office information systems Information systems that support and help coordinate knowledge work in an office environment by handling documents and messages in a variety of forms—text, data, image, and voice.

OLAP (On-Line Analytical Processing) Software that assists in fast analysis of data stored in databases or data warehouses across multiple dimensions.

On-line processing Completely processing each transaction immediately upon its entry.

Open systems Systems that can operate in various hardware and software environments (as opposed to proprietary systems, limited to the environments of their vendor).

Operating system Systems software that manages all the resources of a computer system and provides an interface through which the system's user can deploy these resources.

Operational audit An appraisal of how well management utilizes company resources and how well corporate plans are being carried out.

Operational management Performed by supervisors of smaller work units, concerned with planning and control of short-term (typically, a week to six months) budgets and schedules.

Optical character recognition (OCR) scanner Combination of hardware and software that scans and recognizes printed or typed text and various codes, and enters the corresponding characters into computer memory.

Organization A formal social unit devoted to the attainment of specific goals.

Organizational memory Means by which knowledge from the past exerts influence on present organizational activities. Increasingly, elements of the organizational memory are contained in the software and in the data and knowledge bases of the corporate information systems.

Organization chart Diagram presenting the arrangement of work positions in an organization.

Organizing Establishing an organizational structure for performing business activities.

Outsourcing Contracting out some of the goods or services previously produced by the firm to specialized providers. In information services, the practice of contracting out the operation of a firm's data centers, telecommunications networks, or applications development to external vendors.

Packet switching Transmitting a message in a telecommunications network by dividing it at the source into fixed-length segments, called packets, which also include bits identifying the receiver.

Palmtop (handheld) computer A diskless microcomputer with limited functionality weighing around one pound.

Parallel operation A conservative conversion method, whereby the old and the new information systems are operated simultaneously until sufficient confidence is gained in the new system.

Parallel processing Computer design that relies on performing a large number of operations simultaneously.

Patent Method of protecting *intellectual property* that protects a non-obvious discovery falling within the subject matter of the Patent Act.

Pen-based notepad Microcomputer with a liquid crystal display (LCD) screen built into its top panel on which the user provides input with a pen-like stylus.

Peripherals In a computer system, input and output devices, as well as secondary storage devices, such as disks and tape drives.

Personal computer See *microcomputer.*

Personal digital assistant (PDA) Pen-based microcomputer using wireless telecommunications to communicate with larger machines in order to send and receive E-mail and launch intelligent agents into telecommunications networks.

Personal information management (PIM) packages Personal productivity software that assists its user in tracking tasks, people, projects, and ideas.

Personal productivity software Applications software that enhances its user's performance on a specific range of common tasks (for example, spreadsheet programs).

PERT/CPM Method of scheduling systems development or maintenance activities and controlling the project.

Phased conversion Introducing the new information system in incremental stages, which are divided by function, organizational units served, the hardware on which the new system will reside, or some other factor.

Physical design Producing a complete specification of all system modules and of interfaces between them, and performing the physical design of the database (compare *logical design*).

Physical schema Description of the physical layout of the database in secondary storage.

Physical view of data The way the data is represented in secondary storage (opposite of *logical view of data*).

Pilot version Conversion method that relies on introducing a part of the information system into one carefully designated organizational area, learning from this experience, and then introducing the complete system.

Pixel One of the grid of dots used to represent an image in computer graphics (for "picture element").

Planning Establishing goals and selecting the actions needed to achieve them over a specific period of time.

Plotter Output device used to produce engineering drawings and similar graphical designs.

Pointing device Input device used to identify a position on a computer screen, such as a mouse.

Portability Ease with which the information system can be moved to a different hardware or systems-software platform.

Portfolio approach Assembling a set of application development projects whose overall degree of risk and expected payoff is appropriate for the firm.

Postimplementation review Final stage of system development life cycle, whose objective is to assess both the system and the development methodology.

Precision of information Degree of exactness with which the reality is described; precision of numerical information is the number of significant digits.

Primary key Field (or fields) whose value identifies a record among others in a data file.

Privacy Right of individuals to retain certain information about themselves without disclosure and to have information about them collected with their consent protected against unauthorized access.

Private branch exchange (PBX) An electronic switchboard that interconnects an organization's telephones and provides connections to the public network.

Procedures Policies and methods to be followed in using, operating, and maintaining an information system.

Process innovation Developing new processes to manufacture products or deliver services (contrast with *product innovation*).

Product innovation Development of a new product or service (contrast with *process innovation*).

Processor See *central processing unit.*

Professional support systems Information systems supporting the performance of tasks specific to a given profession.

Programmer An information systems professional who develops, that is, codes and tests the programs that satisfy the requirements established by systems analysts and the design specifications developed by systems designers.

Programming Writing instructions for computer execution and testing the written code to ensure that it performs according to the specifications developed during system analysis and design.

Prototype A preliminary working version of an information system application (or of one of its parts) that is built quickly and inexpensively, with the intention of learning from it and modifying it.

Prototyping Developing successively more complete *prototypes* of the information system and thus obtaining a functional specification of what the intended system is supposed to do and, possibly, evolving the prototype into the system to be delivered to the users.

Pseudocode Code describing program logic to a human rather than to a computer.

Public-key encryption *Encryption* relying on two keys to ensure secure transmission (i.e., a public encoding key and a secret decoding key).

Query language A fourth-generation programming language used to retrieve data from databases.

Radio transmission Wireless communications technology that transmits voice or data over the air using a lower frequency band than microwaves.

RAID (redundant array of inexpensive disks) Secondary storage device that packages a number of smaller disks into a single unit, to achieve high speed and reliability.

RAM (random-access memory) Semiconductor chips that make up the main memory of a computer. It takes the same amount of time to access any (randomly) chosen memory location in RAM.

Rapid applications development (RAD) A systems development methodology based on evolving a system prototype into an operational system.

Real-time processing systems Systems that respond to an event within a fixed time interval; used, for example, in manufacturing plants or to collect data from several pieces of equipment in a laboratory.

Record Component of a database which describes a real-world entity. A record consists of fields that describe the attributes of the entity.

Regression tests Set of test cases used to revalidate the information system following each maintenance procedure.

Relation Data table used in the *relational data model*.

Relational data model Representing the data in a database as a collection of tables, with two tables related by the columns whose values are drawn from the common domain.

Reliability Probability that the information system will operate correctly; that is, according to specifications, over a period of time. It may also be defined as the mean time between failures.

Report generator Software that enables its user to produce a report without detailing all the necessary processing steps.

Reprographics Reproduction of multiple copies of documents.

Request for proposal (RFP) List of requirements and questions sent to the potential suppliers of software packages or other goods or services.

Requirements specifications Detailed specification of what an information system will do when implemented.

Responsibility reporting A principle according to which managers receive reports within their specific area of responsibility.

Reverse engineering Developing analysis and design specifications from the program code.

RISC (reduced instruction set computers) Microprocessors with high processing speeds achieved thanks to limited instruction sets.

Risk assessment Methodical evaluation of the probability of losses due to security exposures and of the extent of these losses.

ROM (read-only memory) Semiconductor memory chips whose contents cannot be changed.

Router Hardware and software that interconnects two telecommunications networks of different types.

Rule-based expert systems Expert systems in which the knowledge is represented by production rules (IF condition - THEN action).

Salesforce automation Equipping salespeople with portable computers tied into the corporate information systems.

Satellite transmission Form of microwave transmission in which the signal is transmitted by an earth station to a satellite which rebroadcasts the signal to the receiving station.

Schema Logical description of the entire database, showing all the record types and the relationships among them.

Scores-and-weights method Evaluation technique for software packages (or other goods and services) that combines the scores of the package's attributes with the weights users assign to these attributes.

Search engine A World Wide Web facility that maintains its own information about the documents available on the Web.

Secondary storage Large-capacity, relatively inexpensive, long-term storage devices (such as disks) in computer systems.

Security of an information system Integrity and safety of the system's resources and activities.

Sequential access Accessing data records in the order they are stored.

Sequential file organization Storing records in the order of their primary key values.

Server Computer dedicated to making a specific resource available through a telecommunications network to other computers and terminals.

Shell (1) an *expert system* without a knowledge base; (2) in disaster recovery, a computer-ready building, available to accept computer equipment on very short notice.

Signal compression In telecommunications, the reduction of the need for channel capacity by removing redundancies from the signal.

Smart card Plastic card that carries data on a built-in semiconductor chip, or on a laser-optic or magnetic strip.

Sociotechnical design Balancing the technological approach to achieving higher productivity with the consideration of the social and human aspects of technology.

Software Programs that control the operation of a computer system (contrasted with *hardware*).

Software metrics Techniques for measuring the attributes of software and techniques for measuring the attributes of the software development process (e.g., its productivity).

Software piracy Illegal copying of computer software.

Software quality assurance Techniques aimed at producing a reliable software product that satisfies user requirements and organizational objectives.

Source data automation Direct data entry in a computer-readable form (for example, as bar code), without keyboarding.

Spreadsheet Applications software that enables the user to manipulate data represented in a grid of rows and columns.

SQL (Structured Query Language) Data-definition-and-management language of relational databases.

Stakeholders Groups of people who can affect the company's ability to achieve its objectives or who are affected by it.

Statistical databases Databases that contain large numbers of personal records, but are intended to supply only statistical information (such as the U.S. Census database).

Steering committee A high-level unit for establishing the organization's information services policy, whose members are executives representing the major functions or business processes of the organization.

Strategic information systems Systems that assist a firm in realizing its long-term competitive goals and in seeking competitive advantage.

Strategic management Carried out by top corporate executives and corporate boards, responsible for setting and monitoring long-term directions for the firm for three or more years into the future.

Structure chart Graphical tool that specifies the modules that the program will consist of and the interfaces between them.

Structured analysis A systems analysis methodology relying on a graphic description of the system as interacting processes that transform input data into output data, with the use of *data flow diagrams*.

Structured design Specifying the structure of the programs in the information system in such a way that the system will be relatively easy to program and modify.

Structured programming Coding the program by relying on a small number of simple programming structures for organizing its logic. This makes the program code relatively easy to understand, test, and modify.

Subschema Portion of the database *schema*, defined for the needs of specific groups of users or applications.

Supercomputer The most powerful computers, able to carry out billions of arithmetic operations per second.

Switch Device that establishes connections between nodes that need to communicate over a network.

System Set of components (subsystems or elementary parts) that operate together to achieve a common objective (or multiple objectives).

System analysis Analysis of the problem or opportunity to be addressed with a proposed information system.

System design Design of the information system to meet the requirements specifications developed during the system analysis.

Systems analyst An information systems professional who analyzes the user's information requirements, develops system prototypes, develops requirements specifications for information systems, and often also designs these systems.

Systems designer An information systems professional who translates requirements specifications of what the system is expected to do into high-level specifications for the system components.

Systems development life cycle Process of information systems development that consists of four conceptually different stages: systems analysis, systems design, programming (coding and testing), and installation.

Systems software Programs that manage the resources of the computer system and simplify applications programming.

Tactical management Performed by middle managers (for example, department heads or plant managers), who are responsible for the acquisition and allocation of resources for projects according to tactical plans, set out for one or two years.

Tangible benefits Benefits that are easy to express in financial terms.

Technical workstation A powerful microcomputer that typically is used as a *server* or supports industrial design with high-resolution graphical processing.

Telecommunications Electronic transmission of information over distances; also the means of this transmission.

Telecommunications monitor Systems software that processes incoming messages, passing them to the appropriate application programs, and accepts outgoing messages from the applications in order to transmit them into the network.

Telecommunications network An arrangement of computing and telecommunications resources for the communication of information between distant locations.

Telecommuting Working in a *virtual workplace*, outside of the corporate premises.

Teleconferencing Facilities enabling people at remote locations to hold a meeting during which they can communicate by voice, text, or images.

Terrestrial microwave transmission Long-distance telecommunications by means of microwave signals traveling on the surface of the earth.

Testing Executing the information system components, and the entire system when available, for the purpose of finding errors.

Text information management systems Information systems that store textual databases and support access to the electronic documents based on the keywords assigned to them.

Time-based competition Business competition in which those first to the market with a new product or service have a chance to preempt the market.

Time-sharing computer systems Systems providing interactive processing by allocating a short time slice for the use of the server to each user in turn.

T1 carrier A digital system for telecommunications.

Total quality management (TQM) Management technique for continuously improving the performance of all members and units of a firm to ensure customer satisfaction.

Trade secret *Intellectual property* protected by a license or a nondisclosure agreement.

Transaction Elementary activity conducted during business operations, such as merchandise sale, airline reservation, credit-card purchase, or inquiry about inventory.

Transaction log List of all transactions processed during a system run.

Transaction processing systems Information systems supporting operational data processing by processing business transactions.

Transborder data flow Transmission of data across national boundaries; restricted by some countries.

Transnational strategy Strategy of *multinational corporations* under which the overseas components are integrated into the overall corporate structure across several dimensions and each of the components is empowered to become a source of specialized innovation.

Trojan horse method Security threat accomplished by concealing within an authorized program a set of instructions that will cause unauthorized actions.

Twisted pair A communications medium consisting of a pair of wires.

Uninterruptible power supply (UPS) Independent power source that supports continuous operation of an information system in the case of failure of the power supply from the electric utility.

Usability Ease with which the intended users can use the information system, which is highly dependent on the proper *user interface*.

User interface Means by which a user interacts with the computer system.

Value-added network (VAN) A telecommunications network that provides services over and above those provided by common carriers.

Value-added vendor Firm that leases facilities from the *common carriers* and provides specialized telecommunications services to its own customers.

Value chain Chain of activities during which a firm adds value to its input materials.

Vertical packages Applications software that assists users within a specific industry segment.

Very large-scale integration (VLSI) Manufacturing technology that makes it possible to place millions of semiconductor devices (for example, transistors) on a single silicon chip.

Very small aperture terminals (VSATs) Relatively inexpensive and unobtrusive antennas for *satellite transmission*.

Videoconferencing Technology that enables the participants to see and hear one another at a distance.

Virtual memory Seemingly expanded capacity of the main memory of the computer, achieved by keeping in the main memory only the immediately needed parts of programs, with the complete programs kept in secondary storage.

Virtual organization Organization whose structure is to a large degree created by the use of information systems rather than with ownership or lasting organization charts.

Virtual private network Purchased guaranteed access to the telecommunications facilities with specified capabilities, such as transmission speed and access points.

Virtual reality systems Hardware and software that immerse the user in three-dimensional artificial worlds, creating an illusion of an alternative reality.

Virtual workplace Any place outside of the corporate office where a worker can perform his or her tasks with the assistance of information technology and, if desired, in communication and collaboration with other workers.

Visual programming Rapidly building applications by dragging the icons representing software objects with a pointing device (such as mouse) and dropping them in the appropriate place in the program.

Voice-data entry Relying on the devices that can accept spoken input.

Voice mail Technology for storing and forwarding voice messages converted to digital form.

Walkthrough Review by a small group of people of a system development product (such as a data flow diagram or module code) presented by its author.

"What-if" analysis Developing scenarios for solution with the assistance of information systems (usually *decision support systems*).

Wide area network (WAN) Telecommunications network that covers a large geographical area.

Word Largest number of consecutive *bits* that can be accessed at one time in the computer's main memory.

Word processing software Personal productivity software that facilitates entry, storage, manipulation, and printing of text.

Workflow system Information technology that supports document-based organizational processes by automatically routing electronic documents over the computer network to the appropriate workers for their contribution.

World Wide Web Collection of hyperlinked multimedia (text, photos, graphics, voice, moving images) databases stored in computers known as servers all over the world and accessible via the Internet.

WORM (write-once-read-many-times) Optical disk drives that enable users both to read and append information until a cartridge is full. However, the information written on the disk cannot be altered.

X terminal Workstation with a limited processing capability, used to access services provided by other computers to which it is connected.

Yield management Maximizing the revenue from a perishable commodity, such as an airline flight or a hotel-room night.

Index

NAME INDEX

ORGANIZATION INDEX

SUBJECT INDEX